# Therapeutic
## Expedition

# Therapeutic
# Expedition

### Equipping the Christian Counselor for the Journey

## JOHN C. THOMAS & LISA SOSIN

NASHVILLE, TENNESSEE

Therapeutic Expedition:
Equipping the Christian Counselor for the Journey

ISBN: 978-1-4336-7236-1

Published by B&H Publishing Group
Nashville, Tennessee

Dewey Decimal Classification: 158
Subject Heading: COUNSELING\APPLIED PSYCHOLOGY\
COUNSELORS—TRAINING OF

Printed in the United States of America

6 7 8 9 10 11 12 • 18 17 16 15 14

VP

# Contents

The video vignettes are available at http://www.bhpublishinggroup.com/therapeuticexpedition.

| CHAPTER | Video Vignettes Focus |
|---|---|
| Preface | None |
| **Section 1 Introduction** | None |
| 1: The Foundation of Helping | None |
| 2: The Fundamentals of Helping | None |
| 3: The Hazards of Helping | None |
| 4: The Person of the Counselor | |
| **Section 2 Introduction** | None |
| | None |
| 5: Basic Skills: Creating a Connection | Attending Skills<br>Setting Up the Room<br>Empathy/Reflection Skills |
| 6: Basic Skills: Exploring the Problem | Questioning<br>Paraphrasing<br>Clarification<br>Summaries |
| 7: Basic Skills: Giving Feedback | Feedback<br>Interpretation<br>Confrontation<br>Self-Disclosure<br>Immediacy<br>Silence<br>Pacing |
| 8. Basic Skills: Terminating the Counseling | How to End Therapy<br>How to Make a Referral |
| **Section 3 Introduction** | None |
| 9: Managing the Counseling Session | Ethical Introduction<br>Goal-Setting |
| 10: Conducting an Assessment | Bio Assessment<br>Psycho Assessment<br>Social Assessment<br>Spiritual Assessment |
| 11: Case Conceptualization and Treatment Planning | None |
| 12: Strategies for Bringing About Changes | None |
| 13: General Helping Strategies | Recommending Homework<br>The Use of Metaphor |
| 14: Spiritual Strategies | None |
| 15: Professional Issues in Counseling | None |

# Acknowledgments

Tackling the arduous project of writing a professional textbook is not possible without being taught, helped, influenced, inspired, advised, and assisted by others. Those who have crossed our paths in the years since we entered into the counseling field are too numerous to mention individually, though all have contributed in some way. Collectively we would like to thank each of the professors, counselors, supervisors, and researchers who have helped us shape our opinions into a serviceable form. We would also like to express our grateful thanks to the many counselees who have all contributed in ways both small and large to the content of this textbook. Like many, we have learned—and continue to learn—the most from those whom we have sought to help.

We are especially indebted to the leadership of the Center for Counseling and Family Studies department of Liberty University. Thank you, Dr. Ron Hawkins, for your gracious spirit and mentoring in both shaping the primary author's training and supporting the project. We also are grateful to Dr. Scott Hawkins, Dr. Victor Hinson, and Dr. Denise Daniel for their endorsement of the project. We have been heartened by the support we have received from our university. Our colleagues were also an excellent source of encouragement and advice.

Several people contributed to shaping the manuscript and reviewing it for reference accuracy. Greg Mears, Brandon Moore, Anna Moore, Chuck Rodgers, Denise Thomas, Johnny Baker, Kristen Sherett, and Jesse Loftus provided invaluable help by checking the citations and references. Denise Thomas reviewed portions of the manuscript, was a writer of the scripts for the DVD, and performed as one of the counselors in the vignettes. She skillfully handled so many aspects of the project that it would not exist without her.

We consider ourselves to be very fortunate authors to have B&H as our publisher. We are grateful that they believed in us. We express sincere love to Jim Baird and Dean Richardson for the countless hours they poured into this project.

I (John) would like to express my heartfelt appreciation to my wife and best friend, Denise, whose contributions to this work are indescribable. Thank you, Denise, for doing all you do, so much of which goes unnoticed. Our children, Katie and Stephen—both the joy of my life—inspired me to continue. Even my two dogs provided unconditional love when writer's block interfered with progress on the manuscript. And thanks to my dear friends Don and Lorie Marsh and the members of our Sunday school class, Transitions, for providing a safe sanctuary to share personal concerns, for their prayerful intercessions, and encouraging words and touches. They are indeed the world's best cheering squad! To God be all the glory.

I (Lisa) consider it a great honor and privilege to join Dr. John C. Thomas in this invaluable project. I have found his commitment to excellence in the field of soul care, his desire to glorify and rightly represent God, and his devotion to this work a testimony to who he is as a person. Thank you, John, for inviting me to share in this project. I have learned so much. I also thank the King of all counselors for continuing to "make the path straight" during this journey. And I am indebted to David, Tim, and Josh for their love and support in all that I am and do. To friends and family, who are always present with grace and truth abounding, you give life on the fallen planet a tinge of glory. Thank you, all!

# Preface

Our objective in this preface is threefold. First, we want to put our work in context and orient you to the heart of the book. The book has been birthed through our experience, representing over 50 years of counseling with a wide variety of problems and populations. This work is the byproduct of our labors of culling material from a wealth of information that will be relevant to your learning. It is both theological and psychological in orientation. Second, we want to give you an overview of the structure of the book. It is a forest perspective rather than an examination of the individual trees that comprises the landscape of this text. Third, we want to highlight a number of special features we have incorporated in this text, designed to enhance your learning. While learning is a byproduct of a person's effort, how the material is presented can either maximize or hinder the process. We trust that our approach will lead to your ability to master this material; we simply ask for you to give your best effort.

## THE BACKGROUND AND HEART OF THE TEXTBOOK

When we talk with students about the reasons that led them to choosing the helping profession, we typically hear comments like, "*I want to help others*" or "*I feel called and gifted to work with wounded people.*" The words vary, but the meaning is similar; people are drawn to the helping profession because they want to help others. Therefore, one of the most important courses in a counselor-training program is one that teaches the basic counseling skills and therapeutic interventions. In a helping-skills course students learn the core skills of the helping process. A helping-skills course should be a practice-oriented, hands-on experience in which students have the opportunity to see the skills performed and then practice performing those skills themselves. The goal is to equip students with the basic tools to conduct interviews, build a helping relationship with their counselees, understand the counselees' problems, plan treatments, and employ effective strategies. These skills form the foundation of the entire helping process.

Such a course requires a quality textbook. A number of well-respected textbooks provide excellent training in basic counseling skills. For example we have found highly useful information in Cormier and Cormier (1985), Egan (2007), Sommers-Flanagan and Sommers-Flanagan (2003), Young (2010), Ivey and Ivey (2003), to name a few. Because of our Christian faith, however, we prefer to use quality textbooks that have a solid and clear biblical worldview; one that integrates psychological principles and theological truth. Although the books mentioned give students solid training in the helping skills, none presents a biblical worldview approach to the skills of the helping profession.

We anchor our consideration of helping to a biblical worldview. We are unabashedly believers in the inerrancy and inspiration of Scripture. We are simply captured by the Word of God. While some would consider such a belief nonacademic or foolish, we gladly and proudly wear that label. After all the Bible says God has chosen the foolish things of the world to shame the wise and the weak things of the world to shame the things that are strong (1 Cor 1:27, NASB). We position our views on the platform of biblical truth. The philosophy on which counseling is built matters greatly. For this reason we contend that a biblical worldview aptly anchors the counseling techniques and skills in God.

*The Therapeutic Expedition: Equipping the Christian Counselor for the Journey* has been developed on the premise that the study of helping skills is essential for everyone seeking a career in counseling. It does not matter whether the career unfolds in the arena of a state-funded agency, private nonprofit, private practice, school system, or church. It does matter that the person is prepared to work with counselees challenged by the marks of a broken and fallen world.

The aim of this text is to help today's students become effective counselors in an ever-changing world. We are continually bombarded by a pace of life that is faster than ever before, an economic forecast that is gloomier, diseases that are deadly and resistant to modern medicine, and the ever-present fear of terrorism. People value choice, independence, autonomy, and a version of tolerance. Such values are not necessarily good, of course, because they can lead to self-protection, sinful choices and behavior, the embracing of things once deemed wrong, an attack on what has traditionally been viewed as right, and greater antagonism toward believers. Today's world is increasingly moving away from the Judeo-Christian God. As a result, people are more physically threatened and more psychologically unhealthy. Not surprisingly counselees are bringing to us a greater degree of pathology and are bearing many more problems than those who came to our offices decades ago. As you enter the profession, you must be well equipped to embattle the brokenness in people's lives.

## OVERVIEW OF THE TEXT

We have created this book to help prepare you to be an effective helper. It is a practitioner's book that initiates your learning journey in the study of the counseling relationship and techniques that promote change. You might be enrolled in an undergraduate or graduate counseling program in a Christian college or university. Perhaps you are getting your education in pastoral counseling through a seminary. Regardless of the setting or your desired role in the helping profession, *The Therapeutic Expedition* includes selected topics to meet the needs of instructors and professors teaching a course in this area.

When writing a textbook of this sort each chapter becomes an artificial compartmentalization of one aspect of the world. Of course one text cannot adequately address all the factors, skills, and strategies of helping. Entire texts could be written, and have been written on many of this textbook's topics. Yet we have chosen to make this work as comprehensive as possible without being unwieldy in length. We have focused primarily on foundational counseling skills and basic spiritual strategies.

This book is unique in both format and content. We have divided the text into three sections that overview the helping journey. Section 1 ("The Heart of the Helping Process"; chaps. 1–4) provides the foundation and overview of the helping journey. Chapter 1 ("The Foundation of Helping") examines the foundation of the journey, which we root in a biblical worldview. While we advocate a bio-psycho-social-spiritual approach to helping, the most critical aspect is grounding our approach in the Scriptures. We attempt to relate the skills and techniques of helping to worldview topics. In chapter 2 ("The Fundamentals of Helping") we explore the counseling process as a whole. The chapter addresses such key issues as the value, definition, and effectiveness of counseling. We also delineate how counseling is both an art and a science and discuss how your intentions are integral to the helping process. We conclude that chapter by acquainting you with the role of technique in counseling. In chapter 3 ("The Hazards of Helping") we examine the risks associated with making the therapeutic journey. Unfortunately the journey of counseling is not risk free; it poses threats to both the counselor and the counselee. We conclude this section in chapter 4 ("The Person of the Counselor") with a discussion of the primary instrument in helping, namely, you. The Holy Spirit is an energizing factor in helping counselees change, and the Holy Spirit works through the knowledge, words, and behavior of the counselor. The greater the counselor's awareness of the strengths and possibilities he possesses the more effective he can be in the work of counseling. We believe that this is an absolutely critical chapter in your development.

Section 2 ("Basic Helping Skills"; chaps. 5–8) equips you with all the fundamental skills of helping. These chapters are clearly a focal point of interest, because ultimately counselor competence means being equipped to help people. These skills help you relate to the counselee, explore the counselee's concerns, and facilitate the dialogue. In chapter 5 ("Basic Skills: Creating a Connection") we describe one of the most important aspects of the counseling enterprise, the helping relationship. In this chapter we delve into those skills that facilitate a therapeutic bond and relationship between the helper and the counselee. In chapter 6 ("Basic Skills: Exploring the Problem") we introduce you to the universally accepted skills of helping. We discuss how to ask questions, paraphrase, clarify, and summarize. Chapter 7 ("Basic Skills: Giving Feedback") highlights those skills that move the counseling process forward. This chapter equips you in the use of giving feedback, interpretations, and confrontation. We guide you in the appropriate use of self-disclosure and silence. Then we discuss how to deal with issues as they arise in the counseling relationship and how to pace the session. The last chapter in Section 2 teaches you how to end the counseling process. Chapter 8 ("Terminating the Counseling") overviews the importance of appropriately terminating counseling. We cover such issues as the function of termination, types of termination, how to make a referral, and techniques and interventions that effectively end the helping relationship.

The final section ("The Helping Process") is comprised of seven chapters that help you apply your counselor skills to the tasks of helping (chaps. 9–15). In chapter 9 ("Managing the Counseling Session") we seek to equip you with the how-tos of each session. First, we present a model for your work, known as the AIM model. We then provide an overview of how a counseling session is sequenced and discuss the importance of giving an ethical introduction in your first counseling session. Chapter 10 ("Conducting an Assessment") is an overview of the importance of assessment and gives you basic assessment techniques to collect counselee information. Chapter 11 ("Case Conceptualization and Treatment Planning") teaches you how to make sense of the information you gather from your counselee. This chapter helps you gain a clearer understanding of what is happening with the counselee. Chapter 12 ("Strategies for Bringing About Changes") is organized around questions associated with change. If you do not understand how people change and what people need to change, you will flounder in your counseling work. In chapter 13 ("General Helping Strategies") we provide techniques that are broader in scope than the techniques covered in previous chapters. These techniques are relevant and profitable to incorporate into the counseling enterprise and will greatly assist you in making the most of your counseling time. These include such techniques as humor, metaphor, and homework. Chapter 14 ("Spiritual Strategies") suggests a range of techniques that specifically target a counselee's spiritual dimension. These techniques could be conceptualized across many orientations, but spiritual change is their focus. We end the text with important information related to becoming a professional counselor. Chapter 15 ("Professional Issues in Counseling") addresses the fact that we are engaging in activities that involve ministry but that are also linked to a professional field. We look at professionalism, ethics and legal issues, diversity, and your development as a counselor.

A number of practical items are included in the appendixes. These include the American Counseling Association Code of Ethics (2005) and the American Association of Christian Counselors Code of Ethics (2001), sample forms that can be used in your counseling work, and an assortment of handout-like materials that you may find useful in your therapeutic work.

## SPECIAL FEATURES

Teaching and learning the skills of helping may be likened to a journey. In his book on helping, Young (2005) wrote, "An overarching metaphor is . . . that learning the art of helping is a journey with a beginning but no real end point. Those who embark on the quest find it to be a lifelong process of discovery rather than a destination" (p. v). In keeping with this thought we chose to approach this text from the process of a therapeutic journey— whether you are teaching counseling skills, supervising novice counselors, or learning the art of helping, you find yourself on a journey. This book is but one vehicle for taking that journey.

This textbook is intended to help counselors-in-training acquire and refine a repertoire of effective helping skills. Providing a theoretical rationale for the helping skills and strategies is limited since such material is covered in counseling theory textbooks.

One special feature of this textbook is its emphasis on practical application of the skills and techniques. To give you the greatest opportunity to learn, each chapter begins with chapter objectives and a brief outline of the chapter, and the content of each chapter includes figures and tables with the technique guidelines spelled out, and chapter activities. The chapter activities serve as the workbook component of the text. Your professor might want you to complete the activities in a Word document that can be submitted as an assignment, or he might simply have you review them yourself. In addition a PDF version of the questions is available at the Web site. Professors might choose to have students print the workbook and write out their answers as proof of doing original work.

Another special emphasis in this text is the focus on the psychological, interpersonal, and theological sides of the helping enterprise. We do not intend to minimize the saliency of the biological approaches to helping. Our focus is to equip counselors of all kinds with the necessary skills to meet counselees where they are rather than to account for those issues that are not under the purview of a counselor.

Along with the activities, we have created video vignettes to illustrate the effective use of certain skills. The video vignettes are designed to interface with the material from selected chapters and to work conjointly with the chapter activities. We recommend that after you have studied the chapter you watch the video vignettes associated with that chapter. (The video vignettes are available at http://www.bhpublishinggroup.com/therapeuticexpedition.)

Even though this book has a clinical orientation, we have chosen to use the term *counselee* rather than *client* or *patient* to denote the one we are helping. Terms like *client* and *patient* are typically associated with a stronger mental-health focus as opposed to counselee, which has broader appeal.

Creating this textbook has been a long journey for us. We hope that it will provide meaningful and practical guidance to you as you attempt to learn the skills and processes that are effective with hurting people. The therapeutic expedition is a journey that traverses difficult terrain and exposes undeveloped territory. We wish you the best as we embark on this therapeutic journey.

John C. Thomas, Ph.D., Ph.D.
Lisa Sosin, Ph.D.

# Section 1

# The Heart of the Helping Process

**A** good counselor is like a seasoned guide who artfully and skillfully leads lost, wayward, confused, frightened, or disheartened travelers (counselees) on a transformational journey to the place they (counselees) want to go. They have a destination in mind, a challenge to master, a dream to fulfill, and it is calling them to take up their gear and get on the trail. Many are weary, if not broken, void of hope, lost in darkness and perplexity. Some are bewildered and disheartened, travailing the same worn paths that have led them only to destruction. Others are hungry physically, mentally, emotionally, and/or spiritually; lost on a sea of relations with whom they are unable to connect. They have used up their reservoir of resources trying to cross a seemingly tumultuous and endlessly expansive terrain. They know that they need help, yet they are ambivalent about embarking, keenly aware that the expedition will be costly and that they will be like sojourners in unfamiliar lands. Some fear that it is a journey so threatening and arduous that stepping on the trail is like stepping into the abyss. Yet they know they must step off, and as a result of their courage and humility they have called on you to lead the way. This book is about equipping you for their journey.

The first section of the text contains four important chaps. In chap. 1 we focus on critical foundations by exploring the significant relationship between a counselor's worldview and his helping. The focus is on the importance of worldview, the components of worldview in general, and a biblical view specifically, and the connection between one's worldview and his skills and techniques.

Chap. 2, "The Fundamentals of Helping," addresses the value and effectiveness of helping. An explanation of counseling as both a science and art is provided as well as a discussion on the importance of counselors working from an explicit model. The chap. closes with an exploration of counselor intention and the noteworthy place of technique in the counseling process.

The counseling journey has risks. For that reason chap. 3 addresses the hazards of helping that can befall both the counselee and counselor. A special focal point of this chap. is helping you learn how to appraise and avoid the hazards.

Chap. 4 spotlights the person of the counselor. Counselor characteristics, development, and attitudes that affect the counseling process are presented. Highlighted is how the counselor becomes the person God has called him to be as a representative of Himself in the therapeutic relationship.

Thinking again about counseling as an expedition, I (Lisa) recall my days of leading young people on self-discovery journeys. Each youth had a mission in mind: to conquer their fears, to push through their limits, to recognize their strengths. I and the group of explorers were working as one to reach their goal: the last mile, the opposite side of the lake, the other end of the mountain. This was their chosen event, this was their goal, and this was what they wanted to do. They needed a knowledgeable guide, but it was their expedition, their hard efforts, their character-growth opportunity.

I recall awakening in the mornings on Lake Michigan, preparing gear with the only hint of day the slight edge of scarlet cutting across the still-blackened sky. With stars receding I lifted up each element of the coming day to the One who keeps the paths straight, to the One without whom nothing of lasting value could emerge from the passage. The three days before me meant leading a group of insecure fourteen-year-olds, girls and boys, biking for miles and miles and miles along the Michigan shoreline. We traversed hiking trails, taking up canoes against the battering of winds, the torrents of rain, the harshness of sun, and whatever other wild mysteries awaited us from within and without. These were three days of pushing through, three days of providing comfort, direction, protection, encouragement, boundaries, parameters, guidance, food, drink, fun, and bug repellent. My job was to "shepherd" them and God's job to bring forth the fruit. Some made it through the passage—the motivated, committed, and hardworking ones. Others dropped by the wayside here and there, picked up by the van appointed for those who could no longer travail. They were not yet ready, willing, or able.

You and your counselees are on a similar expedition. We pray that as you study how to guide others successfully, you will abide as close to the one true Guide as possible. As you do, He will guide *you*, and through you

He will do great and wonderful things that you could not have asked for or imagined. May your days of leading others be as filled with joy and awe as ours have been.

## Chapter 1

# The Foundation of Helping

*"Psychological, social, and political revolutions have not been able to transform the heart of darkness that lies deep in the breast of every human being. Amid a flood of self-fulfillment, there is an epidemic of depression, suicide, personal emptiness, and escapism. . . . So obviously the problem is a spiritual one. And so must be the cure"* (Dallas Willard, 1988, p. viii).

*"I observed everything going on under the sun, and really, it is all meaningless—like chasing the wind. What is wrong cannot be made right. What is missing cannot be recovered"* (Eccl 1:14–15, NLT).

*"And these are but the outer fringes of his [God's] works; how faint the whisper we hear of him! Who then can understand the thunder of his power?"* (Job 26:14, NIV).

## CHAPTER OBJECTIVES

» To highlight the importance of worldview to helping

» To delineate the key components of worldview

» To elucidate the importance of having an accurate worldview

» To explain the components of a biblical worldview

» To connect worldview to skills and techniques

## CHAPTER OUTLINE

Russ grew up in a Christian home, with parents who came from a strong faith tradition. Around 10 years of age, Russ found that a department store catalog offered opportunities to see women in their underwear, lingerie, and bathing suits. From his first look he was hooked. It didn't take long before Russ saw his first pornographic magazine when a neighbor boy took one from his father's stash. The pornography was taken to a new level when Russ discovered masturbation. These activities stayed with Russ through high school and into Bible school. While in Bible college Russ met a beautiful young freshman, Carol—the daughter of missionaries—who he thought offered the promise of control over his sexual urges. After graduation Russ and Carol married and set off on their honeymoon. To his amazement, the wedding night failed to live up to his expectations. Soon Russ was masturbating to fantasy images of girls he had met and ones he saw on TV. Knowing that his position on a church staff could be jeopardized by buying pornography, Russ avoided it until he discovered it on the Internet. Through the Internet Russ's acting out progressed rapidly.

After the birth of their first child Russ developed a close relationship with a girl, Beth, in the youth group. Beth had not talked to her father in years since he was arrested for sexually abusing Beth and her sister. Russ provided a much-needed male role model in Beth's life. He met with her often, offering counseling and encouragement. When Beth went off to a Christian college, they stayed in touch. When she returned home for Christmas, she met Russ at his office where they talked for hours. Russ never believed he was capable of being sexual with her, but he did. Their sexual encounters happened regularly over the holidays and continued into the spring semester. When he could arrange it, they would meet halfway at a motel where they would have sex. Just before the spring semester ended, Beth paid Russ a visit to report that she was pregnant with their child. Instantly Russ knew his world had collapsed. Nothing would ever be the same. Carol learned of the pregnancy and moved out. Russ resigned from his job as youth pastor as the entire church community learned of the affair.

Jennifer was a 40-year-old wife and mother. She and her college sweetheart, Ben, had been married 16 years and had a wonderful relationship; the kind of relationship that many women envied. Jennifer and Ben worked with young married couples in church, taught premarital courses for the pastor, and were active members of the church choir. Their three children were beautiful and sweet, ranging from 13 to 6 years of age. One weekend, following a choir rehearsal for their church Easter cantata Ben and their oldest girl were traveling to a piano concert while Jennifer and the two children went in an opposite direction for their middle son's swimming event. Jennifer enjoyed watching her children compete in their sports and musical activities and would often get lost in the experience as she reminisced about her own swimming competitions; a swimming career that left her highly decorated. While lost in the nostalgia of her past successes, her cell phone rang. Nothing could have prepared her for the news that her husband and oldest daughter had been killed by a drunk driver while driving to the concert. In one split moment Jennifer lost her lifelong companion and friend and one daughter.

Sam is an 11-year-old, fifth-grader who has been diagnosed with Attention Deficit Hyperactivity Disorder (ADHD) by his pediatrician. Recently Sam has been misbehaving to the point where neither his mother nor his teacher could handle him. Sam's mother had raised him with little help from her former boyfriend, who broke up with her when he learned she was pregnant. With stretched finances and lack of support, Sam's mother was at her wits' end. She was bothered by her ranting and raging while at home, but felt that she could not control him anymore. She knew it was not good for Sam to see her being frequently abused by her new live-in boyfriend, but Sam had to get control of his behavior if she was to survive.

Cases like Russ, Jennifer, and Sam are a few of the types of counselees you will encounter through your counseling. They each pose their own challenges because their backgrounds, personalities, circumstances, presenting problem(s), resources, and goals make them unique. Thus, counselors need a wide range of knowledge, skills, and abilities if they are to provide effective help. A recipe approach to counseling does not work. What works with one counselee and problem might be disastrous with another (Corey, 2005). The greater your ability to conceptualize cases and the more tools you possess in your "helping bag," the greater the likelihood that desired change will occur in the counselee's life. The bottom line is that effective counselors need a strong base of counseling skills that can be adapted as necessary to meet the needs of counselees.

We have orchestrated this textbook to outfit you with the requisite gear to lead counselees of all shapes and sizes. It is not a textbook *about* counseling, but a manual on *how* to counsel. It is a skills-oriented resource that provides a boot camp experience in the helping skills. Throughout the textbook and in the chap. activities, you will be oriented to and drilled in the knowledge, skills, and strategies that will equip you to help counselees like Russ, Jennifer, and Sam. *The Therapeutic Expedition* is about helping people make their personal journey of change and healing. Simply put, our task in this textbook is helping you to help people.

We have chosen to begin the instructional journey by laying the foundation on which you can develop a repertoire of helping skills and strategies. Your personal worldview lays the foundation and orients you on how to counsel. To that end, this chap. describes aspects of a worldview. The accuracy of a worldview is measured by how closely it aligns with biblical truth. Also your worldview interfaces with helping skills and techniques. We will look beneath the surface of *what is done* in counseling to *why it is done*. Thus we will view the components of a worldview in general before seeing what constitutes a biblical worldview.

## THE HELPING HOUSE

In addition to our major metaphor of the therapeutic expedition, we will employ other metaphors throughout the book. The metaphor of a house nicely depicts the role that worldview plays in our counseling skills and strategies (see Figure 1.1).

All buildings are designed and constructed with a particular purpose in mind. A house serves a purpose very different from an office building, for example. Both buildings might be aesthetically pleasing, but the design, construction materials, occupancy, and use of the space differ dramatically. Houses are primarily designed and built to provide sanctuary from the elements, a dwelling, and a place that connects us to a particular location (e.g., "I live at 1985 Hudson Street"). Our helping house captures who each one of us is as a counselor because the house is designed to serve the purpose of helping people.

Foundations are not the focal point of the house; in fact great care is often devoted to disguising them (by masonry brick work and landscaping, e.g.). Foundations simply do not contribute to the architectural aesthetics of a building. Yet without a suitable foundation the building will be unsafe, and its architectural merits will rapidly fade. The foundation is not designed to capture an observer's attention. Rarely, if ever, is it a key factor in choosing a home to purchase. To the architect and builder, however, the foundation is a matter of high importance because it bears the load of the entire structure. A proper foundation can mean the difference between a stable structure and one with constant problems and high maintenance. Thus architects and contractors know that the most crucial element in building a house is the foundation. It is the platform on which the entire structure is built. The soil, topography of the property, depth of the foot- ings, quality of material and construction, size, and shape of the founda- tion are key variables that impact the entire structure.

Your worldview is like the foundation of a house. It is the platform on which you build your life. And it is the foundation on which you construct

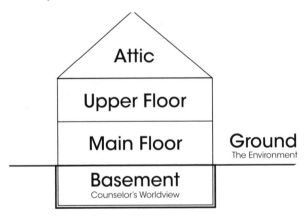

Figure 1.1: The Helping House

your helping efforts. Every counseling theory, model, conceptualization skill, and therapeutic intervention is intricately related to your worldview; that is, your worldview is the foundation on which everything that occurs in counseling is built.

Reflect on the three cases that were described at the beginning of this chap. How would most traditionally trained counselors approach each counselee? In the case of Russ, a helping professional might use Motiva- tional Interviewing, known as MI (Miller & Rollnick, 2002), and cognitive-behavioral therapy, known as CBT (Beck, 1976; Burns, 1999), and encourage 12-step recovery meetings (Carnes, 2001) to address his sexual addiction. Likely the counseling goal would be to stop compulsive sexual behavior. Russ's behavior would probably be seen as a problem because it is causing significant distress for him and those closest to him. Many traditional forms of counseling seem to use a "violation of personal standards" as the basis of determining the appropriateness or inappropriateness—or "rightness" or "wrongness"—of a behavior. In spite of the subjective basis of morality, many such programs still encourage 12-step meetings as part of the treatment plan. If so, it is possible that the counselor would embrace the value of spirituality in recovery. By participating in a 12-step program, the hope would be that Russ will connect to a higher power of his choosing to fill the spiritual vacuum of his life.

In contrast biblically grounded counselors realize that their own life needs to be Spirit-filled and that their counseling theory, model, and theology must be informed by biblical truth. A counselor whose worldview is shaped by biblical truth might also use MI (Motivational Interviewing), CBT (Cognitive-Behavior Therapy), and 12-step meetings to help Russ.[1] A biblical worldview has less impact on the counseling approach than on what is believed about how people function and what is critical to helping them. For the biblically oriented counselor the overarching therapeutic goal would be to do more than stop compulsive sexual behavior, though that would be a first priority. Ultimately the goal would be to see Russ restored and reconciled to God through Christ Jesus. The counselor would hold that Russ needs to find his identity in Jesus Christ. Whereas many sexual addiction treatment approaches advocate the incorporation of spirituality, a biblical worldview would clearly define it. Spirituality would not be subjectively determined and measured according to what "feels right" or to a "higher power of one's own choosing." Specifically spirituality would be defined according to biblical truth and the Higher Power regarded as God. Thus a biblical worldview provides focus and clarity to what constitutes true spirituality and the "higher power." Spirituality is by biblical truth, not determined by a counselee's notion.

Moreover, Russ's behavior is viewed as sinful because it conflicts with God's standards. Yet at the same time Russ's behavior would also be considered redeemable because of the unmatchless grace of God (cf. McMinn, Ruiz, Marx, Wright, & Gilbert, 2006). If MI or CBT are employed, they

---

[1] **Informed consent** would be necessary to incorporate a biblical approach to Russ's counseling. (This note is particularly critical for counselors who are Christians and work in secular settings.)

would be used to help Russ find the right motivations for change (which would include honoring Christ) and go beneath the surface of his sexual compulsiveness to issues of intimacy with God and others. If cognitive therapy is used to dispute Russ's "irrational" core beliefs, the counselor would counter faulty beliefs by Scripture.

So, a biblical worldview does not so much change the nature of the edifice. Rather, it provides clear blueprints for how the edifice should be shaped, provides definition to the appearance of the house, and direction for how the house should be used. In comparison with other worldviews a biblical worldview provides specific content to and clarity for the counselor on how counseling is to unfold.

Clearly we are making some sweeping generalizations with how both traditional and biblically grounded counseling approaches might be implemented. Our main point is not what is or is not included or how various components of the treatment plan are delivered. Rather our point is that the counselor's worldview influences many of these decisions.

## THE NUTS AND BOLTS OF A WORLDVIEW

Guides must be experts at map reading. They must know how to navigate the terrain and find the right path toward their destination. An inaccurate or poorly defined map could be disastrous, resulting in injury or death. Guides want a map they can read and one they can rely on.

Just as an expedition guide needs a map to help him arrive at a destination he has never been to before, everyone needs a map to provide direction for life. Many people go through life with no clarity of where they are going and why. The map they follow is of their own making. Few of us would ever follow a map constructed by someone who has never charted the territory. Yet that is exactly what many people do in many areas of life. They construct their own map based on what "feels" right to them; it is intangible and subjective, built in accord with their own values and beliefs.

We believe, however, that centuries ago God gave us a map, the Bible, to objectify the process and clearly mark the trail. God's Word helps us understand the terrain of life and gives us a clear picture of what life is about. Since God is the Creator of life, He knows the territory; He and He alone is in a position to lay out the map.

The map for life and for counseling is one's worldview. So our concern in this section is to delineate the nature of a worldview. A clear worldview is one in which you are both self-aware and intentional in its construction. For us an accurate worldview is one that is most compatible with the map—the Bible. When you have a worldview that is biblically based and when you are aware of how it influences your helping efforts, you have the foundational gear to guide a counselee on a healing journey. Our intent is not to limit an understanding of truth to only the Bible, however. Truth can be discovered through God's general revelation of nature (i.e., science) and through the working of the Holy Spirit. We want to spotlight, however, the Bible as the basis of truth. We begin this process by discussing the importance of a worldview.

## The Importance of a Worldview

Suppose an expedition guide chooses to "feel" his way through the wilderness rather than follow a map. A well-trained guide might be able to trust his instincts to guide his passengers to their destination. In essence the guide is actually relying on an internal map to feel his way through the wilderness. A tangible map clearly provides orientation and direction, but for a well-trained guide it might only confirm what the guide knows intuitively.

Each one of us has an internal map that consciously or unconsciously provides direction to life. Typically we do not consciously think about our map; we rely on our instincts and intuition to navigate the terrain of life. Our internal map contains the assumptions, beliefs, and principles on which we build our lives. This map reflects what philosophers and theologians refer to as "worldview." Being conscious of and understanding one's worldview is essential to making wise decisions—both personal and professional decisions. Clinically speaking counselors can harm a counselee (see chap. 3, "The Hazards of Helping") when unaware of the worldview that supports their helping efforts.

The reason one's worldview carries so much power is that it is the attempt to answer key questions about life. Where did I come from? Why am I here? What is my purpose in life? What can I know, and how do I know it? How certain can I be about life? What happens when I die? These questions are some of those answered by a person's worldview. The English word *worldview* is derived from the translation of the German word *Weltanschauung*. While that word is a mouthful if you don't speak German, it refers to the essence of living. A worldview is the essence of living because it is a life map, a means of organizing all of life.

Many philosophers, theologians, and other theorists have sought to more concretely define worldview. Nash (1992) defines it as "a set of beliefs about the most important issues in life . . . a conceptual scheme by which we consciously or unconsciously place or fit everything we believe and by which we interpret and judge reality" (p. 16). In his book *The Universe*

*Next Door,* Sire (2009) referred to it as each person's belief in what is "reality real." He defined worldview as

> a commitment, a fundamental orientation of the heart, that can be ex-
> pressed as a story or in a set of presuppositions (assumptions which
> may be true, partially true or entirely false) that we hold (consciously
> or subconsciously, consistently or inconsistently) about the basic con-
> stitution of reality, and that provides the foundation on which we live
> and move and have our being (p. 20).

Sire rightly sees worldview as rooted in the heart; he places it as the foundation on which the scaffolding of our presuppositions are built. In an
essay on worldview Olthuis (1989) provides a comprehensive definition of
a worldview, but he adds that a worldview may be so "internalized that is
goes largely unquestioned" (p. 29). Olthuis adds, "It is the integrative and
interpretative framework by which order and disorder are judged; it is the
standard by which reality is managed and pursued; it is the set of hinges on
which all our everyday thinking and doing turns" (ibid.).

A worldview is intensely practical because it is each person's theory
about the world. It is the big picture that directs daily decisions and actions (Colson & Pearcey, 1999, p. 14) because it provides an interpretive
framework to make sense of the data of life and of the world (Geisler
& Watkins, 2003). In fact it is the philosophical structure that permeates
our entire consciousness. You cannot help but perceive and interpret the
world through the lens of your worldview. Even the words of this page and
text are being filtered by your worldview. A worldview will control the
way you think, make judgments, and decide what is right and wrong. In
short it is the navigational map from which each person makes his journey
through life.

The content of one's worldview is in the form of presuppositions and
suppositions that are philosophical, psychological, and theological in nature. Presumptions are beliefs that each person presumes are true in the
absence of evidence from other sources to verify them. Inherent in the idea
of belief is the assumption that we hold reality. To phrase it another way, "I
am as certain about my belief being real as I am about the chair on which
I'm sitting."

At the core of a person's worldview is a set of beliefs about human beings, the world, and God (Bufford, 2007). These beliefs rest on what we
believe to be the truth about these core categories. For you to say that God
exists and that He loves you is to express a mental assertion of what you
believe to be true. Thus a belief is not in and of itself truth; rather a belief
is only an assumption of what is true (see Figure 1.2).

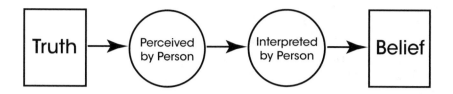

Figure 1.2: The Relationship of Truth to Belief

While we hold that there is absolute truth, no one person possesses it absolutely. We can apprehend large portions of truth, but once we ponder what is true, we begin to distort the true essence of the truth. The worldview you possess is not truth, but it contains truth. Each person's aim needs to be having as much truth as possible in order to live as effectively as possible. The more conscious and intentional we are in the formation of a worldview the more likely it will support the stress of life.

Your worldview is foundational to your life; you simply cannot exist without one. A worldview is as much a part of being human as our beating hearts; just as our heart gives life to our physical body, our worldview gives life to our nonphysical being. If you are constructing a foundation for a building, you want to know what material you need. So we provide a materials list in the next section.

## The Raw Material of a Worldview

Philosophically a worldview is constructed out of four raw materials or subject matters (see Table 1.1). The subject matters encompass broad philosophical (including psychological and theological) concepts that speak to questions central to living: (a) cosmology, which includes physics and metaphysics, (b) epistemology, (c) teleology, and (d) axiology. These philosophical terms are actually very practical. Together these subjects encompass the full spectrum of reality. Cosmology includes such issues as the origin and nature of the universe, life, and mankind. It includes such subjects as physics (i.e., the physical world) and metaphysics (i.e., what is beyond the physical world). Cosmology seeks to answer the question "Where did I come from?" Evolution and creationism have been at odds for more than a century and the debate will continue. The reason for the debate is that cosmology also raises the question, "Is there a God?" To address the question of our origin, we must raise the question of the existence of a God.

Table 1.1

*Four Components of a Worldview*

| Worldview Component | Focus | Key Questions |
|---|---|---|
| Cosmology | Totality of Reality; Physical and Nonphysical Reality | • Where did I come from?<br>• Is there a God? |
| Teleology | • Purpose<br>• Meaning | • Why am I here?<br>• Where am I going? |
| Epistemology | • Knowledge<br>• Truth | • What can I know for sure?<br>• How can I know it? |
| Axiology | • Morality<br>• Values | • Why do I do what I do?<br>• How do I live? |

Teleology refers to the beliefs about meaning and purpose of the universe. Obviously, this philosophical concept addresses the question, "Why am I here?" The origin of mankind (cosmology) sets the stage for questioning "Why are we here?" Whereas the first question asks about the basis of our existence, the second question asks about the purpose and meaning of our existence. In addition to attempting to understand why we are here, teleology also raises the question, "Where are we going?" Knowing our purpose naturally leads us to question our destiny.

Epistemology is concerned with the study of the nature, sources, and limitations of knowledge. It asks the fundamental question, "How do you know what you know?" Epistemology deals with the philosophical side of knowledge; that is, how do you know whether something is true or not. It speaks to the question, "What can I know for sure?" Even that question cannot be asked without considering whether there is an answer or not. So if you are to know anything, how do you go about knowing it? Philosophers have held to one of two views on epistemology: empiricism and rationalism. Empiricism claims that sense experience is the ultimate source of all knowledge. In contrast, rationalism contends that reason is another means by which to gain knowledge. Empiricism is the basis of the scientific method. A third epistemological view claims knowledge can be obtained through revelation as well as through experience and reason.

Axiology deals with how we should live. It includes issues of right and wrong, morality, and ethics. Axiology addresses the questions, "Why do I do what I do?" and "How should I live?" Specifically axiology asks if moral laws that govern the universe exist. "How do I know what is right and wrong?" "How are human problems understood?" Think of all the issues in our world today that hang on the question of whether it is right or wrong, such as abortion, euthanasia, capital punishment, homosexuality, sex outside of marriage, to name a few hot topics. All those issues find their way into the counselor's office. Traditional theorists believe that a counselor should not impose his values on a counselee, and we agree. But while imposing one's values is inappropriate, the influence of a counselor's values is inevitable. One simply cannot be value-neutral. Many theorists take the nonimposition principle further by arguing that the counselee must decide for herself whether it is right. Based on our view of epistemology and axiology, we do not believe a person's moral judgment is the best standard for deciding what is right in moral issues. No one ever says that a person needs to decide if raping another is right for himself; that would be absurd. Hurting another person is wrong. But how do people arrive at that belief that it is wrong to do something if it harms another? The question of what is the standard of morality brings us to the center of axiology.

Cosmology, teleology, epistemology, and axiology are the four raw materials that comprise the foundational walls of your helping house. Each of these subject matters identifies operating systems that are highly interdependent and interactive with one another. Much as a foundation needs to be tied together, so must the components of a worldview relate. Every worldview—whether naturalism, postmodernism, Buddhism, materialism, biblical Christianity, or some other worldview—attempts to give answers to those four major questions: "Where did I come from?" "Why am I here/where am I going?" "What can I know for sure?" "Why do I do what I do/how do I live?"

The importance of realizing the scope and depth of a worldview is to highlight how central it is in how you and your counselee see the world and life. A key question levied about a person's worldview, especially when it is a biblical worldview, is whether anyone can possibly know if it is accurate or true (i.e., epistemology). We will address that in the next section.

Each person's internal map is shaped by a number of life experiences, all of which are relative and subjective sources of "truth." A tangible map does exist to form and shape our internal map with absolute truth; that map is the Bible. The psalmist wrote, "Your word is a lamp to my feet and a light for my path" (119:105, NIV). God's Word provides truth for our worldview. If a person views the Bible as life's tangible map, she can build her life on truth rather than distortions and lies. We will come back to this point later.

## The Accuracy of a Worldview

When using a map to find a destination, we make the assumption that the creators of the map accurately depicted the territory. Many have had the experience of following their GPS to find a particular location only to realize that it did not get them to where they wanted to be. They accurately followed the promptings of the woman's voice on the GPS, but something was awry in the programming that unwittingly led them to the wrong place. Much as a poorly constructed map or impoverished GPS will not get you where you want to go, a poorly constructed worldview will lead you in places you do not want to go and will prevent you from getting places where you need to be.

The question is not if you have a worldview, but what is the quality of its content? The content of your worldview will determine the way you counsel. Thus distorted content in your worldview will lead to inconsistent and incoherent helping. Just as poor material in concrete will weaken a structure, nontruth in a worldview will weaken the way you live and the way you counsel. The key question then is how accurate is the substance of your worldview?

As mentioned earlier, no one can be 100 percent accurate; our worldviews have distortions of the truth, they omit some truths, and they have outright lies in them. No worldview is completely true, and yet no worldview is completely inaccurate either. Nuggets of truth and lies abound in everyone. Virtually all writers convey truth; how much truth is the key question. Truth does not require that it comes from the Bible or Christian writers. One of my (John's) apologetics professors said, "Truth is truth, no matter who perceives it" (Dr. Gary Habermas, personal communication, April 15, 1984). Though many people do not like to consider the possibility that they might be wrong, a wise person asks, "How accurate is my worldview?" The bottom line is whether your worldview is grounded in truth. The more our worldviews align with absolute truth, the better off we will be.

The issue of determining the accuracy of our worldview raises two important challenges. One significant challenge is honestly exploring, examining, and questioning your assumptions and presuppositions to determine their accuracy. To accomplish the first challenge you must rise to the second challenge. You cannot determine if your worldview is accurate unless you have a valid and reliable measure of truth. It will not matter how much time you devote to self-examination if you are using falsehoods as your measure. You simply cannot gauge the accuracy of your worldview without an exact measure or standard; that is, without a true and reliable measuring device. Thus a standard of truth that will most accurately measure your worldview needs to be intentionally pursued and chosen.

The challenge of examining one's worldview naturally leads to two central worldview questions: "Does a true measure of truth exist?" "If so, where can I find it?" From our point of view the most important issue in worldview is the standard by which truth is measured. Broadly speaking one of three standards is used to determine the accuracy of one's worldview. For many people, *self* is used as the standard of truth. If something feels right or seems true to self then it is deemed true and right. Yet self as a measure is subjective because each person decides for himself what is truth. This is known as relativism.

Another standard is *society*, which could be referred to as "the court of public opinion." The populace decides what truth is, thus what is common (the norm) is the determining factor. What is true is determined by others more than by oneself. Truth, then, is relative. Truth is determined by commonly held beliefs, though each person's individual "truth" may differ. In both the self as standard and society as standard, truth does not exist so much in reality as it exists in one's subjective mind.

A third standard for truth is a *religious source*. Some would advocate that Buddha, Confucius, Islam's Qur'an, or the Bible is the basis of truth. In contrast to self and society as standards of truth, this measure is objective because the source does not change nor is it capricious. A Christian worldview uses Scripture as a reference for truth claims (Bufford, 2007). It is our contention that the Bible stands apart from all other religious sources.[2] We believe that the Bible is the true source of truth because God exists (presupposition 1) and has revealed absolute truth in the form of Scripture (presuppositions 2 and 3). From this we will examine the presuppositions of what constitutes the content of a biblical worldview.

### The existence of God (presupposition 1).

Cosmology and metaphysics raise the question of whether God exists. All worldviews include beliefs about the existence of a god or God. Worldviews deal with the questions, Does God exist? What is the nature of God? Some worldviews question whether God exists and if He does what is He like, how can we know Him, and what does He want from us? In contrast with an atheistic worldview, which denies the existence of God, a biblical worldview affirms the existence of a creator God. Viktor Frankl (1959),

---

[2] An apologetic for the inerrancy of Scripture is beyond the scope of this book. Students are encouraged to read the following: N. L. Geisler (1980), *Inerrancy* (Grand Rapids, MI: Zondervan) and R. P. Lightner (1997), *A Biblical Case for Total Inerrancy: How Jesus Viewed the Old Testament* (Kregel Academic & Professional).

world-renowned psychiatrist and survivor of Auschwitz and three Nazi death camps, believed awareness of God, whether conscious or unconscious, is universal.

| Table 1.2 |
| --- |
| *Biblical Worldview Presuppositions* |
| |
| Presupposition 5: Fallen Creation |
| Presupposition 4: Biblically Based Anthropology |
| Presupposition 3: Existence of Revelation |
| Presupposition 2: Existence of Absolute Truth |
| Presupposition 1: Existence of God |

A biblical worldview assumes, at the most basic level that (a) God exists, (b) God is eternal, (c) God is immutable, (d) God is sovereign, (e) God is creator, (f) God is immanent, and (g) God is relational. We have formed seven key aspects of God's nature into an acrostic **CREATES** (see Table 1.3) to help you remember the points.

| Table 1.3 |
| --- |
| |
| **C** = **Creator** of everything |
| **R** = **Relational** in the Godhead |
| **E** = **Eternal**, without beginning and end |
| **A** = **Abiding** because He is immutable |
| **T** = **Transcendent** because He is outside and above all that is |
| **E** = **Ever-present** because He is immanent |
| **S** = **Sovereign** ruler of all |

First, God is **Creator** ("C") (Ps 19:1; Acts 17:26). God created everything ex nihilo, that is, out of nothing. He literally spoke the world into existence (Gen 1:3,6,9,14,20,24,26). According to Scripture, God affirmed the goodness of physical reality (Gen 1:31). Because God designed the world with natural order, there is regularity and the ability to learn about it from science. The belief that God is Creator intricately and intimately ties Him into His creation. From this belief proceed meaning and purpose.

God is a **Relational** ("R") Being who created mankind (see presupposition 4) to be in relationship with Himself and with others. God consists of three distinct persons (Father, Son, and Holy Spirit), while being one indivisible God (Gen 1:26–27; Matt 28:18–19). God is a social Trinity who enters into relationship with His creation, humanity. In fact Jesus is referred to as "God with us" (Isa 7:14; Matt 1:23). God is a dynamic living entity whose sovereignty does not mitigate His sociability toward His creation. As such, He is the God of love (Rom 5:8; 1 John 4:8–10).

Next, God is **Eternal** ("E"). First, God exists; He is eternal and infinite. Nothing is more central to a worldview than the existence of God. God is transcendent and His presence is everywhere (Jer 23:24). In every level of reality He exists fully and completely. His existence is such that He cannot be comprehended by human concepts and ideas (Erickson, 2001). God has no beginning and no end. He has not evolved; He has always existed. He is the "I am that I am" (Exod 3:14). God is self-existent and eternal.

God also is **Abiding** ("A"). God does not change; He is immutable (Mal 3:6). As James 1:17 says, there is no variableness with God. Simply put, God cannot grow, improve, or become better or worse.

The next two characteristics of God deal with His relationship with His creation. First, God is **Transcendent** ("T"), that is, He is above and beyond everything including the world (2 Chr 2:6; Pss 97:9; 18:5; 139:7–12; Isa 66:1; Jer 23:24; Eph 4:6; Heb 4:13). The belief in God's transcendence separates a biblical worldview from a number of other worldviews, such as pantheism. "Transcendent" means that God is not the world; He is beyond it. The prophet Isaiah said, "'For my thoughts are not your thoughts, neither are your ways my ways,' declares the LORD. 'As the heavens are higher than the earth, so are my ways higher than your ways and my thoughts than your thoughts'" (Isa 55:8–9, NIV). God is limitless in time, power, and energy. He is able to do all things (Ps 115:3; Matt 19:26; Luke 1:37).

God is also **Ever-present** ("E"), that is, He possesses what theologians refer to as immanence, which means that God is present and active in creation. He is at work in and through natural processes (Erickson, 2001). Immanence literally means, "to be within" or "near" in relation to God's standard (Geisler & Watkins, 2003). God exists in creation as the Sustainer of the universe (Job 33:4; Ps 65:9–13; Col 1:17), and He is always present with His creation (Jer 23:23–24; Luke 17:20–21; Col 1:27; 1 John 5:11–12), though He is not part of it (pantheism) and is distinct from it. To hold to God's transcendence and deny His immanence is to arrive at deism, but to affirm his immanence and deny His transcendence is to advocate pantheism, both of which are wrong (Erickson, 2001; Geisler & Watkins, 2003).

God is **Sovereign** ("S") (Isa 6:1–5; 55:8–9). The universe, and in fact all that is, is governed by God's laws, which ensure balance, harmony, and unity (e.g., physics, metaphysics, and cosmology). Specifically a biblical worldview asserts that God created all that exists, is sovereign over all (Gen 1–2; 1 Tim 4:4–5), and that He exists outside and above it all. Moreover, as the sovereign God He is one but the one and only God. Moses proclaimed, "Hear, O Israel: the LORD our God is one LORD" (Deut 6:4, KJV). As Sire (2009) writes, "So God is the one prime existent, the one prime reality and . . . the one source of all other reality" (p. 28).

When we seek to understand the nature and scope of God, we do so from a finite perspective. Getting a sense of the character of God is essential to developing an accurate understanding of humanity. A belief in the existence of God relates to counseling skills and techniques in and through the person of the counselor. The existence of God affects the helping relationship in ways that mirror the relationship of the counselor to the counselee and in the reality that God exists for both the counselor and the counselee. For instance just as God exists outside our system—as well as existing within—so too the counselor exists outside of the counselee's world.

### The existence of absolute truth (presupposition 2).

Philosophers have long pondered whether knowledge about the world and of things of the world is possible. As noted earlier, epistemology deals with questions about the nature, scope, and limits of knowledge and truth. Can one know anything? Does truth exist? If so, is truth absolute or relative? What are the proper roles of reason and sense experience in knowing? The answers to these questions are critical to the formation of a worldview.

A biblical worldview assumes that absolute truth exists and that it is independent of one's denial or affirmation of it. In fact truth is the cornerstone of a biblically based worldview (John 14:6). Moreover, a biblical worldview asserts that God is the author of all truth (Ps. 31:5b; John 14:6; 16:13; 17:3,17; 1 John 5:20). In contrast to God, the author and epitome of truth, Satan is the father of lies. Since God is the author of all things and since He cannot change, then truth is immutable as well (cf. Mal 3:6; Rom 11:36).

From a biblical worldview perspective, reason, revelation, and scientific method all play a valid role in the search for truth, allotting a congruence between Scripture and psychology (Carter & Narramore, 1979; Entwistle, 2004a). This being the case, then all truth is objective, absolute, and "knowable" in both creation and in the Word of God. In short "all truth is God's truth." The law of gravity is God's truth just as is the reality that we are born sinners. Because of the unity of truth and the fact that truth exists in multiple places, there are a number of means to which to come to truth. Clearly the Bible speaks to issues that one cannot find by other means. Only through the Bible can one come to understand how much God loves the world.

Closely connected to the question of truth are questions related to morality. Do moral laws exist, and if so on what basis do they exist? Is morality relative or is it universal? These are questions related to axiology and are generally associated with the issue of truth. The Bible directly speaks to issues of morality. Defining what is sin and providing clarity to what is right and wrong are clearly communicated in God's Word.

The presupposition of absolute truth and moral law rivals postmodern relativism. Groothuis (2000) contends that postmodernism disregards the existence of a discoverable truth. Truth equates to what one believes (relativism) or to what works (pragmatism). However, for one to know anything, truth must exist and truth must be stable. Truth is not a byproduct of perception; it exists in reality. For example since science is about the pursuit and discovery of knowledge, it assumes that there are objective truths in the world that can be discovered and proven. If absolute truth does not exist, it would be impossible to do science.

The belief in the existence of absolute truth strongly connects with the use of counseling skills and techniques. Professional counselors talk about the importance of doing evidence-based treatments (Leong, 2008; Woody, Detweiler-Bedell, Teachman, & O'Hearn, 2004). Wise counselors employ those approaches and techniques that research has indicated produce the best results. When mainstream counselors seek to build their approach on evidence-based treatments, they are advocating that counselors employ strategies that are based on "truth." The rationale is that one should use only techniques that have proved to be effective through scientific inquiry. In a world that questions truth, being urged to adhere to research findings is interesting. For Christians, the idea that strategies should be built on truth is not a foreign concept. Christians committed to honoring God's Word realize that while evidence-based treatments are worthy of being utilized, philosophical underpinnings of one's entire approach should also be evidence-based, that is, based on truth.

Christian counselors must not only deliberate about the types of approaches and techniques they use in light of the research; they should also note how those approaches and techniques mesh with a biblical worldview. In our view nothing is more important than establishing a scaffolding of evidence-based truth from God's Word. While apologetics can demonstrate through reason that the Bible is true, that is not within the scope of this project. We simply make the supposition that the Bible is true, that truth can be known, and that truth culled from the Scriptures is relevant to the way we counsel.

### The existence of revelation (presupposition 3).

Entwistle (2004a) observed that truth is revealed in two "books": "God's truths are revealed in the book of God's word (scripture) and the book of God's work (creation)" (p. 229). From the book of God's Word two broad truths are evident: God spoke and God created. The epistemology of a biblical worldview begins with the presupposition that the Scriptures are inspired, inerrant, and authoritative (cf. John 17:17; 2 Tim 3:16–17). Being guided by the Holy Spirit, the authors penned the original manuscripts; thus the Bible perfectly records God's heart in each word (cf. 2 Pet 1:20–22). Therefore the Bible is one's final authority. For counselors, it is the standard against which all philosophies and techniques are measured (Shields & Bredfeldt, 2001).

Also God's Word is instructive on matters that pertain to life, and His Word is foundational to our growth (2 Tim 3:16–17). Extrapolating from this truth, Adams (1986) claims that 2 Tim 3:16–17 teaches that the Bible is all-sufficient, thus making psychology unnecessary. Commenting on this claim Jones and Butman (1991) assert that 2 Tim 3:16–17 simply teaches that Scripture is useful or profitable for teaching, rebuking, correcting, and training in righteousness. Although the Bible is inspired and instructional, it is not "all-sufficient" as the only source of truth (Entwistle, 2004a). It is God who is all-sufficient (Jones & Butman, 1991). One should not confuse the God who spoke the Word with the spoken word. To what the Scriptures speak to we should hold as authoritative and true; but we should not make the Bible speak to things it does not address. Yet as written revelation it is the platform of truth. In sum, the Bible is the epistemological base for all worldview components. Since the Bible is the base for our worldview, it is sufficient.

The second "book" or basis of epistemology is creation (Entwistle, 2004a). God's creation is a natural form of revelation; it reveals His design of the universe. Physical laws exist because an intelligent God customized a universe that reflects divine order. There is predictability in the world because God ordered it; thus science is possible because we do not live in a random or chaotic world.

Yet, we must recognize that the Scriptures, science, and illumination are filtered through human perception and interpretation, which are highly fallible processes. While absolute truth exists, no one holds it absolutely! We must validate our perceptions of truth rather than arrogantly asserting that we possess it.

In applying this to the helping profession it is important to consider whether a counseling issue, goal, or technique has any connection with biblical truth. Shields and Bredfeldt (2001) recommend that the counselor evaluate everything as to whether it is directly supported by and theologically consistent with Scripture. Does the Bible directly address the concept or issue? Is there a direct or doubtable conflict with Scripture? The Christian counselor must follow biblical directives if God is to intervene in counselee situations.

Goals are but one significant aspect of the change process that has biblical relevance; they deal with the direction of change (Adams, 1986). Does what the counselor seeks to help the counselee do mesh with biblical principles? Does the counselee's desired outcome seek symptom relief or transformation? We will discuss goals in more detail in chap. 9 ("Managing the Counseling Session").

Unlike goals, techniques are often biblically neutral. Techniques typically neither clash nor confirm biblical truth. For example the techniques of attending, paraphrasing, reflective listening, and empty chair are but a few of the helping strategies that are biblically neutral. They are not drawn from Scripture, but neither do they move people away from God. A technique does not have to be in Scripture for it to be valid, but it cannot be in conflict with Scripture either. The purpose behind using the technique is generally far more critical than the technique itself.

### Biblically based anthropology (presupposition 4).

Without doubt a person's belief about the nature of humanity is central to his personal and professional ideology. Lewis and Demarest (1996) hold that one's beliefs on the nature of mankind influences inquiries regarding the origin of the soul and whether mankind is inherently good or evil. This presupposition is so critical that we will flesh it out in four tenets.

*Anthropological tenet 1: The origin of mankind.* The two competing worldviews on the issue of mankind's origin are evolution and creation. In contrast to the widespread evolutionary paradigm, Scripture reveals that mankind was created in the image of God.

The foundation of an anthropology is that mankind is made in God's image, the imago Dei (Gen 1:26–28; 2:7; 9:6; Job 34:14–15; Eccl 12:7; Col 3:10). God Himself formed mankind out of the dust of the earth and breathed into his nostrils, making him a living soul. Lints (1993) states,

"The imago Dei provides a theological bridge between peoples of apparently different cultures and times, even different places in redemptive history" (p. 313). Being created in God's image forms a bond that unites human beings and reflects their uniqueness in creation.

*Anthropological tenet 2: The nature of mankind.* The psalmist wrote, "What is man that you are mindful of him, the son of man that you care for him?" (Ps 8:4, NIV). Understanding the nature of humanity as being created in God's image is no small task. We are beautifully and wonderfully made, yet complex.

Eight corollaries stem from our being made in God's image. First, because we are created beings, life is sacred. Every counselee who walks in your office bears God's image, and as such reflects His glory. You are not treating a diagnosis; rather you are helping a God-image bearer.

Second, being created in the image of God is the basis of human dignity (Gen 9:6). One reason we seek to do no harm and benefit our counselees is that each person is an image-bearer. If a person were to defame a statute of a king, it would be as if he had defamed the king himself. Likewise when we harm an image-bearer, we are marring God as He is represented in human form.

Third, because of our creation in God's image, each human being has inherent value. The psalmist said that we are made slightly lower than the heavenly beings (Ps 8:5, NIV). In fact being made in God's image is what gives us value. If we are only the byproduct of evolution, we have no value other than what one deems you have. A biblical worldview acknowledges that human value is rooted in our design and our Designer. You will encounter counselees whose problems you will find appalling. Yet even those counselees have inherent value because they bear God's image. Behavior and motivations can be deplorable, but each person's essence has immeasurable value.

Fourth, because we are made in God's image we are spiritual beings whose hearts are dead without Christ. Each person's heart has been formed by his experiences and choices he has made. How a person interprets reality, reacts to situations, and behaves ultimately flows out of the heart. Paul wrote, "Do not conform any longer to the pattern of this world, but be transformed by the renewing of your mind" (Rom 12:2, NIV). Transformation of the heart is man's most basic need.

Further just as God is relational, so are we. A biblical worldview that is rooted in creation includes a belief that we are relational beings. Thus because we bear God's image, each person has an inherent need to be in relationship. Out of perfect community with one another, the Godhead (God the Father, God the Son, and God the Holy Spirit) created the human race also to live together in community. Therefore God invites people to be part of divine and human relationships (Icenogle, 1994). The Bible illustrates this reality in the creation account. Following the forming of Adam, God said, "It is not good for the man to be alone. I will make a helper suitable for him" (Gen 2:18, NIV). People are wounded in relationships, and they need to be healed in relationships with their fellowman and with God. You are a representative of God to your counselees, and your ability to establish a helping relationship with them will determine your effectiveness (see chap. 5, "Basic Skills: Creating a Connection").

Sixth, being created in God's image is the basis of our meaning. Because we are made by God and for God's good pleasure, we have inherent meaning. Frankl (1959) noted that much of modern neurosis, discontent, and anxiety can be attributed to the will to find meaning. He believed that meaning could be found in every moment of living. Though Frankl discussed three means of finding meaning, he did not speak to the fact that meaning derives from the fact that we are made by our Creator. Our meaning flows from Him and through Him. The human race is not the result of a random act of nature. Rather we are the masterpiece of a loving Creator who fashioned us according to His divine plan. Only through a relationship with God can mankind find true meaning and purpose. This is not meaning or purpose in the existential sense (cf. Bugental, 1965; Yalom, 1980), that is, relativistic and subjectively self-derived, but rather an objectively based meaning and purpose derived as a result of being in relationship with God. Warren (2002) states that the Creator Himself reveals our purpose. As Solomon noted, "Life in the world has significance only when man remembers his Creator" (cf. Eccl 12:1, NIV). From a biblical teleological point of view, the meaning of human existence cannot be established without a reference point outside of man. God gives meaning to His creation; without God mankind can only look to self for meaning and purpose. Without God's true meaning and purpose, mankind is enslaved to a void that he cannot fill. Only God can fill the void and provide meaning in place of meaningless. Thus the first point of a biblical anthropology is that human beings are created in God's image and so they have inherent meaning.

Seventh, being created in God's image includes the gift of free choice. Into the fabric of human existence is woven the principle of free choice tied to responsibility. Evil, and the resulting pain and suffering, became a part of human existence when man chose to exchange the truth of God for a lie, worshipping the creature or creation instead of the Creator (Rom 1). To have true free will man must possess the faculties to enable him to choose between good and evil. Though mankind is capable of choosing since the Fall, the curse of sin produces wrong motivations and choices. We are wholly unable to do what is pleasing to God. We are no longer capable of distinguishing good from evil in that the former has become corrupted and the latter predominates. The Fall has so blinded us that we prefer evil, though few of us would constitute what we are doing as such. The problem is not an inability to exercise our wills, but a total inability to will good (i.e., holy volition). Human choices are made as expressions of the heart. The distressing situations people are in flow out of their choices or those of others. Willard (2002) expresses it well when he says, "The spiritual place within us from which outlook, choices, and actions come has been formed by a world away from God. Now it must be transformed" (p. 14).

Eighth, the image of God that everyone bears is a distorted and twisted image; man is inherently sinful (Gen 3). For that reason Francis Schaeffer called us "glorious ruins" (cited in Winter, 2008). Through Adam and Eve's choice to rebel against God's authority (see Gen 3), the human heart of everyone is infected with this rebellious malady of distrusting God, manifested in disobedience to his laws (i.e., sin). Whereas God's creation was good (Gen 1–2), man's "creation" was sin (Gen 3).

Sin is both a trait and a state. "Trait sin" is our sin nature; we are inherently sinful and born spiritually dead (cf. Rom 6–8). Every aspect of humanity is fallen, that is, each part of our soul is corrupt. Sin is fused into our genetics. As a result our physiology, cognitions, emotions, and actions are distorted in ways that are peculiar to themselves, yet without destroying our imageness. Sin has physical, cognitive, emotional, social, and spiritual consequences, and at times these consequences are particularly severe (Rom 1:18–19). Through life, each one becomes more damaged by sin so that each one may be more or less maladaptive or dysfunctional. From our infancy we engage in sinful choices, a manifestation of "State sin," that is, the experience of sinning. State sin speaks to the act and acts of sinning.[3] Sinful acts include such behaviors and inner states as lying and the desire to deceive, adultery and lust, stealing and envy or greed, murder and hate, to name a few. A biblical worldview first puts the emphasis on the trait of sin, dealing with a person's spiritual deadness and separation from God. Then the acts of sin or being in a state of sinning are addressed.

---

[3] McMinn, Ruiz, Marx, Wright, and Gilbert (2006) use the term "state sin" to describe the human condition of sin (our trait sin) and "act sin" (our state sin) to describe the act of sinning.

*Anthropological tenet 3:* The need of mankind. One of the most significant anthropological tenets of a biblical worldview is the fact that God has provided a remedy for mankind's trait sin and state sin. Following man's birthing of sin that corrupted and damned himself and creation, God initiated a plan of redemption to (a) provide a fulfillment of God's purposes for relationship with His creation (Lints, 1993) and (b) to reconcile mankind back to Himself. Sin caused separation from God, but redemption brings us back into a relationship with Him. Just as sin entered into the world by one man, restoration and righteousness are also by one man, Jesus Christ (Rom 5:12). Motivated by His great love for His creatures, God made it possible for man to again be in relationship with Him. "For God so loved the world that he gave his one and only son, that whoever believes in him shall not perish but have eternal life" (John 3:16, NIV). As a demonstration of God's unfathomable grace, Christ became that one man who offered Himself as the perfect sacrifice to redeem fallen mankind. Because of Christ's death and resurrection He can offer redemption to mankind, but salvation is applied only to those who place their trust in Him (Rom 3:25; 5:10,18; Col 1:20–22; Heb 9:26–28; 1 Pet 1:3).

Redemption saves mankind from the consequences of the Fall, but it also imparts the capacity to live a spiritual and abundant life (John 10:10). God has a twofold purpose in redemption: to relieve the believer of the burden and weight of sin and to compel him toward a fuller life.

Reconciliation with God has a powerful connection with reconciliation between people (Icenogle, 1994). Through faith in Jesus Christ we can be in relationship with God, and begin to enjoy the balance, harmony, and unity the life of a disciple cultivates. "Thereafter, faith is a keeping open of the soul, so that Christ can come in with the blessing and take possession and fill all. Accordingly, faith becomes the most fervent and unbroken communion betwixt the soul in which Christ obtains His place and Christ Himself, who by the silent, effectual blessing of the Spirit is enthroned in the heart " (Murray, 1984, p. 88). The counseling relationship provides an ideal place for such cultivation of communion to take place.

As McMinn (1996) wrote, "Understanding sin gives meaning to redemption" (p. 266). Also the converse is true; understanding redemption gives meaning to sin. No matter how maladjusted, wounded, lost, or evil your counselees seem, they are redeemable. We are capable of any sin under the "right" circumstances, but also nothing is beyond the penetrating power of God's redemptive grace; He specializes in the impossible (Luke 1:37). The final authority is neither psychology nor theology but Christ Himself. The integration of theology and psychology is analogous to the operation of the body of Christ in that both are vital and necessary members of that body, independent yet dependent on one another, but in subjection to the head of the body, who is Christ (1 Cor 11:3).

Jesus was not interested in bringing about change in humanity through social institutions or other outer forms of man's existence. Instead, He sought to bring about change from the inside out. He focused on changing people's ideas, beliefs, feelings, habits of choice, and distortions of reality and truth. In our thoughts God first begins to unlock the truths of Christ's words by the work of the Holy Spirit, providing the basis for choosing to become more closely realigned with God and his ways (Willard, 2002). By God's grace and good will we are able to be freed from our enslavement to sin and its consequences, as well as the confines of the flesh.

The Bible is filled with promises for those who place their hope in God (Pss 31:24; 71:5). The Scriptures place a great emphasis on the importance of hope for human coping. Perhaps one of the most powerful verses that reflect the mind of God in relation to this matter is Jer 29:11, "'For I know the plans I have for you,' declares the LORD, 'plans to prosper you and not to harm you, plans to give you hope and a future'" (NIV).

*Anthropological tenet 4: The motivation of mankind.* The basic motivation for the nonbeliever is the desire to search after the truth (Rom 1:16–20). This existential vacuum is God-shaped. For the believer the motivation is to become holy (cf. Lev 19:2; Gal 2:20; Eph 1:3–4); and this requires self-denial (Gal 2:20–21; Eph 4:20–24). Self-denial properly aligns us with God, and it also gives us the proper attitude toward others. We are to view others as image-bearers of God. Self-denial toward God is expressed by commitment to His will. Such commitment properly understood and acted on helps us bear adversity, knowing it is God at work in our lives doing what is good for us according to His good intention and kind will (Phil 2:12–13).

Biblical anthropology has implications for counseling in general and for the use of skills and techniques in particular. First, these tenets illuminate the nature of the counselor-counselee relationship. Because we are created in God's image, we engage in an incarnational relationship with our counselees. And because spirituality emanates from God, each counselee encounter is a spiritual one. Each counselee who walks into your office came of his own free will. A counselee might say that he was coerced into counseling, but he chose to come to avoid more adverse consequences. Your responsibility as counselor is not to get the counselee to do what is right; the counselee must decide what he will do. Effective counselors know how to interact with counselees so they can tip the balance in favor of what seems to be the wisest or most prudent decision. Do not attempt to make decisions for any counselee; this violates this aspect of mankind's creation. Your use of skills and techniques must be employed in ways that respect the freedom of the counselee. Coercion by a counselor is uncalled for.

Many counseling theorists warn against the counselor using influence to coerce counselees to do what the counselor thinks best (Ivey & Ivey, 2003; Miller & Rollnick, 2002; Young, 2010). In fact when incorporating spiritual interventions (see chap. 14, "Spiritual Strategies"), you must be ethically responsible by being aware of your own emotions, opinions, attitudes, values, beliefs, and behavior; avoiding countertransference and the development of a dual relationship (AACC 2004 [see Appendix B]; Richards & Bergins, 2005).

Counselees bring their brokenness into your office. You will work with people who have made sinful choices and/or who have been wounded by other people's sinful choices. Your counseling skills and techniques must account for people's brokenness, defenses, self-protection, insecurities, vulnerabilities, and limitations. Much as Adam and Eve's sin led them into hiding and blaming, counselees will require skillful questions in a safe environment to come out from behind their defensive and self-protective "fig leaves." Getting to the truth and root of a problem is not an easy task. Counselees will distort, delete relevant information, and overgeneralize.

In a spirit of love and acceptance, recognize the impact that both trait sin and state sin have on a person spiritually, mentally, emotionally, and physically. McMinn and Campbell (2007) define sin as disobedience that warps one's personal identity, needs, wants, and relationships. People often experience turmoil when they recognize that what they desire is inconsistent with God's truth and with what is right. Jones and Butman (1991) refer to this experience as compound and conflicting motivations.

The counselor must model what a redemptive relationship with Christ is like (McMinn, 1996). Thoughtfully integrating a biblical worldview and sound psychological principles is necessary because people who seek counseling suffer in meaningful ways and need to be cared for as persons; not just treated as a set of symptoms (Sperry & Shafranske, 2005). Through experiencing the counselor's love, grace, and mercy and being related to as a person, the counselee gets a sense what it is like to be rightly related to Christ. Each counselee must be approached with grace. The counseling relationship can help draw the counselee into an experience of grace, thereby paving the way for self-reflection, confession, and repentance. This encourages the counselee to recognize his or her need for God's deliverance (McMinn, 1996).

### A fallen creation (presupposition 5).

The Scriptures not only elaborate on the problem and hope for mankind; they also address the fact that the world is fallen. Biblical truth communicates the fact that creation has been corrupted. Because of sin, humans, God's image-bearers, are corrupted and so is His entire creation (Eccl 1:15; Rom 1:18–32; 8:20–22). Because of the sin of disobedience, an antagonistic relationship commenced between mankind and his environment. Rather than being the benevolent steward of creation, people tend to further disturb his environment even as the environment extends its own corruption to man.

Because the physical world is fallen, science will never be the perfect means of knowing truth or knowing God. Pain, suffering, and stress will be constant companions to mankind's existence. What is broken in this world cannot be repaired through human agency. God is sovereign over His creation and will one day restore it (Exod 15:18; Deut 32:39; 1 Chr 29:11–12; Job 9:12; 12:10; Pss 22:28; 33:11; 115:3; 135:6; Rev 19:16).

The presuppositions that we have presented reveal that mankind's basic problem and dilemma is a spiritual one. Thus psychological strategies and interventions alone are in a sense treating the symptoms of the problem rather than the problem itself. Of course counseling can bring relief and can support counselees in meeting their temporal goals, but without a spiritual perspective, it is relativistic and devoid of spiritual depth. Psychology alone can only bring temporary and transient relief and may tend merely to supplant symptoms. Without the implementation of a biblical worldview that addresses the totality of mankind's issues, counseling efforts are merely palliative. Failing to integrate biblical truth into a psychological understanding of humanity and into the counseling approach leaves the doors open wide to an erroneous understanding of man and to erroneous approaches, concepts, and treatments in counseling.

Your worldview is the meaningful "center" to what you will do in your counseling. For example, your worldview will influence the target or purpose of counseling. What you believe is your purpose as a professional helper will dramatically shape how you work with counselees. Counseling skills and techniques are nothing more than the arrows you use to hit the target you have identified. If your target is off, your choice of techniques will ultimately prove ineffective. And, if you have the right target in sight but you choose the wrong arrow, your purpose will not be met.

## Summary

The most important foundation for counseling is the counselor's worldview and the counselee's worldview. The counselor and counselee each brings a personal worldview into the helping relationship (see Table 1.4). The counselor's worldview consciously or unconsciously informs the counselor on how to counsel. The counselee's worldview influences life goals, suffering, therapeutic goals, and more. At times the worldviews of the counselor and counselee match famously. Far too often, however, there is a mismatch between the two.

In addition to the level of congruence between the counselor and the counselee's worldviews is the level of congruence between the counselor's worldview and the map—the Bible (see figure 1.3). Because we believe the Bible is truth, whether it is explicitly evident in the session or implicitly present as a backdrop to the counselor's work, the foundation of the counselor's skills and techniques is strong and stable.

## THE ULTIMATE GUIDE: THE ROLE OF CHRIST IN COUNSELING

Setting a standard for Christian professional counseling, the American Association of Christian Counselors (AACC) Code of Ethics (see Appendix B) lists Jesus Christ as its first foundation: "Jesus Christ – and His revelation in both the OT and NT of the Bible – is the pre-eminent model for Christian counseling practices, ethics, and care giving activities" (p. 4).

Table 1.4

*Relationship of Worldview Components and Biblical Worldview to Helping Skills*

| Worldview Component | Biblical Worldview Content | Relationship to Helping Skills and Techniques |
| --- | --- | --- |
| • Cosmology | Existence of God | • Gen 1 and 2<br>• Existence of God gives provision of incarnational relationship (John 1:1–18; 15:1–5)<br>• Connects with skills and techniques in the "person of the counselor"; who is transcendent "above" the counselee, yet fully present and active |

Table 1.4 (cont.)

*Relationship of Worldview Components and Biblical Worldview to Helping Skills*

| Worldview Component | Biblical Worldview Content | Relationship to Helping Skills and Techniques |
|---|---|---|
| • Epistemology | Existence of Absolute Truth | • Truth is anchor for the soul (Heb 6:19); it exists both implicitly and explicitly in the counseling relationship<br>• Right and wrong way to engage skills and techniques (e.g., there is a knowable means of building rapport)<br>• Social justice issues with counselees |
| • Epistemology | Existence of Specific Revelation – Scripture (2 Tim 3:16–17; Heb 4:12) | • Counselor is rooted in Scripture; implicitly brought to counseling because of the nature of truth<br>• Cognitive-behavioral strategies find "rationality" in Scripture because truth exists<br>• Counselor reveals self – skill of self-disclosure |
| • Cosmology<br>• Epistemology | Existence of General Revelation – Creation (Gen 1–2) | • Benefit from social science research; empirical based findings<br>• The role of the environment in assessment |
| • Epistemology | Anthropology: Mankind Created in God's Image (Gen 1–2) | • Counseling relationship is an incarnational relationship<br>• Spiritually attached to God; counselor relates spiritually as well as socially to counselee<br>• Multiculturalism – both genders and all races derived from God |
| • Cosmology<br>• Teleology | Anthropology: Mankind Has Value (Ps 8:9) | • Treat counselee ethically (e.g., informed consent)<br>• Offer respect, seek to do no harm, accept, and love your counselees<br>• Counselees deserve being attended to through the use of attending skills<br>• The value of people sets the stage for termination skills to end counseling relationship |
| • Cosmology<br>• Teleology | Anthropology: Mankind Is a Spiritual Being | • Spirituality is added to the bio-psycho-social assessment and treatment plan<br>• Spirituality is at the heart of the person, not just a component of the person.<br>• Counseling relationship is also a spiritual relationship<br>• Techniques must address spirituality |

Table 1.4 (cont.)

*Relationship of Worldview Components and Biblical Worldview to Helping Skills*

| Worldview Component | Biblical Worldview Content | Relationship to Helping Skills and Techniques |
|---|---|---|
| Cosmology Teleology Axiology | Anthropology: Mankind Has Free Will | • Informed consent<br>• Agenda setting<br>• Collaboration<br>• Consider motivation of counselee<br>• Responsible to them, not for them<br>• The counselee has freedom to make choices; the Holy Spirit can work in them to accomplish God's will |
| Cosmology Teleology Axiology | Anthropology: Mankind Is a Relational Being | • Importance of incarnational relationship<br>• Assess social supports<br>• Assess social skills<br>• Born and formed through attachment<br>• Avoid creating dependency<br>• Intervene systematically; use social strategies |
| Cosmology Teleology Axiology | Anthropology: Mankind Is Fallen and Sinful | • Need for change<br>• A problem with evil; demonic influences and incorporation of evil into every piece of fabric of this world<br>• Bio-psycho-social-spiritual weaknesses<br>• Counselee sinfulness and flesh impact effectiveness of counseling<br>• Depraved without Christ<br>• Need accountability; basis for ethical guidelines to govern and regulate professional behavior<br>• Understand and appreciate the power of pathology<br>• Ability to self-deceive; sin / flesh create blindness to one's deficits and strengths<br>• Fear requires creating a safe haven<br>• We relate through woundedness<br>• Counselor woundedness (baggage) can hamper the counseling; have self-awareness<br>• Both the counselor and counselee can be harmed through helping; have self-awareness<br>• Counselees need supervision and consultation to examine their own hearts<br>• Goals will not typically be godly<br>• Bring truth to tension between their current state of brokenness and where they can be in Christ<br>• Employ techniques that target different domains that are affected by sin / weakness; holistic<br>• Generational context |

Table 1.4 (cont.)

*Relationship of Worldview Components and Biblical Worldview to Helping Skills*

| Worldview Component | Biblical Worldview Content | Relationship to Helping Skills and Techniques |
|---|---|---|
| Cosmology Teleology Axiology | Anthropology: Mankind Can Be Redeemed | • Vision for what counselee can become<br>• Counselor needs to have hope and be patient; trusting God to work. Luke 1:37, nothing is impossible with God<br>• Skills and techniques springboard from re-demption; help counselee find healing through the pain<br>• Goals can be structured to bring about growth, not just healing<br>• Sin and redemption create a need for confession and repentance<br>• Employ strategies that target each aspect of the fallen person in order to redeem it |
| Cosmology Teleology | Creation Is Fallen (Rom 8:22) | • Science is not perfect, thus it is not true truth<br>• Environment is corrupted; must structure therapeutic environment to optimize change<br>• Some things cannot be changed; must help counselee cope (Eccl 1:15)<br>• The counselee and counselor can be harmed through helping |

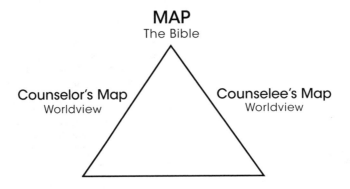

**MAP**
The Bible

**Counselor's Map**
Worldview

**Counselee's Map**
Worldview

Figure 1.3: Counselor and Counselee Worldviews
in Relationship to the Bible

The starting place for learning how to counsel is to look to the ultimate Guide, Jesus Christ. He is "the way, the truth, and the life" (John 14:6). He is life because He is God. And Jesus is the way because He is the doorway to God (John 10:7), the "ultimate Guide" to bring restoration to and connection with God.

Jesus Christ is also the truth (cf. Jer 42:5; Rev 3:7,14; 6:10). According to Bryant and Krause (1998), the word "truth" refers to the opposite of falsehood; truth is when a stated proposition matches factual reality. The opposite of this was what merely "seemed" to be a certain way, only an appearance. Appearances might change, but truth does not. Jesus Christ is the definitive and perfect Word expressing who God is; He is true, pure, and a reflection of the facts. He does not change nor is He merely an image of truth; He *is* the truth.

Jesus is also the life. He provides the ultimately longing for every heart, namely, satisfaction and contentment in life. Christ's life-giving Spirit gives life to the dead (cf. Deut 30:20; Josh 3:10; Ps 36:9; Jer 10:10; John 1:4; 5:25–29; 10:10; 11:23–26; Col 3:4; 1 John 1:1–3; 5:20).

Through Him we provide incarnational guidance to our counselees. From Christ, the living Word (John 1:1–18), we develop a worldview that becomes the basis of the way we approach life and the foundation for doing the work of counseling. From our worldview our skills and strategies are conceptualized, internalized, and energized.

## CHAPTER SUMMARY

Most people are drawn to the field of counseling to help people with their suffering. The Bible addresses the questions of the origin and meaning of the universe; provides an explanatory framework for understanding the origin of mankind, the meaning of mankind, the problem and hope for mankind, and the problem with the world. The Bible is a complete and comprehensive source of knowing how to approach life and how to work with counselees. Without doubt the Bible is a necessary component to your counseling gear. It will ground you and orient you to the ultimate Guide for your therapeutic journey.

So often counselors who are Christians enter the helping profession with multiple worldviews (consciously or unconsciously) and await the dynamics of the relationship to unfold before deciding which worldview to use as the underpinning of the counseling process (Trozer, personal communication, October 16, 2009). It is critical that you adopt a biblical worldview to guide your work.

While the Bible is a necessary element in your counseling work, the wise counselor knows how to cull from the psychological world the knowledge that will augment the helping process. This does not mean that the Bible is insufficient; it means that psychology offers specific content that informs counselors how best to intervene. Ministers develop their sermons from the Scriptures. They know how to make use of sermon helps such as commentaries, Bible dictionaries, and other resources. Most ministers, however, learned how to preach by reading homiletic books, books that help ministers know how to develop and deliver sermons. Such books teach ministers principles of persuasive speaking and even make use of learning theories. The use of such books does not negate the prominence of Scripture in the sermon; instead it augments the minister's knowledge, ability, and skills in preaching. Likewise, using counseling textbooks to prepare yourself in how to counsel does not diminish the role the Bible plays in the helping process.

The crux of the issue is that being technically proficient in the practice of helping is not sufficient nor is having techniques that have been found to be correlated with successful outcomes. Both technical proficiency and evidenced-based strategies are important, but of greater concern is the worldview from which we operate. The benefit of counseling that is biblically based is that life issues are confronted with open acknowledgment of a Creator, His values, His perspective, and His ability to redeem and restore.

## CHAPTER 1 ACTIVITIES

Directions: Prayerfully and carefully complete the following questions/activities related to the content of this chap.

1. In this chap. we learned that distorted content in our worldview can lead to inconsistent and incoherent helping. Therefore a key question we must ponder is how accurate is the substance of our worldview? As a means of exploring your worldview, define in your own words the terms cosmology, teleology, epistemology, and axiology (which are the four raw materials that comprise the foundational walls of your "helping house") and answer (about yourself) the questions related to them (depicted in the chart below).

| Worldview Component | Focus | Key Questions |
|---|---|---|
| Cosmology | Totality of Reality; Physical and Nonphysical Reality | • Where did I come from?<br>• Is there a God? |
| Teleology | • Purpose<br>• Meaning | • Why am I here?<br>• Where am I going? |
| Epistemology | • Knowledge<br>• Truth | • What can I know for sure?<br>• How can I know it? |
| Axiology | • Morality<br>• Values | • Why do I do what I do?<br>• How do I live? |

As helpers representing the Lord Jesus Christ it is our utmost responsibility to be sure our worldview aligns with biblical truth. Does yours?

2. An accurate view of God is at the heart of what we do as counselors. Use the acrostic below to define in your own words these attributes of God and then discuss how they relate to your own experience and knowledge of God:

> **C = Creator** of everything
> **R = Relational** in the Godhead
> **E = Eternal**, without beginning and end
> **A = Abiding** because He is immutable
> **T = Transcendent** because He is outside and above all that is
> **E = Ever-present** because He is immanent
> **S = Sovereign** ruler of all

How could remaining aware of these attributes of our heavenly Father influence your work as a counselor? What is your plan for abiding in Him and allowing Him to be your ultimate Guide?

3. What does the following statement mean: When mainstream counselors seek to build their approach on evidence-based treatments, they are advocating that counselors employ strategies that are based on "truth"?

4. According to this chap. what are some questions we can ask ourselves to determine if particular counseling strategies and techniques are congruent with biblical teachings?

5. Elaborate on the following statement by adding at least two more sentences to it:

"The human race is not the result of a random act of nature. Rather we are the masterpiece of a loving Creator who fashioned us according to

His divine plan. It is only through a relationship with God that mankind can find true meaning and purpose."

6. What did Francis Schaeffer mean when he referred to man as "glorious ruins"?
7. What is the difference between state sin and trait sin? As McMinn (1996) wrote, "Understanding sin gives meaning to redemption" (p. 266). What does this statement mean?
8. How can the counselor model what a "redemptive relationship with Christ" (McMinn, 1996) is?
9. Write a brief letter to your future counselees (not one you will actually send) that describes your worldview and discusses your commitment to live your life, including your work as a counselor, rooted and grounded in the Christian worldview.

## Recommended Reading

Geisler, N. L., and Watkins, W. D. (2003). *Worlds apart: A handbook on world views* (2nd ed.). Eugene, OR: Wipf & Stock.

These authors provide an evangelical overview of the prominent worldviews: deism, pantheism, panentheism, finite godism, polytheism, atheism, and theism.

Sire, J. W. (2009). *The universe next door: A basic worldview catalog.* Downers Grove, IL: InterVarsity Press.

Sire's work is an excellent resource on the worldviews: Christian theism, deism, naturalism, nihilism, existentialism, Eastern pantheistic monism, the New Age, and postmodernism. He does an excellent job in describing each worldview and comparing it with the biblical worldview.

# Chapter 2

# The Fundamentals of Helping

*"Christian counseling must be a biblical-clinical process that facilitates case-wise counselee satisfaction. It is built on the sure foundations of Scripture, dependent on the inspired leading of the Holy Spirit, and selectively using the best of helping ministry resources and the bio-psycho-social sciences"* (Clinton & Ohlschlager, 2002b, p. 51).

*"And we urge you, brothers, warn those who are idle, encourage the timid, help the weak, be patient with everyone"* (1 Thess 5:14, NIV).

## CHAPTER OBJECTIVES

» To delineate those factors that speak to the value of helping

» To discuss those factors that make helping distinct from other related concepts

» To present information that supports the effectiveness of helping

» To explain how helping is both a science and an art

» To highlight the importance of adhering to a counseling model

» To discuss how a counselor's intentions are integral to the helping process

» To discuss the value and place of techniques in the helping process

## CHAPTER OUTLINE

THE VALUE OF HELPING
    Relief from Personal Pain
    Self-Awareness
    The Facilitation of Hope
    Changing Behavior
    Making a Difficult Choice
    A Sounding Board
    Personal Support
    Enhancing Communication
    Personal Growth
    Growing Spiritually

THE DISTINCTIVENESS OF HELPING

FOUR LEVELS OF HELPING
    Counseling Is Distinct from Guidance
    Counseling Is Distinct from Discipleship
    Counseling Encompasses the Total Person
    Counseling Is Distinct from Psychotherapy

THE EFFECTIVENESS OF HELPING

THE ART OF HELPING

THE ROLE OF A COUNSELING MODEL

COUNSELOR INTENTIONS

THE ROLE OF TECHNIQUES
    Rationale for Using Techniques
    Guidelines for Using Techniques

CHAPTER SUMMARY

CHAPTER 2 ACTIVITIES

---

What is counseling? Will people make appointments to see a counselor? Does counseling work? How does a counselor try to help? These questions are a few that relate to the fundamentals of helping. Practitioners need to have a big picture of their service in order to be effective in providing that service.

In this chap. we will examine the practice of professionally coming alongside those who are in need of healing and change. The chap. focuses on the value, distinctiveness, and effectiveness of professional helping. The formulation of a general counseling model will be offered along with the identification of the role that techniques play in the helping process.

## THE VALUE OF HELPING

Finding wise counsel has always been a valued service. Since the garden of Eden, the need for help in responding to life situations has been universal. People helpers have run the gamut from tribal wise men, shamans, exorcists, priests, ministers, physicians, to professional helpers. In today's world helping is highly regulated and limited to practitioners with specialized training. Experts in the field of counseling and psychology have pointed out that the need for counselors will always exceed the supply (Albee, 1968). A survey of approximately 10,000 adults showed that one of four Americans meets criteria for psychological disorder in any given year and that slightly less than half of all the people in the United States will suffer from a psychological disorder over the course of their lifetimes (Talan, 2005).

The reason is that brokenness is everywhere. All levels of society are ravaged by the effects of sin. The mark of the Fall is ubiquitous. A fallen world interacts with and is influenced by sinful people. The more sin is experienced in the world or people, the more society seems to express its sinful side. People are struggling with the fast pace and rapid changes in our society. Individual physical, mental, and emotional health have suffered. Relationships are fragmented or broken in pieces.

Ultimately the spiritual void built into every soul is never fulfilled because people look for wholeness in all the wrong places. Clinton and Ohlschlager (2002a) capture the essence of our times in these words: "Instead of confronting problems, people, and systems, they escape into private, secret, and desperate worlds of designer drugs, pornography, sexual addiction, gambling, shopping and mindless consumerism, idolized sports, rampant violence, and even suicide" (p. 13). The need for trained people who are adequately equipped to address the myriad of problems confronting our society has never been greater.

People's view of counseling is influenced by many factors. The media dramatically influences our notions of the value of counseling and of what a counselor is like. In the 1970s comedian and actor Bob Newhart played a psychologist on a television program. Portions of the show included humorous interchanges between Bob and his counselees. Counseling seemed to have no more value than providing voyeuristic humor. In the church, preaching and pastoral comments might positively or negatively stimulate images of the legitimacy of counseling. Depending on the pastor's own theological persuasions and preferences, the value of counseling perceived by the church's members may depend on the opinions of authority figures.

Whether from secular sources, media, family, friends, or church, almost everyone has an opinion of counseling. To some, the value of counseling is seen as similar to the value of insurance. Writing a check for hundreds or thousands of dollars for home insurance or car insurance is an economical stretch for many. Coupled with the financial burden is the fact that most people fail to benefit from the investment of dollars. Seemingly one is simply giving money away. However, when your home is robbed or destroyed by fire or when your car has been in an accident, the value of insurance is not questioned. When people have a significant need that they have been unable to solve on their own, they are more likely to seek counseling help. Thus the value of counseling is inseparably linked to the desired outcomes that prompt an appointment.

So exactly what leads people to seek counseling? Research seems to indicate that only about one-third of people who need counseling actually receive it (Andrews, Hall, Teesson, & Henderson, 1999), and it is often the last resort for many (Lin, 2002). But for those who do present themselves to a counselor, there are a variety of motivators. The following are reasons people seek a counselor.

### Relief from Personal Pain

People seek a counselor out of their own volition or due to the urging of another individual or at the behest of the state. Regardless of the referral source, however, the underlying motivator is often some form of pain. The personal distress one feels over a lost relationship, the frustration felt by dealing with an irresponsible family member, the demoralization from struggling with a mental-health problem, or having one's capacities for responding to life's demands taxed by trying to hold everything together— all these bring personal pain. The bottom line is that people seek counseling when something in their lives is awry. They might be experiencing wounds from the past or wounds from the present, but either way there is a desire to feel better. When we come alongside such people, we are attempting to understand their inner world and hoping to help them find ways to manage their lives more effectively so that they can find a sense of rest. For people who seek counseling out of a demand for relief, the value they attribute to counseling comes from getting someone to make the pain go away.

## Self-Awareness

Counseling can help people discover their inner self. It can help them see blind areas in their lives. Through counseling, people can discover the deep-seated beliefs, attitudes, and expectations that drive their behavior. Like a professional athlete who benefits from the observant eyes of an experienced coach, counselors offer counselees a fresh and expert perspective on their lives. Counselors provide new ways of looking at behavior and promote the development of necessary skills that are lacking. With a counselor who is gifted at facilitating insight, people can unearth those foundational processes and bring them into the open where they can be more rationally evaluated. In the context of the helping relationship, counselees can recognize how internal issues impact their lives. The helper can facilitate the counselee's examination of basic assumptions about oneself and one's relationships to others. For those desiring self-awareness, the value of counseling comes from the help they receive in knowing themselves in a deeper and more realistic way.

## The Facilitation of Hope

Hope is critical to a satisfying and abundant life (Prov 13:12). Because the present is a link between the past and the future, a person with a painful past often views the future with skepticism and fear. Hope begins with the counselee believing that it is possible for his future to be different from the past. It is a belief in the possibility of change (Gal 2:20; Rom 6:4). The value of counseling is also found in the counselor's ability to foster hope (Yalom & Leszcz, 2005). Counselors can encourage the counselee to believe that God is still at work in the person and will complete His good will (Phil 1:6; 1 Thess 5:23–24) and that God holds a special plan and promise for the future (Jer 29:11).

People anchor their hope in all sorts of things, and when that hope is misplaced, stolen, or lost, it creates a vacuum that leads many to consult a counselor. The absence of hope is evident in a loss of direction and despair. People who are hurting, particularly those who have struggled for years, believe that the future will be a continuation of the past. They cannot grasp that life can be richer and more meaningful than it has been. In contrast with despair that the future will be a continuation of the past, hope brings the belief that the future can offer new life. Often the first challenge a counselor will face is helping the counselee give up self-defeating logic. Despair and hopelessness have become the soothing companions of many counselees. When you can help a counselee believe that things can be better, the seeds of hope start to germinate.

The counselee can experience hope by interacting with a counselor who is respectful, sensitive, accepting, competent, and hopeful. One way counselors can encourage hope is by getting the counselee to make even the smallest change. Even the most nominal change can give the sense that something is being done and that things can change.

In our opinion nothing offers hope more than the understanding that God can do the miraculous (Luke 1:37). He can raise the dead, calm hurricane-like forces, restore functioning, and transform lives. This is rooted in the eternal hope that believers possess. Paul said, "If in this life only we have hope in Christ, we are of all men most miserable" (1 Cor 15:19, KJV). The fact that Jesus has defeated the evil one and death (v. 17) facilitates a hope that is securely rooted in the future but experienced in the present. Regardless of the source of hope, the value the counselee will place on counseling will arise out of a restored sense of hope.

## Changing Behavior

Counselees often report that their presenting problem is some troubling behavior. This might be a compulsion or addiction, or it might be related to an emotional reaction such as rage or avoidance. Regardless of the behavioral concern, the desired hope is for control, change, or the acquisition of a new skill.

Many behavioral patterns are learned and can therefore be unlearned. Also behavioral problems have cognitive and spiritual roots that must be targeted if the behavior change is to become permanent. By targeting the counselee's beliefs, attitudes, values, and actions and by modeling healthy patterns, the counselor can help counselees make the needed changes in their lives. By examining and challenging the counselee's life assumptions the helper can generate change in the counselee. You can help counselees learn new skills that replace deficit or obsolete ones. For those seeking behavioral change, the value of counseling is in receiving help for obtaining control or changing the behavior.

## Making a Difficult Choice

Counselees sometimes report that they desire counseling because they face key decisions that need to be made. The decision might involve entering or ending a relationship, changing a career, or confronting someone. But by the time people contact a counselor they generally have had a lot of input about the situation. Counselees sometimes need someone to help them sort through the mass of input or consider other alternatives. When the need is decision-making, the value of counseling is in having an unbiased person assist them in making a difficult decision.

## A Sounding Board

Counseling provides an opportunity to meet a person in a one-to-one relationship so that the person can talk about personal and private matters. This enables the individual to have his situation viewed from a neutral "third-party" perspective. People want a trained person who is not invested in the outcome to hear their ideas and feelings and help them sort them out. To accomplish that objective, such people will need to be willing to self-disclose to the helper.

Novice counselors often think of self-disclosure as a counselor skill (see chap. 7, "Basic Skills: Giving Feedback"), but all counseling begins with some level of counselee self-disclosure. In the helping profession self-disclosure is a process whereby a counselee verbally reveals private feelings, thoughts, beliefs, or attitudes to another person (Leaper, Carson, Baker, Holiday, & Myers, 1995). Research shows that self-concealers (people who choose not to verbally disclose personal information to another) were three times more likely not to have sought counseling when they were experiencing a problem (Cepeda-Benito & Short, 1998). Thus a person's comfort with self-disclosure, in particular emotional disclosure, is indicative of an individual who is more likely to voluntarily seek help when a need arises. The ability of the helper to create a safe haven (see chap. 5, "Basic Skills: Creating a Connection") so that the counselee can explore personal issues will ultimately impact the counselee's value of the counseling.

## Personal Support

Everyone needs support from time to time. Think of Moses trying to keep his arms in the air so that the people of Israel could be victorious in a battle with the Amalekites. When he lowered his heavy and fatigued arms, the people of Israel started to lose. Moses needed the support of Aaron and Hur to help him hold his arms up so that Israel could prevail (Exod 17:10–13). Counselees sometimes need nothing more than support for their burden (Gal 6:1–2). They need a trusted and credible person to encourage them and to be present with them during difficult times. People come to counseling to figure out what resources are available that can be used to help them get through particular difficulties. When a person feels alone or overwhelmed, counseling can be valuable in removing the sense of isolation and in sensing that the burden is lighter.

## Enhancing Communication

One of the most significant benefits of counseling is that the process of helping highlights the significance of communication in relationships.

Research shows that problems with communication are a significant factor in marriage problems (Zargar & Neshat-Doost, 2008), family issues (Goodman, 2007), workplace concerns (Duddle & Boughton, 2009), and church dynamics (Stewart, 2008). Improving our ability to communicate can literally affect every domain of our lives. As a rule people typically want to be understood more than they want to understand. Both have a place. More often, counselees need to learn how to listen and give others a sense that they have been truly heard. One of the greatest gifts we can give others is giving them the sense they are understood. Also counselees have to learn to express themselves too. One significant communication area from which many counselees can benefit is learning how to identify their feelings and to express them in appropriate and effective ways. Many counselees only know how to express a particular feeling like sadness, guilt, or anger, and they do so in inappropriate ways. Counselees also need to learn how to communicate their thoughts and attitudes in ways that are truthful and honest. The better we understand people and can communicate, the more effective our witness for Christ can become and the more our relationship can be characterized by godly love. The value of counseling is found in improved relationships.

### Personal Growth

Counseling is a vehicle by which to help others attain the life God has intended us to experience (John 10:10), a life that we can more fully enjoy, appreciate, and share with others. The desire to become a better person motivates more than a few to seek counseling. Thus one value of counseling is that it helps counselees become the sort of persons they desire to be and allows them to more deeply enjoy the people God has placed in their lives. Through life we experience situations that cause us to "work out [our] salvation" (Phil 2:12). In the case of people desiring or needing to grow, the value of counseling is in the realization of a newer self.

### Growing Spiritually

Most surveys of Americans indicate that religious people typically turn to their clergy first before seeking assistance from professionals (King, 1978). Yet when they do go to a professional counselor, there is the potential for spiritual growth and discipleship there too.

Perhaps the greatest value of counseling is that it can help people become more Christlike (Rom 12:1–2; Eph 4:14–16; 2 Pet 3:17–18). Counseling is not a substitute for discipleship, but it can promote spiritual development through the vehicle of pain. By addressing issues that block or hinder a person's new life in Christ, people can learn to put off old ways of living and develop godly traits such as holiness, righteousness, love, joy, peace, longsuffering, patience, humility, mercy, kindness, self-control, and goodness (Gal 5:16–26; Eph 4:22–32; Col 3:8–17). As counselees grow in their spiritual walk, they learn how to deal with their current problems and they also become better prepared for future challenges.

One specific way counseling can encourage spiritual growth is by helping counselees develop a theology of suffering. Through counseling, we can help others see how they can use their personal suffering to experience Christ more completely (cf. 2 Cor 1:1–8). Whereas discipleship relationships exist for mentoring a person to grow in his knowledge of the Word of God, counseling relationships exist for transforming concerns and deficits into godliness. Paul wrote in Col 1:28 that his ministry with people was to promote spiritual maturity. A spiritually mature person knows his ultimate purpose in life and lives life in a conscious awareness of worship and service. Grounds (1976) suggests that the ultimate goal of counseling should be to help our counselees develop holiness, not happiness, to find spiritual health not just emotional, mental, or physical health. The primary aim of Christian counseling is to help people love God and others with all of their heart, mind, and soul (Evans, 1986). Counseling provides a place to apply biblical truths to personal and private issues so that the person can grow in Christ. For the Christian, the ultimate value of counseling is that it is a vehicle to achieve a connection with God that was previously considered impossible.

When someone makes the decision to see a counselor, he usually has a high degree of demoralization and despair. In other words, those we are called to help come to counseling with a number of misgivings, and for understandable reasons. People do not find it easy to ask for help or accept assistance that is offered. Most people cannot readily be fully open with someone they do not trust or do not know. At times, problems may seem too overwhelming, too large, or too shameful to share. The idea of going to a counselor can make believers question their faith or spiritual maturity. Regardless of the desired outcomes that might prompt a counselee to seek help, it is often helpful for the counselor to point out the value of the process.

Some biblical counselors have contested that there is no such thing as "Christian psychology," and that any approach to counseling that is not biblically based and biblically oriented is sin (Adams, 1970; Hathaway, 2005). As committed conservative Christians ourselves, we wholeheartedly endorse the value of the Scriptures. God's Word is inspired (2 Tim 3:16–17) and without error. It does not simply contain truth; it is truth. We could never speak ill of an approach that heralds the weight and worth of Scripture. At the same time, however, we do not believe that counseling must be limited to biblical verses or directives. In our combined years of counseling services we have not known one Christian who moved away from God *as a result* of the counseling. Of course, counselees have exercised free will and chosen paths that we would not endorse. Their choices were not the byproduct of "unbiblical" counseling. Our experience has been that God has used our work, and that of other similarly committed Christian professionals, to draw lost ones to Himself, redirect misled ones back to Him, and spiritually strengthen others who waivered or were weak. We credit any changes to the Lord's doing (see chap. 12, "Strategies for Bringing About Changes") and not the work of our hands. A pastor who is well-grounded in theology, skillful in the exposition of Scriptures, and well trained in the delivery of sermons can more effectively persuade parishioners. Salvation and sanctification are the work of the Holy Spirit, not the pastor. Likewise counselors who are well grounded in theology, skillful in the knowledge and philosophy of counseling, and possess prowess in helping can more effectively facilitate spiritual and psychological transformation in their counselees.

In summary the value the counselees see in counseling is inherently and inextricably tied into the reason help was sought. It is thus a subjective appraisal by the counselee. Yet the value of counseling is not solely linked with its outcomes. We believe that counseling is valuable because it is a tool that God can use to accomplish His purposes. It is a most intimate way to help someone wrestle with the practical truths of Scripture and help them apply those truths.

## THE DISTINCTIVENESS OF HELPING

The field of counseling has emerged from many other disciplines. Kottler and Brown (1992) indicate that it is a hybrid of knowledge from fields of study such as psychology, sociology, family studies, psychiatry, education, and philosophy. The first paid helpers were doctors and philosophers, though the clergy had offered counsel for centuries.

Each of us (John and Lisa) has provided guidance, advice, and counsel to others at some point in our lives. Hopefully armed with common sense and a solid knowledge of the Bible we have engaged in casual helping encounters with family members, friends, co-workers, neighbors, and fellow parishioners. Sitting over a cup of coffee in a restaurant or relaxing in someone's family room, we have listened to the stories of others and offered our ideas to help them in some meaningful way.

Although these activities represent coming alongside of people who are in need of help, they are not what we think of when talking about professional Christian counseling. This section considers how counseling with a trained helper is distinct from other forms of helping.

Counseling differs from friendship in a number of significant ways. First, counseling is a contracted and professional relationship, whereas friendships are social. In a professional relationship those we help schedule appointments, complete forms, pay for services, and have a level of expectation about the professional services they will receive. These factors are not present within a friendship.

Second, because counseling is a contractual relationship, it is typically a limited relationship. It is an ad hoc relationship to address personal concerns. The goal of counseling is to help the counselees get to the point that they do not need to see the counselor again. Friendships are timeless and thrive in good and bad times.

Friendship dialogue typically involves two or more people mutually exchanging information, ideas, thoughts, and feelings. In contrast, counseling is a one-way conversation in that the focus is always on the counselee's concerns and is also characterized by a higher level of intensity. In the helping process ideas are developed at a slower pace, felt at a deeper level, and carefully weighed (Patterson & Eisenberg, 1983).

Another distinction between counseling and friendships is that people normally select their friends. We are drawn to certain types of people and repelled by others. In contrast, counselors do not have the same ability to choose whom they will help. Limiting our therapeutic work to only certain types of people is poor business and ineffective ministry. In fact failure to help some to come to us could fall in the parameters of unethical practice (Corey, Corey, & Callanan, 2007). It is not uncommon for counselors to avoid certain types of problems, and there are certain people they work with more easily than others. Some counselors lack the skills and competency to effectively help in every case. But being a professional helper involves a commitment to provide quality care to all kinds of people.

Friends typically offer advice out of their personal experiences. Friends do not approach their friends' circumstances or problems from a theoretical understanding of human behavior that is linked with strategies aimed at addressing the key issues. Professional helpers have been trained in understanding human behavior. They are experienced in knowing what tools to use and when.

The sole purpose of the counseling relationship is for the recovery of the counselee (Herman, 1997). The counselee therefore enters into the helping relationship at a disadvantage. The power inherent in the counselor's position makes possible the exploitation of the counselee. The counselor should seek to gain nothing out of a relationship other than to know that she is living out her calling before God.

Finally professional helpers operate from a neutral perspective rather than having the personal investment of a friend. The lives of a professional and the counselee only intersect in the sanctum of the helping office. In contrast, the lives of friends intersect in many ways beyond the troubling situation being discussed.

## FOUR LEVELS OF HELPING

Just as professional helping is distinct from friendship, also particular distinctions exist within the helping relationships. Although each of the following levels of helping relationships is discreet from the other, they all have the common goal of seeking to produce some level of growth and maturity. Figure 2.1 depicts the four kinds of helping: Guidance, Discipleship, Counseling, and Psychotherapy. In Table 2.1 the four kinds of helping are compared on several key components.

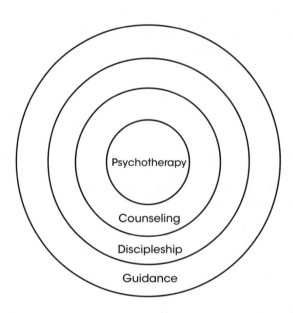

Figure 2.1: Four Types of Helping Relationships

Table 2.1

*Comparison of Helping Relationships*

| Type of Helping | Importance of Relationship | Function | Primary Strategies |
|---|---|---|---|
| Guidance | Low | Problem-Focused | Instruction Problem-Solving |
| Discipleship | High | Developmental-Focused | Bible Study Modeling |
| Counseling | High | Issue-Focused | Encouraging Motivation Skill Development |
| Psychotherapy | High | Process-Focused | Insight Resolution of Inner Conflicts Healing |

## Counseling Is Distinct from Guidance

Guidance has a significant role to play in the counseling process, but it is distinct from counseling in that it focuses only on providing practical direction and information. Guidance can take many forms. For example sharing ideas about enriching a relationship, methods for dealing with depression, or strategies for coping are all forms of guidance.

The concept of guidance has its roots in the Bible. Proverbs 13:14 says, "The teaching of the wise is a fountain of life, turning a man from the snares of death" (NIV). The Christian counselor is committed to using information to bring about meaningful change.

The Greek New Testament uses two words that capture the function of guidance: *boule* and *gnome. Boule* refers to resolving, deciding, or deliberating on a course of action; *gnome* presupposes knowledge and is concerned with intention, consent, will, purpose, and judgment (Bauer, Arndt, & Gingrich). The main thrust of the biblical uses of guidance is in problem-solving and making the right decisions; it is a problem-oriented focus. The ultimate objective of guidance is an informed person. Although such activities have their place in counseling, the work of counseling extends beyond guidance.

## Counseling Is Distinct from Discipleship

A second form of the helping relationship that is specific to activities of Christians is discipleship. Discipleship is an interpersonal and interactive process of helping someone apply biblical truth for the purpose of producing spiritual maturity. In the work of discipleship a counselor incorporates guidance with scriptural doctrine and principles to help facilitate spiritual transformation in the counselee's life. The relationship between the discipler and the disciple is one of teacher to learner. The focus of discipleship is to promote spiritual growth, with the ultimate objective of producing Christlike maturity.

## Counseling Encompasses the Total Person

The last two types of helping, counseling and psychotherapy, capture the true essence of what it means to "come alongside." The similarities between the two are such that distinctions between the two are artificial and serve little function (Patterson, 1986). For instance both focus on addressing inner life issues and how they block or hinder the person from functioning well. From a biblical perspective both counseling and psychotherapy can be used to work on those inner-life issues that interfere with the person becoming like Christ.

In a Christian context, counseling carries guidance and discipleship to a deeper level by exploring how personal issues relate to life. Guidance, discipleship, and counseling all deal with wellness, growth, and development. However, counseling, unlike guidance and discipleship, also addresses a person's personal problems. From this point of view counseling is primarily issue-oriented. As a dynamic approach it seeks to prevent and relieve problems that result from the human condition. Counseling is a comprehensive attempt to help a counselee with the myriad challenges of living. Counseling is a specific activity that is agreed on by two parties, forming a contractual relationship.

Like guidance and discipleship, the function of counseling is found in Scripture. According to Minirth (1977), there are at least five words in the New Testament that speak of the concept of "counseling": *parakaleo, noutheteo, paramytheomai, antechomai,* and *makrothymeo.* All five of these appear in 1 Thess 5:14 and are relevant to the ministry of all believers. In particular, however, the two primary biblical words that seem to capture the essence of biblical counseling are *parakaleo* and *noutheteo.* We think of them as two sides of a helping coin.

*Parakaleo* means "to be called alongside, to support, and to encourage" (Bauer, Arndt, & Gingrich, 1979). The term is translated "consoling," "strengthening," and "encouraging" (1 Thess 3:2; 4:18), "begging" or "beseeching" (1 Cor 1:10; 4:16), "consoling" (Luke 2:25), and "exhorting" (1 Thess 2:3). The same word is used to speak of the Holy Spirit and His ministry in our lives. This side to counseling is supportive, encouraging, and motivational. It may be either directive or nondirective, allowing the counselee to come to her own conclusions.

The other side of the helping coin involves the Greek word *noutheteo*, which means "to warn," "to admonish," "put sense into," or "to confront" (Bauer, Arndt, & Gingrich, 1979). The key idea is to redirect an individual to a different path. Dr. Jay Adams (1970) developed an entire approach to counseling, called *Nouthetic Counseling*, based on this one word. When thinking about the ministry of *noutheteo* many think of direct confrontation, but the word also includes confrontation that is nondirective and gentler. For example a nondirective form of confrontation is illustrated in the story of Nathan confronting David with his sin of adultery and murder (cf. 2 Sam 12:1–9). Nathan built the confrontation into a story that led to David's admonishing himself.

## Counseling Is Distinct from Psychotherapy

The fourth type of helping relationship that includes the concept of "coming alongside" is psychotherapy. From a Christian point of view psychotherapy incorporates all helping types. Some writers do not distinguish between the terms *counseling* and *psychotherapy*; in fact many people use the words interchangeably. However, a technical difference between the two forms of helping is that psychotherapy takes the counselee to a deeper level than counseling. Psychotherapy explores and intervenes with aspects of the personality structure. Psychotherapy addresses the internal and external processes that stimulate behavior. From a Christian view the objective of psychotherapy is to apply the truths of Scripture in conjunction with psychological principles in treating behavioral and emotional problems by penetrating beneath the surface and exploring their origins. Although the ultimate aim of psychotherapy depends on the counselor's theoretical orientation, the primary objectives are to help people understand and remove the internal blocks to healthy living, to heal from deepseated wounds, and to develop the ability to understand how their internal workings interact with the world around them.

In the final analysis coming alongside a hurting person is a unique calling to a special kind of helping. Regardless of the level of help being offered, both counseling and psychotherapy represent a distinct profession that requires specialized training.

## THE EFFECTIVENESS OF HELPING

Counseling and psychotherapy research have a relatively young beginning, dating from approximately the end of World War II (Garfield, 1983). Yet the decades since then have generated a frenzy of debate over the question of whether counseling is effective. Since no research design is without its limitations and imperfections, advocates on both sides can easily dismiss the claims of their opponents.

Some artists create more memorable art, some lawyers achieve better results for their counselees, and certain teachers facilitate greater achievement in their students, thus some counselors will achieve better results than others. In fact when I (John) worked as an employee assistance consultant and had to refer employees and family members to therapists, I considered the helper's particular areas of expertise and competence more than other variables (Wampold, 2001).

Two key questions that deal with counseling effectiveness are these: Is counseling effective? If so, how or why? In answering the first question, the preponderance of outcome studies indicate that the majority of people who seek counseling services improve, though some counselees might actually get worse (Howard, Kopta, Krause, & Orlinsky, 1986; Lambert & Cattani-Thompson, 1996; Lambert, Shapiro, & Bergin, 1986; Seligman, 1995; Shapiro & Shapiro, 1982; Smith, Glass, & Miller, 1980). It might seem surprising, in fact unnerving, to think that someone can get worse by having counseling. Yet research does indicate that counseling can produce harm in some individuals (Lambert & Miller, 2001; Rhule, 2005) with estimates ranging from 3 to 6 percent or 5 to 10 percent (Boisvert & Faust, 2003; Lilienfeld, 2007; Mohr, 1995; Strupp, Hadley, & Gomez-Schwartz, 1977). The adverse outcomes might be because of poor treatments, a poor helper, or a poor effort on the part of the counselee. Moreover, some poor outcomes might be because of research design failures. Interestingly research findings indicate that studies with poorer designs tend to be less effective.

In spite of the fact that counseling does not always work, evidence from the majority of findings clearly supports the idea that counseling is profitable. Effectiveness has also been studied from the standpoint of counselee satisfaction. For example a meta-analysis (a study that looks at the findings of many studies) found that the vast majority of counselees were satisfied with their helping services (Hemmings, 2000).

Though the overall effect of counseling is positive, studies do not indicate that any particular school of counseling is better than another (Seligman, 1995). Whether a person adheres to cognitive-behavioral counseling, Adlerian counseling, solution-focused counseling, or some other approach, the effectiveness is relatively the same.

Numerous studies have attempted to understand what factors contribute to a better counseling outcome. Asay and Lambert (1999) estimated that only 15 percent of change was attributable to a specific counseling technique. The other 85 percent of counselees' improvement could be attributed to factors such as the counseling relationship, placebo effects, and other counselee factors. Research strongly suggests that counseling success depends on the individual qualities of the counselee and the counselor and in their interactions, rather than in the therapeutic method (Kim, Ng, & Ahn, 2005; Workman & Williams, 1979). In particular counselee expectations play a role in counseling outcomes. A series of studies showed that counselees who are able to have a meaningful relationship with the counselor do better than those who maintain a superficial interaction with the counselor (Strupp, 1980a, 1980b, 1980c, 1980d). Research suggests that counselee decisions to begin counseling are directly influenced by the help they expect to receive. But counselee expectations also have a downside. Some research suggests that counselee expectations seem to have diminished the quality and effectiveness of counseling (Tinsley, Bowman, & Ray, 1988). Glass, Arnkoff, and Shapiro (2001) concluded that counselees who receive a type of counseling that they believe in and prefer may be more likely to work harder in counseling from the start, to comply with the counselor's recommendations, and not to drop out of the counseling prematurely.

Studies have also sought to examine the "common factors" of most theoretical orientations to understand what counselor factors impact effectiveness (Asay & Lambert, 1999). The term "common factors" refers to the following characteristics: warm support, reassurance, suggestion, credibility, and counselor attention. Research by Sloane, Staples, Cristol, Yorkston, and Whipple (1975) showed that counselees listed the following items as "extremely important" or "very important" in facilitating their improvement: (a) the personality of the counselor, (b) the counselor helping to understand the problem, (c) encouragement to gradually practice facing the things that bothered them, (d) being able to talk to an understanding person, and (e) the counselor helping them obtain greater self-understanding.

Beutler (1991) reviewed variables that contributed to counseling outcomes and concluded that the counselor-counselee match was the strongest predictor of outcome. Research has also suggested that similarities between counselees and counselors regarding attitudes, beliefs, and personal values, expectations toward counseling, coping styles, and self-concept were associated with counseling effectiveness (Beutler, Crago, & Arizmendi, 1986; Nelson & Neufeldt, 1996; Reis & Brown, 1999).

Finally, other factors have been shown to be related to outcome. For example longer-term counseling results in considerably better results (Seligman, 1995).

In summary, the process of helping is effective in the vast majority of cases. Both counselee factors and counselor factors are integral to positive and negative outcomes. Whereas the helper has little control over the counselee factors, we do have the ability to control those counselor factors that optimize the possibilities of improvement.

## THE ART OF HELPING

The ability to come alongside people, and understand them, and empathize with them is both a science and an art. Science brings the harder side and art the softer side to the questions associated with human functioning. Counseling does have a harder side that is emphasized by researchers who seek to understand the science of helping. Systematic and reliable processes can be applied to human behavior and professional helping. In this textbook we seek to provide you with as much of the science of counseling as possible in order to help you become effective in your work. Yet coming alongside hurting people is much more an art than a science.

In considering the softer side of counseling, we focus on two major ways that working with human behavior requires an artful approach. First, we note the difference between objective and subjective experiences, and second, we then compare the helping process to the function of arts.

Counseling is more of an art because it involves more subjective than objective processes. Objective processes, the science side of counseling, are ones that are measurable, quantifiable, and standardized; they are largely free of being contaminated by the scientist. In contrast, a subjective process is one that is highly dependent on what you are told, experience, and understand. Subjective processes are more influenced by the person's perspectives, and so they are more prone to bias. Art is much more of a subjective than an objective process. You can teach people how to do particular techniques, but how the artist puts it together is highly unique and personal. People can look at an art piece and see different things; two viewers can imbue the same piece of art with different meanings.

Also objective processes are much easier to teach and to learn. The procedures for learning a skill are identifiable and standardized.

Surgeons often state that once a particular surgery has been learned, in a relatively short period of time it becomes so routine it is boring. While each patient is a unique system, the fact that every person has similar human systems allows the surgeon to know what he or she is doing and to have the work reduced to a set of procedures. The way surgery is taught gives the surgeon specific procedures to follow in each situation, and the variations are nominal from patient to patient. The surgeon can use an x-ray or MRI to discern and locate a particular mass. As counselors we do not have a routine set of procedures that, once learned, result in competence. Developing the skill of counseling is far more complicated than that. Counseling deals with subjective processes inside human beings that make the understanding and evaluation of what is going on complex. The field of counseling has yet to create a psychological and spiritual x-ray to ascertain such subjective experiences as resentment, pride, or even depression. Whether the skill is assessment, diagnosis, or treatment, the role the counselor as a person (see chap. 4, "The Person of the Counselor") plays in evaluating, understanding, and treating is enormous. Thus counseling is created at the intersection of two subjective human beings.

An artist creates a work to communicate a message to the viewer. Likewise counselors create a dialogue to facilitate a process in the counselee. Art provides beauty to a culture and enriches it. An end result of counseling is to beautify and enrich the individual. An art product is an extension of the artist. Similarly a counseling session is an extension of the counselor. No matter how carefully an educator may be in teaching a particular counseling technique, the practitioner will ultimately assimilate that learning into his own interpersonal style and worldview.

The bottom line is that helping people cannot be reduced to a systematic set of steps and principles. Counseling cannot be reduced to a technology. Counseling is more than a mechanical set of procedures. Even for those skills and techniques that can be taught more behaviorally, they will be expressed through the person of the counselor in a unique way. Good counselors have the ability to creatively use a technique to fit the counselee's frame of reference so that it has the greatest impact. Counselors who understand the art of helping also know how to follow the principles of helping in a myriad of contexts. It is simply impossible to give novice counselors a list of what to do when.

## THE ROLE OF A COUNSELING MODEL

In counseling literature two terms that are often used interchangeably are "counseling model" and "counseling theory." Strictly speaking there is a difference. A theory refers to general principles that are verified by data that explain certain phenomena (Shertzer & Stone, 1974). As such, a theory focuses on the principles that underlie practice rather than just practice itself. George and Cristiani (1981) state,

> When a counselor is baffled by a problem, he turns to theory to enlarge his perspective about the various alternatives. Since a theory's ability to explain what we are doing suggests the value of that theory, it follows that a theory would also suggest what needs to be done when we are faced with a problem (p. 126).

There are many examples of counseling theories in both Christian and secular literature. Popular theories include Gestalt (Perls, 1969; Shepard, 1975), Person-Centered (Rogers, 1961), Rationale-Emotive Theory (RET; Ellis, 1957), Cognitive Theory (Beck, 1972), Behavioral (Skinner, 1938; Skinner, 1974), Psychoanalysis (Freud, 1895), Adlerian (Adler, 1958), Jungian Theory (Jung, 1954a; Jung, 1954b), Interpersonal Theory (Sullivan, 1947; Sullivan, 1953), Reality Theory (Glasser, 1962), Nouthetic (Adams, 1970), and Discipleship Theory (Collins, 1972). Although there are over 400 theories (Corsini & Wedding, 1995), they are not the same. Hansen, Stevic, and Warner (1982) have described five characteristics of a good theory. For the theory to have counseling and therapy merit, each one must (a) be clear, easily understood, and communicable; (b) be comprehensive and supply plausible explanations for a variety of phenomena; (c) be explicit enough to generate research; (d) relate means to desired outcomes, stating specific procedures for achieving an end product; and (e) be effective and useful to the practitioner.

While a counseling theory explains certain phenomena, a counseling model is an explanatory representation of a theory rather than the theory itself (Alvarez & Piper, 2005). It is a system of how various elements fit together. The model is a larger picture of how things work. For example Rationale-Emotive Theory (Ellis, 1957) and Cognitive Theory (Beck, 1972) could be categorized as cognitive models because of their emphasis on beliefs in human behavior. Psychoanalysis (Freud, 1895) and Jungian Theory (Jung, 1954a, 1954b) would fit a psychodynamic model because of their emphasis on deep internal processes. Thus, a counseling model speaks to the focus of the helping and how people find resolution to their concerns.

In summary, counseling theories are based on how someone sees human nature and the environment. A counseling theory provides a systematic way to understand a person's psychological framework, the way problems arise in the person's development, and strategies to help resolve those problems. A counseling model provides a framework that will guide your work. It provides the skeleton on which the counseling processes are attached. As Corey (2005) recommends, counselors should choose theories and models that most closely relate to and reflect their worldview.

A conceptual framework for counseling may be called the counseling stool model of practice (see Figure 2.2). According to this model the practice of counseling has three primary supports. Piano stools were once made with three legs because they were considered more stable than a four-legged bench.

The first and most important leg to the practice of counseling is the person of the counselor. We will discuss this in more detail in chap. 4 ("The Person of the Counselor"), but it is critical to understand that counseling is an extension of the human delivery system. The fabric of your counseling practice is woven together with the kind of person you are, the intelligence you possess, the issues you struggle with, the strengths you can access, and the beliefs and values you claim. Your public self, private self, and professional self are all relevant to the practice of counseling. In fact they are inseparable.

The second leg of the stool is the counselor's philosophy and theory. This support to counseling practice is subjective in that the roots of counseling practice extend into the counselor's theoretical orientation and the philosophical underpinnings of that orientation. In essence counseling is ultimately about philosophy because it deals with the presuppositional level of the discipline. Moreland and Craig (2003) state that philosophy is a "second-order discipline" in that it studies psychology or counseling. Philosophers ask questions, normative questions, about the discipline (e.g., questions pertaining to what should or should not be believed in the discipline and why), analyze and critique the discipline's underlying assumptions, clarify the discipline's concepts, and seek to relate it to other disciplines. Philosophers consider the logic of the discipline, epistemology (the study of knowledge), metaphysics (the study of being or reality), and value theory (the study of values). Each of these branches of philosophy is important to a counseling model. Thus your theoretical orientation (e.g., Nouthetic, Adlerian, Cognitive-Behavioral, Gestalt, Solution-Focused, or Systems Theory) coupled with the philosophical assumptions proceed from the person of the counselor. They shape and guide the way the counselor engages in the helping process. They provide an anchor for making sense of what you are doing as a counselor (Corey, 2005).

The third leg of the counseling stool is the counselor's knowledge and skill. There is an intimate relationship between the counselor's philosophy and theory and the counselor's knowledge and skill. Counselors typically choose theories that are consistent with their model of the world, how they believe things work. A knowledge base is generated that fits the counselor's philosophy. From the basis of your theory and knowledge, you then learn the general skills of counseling (chaps. 5–8) and how to counsel in a way that is consistent with your theory and philosophy.

In the next chap., we will present a counseling model, not a theory, but the bottom line is that your model should be informed by biblical truth, conservative Christian theology, and the scientific findings of psychology. As a counselor, you cannot help what you do not see, and you cannot see what you do not understand. It is through the lens of a theory or model that you make sense of your counselees and know how you need to help them.

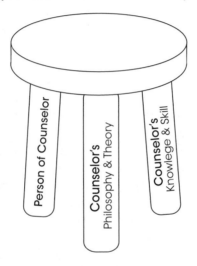

Figure 2.2: The Counseling Stool

## COUNSELOR INTENTIONS

Many novice helpers focus on "what they need to do." The desire is for techniques and strategies that offer promise in helping the counselee. Rather than thinking about particular techniques or strategies, first begin with knowing what it is you want to do. This is what is called "counselor intentionally." By knowing what you want to do or need to do, you can have a clearer sense of what you need to be doing with the counselee. Building off of the work of Hill and O'Grady (1985) and Hill, Helms, Spiegal, and Tichenor (1988) the following counselor intentions and counselee reactions are suggested. The acrostic in Table 2.2 is COUNSELING INTENTIONS to help you remember 19 distinct counselor goals in working with counselees.

## Table 2.2

*Counselor Intentions and Counselee Reactions*

| Intentions | Counselee Reactions |
|---|---|
| **C** = Challenge | "I was shown that what I was saying was not what I was doing." |
| **O** = Oriented | "I got more focused about what I was wanting to do." |
| **U** = Understanding | "I thought the counselor understood what I was trying to say." |
| **N** = Negative thinking | "I came to see how my thinking affected my behavior." |
| **S** = Self-defeating thinking | "I became aware of what and how I thought kept me in the same misery." |
| **E** = Explore | "The counselor asked a lot of questions and got me thinking about things that I had not considered." |
| **L** = Limits | "The counselor explained to me what he could and could not do for me." |
| **I** = Interact | "I really connected with the counselor." |
| **N** = Nurse | "I felt that the counselor really cared about what I was going through." |
| **G** = Goal-setting | "The counselor gave me direction and what I needed to do to arrive at my goals." |
| **I** = Interpretation | "I got a new perspective on another person." |
| **N** = Normalize | "I learned that I was not crazy, that what I was experiencing was normal." |
| **T** = Transform | "I got ideas about what I could do differently and help making those changes." |
| **E** = Encouragement | "I felt like the counselor believed in me." |
| **N** = Negotiate solutions | "The counselor helped me think through and come up with solutions for my problem." |
| **T** = Teach | "I learned something that I did not know." |
| **I** = Insight | "I saw how I really came across to others." |
| **O** = Optimistic | "I felt hopeful about the future that I could change." |
| **N** = Nix relapse | "I learned what triggers my relapse." |
| **S** = Self-control | "I learned how to control my behavior in difficult situations." |

## THE ROLE OF TECHNIQUES

The English word *technique* is derived from the Greek word *techne*, which means "skill." In the helping profession a technique is viewed as a preferred counselor strategy (Thompson, 2003). "Helping skills" refer to the ways counselors attend, listen, understand, challenge, and initiate actions that help the counselees with their personal concerns. The possession of skills or techniques are the mark of a professional.

Yet as important as techniques are to the counseling process, it would be inaccurate to reduce counseling to nothing more than a collection of techniques. Leitner (2007) argues that counseling is not about assembling a bag of tricks or incorporating a formula. A counselor who has acquired many techniques is merely a technician skilled in a "gimmick," according to Thompson (2003): "The counseling experience is much more than the counselor's use of technique; the human dimension of the relationship as well as the readiness and responsiveness of the counselee are also very important" (p. xii). Helping ultimately emanates from the person of the counselor (see chap. 4, "The Person of the Counselor"). The idea is that techniques are to proceed so naturally from the counselor that they seem like authentic responses to the counselee. Of course during the learning process very little is natural. It takes time to become proficient in the use of techniques, but it begins with understanding the nature and purpose of techniques. The purpose of this book is to help you, whether you come from a professional or pastoral perspective, to become skilled and competent in the art of helping.

### Rationale for Using Techniques

Most novice counselors beg to learn techniques. Young (1992) wrote, "At some point in every therapist's academic training, a great thirst for practical methods develops. . . . This urge often comes when our favorite theoretical system appears to become inadequate" (p. 1).

A number of writers have proposed a rationale for the use of techniques in counseling. Jacobs (1992) offers seven reasons for using techniques. They can (a) make concepts more concrete, (b) heighten awareness, (c) dramatize a point, (d) speed up the counseling process, (e) enhance learning because people are visual learners, (f) enhance learning because people learn through experience, and (g) give focus to the session. Rosenthal (1998) offers six additional reasons why techniques are important to effective counseling. First, a technique often allows the counselee to surmount an impasse or sticking point. Second, a technique can renew the counselee's interest in counseling. Third, a technique offers an escape from the mundane experience of counseling. Fourth, a technique can be used as an adjunct to any brand or modality of counseling. Fifth, counselees often report that a particular technique was instrumental in helping them. Sixth, a technique can be extremely effective when applied to a given symptom, difficulty, or disorder.

## Guidelines for Using Techniques

Several keys in employing techniques in the helping process should be borne in mind. As a mnemonic device we have created the six guidelines into the acrostic **SKILLS** (see Table 2.3).

| Table 2.3 |
| --- |
| *SKILLS: Guidelines for Using Techniques* |
| **S** = **Suitable** to the counselee's circumstances and needs |
| **K** = **Keep** it consistent with who you are as a person |
| **I** = the counselor should be **Intentional** |
| **L** = the counselor has **Learned** the technique |
| **L** = **Limit** the use of techniques |
| **S** = **Speak** the counselee's language |

First, the "S" is to remind you to ensure that the techniques are **Suitable** to the counselee's situation and needs. Be flexible, appropriate, and pragmatic in the use of techniques. Because of the diversity of populations that counselors serve, one size does not fit all. Knowing how to use a particular technique with a particular counselee is the mark of a seasoned counselor.

Second, the "K" in SKILL refers to **Keeping** the technique consistent with who you are as a person. Do not use techniques that make you uncomfortable. The best techniques are ones that fit your personality and that are consistent with your values and understanding of human behavior.

The third guideline, "I," refers to being **Intentional** in the use of techniques. Have a clear purpose and rationale in mind for using a particular technique. Although an extension of the counselor, techniques arise out of the counselor's intention. Techniques are the vehicle to accomplish your intention. Thompson (2003) states that incorporating a particular technique in the helping process should be organized around a fundamental principle of treatment and directed toward a specific goal. In other words making techniques intentional means having a clear understanding of what you are doing and why. For example you might ask yourself, "Since I need to accomplish exploration, what is the best technique to employ to get there?" By doing so you are bridging the gap between intent and strategy.

The "L" reminds you to adequately **Learn** the technique before using it. A key guideline is that sound training in a particular technique should precede the use of the technique. Ethical guidelines require that you have competence in the use of techniques. In other words the skillfulness of the counselor is paramount in using the technique.

The second "L" refers to having a **Limit** in the use of techniques. It can be tempting to use techniques at every opportunity because it gives a sense of direction and control over what is happening in the session. Helping someone is not a procedure; it is a healing relationship. The interaction of the counselor and counselee, with the work of the Holy Spirit, can produce real change.

The last letter "S" is to remind you to **Speak** the counselee's language. State the purpose of the technique in language the counselee can understand. And state why you believe the technique is beneficial.

However, techniques do not produce change. Techniques can bring focus to a session and provide insight, but in the final analysis the counselor cannot solve the counselee's problem. The real counselor is the Holy Spirit (John 14:26; 16:12–13), who works to comfort, instruct, and convict.

## CHAPTER SUMMARY

In this chap. we discussed the practice of counseling. We explained how counseling is a distinct type of helping relationship that has value in facilitating wholeness in the lives of broken people. Research supports the view that, given the correct conditions, counseling can be effective. Moreover, God can heal the deep wounds of the human soul.

Becoming effective requires balancing the science and art of counseling. This textbook is designed to help you learn the science of counseling; but the art of counseling cannot be taught. You grow through your own experiences in conducting sessions and through your exposure to seasoned counselors. Most of all, realize that as a Christian counselor the ultimate source of help rests not with you but with the Holy Spirit. We cannot teach you how to do the art of counseling or explain how to be sensitive to the Holy Spirit's leading. Simply remember that it will not be your cleverness in choosing techniques that promotes true transformation. Rather it will be your willingness and ability to be fully present with the counselee and your sensitivity to the Holy Spirit's leading. The next chap. discusses practical aspects of the process of counseling.

## CHAPTER 2 ACTIVITIES

Directions: Prayerfully and carefully complete the following questions/activities related to the content of chap. 2.

1. Suppose you were talking with someone who believes counseling is a waste of time and money. Consider a response to that person who questions the value of counseling. Write out that response in as detailed a manner as possible that would address the person's objections.
2. Discuss the point that you could facilitate hope with a counselee who is so depressed and hopeless that the person believes change is impossible.
3. Review the benefits of counseling discussed in this chap. First, rank the benefits in the order you believe captures the importance of each benefit. Then write the reasons for your top three choices.
4. Describe the reasons you believe counseling is different from helping a good friend and from discipling another believer.
5. Suppose a father questions the effectiveness of helping his rebellious adolescent. He wants you to convince him that his money will be worthwhile. Write your response to the father.
6. In this chap. we described a three-legged stool that comprises the essentials of a counseling model. Describe your thoughts about each leg; in other words create your own model from addressing each of the legs.
7. Write what you believe would be your primary five intentions or goals in working with counselees. Defend your responses.
8. Imagine a continuum that ranges from counselors who believe that change in counseling is more effective if the counselor relates as a person to the counselee to the other end of the continuum where the counselor believes that change occurs through the use of orchestrating it by techniques. Consider where you would fall on that continuum. Write out your rationale for that perspective.

## Recommended Reading

Adams, J. (1979). *A theology of Christian counseling*. Grand Rapids, MI: Zondervan Publishing House.

> Every counselor should at least have an understanding of the nouthetic position as outlined by Jay Adams, a true pioneer in Christian counseling. While his work largely eliminates the need for psychology, he does show how the Bible is relevant to

modern-day problems. We believe every Christian counselor should hold the Bible in the highest of esteem.

Clinton, T., & Ohlschlager, G. (Eds.) (2002a). *Competent Christian counseling: Foundations and practice of compassionate soul care* (Vol. 1). Colorado Springs, CO: Waterbrook Press.

> This book is a comprehensive overview of Christian counseling. It covers the philosophy, theology, and clinical aspects of the counseling field.

Jacobs, E. (1992). *Creative counseling techniques: An illustrated guide.* Lutz, FL: Psychological Assessment Resources.

> This is an excellent resource that contains practical and valuable ideas for working with counselee issues.

# Chapter 3

# The Hazards of Helping

*"Prohibitively, then Christian counselors avoid every manner of harm, exploitation, and unjust discrimination in all counselee-congregant relations. Christian counselors are also aware of their psychosocial and spiritual influences and the inherent power imbalance of helping relationships—power dynamics that can harm others even without harmful intent"* (AACC, 2001).

*"And who will harm you, if you are passionate for what is good? But even if you should suffer for righteousness, you are blessed. Do not fear what they fear or be disturbed, but set apart the Messiah as Lord in your hearts, and always be ready to give a defense to anyone who asks you for a reason for the hope that is in you. However, do this with gentleness and respect, keeping your conscience clear, so that when you are accused, those who denounce your Christian life will be put to shame. For it is better to suffer for doing good, if that should be God's will, then for doing evil"* (1 Pet 3:13–17).

## CHAPTER OBJECTIVES

» To learn how countertransference negatively affects both the counselee and counselor

» To examine the potential hazards to the counselee as a result of counseling

» To understand how counselor issues impact counselees

» To examine the potential hazards to the counselor

» To learn ways the profession of counseling can take an emotional toll on the counselor

» To review means of avoiding the hazards

» To assist the student counselor in applying the principles of this chap.

## CHAPTER OUTLINE

HELPING HAZARDS THAT CAN HURT THE COUNSELEE
    Countertransference
    Projection
    Projective Identification
    Poor Competence
    Unethical Behavior
    Summary

HELPING HAZARDS THAT CAN HURT THE COUNSELOR
    Countertransference
    The Emotional Toll of Caring

AVOIDING THE HAZARDS

CHAPTER SUMMARY

CHAPTER 3 ACTIVITIES

---

N o expedition is without risks. The kinds of risks for any pilgrimage depend on the specific expedition undertaken. Most expeditions involve physical risks and even injuries. A seasoned and experienced guide knows those potential risks, and his training and preparation helps him know how to protect himself and his trekkers from danger. Caring for the trekker begins with informing him of the potential risks involved, and when and how such risks might manifest themselves on the journey.

Likewise many risks are associated with counseling. Yet when people think of counseling, they typically think of help and improvement. Such a perception is generally true, but unfortunately there is a darker side. Though research shows that most people benefit from counseling (Strain, 1999), some people actually get worse and are even harmed. Even the helper is not exempt from possible adverse effects of counseling.

This chap. has a twofold purpose. The information presented in this chap. is intended to show that counseling can be hazardous to the counselee and counselor alike.

## HELPING HAZARDS THAT CAN HURT THE COUNSELEE

Inadvertently the counselor can become a weapon of harm rather than a tool of healing. These harmful effects of counseling can emanate from the counselor's own life or from his professional incompetence. Yet all ethical codes call for counselors to do no harm; to protect the welfare of the counselee AACC, 2004 [see Appendix B]; American Counseling Association (ACA), 2005 [see Appendix A]; American Psychological Association (APA), 2002).

This section examines five potential hazards that can place a counselee's welfare in jeopardy. These threats are countertransference, projection, projective identification, poor competence, and unethical behavior.

### Countertransference

Bob was a 24-year-old counseling intern who worked with children and adolescences at a Christian family counseling center. One morning Bob met with a mother of an eight-year-old boy. Throughout the session the woman was very critical of her son and seemed to have unrealistic expectations for him. Bob concluded that the mother was expecting her son to be perfect and thus felt very protective of the child. He identified with the little boy and noticed that the mother's criticism and demands reminded him of his own relationship with his mother. Soon Bob became involved in a power struggle with the mother. He confronted her demandingness and shamed her about the long-term consequences of her actions. The session ended with Bob frustrated and the mother threatening not to return.

Without a doubt, countertransference is the most well-known hazard associated with the helping relationship. It describes a counselor's own thoughts, feelings, and behaviors in relation to a counselee (Watkins, 1985). Countertransference occurs when a counselor projects his emotional reaction to or behavior toward the counselee (Fauth & Hayes, 2006). Inevitably the counselor's own needs then become entangled in the counseling relationship, interfering with the counselor's objectivity (Corey, Corey, & Callanan, 2007). The reaction might be irrational, interpersonally stressful, and self-defeating but occurs outside the range of a counselor's awareness and/or ability to manage.

The concept of countertransference is derived from a similar process, known as transference that is associated with the counselee. Specifically transference refers to a phenomenon in which a counselee redirects feelings from the past onto the counselor. In reality transference is a part of every relationship. We perceive people not as they really are, but through the filter of our life experiences. We can never bury a feeling that is still alive. Such feelings will resurrect themselves in other relationships that somehow connect with the original experience.

The spark of countertransference originates in the intensity bound up in the counseling relationship, which ignites the counselor's own issues. A female counselor may have unresolved needs to nurture, to foster a dependent relationship, and to be affirmed and validated by male counselees. Or a male counselor may develop sexual feelings toward submissive and vulnerable women because of his unresolved issues from the past. It is not uncommon in sessions with novice counselors to hear comments such as these: "I thought I had my mother [or father, or someone else] in the counseling session," or "I thought about this counselee all the time and worried about him before I went to bed. It was all-consuming." Unless you are aware of these dynamics, counseling will be significantly affected and you will be prone to ethical violations.

Counselors need to be sure they do not harm those whom they are called to help because of their own issues that may get in the way. The power imbalance between the counselor and counselee render all counselees vulnerable to exploitation and abuse (Herman, 1997). Progress in counseling is stunted when counselors use counselees, unconsciously seeking to fulfill their own unmet needs. I (John) supervised a seasoned male counselor who was upset with his young female counselee for making a choice with which he did not agree. It became evident that the older counselor was seeing her as his own daughter, who had made some similarly poor choices. From this supervision session I learned that one never becomes so experienced that personal issues no longer contaminate one's counseling work.

Depending on the unmet needs of the counselor the faces of countertransference can differ dramatically. A few key needs are the following.

### The need to feel powerful.

One of the most devious ways that countertransference occurs is when counselors need to feel powerful. People who have a need to control and feel powerful can be attracted to the helping profession. Some people can come to believe they are in charge of their counselees' lives and either overtly or subtly manipulate their counselees. Giving advice can make someone feel powerful, to feel like an expert who is needed by others. For Christian counselors this dynamic can be disguised behind the mask of "biblical truth." The Bible is absolute truth. The issue, however, is not the imparting of truth, but why the truth is being imparted. The power-needing counselor believes that he or she has the ultimate answers on how the counselee should live. At times the need to feel powerful comes out of deep feelings of vulnerability. When these things occur, counselors have entangled their past feelings with their counselee, believing that controlling the counselee can insulate him from the fear he once felt.

### The need to parent.

Closely related to the power-needing counselor is the counselor who has a need to parent. Unfortunately it is relatively easy for novice counselors to take on a parental role. Many counselees come to counseling because they lack assertiveness and do not trust in themselves. When counselors step into the parental role, they become overinvolved in the counselee's life. They might compulsively give advice and foster a dependency that places a counselee in an inferior position and they replicate many of the dysfunctional issues of the past.

### The need to nurture.

Perhaps the most common way countertransference takes hold of counselors is in the need to nurture. On the surface, wanting to nurture sounds innocuous, but in actuality it is quite insidious. In this form of countertransference counselors view their counselees as fragile and in need of emotional support. This form of countertransference can manifest itself in failing to challenge the counselee or in caressing or soothing a counselee. In the end the problems of the counselee are only perpetuated.

### The need to be needed.

Some counselors believe they are indispensable to their counselees, thereby creating a sense of dependence in their counselees. However, effective counseling helps counselees develop a dependency and reliance on God rather than on the counselor. When countertransference takes this form, counselors maneuver the counselee into a role of weakness as a sick person, a child, or an inexperienced or naïve person. Ironically the counselor actually depends on the counselee to establish and maintain this role.

### The need to be validated.

Counselors with unmet needs for approval subtly or overly manipulate their counselees to obtain acceptance, admiration, and awe. They fear disapproval and rejection. In some cases the counselor might put tremendous pressure on the counselee to get better. Counselees might think they can report only successes to the counselor, not failures. Early in my (John's) career I learned that I had a strong need to receive professional validation from my counselees. Through a particular case I came to realize that I felt overly inflated by counselee compliments. With one particular counselee,

I actually structured the sessions in order to have the counselee praise me for my help. Such desires and behavior are void of therapeutic benefit for the counselee and can never really satisfy the counselor's need to feel affirmed.

### The need to feel safe.

Another form of countertransference is the need to feel safe. Emotionally charged words and behavior occur within the confines of counseling sessions that have the potential to make an anxious counselor feel unsafe. Some counselors are unnerved by their counselee's anger. Something in the counselor's past has caused them to believe that anger is threatening and thus should be avoided. Other counselors might become uneasy when counselees discuss certain sexual experiences, fantasies, or problems. Regardless of the trigger for their uneasiness, the counselor's countertransference poses a threat to the counselee and to the counseling relationship. Counselors might avoid emotionally charged topics, feel insecure in their work, or attempt to elicit reassurance from the counselee. The end result is that the counselee is not helped and the counselor has modeled unhealthy behavior. Of course all counselors will have strong feelings about their counselees. Unethical behavior can occur, however, when these feelings become more about the counselor than the counselee. Recognizing the presence of such countertransference is not always easy. Many of these countertransference forms can be subtle in their manifestation while triggering strong emotions in the counselor. You know your own issues are becoming entangled with those of the counselee when you (a) express a sudden eruption of strong emotion that is out of proportion to the situation, (b) act in nontherapeutic ways, or (c) have distorted thinking.

Particular emotions might be clues to the presence of countertransference such as significant frustration, anger, and resentment; dislike and disgust; shame; feelings of incompetence (i.e., fear they cannot live up to the counselee's expectations); depression; hopelessness, feeling of excessive pride; and romantic feelings. Countertransference might be evident in actions such as blaming the counselee, withdrawing by becoming unavailable or emotionally detached, overstepping boundaries, inappropriate touching, becoming sexual, and inappropriately self-disclosing. Cognitively the counselor's countertransference might find expression in the belief that he or she is responsible for the counselee, that he or she has a Messiah-complex, or that the counselor is unable to help.

The wise counselor is always aware of his tendencies to seek to meet personal needs through the professional relationship. Your responsibility is to know how to distinguish countertransference reactions that are inevitable because of the intensity of the counseling relationship from those that are imposed because of one's own pathology or preoccupation. Novice counselors as well as seasoned counselors need to make use of supervision to explore how personal issues might be playing out in the counseling relationship.

All countertransference reactions, however, are not detrimental to therapeutic progress. Countertransference reactions can provide an important means for understanding the world of the counselee (Arizmendi, 2008; Pattison, 2007). What is of paramount importance is that you recognize your reactions and manage your own feelings. A study conducted by Gelso, Latts, Gomez, and Fassinger (2002) found a significant correlation between a counselor's ability to manage countertransference and counseling effectiveness. Most notable in their findings was the role that emotions played. Counselor trainees were evaluated for their level of insight into their own emotions, their appreciation for the distinction between their own feelings and their counselee's feelings, their ability to manage their own anxieties, and their ability to conceptualize the counseling relationship. Counselors cannot rid themselves of all traces of countertransference or fully resolve key issues from the past. But they can become aware of these reactions and can deal with these feelings in their own counseling and through appropriate ongoing supervision.

Recall the story of Bob from the beginning of this section. Had Bob recognized the connection between his unresolved issues from his own family of origin and his behavior toward the counselee, he could have avoided a power struggle with the mother and maintained his composure through the rest of their counseling sessions together. In his supervision session Bob could have processed his reactions to the counselee's mother and toward his own mother. Countertransference need not be a hazard, but if unchecked it can harm both the counselor and counselee.

A key to managing countertransference is *never* work on your countertransference with a counselee. If you do, you will blur boundaries and put yourself in a risky position. The most damaging and common types of countertransference involve sexual issues. That is one area in which you must *always* guard your heart. Regardless of the type of countertransference, if you are experiencing feelings and/or having thoughts that are relatively intense about the relationship, discuss it as soon as possible with your supervisor or someone else. Keep your work within an ethical framework (see chap. 15, "Professional Issues in Counseling") and honor God in your shepherding care of your counselees.

## Projection

Filtering other people's lives through our own is also noted when a counselor sees his own issues in the counselee. It is as if the counselee is a blank screen on which the counselor creates a self-portrait. Consider the story recounting the reunion of two estranged twins, Jacob and Esau recorded in Gen 33:1–11. Jacob was so fearful of meeting with Esau because of having manipulated their father's blessings that he sent gifts ahead in an attempt to mollify his brother's wrath. Unknown to Jacob, however, was the fact that the gifts were not necessary. Long before their meeting, Esau had forgiven Jacob and was no longer angry with him. Instead of wrath Jacob received Esau's embrace.

We tend to see what we expect to see (Abercrombie, 1989) and may behave toward other people as if they are the people we expect them to be. In the process we send subtle messages about the role the other person is supposed to play with the implicit intent of getting the person to adopt the role (Ryle, 1998). We project an existing mental model on to the present, and may then behave in a way that is appropriate for the internal model, but may be inappropriate to the reality of the present.

## Projective Identification

In projective identification the counselor deals with unacceptable feelings, impulses, or thoughts by falsely attributing them to the counselee. Unlike simple projection, the counselor does not fully disavow what is projected but remains aware of his emotional issues and yet views them as justifiable reactions to the counselee. Often the counselor can induce the very feelings in counselees that were first mistakenly believed to be there, making it difficult to clarify who did what to whom first.

## Poor Competence

Some ways to harm a counselee are by giving poor advice, wrongly interpreting information, or saying something incorrect because of lack of knowledge, unfinished business, or personal values (Meier, 1989). Also a counselee may be harmed if you move too quickly in the counseling sessions, trying to deal with sensitive issues long before the counselee is ready. Conversely you can also do harm if you move so slowly that the counselee thinks that nothing is happening in the counseling session.

## Unethical Behavior

I (John) once spoke with a woman (whom I will call Janice) who had several poor experiences with counselors, mostly male counselors. Eventually she found herself working with a male counselor who seemed different from the others. He was warm, inviting, caring, compassionate, and helpful. As a 20-year-old woman, she yearned for a male figure who would love her and protect her. In the relationship with her counselor she met that man. Unlike other men in her life, he invited her into a relationship of intimate sharing without any ulterior motive. In her counseling with this man, she accomplished more with him than with anyone else with whom she had sought help. Unfortunately because her job required her to relocate, the woman reluctantly needed to end her therapy with this wonderful counselor. At the end of the final session he said to her, "Since this will be your last session with me would you be willing to give me oral sex?" The woman told me that she was literally dumbfounded to the point she thought she could not have heard him correctly. Startled, she asked, "What?" and he repeated his question. In spite of all the positive changes this woman made with this male counselor, it was largely lost because of this man's audacity.

In your work be moral and ethical. It is sad when any counselor is taken before a licensure board or before a church body because of unethical practice. It is especially grievous, however, when it is a Christian counselor. We grieve the Holy Spirit when we sin (Eph 4:30), and we harm the reputation of Christ.

## Summary

When people seek our help, we must do no harm. If a pedestrian is hit by a car, it does not matter whether the driver intended to inflict harm or inadvertently did so. Although our intentions might be noble, we can still do incredible harm if we are not careful. We will give an account for what we do with the people God sends to us for care (2 Cor 5:10). As the counselor, pay attention to what is happening between you and the counselee. By monitoring the process you can minimize the chances of ever doing harm.

## HELPING HAZARDS THAT CAN HURT THE COUNSELOR

Counselors have written extensively about the personal satisfaction and transformative growth that they have gained from their helping work (e.g., Aponte & Winter, 1987; Burton, 1976; Guttman & Daniels, 2001; Kottler, 1994; Sussman, 1992). Helping people with personal problems is a rewarding and positive endeavor (Guttman & Daniels, 2001; Guy & Brown, 1992; Guy & Liaboe, 1986), in which we have the privilege of ministering to the wounded. The joy of seeing people's lives redeemed and restored can make the journey of becoming a counselor an incredible blessing. At the same time helping people can also be a frustrating and negative experience (Kaslow & Schulman, 1987).

Hurting our counselees is clearly something to avoid. All mental-health professional organizations advocate the merits of protecting the counselees' welfare. Equally hazardous is allowing counselees to hurt ourselves. Two key hazards associated with counseling are countertransference and burnout.

## Countertransference

The dynamic of countertransference was discussed in the preceding section with a focus on the harm it can bring to a counselee. Since countertransference stirs up strong emotions in the soul of the counselor, it clearly has the capacity to wreak havoc in the counselor's life. You are vulnerable to harmful effects stemming from countertransference when the activities of the counselee have real potential to threaten your personality or personal stability. We have known of several counselors whose careers were shattered because they allowed their internal reactions to the counselee to take control of their lives. Some made poor decisions or unbiblical choices, or were swept into so much emotional distress that they needed help themselves.

## The Emotional Toll of Caring

Learning to counsel and engaging in the work of counseling is demanding. Moursund (1985) wrote, "Stress is our daily fare; we spend our hours dealing with pain and anxiety" (p. 214). Kottler (1994) discussed the problems of loss of sleep, one-way intimacy, fatigue, narcissism, conflict, and financial problems.

The nature of counseling typically brings together a person who is sensitive and caring with people who share stories of trauma, pain, fear, and losses. Listening to such stories throughout the course of a day exposes caring helpers to the "garbage" of living. Handling suicidal statements, anger directed at the counselor, severely depressed counselees, apathy, aggression, and violence are stressful experiences that counselors typically confront. As a result counseling practitioners often experience significant levels of occupational distress (Ross, Altmaier, & Russell, 1989). Occupational stress can cause ill health, absenteeism, high workforce turnover, reduced efficiency and performance, and burnout (Cushway, Tyler, & Nolan, 1996). Although people experience stress differently, research points to moderate depression, mild anxiety, emotional exhaustion, and disrupted relationships as the common residue of immersing ourselves in the inner worlds of distressed and distressing people (Brady, Healy, Norcross, & Guy, 1995). Clearly there is a range of potential harmful reactions and responses associated with the work of helping.

Smith, Kleijn, and Hutschemekers (2007) identified three hazardous categories of counselor reactions to therapeutic work: traumatic, interactional, and situational. They found that counselors reacting to traumatic events exhibited such reactions as shock, anxiety, feeling overwhelmed, and feeling destabilized. Those experiencing interactional difficult situations exhibited a higher-than-usual level of emotional investment along with feelings of helplessness and being manipulated. And they found that counselors reacting to existentially difficult situations demonstrated a heightened rumination style and increased sense of responsibility.

Counselors may also experience similar feelings toward their counselees because they care for people whose lives have been so affected by a depraved and dark world. In other words since counselors work with suffering people, you will not only contend with the normal stress of working a job, but you will also experience stresses that are unique to the counseling profession (Donat & Neal, 1991; Guy, Brown, & Poelstra, 1990; Prosser, Johnson, Kuipers, & Szumukler, 1997). These may include emotional and personal feelings of encountering the walking wounded, inadequate administrative support, and threats of malpractice suits or ethical complaints. Counselors tend to absorb the pain of their counselees. Caring for hurting people can result in emotional, physical, mental, and spiritual exhaustion. The fallout involves feeling depleted, chronically tired, helpless, hopeless, and even cynical.

Several terms have been used to capture this state of being: *compassion fatigue* (Figley, 1995), *secondary trauma* (Figley, 1995), *burnout* (Freudenberger, 1974), and *vicarious trauma* (McCann & Pearlman, 1990). Each of these terms captures the result of stressors associated with the daily work of counseling, especially the interactions with counselees and colleagues and in the stress associated with the institutions and organizations in which counselors are serving.

The impact of compassion fatigue is widespread. In a study by Meldrum, King, and Spooner (2002) the researchers found that 27 percent of professionals working with traumatized individuals were experiencing *extreme* distress. Overall 54.8 percent were distressed, and 35.1 percent were very or extremely emotionally drained. Identifying the negative impact of caring is not always so straightforward or easy. Figley (1995) suggests that burnout, countertransference, worker dissatisfaction, and related problems mask the issue of compassion fatigue. One of the major implications of compassion fatigue is the loss of one's effectiveness as a helper because of the impaired judgment, impaired decision-making, and the emotional toll of caring. Addressing the fallout of helping is the responsibility of each counselor and also the organization that employs him. Ultimately, however, it is up to each counselor to be a wise steward of his life.

Ironically counselors are often unaware that their counseling work is hurting them. In many cases the process is gradual and insidious. "As counselors devote substantial amounts of time and energy to helping counselees, they may lose sight of their own personal health and the needs of their own families" (Morrissette, 2002, p. 35). The natural care and concern characteristic of counselors and the intense overinvolvement with serious suffering obscures their ability to step back and examine themselves and realize the toll their work is taking on them. Paradoxically many counselors are so ministry-minded, business-minded, or proud to admit that a problem exists. The need to meet financial obligations, obtain a particular financial status, or avoid disappointing someone drives some professionals to overextend themselves.

## AVOIDING THE HAZARDS

The purpose of this chap. is not to create so much fear that you change your professional interest in counseling. Rather the intent of the chap. is to provide a clear reality check to the seriousness of the counseling profession so that appropriate changes and adjustments might be made. Everyone who has driven has come across the sign that says "Road construction ahead." The sign serves as a warning to the hazards that lie ahead. Prudent drivers slow their speed and take precautions to avoid injuring others, themselves, and their vehicles. Without that sign, drivers would hit potholes and other hazards, thereby causing significant damage. In a similar way this chap. is a road sign to warn you about potential hazards down the road. Several actions can be taken on your part to prevent harm.

First, work with integrity. Secular counseling associations have ethical guidelines that require the counselor to do only good and to seek the welfare of the counselee. Integrity is to characterize every Christian counselor. We are to be whole; what we are in public must match what we are in private. When we operate with integrity, we will not make choices that feed the flesh or are harmful to the counselee.

Second, maintain good self-care. The last chap. addresses several steps toward maintaining good self-care. These include (a) deal with known sin, (b) know your weaknesses, (c) take ownership of your life and problems, (d) create balance, (e) take time for yourself, (f) develop a healthy social support system, (g) accept your circumstances and limitations, (h) monitor yourself, and (i) seek help if necessary. According to Corey (2005), personal counseling enhances one's therapeutic impact by helping you "learn to deal with countertransference" (p. 21), which may include overidentification with counselees or "meeting [the counselor's] needs through their counselees" (p. 21). By becoming emotionally, mentally, and spiritually stronger you will develop a resilience against making poor choices and being harmed by helping.

Third, get personal counseling to learn about yourself. We will deal with this issue more in the following chap., but for now, realize its importance in helping you become whole. Sandra Wilson (2001) wrote that "hurt people hurt people." Indeed we are hurt in relationships by people who carry wounds themselves. But it is also true that "healed people heal people." As you deal with your own issues, you are in a stronger position to be an agent of healing.

Fourth, remember that you are responsible *to* your counselee, not *for* your counselee. At times novice counselors misunderstand the concept of responsibility in helping. It is easy to mislabel responsibility and believe you can be responsible for the actions and intentions of others. You can be responsible only *for* yourself, but as stated, you can be responsible *to* your counselee. Do not attempt to assume the role of God in the counselees' lives.

## CHAPTER SUMMARY

Though we are called to help, we may cause harm to our counselees and to ourselves. Years ago Carkhuff and Berenson (1967) said, "Counseling is as effective as the therapist is living effectively" (p. 197). In keeping with the words of the apostle Paul, "And whatever you do in word or deed, do all in the name of the Lord Jesus, giving thanks to God the Father through Him" (Col 3:17, NKJV). In that verse Paul summed up how genuine Christians live. Commit everything you say and everything you do to the Lord Jesus; honor Him in everything, and you will be able to insulate yourself against the hazards of helping.

## CHAPTER 3 ACTIVITIES

Directions: Prayerfully and carefully complete the following questions and activities related to the content of this chapter.

1. List the reasons for countertransference given in this chap. and briefly discuss them. Which one of these reasons will likely relate most to you and why?

2. Since counselors must possess self-awareness, identify two potential reasons that might affect you. Write out why you believe these reasons might pose a risk for you. Then develop a plan to address each reason.

3. Review the ACA's Code of Ethics and the AACC Code of Ethics found in Appendixes A and B.
    a. Name three ways each code addresses the hazards to the counselee.
    b. Name three ways each code addresses the hazards to the counselor.

4. Name four potential hazards that can place a counselee's welfare in jeopardy and describe in detail your plan for ethically managing these in your practice.

5. Discuss two key hazards to the counselor associated with counseling and describe your plan for managing these in your life.

6. Based on your self-knowledge and the feedback from others (ask some individuals close to you), which of these hazards pose the greatest threat to your potential counselees and you?

7. Write a letter to God in which you prayerfully request help for the specific areas you described in questions 1–3.

8. One of the ways to avoid doing harm is to write progress notes as soon as each session is over. Imagine that you just finished a session and as you write your notes, you discover that you reacted ineffectively to a counselee struggling with his faith. Imagine that your counselee shared that he had fears and doubts about his faith and that he was feeling angry with God. Instead of listening to your counselee and providing a "holding environment" so he could explore and understand his feelings, you had immediately started telling him what he should do to shore up his faith and you gave him Scripture verses to help him do so. Looking back, you see that your counselee immediately "shut down," and for the rest of the session he talked about surface things. In fact he was very ambivalent about scheduling another session. What do you imagine you might do to deal with and redeem this error?

9. Who are the people in your life who can serve as supervisors and counselors to you as you deal with potential hazards in your work? If you do not have a supervisor or counselor, prayerfully consider finding someone who can function in this role for you. This work is too important and too potentially dangerous to your counselees and to you, to go it alone.

## Recommended Reading

Skovholt, T. M., and Trotter-Matheson, M. (2009). *The resilient practitioner: Burnout prevention and self-care strategies for counselors, therapists, teachers, and health professionals.* 2nd ed. New York: Routledge.

> This book provides all those who work with people information on how to maintain "self-care" while providing "other care."

Swenson, R. (2004). *Margin: Restoring emotional, physical, financial, and time reserves to overloaded lives.* Colorado Springs, CO: NavPress.

> Counselors can glean much from this work to help them maintain appropriate balance in their lives and to help counselees obtain balance in their lives.

Wilson, S. D. (2001). *Hurt people hurt people: Hope and healing for yourself and your relationships.* Grand Rapids, MI: Discovery House.

> Dr. Wilson's model is intensely practical and relevant to those who counsel. Her insights in human functioning are overwhelmingly comprehensible and infused with biblical wisdom. Her premise is simple: Hurt people do indeed hurt people. She unpacks how that process plays out in different relationships and contexts. Counselors and church leaders alike will find this book powerfully informative.

# Chapter 4

# The Person of
# the Counselor

*"If it is true that those who seek us out are broken, needy, and vulnerable, and if it is true that you and I are called by God to shepherd such people, then we must learn how to shepherd fitly. Furthermore, if it is true that such a task is so serious and awesome because of its potential impact for good or evil in the lives of others, and if it is also true that shepherding selfishly and unfitly grieves the God who has called us, then we had better learn to counsel according to the Master's own heart"* (Diane Langberg, cited in Clinton and Ohlschlager, 2002a, p. 75).

*"Our conscience testifies that we have conducted ourselves . . . in our relations with you, in the holiness and sincerity that are from God"* (2 Cor 1:12, NIV).

## CHAPTER OBJECTIVES

» To highlight the importance of the person as a counselor in the helping process

» To present a taxonomy of counselor characteristics

» To present a taxonomy of counselor development

» To discuss key attitudes that affect the counseling process

» To review characteristics of effective helpers

» To provide students with information on how to take care of themselves

» To provide information on becoming the person God has called you to be

## CHAPTER OUTLINE

A MODEL OF HELPER DEVELOPMENT
   A Taxonomy of Counselor Characteristics
   A Taxonomy of the Person of the Counselor

THE CHARACTERISTICS OF AN EFFECTIVE COUNSELOR
   Love: The Counselor's Belt
   Trustworthiness and Authenticity: The Counselor's Outer
      Garments
   Self-Awareness: The Counselor's Undergarments

THE CARE AND FEEDING OF THE COUNSELOR
   Deal with Known Sin
   Know Your Personal Landmines
   Take Ownership
   Improve Your Coping
   Learning from Your Own Suffering
   Learn to Self-Monitor
   Seek Personal Counseling

CHAPTER SUMMARY

CHAPTER 4 ACTIVITIES

W e (John and Lisa) have each had the experience of hiring a professional guide for a tour we were taking of a national park. Although each guide took the customers to similar points of interest, no tour was the same. Each guide had his own interests, experiences, and insights into the stops along the route. Their personal perspective made the expedition uniquely their own. Besides experiencing various points of interest, we were seeing those points of interests through the eyes of the guides.

What makes counseling so unique is that it is conducted through a unique individual. The counselee's problems are viewed through the eyes of the counselor. What strikes the counselor as important says as much about the counselor as it does about the counselee. Clearly the counselor is the most important ingredient in the helping process (Corey, 2005; Skovholt & Jennings, 2004).

Every profession has its own tools of the trade. Carpenters have their power tools, musicians play their instruments, artists use their pencils, and surgeons operate with their scalpels. One thing that makes the profession of counseling so different is that the counselor himself is the tool (Combs, Avila, & Purkey, 1971; Dewane, 2006). Because the person of the counselor is the means by which counseling occurs, everything about the counselor plays a role in a face-to-face encounter with a counselee (Hardaway, 1976; McMinn & McRay, 1997; Williamson, 1962).

The notion that you, the counselor, are the tool is revealed not only in what is said in the session but also how you act, especially in your nonverbal communication. As the famed family therapist, Virginia Satir (1987) said, "Therapy is a deeply intimate and vulnerable experience, requiring sensitivity to one's own state of being as well as to that of the other. It is the meeting of the deepest self of the therapists with the deepest self of the patient or counselee" (cited in Morrissette, 2002). Similarly Aponte (1994) stated, "Therapy challenges clinicians to use their personal selves effectively within the professional relationship" (p. 3), which means that you need to understand your personal and professional influence on the counselee. Raines (1996) asserts that when we meet people who have suffered "malignant deprivations and losses . . . only the provision of an authentic person will suffice" (p. 373). Therefore in order to be effective in the work of counseling you must become skillful at using yourself and that you become real (Smith, 2003).

As novice counselors learn the trade of counseling, they assume that helping equates with knowledge of theory and techniques. In other words they assume that counseling-related knowledge is both necessary and sufficient to help. The student's focus is outward on the "how to" of counseling. They inquire about how to conceptualize a counselee's situation and what to do in certain situations. Such questions are appropriate and necessary, but they overlook the most important factor in the counseling process, namely, the counselor. The person of the counselor subsumes any theory or technique (Bohart, 2001; Leitner, 2006; Seligman, 1995; Truax & Mitchell, 1971). In fact Corey (2005) contends that the person of the counselor is the main technique. Williamson (1962) writes, "I suggest that the style of living of the counselor himself is an extremely important and effective technique in counseling" (p. 214). Theory and technique alone are insufficient in bringing about lasting change.

For the Christian counselor the importance of the person of the counselor is both apparent and paramount. The Christian counselor is a "signpost" to the person of Jesus Christ (Crabb & Allender, 1997). As a representative of the redeeming and restoring Christ, the counselor reflects His image. In concert with Jesus' incarnate love, the Christlike counselor will find that counselees will strive to imitate behavior that reflects Christ. Paul referred to this principle in 1 Cor 11:1, when he urged his readers to imitate him as he followed Christ.

The Christian counselor is an instrument of the Holy Spirit. Just as the Holy Spirit is the one who comforts, convicts, advocates, and guides, so the Christian counselor becomes an incarnate presence of those activities. The Christian counselor seeks to receive enlightenment from the Holy Spirit of God (Crabb, 1977). God's truth, not your "truth," is the thrust of the counseling process. As the Holy Spirit indwells, fills, and equips you, the counseling will naturally follow from God's absolute truth and principles for living.

Growing into the kind of person who can most effectively help people is a holistic endeavor that taps every facet of living. Since the relationship between the counselor and the counselee underlies every aspect of counseling (see chap. 5, "Basic Skills: Creating a Connection"), it is critical that you understand how the person of the counselor impacts the therapeutic relationship.

## A MODEL OF HELPER DEVELOPMENT

Figure 4.1 provides an overview for counselor skill development (cf. Haber, 1996). The helper's house contains the floor plan for developing the components and skills necessary for being a Christian counselor. Chapter 1 ("The Foundation of Helping") addressed the role of one's worldview in the work of counseling. This chap. focuses on the main floor of the house, the person of the counselor, which encompasses all the experiences, personality, gifts, spirituality, ethics, values, and relational affiliations of the helper. The counselor is the main floor on which counseling is built. To the degree that the counselor is privy to her internal world, then the self-knowledge can be used to enhance the implementation of the skills, orientation, and theology.

In the following four chaps. (5–8), we will delve into the upper-floor story of the helper's house, the level where the basic helping skills "reside." The upper floor of a house is always established on a foundation to give it permanence and stability and a main floor that provides access. In the case of the helper the upper floor is situated on the person of the counselor. As noted above, some people have an easier time learning particular skills, are more inclined to exhibiting certain counselor qualities associated with effectiveness, and employ the skills in a manner unique to them.

The attic represents the counselor's theoretical orientation, which is an expression of the beliefs, values, and knowledge of the helper. The counselor's orientation provides a framework for offering help and addressing the counselee's concerns. We spoke about the counselor's model and orientation in chap. 2, "The Fundamentals of Helping," and we will propose a specific model in chap. 9 ("Managing the Counseling Session").

The attic transcends the entire house. Attics typically store family treasures and artifacts. In the helper's house the attic is filled with the coun-

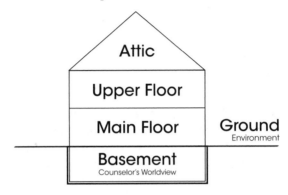

Figure 4.1: The Helper's House:
A Model of Counselor Development

selor's beliefs about the Godhead, mankind, sin, redemption, and hope. A number of these issues were addressed in chap. 1 ("The Foundation of Helping").

The final aspect of the helper's house is the lot on which it resides. Every person exists in an environment. The space on which a person resides includes a street, neighborhood, community, town or city, state, and nation. In this model the helper's house resides within a family context (e.g., nuclear, extended), a work context (e.g., department, organization, employer), a social system context (e.g., friends, acquaintances, community organizations), a professional context (e.g., memberships), a spiritual context (e.g., church, small group, denomination). Each workplace has its own culture that shapes the way work is performed and the expectations of employee behavior. Churches, for example, have a view of the helping profession that can range from favorable to highly unfavorable. The wise helper understands that he or she exists in a web of interlocking systems that seeks a level of influence on the person.

## A Taxonomy of Counselor Characteristics

What counselees prefer in counselor characteristics play an important role in the counseling relationship (Finney, 2004). In light of this fact Beutler, Crago, and Arizmendi (1986) have extensively examined counselor characteristics in order to better understand the role they play in the counseling relationship. As a result of their work they developed a taxonomy of counselor characteristics that fall along two dimensions (Figure 4.2). The first dimension represents characteristics that are externally observed (i.e., objective) to those that must be inferred (i.e., subjective). The second dimension represents those characteristics that cut across situations (i.e., cross-situational) to characteristics that are specific to counseling. Cross-situational traits are those that exist both inside and outside of counseling. Such traits are generic attributes that include the counselor's age, sex, ethnicity, personality, emotional well-being, attitudes, beliefs, and spiritual life. Since these variables are developed independently of counseling, they are called "extra-therapy variables" (Najavits & Weiss, 1994).

The second dimension covers the range of qualities that can be characterized as objective and subjective. Objective qualities refer to those characteristics that do not require the counselor to report them in order to know them. In contrast subjective qualities require that the counselor share them in order for them to be meaningfully known. Beutler and associates (1986) identified subjective counselor traits as encompassing such cross-situational variables as personality and therapy-specific variables.

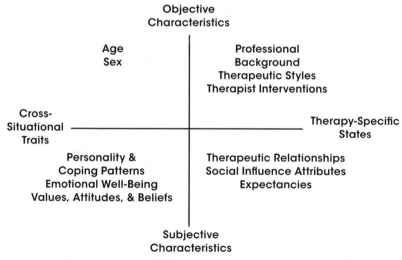

Sources: Beutler, Crago, & Arizmendi (1986), and Beutler, Machado, & Neufeldt (1994)

**Figure 4.2: A Taxonomy of Counselor Characteristics**

## A Taxonomy of the Person of the Counselor

Although a counselor possesses characteristics along both the dimensions as noted by Beutler, Crago, and Arizmendi (1986), counselors obtain most of these characteristics through the development of their entire person. The person of the counselor who is the main floor of the helping house (see Figure 4.1). Bufford (2007) holds that the character, life, and work of the counselor are at the core of consecrated Christian counseling.

> Counseling is most truly Christian when the counselor has a deep faith; counsels with excellence; has a Christian worldview; is guided by Christian values in choosing the means, goals, and motivations for counseling; actively seeks the presence and work of God; and actively utilizes spiritual interventions and resources within ethical guidelines (p. 120).

One means of conceptualizing the person of the counselor is the need to have (a) awareness, (b) skill, and (c) knowledge. These three competent counselor needs form an acrostic "ASK." In this section we will present a taxonomy of counselor development that includes the development of the counselor's head (i.e., knowledge), hands (i.e., skill), and heart (i.e., awareness).

### The head: Developing the knowledge base.

The head component of counseling includes the therapy-specific states identified by Beutler and associates (1986) as well as the cross-situational characteristics of values, attitudes, and beliefs. Since the "head" aspects of counselor training occupy most of the counselor education coursework, we will provide only a succinct overview in this chap.

Like the human brain, this domain has two hemispheres: the counseling-knowledge hemisphere and the theological-knowledge hemisphere. Christian counselors are applied theologians (Wilson, 1990), who possess both the knowledge and skills of their secular counterparts but perceive people and circumstances through a biblical lens. Though we will discuss both of these hemispheres separately, in actuality they form a whole just as the right and left hemispheres of the brain form one brain.

### *Counseling knowledge base.*

Proverbs 20:5 says, "The purposes of a man's heart are deep waters, but a man of understanding draws them out" (NIV). A key to helping others is developing the knowledge and ability to understand and intervene in their difficulties.

The development of a counseling-knowledge hemisphere encompasses every academic component in your educational program. To truly help people, you must have a clear understanding of counseling that includes knowledge of human functioning, theories, and techniques. A counselor's theoretical orientation and understanding of human functioning are integral to providing the best care of wounded souls possible. Counseling theory is to counseling what theology is to the Bible. Theory offers a road map of human functioning and helping, allowing the counselor to understand, predict, evaluate, and improve (Brammer, Shostrom, & Abrego, 1989). The underpinning of any theoretical orientation is a set of beliefs, values, and dispositions that influence how one practices counseling. A number of these factors emanate from the counselor's heart, which will be discussed in detail below. A theory of counseling provides a consistent and coherent perspective on human functioning, human dysfunction, and the mechanisms of therapeutic change. Counseling strategies and techniques follow from the counselor's understanding of these perspectives.

Being able to conceptualize counselee situations and functioning is fundamental to the work of helping (Beutler, Machado, & Neufeldt, 1994). Effective helpers possess clinical wisdom, which includes the ability to accurately assess, understand, and treat counselee difficulties. Knowledge provides a major basis for making sense of the counselee's problem, its roots, and the counselee's needs. Also counselors need to be able to identify a variety of helping strategies that can be tailored to meet the needs of individual counselees. Case conceptualization is discussed in more detail in chap. 11.

Also counselors need to develop other cognitive sets that directly impact counseling. For example Beutler, Machado, and Neufeldt (1994) identified self-efficacy (i.e., the sense that one has the competence to be able to counsel) as a reliable characteristic to use in selecting and training counselors. Effective Christian helpers, however, temper positive self-beliefs and confidence with a humility and dependency on God, who alone brings healing and change.

### Theological knowledge base.

Every counselor possesses a personal philosophy for living and a counseling orientation that includes a philosophical worldview (Arbuckle, 1965). Secular programs typically view life from a humanistic worldview. In contrast, Christian helpers ground themselves in a biblical worldview that forms their philosophy of living. Christian counselors have a solid and explicit biblical worldview that incorporates knowledge of the Scriptures, knowledge of how to study the Bible, and well-formed theological insights on numerous issues related to human functioning.

First, the counselor's theological orientation is established in the truth of God's Word (i.e., special revelation). The Bible addresses the most important aspects of life—its meaning, purpose, and value. The truths of the Bible form the foundation of our understanding of human functioning and of counseling work. Without being able to set our counseling feet on a solid foundation, we will flounder in our work and fail to offer true hope to our counselees. Moreover, any counseling that rests on a foundation other than biblical truths and principles cannot be considered Christian counseling.

Theologically the Bible delineates four core events that capture the story of mankind: creation (i.e., mankind is made in the image of God), the fall (distortion of the image, separation from God, sin, sickness), redemption (the need for spiritual and emotional healing), and the new life in Christ (living for Christ, loving God and others). Understanding these key events and how they relate to human functioning is critical in providing a truly Christian approach to counseling (Clinton & Ohlschlager, 2002a; Crabb & Allender, 1997; McMinn, 1996; McMinn & Campbell, 2007; McMinn & Phillips, 2001; McMinn, Ruiz, Marx, Wright, & Gilbert, 2006).

### The hands: Mastering the art of counseling.

Just as a head is useless without a body, so counseling and theological knowledge alone is insufficient to enable one to come alongside and help hurting people. Knowledge of counseling without counseling skill is like knowing how to drive without ever sitting behind the wheel of a car. So the hands of the counselor become engaged when the counselor practices and applies all that has been learned. Learning how to do it is at the core of counselor training and encompasses both the objective and subjective characteristics of the therapy-specific states identified in the taxonomy of Beutler, Machado, and Neufeldt (1994), including therapeutic style, interventions, relationship-building skills, and theoretical orientation.

Counselors must develop competence and mastery of skills that have been shown to be useful in helping the hurting (Stein & Lambert, 1995; Stevens, Dinoff, & Donnenworth, 1998). One of the most unsettling aspects of an education program for novice counselors is practicing the techniques of counseling. Many counselors in training are apprehensive as they sit face-to-face with their first counselee. Knowing what to say and what to do is daunting. But the only way a person can become a competent counselor is to counsel. There is no substitute for hands-on practice and for receiving focused feedback from an experienced helper.

Learning the skills of counseling is similar to acquiring mastery at any discipline. It requires understanding, practice, sound feedback, and more practice. In other words it takes time to develop into a competent Christian counselor. The results of receiving skill-based training and actively engaging in the process is being prepared to help as many people as possible (Crews et al., 2005; Urbani, Smith, Maddux, Smaby, Torres-Rivera, & Crews, 2002; Zimmick, Smaby, & Maddux, 2000). This entire text is designed to accompany a hands-on approach to counselor skill training. This textbook is dedicated to helping you learn and refine your abilities to develop a helping relationship with your counselees and learn strategies that are useful in bringing about healing and change.

While learning a skill takes time, it pales in comparison to what is involved in growing as a person and developing the cross-situational characteristics (Beutler, Machado, & Neufeldt, 1994).

### The heart: Being a whole person.

A person's head and hands are lifeless without a beating heart. The life of every person lies in a healthy working heart. The heart gives life to the body, and it also facilitates direction and activity. People must have their "hearts in it" for them to pursue some goal passionately. Likewise counseling is more than a mental/behavioral enterprise. Together the head and hands create the scholar-practitioner aspects of counseling, but by themselves they are insufficient in creating an authentic, well-balanced, and godly counselor. Since all cross-situational factors find expression in the counseling relationship, effective counseling ultimately hinges on the person of the counselor.

By the very nature of counseling, it is impossible to contain the counselor's emotional life, spiritual life, experiences, values, and attitudes. Any unresolved issues in your life will come to light in the context of the counseling relationship, creating an interpersonal nightmare (Wallin, 2007). One must see and deal with his own personal needs before he can see the mess in another person's soul with clarity (Crabb, 2003). Moreover, counselees will rarely improve beyond the functioning of their counselors; you cannot take a counselee where you have not been (Corey, 2005; van Deusen Hunsinger, 1995, 2001).

To be effective in counseling, then, one must possess the greatest level of spiritual and psychological health possible. Before you can adequately and appropriately interact with your counselees' issues, you must confront your own sins, secrets, scars, and shortcomings. An unexamined life is a dangerous life, especially when that life so powerfully impacts others, as is true in counseling. Just as the apostle Paul encouraged believers to examine themselves before partaking in the Lord's Supper (1 Cor 11:28), carefully examine yourself before entering into the sacred place of the counseling relationship. Spiritual maturity is the fruit of a self-examined heart.

Writing in the context of group counseling, Yalom and Leszcz (2005) captures the importance of knowing yourself.

> Our knowledge of self plays an instrumental role in every aspect of the therapy. An inability to perceive countertransference response, to recognize our personal distortions and blind spots, or to use our own feelings and fantasies in our work will severely limit our effectiveness. If you lack insight into your own motivations, you may, for example, avoid conflict in the group because of your proclivity to mute your feelings, or you may unduly encourage confrontation in a search for aliveness in yourself. You may be overeager to prove yourself or to make consistently brilliant interpretations, and thereby disempower the group. You may fear intimacy and prevent open expression of feelings by premature interpretations—or do the opposite: overemphasize feelings, make too few explanatory comments, and overstimulate counselees so that they are left in agitated turmoil. You may so need acceptance that you are unable to challenge the group and, like the members, be swept along by the prevailing group current. You may be so devastated by an attack on yourself and so unclear about your presentation of self as to be unable to distinguish the realistic from the transference aspects of the attack (p. 559).

What is true for group counselors is true for individual helpers. Our personal strengths, hang-ups, limitations, and issues are strongly interwoven into the work of helping. As human beings, we bring our personal histories, values, attitudes, interpersonal styles, personal baggage, and emotions into the counseling relationship. We will examine these later in more detail.

### *Counselor history: The forming of the heart.*

A person's life story includes a collection of living memories. A person's history consists of both pleasurable and unpleasurable events that blend together with his or her temperament. These events are primarily interpersonal experiences that give birth to and reinforce personality. Each person's history includes the experiences that shape his values, attitudes, interpersonal style, emotions, and so forth.

In any interpersonal context such as marriage and counseling, both parties bring their personal histories of relational affirmation and injury into the relationship (Leitner, 2007). In the counseling context counselors use the terms *transference* and *countertransference* to explain the impact of relational history in the counseling relationship. More will be said about countertransference later in this chap. Suffice it for now to understand that knowing where you have been and which needs did not get fully met along the way will keep you from tearing down others.

### *Counselor values: The passion of the heart.*

For decades research has shown that counselor values influence the quality of the counseling relationship (Samler, 1960; Walker, 1956; Wrenn, 1957). Values refer to those things that are important to each of us; they are emotionally laden thoughts about goals, ideas, beliefs, and opinions that we hold as special. Values play a significant role in the choices we make. The concept of values is often confused with the concept of morals. The difference between morals and values has not always been clear. According to Grant (1985), "Moral values are distinguished from values in general in that they encompass only attitudes towards other individuals and attitudes towards actions that affect them" (p. 143). In other words morals are more specific than values.

Christian counselors have long heralded the importance of values and the fact that it is impossible to be value-free in counseling. Values permeate every facet of counseling. Garfield and Bergin (1986) stated that progress in developing new and more effective techniques of psychotherapy has obscured "the fact that subjective value decisions underlie the choice of techniques, the goals of change, and the assessment of what is a 'good outcome'" (p. 16). Moreover, the goals of counseling also reflect distinct value orientations (Madell, 1982). For example, one's values determine whether happiness is a legitimate goal for the Christian counselee or whether the use of corporal punishment is considered appropriate.

Counselors, like all people, have stated values and real values. Stated values are those that are cognitively acknowledged about how a person thinks and feels about a particular topic. Real values, however, may not be in concert with those consciously acknowledged. A colleague of mine (John's), who claimed to be a committed Christian, had a stated belief in the sanctity of life. In a counseling session with a pastor's daughter who was pregnant at the age of 13, however, the colleague encouraged the family to consider an abortion because of the social and psychological implications of the 13-year-old daughter having the baby out of wedlock and before she was emotionally equipped to be a parent. The counselor's stated value of the sanctity of life was not as real as she asserted.

### *Counselor attitudes: The perspectives of the heart.*

Attitudes are basically inner positions of the heart, which when activated lead to patterns of thought and actions. Bound up in attitude are our values, motives, and beliefs. A person's perspective on life is directly linked to attitude. We could consider many attitudes, but we will discuss only a few key ones.

*Attitudes about God, Christ, the Holy Spirit, the world, and the Word.* What a counselor believes about God, Jesus Christ, the Holy Spirit, the world, and the Word will impact how he or she frames issues, challenges a counselee, and provides guidance. These doctrines form the philosophical worldview of the counselor. The manifestation of these core beliefs is evident in all aspects of counseling. Counselors have their stated theological beliefs, but they also carry a practical theology that may not reflect their stated beliefs. For example we have known a number of conservative Christian counselors who hold to the notion that "God wants us to be happy." Of course God is not committed to our unhappiness, but His desire for us far exceeds our happiness. Scripture leaves no doubt whatsoever that God wants us to be holy and that we worship Him (Matt 4:10; 5:16; John 17:19; Rom 12:1; 1 Pet 1:16). We are offered an abundant life (John 10:10), but nowhere in the Bible are we encouraged to seek a happy life. The notion that God wants us to be happy seems innocuous at first, but we know of cases where the counselor's attitude that God desires our happiness has been used to recommend such things as divorce, abortions, and even infidelity.

*Attitudes about the calling.* Few callings have the ability to have such an eternally meaningful impact on others as helping. Christian counseling is more than a job or role; it is a divine calling (Crabb & Allender, 1997). Believing that God has called you into the work of helping people will enable you to persevere through difficult times. Following God's call provides immense and profound joy in seeing what God does in the brokenness and shattered lives of people. When you know that God delights in your professional work, you feel a freedom to connect with hurting people and walk with them through their valleys of anguish. In contrast, doubting your calling will lead to chronic frustration, cynicism (which is anger), and burnout. Examining your attitude about your calling means asking yourself these questions (a) Why do I want to be a counselor? (b) What personal needs does it fulfill? (c) What traits and characteristics do I bring into this calling? (d) If I were to do anything else other than counseling, what would it be?

*Attitudes about oneself.* The counselor's attitudes about himself or herself are bound up in counseling. Having positive perceptions of oneself does not mean that one is basing confidence on self rather than Christ. Feeling comfortable in a crowd or a new setting, speaking to a large group, or being able to handle change are some of the factors that relate to attitudes about oneself. The sense that one is able to take on new things is not mutually exclusive with finding identity in Jesus Christ. It is thus important to take stock of one's own self-perceptions.

Two broad sides relate to self attitudes. One side of this factor deals with *personal* attitudes about the self, and the second side relates to *professional* attitudes about oneself.

From a personal perspective what do you really believe about yourself? Who or what do you really depend on for life? Many people want to be counselors because of their own woundedness. Some come from dysfunctional families and others have experienced a deep loss or were abused. Many counselors feel profound shame and find their lives controlled by fear of rejection, failure, abandonment, or betrayal. Christian counselors experience the same problems as everyone else: financial concerns, marital issues, parenting struggles, losses, and changes in mood. Moreover, counselors have God-given needs, many of which can be distorted by their personal history. How we seek to get our needs met has many implications for the counselor. When I (John) was learning counseling, my supervisor noticed that crying women seemed to bring out in me an emotional caretaker role. At those times, I stopped being therapeutic and started engaging in nurturing. As the supervisor and I explored the reason for my behavior, we found its roots in my family dynamics. The bottom line is that counselors bring their own self-perspectives into counseling.

A person's attitudes affect specific factors in counseling. A counselor's perception, beliefs, and feelings about his professional competence will either support or undermine his counseling efforts. At times all counselors feel unsure about what to do or lack the training in certain problem areas. In general, however, it is important to feel comfortable in the role of counselor and to have a sense of one's ability to help hurting people.

*Attitudes about the problem.* A problem that is cast in the counseling session can profoundly impact the heart of a counselor. Some problems are easier to accept than others. Other problems are more heart-stirring. Dealing with people who are experiencing issues about a child moving out is not typically emotionally draining on a counselor. By contrast hearing about how someone was abused, raped, assaulted, or lost a child to death can deeply affect the counselor's emotions. Some counselors will not work with sexual offenders, domestic violence, substance dependency, or a problem with which the counselor is personally wrestling. Careful attention must be given to understand one's own views of particular disorders, problems, and issues.

*Attitudes about the counselee.* What we think about people will ultimately be expressed in how we interact with them. More specifically how we see the counselee before us will translate into the counseling room either positively or negatively. We all know that some people are more difficult to like and even harder to care for. Sometimes, however, our difficulty with a particular counselee says more about us than it does about the counselee. When we find ourselves struggling to like or accept a particular counselee, first begin with self-examination and be open to recognizing that our own issue is at stake.

### Counselor interpersonal styles: The power of the heart.

We were made for relationships, and it is through relationships that we thrive and struggle. Relationships empower us, and knowing how you operate in relationships will enable you to capitalize on your strengths and work on your weaknesses.

We learn how to view ourselves and how to act in relationships because of experiences we have in our families of origin and later because of interactions with others in our family, our social contacts, and our occupations (Bowen, 1966; Kernberg, 1976; Sullivan, 1953). The conclusions we draw and the learning we experience become the scaffolding of our internal working models (Bowlby, 1969, 1973) mentioned in chap. 3. The roles that we assume are shaped by these early experiences (i.e., personal history) as well as the conclusions we make about ourselves, God, others, and the world from those interactions.

The beliefs that we have about other people and ourselves will express themselves in behaviors that have a predictable impact on others (Kiesler, 1996). Some people are rigid, and others are more flexible. Some people desire closeness, while others prefer interpersonal distance. Some open up to people around them, while others are highly reluctant to share their feelings. Some people are warm and inviting, while others are diplomatic and formal.

Effective counselors know how they function in both personal and professional relationships. Assess yourself and understand who you are and how you operate with different kinds of people.

### Counselor baggage: The painful heart.

Out of one's history of life experiences can come various shapes and sizes of baggage that can weigh the counselor down in his personal and professional life. In fact most helpers are attracted to the helping profession because of their personal histories. Some researchers suggest that the counseling profession is disproportionately populated by people who had excessive emotional demands placed on them during childhood (Lackie, 1983; Miller, 1990). For example Lackie (1983) found that over two-thirds of counselors surveyed described themselves as a child only protected by a parent, an overresponsible family member, one with go-between parents, the "good" child, and the bearer of family burdens. Likewise Fussell and Bonney (1990) found that counselors were prone to being in the role of parental caretaker in their family of origin.

Specifically in the counseling relationship our "baggage" can be detrimental to the helping process. For example you might find yourself trying to save a counselee instead of empowering the counselee to use psychological and spiritual resources to save himself (rescuing). Several boundary issues can also occur. For instance you might be prone to give in to demanding counselees by not having secure-enough boundaries. Or you might be too open and transparent with counselees, leading to an enmeshed relationship with the counselee. Boundary issues in your life can also lead to becoming sexual with counselees or overly emotionally involved. Also one can get caught up in the counselee's pain, chaos, and hopelessness.

By not dealing with our own baggage, we might project our own personal or family issues into the counseling relationship (i.e., countertransference) and attempt to solve our own problems in the wrong context (Wallin, 2007). For that reason the emotional and spiritual health of the counselor is paramount. In their review of studies related to counselor well-being, Beutler, Crago, and Arizmendi (1986) concluded that counselor well-being facilitates both the process and outcome of counseling. Later Beutler, Machado, and Neufeldt (1994) concluded that "high therapist distress or disturbance levels may not only prevent counselee growth, but actually induce negative changes" (p. 238).

Imagine taking a trip to a foreign country. If you needed to be able to move around the country, you would limit the amount of luggage you would carry with you (airline limitations aside). Extra baggage is too cumbersome and will weigh you down. Similarly not dealing with your own personal "baggage" will prevent you from fulfilling your divine calling. To be as effective for the cause of Christ as possible, deal with your unresolved issues of abuse, trauma, abandonment, or betrayal.

### *Counselor emotions: The power of the heart.*

The work of a counselor is demanding and draining. In this vein Patterson and Eisenberg (1983) articulate the emotional demands of working with hurting people.

> For the counselor, the related activities of attentive listening, infor-
> mation absorption, message clarification, and hypothesis generation
> require intense energy. Beyond these largely intellectual activities is
> the emotional experience of caring for another enough to be affected
> by that person's emotions without becoming lost in those emotions and
> therefore debilitated as the facilitator (p. 9).

The emotional nature of the counseling relationship requires counselors to be able to regulate their emotions. The intensity of a counselor's
reactions usually surprises novice counselors. Beginning counselors, in
particular, are wise to understand that it is common to be anxious about
helping and experiencing emotional reactions during sessions. Counselors
should not assume that in offering help they will be immune from emotional reactions. Instead, discerning counselors know that they experience
the same range of human emotions and reactions as anyone else (Robbins,
2008). Counselors who accept and tolerate their emotional reactions can
then learn to value emotions as a meaningful connection with the experiences of their counselees.

Counselors who shut off or deny awareness of their own emotional
experiences deny themselves a valuable way to understand their counselees and help them grow. As believers we are not to be pretentious about
anything; we need to face the cold reality of our hearts. Shutting off or
denying awareness of emotions is a defensive strategy by counselors who
typically view their own emotions as unacceptable. Often the message in
their family of origin was that certain emotions were wrong. Generally
these counselors fear that their emotions will overwhelm them, cause them
to lose control, or are sinful and unacceptable.

Counselors who fear their own emotions and the emotions of others will
eventually steer members away from potentially productive topics. They
divert counselees from issues that elicit their own emotions because these
issues cause reactions that make them aware of their own emotional vulnerabilities and needs. Inevitably counselors who cannot accept or tolerate
their own emotions will deprive their counselees of meaningful opportunities to confront their difficult issues.

At times counselors act out of love and can respond to situations with
wisdom, composure, and understanding. On other occasions, however,
counselors may react out of their own emotional issues and their responses may be inappropriate or harmful. If you (a) respond with uncensored
advice without fully understanding the situation, (b) become anxious and
burdened by the counselee's problems, or (c) distance yourself from the
counselee, the result will be ineffective help.

## THE CHARACTERISTICS OF AN EFFECTIVE COUNSELOR

Several decades ago Carl Rogers (1961) wrote,

> But what are the characteristics of those relationships which do help,
> which do facilitate growth? And at the other end of the scale, is it pos-
> sible to discern those characteristics which make a relationship un-
> helpful, even though it was the sincere intent to promote growth and
> development? (p. 41).

The questions asked by Rogers focus on a core issue in counseling, namely, what characteristics contribute to a helpful therapeutic climate? Rogers
(1961) described the process of his theory, Person-Centered psychotherapy,
in one sentence: "If I can provide a certain type of relationship, the other
person will discover within himself the capacity to use that relationship for
growth and change, and personal development will occur" (p. 33). Conservative Christians have typically disregarded much of what Carl Rogers
wrote because of the humanistic foundation on which his theory was built.
Although we too reject the philosophical underpinnings of his counseling
theory, we believe that his approach describes several salient characteristics of effective counseling that squares with biblical teaching. Rogers's
approach to counseling is centered in the belief that certain core counselor
characteristics (i.e., warmth, unconditional positive regard, and genuineness) will help the counselee change. For Rogers these core attributes are
both necessary and sufficient. From our perspective the attributes might
be necessary, but they are not enough to help counselees make needed
changes.

Holmes (2001) said, "What good therapists do with their patients is
analogous to what successful parents do with their children" (p. xi). A
parent's heart for his children evokes something in the parent that touches
the life of the child. Likewise these following characteristics that promote
effective counseling emanate from the counselor's heart. Though each one
has a behavioral manifestation, they are ultimately inner dispositions. As
noted by Jones and Butman (1991), the qualities of the counselor cannot "be reduced to skills or sensitivities that can be turned on or off as
the occasion demands. Indeed this would be the epitome of incongruity"
(p. 273). We will use the analogy of clothing to address the characteristics
of an effective Christian counselor.

### Love: The Counselor's Belt

According to Col 3:14, the belt that brings together all aspects of one's
spiritual wardrobe is love. Biblically the most important attribute of any
relationship is love (cf. 1 Cor 13). In fact the whole Bible can be reduced

to the simple thought that it teaches us how to love God and how to love one another (Adams, 1986).

Ultimately our ability to love comes from God, the source of all love. At the deepest level God is a Lover (1 John 4:8). He is relationally oriented and relationally driven (Jer 31:3; Rom 5:8). If you desire to model godliness to your counselees, demonstrate love in your interactions with them.

When Jesus was asked which OT commandment is greatest, He condensed all the commandments into two principles: "'Love the Lord your God with all your heart, and with all your soul, and with all your mind, and with all your strength.' . . . 'Love your neighbor as yourself.' There is no other commandment greater than these" (Mark 12:30–31, NASB). The apostle Paul also viewed love as the summary of the OT, "the entire law is fulfilled in one statement: You shall love your neighbor as yourself" (Gal 5:14, HCSB). The entire Bible communicates a message of love. In short, love is the measuring stick by which our lives will be judged. Every human being can relate to another on some level, but it is the quality of those connections that are most critical. First John 4:20 further details how one's ability to love is directly connected to that person's relationship with God. The predicament for mankind is that our sin nature causes people to seek personal agendas rather than the interests of others. Sin and self-protection stand in the way of truly loving. Thus an essential element in relationships is an understanding of the nature of love and a demonstration of its power in relating to others.

In our counseling and therapy work, we are called to demonstrate a Christlike love to our counselees. This love is for the counselee's welfare (Sanders, 1997). And this love is seen in how we bear our counselee's burdens (Gal 6:2). Noted Christian author and psychologist Larry Crabb (1977) aptly observed, "The majority of people who are experiencing personal anguish can be tremendously helped by a warm, genuine interest of people who care. When I feel loved my burdens seem lighter" (p. 166). Years ago noted psychoanalyst Arthur Burton (1976) observed the following: "In a society which no longer cares, and certainly does not care deeply for its deviants, the therapist remains the one person who really cares about the atypical, the gauche, the awkward, and the crippled" (p. 134). This sentiment resonates with any counselor who calls himself a Christian.

Paul evinced this sort of love for those to whom he ministered. In 1 Thess 2:8 Paul told the readers that he not only shared God's truth, but in doing so he gave himself to them. In fact he said he gave himself to each one. Many counselees are easy to love. But the measure of your love is not those counselees but the ones who have committed acts that you deplore or those whose behavior is offensive to you or stretches your tolerance. Consider the hard-to-love counselees and what it will take to develop a godly love for them. Even the most loving counselor who has the best of intentions, excellent education and training, and a heart for God will not be able to fully love each and every counselee that sits across from him. Sometimes the struggle to love is due to our own issues getting in the way. For instance it is difficult to love someone who has the same problem you have. At other times it may be difficult to love a counselee whose values differ dramatically from yours. Regardless of the reason each counselee will provide opportunities for you to grow. Prayerfully develop a plan to address those self-imposed limitations, and ask God to help you grow in those areas.

A significant component of love is accepting people for who they are, but not their choices or actions. You are to be a minister of grace; your response to the choices and problems of your counselee are to be filtered through humility and compassion. Be nonjudgmental and accepting of people. View your counselees in the light of God's view of that person. In other words God's perspective is the centering reality in the counseling relationship. You would be wise to see and understand through the eyes and mind of God those you are called on to help. The well-known priest Henri Nouwen (1979) artfully wrote, "For compassionate man nothing human is alien: no joy and no sorrow, no way of living and no way of dying" (p. 41). Although Job's friends were accepting and supportive in being physically present with Job on the ashheap, their dialogue with Job failed to embrace his pain. In fact, much of their dialogue mocked Job's perceptions and feelings (Job 17:2). They sought to convince Job that their interpretation of the "facts" was the correct one, when in fact they were wrong (Job 42:7–12). Job clamored that a man should have the devotion of his friends even if he walks away from God (Job 6:14). Love and acceptance of the counselee create the conditions in which the necessary risk-taking, catharsis, and exploration can unfold. Perhaps Job was able to be bluntly honest in openly expressing his feelings because of the powerful love evident in his friends' willingness to spend seven days and nights in silence on the ashheap. When you respond to counselees with an incredible measure of grace, you provide the lubricant to share truth. Grace provides safety, reduces shame, and allows the counselee to hear truth without self-condemnation. Bringing truth without first creating the space for it will backfire. Not only will "your" truth (by truth here we mean God's truth) be rejected, but so will you.

The reason that displaying biblical love is so important is that as a Christian counselor you represent the Lord. Christian counselors represent His name and His attitude toward them. Counselees may believe that they will be judged or condemned for their actions. Of course others believe that whatever they do, no matter how wrong, God will forgive them, so it is OK.

Often counselees depend on their counselor instead of depending on God. Though this is temporary for some people, others never move beyond their dependency. For whatever reasons, some people are unable to sense that their needs can be met in Jesus Christ. As such, they look to those who identify themselves with Christ for an incarnate sense of what they deeply need through Him; this constitutes the incarnate relationship of the helping process.

In addressing the needs of an increasingly multicultural society, you need be prepared to work with counselees while considering their race, ethnicity, social class, generational differences, gender, sexual orientation, and disability status (Baruth & Manning, 2003; Hall, Guterman, Lee, & Little, 2002). To avoid alienating minority counselees, white counselors need to develop an awareness of their own racial biases and racial identity and to assess their personal levels of readiness before attempting cross-cultural counseling (Chae, 2001; Robinson, 1993, 1999; Robinson & Howard-Hamilton, 2000).

The bottom line is that out of a heart of love the counselor will display empathy, unconditional positive regard, grace, mercy, and acceptance (Keijsers, Schaap, & Hoogduin, 2000). By doing this the counselor will more clearly reflect Jesus Christ through his counseling. When counselees know that you truly care for them and sense that you are there for them, they are more appreciative of the counseling relationship and counseling process. When you can express genuine love, the counselee is influenced toward more loving behavior. Deeply wounded counselees will then find the safety in which to more fully express themselves and experience a taste of the character of God.

## Trustworthiness and Authenticity: The Counselor's Outer Garments

Trust and authenticity basically mean that what you see is what you get. Thus the ideas of trust and authenticity capture the basic outer clothing that a person wears, that is, what is open for the world to see.

Trust must be present in any collaborative therapeutic relationship. Trust and fidelity in the counselor are intrinsic to an effective counseling relationship (Strong, 1968). Counselees will consider trusting the counselor if the latter is known for honesty and integrity, and is seen as sincere and open, with a perceived lack of motivation for personal gain. Counselees judge a counselor's trustworthiness based on reputation (e.g., "My pastor referred me to you; he said that you are a good Christian counselor who could help me"), physical appearance (e.g., "She has an honest face"), and how you interact with them in the appointment (e.g., maintaining confidentiality, keeping promises, accepting feedback, being open). Research findings on trustworthiness indicate that counselors who were introduced to their counselees as highly credible were perceived as more attractive and trustworthy and inspired more confidence than counselors who were presented with a low credibility introduction (Bernstein & Figioli, 1983).

Like trustworthiness, the value of authenticity has been heralded for decades. Jourard (1971) posited that authentic counselors invite counselees to become authentic. He highlighted the value of authenticity in these words.

> I wondered why I was so tense and exhausted; it soon became clear that my exhaustion came from withholding myself from my patient, from my own resistance to authentic being. . . . With this realization, many recollections came, rushing to me patients who had begged me to tell them what I thought, only to be met by my cool, faultless reflection or interpretation of their question or else by a downright lie, e.g., "Yes, I like you," when in fact I found them boring or unlikable. Also, there came to me recollections of instances where I had violated what I thought were technical rules, for example, holding a weeping patient's hand or bursting out laughing at something the patient had said and of patients later telling me that when I had done these things, I somehow became human, a person, and that these were significant moments for the patients in the course of therapy (pp. 145–146).

Authenticity is a powerful concept that begins with God. The Scripture teaches us that God's name is "I am that I am" (Exod 3:14; 34:6). In other words He is that He is; He is authentic. He cannot pretend to be something He is not; He is simply Himself. From His authenticity we are to become authentic with others.

When you are able to communicate authentically, an atmosphere is created which in turn prompts the counselee to behave authentically. When counselees begin counseling, they are usually unauthentic in that they hide parts of themselves and attempt to protect their vulnerable parts from being exposed. By living in a fallen world and having a fallen nature, we are easily conditioned toward conventional unauthentic patterns of response;

our environment induces us to muffle rather than express, to delude rather than to be straightforward.

Being authentic is being able to live with your guard down, to be able to be oneself and not acquiesce to be what you think others want you to be. It means that you are transparent with others. To be completely whole, be aware of the masks that you hide behind and what you are attempting to cover up. Only when you face your reality; that is, your secret sins, dark side, and true motives can you move into the realm of being trustworthy and authentic. Humanity interferes with being fully real because of the risk of being fully known. Avoid hiding your genuine humanness behind a mask of professionalism. As Crabb (2003) writes, "The key is authentic encounter, not professional precision" (p. 67).

The problem of hiding and repressing one's true self and feelings has its origins in Adam. After Adam and Eve sinned, they hid themselves. Ask yourself, What heart issue leads you to conform to others' expectations and to keep your guard up? You can, however, have a desire and commitment to live authentically before everyone. You are most authentically yourself when you become like Jesus Christ. Of course you can never match the level of authenticity in Jesus. If you seek to maintain a certain look or give a certain impression, you will never be fully authentic. The authentic counselor will own up to his own feelings of frustration and of satisfaction in a way that does not violate loving or edifying the counselee. Authenticity also means not shying away from your mistakes. Only God is infallible, and we are not to stand in His role.

### Self-Awareness: The Counselor's Undergarments

Self-awareness refers to a person's insight and understanding of inner feelings, attitudes, beliefs, values, vulnerabilities, inadequacies, and the impact these factors have on others. Tudor and Worrall (1994) defined self-awareness as being "aware of the flow of feelings and sensations within us as we work" (p. 2). The importance of counselors possessing self-awareness is an established value (Deacon, 1996; Grimmer & Tribe, 2001; Johns, 1996; Yalom, 1980), especially in counseling culturally diverse counselees (Baruth & Manning, 1999). Stone and Shertzer (1963) champion the importance of self-awareness to counselor effectiveness: "A true professional knows not only who he should be but also what he is" (p. 346). The value of self-awareness is found in the Council for Accreditation of Counseling and Related Educational Programs (CACREP) standards that require programs to offer its students opportunities to increase self-awareness (CACREP, 2001).

The more self-awareness counselors have of themselves the better they can understand their experiences when counseling. Loganbill, Hardy, and Delworth (1982) state that counselors "who are cognizant of the intricacies of their own personal issues are in a better position to distinguish between what is happening with the counselee and what is happening within themselves" (p. 7). Wallin (2007) writes, "To 'raise' secure patients, we must cultivate the capability for reflection in psychological depth" (p. 4). The Bible places a high premium on self-awareness, urging us to a "ruthless self-examination" (Crabb & Allender, 1997, p. 50). Hebrews 4:12 teaches that one of the roles of the Word of God is to cut into our inner being to reveal what is hidden within our hearts.

Also self-awareness will allow you to be able to maintain composure while working with difficult counselees. Unaware counselors are prone to be swept away by their counselee's emotional tidal waves, which is of no help for their counselees and for themselves.

Like counselees, counselors too differ in their ability and skill of self-awareness. Yet similarly, helpers increase their level of self-awareness by exploring significant themes, patterns, concerns, and issues. To increase self-awareness, Guerin and Hubbard (1987) advocate that counselors examine the role that their family of origin plays in their work: "The relationship experiences in one's own family are the basic training ground for the development of an effective family and/or individual psychotherapist" (p. 47).

Though understanding your personal history is a critical factor in obtaining self-awareness, perhaps the greatest window into your soul is examining how you interact with others. To develop accurate self-awareness, learn to look at yourself as if through someone else's eyes and hear yourself as if through the ears of prospective listeners. The self-aware helper has the capacity to use countertransference as a diagnostic indicator (Marcus, 2007). For example when taking my practicum I (John) learned that strong women evoked certain behaviors from me. As my supervisor and I plumbed the depths of my audiotaped sessions, it was evident that I had unresolved issues that prompted my behaviors. As I matured as a counselor, I learned how to better understand my counselees by monitoring the internal feelings I experienced in the sessions.

Closely aligned with your interactions with others is your emotional life. Your feelings are a barometer of what is going on in your heart. When you get into contact with your emotions you gain a clearer understanding of life and the choices you make.

Without self-awareness you will be unable to grow and see the positive and negative impact of your own behavior on others. As Brems (1993) articulates, "Gaining awareness has to precede modification of behavior and attitudes and can be a painful effort as clinicians begin to recognize that they are not free of recalcitrant prejudicial behaviors and beliefs" (p. 72). Brem is correct in noting that gaining inner awareness is a painful process; it requires us to understand our sins more than we desire. Crabb (1988) stated, "If awareness of what's inside forces me to admit that I'm utterly dependent on resources outside my control for the kind of change I desire, if helplessness really is at the core of my existence, I prefer to live on the surface of things. It's far more comfortable" (p. 16). Crabb further elaborates on the need for self-reflection: "Christ wants us to face reality as it is, including all the fears, hurts, resentments, and self-protective motives we work hard to keep out of sight, and to emerge as changed people" (p. 32). Crabb argues in his book *Inside Out* that we need to gain an awareness of the thirst for God that we have deep within our souls. He believes that understanding and experiencing this thirst is necessary to (a) break bad habits, (b) recognize subtle sin, and (c) develop a passion in our pursuit of God. Readers are strongly encouraged to read Crabb's work in order to develop a fuller appreciation of both the need for self-awareness and the roots of our issues that emanate from beneath the surface of our lives. It is imperative that you use classtime, laboratory work, and field placements as fertile opportunities for personal reflection, evaluation, and growth. For when you possess self-awareness, the counselee is drawn to deeper reflections of himself.

## THE CARE AND FEEDING OF THE COUNSELOR

The ultimate aim of the Christian counselor is not to help the hurting, but to glorify God. One of the best ways each of us can glorify God is to become the person God has called us to be. This section is about ways to minimize our frustration and pain and maximize our satisfaction in our calling.

Maturing in every aspect of life and becoming like Christ will position the counselor to become a better helper. Addressing your personal issues that block your contentment and assuage your service will make you a better helper and will make you more godly. The proper care and feeding of the counselor involves maintaining your personal, psychological, and spiritual hygiene and nourishing your soul.

To fulfill your calling in becoming the person God has called you to (a) deal with known sin; (b) know personal landmines; (c) take ownership;

(d) improve personal coping; (e) learn to use suffering; (f) learn to self-monitor; and (g) seek personal counseling, if needed.

## Deal with Known Sin

Biblically the concept of sin refers to either our Adamic inherent bent to sin (Rom 5:12) or to our wrongful actions and attitudes (Prov 6:16–19; Rom 1:29–31; Gal 5:19–21; 2 Tim 3:2–5). Our sinful nature captures the fact that God credits the original sin of Adam to each member of the human race (1 John 1:8–10). This can be considered as our Sin (capital "S"). Personal sins flow from that sinful nature (Rom 7:17), but are ultimately the result of choices that violate God's standards, as revealed in the Bible. These are our sins (lower-case "s").

Identifying and confronting sin is vitally important. Unless sin is brought to light, it will grow and undermine every aspect of your life. Several simple steps can help you face up to personal sin. God's initial step in dealing with sin is to recognize it. Hearing, reading, and studying God's Word brings your sinful ways to light (2 Tim 3:16–17). For some, the need to confront your sin nature is the starting point. If you have never accepted Christ as your personal Savior by confessing and repenting of your sin, then do so right now. The concepts of confession and repentance are explained in further detail below.

For those who have a personal relationship with Jesus Christ, the flesh will still cause them to sin. Thus the second step, then, is confessing your sin to God (1 John 1:9). The Greek word typically translated "confess" in the English language is the word *homologeo*, which means "to speak the same thing." The idea of confession, then, is to agree with God on the sin. Ultimately all sin is first and foremost an affront against God (Ps 51:4–5), not just against others and ourselves. The third step necessary in facing your known sin is to repent, that is, to make a willful decision to turn from that sin and live for God. The wise follower of God makes it a practice to maintain a blameless conscience (Acts 24:16; Rom 6:6,11,13; 8:13; Col 3:5). The Christian counselor, like any believer, is wise to keep very short accounts of sin and seek to yield himself to the Holy Spirit (Gal 5:22–25). The final step is to make restitution if necessary (Prov 6:31; Luke 19:26).

## Know Your Personal Landmines

Counselors should explore their basic attitudes and beliefs and work to understand them better before engaging in the helping profession. Counselors need to be sensitive to their personal reactions and be willing to reflect on the underlying reasons for them. This ability to be introspective and understand oneself is critical to mature healthy living, and as professionals and Christians we are to be examples of spiritual maturity (Titus 2:1–10).

Self-examination and self-awareness can help you know about your personal landmines. Of course a landmine is an explosive device used in war that the enemy buries underneath the ground. As the enemy advances, it is unaware of the existence or location of landmines. When a soldier unknowingly steps on a landmine, the device explodes, killing or maiming the soldier. Similarly a personal landmine refers to an issue beneath the surface of a person that will either explode or implode when pressure is applied from outside. Many people are unaware of their own landmines.

Only through deep reflection can we unearth our personal landmines and remove them from our lives. Two limitations can occur with self-reflection that will likely prevent you from coming to a better understanding of yourself: (a) not going deep enough in your reflection and (b) not appreciating the depth of your fallenness (Rom 7:23; 8:5–8; Gal 5:16,19–21). In this regard Crabb (1988) writes, "Just a quick glance beneath the surface of our life makes it clear that more is going on than loving God and loving others. It requires only a moment of honest self-reflection to realize that, no matter how much we may have already changed, we still have a long way to go" (p. 29).

Yet surfacing your issues can lead to self-condemnation provoked by an overwhelming flood of shame. Just as you are to be a minister of grace to your counselees, you must apply that same grace to yourself. Though we deserve condemnation, we know that in Christ we are free from condemnation (Rom 8:1). The point is not whether we deserve condemnation because we do; we are all fallen before a perfect, holy, and righteous God. The point is that we can offer the same grace to ourselves that Christ has offered to us.

Mapping out one's own personal journey and understanding one's unmet needs is the primary work of any counselor in training and the ongoing work for all seasoned counselors. Research suggests that some professionals enter the counseling field in order to resolve their own emotional problems (White & Franzoni, 1990) and that there is a high incidence of personal relationship problems, substance abuse, depression, suicide, high anxiety, and sexual contact with counselees (Bermak, 1977; Deutsch, 1985; Stadler & Willing, 1988; Thoreson, Budd, & Krauskopf, 1986). Such behaviors are personal landmines that can lead to personal disaster.

Many questions could be explored in identifying personal landmines, but we will limit our discussion to a few. First, the place to begin exploring for personal landmines is why you are considering entering the helping profession. On the surface most students offer reasons such as these: "I want to help others," "I believe that God has called me to the work," "I have been told that I am a good listener," or "I believe I am gifted to help." Far beneath the surface of those reasons, however, lie stronger motivations that prompt many into the helping profession. Sussman (1992) suggested a list of deeper motivations behind the pursuit of the helping profession. These include the desires to be idealized, to be a nurturer, to be in a dominant position, to achieve safe intimacy. These need-based motivations can ultimately create problems, issues, struggles, and ethical violations. For example a need to please and be accepted might result in the counselor being indecisive and permitting destructive patterns to go on without interruption. The counselor and counselee might settle into a mutually pacifying, mutually dependent prolonging of nontherapeutic work. Another significant need-based landmine is the prey of power. Colby (1951) cleverly capture the seduction of being in a dominant position.

> There is in every healing profession the temptation to play God, and an all-wise, all-powerful-acting therapist may soon run into unpleasant difficulties, just as new-found powers proved heady for the sorcerer's apprentice. A psychotherapist is really not God, nor even a close relative of his (p. 21).

Thus it is imperative for you to examine your personal deep-seated motivation behind your pursuit to be a counselor and to know how these issues might affect your work.

Second, explore how your personal history might affect your work with counselees. Research suggests that the life experiences of counselors can create landmines as they work with counselees. For example Jurkovic (1997) found that counselors who experienced high emotional demands as children might find themselves more vulnerable to a sense of duty to help their counselees. Some counselors have experienced abuse in their past, struggled with addictions, been the victims of crimes, or had significant family issues. These events can taint a counselor's perspective with counselees. I (John) knew a counselor whose husband had a series of affairs and who ultimately left her for someone else. Historically this counselor was excellent with marital problems and had worked with countless cases of infidelity. Following her own husband's disclosure and decision to leave, however, she was unable to maintain neutrality and objectivity with men engaged in affairs. It took her a few months, but she eventually realized how her own personal landmine was affecting her attitude toward her counselees. Healthy counselors recognize their landmines and take appropriate action to address them.

Third, consider in which areas of your life you are most vulnerable. Some counselors are prone to controlling others. One significant landmine is subconsciously attempting to make a counselee over in our own image, rather than encouraging a counselee to become conformed to the image of Christ.

Fourth, consider what triggers your stress. Since counselors are to model healthy coping, it is important to know what situations derail you. Everyone will experience times of personal struggle, but the important thing is to manage those difficult times and prevent them from contaminating your professional life. Counselors are of little value to their counselees if they themselves are overwhelmed by the stresses and strains of life. No one is immune from having issues in their lives that will affect their work as a helper. Wise counselors are exhorted to be alert for the signs of impairment and to seek assistance.

## Take Ownership

No one can change anything he cannot control, and no one is more in control of your choices then yourself. Thus take responsibility for dealing with your personal landmines, "baggage," or areas of weakness in your life. People who take ownership of their lives direct their efforts and actions toward making changes rather than pointing the finger at people or circumstances. In contrast people who do not take ownership feel like victims. They lament about how they were let down or unjustly treated. You need to learn how to recognize and address your personal issues when they are correctable and how to let go of them when no correction is possible. Face up to your problems, weaknesses, issues, strengths, and assets. When you take ownership of your life, you accept the fact that you always have a choice in how to handle problems.

## Improve Your Coping

Counselors are faced with demanding jobs that require the ability to cope well. As discussed earlier, the workload of a counselor can take a toll. There are many stresses in the profession, including handling difficult cases. Research indicates that not all counselors cope with difficult cases well. Orlinsky, Norcross, et al. (2005) conducted a large-scale international study of counselors to evaluate coping strategies for difficult cases. Findings led to the development of three dimensions of counselor difficulties: self-doubt, frustrating cases, and negative reactions to counselees.

To avoid such difficulties, improve your overall coping effectiveness. The question is not *if* you cope with situations, but *how* you cope with them. The word *cope* comes from a Latin word that means to engage in war. Just as some soldiers are better than others, some people are simply better at coping than others. All can improve their coping skills, however.

People who cope well have good mental and spiritual hygiene. They maintain their health through active and preventive means. A few strategies can help you cope well with life's difficulties.

### Create balance in your life.

The work of counselors sets them up to have an outward focus which might result in their paying less attention to their own needs. First, to have balance in your life, you must be willing to set limits. Often novice counselors over-schedule themselves, based on the convenience of their counselees. Second, balance work and play. Work has a way of creeping into our personal lives through rehashing the problems of the day, taking work home, working overtime, and being on call. Saying no does not mean saying never, but it does mean limiting the amount of work invasion. For Christians, work can creep into one's personal life, and ministry activities can overload a person's schedule. The key to balancing work, ministry, and personal time is finding and maintaining leisure activities that can be done alone and with family members. Leisure activities can take many forms, but the key is that such activities provide mini-vacations from the stress of working so closely with hurting people. Leisure activities also provide positive experiences with people who have nothing to do with emotional pain and suffering. Richard Swenson's (2004) book, *Margin: Restoring emotional, physical, financial, and time reserves to overloaded lives* is an excellent resource to read for personal and professional purposes.

### Take time for yourself.

Closely aligned with balance is the need to take time for oneself. The basic principle here is that giving *of* yourself requires giving *to* yourself. Clearly becoming self-indulgent is sin. You are not to become the center of your own world. But neither are you to be machines that minister and work continually without taking care of your basic needs. Become good stewards of yourself. To avoid burnout you need to build in time for charging your battery. Taking time for yourself when under the press of time may seem counterintuitive, but the time lost is often made up by being able to work with renewed energy and efficiency. Even Jesus took time to get alone. Ironically many counselors are willing to give this advice to counselees but unwilling to follow it themselves.

**Accept yourself.**

Research shows that a counselor's self-understanding and self-acceptance affects a counselee's capacity for self-acceptance (Truax & Carkhuff, 1965). Your ability to accept yourself is a critical factor in your ability to help others who are struggling with their own problems. God understands our struggles and meets us at whatever place we find ourselves. He met a sinful woman at a public well (John 4:6–29) and an adulterous woman before a self-righteous mob (John 8:1–11). The gospels record many instances of Jesus loving people in the midst of their ungodly lifestyles (e.g., Luke 19:1–10). Therefore if God loves us and accepts us for who we are and where we are, then we need to realize that accepting oneself is not antibiblical. The fact that God accepts us does not mean that He condones everything we do and everything we are. Out of His boundless love He seeks to grow us into the likeness of His Son. Yet God still accepts us with all our imperfections.

The implication of accepting yourself means that you have an inner comfort; you are at peace with yourself. Then you as a counselor can help put others at ease. If you have ever been the guest in the home of someone who was uptight, you know how it can create uneasiness with everyone. Henri Nouwen (1979) captured this concept when he related the biblical concept of hospitality to the work of ministering to the hurting. To be truly hospitable, Nouwen says, you must feel at home in your own house. When you are comfortable in your own space, you can create a free and fearless place for the unexpected visitor to feel at home.

How can you accept yourself? First, be a real, authentic individual. You cannot fool God regarding your inner life. Second, simply accept yourself and your limitations. There is only one God, and everyone else has significant limitations. Be OK with what you cannot do. Third, remember that such problems do not define you. We are given new natures at conversion (Eph 4:24; Col 3:10), and God views us through the righteousness of Christ (Rom 8:1). Fourth, grieve when bad things happen to others and to yourself. A fallen world has fallen people who do things consistent with the fall. In the words of King Solomon we live in a world where the crooked cannot be made straight (Eccl 1:15).

**Maintain a strong social support system.**

Research supports the power of being socially connected versus being socially isolated. It is possible, however, to be in crowds of people and encounter people regularly and yet still be socially unconnected. Effective counselors have friends who understand the nature of counseling and friends who do not. Both sets of friends are needed and valuable in maintaining a healthy relational support system.

## Learn from Your Own Suffering

Henri Nouwen (1979) contends that until one has suffered he is not equipped to plunge the depths of another's soul. Likewise the great Christian Missionary Alliance preacher and writer from the mid-1900s, A. W. Tozer, believed that all great Christians have been wounded (Tozer, 1996). In other words God often does not use someone greatly until that person has suffered deeply. What we gain in the university of life makes us much wiser and more insightful than what we gain from all our academic courses. Professional training in the helping profession equips people with the knowledge, ability, and skills of competent counselors. But without the benefit of tapping into life experiences, the learning that comes from academic training offers little solace to those who are in the grips of personal suffering.

Of course suffering knows no prejudice (Thomas & Habermas, 2008). Since suffering is not an elective course in the school of life, everyone will experience it at one time or another. What is important for Christian helpers is gleaning the wisdom that can come from the path of personal suffering; the level of this wisdom determines to what depth we can plumb with our counselees (Thomas & Habermas, 2008). In other words suffering is a required course that can greatly benefit others as well as each of us. In 2 Cor 1:3–7 Paul discussed our receiving God's comfort in our suffering so that we then can comfort others. God's desire is to use our suffering to strengthen us and to mature us. Invest in your suffering and use it to encourage others.

## Learn to Self-Monitor

In the counseling field self-monitoring is used in two distinct ways. First, it is used to describe people who monitor their own behavior in relationships in order to give the right impression. In one study mental-health professionals identified "self-awareness/self-monitoring" as the number-one contributor to optimal functioning (Schwebel and Coster, 1998). People who are prone to self-monitor are typically concerned with acceptance. Human nature causes people to attempt to elicit from others responses that confirm their own self-images (Wrong, 1961). In the counseling relationship self-monitoring can affect how the counselee perceives the counselor. Some studies suggest that novice counselors who are high in self-monitoring have a low tolerance to ambiguity. They might also appear manipulative unless their interpersonal styles are tempered. Those individuals who are low in self-monitoring are more at risk of becoming dogmatic or rigid in response to counselees' needs (Haferkamp, 1989). The more self-awareness that counselors develop and the more acceptance they have of themselves, the more effective they will be in their counseling.

Second, self-monitoring is used to describe the process of paying attention to what is happening in one's life internally and externally. Learn to self-monitor your own emotions, values, beliefs, attitudes, and actions so that these reactions do not interfere with your counseling work. This process relates to the concept of countertransference, which is discussed in greater detail in chap. 3.

## Seek Personal Counseling

If counselors are to help others change and grow, they need to be open to changing problematic areas in their own lives and growing in every aspect of their lives. You need to know how to help yourself and how to receive help from others when it is needed. The point is to be willing to do for yourself what you desire to do for your counselees. Just as counselees will seek your services when they need the help of another, you need, when necessary, to be willing to submit yourself to the process of being helped by another.

Personal counseling can help you better understand your motivations, explore how your own needs influence your actions, discover how you use power when interacting with others, and determine if you are prone to using the counseling role to persuade rather than facilitate (Norcross, 2005; Orlinsky, Norcross, Rønnestad, and Wiseman, 2005). By availing yourself to receiving counseling, you can become more aware of how personal problems and unmet needs interfere in your own life. A secondary gain is that it also impacts the quality of counseling and your ability to be a positive model for counselees. The importance of personal counseling for counseling students is so strongly supported by many in the field that it is recommended that counseling students be required to receive counseling (D'Andrea & Daniels, 1992). Based on years of studying counselors who obtain personal counseling, Norcross (2005) writes, "It seems virtually impossible to have undergone personal therapy without emerging with heightened appreciation of the interpersonal relationship between patient and therapist and the vulnerability of a patient" (p. 844).

In addition obtaining personal counseling gives you a greater insight into the role of the counselee (Grimmer & Tribe, 2001). This demonstrates that you believe in the "product" that is offered to others. You need to be willing to "practice what you preach" and obtain help when needed.

Though some theorists recommend that counselors obtain personal counseling (D'Andrea & Daniels, 1992; Yalom, 2002), others believe that the benefits derived from counseling can be woven into supervision aimed at heightening self-awareness (Aponte, 1994). A counseling supervision model prescribed by Aponte (1994) makes use of genograms, interviews with family members, and live supervision to explore the counselor trainee's personal history. After gaining insight into any unresolved issues, trainees are encouraged to obtain personal counseling for help in working through those issues.

Though a number of counselors-in-training can benefit through skilled supervision, many would be served better by the services of a professional counselor, especially when deeper issues have been unearthed. Ironically counselors are often reluctant to go for counseling (Guy, 1987). Yet many problems can be obviated if counselors-in-training work out as many issues before working with counselees. Often, however, working with counselees can create a need to deal with personal issues that result from counselor interactions with their counselees. A counselor's personal issues can evoke countertransference in the counseling relationship and hinder their therapeutic effectiveness. Though the counseling relationship is unique, the normal human reactions a counselor has with other people in his life emerge in the counseling relationship.

## CHAPTER SUMMARY

Counseling is both a personal and a professional encounter. Personally through the vehicle of counseling the counselor expresses his or her beliefs, values, attitudes, and abilities in concert with the counselee. Though the counseling profession attracts noble, kind, and compassionate people, it also attracts people who have a need to help people, people who are wounded, and people who do not know their boundaries.

The effectiveness of counseling hinges on the counselor (Wampold, 2001) and his ability to draw from God. The prophet Daniel aptly captured the power of God in helping people: "Praise be to the name of God for ever and ever; wisdom and power are his. . . . He gives wisdom to the wise and knowledge to the discerning. He reveals deep and hidden things; he knows what lies in darkness, and light dwells with him" (Dan 2:20–22, NIV).

As a Christian helper, be committed to being all God has called you to be. Be committed to grow, mature, develop, and become transformed into the image of Christ. The impact of such maturity is that you will be congruent with what you purport to be and what you say. As Carlson (1976) writes, "Ideally, the range of therapeutic responses represents a person's professional role and personality so that the counselor does not merely act out of a particular helping role but actually possesses the attributes and feelings of that role" (p. 187).

In the process of growing, however, the impact of a wide range of problems encountered in the counseling profession will inevitably produce personal reactions in the counselor. These reactions can interfere with the success of counseling. Moreover, the impact of these reactions can also harm the counselee, as discussed in the previous chap., "The Hazards of Helping."

One means of avoiding doing harm is to be skilled in counseling. The more prepared you are and the more trained you have been, the less likely you will allow incompetence to affect your work. Equipping you in those skills is the focus of the next section (chaps. 5–8) of this text.

## CHAPTER 4 ACTIVITIES

1. Which domains are you more likely to emphasize when helping a counselee change: thoughts, feelings/emotions, behaviors/actions, relationships, and spirituality? Why do you think these domains should be emphasized?

2. Below are several difficult topics and problems that counselors face. Rank each item below, with 1 being the most difficult and 5 being the least difficult or very easy. Then write why you believe those topics or problems will present difficulties for you. What life experiences may have shaped your responses to the items above?

| 1 | 2 | 3 | 4 | 5 |
|---|---|---|---|---|
| Most Difficult | Difficult | Average | Easy | Very Easy |

   a. Abortion ____
   b. Adolescent struggling with sexual orientation ____
   c. Affair ____
   d. Parent experiencing the death of a child ____
   e. Suicidal counselee ____

3. Write the reasons why you want to be a counselor. How do those reasons mesh with a biblical worldview?

4. On a scale of 1 to 10, with 10 being highest, rate how well you know your own heart. What do you believe might be blind spots or what areas of your life have people pointed out to you as a weakness?

5. Identify the areas of your attitudes mentioned in this chap. What areas do you believe you need to strengthen and why? Develop a plan to do so.

6. On the following scale rate yourself on the items below:

| 1 | 2 | 3 | 4 | 5 |
|---|---|---|---|---|
| Very Low | Below Average | Average | Above Average | Very High |

a. I am able to tell the difference between little and big matters: _____

b. I am able to solve problems rather than be overwhelmed by them: _____

c. I am able to get along well with others who are different from me: _____

d. I am able to accept responsibility for my actions: _____

e. I am able to maintain self-control under stress and pressure: _____

f. I usually seek approval and affirmation from others, and I am afraid of criticism: _____

g. I tend to isolate myself from and am afraid of people in authority roles: _____

h. I am rarely able to appreciate my own accomplishments: _____

i. I tend to mistrust my feelings and the feelings expressed by others: _____

j. I tend not to trust people easily: _____

k. I tend to feel that I am being taken advantage of by others; I often feel victimized: _____

l. I tend to take myself too seriously, and I view all of my relationships just as seriously: _____

m. I usually feel frightened or stressed when I am in the company of an angry person: _____

n. I usually feel guilty when I stand up for myself or take care of my needs instead of giving in or taking care of other people's needs: _____

o. I have problems with compulsive behavior (e.g., drinking, drug use, smoking, gambling, sex, food, shopping): _____

p. I tend to attract people who have problems with compulsive behavior (e.g., drinking, drug use, smoking, gambling, sex, food, shopping): _____

q. I have a tendency to be impulsive and to act quickly before considering alternative actions or possible consequences: _____

r. I tend to judge myself without mercy. I am my own worst critic, and I am harder on myself than I am on others: _____

s. I tend to feel more alive in the midst of a crisis, and I am uneasy when my life is going smoothly: _____

t. I continually anticipate problems: _____

u. I deal with problems by staying busy and avoid having to face them: _____

v. I tend to have difficulty having fun. I do not play or relax enough: _____

w. I tend to be attracted to others whom I perceive to have been victims, and I tend to develop close relationships with them. Consequently I often confuse love and pity, and I tend to love people I can pity and rescue: _____

x. I tend to need perfection in my life at home, school, and/or work. I typically expect perfection from others in my life: _____

y. I tend to feel confused and angry at myself, not in control of my environment or my life, particularly when stress is high: _____

z. I tend to deny that my current problems stem from my life. I also tend to deny that I have feelings from the past that are impeding my current life: _____

Review your responses above. Identify those that are either on the higher or lower end of the continuum. What do they say about you? Share your responses with another person in your class. What do each of you learn from processing each other's responses?

7. Spiritual Evaluation:

| 1 | 2 | 3 | 4 | 5 |
|---|---|---|---|---|
| Not At All | Partly | Unsure | Definitely | Very Definitely |

a. I believe God has called me into the work of helping.

b. God seems very impersonal to me.

c. God is difficult to please.

d. I have never really lived out my faith as I believe God wants me to.

e. I find it easier to be a Christian if I follow rules rather than living in grace and finding God's will in the gray areas.
f. I depend on God as I live my life.
g. Those who know me can tell that I live out my faith.

## Recommended Reading

Ortberg, John (2009). *The me I want to be: Becoming God's best version of you.* Grand Rapids, MI: Zondervan Publishing House.

> Pastor, speaker, and author John Ortberg provides another critical work that fosters personal spiritual reflection. If you need to learn how to live out the Spirit-filled life, then Ortberg's book will give you great insight and challenges. The way of the cross requires brokenness and each believer must learn how to turn brokenness into Christian victory.

Tan, S. Y., & Gregg, D. (1997). *Disciplines of the Holy Spirit: How to connect to the Spirit's power and presence.* Grand Rapids, MI: Zondervan Publishing House.

> Two therapists and scholars collaborated on a work that addresses the role that the Holy Spirit plays in a dynamic, close walk with God. They address how the Holy Spirit wants to energize each believer's life. They explain how a yielded life promotes powerful transformation.

Tozer, A. W. (1977). *That incredible Christian.* Beaverlodge, AL, Canada: Horizon House.

> Each chap. in this book is power-packed. You will find a wonderful use of literary paradox as Tozer discusses "the incredible Christian." It is an outstanding work to examine what living for Christ is truly about.

Willard, D. (1988). *The spirit of the disciplines.* New York City, NY: HarperCollins.

> Dallas Willard is a brilliant Christian thinker and author who has the ability to challenge readers on their spiritual journey. In this work he provides keys to transforming yourself through the practice of the spiritual disciplines.

# Section 2

# Basic Helping Skills

**A**s therapeutic guides, we need to be properly equipped to lead counselees safely and effectively on the journey. This section of the *Therapeutic Expedition* is dedicated to outfitting you with the requisite information and skills you need to be effective in the helping profession. Chaps. 5–8 discusses fundamental skills of the helping profession, beginning with knowing how to skillfully use yourself.

Whereas chap. 4 focused on your *being*, chaps. 5–8 focus on your *doing*. In chap. 5 we delve into the foundation of helping, the therapeutic relationship. The purpose of counseling is not to create a connection but to address the counselee's deficits and developmental needs. In short, counseling is about instigating profitable counselee change. Understanding the process change and the mechanisms of change are instrumental to being an agent of change. The prophet Jeremiah scolded the religious leaders for healing the wounds of God's people superficially (Jer 6:14). Trusted guides not only have the human qualities that engender trust, but they also have a skill set that makes them credible. Likewise, they are experts in creating a sanctuary of safety. Establishing a relationship with counselees that fosters openness, vulnerability, and the ability to redress personal difficulties is of utmost importance.

Chap. 6, "Basic Skills: Exploring the Problem," discusses how to effectively explore your counselees' concerns. These skills include the art of asking questions, paraphrasing, clarifying, and using summaries. Such skills are considered fairly universal, and will serve you well in your efforts to help. Being proficient in these skills will increase your confidence, give you a sense of competence, and improve your helping effectiveness.

In chap. 7 we focus on those skills that help facilitate change, the skills of feedback, interpretation, confrontation, self-disclosure, immediacy, silence, and pacing. It provides a case example to assist you in seeing how the skills are applied.

Counseling begins with a destination in mind too. As we have seen, the goals that are established early in the helping process are hopefully realized and the need for help wanes. Learning how to end the counseling process is as important as knowing how to initiate it. In chap. 8 ("Basic Skills: Terminating the Counseling") we discuss the skills that facilitate the best ending to the process. We address such issues as the function of termination, kinds of termination, how to make a referral, and techniques and guidelines in appropriately ending the counseling.

Just as a wilderness guide will tailor her equipment to the environment in which she is working, you too must tailor the therapeutic skills to the environment and populations with whom you will be working. It is your responsibility to be prepared, equipped, and outfitted for the therapeutic journey. These next four chaps. will give you the fundamental knowledge and skills, but it is your job to become proficient at using them.

## Chapter 5

# Basic Skills: Creating a Connection

*"If Christ lives in us, controlling our personalities, we will leave glorious marks on the lives we touch. Not because of our lovely characters, but because of his"* (Eugenia Price, quoted in Manser [2001], p. 37).

*"Anyone who has entered the darkness of another's pain, loss, or bewilderment, and who has done so without the defenses of a detached professionalism, will know the feeling of wanting to escape, of wishing they had not become involved"* (Campbell, cited in Leech [1989], p. 35).

*"Instead we were gentle among you, even as a nursing mother nurtures her own children. We cared so much for you that we were pleased to share with you not only the gospel of God but also our own lives, because you had become dear to us"* (1 Thess 2:7–8, HCSB).

## CHAPTER OBJECTIVES

» To discuss the process of skill development

» To overview the basic helping skills

» To discuss the benefits and risks of the skills

» To discuss the differences between content and process in counseling

» To discuss a continuum of counseling skills from nondirective to directive

» To provide easy-to-remember guidelines on how to implement the skills

» To explain the origin and role of the helping relationship in the healing process

» To present the value of a strong therapeutic relationship

» To provide an overview of rapport skills

» To relate rapport skills with active listening

» To consider the development of active listening in three parts

» To provide an overview of attending behavior

» To explain the importance of communicating empathy through reflecting

» To discuss the use of minimal encouragers in active listening

» To provide opportunities for students to develop these skills through directed activities

## CHAPTER OUTLINE

Remember the process you went through in getting a driver's license? Having a license and being free to go where one wants without having to be driven by parents or a friend is a welcomed milestone, a rite of passage in our American society. But obtaining a driver's license is not without its obstacles. The privilege of driving requires that you can prove your ability to drive safely. The fact that you had been exposed to the mechanics of driving as a passenger for over fifteen years did not exempt you from taking classes, student driving, passing a test, and demonstrating proficiency.

You likely remember spending hours studying the driver's manual in order to get your learner's permit and have the restricted right to drive. Seeing others drive and knowing the rules of the road are different from actually driving a car. Taking the first trip around the block typically begins with the car lurching forward and then coming to an abrupt stop. New drivers must learn the feel of depressing the accelerator and brake so that starting and stopping are smooth and seemingly effortless. Maintaining a straight line on the right side of the road is yet another task that requires patience and practice. Each time you drive you learn more, gain experience, and benefit from your mistakes. Practice equips the driver with knowledge and ability in handling particular road situations, responding to the carelessness and recklessness of other drivers, and navigating the roads. The more you practice, the more you develop competency in driving. Of course some learners pick up the skills more quickly than others. The mastery of driving is at different rates for each learner and ultimately the level of skill that is developed might also be different, but the outcome is the same—being able to drive safely, naturally, and without much thought.

Likewise mastering the skills of counseling takes practice, perseverance, and time. Most experienced counselors give little thought to each and every response they give their counselees. The nonverbal behavior and verbalizations are expressed naturally. Developing the confidence of an experienced counselor is not learned in a classroom; it is honed in the counselor's chair. You can study numerous counseling and therapy textbooks and watch countless DVDs of experienced counselors conducting therapy sessions, but nothing replaces sitting across from actual counselees and applying what you have read and learned. As you counsel more counselees, encounter more problems, and deliver more solutions, the more normal and natural counseling becomes.

## MODEL OF HELPER DEVELOPMENT

We have already discussed the Helper's House in previous chaps. (see Figure 5.1). The helper's house contains the floor plan for developing the components and skills necessary for being a Christian counselor.

The focus of this chap. is on the upper floor of the helper's house. In your home you have rooms of different sizes, each with a distinct purpose. The kitchen is used for food preparation and storage, the bathroom for hygiene purposes, and the family room for relaxing and socializing.

Likewise, the helper's upper floor contains different skill sets for unique and distinct purposes. Various authors label the set of skills differently, but the distinct purposes are relatively the same.

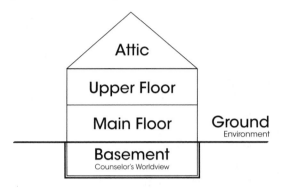

Figure 5.1: The Helper's House:
A Model of Counselor Development

In the next several chaps. we will describe the rooms associated with the helper's main floor. This floor represents the basic skills of being a counselor. Whether learning to drive, play an instrument, or acquire a second language, you break down the overall skill of performing the activity into bite-sized components. The mastery of any skill is acquired by learning the fundamentals of the skill and then building on those rudimentary skills block by block until proficiency is achieved.

This chap. focuses on the basic skills of the counseling expedition. The first set of skills helps the counselor connect with the counselee. These skills include attending skills; empathy skills; immediacy, which involves dealing with issues as they arise in the counselor and counseling relationship; and pacing the helping process.

A second set of skills helps you explore the counselee's presenting concerns and issues. The skills of exploration include asking questions, using paraphrase, asking for clarification, and using summaries.

The third set of basic skills pertains to facilitation. Once a counselee's presenting concerns are explored, you need to have skills to facilitate growth. Skills that help you engage counselees and move them through the journey include giving feedback, making interpretations, confronting, and being silent. Before moving into each of the counselor skill sets it is important to understand that these basic counselor skills target either content or process.

| Table 5.1 *Functional Allocation of Counselor Skills* | | | |
|---|---|---|---|
| | **SKILL SETS** | | |
| **Skills** | **Connection** | **Exploration** | **Facilitation** |
| Rapport | **P** | S | S |
| Safe Haven | **P** | S | S |
| Attending | **P** | S | S |
| Reflection | **P** | S | S |
| Minimal Encouragers | **P** | S | S |
| Questions | S | **P** | S |
| Paraphrase | S | **P** | S |
| Clarification | S | **P** | S |
| Summary | S | **P** | S |
| Feedback | S | S | **P** |
| Interpretation | S | S | **P** |
| Confrontation | S | S | **P** |
| Self-disclosure | S | S | **P** |
| Immediacy | S | S | **P** |
| Silence | S | S | **P** |
| Pacing | S | S | **P** |

P = Primary function; S = Secondary function

## CONTENT VERSUS PROCESS IN COUNSELING

It is important to distinguish between content and process when counseling (see Table 5.2). Content refers to the topic or subject matter being discussed, to the actual message of the counselee's words. Process refers to the delivery of the subject matter, the way things are said.

Whereas content refers to what the counselee says, process emphasizes how the counselee says it. Content is the information being presented, but process is the manner or sequence of events through which the content is delivered. Content is what people talk about; process is how people interact and relate. Content includes only the words that a counselee uses to give a message, but process also includes the things a counselee leaves out of his message and the nonverbal communication that accompanies the words. Perhaps the most important distinction between content and process is that the content can deceive but the process cannot. People are typically aware of the content they are presenting, but less aware of how they are presenting it. Whereas people can have conscious control of the content, they are typically unable to control the process.

### Table 5.2
*Comparison of Content and Process in Counseling*

| Content | Process |
| --- | --- |
| Subject matter | Delivery of the subject matter |
| The what of a message | The how of the message |
| Counselee's words | How the counselee says the words |
| Only what the counselee says | Includes what the counselee does not say |
| What people talk about | How people relate and interact |
| People have awareness of the content | People are typically unaware of the process |

Thus content is able to be distorted, disguised, and manipulated. Anyone can deceive another person with words. In contrast, however, process reveals the true agenda of the heart. It is the cue to what someone really wants. When I (John) was doing my master's practicum, I had the opportunity to have lunch with my supervisor. As my supervisor, another student, and I were on our way to a restaurant, an interaction occurred that literally caught me off guard. My supervisor was sharing something personal. After he finished, I made a joke of something he had said. Immediately my supervisor stopped and lovingly asked me, "Why do you push people away with your humor?" As a master counselor, my supervisor had tapped into my process. Certain topics by particular people generated a discomfort in me. A pattern in my life that I was totally unaware of before that exchange was that when an authority figure, whom I highly respected, shared so personally with me it triggered feelings of insecurity or fear. He had worked with me over a number of months and had identified a process in me that related to my way of interacting with others. This exchange allowed my supervisor an opportunity to challenge my process. He accurately read my process, and in his response he ignored my attempt at humor to speak to my heart and the dynamic of my interaction. That is the difference between content and process.

Focusing on the process often yields much more valuable information than the content the counselee says. Experienced helpers know the truth in the adage, "Actions speak louder than words." Whereas the content can change from topic to topic, the process remains the same. People are primarily the same across settings and are unaware of their true agendas and intentions. Attending closely to the process of what is happening in counseling is often more revealing than the words.

## THE NONDIRECTIVE AND DIRECTIVE
## CONTINUUM OF HELPING SKILLS

One way to conceptualize the various helping skills is on a continuum from nondirective to directive. Helping skills that are prone to being directive involve the counselor taking an active approach in obtaining specific information and speaking to the counselee's life situation or story. In contrast nondirective skills are less restrictive on the counselee. Nondirective techniques allow the counselee a greater freedom of expression. The emphasis in using nondirective skills is getting the counselee to open up. When a counselor uses nondirective skills, he is attempting to tap into the counselee's perceptions, thinking, emotions, attitudes, and values.

Table 5.3 depicts counseling skills along a continuum. The numbers associated with points along the continuum are relative as is the actual location of each skill on the continuum. How the counselor employs the specific skill in the counseling process will ultimately determine the level of directiveness or nondirectiveness of the intervention.

Table 5.3

*The Nondirective and Directive Continuum of Helping Skills*

| ← Nondirective | | | Directive → | | |
|---|---|---|---|---|---|
| 0 | 2 | 4 | 6 | 8 | 10 |
| Silence | Reflective Listening | Indirect Question | Open-ended Question | Closed-ended Questions | Provocative Question |
| | | Paraphrase | Rhetorical Question | Self-disclosure | Leading Question |
| | | Summary | Clarification | Interpretation | Punishing Question |
| | | | | Immediacy | Feedback |
| | | | | | Confrontation |

The following sections will expound on each of the basic helping skills. Judicious counselors are aware of the level of directiveness associated with each skill and are cognizant of the specific purpose in choosing a given skill.

## SKILL SET OF CONNECTION

The foundational counseling skill set involves the attitude, knowledge, and behaviors that establish a connection with the counselee. The skills set that contributes to a working alliance with the counselee is known as "rapport skills." To create rapport you need to understand those major variables that lead to a productive counseling relationship. In this chap. we will address how counselors can establish a strong helping relationship with their counselees. Understanding and mastering these skills is the hallmark of successful counselors. We will begin by discussing the value of connection, the importance of the having a solid connection with a counselee, and the specific skills that contribute to a helpful therapeutic relationship.

### Created for Connection

From the beginning God set in motion certain divine and human realities that are uniquely imaged and reflected where two or more people come together (Icenogle, 1994). Since eternity past God existed in community and desires "face-to-face" relationships with His creation.

God is a relational God who lives in perfect relationship as God the Father, God the Son, and God the Holy Spirit. In giving us His image God put in us a craving to relate, first to Himself and then to others. He created us as relational beings.

Through relationships we are born, shaped, and exist. As a result, relationship is central to life; it is in our nature to seek and need connection with others in order to thrive. But being in relationships is not the important thing. Instead, *how* a person is in relationship determines his or her physical, emotional, and spiritual health (Mortensen, 2008). In other words it is the quality of one's relationships that is of ultimate concern.

The value God places on relationships is evident from Genesis to Revelation. The characteristic quality of our relationships is best captured by the words of Jesus.

> Jesus said unto him, Thou shalt love the Lord thy God with all thy heart, and with all thy soul, and with all thy mind. This is the first and great commandment. And the second is like unto it: "Thou shalt love thy neighbor as thyself." On these two commandments hang all the law and the prophets (Matt 22:37–40, KJV).

Nearing the end of His earthly ministry, Jesus once again educated His disciples about the way they needed to be with others. He said, "A new commandment I give to you, that you love one another, even as I have loved you, that you also love one another. By this all men will know that you are My disciples, if you have love for one another" (John 13:34–35, NASB). Jesus' claim that loving one another was a new commandment was not technically correct because the commandment was first mentioned in the OT (Lev 19:18). Obviously Jesus did not mean that the command- ment was new in its creation. Rather He was referring to the fact that it was new in its context. Throughout the centuries of the OT obedience to the Law indicated whether one was a genuine follower of the Lord. But Jesus introduced a new paradigm, a new litmus test to determine the genuineness of a person's faith. The new context is no longer obedience to the Law; instead it is loving others. A person's ability to demonstrate godly love in relationships is the evidence of his faith. In other words God gauges your spirituality through relationships. A person's interpersonal behavior is at center stage of his faith. Loving God and others, made evident by one's actions and attitudes, is the measure of Christlikeness.

A significant context in which to fulfill that commandment is the church, the body of Christ. Throughout the epistles the church is described as a body of believers who are to dwell together in unity (cf. 1 Cor 12; Eph 1:21–22; Col 1:18). Moreover, the NT includes approximately 55 "one anothers" specifying exactly what loving others looks like. The connec- tion we have with others through the body of Christ provides a central relational context to meet the life needs of its members.

A person's need for and value of connection is rooted in our design; it is through relationships that we are formed into the people we come to be. We are wounded in relationships, and we must heal in relationships. So counselors should be experts in establishing healing connections with their counselees (Waehler & Lenox, 1994). In fact research strongly supports the belief that the relationship between the counselor and the counselee is likely the most central component to counseling effectiveness (Fitzpat- rick & Irannejad, 2008; Kivlighan, 2007). In other words your ability to establish a healing connection with each counselee is critical to counseling success.

The connection you establish with your counselee is the cornerstone on which the entire counseling structure is built (Halverson & Miars, 2005; Holmes, 2001). Virtually all counseling theories view the helping relation- ship as integral to outcome, though different words are used to describe it, and some authors place more emphasis on it than others. Kottler and

Brown (1992) commented on the centrality of the relationship between the counselor and counselee:

> Regardless of the setting in which you practice counseling, whether in a school, agency, hospital, or private practice, the relationships you develop with your counselees are crucial to any progress you might make together. For without a high degree of intimacy and trust between two people, very little can be accomplished (p. 64).

The helping relationship is key to accomplishing meaningful work with a counselee. Although creating a connection is not an end goal, it is the means to accomplishing other goals. The bottom line is to become an expert at creating, sustaining, repairing, and using the helping relationship to facilitate change in the counselee. Research shows that the helping relationship is a central factor in successful counseling (Hubble, Duncan, & Miller, 1999). In fact some studies report as much as 30 percent of counselee change is attributable to variables inherent in the helping relationship.

The bond that occurs between the counselor and counselee is known as rapport, which is the construct that describes the solid connection between the two. Rapport is the sense that one is in sync with the counselee; it includes the concepts of goodwill, confidence, trust, and caring. Many theorists have emphasized the centrality of the therapeutic relationship. Carl Rogers's (1961) Person-centered therapy is rooted in the ability of the counselor to establish a helping relationship with the counselee. Buber (1970) speaks of the I-Thou relationship as a spiritual reality that arises and exists in the therapeutic encounter. The I-Thou relationship emerges as two people share openly and authentically.

From a biblical worldview perspective rapport is seen in the Trinity, in the persons of the Godhead. The relationships between the three persons of the Trinity are the perfect model of rapport. The relationships between the Father, Son, and Holy Spirit are sustaining, trusting, and harmonious. Unity of purpose creates a climate that allows each person of the Godhead to be effective in carrying out His function. This eternal and immutable rapport allows them to be all of who they are.

The helping relationship in counseling becomes an incarnational relationship in which counselees are exposed to what God is like. It is a context for a counselee to receive love, a need that is deep within every human heart. Rapport also enables counselees to learn their true identity; they begin to understand that their worth comes through their irreplaceability. Also rapport can help counselees sense that God made them in His image for a special plan and purpose that only they can accomplish. In other words counselees can gain insights by the way they are viewed and treated by the counselor. As Henri Nouwen (1979) suggested, the hospitable host pays attention to the needs of his guest. Viewing our counselees as guests and seeing them through Jesus' eyes will facilitate the counselee's perception that God might perceive them in the same way. This "incarnational relationship" is akin to what McMinn (1996) calls "redemption in counseling" (p. 259). To enter into this incarnational relationship with your counselees, develop the capacity to be Christlike before them. A number of counselees you will encounter will test your patience. During those times counselors often need to maintain a Christlike presence. As you sit at the feet of the Master through your own personal time with Christ, you learn His ways and become more like Him. No amount of training can replace what your personal devotional and worship time contributes to the counseling relationship. The ability to offer the power of a godly presence requires that we be fed at God's table.

## Learning How to Build Rapport

Rapport skills include conditions, attitudes, and behaviors that lend themselves toward establishing a solid helping relationship. With some counselees the establishment of rapport seems instantaneous and effortless (Dinkmeyer, Dinkmeyer, & Sperry, 1987; Gilliland & James, 1988). In most cases, however, building that connection with the counselee takes time. To establish and maintain a solid therapeutic relationship it is important to (a) create a safe haven, (b) establish presence with the counselee by actively listening, and (c) communicate empathy.

### Rapport skill 1: Establishing a safe haven.

One reason rapport is critical to counseling success is that it is the basis of human development. From an attachment perspective (Ainsworth, Blehar, Waters, & Wall, 1978; Bowlby, 1940; Bowlby, 1969; Bowlby, 1973; Bowlby, 1980), the safe haven that can exist between an infant and caregiver can be viewed as rapport. Within the context of the primal relationship a child learns how to explore, experiment, and draw conclusions about life. When the relationship between the child and caregiver is both stable and secure, the child views the caregiver as a safe haven. In contrast an unpredictable relationship between the caregiver and child can produce an anxious and ambivalent child who is afraid to explore and experiment. In such cases the caregiver is not perceived as a safe haven. For the child a safe haven is a place of refuge. It is a place that ensures the child that basic needs will be met, that wounds will be cared for, and there is no reason to fear abandonment.

The connection between the counselor and the counselee will either facilitate or hinder exploration, experimentation, and growth (Wallin, 2007). Establishing a safe haven for the counselee means creating an atmosphere that promotes a sanctuary for vulnerability and growth (Holmes, 2001). The counselee senses that the counseling office is a safe place and that the counselor is a safe person. The counselor's presence becomes a homestead of rest, reflection, and recovery.

When the counselee sees the helping relationship as a safe haven, free disclosure is more likely to occur. A secure and stable helping relationship allows counselees the opportunity to struggle, fail, and learn without fear of losing the relationship. In a world that places a premium on self-sufficiency and independence, requesting help is a significant act of courage for many people. Seeing a counselor is an admission that they cannot handle their problems on their own. So many people who go to a counselor feel like a failure.

In order to expose vulnerability, counselees need to feel safe and secure (Wallin, 2007). Without a safe haven counselees cannot openly face their struggles. Counselors promote a climate of safety by providing a framework for expectations for the counselee. One significant framework is assuring the counselee that his personal information will be held in confidence. The counselee needs to be assured that the helper is not sharing with others anything that is shared in the sessions unless legally mandated to do so. Counselors should also provide safety by informing counselees that human problems and struggles are viewed as a normal part of a fallen world.

The conditions that engender this safe haven for counselees are both tangible and intangible (see Table 5.4). Tangibly, you can foster a safe haven by paying attention to the counseling setting. The environment in which counseling occurs can enhance or diminish one's capability to listen actively. Over the years we have counseled in less than desirable settings, including cars, planes, gymnasiums, church pews, restaurants, and park benches, to name a few. Though counseling can take place anywhere at any time, it is best to optimize the setting so that a safe haven is facilitated. The counselee will give attention to the location of the office, the decorations, the orderliness, and the smells. The environment will communicate that this is a comfortable or uncomfortable place and whether it is a scary or safe place.

Focusing on the tangibles in the environment can be well worth the time and effort. Obviously the most comfortable setting improves the chances that the counselee will relax enough to open up. Using comfortable chairs and fabrics and finding the best room temperature are typically within the counselor's control. Any distractions should be removed or minimized. Ensuring that the counselee has privacy without the fear of interruptions allows for the free expression of thoughts and emotion. Examples of distractions include outside conversations, radios, people knocking on the door, telephone and cell phones ringing, and office clutter. We have worked in settings where we could hear every word that was being said in an adjoining office. I (John) have counseled where the sounds of heavy construction outside the window were loud and constant. Hearing the counselee, let alone staying focused, was physically and emotionally draining. Extraneous noise and interruptions can quickly erode the work you have been doing to facilitate counselee disclosure. Of course, emergencies do happen, and occasional interruptions are unavoidable. Taking phone calls or people knocking on the door during sessions are generally preventable. A simple "Do not disturb" sign and turning off the ringer works wonders. To the extent possible, find office settings with thick walls and doors that restrict sound.

## Table 5.4
### *Conditions That Work Against a Safe Haven*

| Tangible Conditions: The Counseling Setting | Intangible Conditions: The Counselor Responses |
| --- | --- |
| Lack of Privacy | Disrespecting the counselee: judging, criticizing, moralizing |
| Distractions | Dismissing the counselee: diverting the conversation, patronizing |
| Uncomfortable chairs, poor room temperature | Directing the counselee: trying to fix the counselee |
| Dirty space, disorder in the office | Listening to confirm one's observations |
| Unprofessional and inappropriate amenities | |
| Unprofessional and inappropriate dress | |

Another tangible element is how the counselor dresses. As a rule how one dresses should reflect his personality, and it should be appropriate for his professional role. Counselors who work in a large urban setting should dress like the counselees who come to the office. Counselors in rural settings might need to dress differently. If an adult comes from his job dressed in a blue-collar uniform, a counselor wearing a suit and tie or a tailored dress might make the counselee feel uncomfortable. As a rule, clothing that is professional-looking, clean, comfortable, and appropriate to your setting will facilitate building rapport.

Create a relaxing and comfortable feeling in your office facilities. Of course the facilities do not have to be luxurious; simply paying attention to the cleanliness, orderliness, and amenities of the space will suffice. Remember that your office space becomes an extension of yourself. People's offices provide insights into their personality and how serious they approach their work. Think of the difference you imagine in these two counselors. One counselor has photos of her family on the desk, interesting pictures and degrees on her walls, and plants and artifacts in the office. In contrast another counselor has only a few photos on a wall of his office to break up the dead space. Piles of paper are on the desk and file folders are stacked on the floor near the desk. The furniture is worn and uncomfortable. What thoughts do you have about each of the counselors?

Your working space and dress can help you maintain your professionalism, provide a sense of relaxation, and not distract you from the work you are to provide.

These tangible conditions can certainly help establish a safe haven, but more important, they are the intangible qualities of the counselor's attitude and behavior, often referred to as "core conditions" (Rogers, 1951; Young, 2010). We spoke about these attitudes and behaviors in chap. 4 ("The Person of the Counselor"), but it is worth noting again that how the counselor interacts with the counselee will impact perceptions of safety. The counselor "core conditions" demonstrate respect and compassion for the counselee (Kottler, 2004), thereby facilitating the establishment of rapport. Remember that who you are and how that is expressed and experienced by the counselee will impact rapport and the creation of a safe haven more than anything else. Damage that is done through counseling does not typically result from what is said, but how the counselee is treated. Your behavior must be accepting and nonthreatening; remember you are a minister of grace. Your goal is to help people understand themselves, to equip them with the tools necessary for managing their circumstances and emotions, and to help move your counselees forward in their spiritual lives. Elements that block a safe haven are disrespecting the counselee, dismissing the counselee, and trying to fix the counselee. Obvious and blatant disrespect of a counselee violates the ethical principle of protecting the counselee's welfare, but subtle forms of disrespect are no less damaging. You might think that a counselor dismissing a counselee is rare, but it occurs more often than many people think. You can inadvertently disrespect counselees when you judge, criticize, or moralize. Job lamented that his counselors mistreated him through their judgments of his spiritual condition (Job 16). When a counselor diverts a conversation because the topic touches too close to home or when the counselor reassures a counselee that "it will be OK," the net result is that the counselor has minimized the counselee's emotional state. Such behavior is disrespectful.

Attempting to fix the counselee's situation as if the job were like repairing a broken water pipe takes the responsibility and opportunity for growth away from the counselee. In an attempt to help the counselee novice counselors might say something like, "If I were you, I would . . ." or "I know someone who had a similar problem, and she got over it by . . ." In reality, however, such responses derail the focus on helping the counselee mature from the experience. It also can feed the counselor's ego.

Another intangible condition to avoid is listening to confirm your own observations. Counselors ought not think they know what another person's true problem might be. Unfortunately people tend to believe that certain cues are linked to particular problems. As a result, it becomes easy to find evidence to support the working theory. Although the hypothesis might be correct, it is important to stay open to alternative explanations in order not to miss information that would disconfirm the working theory. Often counselors operate out of their own issues or are riding their own hobby horse when they assume that they know what a counselee is experiencing. Stay open to possibilities early in the counseling process. If you think you know, look specifically for information that might disconfirm your thoughts in order not to convey a false diagnosis or give a wrong explanation.

The first skill in building rapport is simply providing a safe atmosphere that is conducive to open communication. The particulars will differ from counselor to counselor, but the objective is to create a safe haven for the counselee and counselor to address the counselee's issues. In the context of safety counselees can feel free to redress their disturbances, failures, and interpersonal traumas. Through sensing that there exists a safe haven, emotional needs can find fulfillment, wounds can experience reparation, new internal models of self and others can be developed, and developmental impasses can be removed. Most importantly Christian counselees maximize their ability to utilize faith as a resource in their recovery.

**Rapport skill 2: Active listening skills.**

Every child has heard his parents say, "You are not listening to me." Early in my marriage my wife told me (John) that I was not listening to her. At times she would try to talk with me when I was watching TV, or reading, or at my computer. Although I had heard what she said and could practically repeat it back to her word for word, my wife never appreciated my raw ability to multitask. She assumed that I was not listening to her. I was a trained counselor armed with active listening skills and was incredulous about being told that I was not listening. But soon I realized that I was violating every rule and principle of effective listening. The foundation of every relationship is the ability of each person to create a sense that the other is truly being heard; a need all people possess. A treasured gift I could give my wife was my full attention.

Coming alongside a hurting person requires that counselors establish a strong alliance with that person by actively listening to his stories (McMinn & Campbell, 2007). Gratton (1992) expounds on the spiritual aspects of listening. She says that counselors must listen in such a way that the counselee willingly reveals the deepest part of his or her soul. "We must listen for echoes or hints of that call in the concrete aspects of the person's life situation" (p. 71).

When counselors pay attention to their counselees' need to have their stories heard, rapport is established. Actively listening tells the counselee that he or she really matters. Many writers agree that the most significant skill in establishing a therapeutic relationship is active listening (Edwards, Peterson, & Davies, 2006; Harper, 1996). Even more than advice-giving, no concept is more closely associated with effective counseling than listening.

The Bible speaks often about the value of listening. God created us with a deep yearning to be heard and understood. Perhaps no verse is more relevant for counselors than Prov 18:13, "He who answers a matter before he hears it, it is folly and shame to him" (NKJV). James also placed a high priority on listening: "be quick to listen, slow to speak and slow to become angry" (Jas 1:19, NIV).

Active listening is much more than appearing to listen or even hearing the verbal message. It implies listening with deep understanding and communicating that understanding appropriately. Active listening (a) helps the counselor receive and respond to the entire content of the counselee's communication, (b) helps the counselor get at the deeper issues, (c) helps the counselee listen to himself, and (d) earns the counselor the right to lovingly and caringly challenge the counselee. Acquiring the skill of active listening means that the counselor develop three specific skills that form the acrostic ARM: A = *Attending* skills, R = *Reflecting* skills, and M = *Minimal* encouragers.

### Active listening skill 1: Being present in body through attending skills.

In Gen 3, following Adam and Eve's sin of disobedience, God came to them. One might expect God to demand that Adam and Eve present themselves before Him. God was clearly in the position to get them to come to "His office," so to speak. But this was not the case. At their time of greatest need God brought His presence to Adam and Eve; He sought them out.

God sent His Son in the form of flesh to be present with us and to redeem our brokenness. Jesus Christ "dwelt among us" (John 1:14). The Greek word for "dwelt" means "to tabernacle" or "to be present." Man's need for redemption from sin required that Jesus Christ be present with us. God once again came to mankind to address a need; He became physically present to us.

First, your presence is an active investment in the lives of those who are wounded and broken. To be fully present with counselees, do not call attention to your titles, positions, and training. The quality of your presence with the counselee is what matters most. Nonverbal behavior is a powerful form of communication because it reveals your heart (Likowski, Mühlberger, Seibt, Pauli, & Weyers, 2008). From our earliest moment on earth every human begins receiving and sending nonverbal messages. As a nonverbal communicator, the body can be used as a tool to facilitate rapport. Positioning your body so that you give all your attention to your counselee invites open dialogue (Bolton, 1979). Counselors refer to this process as an "attending" skill.

The concept of coming alongside a counselee is referred to as establishing a "therapeutic relationship" or developing a "therapeutic alliance." This requires maintaining a balance between closeness and separateness (Leitner, 2007). As Teyber (2006) notes, effective counselors use the counseling relationship to foster growth and to encourage positive change. In fact the quality of the counseling relationship is a critical factor in obtaining positive outcomes (Asay & Lambert, 1999).

Attending skills can accomplish four important counselor outcomes. First, attending is a posture of involvement, demonstrating that you are present. All of us have had the experience of talking with someone who is not really present (recall the story of John not listening to his wife). While we are attempting to share something we consider important, we notice that the person is looking around or gazing at something else. Perhaps the person's body is slightly turned away from us. Whatever the case, such behavior indicates that the person might be physically present but psychologically absent. To be the best counselor possible, be sure to communicate psychological presence. This is accomplished through your physically attending to the counselee's presence. To establish rapport through active listening, be fully there. When you truly come alongside, you are "being with" your counselees in such a way that they experience your physical and psychological presence.

Second, attending to the counselee says that you are interested in what is being said. Your interest is conveyed not only by the words you use, but also in facial expressions, body posture, inflections, and gestures (Kopp, 1989). Counselees are checking out their counselor, just as counselors evaluate their counselees.

Third, attending equalizes the power inherent in a counselor-counselee relationship. By virtue of your role as the helper, a sense of power is imbued to that position. But attending levels the playing field by demonstrating that the interest of the counselor is in the counselee; it creates a relationship without any demands. Attending reflects a willingness to know the counselee and to be known yourself (Moursund & Kenny, 2002).

Fourth, attending augments your effectiveness. Wise counselors seek to arrange things in such a way that they increase their ability to influence the process and the counselee toward the agreed-on goals. By sound attending, you invite open dialogue and create a therapeutic connection, which leads to better outcomes (Asay & Lambert, 1999).

An acronym known as **SOLER** (Egan, 2007), that has been used for decades, can remind a beginning counselor of the physical positioning that communicates physical and psychological presence. The positions should be natural, not overdone.

The "S" in SOLER refers to facing the counselee by **Sitting squarely**. "Turning away" signifies that someone has chosen not to involve himself with another person, but, "turning to" another communicates a willingness to be present and involved with that person. To attend, then, requires that you orient your body both literally and figuratively toward the counselee. One aspect of sitting squarely is establishing appropriate proximity. Every person has his own sense of "personal space," but there are some general guidelines to bear in mind for all situations. For example the space between friends is typically small because friendships are familiar and comfortable. Friends often share more personal information with each other, so being close limits the ability of others to "easedrop" on a private conversation. In contrast, the space between strangers might be greater because of the minimal trust inherent in all new relationships. In North

American culture distances closer than 18 inches are considered appropriate only for people who have an intimate relationship (Hall, 1966). Thus your physical proximity to the counselee communicates a willingness to engage the counselee personally, yet without smothering or being intrusive. According to Egan (2007), squarely facing a counselee communicates the point, "I'm with you right now."

The "O" in SOLER stands for maintaining an **Open** posture. For example, sitting with folded arms may communicate coldness, defensiveness, or disgust. Sitting behind a desk might communicate a distant and authoritative posture toward the counselee. Having an open posture invites the counselee to be open and to share concerns freely. Openness conveys a sense of acceptance of the counselee. Sitting in an open posture with a counselee communicates the point, "I'm open to you right now" (Egan, 2007).

The "L" in SOLER refers to **Leaning** toward the counselee. When we lean away from someone, we are typically indicating our wariness, distrust, disagreement, disengagement, or boredom. Lovers who are situated across from each other often lean toward each other because of the intimate nature of their relationship. Leaning toward a counselee communicates the specialness of the counseling relationship and your interest in the person. It demonstrates that you are giving energy and attentiveness to the counselee and no one else. Properly leaning toward the counselee communicates, "I'm interested in you and in what you have to say."

The "E" in SOLER conveys the importance of **Eye** contact. You need visually to attend to your counselee. Maintaining good eye contact does not mean staring the counselee down. Rather, good eye contact means focusing on the counselee's face and occasionally shifting the focus to other parts of the body. Visually assessing a counselee's breathing or skin coloration can help you ascertain the counselee's level of anxiety. A restless or bouncing leg might suggest anxiety or impatience. Poor eye contact on the part of the counselee could signal boredom, embarrassment, submissiveness, or even anger, and frequent shifting in a chair or changes in posture may indicate disinterest or anxiety. Eye contact that is directed to the counselee communicates that your attention is where it is supposed to be. Like the other aspects of SOLER, proper eye contact sends the message, "I'm interested in what you have to say."

The "R" of SOLER highlights the need to be **Relaxed** or natural in one's nonverbal behavior. For novice counselors, this might be the most difficult part of attending because of the insecurity that comes from being inexperienced. In practicum and internship experiences, counselees are aware of the novice status of their counselor. In such circumstances counselees typically understand the counselor's anxiety, though they still do not appreciate it. Though nominal counselor anxiety can hinder the process, excessive anxiety can block therapeutic progress. Such counselor insecurity indicates that the counselor's focus is on himself rather than the counselee. On the other hand a counselor who is relaxed demonstrates interest in and focus on the counselee. The counselor's relaxed posture communicates a sense of peace in being with the counselee and confidence in one's abilities and services. Being relaxed allows you as the counselor to stay grounded and in contact with yourself and aware of the messages your body is communicating. A relaxed posture tells the counselee, "I'm comfortable being with you."

The attending behaviors described above must be weighed against cultural factors. In general North Americans would agree that these guidelines are appropriate in demonstrating active listening. Some cultures, however, would not find these guidelines useful and might even consider them offensive. For example the Native American culture has adopted many North American attitudes. In most situations facing a person squarely, adopting an open posture, and maintaining eye contact are considered appropriate. When listening to elders, however, the younger person would typically maintain a submissive posture, with eyes averted as a demonstration of respect. Some Caucasians might interpret this as a lack of respect, whereas in Native American culture the opposite is true.

Also, racial and gender differences factor into the establishment of rapport. Research on the influence of race and gender on the counselor-counselee relationship has been mixed. In the case of race some studies suggest that racial similarity facilitates rapport (Banks, 1971; Hall, Guterman, Lee, & Little, 2002; Pinchot, Riccio, & Peters, 1975), but other studies suggest that different variables eclipse racial matching (Wintersteen, Mensinger, & Diamond, 2005; Ortega & Rosenheck, 2002). In contrast to studies on race, research exploring the role of gender matching has been fairly consistent in pointing to same-sex counseling relationships as preferable (Hall, Guterman, Lee, & Little, 2002; Wintersteen, Mensinger, & Diamond, 2005).

It is impossible not to communicate. Your body is always communicating messages to others. Be intentional in ensuring that you are sending the types of messages that will enhance not diminish your effectiveness. You are physically present with your counselees when you pay careful attention to their words, behaviors, and intentions. Ultimately your full presence is needed to understand their experience and to communicate that understanding verbally and nonverbally.

While the SOLER skills provide nonverbal factors associated with attending, matching a counselee's "representational system" focuses on how dialogue can facilitate attending. According to Bandler and Grinder (1975) and Grinder and Bandler (1976a) people process their experiences through five sensory channels or "representational systems." Each system is a way a person can represent, code, store, and give meaning or language to experiences. We use all our senses in experiencing our world, but primarily we rely on one or two systems to represent an experience. Each system has vital information that impacts how we might interpret a life event. These representational systems include visual (what we see), auditory (what we hear), kinesthetic (what we feel tactically), olfactory (what we smell), and gustatory (what we taste). In the helping process the visual, auditory, and kinesthetic modalities (gustatory and olfactory are typically included with kinesthetic) are the most important. A clue to a counselee's preferred type of processing is found in the words used to describe an experience. The words we use reflect what particular system is primarily in operation for that experience. Table 5.5 gives a list of words related to each of the three key representational systems (Lankton, 1980).

Visual processing creates internal images and pictures. A visual person will use words like those in the visual column. For example counselees processing visually might describe their experience in the following ways: "I see what you are saying" or "From my point of view" or "I want a different perspective" or "I can shed some light on the matter" or "Things are looking up."

Table 5.5

*Words Associated with Visual, Auditory, and Kinesthetic Modalities*

| VISUAL | AUDITORY | KINESTHETIC |
|---|---|---|
| See | Listen | Feel |
| Clear | Yell | Touch, Touchy |
| Focus | Tell, Told | Pressure |
| Picture | Talk | Hurt |
| View | Hear | Pushy |
| Perspective | Ears | Grasp, Get hold of, Handle |
| Bright | Discuss | Relaxed |

Table 5.5 (cont.)

*Words Associated with Visual, Auditory, and Kinesthetic Modalities*

| VISUAL | AUDITORY | KINESTHETIC |
|--------|----------|-------------|
| Show | Shout | Sense |
| Colorful | Loud, Noisy | Experience |
| Glimpse | Call | Firm |
| Illustrate | Tune in | Walk through |
| Insight | Resonate | Heavy |
| Outlook | Question | Move |
| Vision | Language | Rough |
| "Now look" | "Now listen" | "You know" |

Adapted from Lankton (1980), cited in W. H. Cormier & L. S. Cormier (1985), *Interviewing strategies for helpers: Fundamental skills and cognitive behavioral interventions* (2nd ed) (Pacific Grove, CA: Brooks/Cole).

People who process using the auditory mode represent their experience in internal dialogue, words, and sounds. To recall a conversation that you had yesterday you would need to use your auditory mode. A person who processes an event using the auditory system will express his thoughts with such statements as "I hear what you are saying" or "I can call attention to it" or "We're on the same wavelength" or "I'm at a loss for words" or "That strikes a chord with me" or "He was talking gobbledygook."

Processing in the kinesthetic mode leads to somatically felt experiences. Remember a time when you felt powerful and special. A counselee who represents an experience kinesthetically might say: "I can hold onto that" or "I'm in touch with what you are saying" or "I've got a handle on it" or "Get a grip on yourself" or "One step at a time" or "I need something concrete" or "I'm ready to tackle the problem head-on" or "I'm trying to keep things in balance" or "She rubs me the wrong way" or "I feel it in my bones" or "That was a sticky situation."

Though not part of conscious awareness, each person has a primary representational modality that processes each life experience. When learning a new skill, some people prefer to see it or imagine it being performed, but other people need to have it explained to them in detail, and still others need to get a feel for it (Ellerton, 2005). The words a counselee uses reveal how he is experiencing a situation. When you listen for the kinds of words counselees are using, you may not be able to tell what the person is thinking, but you can have a good idea of how the counselee is thinking.

Moreover, counselors who can phrase their responses in such a way that they match the counselee's representational system enhance rapport (O'Connor & Seymour, 2002). In other words you are wise to speak the counselee's language. For instance if the counselee says, "What you are suggesting doesn't feel right to me," the counselor could respond with kinesthetic language such as "Let's touch on the points another way." Suppose a counselee says, "I cannot listen to another thing that person has to say." Rather than you saying, "You must feel really hurt and angry right now," you can use auditory language in your response and say: "You simply cannot talk about it with her." Suppose a counselee says, "I can still see the look on his face when he told me that he was leaving." If the counselor responds with "You can feel the experience right now," the counselor is crossing representational systems. The counselee is using visual mode, and the counselor is responding in the kinesthetic mode. A better response might be, "His look illustrates the deep pain you feel inside." In this response the counselor begins with the counselee's primary system (visual) and then links it with the kinesthetic experience of the event.

Matching a counselee's representational system or verbal matching is associated with neurolinguistical programming (NLP). The research related to NLP in general and to verbal matching in particular has been mixed (Elich, Thompson, & Miller, 1985; Heap, 1988; Sharpley, 1987). As a result of the research findings the theory was reformulated (Grinder & Bostic St. Clair, 2001). Nevertheless some studies do suggest that verbalization matching might positively augment rapport. In a dissertation study Brockman (1980) compared participant reactions to different counselors. One matched the counselee verbally and the other did not. Results showed that participants preferred counselors who matched them verbally over those who did not. Though research support for this method of attending is not as impressive as we would desire, it makes sense to speak the counselee's language as much as possible. No research shows that matching a counselee's representational system harms rapport.

### *Active listening skill 2: Reflecting skills to communicate empathy.*
Another component of active listening is the ability to reflect back the counselee's message you are taking in. Put another way, reflecting empathically means that the counselor responds affectively to the counselee. Connecting with a counselee empathically through their feelings can be significant in the counseling process. The value of counselee's having their feelings honored has been noted by Teyber (2006). Often counselees

have experienced poor responses to their feelings by others. Empathic listening honors your counselee, creates a safe haven, deepens your rapport, and facilitates much insight.

Research supports the fact that empathy is a fundamental part of the counseling process (Carlozzi, Bull, Eells, & Hurlburt, 1995; Hartley, 1995), and that is consistent with most theoretical orientations. The most notable theoretical orientation that uses empathy is person-centered therapy (Rogers, 1951). In fact Rogers (1951) is credited with introducing empathic understanding as a core condition of counseling. He defined it as the counselor's ability to "enter the counselee's phenomenal world—to experience the counselee's world as if it were your own without ever losing the 'act if' quality'" (p. 284). While secular theorists became enamored with Rogers's wisdom of using empathy to counsel, the Bible had long before conveyed the value of empathy.

While the word *empathy* is never used in the Bible, it is the very heart of the gospel message. The apostle Paul captured the notion of empathy when he described Jesus assuming the role of a servant and being made in our likeness (Phil 2:7). Paul urged believers to "rejoice with those who rejoice; weep with those who weep" (Rom 12:15, HCSB). The writer of Hebrews told his readers to "remember the prisoners, as though you were in prison with them, and the mistreated, as though you yourselves were suffering bodily" (Heb 13:3, HCSB). The apostle John wrote that "the Word became flesh and dwelt among us" (John 1:14, NKJV); in other words God empathized with us by becoming one of us. Jesus was not merely sympathetic to our need; He also empathized with us by becoming our High Priest who is touched with our pain (Heb 4:15). Interestingly Henri Nouwen (1979) wrote that we cannot help a person who is suffering unless we enter their pain. Though we cannot literally enter their pain the way God entered our pain, we can—as Heb 13:3 states—enter their pain *as if* it were our own. That is empathy at its best.

Nouwen's comment goes to the heart of the very meaning of the word *empathy*, which comes from a German word that means "to feel into" or "to feel with." The idea of empathic understanding is responding to the counselee with sensitivity. Brammer and Shostrom (1982) state that empathy is "an attempt to think with, rather than for or about the counselee" (p. 160). Gladstein (1983) described it as feeling as if one were in the other person's shoes. Perhaps one of the most comprehensive definitions of empathy is by Baron-Cohen (2003).

> Empathizing is the drive to identify another person's emotions and thoughts, and to respond to them with an appropriate emotion. Em-

> pathizing does not entail just the cold calculation of what someone
> else thinks and feels (or what is sometimes called mindreading). . . .
> Empathizing occurs when we feel an appropriate emotional reaction,
> an emotion triggered by the other person's emotion, and it is done in
> order to understand another person, to predict their behavior, and to
> connect or resonate with them emotionally (p. 2).

Baron-Cohen's definition conveys the biblical notion of truly loving others as we love ourselves. It wonderfully captures the fact that all believers are to rejoice with those who rejoice and weep with those who weep (Rom 12:15). In the context of counseling the empathic counselor communicates a deep and accurate understanding of the counselee's feelings, actions, and thoughts.

Bohart and Greenberg (1997) wrote an entire volume on empathy and other authors have proposed different levels of empathy. In its most basic and simplest form empathy is the ability to be sensitive to other people (i.e., compassion and comfort with intimacy), the ability to understand the experiences and perceptions of another person (i.e., cognitive empathy), and the ability to feel what other people are experiencing (i.e., affective empathy). The wise counselor is aware of and tuned to the counselee's inner world. Through connecting skills the counselor's task is to sense, respond to, and follow what the counselee is experiencing.

In chap. 4 ("The Person of the Counselor") we addressed characteristics of effective helpers. To that list we could add the ability to be comfortable with psychological intimacy (Dunkle & Friedlander, 1996). Your ability to tolerate emotional closeness and vulnerability with another person will depend largely on your own temperament, background, and family dynamics.

Counselors must also seek to understand what is going on in the life of the counselee. In fact research has linked a counselor's cognitive empathy ability with positive counseling outcomes (Duan & Hill, 1996). Research has also found that a counselor's level of cognitive empathy is related to his level of cognitive complexity (Lutwak & Hennessy, 1982) and ego development (Carlozzi, Gaa, & Liberman, 1983).

Whereas cognitive empathy deals with the counselor's intellectual understanding of the counselee, affective empathy deals with the counselor's ability to feel the counselee's emotions. Egan (2007) speaks of two distinct degrees of affective empathy: (a) *primary empathy* and (b) *advanced empathy*. Primary empathy focuses on the counselee's feeling by identifying and labeling them. When counselors express primary empathy, they are communicating that they understand the major themes in their counselee's story. Primary empathy facilitates rapport, openness, and trust, and helps counselees explore themselves and their problem situation. Advanced empathy is characterized by helping counselees see beyond the surface issues. It offers counselees a deeper level of insight and understanding into their issues, concerns, and life themes. Advanced empathy is expressed when the counselor accurately conveys his understanding of what the counselee implies or infers in order to draw out implications of the issue. Whereas primary empathy helps a counselee see the apparent issues more clearly, advanced empathy helps the counselee get in contact with these issues. It is helpful to ask yourself, "What is the core message of what the counselee is saying?" By doing so, advanced empathy adds to the counselee's self-awareness.

Let's suppose you were counseling Robert who is seeking to improve his marriage. When he arrives at the office for his scheduled session, he seems upset. When you remark on the fact that he looks distressed, he relates to you the following story. As he was leaving work on Friday, his boss handed him some work that needed to be done right away. When Robert protested that he had other plans for the evening, his boss insisted that this project required his immediate and full attention. Robert says to you that he had intended to surprise his wife by taking her to her favorite restaurant that evening. Because of his new assignment he decided that he had better work on the project; he determined that the consequences for not delivering it to his boss on time would be far worse than neglecting his wife on this one occasion. Robert worked several extra hours on Friday night and continued to work on the project all weekend. Ultimately he completed the project late Sunday night.

On Monday Robert handed the finished product to his boss with a comment that it took him all weekend but he got it down, hopefully to the boss's satisfaction. Robert's boss took the report and set it aside without looking at it, commenting, "Now I have two weeks to review this before I present the proposal." Robert left the office in a quiet rage.

| | |
|---|---|
| **Counselor:** | *Wow, you sound angry!* (primary empathy) |
| **Robert:** | *I am! I worked all weekend and he didn't even look at it!* |
| **Counselor:** | *What was it about working all weekend that upsets you the most?* |
| **Robert:** | *I gave up my specially planned evening with my wife in order to make life convenient for my boss!* |

| **Counselor:** | *It sounds like you are worried that your attempt to communicate to your wife how important she is to you was derailed by your boss's demand.* (advanced empathy) |
|---|---|
| **Robert:** | *Exactly! We are struggling right now, and I wanted to take the time to tell her how special she is to me. My boss ruined that opportunity and to make matters worse; now we are fighting about the time that I spent working this weekend!* |

Some people are more predisposed to being empathic than others; for such people expressing empathy comes more naturally. Such people have what is known as *emotional intelligence*, which involves the ability to perceive and express emotion, to access and assimilate emotion in thought, to understand and analyze emotion, and to regulate emotion (Mayer, Salovey, Caruso, & Sitarenios, 2001). If your expressions of empathy do not come naturally, work hard to develop emotional competence in relating to others. Even if you sense that you lack emotional intelligence, listening empathically and reflecting that understanding back to the counselee is an acquired skill. Although some students acquire the skills to communicate empathy more easily than others, most students need great patience and sufficient time to master this skill. Virtually everyone can learn to understand what someone is really saying and can express that understanding in a meaningful way. Mastering the art of empathic responding, however, takes time and patience.

One of the main reasons students struggle with this skill is that they naturally gravitate toward solving the counselee's problem. When the counselee's emotional self-discovery is neglected, successful treatment outcomes are diminished. Developing reflective listening requires trusting that reflecting the counselee's thoughts, feelings, and meanings will be the best vehicle to help the counselee make necessary changes. People want to know that another person truly understands before they are willing to drop their guard. Empathic listening contributes to the safe haven needed by counselees to freely disclose, explore, and experiment. Counselors need to trust that counselees can eventually come to the place where they need to be in order to grow from their problem(s). Changing people is the work of the Holy Spirit, not the work of the counselor. The counselor's job is to facilitate the processes by which the Holy Spirit can work on the heart of a counselee in order to produce change and growth. It has amazed us over the years of our counseling work how using this technique brings the counselee to the place where we were hoping to lead them.

Counselors need to avoid believing that they are responsible *for* the counselee. Rather the counselor should realize that he is only responsible *to* the counselee. We are not to assume responsibility for our counselees. We are called to serve the Lord by helping people, but that does not mean that we alone are responsible to change them.

Whereas trusting this technique is a matter of your belief system (i.e., the head and the heart of the counselor), learning how to reflect that understanding back to a counselee is an acquired skill (i.e., the counselor's hands). Everyone can learn to understand what someone is really saying and express that understanding in a meaningful way. Mastering the art of reflective listening, however, takes a lot of time and patience for most people.

Developing the skill set for empathic reflective listening can be mastered by learning seven steps that form the acrostic **EMPATHY**.

| Table 5.6 |
| --- |
| *Empathic Listening Steps* |
| **E** = **Explore** your inner world |
| **M** = **Move** into your counselee's internal world |
| **P** = **Personalize** the counselee |
| **A** = **Assess** nonverbals and what is said and not said |
| **T** = **Translate** the counselee's message into an empathic statement using feelings |
| **H** = **Hear** from the counselee if you are correct |
| **Y** = **Yield** to the counselee's response |

"E" means **Explore** your inner world. To develop the skill of empathic listening, know what is happening inside yourself. In other words it is important to possess self-awareness, as we noted in an earlier chap. As internal experiences are felt, become mindful of your own mental and emotional states. In empathic listening suspend and inhibit your own perspective (Goldman, 2006).

Some people who seek to be helpers struggle with intimacy. As such they regulate their closeness to counselees. To become comfortable with reflective listening you must desire to connect and feel comfortable being close to the counselee, that is, you must desire to be fully present with the person.

Another internal experience that many helpers face is the need to "do it right." You must deal with your fear of doing it wrong. Giving an empathic response is not about devising a clever response. Being fully focused on the counselee means you are not focusing on your needs. Moreover, providing empathic responses to counselees means accepting them with a nonjudgmental attitude. If you think, "I cannot believe he did that" or "She should have known better," you will never be able to empathize. We all fail, we all make mistakes, and every person sins (often repeating the same sin). Thus getting the log out of your own eye (Matt 7:3–5) will help you see the counselee as no worse than you. You will see the counselee as a fellow sojourner, struggling to deal with the sin nature, the flesh, and a fallen world.

"M" stands for **Move** into your counselee's internal world. It is dangerous to move into someone else's life when you do not know yourself. Once you have gained insight into your own issues, hang-ups, limitations, and strengths you are in a position to explore the heart of another.

Truax and Mitchell (1971) wrote much about the core conditions of an effective counseling relationship. They spoke to the power of adopting the counselee's internal frame of reference.

> As we come to know some of his wants, some of his needs, some of his achievements, and some of his failures, we find ourselves living with the other person much as we do the hero or heroine of a novel. . . . We come to know the person from his own internal viewpoint and thus gain some understanding and flavor of his moment-by-moment experience (p. 315).

The counselor steps into the counselee's internal world by understanding the counselee's feelings while seeking to reflect the experiences, attitudes, and beliefs underlying those feelings. When Jesus stepped into our world, He did not do so to understand our experience but to communicate that understanding. He knew what it was like to be human. Because of our humanness, however, we could not fathom God's understanding our plight until He became like us. In a similar way communicate your understanding to the counselee so that the counselee can experience being understood.

To be able to understand what others might be experiencing, counselors need to have an accurate theory of the mind. Theory of the mind refers to the ability to infer other people's mental states (Malle, 2005). Although different theories exist, it is believed that a person's own self-awareness helps him infer what is behind other people's behavior (Astington, 1996). The counselor's theory of the counselee's mind is the foundation to primary and advanced empathy. Moreover, it entails the ability to communicate that understanding accurately (Baron-Cohen, 2005).

Beginning counselors find it difficult to connect the counselee's non-verbal behavior and words into an affective experience. When feelings are noted, however, it is important to follow the counselee's pain. The pain will take you into the counselee's inner self or, as the Bible refers to it, the "heart." As you are aware of your own emotional experiences, you will become comfortable in following the counselee's feelings.

It takes time for some counselees to see the counseling relationship as a safe haven. Create the therapeutic space within which safety exists for the counselee to risk thinking about doing things differently. This safety is a consequence of the counselor's ability to connect; it can be compromised if the counselor either neglects this skill or uses it inappropriately. When you use the reflection of feeling skills to enhance the counselee's self-awareness too quickly, the counselee might also feel threatened, become defensive, and abandon treatment.

"P" means **Personalize** the counselee. A popular metaphor regarding understanding others is the idea of walking in another person's shoes. Step inside the counselee's reality and attempt to experience it as if it was happening to you. Silently ask, "How would I feel if this were happening in my life?" Many individuals have common reference points, life experiences that are similar. One example of this is that most people have experienced a significant loss. When a counselee begins to discuss the death of a loved one, counselors might recall how it felt when it happened to them, and verbally reflect those feelings to the counselee, by saying, "You feel rejected and abandoned." If a counselee's spouse left the marriage, an appropriate reflection that might come from your own perspective might be "You feel lost and lonely." Whatever emotions you might become aware of in the moment or recall from your past could be appropriate for the counselee. However, what the counselee is feeling may be dramatically different from what you have experienced. The counselor must see the experience not from his viewpoint, but from the viewpoint of the counselee. Loving others as we want to be loved does not mean the same actions that communicate love to us are what we are to do for another person. Rather our love is to reflect a desire to meet the needs of the other person just as we want our needs met. If you have never been physically abused by a parent, it might be easy to judge a counselee who now distances himself from his own children. You might think, "I would never distance myself from my children; I could never do those things to my kids." While that might be accurate, neither have you been abused by a parent. Perhaps this parent is distancing himself as a protective measure; a way to avoid hurting his own children the way he was hurt. Be humble and recognize that a counselee's behavior is part of a larger context. Your affective reflections account for the counselee's frame of reference, not yours. This again reinforces the need for each helper to explore his own internal world.

"A" is **Assess** nonverbals and what is said and not said. We have been trained from childhood to respond to what is said, not to what we observe. Yet when people are emotional, the greatest information is often found in their nonverbal communication. For example a counselee's vocal modulation may be absent or extreme, intonation may be flattened or heightened, the counselee might sigh, or there might be unusual pauses in what the counselee is saying. Eyes may be wet or downcast, shoulders might be slumped, teeth might be clenched, or the counselee's arms might be crossed. "You are feeling overwhelmed and lifeless by the loss of your husband" might be an appropriate counselor reflection for the counselee who has had a relationship end and is sitting slumped with downcast eyes unable to speak.

We will discuss the use of the mental status exam in chap. 10 ("Conducting an Assessment"), which includes observing the counselee's signs and symptoms. Beyond observation of nonverbal communication, however, also listen to how the counselee speaks and what seems to be missing from the content of the message. Remember that counselees often use feeling words to describe their internal reality. They might share with the counselor that the abrupt end of an important relationship leaves them feeling "unhappy." When the counselor reflects a feeling that has a meaning similar to the emotion identified by the counselee (for example "There is a lot of sadness in this for you"), the self-awareness of the counselee is enhanced. Continually ask yourself what the counselee is feeling and what the counselee needs and wants.

Feelings can be identified in a variety of ways: (a) single words such as "I feel good"; (b) phrases such as "I'm on top of the world"; (c) behaviors such as "I feel like hugging you"; and (d) implied in expressions such as "I feel I'm first on her list" (e.g., joy), "I feel I'm going to get it this time" (e.g., fear), "I'm feeling dumped on" (i.e., anger), and "I'm feeling stereotyped" (i.e., resentment). The key in assessing the counselee's core message is to read between the lines and to look for and follow the pain in the counselee's heart. While our cognitions are the foundational aspect of our makeup, emotions are neurological. That is, emotions are physiologically wired in our brains. Whether we like it or not and whether it makes for good preaching or not, our emotions in particular and feelings in general are a stronger predictor of what we come to believe about the world and what we do.

"T" stands for **Translate** the counselee's message into an empathic statement using feelings. The feeling-word vocabulary of many beginning counselors is often limited. As a result, they risk falling into the habit of selecting their reflections of feelings from a limited menu of words. Appendix I gives a list of feeling words that can assist the counselee and counselor alike in labeling emotions. Some counselees may not develop an ability to express their inner emotional reality in healthy ways, and may be limited to acting out their emotions physically, sometimes with devastating consequences. Often counselees will tell the counselor how they do not feel. They will make statements such as, "Well I don't feel good about it." In cases like this the counselor may simply reflect any emotions that are the opposite of the emotion the counselee has rejected. An example would be, "You're feeling bad and worried about this situation." In addition behind every complaint is a wish, and the wise counselor listens for what the counselee wants and needs. "Sounds like you really want him to . . ." or "You deeply wish that he would . . ." Under the best of circumstances, the reflection of covert emotions is difficult. By definition, covert feeling is outside the counselee's awareness, and counselors-in-training are often fearful that they will not identify a hidden feeling correctly. This desire to be right can lead to minimizing or omitting feeling skill, and limit the effectiveness of the counselee's counseling experience. Early in counseling it is best to choose more gentle feelings. A counselee who shares about something his spouse did that really upset him might rebuff the following counselor response, "You are angry at her." While the reflection might be correct, the counselee might not be ready to accept that label because of how anger is viewed. More gentle responses that would be more palatable for the counselee might include "You are frustrated with her" or "You feel put out with her" or "When she made fun of you in front of your friends, you felt embarrassed and got upset with her." Another means of offering empathy is to use what we call the *empathy formula*. The formula is comprised of two parts and is simple and straightforward. You first begin with a "You feel . . ." sentence. It is important that you get into the right family of emotions with the right intensity. Then the second part is added, "because" followed by your mentioning the experience, event, behavior, or internal processes that give rise to the feelings. For example, "Eric, you're afraid because it seems that every time you have taken a risk it has resulted in disaster. You have no reason to think that this will be any different."

"H" means **Hear** from the counselee if you are correct. From the reflection of feeling, one of two things will happen. The counselee will or will not accept it. If the reflection fits, the counselee will usually endorse it by continuing to share or even acknowledging with "yes" that the reflective response resonates. If the response does not fit, the counselee will deny it, and usually follow up by telling the counselor what he or she believes the correct feeling to be. Knowing this about counselee behavior allows the counselor-in-training to acquire a comfort level with this technique. When coupled with the understanding that what the counselee is not feeling may be as important as what is being felt, the counselor is helped in determining the counselee's self-discovery.

"Y" is **Yield** to the counselee's response. Sometimes a counselee will argue with your response. Even though you might be correct, the counselee might not be ready to accept hearing the statement as you worded it. True, people know themselves better than anyone else, but it is also true that people can be blind to their own issues or resist hearing the truth. Regardless of the reason, if the counselee rejects your response, accept it; while it may be tempting to defend your response, that will likely create a power struggle and diminish rapport. No matter what, the counselee heard your comment and it will have an impact. Remember that when you use the reflection of feeling skill, the counselee can benefit even when the reflective response does not resonate with him.

What follows are two examples of counselor responses to a particular counselee statement. Read the counselee and counselor statements below and determine whether Counselor A or Counselor B is providing the best empathic reflective statement.

> **Counselee:** *It hurts so bad when I think that we were so close to getting married. I wanted him to be my husband more than anything in the world, but he doesn't want me anymore.*
>
> **Counselor A:** *It hurts really badly now, but in time it will not hurt anymore. You can find someone else.*
>
> **Counselor B:** *Thinking about your fiancé breaking up with you brings up feelings of sadness and a strong sense of rejection.*

Counselor A is attempting to help the counselee feel better by focusing on the fact that painful feelings are typically temporal. Though Counselor A begins with an empathic response, it fails to affirm the counselee's experience. If you have ever lost someone special to you, you know that hearing that a loss will hurt less with time is not comforting or helpful. A truly empathic response acknowledges the full range of feelings. In contrast Counselor B knows that there is great therapeutic value in being able to process feelings out loud. This response is truly empathic because it captures the two key points of the counselee's statement: the hurt and not being wanted.

Consider another example:

**Counselee:**     *I wish had listened to my wife. If only I had not insisted that we drive through the night, the accident would not have happened and she would be alive.*

**Counselor A:**   *You feel as if your whole life has been ruined by this accident.*

**Counselor B:**   *It sounds as though you feel responsible for your wife's death because you failed to take her advice.*

Counselor A is focusing on how the accident has affected the counselee's life, rather than on the counselee's sense of responsibility for the death of his wife. While the decision to drive through the night was ill-advised, it was not a deliberate act with the intent of causing injury to his wife. Counselor A is ignoring the counselee's sense of guilt and moving in a direction that emphasizes only how the past is influencing his future, without any regard for the counselee's feelings about his role in the death of his wife. However, Counselor B recognizes the guilt that the counselee feels and the active part that such an emotion plays in his contemporary existence. By accurately empathizing with the counselee, Counselor B is opening the door for further exploration of this individual's grief and the possibility of moving beyond it.

| Table 5.7 |
| :--- |
| *Key Questions* |

| | |
| :---: | :--- |
| 1. | Am I allowing the counselee to do most of the talking? |
| 2. | Am I jumping to conclusions because of my own life experiences? |
| 3. | Am I facilitating the counselee to make his or her own decisions, or am I attempting to steer the person to what I believe is the right decision? |
| 4. | Am I allowing the counselee to have ownership of his or her own problem? |

### Active listening skill 3: Minimal encouraging skills.

Whereas attending skills require a physical presence expressed through the counselor's body, minimal encouraging skills (the "M" in the acrostic "ARM") require a mental presence expressed through the counselor's words and even nonverbal communication. Minimal encouragers demonstrate a counselor's active listening by stating that the counselee's disclosures are being tracked. Minimal encouragers typically occur naturally and outside of most people's awareness. The objective of minimal encouragers is to stimulate more conversation from the counselee with the minimum amount of interruption by the counselor. Minimal encouragers can facilitate counseling by helping clarify confusing content and getting the counselee to expound on what is being shared.

These skills comprise both verbalizations and nonverbal behavior that include sounds, words, short phrases, and head nodding that encourage the counselee to keep talking. For example when the counselor makes such sounds as "uhm" and "hmm," uses words such as "OK," "I see," "and then," "so," "really," "yes," "say more about that," or even repeats the last word or two of the counselee, the counselor is hoping to communicate that he or she is listening and desires to hear more information. A major pitfall of counselors-in-training is finding the balance between using them too much, which can communicate impatience, or using them too little and giving the impression of not being present.

## CHAPTER SUMMARY

Competent helpers are experts in conversation, both verbal and non-verbal communication. They know how to attend to what the counselee is saying, to listen, and to communicate understanding. They know how to encourage the counselee to share and express feelings, clarify the problem or concern, deal with the problem, and have some guidelines about what to do when strong feelings are expressed.

Though establishing rapport can be a painstaking process, it is essential for giving help. Master the ability to establish a strongly connected therapeutic relationship in order to communicate that you are genuinely interested in helping the counselee. Your ability to connect is pivotal and foundational to the counseling process. As Yalom and Leszcz (2005) write, "Psychotherapy is both art and science; research findings may ultimately shape the broad contours of practice, but the human encounter at the center of therapy will always be a deeply subjective, nonquantifiable experience" (p. xv).

The two broad skills that comprise connecting or rapport include (a) creating a safe haven and (b) active listening. A safe haven provides a sanctuary for the counselee to become vulnerable and grow. By attending to the tangible and intangible conditions of counseling, a safe haven can be established.

Rapport is also established when the counselor actively listens. This skill set requires that you attend physically, reflect affectively, and minimally encourage the counselee to communicate. Professional counselors listen well, and they hear nuances in the counselee's communication that are beyond the awareness of most others. Listen deeply as if to give the impression that you seemingly read minds and know what people are thinking. Through the relationship with the counselor the counselee can gain a taste of God's love, righteousness, grace, and mercy. As counselees find a connection with their counselor, they sense what it is like to have a secure relationship with Christ. Counselors must provide presence to those to whom they are called to minister.

## CHAPTER 5 ACTIVITIES

1. Describe the difference between content and process in counseling.
2. Review the scriptures and find five verses (write them out along with their "addresses") that speak to the value that God places on relationship.
3. How does the therapeutic relationship hold the potential to provide an "incarnational" relational experience for the counselee and why is this important in counseling?
4. Name three people in your life who provide you with a "safe haven." What are the qualities of these persons and the relationship they offer you that makes them safe people for you?
5. Name and describe the tangible and intangible conditions that work against providing a safe haven for counselees.
6. Read through the book of Proverbs and find seven verses related to the importance of being cautious with the use of the tongue. How can you apply these verses to your own family relationships? How can you apply these verses to your therapeutic relationships?
7. Describe in detail the skills discussed in the section entitled "Active listening skill 1: Being present in body through attending skills." Include a description of the SOLER model and how to attend through Representational System Matching.
8. Describe in detail the skills discussed in the section entitled "Active listening skill 2: Reflecting skills to communicate empathy." Utilize the acrostic "EMPATHY" in your description.

9. What are the key questions (provided in this chapter) that we should ask ourselves during counseling sessions to help keep us on track in terms of listening?

10. Share about a time when you felt listened to while discussing your feelings with someone you know. What was this person doing that lead to these feelings? How might experiences like these influence how a person experiences God?

## Vignette Questions

### Vignette 1
### Attending Skills

1. Based upon the first vignette, what issue brought the counselee to see the therapist? How do you think the counselee felt at this point in the session?

2. Did the therapist connect with the counselee? How would you characterize the relationship between the therapist and the counselee?

3. How did the counselor's behavior(s) shape the counselee's view of him?

4. What concepts of connecting could be improved in this demonstration?

5. Can the therapist repair the counseling relationship at this point? If yes, how would he go about doing so?

### Vignette 2
### Empathetic Listening

1. In the second vignette, what do you think this experience was like for Charlie? Do you think that he feels "heard"? Why or why not?

2. If you were Charlie, would you have felt comfortable? If you answered "yes," what did the counselor do that made you feel at ease? If you answered "no," what did the counselor do that made you uncomfortable?

3. Where did the counselor use EMPATHY (support your view by identifying which letter of the acronym was used and explain why it applies)?

4. Why do you think that the use of sarcasm was interpreted in the vignette as "detaching from reality"?

## Recommended Reading

Clarkson, P. (2009). *The therapeutic relationship* (2nd ed.). Philadelphia, PA: Whurr.

> Although primarily based in psychodynamic theory, Clarkson provides a very insightful perspective into the counseling relationship. Through the book she unpacks five aspects of the helping relationship: the working alliance, transference, reparative/developmentally needed, person-to-person, and transpersonal relationships.

Martin, D. (1999). *Counseling and therapy skills*. Prospect Heights, IL: Waveland Press.

> Though a secular book, Martin provides helpful instruction on how to be empathic with counselees. It is a practical book that is geared to the novice counselor.

Nichols, M. (2009). *The lost art of listening*. New York City, NY: Guilford Press.

> Nichols does an excellent job of providing a behind-the-scenes look into the listening habits of people. He centers his discussion in the context of relationships and faces questions such as why people listen. The book is full of stories to help the reader grasp the concepts and quizzes to help readers test how well they are learning.

## Chapter 6

# Basic Skills: Exploring the Problem

*"Christian counselors promote healing as they help counselees to solve problems . . . They also promote healing as they help counselees grow in faithfulness and vitality of Christian discipleship . . . [Change in] Christian counseling . . . embodies the dual nature of freedom—freedom from condemnation, trauma, and other problems, and freedom to act as Christian disciples in the world"* (Craigie, 1994, p. 214).

*"Whatever your hand finds to do, do it with all your might, for in the grave, where you are going, there is neither working nor planning nor knowledge nor wisdom"* (Eccl 9:10, NIV).

## CHAPTER OBJECTIVES

» To equip students with the ability to explore counselee concerns and issues

» To develop the ability to ask appropriate and meaningful questions

» To learn when and how to paraphrase counselee statements

» To learn how to ask counselees to clarify what is being said

» To learn how to conduct summaries throughout the counseling process

» To provide opportunities for students to further their exploration skill development through learning activities

## CHAPTER OUTLINE

---

In chap. 5 ("Basic Skills: Creating a Connection"), we laid the foundation for understanding helping skills. We discussed the importance of understanding where a particular skill falls on a continuum of nondirectiveness to directiveness. The difference between content and process was also explained with the point that the key to counseling is focusing on process rather than on content. Most importantly we discussed the first skill set in becoming an effective helper, namely, creating a connection with your counselee.

In this chap. our intention is to build on the substance of a solid helping relationship by equipping you with key skills in offering effective counseling. The next set of skills we will address is Exploration Skills (see Table 6.1; the same as Table 5.1). These skills are also illustrated in the DVD that accompanies the text. It is important that all counselors master these basic skills.

## SKILLS OF EXPLORATION

Skills of exploration comprise the activities that counselors employ in order to understand the counselee's concerns and issues. By inquiring into your counselee's concerns, you can better grasp the reason for his interest in counseling and what he wants to happen in order for counseling to be considered effective. We will begin with the most basic of these skills, the skill of questioning and then move to paraphrasing, clarifying, and summarizing.

| Table 6.1 | | | |
| --- | --- | --- | --- |
| *Functional Allocation of Counselor Skills* | | | |
| | **SKILL SETS** | | |
| **Skills** | **Connecting** | **Exploring** | **Facilitating** |
| Rapport | P | S | S |
| Safe Haven | P | S | S |
| Attending | P | S | S |
| Reflection | P | S | S |
| Minimal Encouragers | P | S | S |
| Questions | S | P | S |
| Paraphrase | S | P | S |
| Clarification | S | P | S |
| Summary | S | P | S |
| Feedback | S | S | P |
| Interpretations | S | S | P |
| Confrontation | S | S | P |
| Self-Disclosure | S | S | P |
| Immediacy | S | S | P |
| Silence | S | S | P |
| Pacing | S | S | P |

P = Primary function; S = Secondary function

## The Skill of Questioning

Questions are regarded by experts in counseling techniques as a major tool of the counselor (Egan, 2007; Ivey & Ivey, 2003; Patterson & Eisenberg, 1983; Sommers-Flanagan & Sommers-Flanagan, 2003). Helping people requires going beyond listening. Wise counselors probe into areas of the counselee's life that are associated with various problems or issues. Without the skillful use of questions a counselee's problems cannot be fully and accurately assessed.

This section explores the nature, power, and kinds of questions employed in the counseling process. We will present limitations and pit-falls of using questions and provide guidelines for effectively using questions to facilitate counseling goals.

## The Nature and Power of Questions

The use of questions comes early in mankind's history. Questions were first used by God when He sought out Adam and Eve and questioned them about their sin (Gen 3:9,11,13). God also asked questions of Cain following his murder of Abel (Gen 4:6–7,9–10). Questions have a powerful role in our lives. Used appropriately, questions can facilitate positive counseling outcomes.

Questions offer a number of advantages over other helping techniques. First, questions can provide a systematic framework that guides the counseling process (Ivey & Ivey, 2003). They facilitate the counseling session, keeping the session moving forward, unfreezing frozen dialogue, and guiding the counselee back on course. Questions such as these can help facilitate the counseling process: "What would you like to talk about today?" "What do you hope to accomplish in coming to see me?" "At the end of the last session, you agreed to journal. How did that go?" "Earlier we were talking about your fear of failing and somehow we got sidetracked. Are you open to talking more about that fear?"

Similarly, effectively employing the use of questioning enables you to explore the counselee's problem more fully. Questions can help counselors understand their counselees' situation and help each counselee to give the fullest possible descriptions of their experiences. Questions such as these can help enrich the counselee's story: "What happened next?" "What is a specific example of that?" "What else comes to your mind?" "How did you feel when that happened?"

Even when counselees are being cooperative, they do not always give all the important information the counselor needs. Sometimes the only way to obtain the information is by asking questions. Thus prudent questions allow counselors to fill in what seems to be missing from the counselee's story. The following are attempts to get important pieces that are missing from the story: "How long have you been feeling depressed?" "You said that you left when your wife started attacking you, but what did you say before you left?" "What might we have missed so far?" When the story is unclear or when you are confused, questions can also help clarify what the counselee is saying.

Questions can also help open up new areas of exploration. For example, "It would help me to know about your family. What are some important things that stand out about your family?"

Another powerful use of questions is to challenge a counselee. When God said, "Adam, where are you?" He was not unaware of Adam's whereabouts. God's question was a means of making Adam admit that he was trying to hide from God and Eve. The writer of Proverbs aptly noted, "As iron sharpens iron, so one man sharpens another" (27:17, NIV).

## Kinds of Questions

Questions can be grouped into various categories depending on the nature of the inquiry. One category is questions that solicit two types of answers: open-ended versus closed-ended questions. A second category includes direct questions versus indirect questions. A third category includes questions that are best avoided, such as leading questions and double questions. A fourth category is comprised of questions that attempt to provoke thought. These include projective questions, rhetorical questions, and hypothetical questions.

### *Open-ended versus closed-ended questions.*

Broadly speaking, two types of questions are used by counselors: open-ended questions and closed-ended questions (see Table 6.2). Each type of question reflects what the name implies. For example, open-ended questions encourage the counselee to elaborate; that is, open-ended questions "open up" the counselee's response. Closed-ended questions, on the other hand, close down the counselee's response. The counselee is limited in his response to the question. In other words the open-ended question is broad, and the closed-ended question is narrow.

Closed-ended questions are asked in ways that limit the counselee's response to only a few words at best. Questions that begin with words such as do, can, is, did, and are can usually be answered with "yes" or "no" responses. Some examples of closed questions are these:

- "So it seems the problem is that your son needs to change his friends. Is that correct?"
- "Are you having financial problems?"
- "Did you tell her that you loved her?"
- "Can you think of a time when he hurt you?"

An open-ended question is worded in such a way that it elicits as much information as possible. Typically these questions begin with words such as what, how, when, where, or why.

As a rule, what questions tend to elicit facts and information, how questions are aimed at obtaining a process or sequence, and why questions often prompt reasons and intellectualizing (Ivey & Simek-Downing, 1980). Why questions typically elicit defensiveness and thereby diminish rapport. Sommers-Flanagan and Sommers-Flanagan (2003) explain that why questions produce one of two responses. One response is "Because" followed by an explanation. Another response is "Why not." If the counselee feels attacked, he or she might seek reassurance from the counselor about the behavior in question. Why questions might help a counselee take a more in-depth look at certain patterns or motivations, but in general the counselee tends to avoid them.

Open-ended questions vary in the level of openness needed by the counselee to answer adequately. Sommers-Flanagan and Sommers-Flanagan (2003) note that questions "do not uniformly facilitate depth and breadth of talk from counselees" (p. 83). Questions beginning with the word when and where typically result in information about time and place, whereas who questions identify people. Sometimes open-ended questions are not asked in the form of questions at all. Sometimes a counselor's request may be worded in the form of an "invitation." For example, "I am wondering about the way you typically deal with loss" or "Tell me about the way you deal with loss." These statements are open-ended in that they allow the counselee total freedom to describe his experience, but they are worded in a way that prevents the counselee from facing an inquisition. If you have played the game "Twenty Questions," you can appreciate the fact that you do not get a lot of information simply by asking questions.

### Table 6.2
*Comparison of Open-Ended and Closed-Ended Questions*

| Open-Ended Questions | Closed-Ended Questions |
|---|---|
| Broad | Narrow |
| More enrichment response | More specific response |
| Invites counselee to dialogue | Curtails dialogue |
| Solicits views, opinions, thoughts, and feelings | Solicits facts |
| Facilitates rapport | Hinders rapport |

In considering the difference between open-ended and closed-ended questions, compare the two sentences below:

- "Do you have a good relationship with your husband?"
- "Tell me about your relationship with your husband."

In both sentences the topic is identical. The responses the counselee will likely give, however, will be dramatically different. In responding to a closed-ended question, a counselee will typically limit his response. The second question, in contrast, invites dialogue. It does not assume any particular quality to the relationship the counselee had with his parents.

Does this mean that only opened-ended questions should be used? No; each kind of question has its intended purposes. Open-ended questions are best used (a) to stimulate conversation from the counselee, (b) to encourage the counselee to express himself more fully, (c) to obtain fuller descriptions of the counselee's experience, and (d) to foster the interactive nature of the counseling relationship. Most counseling sessions begin with the use of an open-ended question. For example "What led you to decide to see a counselor?" or "What is your goal for coming to see me?"

Closed-ended questions are purposeful when the counselor wants to (a) obtain specific information; (b) determine whether specific behaviors, symptoms, or signs are present; (c) restrain an overly talkative counselee; and (d) narrow the topic of discussion. The intentional helper chooses those techniques and methods that will optimize outcome.

### Direct versus indirect questions.
Direct questions are those that are clearly a question; they are direct queries. By contrast indirect questions are actually statements that imply a question. Indirect questions do not "feel" like questions.

Compare the paired sentences below.

Table 6.3

*Comparison of Direct and Indirect Questions*

| Direct Questions | Indirect Questions |
| --- | --- |
| "How does it feel being married?" | "I'd love to hear about what it feels like being married." |
| "What was your home life like?" | "Tell me about your home life." |
| "What was it like losing your mother at such a young age?" | "I'm wondering what it was like for you to have lost your mother at such a young age." |
| "In the two months you have been coming here, what progress do you think you have made?" | "You have been coming to see me for two months. I'm curious about the progress you think you have made." |

### Scaling questions.
A useful close-question is to have the counselee respond to identify an experience with a number. Scaling questions are designed to obtain a

subjective assessment from the counselee by using a scale from either 1 to 10 or 1 to 100. For example "On a scale of 1 to 100, with 100 being the most anxious you have ever been, what number best captures how anxious you have been since our last session?" There is no limit to the types of scaling questions you can create.

### Questions that should be avoided.

*Leading questions.* Anyone who has watched courtroom scenes on television has heard the statement from an opposing attorney, "He is leading the witness." That is the idea behind leading questions.

A leading question is more closed than a closed question. It suggests the type of answer the counselee is seeking and assumes an answer. These are examples of leading questions: "Did your father abuse you?" "Did you think about looking for a new job?" "Don't you agree that he really does love you?" "Isn't it true that you wanted to get yourself fired?" "No one would end a marriage unless she knew why, would she?" "Wouldn't you rather get what you want than have what you don't want?" "You probably thought that nothing would change?" Some leading questions are more inquisitive than interpretive. "Did your father abuse you?" might actually help clarify the counselee's story, but it also can be implying what you think is happening. A question such as, "Don't you resent your father for abusing you?" calls for an interpretation of the counselee's experience. The question is simply the vehicle in which to deliver the interpretation. A better feedback would be to state, "I find myself wondering if you resent your father for abusing you." In this way the counselor owns his view of the counselee's story. Many counselors follow such an interpretive statement with, "Does that fit for you?" or "How does it feel hearing that?"

*Double questions.* An example of a double question is this: "What was it like growing up in your household? In other words what was discipline like?" The counselee does not know which one to answer, so he will ignore one of the questions and answer the other. In this example the counselee will likely only address how his parents disciplined. Double questions are both confusing and limiting.

Another type of double question is when the helper includes two alternatives in a question. For example "Were your parents strict or permissive?" "Were you able to remain sober, and did you go to Alcoholics Anonymous?" "How would you describe your sex life? Can you talk about sex with your wife?" Every counselor likely uses double questions occasionally, but skilled helpers rarely do so intentionally.

*Punishing questions.* The punishing question is a form of confrontation in which the counselor posits a question to highlight a discrepancy or inconsistency. The punishing question requires more than the words, but the counselor's tone of voice also communicates shame and condemnation. For example "Why did you say that?" "What were you thinking when you hit her?" "Don't you think you should have known better?" The questions have nothing to do with exploration; instead they focus the counselee's attention on what the counselor considers blameworthy behavior.

### *Other types of questions.*

*Provocative questions.* At times counselors desire to stimulate counselees to consider different ideas or implications of their thinking, or to challenge their thinking. Provocative questions can assist you in challenging the counselee to think constructively.

*Projective questions.* Sometimes counselors ask "What if" questions. These are questions that ask counselees to speculate and allow exploration of motivations, dreams, thoughts, feelings, and behaviors. Projective questions are a form of open-ended questions designed to get the counselee to consider various possibilities. Through the response the counselor gets a glimpse into the counselee's values and judgments (Sommers-Flanagan & Sommers-Flanagan, 2003). These are examples of projective questions: "What would you do differently?" "How would things be different if you stopped drinking?" "If you were to wake up tomorrow and a miracle occurred during the night that eliminated your problem, what would be some of the first things you notice?" (De Shazer, 1988).

*Rhetorical questions.* Rhetorical questions are inquiry statements not meant to be answered. The purpose of a rhetorical question is to provoke thoughts. Rhetorical questions can help the counselee face an undeniable truth.

*Hypothetical questions.* When you use the word *would* early in a question, you are forming a hypothetical question. Hypothetical questions can be used to encourage the counselee to discuss the "what ifs" of a situation. For example "What would you do if she left?" or "How would you handle it if you find out that your son is lying?" Prompting the counselee to consider possibilities helps in problem-solving and planning for contingencies.

### Limitations and pitfalls of questioning.

The use of questions in the counseling process is both powerful and advantageous. Yet questions are not without their limitations and pitfalls. As with any technique, there is a downside to asking questions. This section explores some of the pitfalls and limitations of using questions.

First, some helpers wrongly assume that if asking questions is good, the more they ask the better. Counselors can easily begin to bombard the counselee with questions, which might put the counselee on the defensive or cause him to think he is being grilled. When inexperienced counselors do not know what to do, they typically think of a question. The more you develop a broad base of helping skills, the more choices you will have in facilitating the counseling process. In addition, when the counselor and counselee differ in their cultural roots and experience, questions can be problematic. When the cultural difference is significant, the counselee might not trust the counselor who asks too many questions or questions about certain topics. Cultural differences usually mean that a strong level of rapport needs to be established (see chap. 4, "The Person of the Counselor"). If a counselee's background differs dramatically from yours, more time may be needed to develop rapport (Raines & Ewing, 2006). Rapid-fire questions will not facilitate the development of rapport and can damage the counseling relationship. Research indicates that men ask more questions than women counselors (Ellis, 1997). If the desired counseling goals can be accomplished without the use of questions, it is better to avoid asking questions.

The most obvious pitfall of using questions is that the counselor takes control of the counseling session. When you ask a question in any context, you put yourself in the position of controlling a conversation (Sommers-Flanagan & Sommers-Flanagan, 2003). By their very nature questions are intended to obtain information from another person. Asking questions can cause the counselee to wait on the counselor to direct the conversation. Since counseling is a collaborative process in which the counselee takes the counselor in directions that will reveal the heart of the problem, taking charge of the content can be counterproductive.

Another pitfall of asking questions is that they can interrupt the flow of a counselee's story. They can direct the counselee from a particular pathway of discussion to a different path altogether, potentially leading to the missing of relevant information. In particular, closed-ended questions can derail a counselee from her story, by making her feel interrogated. As a result the counselor will miss learning about things that are relevant and important to understanding the counselee.

A significant danger in using questions is asking double questions, leading questions, and punishing questions. As noted above, these types of questions are best avoided.

Also ask questions carefully and selectively. People in some cultures might perceive a particular question as invasive or inappropriate. For example, a challenging question from a more youthful counselor may be interpreted as disrespectful by people in many Asian cultures, where both elderly men and women have earned the respect of younger individuals because of their age (Elliott, Di Minno, Lam, & Tu, 1996).

### Guidelines for using questions.

This section discusses guidelines to help you know when and how to use questions in the counseling process.

The "P" in the word **PROBE** refers to **Probing** awareness. Be aware that you are asking questions. We have noticed in our supervision of novice counselors that they too often fall into the habit of asking questions, often closed-ended questions, but they are not aware that they are doing so.

| Table 6.4 |
| --- |
| *PROBE CLIENT: How to Use Questioning* |
| **P** = **Probing** awareness |
| **R** = **Refrain** from asking questions if possible |
| **O** = Use **Open-ended** questions |
| **B** = Be **Brief** in asking questions |
| **E** = **Eschew** double, punishing, and leading questions |
| **C** = Use **Closed-ended** and **Clarifying** questions for specifics |
| **L** = **Limit** why questions |
| **I** = Be **Imaginative** in asking questions |
| **E** = **Evade** asking too many questions to less-verbal counselees |
| **N** = Develop the **Nerve** to probe sensitive areas |
| **T** = **Tolerate** the counselee's processing |

The "R" refers to **Refraining** from asking questions if possible. Challenge whether the questions you are about to ask need to be asked. You can employ a myriad of other techniques to facilitate open dialogue such as paraphrases and indirect questions (e.g., "Say more about that" or "Tell me about . . ."), reflective listening (discussed in chap. 5, "Basic Skills: Creating a Connection"), or minimal encouragers (chap. 5). The more you develop the full repertoire of counseling skills, the easier it will be to avoid relying too extensively on asking questions.

The "O" refers to using **Open-ended** questions as much as possible. Questions such as these are geared at providing more focused dialogue without limiting the counselee to specific responses: "What happened next?" "What impact did that have in your life?" "What are some things you've thought of trying?" "How did that change your relationship with your mother?"

The "B" refers to being **Brief**. Counselors need to develop the ability to be as succinct as possible in asking questions. Novice counselors often ramble in using verbal techniques. When asking a question, the inquiry can easily get lost in the mass of words.

The "E" refers to **Eschewing** double questions, leading questions, and punishing questions. Practice asking single questions that do not assume an answer or seek to shame a counselee.

Another useful acrostic is the word CLIENT.

The "C" refers to asking **Closed-ended** and **Clarifying** questions when you need to find out certain symptoms or signs the counselee is experiencing, when open-ended questions have not given the needed information. For example, if you asked the counselee to tell you more about her sleeping and you find out that the sleeping is disrupted but not how, you might need to ask, "Are you waking up in the middle of the night and unable to go back to sleep, or is it that you have more trouble falling asleep in the first place?" or "Tell me what you mean by 'disrupted'?" Also ask for clarification when you do not understand what the counselee is saying. Make it clear that the question is because of your own confusion. For example "Are you saying . . . ," "Did you mean . . . ," and "I'm sorry, but did you say that . . ." are attempts to make sense of the counselee's story when you are uncertain what the counselee means or if the counselee worded his story in a way that could mean more than one thing.

The "L" refers to **Limit** why questions. In general asking why questions are rarely productive because people interpret them as communicating disapproval or displeasure. As a result people typically respond to why questions defensively. A question that begins with why can be used to seek additional information or to ascertain a person's rationale, but the connotations it produces make it less than desirable.

Be **Imaginative** ("I") in asking questions. All too often counselors fall into a routine of phrasing questions in the same way. They may begin most of their questions with what or how, which limits the ability to gather other information about the counselee's experience.

"E" reminds you to **Evade** over-questioning less verbal counselees. Some counselees are very verbal, whereas others are less talkative. Both provide challenges to helpers. With a less-verbal counselee it is easy to fall into the trap of asking questions in order to get the information needed. Often using silence (which will be discussed later in the chap.) is a way to address quieter counselees.

Develop the **Nerve** ("N") to explore difficult areas, but do so respectfully. You need to approach sensitive areas respectfully and carefully. Counselors typically ask questions about the personal and private areas of a counselee's life, including sexual functioning, abuse, and the like. If the counselee avoids or refuses to answer a question, do not force it or shame the counselee. There is a place to confront, but early in the counseling process allowing the counselee as much latitude as possible will more likely result in a trusting counseling relationship. At the same time you might need to consider your own comfort level in probing into areas that are generally taboo in social relationships.

The "T" refers to **Tolerating** the counselee's processing of the question. In other words be patient and wait for an answer. Allow the counselee time to respond without asking another question, while the counselee is thinking how to answer the first question.

In summary, questions used with care can be a highly productive and effective means of helping a counselee. Questions can help or hinder the counseling process. From a positive point of view, questions can be viewed as appropriate, stimulating, or challenging. Negatively, some counselees may consider particular questions as intrusive, inappropriate, disrespectful, or rude. Counselors in training should consider how their use of questions fits with their natural style (Ivey & Ivey, 2003).

## The Skill of Paraphrasing

Simply stated, in a paraphrase the counselor uses her own words to capture what the counselee says. A good paraphrase is free of advice, judgments, and commentary. Instead, a paraphrase involves the counselor selectively gathering the counselee's key ideas, translating them into his own words, and feeding them back to the counselee (Cormier & Cormier, 1985). From the counselee's point of view his message contains facts about a situation or person. The counselor knows, however, that what the counselee considers facts are often a constellation of the counselee's perceptions, judgments, and opinions. A paraphrase seeks to reveal what the counselor is hearing. Young (2010) says a paraphrase as simply a distillation of the counselee's message.

### The purposes of paraphrasing.

First, an accurate paraphrase clearly communicates to the counselee that what is being said is being heard and understood. Ivey and Ivey (2003) point out that often counselees have complex problems that few if any people in their social circle have demonstrated interest in accurately hearing and exploring. Using a paraphrase assures the counselee that he is truly being heard.

Another purpose of paraphrasing is that it can cause counselees to focus on the content of their message. Because paraphrases are predominantly a technique that is cognitively oriented rather than affectively oriented, it highlights the content of the counselee's dialogue when addressing the counselee's feelings would be counterproductive.

A well-timed paraphrase can move a counselee back onto the subject when he or she has veered (Cormier & Cormier, 1985). A good paraphrase can let the counselee know that they have been heard and that there is no need to repeat telling the same story.

Paraphrasing is best used when the counselee says something that is important. It can encourage the counselee to elaborate on a key idea or thought (Cormier & Cormier, 1985). A paraphrase can help a counselee direct his attention to a particular event, behavior, thought, attitude, or value.

Also a paraphrase can facilitate exploration and can encourage the counselee to enrich her story without having to inquire (Ivey & Ivey, 2003). The paraphrase does not include the pressure that might be felt with a question, yet it has many of the advantages inherent in asking a question.

### How to use paraphrasing.

The following acrostic **PHRASE** provides six guidelines on effectively employing paraphrase in counseling (see Table 6.5). The first step in becoming competent in using the paraphrase skill is to **Perceive** ("P") the content of the message accurately. A paraphrase is the counselee's message stated in your own words. A paraphrase helps you restate what the counselee is telling you. Carefully attend to the counselee's message by listening and observing what and how the counselee is communicating. In chap. 5 ("Basic Skills: Creating a Connection"), we spoke about attending and active listening, skills that are linked to paraphrasing. Some counselors find it helpful to silently restate what the counselee is saying.

Table 6.5

*PHRASE: How to Use Paraphrasing*

| |
|---|
| **P** = **Perceive** the content of the message |
| **H** = What is the **Heart** of the message |
| **R** = **Rephrase** the counselee's message in your own words |
| **A** = **Assess** the timing of the paraphrase |
| **S** = Make your **Statement** |
| **E** = **Evaluate** the accuracy of your paraphrase |

The second guideline is to focus on the **Heart** ("H") of the counselee's message. As counselees share their stories, particularly verbose counselees, it is easy to get lost in a volume of information. One way of getting to the heart of the counselee's message is to ask yourself what key message is in the counselee's content? What event, person, object, or idea is paramount?

If you believe a paraphrase is timely, **Rephrase** ("R") the counselee's message by condensing it in your own words. But the point is not to parrot what the counselee is saying. When you go through a drive-in to get your meal, you want the worker to state your order back to you to be sure it is correct. A paraphrase is not a repetition of the counselee's words, but a rephrasing of the words. As you form the paraphrase, remember to be succinct. Too much information might result in the counselee losing her place in her story. In addition to rephrasing the counselee's content, carefully choose the beginning words for your paraphrase. Paraphrase statements typically begin with words such as these:

- "So you think . . ."
- "What I hear you saying is . . ."
- "You envision . . ."
- "It sounds like . . ."

After you have the heart of the counselee's message, **Assess** ("A") whether a paraphrase is the appropriate response. Determine if a verbal response is necessary to the story or whether simply tracking what the counselee is saying would be wise. It is easy for counselors, especially novice counselees, to become too verbally active early in the counseling process. Interventions need to be well timed and appropriate to the context and the situation. No intervention should derail a counselee from his story or take the focus off the counselee. Typically intuition, discernment, and experience help you know whether to use a paraphrase.

With the wording firmly in your mind, use the "S" in PHRASE to remember that paraphrases involve making the actual **Statement** to the counselee. Verbalize the paraphrase to the counselee so that it is delivered as a statement, not a question. Raising your voice at the end of a sentence implies a question rather than a statement. Paraphrases are always used as a statement. In addition be brief in your paraphrase. The more words you use the less meaning they have for the counselee.

The final step in the process is to **Evaluate** ("E") the effectiveness of the message. If your paraphrase fits, the counselee will verbally or nonverbally confirm its accuracy and helpfulness. If the paraphrase seems off base to the counselee, the counselee will verbally or nonverbally inform you that you missed the mark.

In summary, remember that a paraphrase is not parroting what the counselee said. It is incorporating the counselee's key ideas in your own words.

## The Skill of Clarification

Crabb and Allender (1997) point out that one of the greatest obstacles to effective listening occurs when you believe you know what another person is trying to say. "Language is like a multifaceted jewel: just as the colors change when the gem is turned in light, so new shades of meaning become apparent every time we consider someone's words from another angle" (p. 126). The skill of clarification helps the counselor look at different facets of the jewel.

The skill of clarification also demonstrates that the helper is listening but still needs to understand better what the counselee is saying. Clarifying responses can (a) check the accuracy of what you heard the counselee say, (b) clear up vague and confusing messages, and (c) encourage more counselee elaboration.

As a rule, counselors ask for clarification in the form of either an openended or closed-ended question. Some examples of clarification responses include are these:

- "What exactly does your father have to do with this situation?" (open-ended)
- "Do you mean he never supports you?" (closed-ended)
- "Are you saying that she wanted to move out but you convinced her not to?" (closed-ended)

To employ the use of clarification make use of four steps that form an acrostic **CARE** (Table 6.6). The first step is identifying the **Content** ("C") of the counselee's message and determining what is vague, confusing, or missing from the counselee's message. When the counselor hears what seems like distortions, deletions, and generalizations (Bandler & Grinder, 1975) in the counselee's story a clarification question might be asked to make better sense of what is being said.

Second, determine an **Appropriate** ("A") response to clarify the message. In doing so, consider how to request the needed information. Brammer (1973) suggests that counselors be honest about their confusion when giving their response. For example you might say, "I'm sorry I could not make out what you were saying. I thought I heard you say that you wanted to break off the relationship."

Third, after the **Response** ("R") is formed, the counselor intervenes in the counselee's disclosure. Also use your voice to deliver the clarification as a question rather than a statement.

Fourth, the counselor **Evaluates** ("E") the effectiveness of the clarification response. To do this, carefully listen and observe how the counselee responds to the clarification question. If the clarification response is effective, the counselee will elaborate on the message to give missing information or to explain the ambiguous part of the message (Cormier & Cormier, 1985). If the response is not effective, the counselee will ignore the counselor's question or simply not respond. At times the counselee will continue to give messages that omit certain facts.

In summary, using clarification helps avoid drawing assumptions and false conclusions. Clarification provides necessary information to make sense of what the counselee is saying and to verify what is being heard without jumping too quickly to conclusions. Clarification typically employs the use of an inquiry to better understand the counselee before moving forward in the process.

Table 6.6

*CARE: How to Use Clarification*

**C** = What is the **Content** of the message

**A** = What is the **Appropriate** response

**R** = **Respond** with the clarification inquiry

**E** = **Evaluate** the accuracy of your clarification inquiry

## The Skill of Summary

The use of summary is similar to paraphrasing, but it involves pulling together more pieces of information. A summary distills everything the counselee has said in the session up to that point; it is a recap of the counselee's story. Young (2010) states that a summary can include any— and we would add all—of the following: (a) content; (b) major feelings; (c) issues, meaning, and themes; and (d) future plans.

### The purposes of summary.

Summaries can provide a message to the counselee and can help move the counseling process along. Summaries serve several purposes. First, like paraphrases, summaries tell the counselee you have been paying attention and following what is being said. Using a summary also identifies a common theme or pattern. Cormier and Cormier (1985) point out that counselees express many messages throughout the counseling session that have consistencies or patterns, referred to as themes. You can respond to apparent themes by using a summary. A summary can also be used to interrupt excessive rambling and bring the counselee back from tangents (Cormier & Cormier, 1985).

Summaries can also facilitate the counseling process. First, summaries tie together multiple elements of a counselee's message by bringing focus to what has transpired. Second, a well-timed summary can challenge a counselee to explore an issue more thoroughly. Third, as Egan (2007) suggests, summaries can be used when the counseling session has stalled and when the counselee is stuck. Fourth, summaries can provide "psychological breathing space" for sessions that are moving too quickly (Cormier & Cormier, 1985). Fifth, a summary can review the counselee's progress as a means of highlighting what the counselee has accomplished and what the counselee still has left to face (Cormier & Cormier, 1985). Sixth, like bookends, summaries can bridge the current session to the previous appointment. For example,

> "Last session we discussed the struggles you were having with your supervisor and the fear you have over the possibility of losing your job. You also shared with me your concern that your wife had distanced herself and turned your children against you. We ended our session by agreeing that you would journal your thoughts and feelings in prayer letters to God."

Summaries are helpful in concluding a session. A summary that signals to the counselee that the time of the appointment is nearing an end can serve as a statement about the time winding down and as a recap of the session. Consider the following example:

> "Before we close our time together, I want to see if I'm able to capture the key points of our conversation. Because your company is considering a merger, you believe there is a likelihood of your losing your job. If that were to occur, you and your wife have not put away enough money to make ends meet. A more significant issue, however, seems to be that you do not believe you could handle being told that you no longer had a job; it would be a huge blow to you. On top of that, you are also concerned about the chances of getting another equally paying job. How does that fit?"

Intuitively a summary at the end of an appointment makes sense. Just as a research paper has a conclusion, using a summary statement at the end of the counseling time can help the counselee transition back to his life. Also summaries provide a means of transitioning from one topic to another or capturing a lot of information that has been explored. An example of this use of a summary follows:

> "Before we move on, I want to make sure I understood you correctly. Your boss told you that the company might merge with a larger organization. That has created a lot of uncertainty around the office. You also fear that you could be on the 'hit list' if people were to lose their jobs."

Whether used throughout the helping process, the beginning, or the end of a session, summaries provide a highly valuable role, but there is not a one-size-fits-all summary. The counseling situation at hand will require the counselor to fashion a summary appropriate to the context and for a unique purpose. The following section examines the kinds of summaries counselors can use.

### Kinds of Summaries.

Young (2010) identifies four kinds of summaries: (a) focusing, (b) signaling, (c) thematic, and (d) planning. A focusing summary is one that directs the counselee's focus onto the major themes and issues. It can be used to capture information from previous sessions or capture what has occurred in an opening session. According to Young (2005), a focusing summary "places the spotlight on the counselee's responsibility for the problem, and reminds the counselee of the goals" (p. 161). Young shares an example of a focusing summary from a first session that was intended to get the counselee on track at the very beginning:

Table 6.7

*Kinds of Summaries*

| |
| --- |
| **Focusing** – directs counselee to major themes and issues |
| **Signal** – informs counselee that the counselor is on the same page |
| **Thematic** – provides an interpretation of a pattern of content, emotions, and meanings |
| **Planning** – reviews the counselee's progress, plans, and commitments |

> "Let's review what I know so far. Your mother called and made this appointment for you because you were arrested about a month ago for public intoxication. One of the conditions of your probation is that you receive help for your drinking problem. Your probation officer referred you to our agency. So you're here to do something about the problems you've been having with alcohol. Is this correct?" (pp. 161–62).

A second kind of summary, a signaling summary is employed in the middle of a session to inform the counselee that the counselor understands what the counselee has shared thus far. A signaling summary can tacitly tell a counselee that it is OK to move onto another topic because the counselor has a firm grasp of the current topic.

A thematic summary is an advanced reflecting technique that demonstrates that the counselor is able to make connections and bring together the content, emotions, and meanings (Young, 2010). In a way this kind of summary provides feedback to the counselee and might be viewed as an interpretation of the counselee's situation. A theme can be defined as a pattern of content, emotions, or meanings that finds repetition in the counselee's life and expression in the counselee's story. Young offers the following examples of thematic summaries.

> "Two issues seem to keep coming up. One of them is the anger you feel in a number of different close relationships (emotional or feelings theme), and the other is your sense that you haven't been able to reach your potential in your career (content theme)" (p. 162).
>
> "As you have been talking, I seemed to notice a pattern, and I'd like to check it out. You seem to want to end relationships when they begin to lose their initial excitement and romance (content theme)" (p. 163).
>
> "From everything we've talked about over these past few weeks, one major issue seems to be that, over and over again, you hesitate to make a commitment to a career or to a relationship or to take any important action because you are afraid you might let your parents down by failing (meaning theme). Is that right?" (p. 163).

The last kind of summary described by Young (2005) is planning summaries. The counselor uses a planning summary to review the counselee's progress, plans, and commitments made during the session. Young states that the planning summary serves as a bridge to closing the session. He offers the following examples.

> "Well, it seems like we've identified several things in the first session that we want to pursue. First, you are unhappy with the way you tend to become overly dependent on your friends. You want to follow your own interests. In fact, you want to get to know yourself better. With this in mind, we thought about your entering a counseling group. . . . Besides that, you'd like to identify some goals for your career. That is something you and I can begin to work on right away. We'll set up an assessment program and talk more about this in the next several weeks. How does all this sound?" (p. 163).
>
> "Let's recap what we have talked about so far. On the one hand, you have accomplished your financial goals, but you are far from satisfied with your relationships with friends and family. You have said that this

> is because you are not very assertive. It sounds as if this is the area
> we need to discuss in our next session. What do you think?" (p. 163).

The main point of using a planning summary is to remind counselees of things that have transpired during a session and to reinforce the things that they have agreed to earlier. In this way a planning summary creates a verbal contract with the counselee as to the agreed-on "go-dos."

### Guidelines for using summaries.

Creating summaries is similar to using paraphrases. Using the paraphrase acrostic **PHRASE**, we offer six guidelines for creating different kinds of summaries. First, **Perceive** ("P") and recall the counselee's message or series of messages. It is one thing to capture the counselee's message in a paraphrase since the amount of information is much more limited. It is quite another endeavor for the counselor to pull together the large pieces, themes, and patterns into a coherent whole. Thus work hard to maintain the focus throughout the session in order to know what to say when.

Table 6.8

*PHRASE: Guidelines for Using Summaries*

**P = Perceive** and recall the various messages

**H =** What is the **Heart** of the messages

**R = Recap** the counselee's messages in your own words

**A = Assess** the timing and type of summary

**S =** Share your own **Statement** with the counselee

**E = Evaluate** the accuracy of your summary

Second, seek to get at the **Heart** ("H") of all the pieces of the counselee's message. Cormier and Cormier (1985) recommend that the counselor identify any apparent patterns, themes, or multiple elements of these messages by asking questions like "What has the counselee repeated over and over?" or "What are the different parts of this puzzle?" The counselor is listening for messages that the counselee has repeated through the counseling session or sessions.

Once you have made the decision to summarize and you have chosen the kind of summary appropriate to the context, **Recap** ("R") the messages. Cormier and Cormier (1985) recommend using the personal pronoun "you" or the counselee's name in forming the summary. For example "You seem to be feeling . . . ," "I sense that you . . . ," "In listening to you share about your mother, it sounds as if . . . ," or "Bob, you have been repeatedly sharing with me about the sadness you feel over . . ." Then choose the words that describe the theme or tie together multiple elements.

Once the heart of the conversation has been pinpointed, **Assess** ("A") whether it is the appropriate time for a summary and if so, what summary would be most beneficial. If you believe that a summary will be beneficial, then determine the kind of summary that will accomplish the greatest gains. In other words seek to focus the counselee, signal the counselee, address a theme or pattern in the counselee's messages, or use a planning summary to review progress and agreements.

The fifth step in the process requires that the counselor share the summary **Statement** ("S") with the counselee. Then when it has been said, **Evaluate** ("E") its accuracy and effectiveness by observing and listening. Like any tool in the hand of the counselor, summaries can be overused or ill-timed. Ultimately learning from successes and poor outcomes will help the counselor master the skill of summary.

## CHAPTER SUMMARY

Skilled helpers know how to explore their counselees' concerns in such a way that they begin to grasp the situation fully and in a way that provides new insights for each counselee. Perhaps no skill is more associated with counselors than the skill of questioning. Helpers know how to ask questions and ask the right kinds of questions to unearth the necessary information. Counselors also know how to paraphrase counselee statements and ask for clarification when needed. A skill often neglected by counselors is the ability to summarize what the counselee has said. Wise counselors know what bits of information to pull together to capture the themes and issues of what was discussed.

The next chap. will delve into the third skill set, Facilitation Skills. These skills help counselors further the counseling process. As the Counselor Skill table shows (Tables 5.1 and 6.1), each skill set has primary and secondary functions in the counseling process. It is important for the counselor to learn the timing of these skills. Most of that skill development will occur during your practicum and internship, but for now think about how you respond to counselee statements.

## CHAPTER 6 ACTIVITIES

1. Describe the nature, power, and types of questions employed in the counseling process.

2. What is the difference between open ended and closed ended questions?
3. What is the difference between direct and indirect questioning?
4. Create a simulated dialog between a counselor and counselee that uses one of each of the questions in numbers 2 and 3 above.
5. What are the questions you should avoid using in counseling and why?
6. What is provocative questioning and provide an example of each type given in the chapter.
7. Use the acrostic PROBE COUNSELEE to describe the guidelines for using questions effectively in counseling.
8. What are the guidelines for effectively using the skills of paraphrase, clarification, and summary in counseling? Provide a simulated example of the use of each of these skills in the context of one therapeutic encounter.
9. How might you draw upon your relationship with Christ while utilizing the skill of questioning with counselees?

## Vignette Questions

### Vignette 3
### Questions

1. In the third vignette, what type(s) of questions did the counselor ask? Explain your response in light of the material you are currently learning.
2. Describe the relationship that the counselor established with the counselee. Did it help the counselee explain the reason that she came to therapy?
3. How do you think that the counselor's use of questions impacted the counselee?
4. Discuss the counselor's use of questions. Were any fundamental counseling guidelines violated during his interaction with counselee?
5. What could the counselor have done to elicit information that would benefit the counselee and at the same time establish rapport with her? Explain your reasoning.

### Vignette 4
### Questions, Paraphrasing & Summaries

1. In the fourth vignette you saw a number of exploration skills demonstrated. How can information be obtained from a counselee without the use of questions?

2. How did the counselor use information gathered from dialoguing with the counselee to shape her questions, paraphrasing and summaries?
3. What is the difference between paraphrasing and summarizing?
4. Is the use of questions an advantage or disadvantage in the counseling session? Explain your answer.
5. How do you think the counselee felt during the session? What was it about the session that made it possible for her to feel this way?

## Recommended Reading

Rosengren, D. B. (2009). *Building motivational interviewing skills: A practitioner workbook*. New York City, NY: Guilford Press.

> This is an excellent resource on how to incorporate motivational interviewing into your counseling repertoire. The author provides user-friendly and concise explanations to the core competencies of motivational interviewing along with practical exercises to help readers learn the skills.

# Basic Skills: Giving Feedback

*"We must lead with our ears into the particular story of someone's life. Curiosity begins the process. But not empathic curiosity. Our purpose is not merely to hear what another is feeling. We want to discern what the forces of darkness have been deceitfully saying . . ."* (Crabb, 2003, p. 139).

*"He who answers before listening—that is his folly and his shame"* (Prov 18:13, NIV).

## CHAPTER OBJECTIVES

» To acquaint you with the basic skills of facilitation

» To help you understand the purposes, limitations, and pitfalls of giving feedback

» To help you learn how to provide effective feedback to counselees

» To learn the benefits, limitations, and pitfalls of interpretation

» To help you learn how to provide effective interpretation to counselees

» To learn how to confront counselees effectively

» To learn how to effectively and appropriately self-disclose personal information to counselees

» To learn how to talk with a counselee about what is happening in the counseling relationship

» To learn how to manage and use silence in a therapeutic manner

» To provide guidelines to help you manage the session and pace the counseling

## CHAPTER OUTLINE

THE SKILL OF FEEDBACK
General Purposes of Feedback
Limitations and Pitfalls of Feedback
Guidelines for Giving Feedback

THE SKILL OF INTERPRETATION
Benefits of Interpretation
Limitations and Pitfalls of Interpretation
Guidelines for Giving Interpretation

THE SKILL OF CONFRONTATION
The Need and Value of Confrontation
Limitations and Pitfalls of Confrontation
Guidelines for Using Confrontation

THE SKILL OF SELF-DISCLOSURE
Benefits and Hazards of Self-Disclosure
Kinds of Self-Disclosure
Guidelines for Using Self-Disclosure

THE SKILL OF IMMEDIACY
Kinds of Immediacy
Risks Associated with Immediacy
When to Use Immediacy
Guidelines for Using Immediacy

THE SKILL OF SILENCE
The Role of Silence in Helping
Kinds and Purposes of Silence
Benefits and Risks of Silence
Guidelines for Using Silence

THE SKILL OF PACING

CASE TO ILLUSTRATE THE SKILLS OF HELPING

CHAPTER SUMMARY

CHAPTER 7 ACTIVITIES

The previous two chaps. discussed two sets of skills needed for effective counseling. The chaps. considered how to establish a helping relationship and how to understand the counselee. These skills are absolutely essential in any counseling context. In addition counselors need skills that will help them move the counseling into deeper areas of the counselee's life. Skills in giving feedback can help move the counseling forward. They can promote connection and give further information about the counselee or the problem, but they are primarily targeted at engaging further depth.

This chap. recounts the knowledge needed to master seven critical helping skills that can move a session along. These skills of facilitation include giving feedback, interpretation, confrontation, self-disclosure, immediacy, silence, and pacing. See Tables 5.1 and 6.1 in chaps. 5 and 6.

## THE SKILL OF FEEDBACK

Feedback is a term borrowed from electrical engineering by Kurt Lewin (Yalom, 1980). Just as output can give "feedback" to a system, so a person's communication can be "feedback" by another party as information. In the helping context, feedback is the verbal and nonverbal responses you make to the counselee as you process the information you have received from listening and observing. This skill allows the helper to address the counselee's actions, beliefs, feelings, values, and attitudes. According to Turock (1980) human communication involves an attempt to influence others for several purposes: (a) to create certain feelings, (b) to generate certain beliefs, (c) to produce certain intentions, and (d) to elicit certain behaviors. Receiving feedback is an inevitable part of life, and the counseling office is no exception.

No one goes through life without receiving feedback, both wanted and unwanted. Parents, teachers, friends, and other authority figures are all sources of feedback. Some feedback we receive is encouraging and positive. So we welcome this kind of feedback. But if all feedback we received was positive, we would not get information needed to promote our growth. Growth-producing feedback offers us opportunities to address weaknesses and liabilities. Of course not all feedback is the same. Some of the feedback we receive is given out of a commitment to our well-being. Other times, however, we receive feedback that was intended to wound us, not to benefit us. Regardless of the giver's intent, how we receive feedback is more important than its intended purpose. Even well-meaning and sound feedback can be conceived as negative.

Obviously giving feedback is much easier than hearing it, especially when it is targeted to our vulnerable sides. Because one of the goals of a counselor is to help the counselee grow, it is necessary to know the purposes of feedback and to be skilled at giving it.

### General Purposes of Feedback

Words are powerful. They can heal and they can harm. Proverbs states that "death and life are in the power of the tongue" (18:21, NASB), "a soothing tongue is a tree of life" (15:4, NASB), and "pleasant words are . . . sweet to the soul and healing to the bones" (16:24, NASB). We are to harness the power of words for a specific purpose. No technique is more bound to our words than feedback.

Broadly speaking there are two kinds of feedback: reassuring and reformative. Reassuring feedback reinforces characteristics, qualities, and attributes of the counselee that the counselor wants to solidify and stabilize. "What impresses me the most about you is your willingness to take risks in reaching out to others" is an example of reassuring feedback.

Reformative feedback is typically received less favorably by most counselees. When you employ reformative feedback, the goal is to redirect the counselee back to a physical, psychological, or spiritual healthy standard. The Christian counselor's communication, whether in the form of feedback or otherwise, is to be targeted toward healing. According to Proverbs "The tongue of the wise brings healing" (Prov 12:18, NASB). "When you were meeting with your accountability partners regularly, you seemed to have had more success in refraining from looking at pornography." By connecting the counselee's success with avoiding pornography with working with his accountability group, the counselor's feedback is encouraging the counselee to continue with his accountability partners.

### Limitations and Pitfalls of Feedback

Hearing personal feedback is never easy. Feedback can backfire if the counselee is not ready to hear it. Thus counselors need to be aware of the fact that feedback can jeopardize the counseling relationship and confuse a counselee.

With some counselees the counseling relationship is always fragile. Their personal makeup predisposes them to be hypersensitive to any "negative feedback." No matter how sensitive and careful a counselor may be, the counselee might feel wounded by feedback. Counselees might terminate counseling, reject the counselor, or become resistant to hearing anything else from the counselor.

In other cases the counselor may use poorly chosen words in the feedback, has countertransference that prompts feedback that is more about the counselor than the counselee, or simply gives ill-timed or misplaced feedback. Even with fairly stable counselees, the counselor can damage the helping relationship beyond repair or to the point that the counselor will need to work hard to repair it.

Feedback can also confuse a counselee if the preparation work has not taken place. Thus the counselor might earn the right to give feedback. As the relationship between the counselee and you further develops, the counselee is in essence depositing tokens in the helping relationship "bank." Sufficient deposits protect the counselor from going into the red with a significant withdrawal from painful feedback. The counselor who has adequate deposits is more likely to be viewed as committed to the counselee's well-being.

## Guidelines for Giving Feedback

Patterson and Eisenberg (1983) suggest thinking about a recent time when you received feedback. How was the feedback given to you? How did you perceive the giver's attitude and agenda in giving it? Was it welcomed or unwelcomed? What was your internal experience in hearing the feedback? Patterson and Eisenberg also suggest processing feedback that you have received that was encouraging.

To help you give feedback that will benefit your counselees we offer the following mnemonic device: **FEEDBACK** (see Table 7.1). The "F" stands for the fact that hearing feedback is **Fear-inducing**. In short, no one likes getting feedback. Whether the feedback we receive is welcomed or not, receiving it usually produces some level of resistance. Our natural inclination is to defend ourselves, particularly against any negatively perceived feedback. It is important for you to be sensitive to this fact when offering feedback. Moreover, remember that feedback's purpose is to be helpful to your counselees by giving them useful information.

The second guideline, "E," means to **Earn** the right to give feedback. In the next chap. we will discuss the building of a trusting and helping relationship with counselees. Once you have established rapport and the counselee believes that you understand his situation, only then are you in a position to begin giving feedback. The counselee needs to perceive you as credible in order to go through the experience of hearing and assimilating feedback.

The next "E" is to **Encourage** the counselee to comment on and expand on the feedback. The counselee might either agree or disagree. Allow him to wrestle with it in front of you and to explore it by discussing and relating it to daily life (Egan, 2007). Remember that your feedback is your own perception and not necessarily the ultimate truth. The feedback says as much about you as it does about the counselee.

| Table 7.1 |
| --- |
| *FEEDBACK: Guidelines for Using Feedback* |
| **F** = hearing **Feedback** is **Fear-inducing** |
| **E** = **Earn** the right to give feedback |
| **E** = **Encourage** the counselee to comment on and expand on the feedback |
| **D** = use **Direct** feedback |
| **B** = be prepared for the counselee to **Block** the feedback |
| **A** = **Allow** time for the counselee to reflect but be determined |
| **C** = give feedback **Cautiously**, **Carefully**, and **Calmly** |
| **K** = focus on only one **Key** issue |

Use **Direct** ("D") rather than guarded or obscure feedback. Direct feedback has several characteristics. First, it means that the message is clear. Before sharing feedback with a counselee, be very clear on the exact message you are trying to give and be secure in delivering the message. Ambiguous and faltering feedback will be met with confusion and resistance. Feedback that is given by an insecure counselor will raise suspicion and might prompt a more competitive and aggressive response from a counselee. Be clear about what the feedback is that you want to give. Second, direct feedback is focused and brief and to the point. Avoid lengthy explanations in your feedback. Third, direct feedback does not mean being harsh. Do not confuse directness with being judgmental. God calls us to be "speaking the truth in love" (Eph 4:15). Fourth, effective feedback is delivered descriptively. For example saying to the counselee, "You are irresponsible," labels behavior but provides no specific focus. Instead it is better to tell the counselee, "I understand that you are busy, but when you fail to call and cancel an appointment at least 24 hours in advance, something you agreed to when you signed the Consent to Treatment form, I feel disrespected." Jacobs (1992) recommends that feedback be directive in the following ways:

- "I understand what you are getting at. Now what do you want to do about it?"

- "I understand that he is horrible, but it really doesn't help me to hear more stories about him. I think we need to look at how all of this is affecting you today."

When you want to give feedback, be prepared for the counselee to **Block** ("B") it. It is best to approach the giving of feedback with the idea that it will likely fall on hard ground. No matter how fertile the counselee's heart, hearing feedback is difficult. In particular, we are all especially prone to resist any feedback that does not fit with our own self-perceptions. If a counselee sees herself as self-sacrificing, it will be difficult for her to hear that she is actually self-centered. The counselor is not to argue with the counselee or force-feed feedback. Most of the time it is better to present feedback in a tentative and humble manner. For example, "I am not sure if this is the case, and I am interested in what you think, but did you notice that you focus back on what your wife is doing each time I ask about you what you are doing. Do you see that too? What do you think might be going on here between us?"

**Allow** ("A") time for the counselee to reflect on the feedback, but be determined. As seen in the previous principles, much of feedback is resisted particularly at the time it is received. Some feedback might be incorporated at a later time if it is not too far out of our own self-perceptions. Feedback that is inconsistent with our self-image might eventually be received, but the counselee needs a lot of time to assimilate it. Jacobs (1992) uses a boxing analogy to address the need for the counselor to have determination in helping a counselee. He states that some counselors only know how to jab and when the counselee does not change, the counselor jabs more. Eventually the counselor realizes that other punches are needed. So he throws combination punches, knockout punches, and other punches. He then notes that when the counselor gets the counselee "on the ropes" and the counselee says "ouch," some counselors back off as if to say, "Sorry, I didn't mean to hurt you." Jacobs argues that counselors need the determination to stay with the counselee and keep the punches coming as necessary because people do not change easily.

The "C" in the acrostic refers to giving the feedback **Cautiously**, **Carefully**, and **Calmly**. Offer feedback cautiously and carefully, making sure the time is right. The best feedback in the world will have little impact if the counselee is not ready to hear it. So be judicious and wait until the counselee is ready and open to new ideas in order to increase the likelihood that the feedback will be effective. Proverbs 25:11 says, "Like apples of gold in settings of silver is a word spoken in right circumstances" (NASB). Timeliness and attention to the degree of feedback that the counselee can handle is a treasure. But too much at the wrong time will be lost before it can benefit the counselee. The other part of the "C" is to remind you to be calm in giving feedback. The higher the level of your emotional arousal (e.g., anxious, angry) the more likely the feedback will be met with resistance. Your presence and words are to be experienced by the counselee as safe and soothing so that feedback is easier to assimilate. Thus do not overwhelm the counselee before he or she is ready.

The final guideline in giving feedback to a counselee is to focus on only one **Key** ("K") issue. Most counselees can handle only one issue at a time. The counselee needs to be able to experience the full impact of the focused and specific feedback without getting lost in a maze of ideas. Giving feedback on too many issues will overwhelm the counselee and will result in his being demoralized. Give appropriate feedback in a timely way.

In summary, receiving feedback from a trusted individual is a gift. Proverbs 27:6 says that the wounds of a friend are intended to help. Feedback is a critical skill for Christian counselors. Effective helpers know how to use feedback in a skillful way in order to make it as beneficial for the counselee as possible.

## THE SKILL OF INTERPRETATION

Baruth and Huber (1985) define interpretation as explaining "connections among seemingly isolated information (in the counselee's view) from the counselee. In doing so, the counselee is offered a different perspective on his or her concerns" (p. 160). In the simplest sense interpretations refer to alternative explanations or insights into one's situation or behavior. The counselor attempts to give meaning, significance, or a rationale for an experience in the counselee's life. When a counselor posits an interpretation, he or she is basically saying "This is how I see your situation" (Sommers-Flanagan & Sommers-Flanagan, 2003, p. 74). When using the skill of interpretation, the intent of the counselor is to explain rather than merely describe a counselee's behavior and to change a counselee's frame of reference in a therapeutic direction. Patterson and Eisenberg (1983) state that helpers know they are interpreting when the word *because* is used. The skill of interpretation lies on the directive side of the continuum and is generated from the counselor's own frame of reference (Ivey & Ivey, 2003).

Christian counselors seek to understand the motivations of their counselee's actions. To do so requires that you draw on your observations, experience, understanding of biblical principles, and view of human-behavior dynamics to make sense of the counselee's situation. Thus interpretations arise out of the counselor's conceptions of the counselee and his situations.

In light of the relationship between interpretation and the counselor's understanding of human behavior, no helping skill is more dependent on your theoretical orientation and philosophical/theological underpinnings. Whether you endorse a nouthetic, Adlerian, cognitive-behavioral, or some other approach determines how you conceptualize the counselee's problems and how you strategize to intervene. Thus learning as many theories as you can and developing your own clear understanding of human functioning is critical to effective helping.

Counselor interpretations have been a controversial topic for nearly a century. Proponents of traditional counseling approaches such as psychodynamic, Adlerian, Jungian, and cognitive-behavioral counseling value the use of interpretation. In contrast those who adhere to an experiential approach such as person-centered and Gestalt devalue the role of interpretation, believing that it may block awareness and growth.

Moreover, though we do not believe that God's Word proposes a specific model for counseling, it does include a wealth of information about how people function. We address these issues in greater detail in chap. 11 ("Case Conceptualization and Treatment Planning"). It is critical that the practical aspects of counseling are consistent with the counselor's philosophical and theological beliefs.

## Benefits of Interpretation

The benefits to the counselee from the effective use of interpretation can range from greater self-understanding to release of emotions. Even though counseling theories value the benefits of personal insight differently, there is no harm in being able to truly see oneself. Interpretation allows counselees to see themselves through another person's eyes, especially a person who is trained in understanding human behavior. Jesus often interpreted the behavior of people. For example He often exposed the values and beliefs of the scribes and Pharisees (Matt 9:1–7; 12:22–30; John 8:3–11) and of common individuals with whom He came in contact (John 4:17–18).

Interpretations help counselors gain a fuller understanding of their counselees. Counselees might respond with tears, "ah-ha," silence, or denials. Regardless of the counselee's response, the heart is exposed so that the counselor can better understand the internal workings of the counselee.

Another benefit of interpretation is that it can contribute to the development of a positive helping relationship. It can reinforce counselee self-disclosure, enhance the credibility of the counselor, and communicate the helper's attitudes toward the counselee (Claiborn, 1982).

## Limitation and Pitfalls of Interpretation

Perhaps the greatest danger of employing interpretation is scarring the helping relationship. If your interpretation is inaccurate, imprecise, or abusive, irreparable damage can be done to the relationship with the counselee. Some counselees will perceive the counselor as insensitive or incompetent even if the counselor delivered the interpretation appropriately, timely, and accurately.

One significant limitation of interpretations is that they are intimately tied to theory. How you view human behavior will determine your understanding of the counselee and the nature of the subsequent feedback to the counselee. Theories both help explain behavior and limit explanations of behavior.

## Guidelines for Giving Interpretation

Many of the guidelines associated with giving feedback are also relevant for interpretation. The following nine guidelines, formed in an acrostic **INTERPRET** can be helpful in offering an interpretation.

---

Table 7.2

*INTERPRET: Guidelines for Giving Interpretation*

**I = Incorporate** the use of interpretation cautiously

**N =** what does the counselee really **Need**

**T =** link interpretation to your **Theory**

**E = Earn** the right to give an interpretation

**R =** have a **Rationale** for the interpretation

**P =** have a **Positive** goal in mind

**R =** use **Relative** language

**E =** Give your **Explanation**

**T = Test** the accuracy of your interpretation

---

First, be sure to **Incorporate** ("I") the use of interpretation cautiously. Many counselors get enthusiastic about interpretations. It is as if a puzzle has been solved, and the adrenalin that can generate can cloud a counselor's judgment in whether to share it.

Second, the letter "N" can remind you to focus on what the counselee really **Needs**. Offering an interpretation can be easier than continuing to explore the counselee's feelings. Make sure an interpretation is the best choice.

Third, anchor your interpretations in your **Theory** ("T"). Interpretations must fit with your concept of human behavior.

Fourth, you will need to **Earn** ("E") the right to give interpretations. Credibility and being respectful gives you the right to give interpretations. Like feedback, do not give interpretations until you have credibility with your counselee and your counselee believes that you understand.

Fifth, have a clear **Rationale** ("R") for the interpretation. It is not wise to offer an interpretation until you have adequately done your homework. Typically it takes many sessions to fully assess the counselee and have enough information on which to base an interpretation.

Sixth, have a **Positive** ("P") goal in mind when using interpretation. The purpose of an interpretation is to facilitate counselee awareness and insight, and to lead to growth and change. Interpretations are not meant to be punitive. If possible, incorporate humor with your interpretation.

Seventh, use **Relative** ("R") language. When giving an interpretation to a counselee be tentative and do so in approximate ways (Egan, 2007). Beginning the interpretation with such words as "Could it be that . . . ," "I'm wondering if . . . ," "Is it possible that . . ." helps to couch the interpretation as a matter of the counselor's perspective, not as fact. A counselor might pose an interpretation as follows: "I'm wondering if the reason you storm out of the room when you and your wife are arguing is because of your fear of hitting her again."

The eighth guideline to adhere to in offering interpretations is to use the "E" to remember that while you need a sound rationale for the interpretation, it is only your **Explanation**. It is one perspective on the counselee's behavior. Since interpretations arise out of your theory, they are limited by the parameters of the theory's explanation of human behavior and your professional judgment.

Ninth, the "T" is to **Test** the impact of the interpretation. All feedback is best assessed for its impact on the counselee and its accuracy. Depending on the depth of the interpretation, it might take time for the counselee to process and assimilate it. Be willing to provide follow-up discussion and clarification to help the counselee assimilate its meaning. If the counselee rejects the interpretation, do not argue or press the issue.

## THE SKILL OF CONFRONTATION

In counseling the idea of confrontation involves raising counselee awareness of information being overlooked or distorted. The word *confrontation* itself has an unfavorable reputation with most people and even a dubious reputation in the counseling field. The word is regarded in the literature both positively and negatively. Positively it is viewed as an effective means of noting counselee incongruencies, drawing attention to alternative ways counselees might perceive themselves, or influencing counselees toward new behavior (Strong & Zeman, 2010). Some professionals do not like confrontation because they believe it (a) implies imposing one's mindset on another, often aggressively, (b) harms counselees and (c) is judgmental (Miller & Rollnick, 2002). True, it has the potential of generating counselee resistance and defensiveness. In short, confrontation can destroy a counselee-counselor relationship. Research lends support to this view because findings show that consistently using confrontation diminishes outcomes (Miller, Benefield, & Tonigan, 1993).

Though confrontation might not be held in the highest regard among many in the helping profession, proponents of nouthetic counseling argue that the use of confrontation in helping people is biblical (Adams, 1970; Adams, 1979). In fact they refer to their approach as "biblical counseling" because they believe that the Word of God is totally sufficient for all counseling needs (Adams, 1970). They point out that nouthetic counseling is derived from the biblical Greek word, *noutheteo*, translated "admonish," "correct," "rebuke," "warn," or "instruct." They base the approach on Acts 20:31; Rom 15:14; Col 1:28; and 2 Tim 3:16–17. Dr. Jay Adams, founder of nouthetic counseling, speaks to the value that confrontation plays in the helping process. He argues that Paul "nouthetically confronted" people on a day-by-day basis. He believes that confrontation is central to the work of the ministry because people have problems, face obstacles that must be overcome, and engage in things that are wrong (Adams, 1970).

Though nouthetic counselors do not advocate a harsh form of confrontation, their approach is highly directive. The nouthetic counselor embraces the role of "prophet" with counselees. In other words since forthtelling the truth of Scripture is essential to this approach, nouthetic counselors rely on confrontation.

While many professional counselors do not hold to the centrality of confrontation as do nouthetic counselors, many now believe that confrontation has a significant role in the helping process (Cormier & Cormier, 1985; Egan, 2007; McMinn & Campbell, 2007; Strong & Zeman, 2010; Young, 2010). Often in the helping profession theory and practice are not adequately related. What is believed to be appropriate or not in theory might not be what actually takes place in counseling sessions. For example counselors-in-training might assume that confrontation should be avoided. But research shows that highly educated professional counselors incorporate the use of confrontation more than counselors-in-training

(Tracey, Hays, Malone, & Herman, 1988). Experienced counselors intimately know the need to confront, realizing that at times counselees need to be challenged.

For many counselors, including Christian helpers, the connotations associated with confrontation need to change. Augsburger (1973) provides a different perspective on confrontation; he suggests combining the concepts of "caring" and "confronting" to create the term "care-fronting." The idea of care-fronting is to be sure the counselor is genuinely caring while at the same time he is willing to use "fronting" for the purpose of fostering counselee growth. Augsburger believes that a genuine relationship requires the ability of a person to confront with truth and affirm with love. He writes, "Truth with love brings healing. Truth told in love enables us to grow. Truth in love produces change. Truth and love are two necessary ingredients for any relationship with integrity" (p. 20).

Counselors should and can combine being compassionate with encouraging counselees to examine apparent contradictions and discrepancies. Regardless of what it is called, the idea of confrontation in the context of counseling is to focus the counselee's attention on behaviors, thoughts, attitudes, or values that require closer examination. The purpose of confrontation is to create forward movement (Shulman, 2009). Therapeutic movement is generated when a counselor uses confrontation to highlight discrepancies in the counselee's life and to challenge self-defeating patterns. Ivey, Ivey, and Zalaquett (2010) state that "although all counseling skills are concerned with facilitating change, it is the clarification and confrontation of discrepancies that acts as a lever for the activation of human potential" (p. 241). The purpose in confronting a counselee is to help him see himself more clearly and to consider making necessary changes. Egan (2007) defines confrontation as a means of helping counselees to "develop new perspectives and to change both internal and external behavior even when they show reluctance and resistance to doing so" (p. 186). Ivey and Ivey (2003) state that confrontation is "not a direct, harsh challenge." Then they add,

> Think of it, rather, as a more gentle skill that involves listening to the counselee carefully and respectfully and then seeking to help the counselee examine self or situation more fully. Confrontation is not "going against" the counselee; it is 'going with' the counselee; seeking clarification and the possibility of a new resolution of difficulties. Think of confrontation as a supportive challenge (p. 225).

Ivey and Ivey thus recognize the need to confront lovingly, to walk alongside the counselee rather than pulling him like a farmer dragging a reluctant donkey into a barn. In other words confrontation can be used to challenge counselees to look at themselves.

## The Need and Value of Confrontation

One of the reasons people come to counseling is that they are "stuck" (Perls, 1969). They are unable to move forward because they do not know in which direction to go, they have limited alternatives, or they are moving in different directions simultaneously.

Egan (2007) prefers to use the word "challenge" rather than confrontation in light of how confronting has been abused in the past. He sees the role of confrontation as challenging counselees to look at their inconsistencies. He also recommends that counselors confront unused strengths more than counselee weaknesses. In other words perceptive helpers challenge counselees to consider the assets and resources they have but fail to use.

Ivey and Ivey (2003) categorize confrontation among their "influencing skills" because it causes counselees to examine core issues. They believe that when confrontation is used skillfully and nonjudgmentally, counselees are challenged to talk in more detail and to resolve their problems and issues. Because of its provocative value, Ivey and Ivey view it as one of the most powerful counselor skills.

As noted by nouthetic counselors, there is clearly a biblical basis for confrontation. Consider the story of David who committed adultery and conspired to murder. The prophet Nathan confronted him with a story that exposed David's deeds to his own heart (2 Sam 12:1–15). Paul admonished believers to confront those who are unruly (1 Thess 5:14), and the writer of Hebrews challenged believers to provoke (lit., "stir up") other believers to good works (Heb 10:24). Jesus confronted Peter (cf. Matt 16:23), Judas (Matt 26:20–25), money changers (Mark 11:15–18; John 2:12–22), and the Pharisees (Matt 23). Biblically, confrontation was used with those who followed God or Christ and those who did not. It was used to challenge people to recognize their sin, to label their sin, and to challenge people to their best.

Patterson and Eisenberg (1983) capture a number of possible discrepancies that counselors might need to address through the use of confrontation. First, discrepancies can exist between the counselee's perceptions and accurate information. "We act on the basis of what we believe to be true, and when our beliefs are inaccurate we can act in ways that are self-defeating" (Patterson & Eisenberg, 1983, p. 76). For example Robert experiences a frustrating day at work and has been mulling over a work-related problem to which he sees no solution on his drive home. He walks through the door with a scowl on his face as he continues to contemplate the issue. His wife, Susan, having seen Jennifer's, their newborn daughter, first smile, is eager to share the news and greets him enthusiastically at the door. Robert barely acknowledges her warm greeting and recitation of the exciting event, choosing instead to head to his home office to resolve the problem that is on his mind. Susan is upset. She sees Robert's preoccupation as an uncaring attitude about Jennifer's development and insensitivity to her excitement. Robert interprets Susan's greeting as insensitive to the stress he feels; in his mind she should give him some time to unwind instead of "pouncing on him" as soon as he opens the door. The evening is spent in silence as both spouses bitterly recount in their minds the "selfishness" of the other.

A second discrepancy can occur between the counselee's perceptions and actions. The counselee might say that he sees a situation one way, and yet act in a way that is contradictory to that perception. The next day Robert and Susan finally discuss their feelings about the events of the previous evening, acknowledging how they felt and taking responsibility for their role in it. Robert promises to set aside work when he comes home, at least until Jennifer's bedtime; Susan promises to allow Robert a few minutes to "unwind' when he first gets home before she engages him in conversation. Throughout the ensuing week when Robert comes home, he immediately leaves to "go out with the boys" or retreats to his office to finish work that he brought home with him. When confronted by Susan about their agreement, he shrugs it off by saying that the stress is becoming too much and he has to get the work done and "blow off some steam" in order to stay healthy. Susan is furious; his needs are being met, but hers are not; it seems that he is "saying one thing and doing another."

Discrepancies can also emerge between a counselee's wants and actual results. "Self-defeating patterns are persistent actions that either fail to satisfy an important want or bring about unwanted consequences" (Patterson & Eisenberg, 1983, p. 77). Frustrated by Robert's inattention and selfishness, Susan begins to frequently "remind" Robert about his responsibilities to her and their daughter. He responds by spending more time out with his friends in order to avoid a confrontation with Susan. Irritated by Robert's response to her nagging, Susan begins to avoid Robert's sexual advances. The emotional distance between them continues to grow.

Fourth, discrepancies can exist between the counselee's verbal and body messages. Perls (1969) held that people cannot easily hide their internal truths from being expressed in body messages. I (John) was counseling with a young girl whom I was trying to get to open up. The mother looked at the daughter and said "Honey, you can tell him anything you want to," while shaking her head no. There was a clear mixed message being sent.

Discrepancies can also occur between the counselee's actions or ideas and the counselor's judgments. Counselors might challenge irrational thinking in order to provoke the counselee to think about things differently. Patterson and Eisenberg (1983) also state that discrepancies can occur in how counselees view themselves and how counselors view the counselees. A counselee might see himself as open, while the counselor views the counselee as closed. A counselee might not think she is living in self-pity, but the counselor may view the counselee as living as a perpetual victim.

Young (2010) presents three reactions of counselees to confrontation. First, a counselee may deny that a discrepancy exists. The motivations behind the denial might include the counselee wanting (a) to discredit the counselor, (b) to change the topic, (c) to find support elsewhere, or (d) to falsely accept the confrontation.

Second, a counselee may choose to accept part of the confrontation and reject the rest. Sometimes counselees can agree that part of a confrontation is correct, but they do not accept all aspects of the confrontation. Rather than arguing about the denied part, the counselor can work on the agreed-on part.

The third level of confrontation is one in which the counselee fully accepts the confrontation. The counselor can process the counselee's realization of the discrepancy with the goal of helping the counselee deal with it.

## Limitations and Pitfalls of Confrontation

Of all of the techniques in counseling, confrontation has the greatest potential for harm. It has been called the "thermonuclear weapon" of counseling (Young, 2010). No skill has been more abused or contains more landmines than confrontation.

The provocative nature of confrontation can provoke either counselee growth or counselee opposition. Just as dynamite can be used to clear roadblocks or to destroy buildings, so confrontation can challenge counselees to examine issues or blow up the counseling relationship. Experts in using dynamite know that it must be handled with care because of its potential for destruction. Likewise confrontation in counseling must be handled with respect because of its power to wound and to heal.

Confrontation will be abusive when it is delivered poorly. Abuse occurs when counselors are harsh or punitive or overuse confrontation. When counselees perceive that the counselor is hammering them and forcing them to admit something they have no desire to say or do, their defenses become engaged. Few helpers view their behavior as abusive, but it can occur more easily than they think. Consider the example:

> Abusive: "Charlie, you seem to say one thing and do another. How can you say you love God when you are being sexual with your girl-friend?"
>
> Non-abusive: "Charlie, earlier you shared about your desire to have a godly life, which truly blessed me. Yet you also talk about your sexual relationship with your girlfriend as important to you. I'm struggling to make sense of those two desires."

In the first example above the counselor targeted the value-behavior discrepancy but delivered it in a way that seemed to throw it in the counselee's face. In the second statement the counselor also targeted the value-behavior discrepancy, but did so in a softer way. The counselor made the two opposing desires something that he or she could not reconcile, thereby handing it back to the counselee to face.

When moving into confrontation territory, be aware of the many land-mines that exist. The most explosive landmines include being perceived as insensitive, judgmental, and even intolerant. Studies indicate that confrontation has been found to evoke counselee resistance (Miller & Rollnick, 2002; Patterson & Forgatch, 1985), is associated with poor outcomes (Miller, Benefield, & Tonigan, 1993), and requires more caution in working with people with various cultures (Eng & Kuiken, 2006; Ivey & Ivey, 2003).

## Guidelines for Using Confrontation

Confrontation is not giving a message to a counselee; it is also a process by which to help the counselee move forward. Ivey and Ivey (2003) state that "the skills of questioning, observation, reflective listening, and feedback loom large in effective confrontation" (p. 225). The skill of confrontation is never used in isolation from other counselor skills. The acrostic **CONFRONT** presents eight guidelines to remember when using confrontation (see Table 7.3).

Table 7.3

*CONFRONT: Guidelines for Using Confrontation*

**C** = **Cautious** in using it

**O** = **Obtain** the right to use confrontation

**N** = use a **Natural** delivery

**F** = have a **Foundation** to support the confrontation

**R** = **Remove** the stigma

**O** = examine the **Outcomes** of changing and not changing

**N** = **Name** the confrontation

**T** = **Test** the impact and accuracy of the confrontation

The "C" in the word CONFRONT refers to being **Cautious** in employing confrontation. Consider whether confrontation is the most appropriate response. Our experience suggests that novice counselors often confront too soon, too much, and too casually. If there are other ways to address the inconsistencies and discrepancies, they might be preferred. If you are feeling angry toward your counselee, it is important to stay in the role of facilitator. Confronting when you feel strong emotions toward the counselee will harm the counseling relationship and create resistance in the counselee. Also, consider the timing of any confrontation. In driving a car with a standard transmission, it is possible to shift too early or too late. Either way there is a problem. The road conditions and the vehicle interact to determine when it is best to shift. Further, when you come to road construction and a torn-up highway, you slow the car down and move forward with caution. When you get through the hazardous conditions, you can once again resume your speed. In counseling some counselees are so torn up that you must proceed with extreme care, whereas other counselees are immediately open and responsive. Paying attention to the counselee's conditions can help you know at what pace to proceed.

The "O" is to remind you to **Obtain** the right to use confrontation. As noted with earlier skills, one must earn the right to confront. Confrontation is most effective in the context of a strong helping relationship with the counselee. As McMinn (1996) notes in describing the therapeutic relationship, "It is easy to discount the words of strangers. But as a counseling relationship deepens and as trust is established, words of confrontation are taken more seriously" (p. 149). The goal is to help the counselee not feel ashamed about what you are confronting. Also it is always inappropriate to take your own frustrations and anger out on the counselee.

Use the "N" to remember to use a **Natural** delivery in confronting. When people think of confrontations, they imagine someone raising his voice and using more forceful gestures. But wise helpers confront by being as natural and normal as they are with other skills. Confrontations can vary in intensity from gentle to strong, from subtle to obvious. Yes many counselees think that their counselors' messages are delivered in a harsh and aggressive manner. Miller and Rollnick (2002) point out that there is no evidence that stronger confrontations benefit counselees, even substance-abusing counselees. It is thus wise to begin with more gentle confrontations. Confrontations should never be phrased as ultimatums. More subtle forms of confrontation should always be used.

Seek to offer a confrontation in a way that the counselee will most likely accept it (Young, 2010). Berenson and Mitchell (1974) analyzed research related to confrontation, and they found that (a) helpers who had a higher level of responsive skills confront in a different and more effective manner than those who possess low levels of responsive skills, (b) there are different kinds of confrontation that are effective when employed in a certain sequence, and (c) confrontation alone is inadequate. For example you can offer a more gentle form of confrontation that directs the counselee's attention to look at what they are truly experiencing. A counselor might say to a husband, "You seem irritated with your wife." Making the statement in a tentative manner ("You seem . . .") allows the counselee to view the feedback as an opinion. If the counselee is indeed furious with his wife, he can raise the level of emotion ("No, I'm not irritated; I'm furious!") that still validates the counselor's perception without risking a stronger emotion than a counselee is ready to hear.

The "F" refers to having a **Foundation** to support the confrontation. Be able to support your confrontation clearly. Before confronting be sure you can back up your observations with examples. For this reason, Ivey and Ivey (2003) advocate that counselors observe and listen to accurately perceive the counselee's mixed messages, discrepancies, and incongruity.

The fifth guideline is to **Remove** ("R") the stigma from the confrontation. Another way to offer a confrontation is through owning the experience yourself. In the case above a male counselor might tell a husband, "Perhaps you feel like I do when my wife does that—controlled." You can remove the stigma from the counselee's experience by admitting to having similar experiences.

The "O" stands for evaluating the **Outcomes** of changing and not chang-ing. Explore with counselees the consequences of remaining the same. The motivational interviewing approach (Miller & Rollnick, 2002) pro-vides rich techniques on how to help the counselee evaluate the potential future outcomes.

The "N" reminds you to **Name** the discrepancy. Name and identify the confrontation in a way that helps the counselee see and accept it. Cormier and Hackney (2008) recommend that counselors structure a confrontation by saying, "You said . . . but look." Young (2010) recommends using the "On the one hand . . . but on the other hand . . ." as a structure that lays out the discrepancy. In either case the counselor provides both sides of the discrepancy. In the first part of the confrontation the counselor reminds the counselee that he or she has a stated goal, desire, or plan. This is followed by the counselor noting a discrepancy in the counselee's behavior. For example, "You said you wanted to improve your relationship with your wife, but you continue to commit to various work projects and community activities that take you out of the home." In this example the counselor is highlighting the discrepancy between what the counselee stated he want-ed and what he is actually doing and which is working against his goal. A simple and direct communication works best (Patterson & Eisenberg, 1983). Being vague and unclear in the message will likely breed confusion and resistance as you and the counselee have to sort out what you were saying and what you meant to say.

The last guideline is to **Test** ("T") the accuracy and impact of the con-frontation. Carefully evaluate the counselee's response to the confronta-tion. As a rule it is sensible not to push your observations on the counselee. As with any form of feedback, it might take time for the counselee to be able to process and assimilate the information. If the counselee rejects the message of your confrontation, back away from it and validate the coun-selee's response.

## THE SKILL OF SELF-DISCLOSURE

A pioneering proponent of the value of self-disclosing is Sidney Jourard (1971). He described self-disclosure as making oneself known to another person by revealing personal information. As it relates specifically to the helping professions, it has been defined as "a conscious, intentional tech-nique in which clinicians share information about their lives outside the counseling relationship" (Simone, McCarthy, & Skay, 1998, p. 174). Sim-ply stated, self-disclosure means the counselee learns personal informa-tion about the counselor. Because of the counselor crossing a professional boundary to share personal information, Kelly and Rodriguez (2007) describe self-disclosure as a relaxation of therapeutic boundaries.

Research has shown that counselors who disclosed information about themselves were viewed more favorably than nondisclosing counselors, regardless of the preferences held by the counselee (VandeCreek & Angstadt, 1985). Self-disclosure can improve the comfort level of adolescent counselees (Simone, McCarthy, & Skay, 1998), promote reciprocal disclosure (Curtis, 1982), and build rapport (Kelly & Rodriguez, 2007). But the value that counselors place on self-disclosure depends on their theoretical orientation. For example the use of counselor self-disclosure has been scorned by some psychoanalytic theorists (Bianco, 2007; Curtis, 1982; Demetri, 2006; Hansen, 2008; Yahav & Oz, 2006), but is highly regarded by humanistic therapists (Bianco, 2007; Hansen, 2008; Jourard, 1971; Rogers, 1951; Truax & Carkhuff, 1967). Thus "the counselor's" theoretical orientation affects whether self-disclosure is used, and if so how.

## Benefits and Hazards of Self-Disclosure

As with any skill, counselors need to be aware of the pros and cons of using self-disclosure. Research on self-disclosure is mixed, with some researchers suggesting that it is helpful and others that it is harmful (Stricker & Fisher, 1990). In the right circumstances self-disclosure offers several notable benefits.

The use of self-disclosure creates the hazard of potentially steering into one of two ditches. One ditch is being too private and reserved. The other ditch is being overdisclosed and too self-revealing (Murphy and Strong, 1972). If you are too private, it will be difficult for you to be seen as authentic, genuine, caring, and compassionate. If you are too revealing, the counselee might feel devalued and may sense that the focus of therapy is on you, the counselor. In fact excessive or inappropriate self-disclosure has been regarded as an unethical boundary violation (Candill, 2003). Glass (2003) has distinguished between a "boundary violation," which is unethical and a "boundary crossing," which allows the helper to use himself appropriately to facilitate the counseling.

Yet on the other hand a number of positive reasons suggest using self-disclosure in the counseling relationship. First, self-disclosure might help a counselee feel more comfortable in opening up to a counselor (Anderson & Andersen, 1985; Chittick & Himelstein, 1967; DeForest & Stone, 1980). As you share personal and private information with the counselee, you normalize the activity of sharing. Actually self-disclosure is a form of modeling in which the counselor demonstrates how opening up works (Egan, 2007). In other words counselor self-disclosure breeds reciprocity.

Second, counselor self-disclosure helps the counselee know that he or she is not alone, that other people experience similar issues. It can help the counselee not split the world into good and bad, but to realize that suffering is experienced by every human being (Thomas & Habermas, 2008).

Enhancing rapport by building a stronger helping relationship is another benefit of self-disclosure (Rogers, 1951; Jourard, 1971; Truax & Carkhuff, 1967). Research has shown that helpers often self-disclose more to counselees who face greater difficulties in order to enhance deeper rapport with them (Kelly & Rodriguez, 2007).

Fourth, self-disclosure can also help counselees gain self-awareness into their interpersonal impact on others (Anderson & Andersen, 1985). When you share how the counselee's behavior impacts him, it gives the counselee insight into how people in normal situations might also perceive them. Counseling provides a unique context in which counselees can obtain this feedback or at least receive it in a way they can process.

Another justification for using self-disclosure is that it can humanize the counselor (Cormier & Cormier, 1985). The role of the counselee is to share personal information that might be considered embarrassing, shameful, and demoralizing. In addition, some counselees idealize the counselor, believing the counselor to be more spiritual or healthy. So when you share carefully selected personal information, you can normalize the counselee's struggles, neutralize the shame, and demonstrate that you are a fellow sojourner in this life. Inherent in the doctrine of original sin is the premise that we are all broken humans slogging through life's challenges together. One person struggles in one way, and another in different ways, but we all live in a constant state of original sin" (McMinn, 2008, p. 40).

Helping the counselee develop a new perspective (Egan, 2007) is another benefit of self-disclosure. By hearing how another individual has handled a similar situation, the counselee may be able to recognize and assimilate a different approach than they had previously considered. The recognition that a different option exists may allow the counselee to be open to the possibility that even more alternatives exist beyond those already in their view.

Another benefit of self-disclosure is that it creates a more collaborative relationship between the counselor and the counselee. Self-disclosure allows you to share therapeutic control with the counselee (Anderson & Andersen, 1985).

Counselees who are seeking a qualified helper might want to know about the counselor's training, orientation, and specific skills. This is one of the easiest areas to share since it is not as personal as other areas of the counselor's life. We have been asked to share with counselees information about our degrees, professional experience in counseling or with a specific population, and whether we are comfortable dealing with certain issues. If you are not comfortable in self-disclosure, you will likely inhibit therapeutic rapport.

While self-disclosure can be beneficial, it also has hazards. The most significant hazards arise out of being incompetent in the use of self-disclosure. Poor skill implementation might communicate that you lack discretion, are consumed with yourself, are untrustworthy, or worse, are seen as needing more help than the counselee.

Another hazard is that you might operate under the misguided assumption that what worked for you will work for the counselee. Some helpers approach people's problems as machines that can be fixed. But counseling is a human encounter. The goal is to facilitate a process to help the counselee; to allow God to do the work in bringing about change and transformation. It is not your responsibility to save people any more than it is to fix them. Be humble as you approach counselee issues.

Segal (1993) describes several hazards that have led him to believe that self-disclosure should be avoided because (a) it takes the focus off the counselee, (b) it can be a means of avoiding a painful or serious issue, (c) it can prevent confrontation of issues about the counselee's belief that the helper is incompetent, (d) it is difficult to predict how the counselee will interpret it, (e) it causes the helper to cross professional boundaries, and (f) it can reduce the helper's ability to empathize. Also psychoanalytic theorists believe that self-disclosure contaminates the transference process, exacerbates counselee resistance, and communicates that the counselor provides the ideal standard (Anderson & Andersen, 1985). Certainly mindfulness and caution are needed when utilizing self-disclosure.

## Kinds of Self-Disclosure

It is impossible not to communicate information about yourself. Anderson and Andersen (1985) discuss several kinds of self-disclosure, each one being more intimate than the one before it. The first kind of self-disclosure is demographic information, which is related to sex, age, race, build, attire, attractiveness, and others. This is the most superficial level of self-disclosure. Most of the information available through public self-disclosure is not things the counselor would typically try to hide.

The second kind of self-disclosure is professional identity. Counselors automatically self-disclose messages to the counselee about themselves with every word, look, movement, and emotional response (Strong & Claiborn, 1982). In addition, the counselor's attire, office décor, sitting position, and whether there are diplomas and awards on the wall, all convey information about your professional identity. You might also share specific areas of your expertise, areas of counseling in which you are competent.

A third kind of self-disclosure involves your worldview. We telegraph so much about ourselves that it is impossible to control it consciously. What you focus on, how you respond to different statements or behaviors, whether faith disclosures are shared—all of these actions communicate much about how you see and view the world.

A fourth kind of self-disclosure involves the counselor's attitudes and beliefs (Anderson & Andersen, 1985). Such information will become evident in the ideas and opinions you offer and how you react to counselee behaviors and statements.

Counselors also disclose themselves through their emotional responses (Anderson & Andersen, 1985). You can disclose "self-involving" emotions that identify your feelings about or reactions to counselee statements and/or behaviors and "self-disclosing" statements in which you share personal experiences. Self-involving disclosures are based more on the "here and now" than are emotional disclosures. In other words self-involving disclosures are expressions of immediacy. Anderson and Andersen (1985) offer the following examples:

> Self-involving: "I feel happy for you right now."
> Self-disclosing: "That reminds me of my relationship with my mother."

Anderson and Andersen (1985) discuss another type of self-disclosure, which they label "personal experiences of the counselor." They state that this kind of self-disclosure is typically what most people think of when they hear the term "self-disclosure." It refers to any disclosures in which the helper shares an experience that is outside the counselor's professional life. In this kind of self-disclosure counselors share their own experiences, behaviors, and feelings with a counselee that would otherwise be private (Edwards & Murdock, 1994). You might disclose such topics as disorders and relationship issues and how you have coped with particular situations.

Another kind of self-disclosure involves the sharing of information about your life, behavior, or consequences. This kind of self-disclosure accomplishes several things: (a) provides a model for the counselee to follow, (b) fixes a goal in the counselee's mind, and (c) gives the counselee permission to behave in a particular manner. For example the counselee may respond to the counselor, "I see you carrying a heavy burden" or "There is a glow that seems to be emanating from you as you share about this new relationship."

## Guidelines for Using Self-Disclosure

Eight guidelines can help you regulate your use of self-disclosure. These guidelines are in the acrostic **DISCLOSE** (see Table 7.4). The **Depth** ("D") of the self-disclosure depends on the counselee. This means that when self-disclosing the counselor should match the counselee's content and mood. Cormier and Cormier (1985) share the following as an example:

| | |
|---|---|
| **Counselee:** | *I just feel so down on myself. My husband is so critical of me, and often I think he's right. I really can't do much of anything well.* |
| **Counselor:** | *There have been times when I've also felt down on myself, so I can sense how discouraged you are. Sometimes too, criticism . . . has made me feel even worse, although I'm learning how to value myself regardless of critical comments.* |

In this example the counselor's self-disclosure parallels the counselee's content and overall mood associated with that message. However, it is important to begin with nonintimate disclosure. Being too intimate in self-disclosure can be a problem for some counselees. It also helps prepare the counselee for more intimate details later if the situation calls for it.

Table 7.4
*DISCLOSE: Guidelines for Using Self-Disclosure*

**D** = the **Depth** of the self-disclosure depends on the counselee

**I** = make sure it is **Intended** to meet the counselee's needs

**S** = keep your disclosure **Specific** and focused

**C** = put self-disclosure in the informed consent **Contract**

**L** = **Limit** the depth of your personal disclosures

**O** = Make sure it is the right **Occasion** for the self-disclosure

**S** = more **Self-disclosure** early in the counseling and **Self-involving** later in the process

**E** = be **Economical** in the use of self-disclosure

Make sure that the self-disclosure is **Intended** ("I") for the counselee. Examine your motives to make sure that the counselee's interest and needs are the driving force of the disclosure. Ask yourself, "How will this benefit the counselee?"

Keep the disclosure **Specific** ("S") and focused. Do not ramble and get into too many details. You are simply creating a bridge to the counselee's experience. Share only as much information as necessary to fulfill that intended purpose.

Egan (2007) recommends that you make self-disclosure part of the counseling **Contract** ("C"). Whether this is part of the informed consent or discussed as part of the introduction at the beginning of the first session, counselors can inform counselees that they sometimes share personal information as a means of helping the counselee.

**Limit** ("L") the depth of your self-disclosure. Make sure that all disclosures are appropriate and not beyond a level of propriety. You may be tempted to share your personal journey, especially when you can identify with the counselee's struggle. Consider whether the counselee is too vulnerable or too unstable to hear your experiences. As a rule a moderate amount of self-disclosure is related to positive outcomes. But self-disclosure should not disintegrate into swapping "war stories."

Make sure it is the right **Occasion** ("O") for the self-disclosure. The timing of self-disclosure is important; in other words determine if the therapeutic situation calls for it. Sharing information too early in the counseling relationship might confuse counselees about the nature of the professional relationship or wrongly switch the focus away from the counselee's situation.

The "S" is to structure more **Self-disclosure** early in the counseling process and **Self-involving** disclosures later in the process. It is more helpful to use self-disclosure when you share information about yourself earlier in the counseling relationship. As the relationship becomes more established, offering more disclosures can help meet treatment goals.

The final guideline is to be **Economical** ("E") in the use of self-disclosure. Do not overuse self-disclosure. Some counselors share too much too frequently (Egan, 2007). Consider whether other techniques might be more beneficial than self-disclosure (Simone et al., 1998). Harrington (2001) provides a list of excellent alternative counselor responses to self-disclosure (see Table 7.5). These alternative responses include the use of reflection (see chap. 5, "Basic Skills: Creating a Connection"), deflection and clarifying, obliquely confirming, and becoming the counselee's ally.

Table 7.5

*Alternatives to the Use of Self-Disclosure*

| ALTER-NATIVES TO SELF-DISCLOSURE | REFLECT | DEFLECT AND CLARIFY | OBLIQUELY CONFIRM | BECOME AN ALLY |
|---|---|---|---|---|
| *Are you married (coupled, single, divorced, widowed)?* | It sounds like you have a problem with an important relationship. | Tell me about your relationship. How can I be helpful to you? | Relationships are very important to me. | I try to be very supportive of people in significant relationships. |
| *Do you have children?* | It sounds as if you have a problem that involves children. | Tell me about your children. What is it about them that is bothering you? | Children are important to me, and I also understand that they can be challenging. | I am an advocate for parents and for children. |
| *Have you ever had this problem? Or Are you a recovering alcoholic, (or _____ problem)?* | It sounds as if you want to know if I can understand your problem. | I'd like to hear more about you. Help me to know more about what you're struggling with. | It is true that I, just like everyone else, have had to face difficult times before. | I'm very aware of how people with this problem struggle. |
| *How old are you?* | You want to know if I can relate to someone your age. | Tell me what matters to you about age. How is age important to you? | I'm aware of how important it can be to feel as if I can relate to someone close in age. | People of all ages are really important to me. I try to relate to all age groups as well as I can. |
| *Will you call me sometime?* | No, but it sounds like you wish that we could maintain contact. | No, I can't call you back, but let's focus on what we can talk about right now. What would be helpful from someone who could talk with you on a more regular basis? | No, I can't call you back, but I can relate to the feeling of wanting a comforting and supportive person in life. | It's really important to me for every person to have a good support system. While I can't call you back, I want to help you expand your support. |

Table 7.5 (cont.)

*Alternatives to the Use of Self-Disclosure*

| ALTER-NATIVES TO SELF-DISCLOSURE | REFLECT | DEFLECT AND CLARIFY | OBLIQUELY CONFIRM | BECOME AN ALLY |
|---|---|---|---|---|
| *Are you a Christian (Jew, Muslim, etc.)? Or where do you go to church?* | It sounds like your faith is very important to you and you want me to understand. | I'm really interested in your faith. Tell me about how your spirituality is important to you. | A guiding belief system or a set of values is important to me. | I know how important a belief system is to all people and I really want to understand yours. |
| *Will you pray with me?* | I'm sensing that you are really needing my support. | What would your prayer be for yourself? | I believe in the importance of prayer, contemplation, and reflection. | Many people find comfort in prayer, contemplation, and reflection, and I really support that. |
| *Where do you live?* | You're curious about where I live. | What is important to you about knowing that? | Having a sense of community and belonging to a neighborhood is important to me. | I really believe in the concept of community for all people. Help me to know about yours. |
| *Can we go to lunch (or meet) some-time?* | No, but it sounds like you wish that we could meet in person. | No, we can't meet, but I'd like to know more about the supportive people in your life with whom you could meet. | No, but I like knowing that I have someone in my life to meet with. Let's try to find out how you can strengthen your support system. | No, but having a trusted and nonjudgmental listener is a gift. I'd like to earn your trust as we continue our work together |
| *What do you think about this issue?* | You want to focus on my thoughts about this. | What are your thoughts about this issue? | I have some thoughts about this issue, but the most important thing to me right now is your thoughts. | Everyone has thoughts and feelings about life's challenges, and I really want to help you find your way through your thoughts. |

Taken from J. A. Harrington "Self-disclosure: Temptations and alternatives" (paper presented at the SACES Conference, Athens, Georgia, October 27, 2001). (judithharrington@worldnet.att.net)

## THE SKILL OF IMMEDIACY

Of all the helping skills we have discussed thus far, none is more important to the counseling relationship than immediacy. In fact Wheeler and D'Andrea (2004) considered immediacy "one of the most important skills" in the counselor's tool bag.

The reason for its importance is that it addresses the dynamics occurring between the counselor and the counselee. While the counselee is experiencing what the counselor is like and deciding if the counselor can be trusted, the counselor is also having internal reactions to the counselee. Issues will arise out of the relationship between the counselee and the counselor. These realities that emerge in the counseling relationship can be processed through the skill of immediacy (Carkhuff, 1969a; Carkhuff, 1969b).

What is immediacy? Various definitions have been suggested. According to Patterson and Eisenberg (1983), immediacy occurs when the counselor tells the counselee personal and "immediate reactions to the counselee" (p. 34). Turock (1980) states that it involves a counselor's understanding and communicating of what is going on between the counselor and the counselee within the helping relationship, particularly the counselee's feelings, impressions, and expectations, as well as the needs of the counselor (p. 168). Hill and O'Brien (1999) say immediacy refers to the counselor "disclosing immediate feelings about self in relation to the counselee or the therapeutic relationship" (p. 236). Gerald Egan (2007) describes immediacy this way:

> Helpers are willing to explore their own relationships with their counselees ("you-me" talk)—that is, to explore the here-and-now of counselee-helper interactions—to the degree that this helps counselees get a better understanding of themselves, their interpersonal style, and quality of their cooperation in the helping process (p. 40).

The skill of immediacy is a valuable tool in the hands of a competent helper. Carkhuff and Pierce (1977) regard it as the highest level of helping because it focuses on the immediate moment of the counselor and counselee's relationship in order to help the counselee gain more insight into his situation.

Immediacy statements include the counselor's thoughts or feelings about what is going on in the counseling relationship. They might be positively oriented or confrontal. Counselors share their personal thoughts when they cognitively respond to the counselee. Thought-oriented immediacy captures statements that are devoid of the counselor's feelings. Consider these examples: "You worked hard to communicate those feelings with your wife. It took courage to face the truth" or "I've noticed how hard you have been working in our counseling, yet it seems that you are beginning to lose your drive to change." Examples of feeling-oriented immediacy statements include supportive feelings ("I'm so happy that you got the job"), sorrowful feelings ("I'm so sad to learn about your daughter's death"), and finally sentimental feelings ("You have been a delightful counselee to work with, and I will miss our sessions together").

Immediacy can foster counselee growth by redirecting the focus from what is happening outside to what is happening inside, by stimulating more honest communication, and helping the counselee learn ways to handle issues in outside relationships. Because immediacy takes awareness and courage on your part, it can model those beneficial attributes for the counselee (Patterson & Eisenberg, 1983).

## Kinds of Immediacy

Egan (2007) has identified three types of immediacy: relationship immediacy, event-focused immediacy, and self-involving immediacy. Relationship immediacy captures the counselor's ability to discuss the counseling relationship with the counselee. You explore either the way you and the counselee are interacting or how the counseling relationship has evolved. The emphasis is on the relationship as a whole. There are examples of relationship immediacy: "I'm not sure if you are telling me what you think I want to hear or telling me what you truly experienced." "I sense that you and I have a connection . . . one that will help in working through these issues." "It seems as if you are keeping me at arms distance as I try to find ways to help you." Innumerable examples could be given that refer to things that can emerge in the actual helping relationship.

According to Egan (2007), event-focused immediacy, previously referred to as here-and-now immediacy, refers to the counselor's ability to discuss with counselees an interaction that has just occurred. In other words the counselor tries to explore what is occurring in the counseling relationship at that very moment. Consider these examples:

> Counselee (with a frown): "Today was horrible! This morning the kids were being difficult, I spilled coffee on my clothes and had to change, which made me late for work. My boss yelled at me for being late, then gave me a project that normally takes three weeks to do and told me to have it done by Monday. My day just seems to get worse every time I turn around!"
>
> Counselor: "It sounds like you have had a rough day. How do you feel about your circumstances right now?"

In the third kind of immediacy a counselor is using self-involving immediacy when he or she is speaking to the counselee with present-tense personal responses. For example, "It saddens me to think about the fact that you are willing to walk away from this relationship without even trying to see if it can be restored." In this statement you are sharing your immediate heartfelt response to the counselee regarding his decision to disengage from his current relationship.

## Risks Associated with Immediacy

Immediacy involves a level of risk for the counselor (Hazler & Barwick, 2001). Research supports the fact that counselors avoid immediacy issues even when they are brought up by counselees (Turock, 1980). Counselors may change the subject, mislabel feelings, ignore counselee anger, or express disapproval.

Inherent in any communication is the risk of sharing what you are truly thinking and feeling. Such a level of sharing, however, is even more complicated in the counseling relationship. The counselor is in the role of helper, and receiving honest communication from the counselor might not be well received by the counselee. The counselor might be wrong, be viewed as being wrong, derail the counseling session, or be rejected. Some novice counselors fear they are being overly intrusive and overly intimate by sharing their personal reactions to the counselee. The bottom line, however, is that your fears associated with immediacy are a reflection of your countertransference (Wheeler & D'Andrea, 2004). According to Egan (2007) it takes courage for the counselor to use immediacy. Thus place your needs in the background and the counselee's needs in the foreground in order to overcome any interpersonal barrier that hinders the ability to be immediate.

## When to Use Immediacy

Although immediacy is difficult to do in normal social situations, situations occur in the counseling context that makes the use of immediacy a necessary task. In general, immediacy helps you deal with transference and countertransference issues that were discussed in the previous chaps.

Egan (2007) recommends using immediacy in the following situations. First, one situation is when the session is directionless and no progress is being made. In other words immediacy is a wise choice when you and the counselee are at an impasse (Mueller & Kell, 1972). Second, another section is when there seems to be tension between the counselor and the counselee. Counselees can gain insight into their interpersonal style by examining their relationship with the counselor. Third, immediacy can be used when a lack of trust seems to exist in the counseling relationship. Fourth, another situation is when there is a social difference between the counselor and the counselee, evident in being from different social backgrounds or having differing interpersonal styles. Fifth, immediacy can be used when the counselee seems overly dependent. Sixth, another occasion is when counterdependency seems to be blocking the helping relationship. An example of this might be, "It seems that we're letting this session turn into a struggle between you and me. And if I'm not mistaken, both of us seem to be bent on winning." Seventh, you might consider using immediacy when attraction seems to be interfering with the counseling. "It seems we have liked each other from the start, but now I'm wondering if it is getting in the way of working together."

Wheeler and D'Andrea (2004) point out that some experts believe that immediacy is not appropriate until the helping relationship is well established. Yet if counselee issues are affecting the development of the counseling relationship from the start, it might never be established unless the issues are processed.

### Guidelines for Using Immediacy

The counseling literature offers many guidelines to help counselors know how to employ immediacy (Cormier & Cormier, 1985; Egan, 2007; Ivey & Ivey, 2003; Young, 2010). The mnemonic device for implementing the skill of immediacy is **SELF** (see Table 7.6).

| Table 7.6 |
| --- |
| *SELF: Guidelines for Using Immediacy* |
| **S** = remember that **Social** relationships are not the same as professional relationships |
| **E** = **Enlightened** about the process and **Equipped** to address it |
| **L** = **Link** it to yourself |
| **F** = have the **Fortitude** to address it and offer it in the form of **Feedback** |

The "S" refers to the fact that **Social** and professional relationships differ. The most basic obstacle that novice counselors face is to understand the difference between a professional relationship and a social relationship. Wheeler and D'Andrea (2004) state that "intruding," "offending," and "not being liked" are social concepts, but immediacy is a professional concept. What is acceptable in a professional relationship might not be appropriate in a social relationship. Learn to become unencumbered by certain social restraints in the counseling process.

The "E" in SELF refers to the need for you to be **Enlightened** about what is occurring in the relationship and **Equipped** on how to deal with it. Be aware that if what is happening in the counseling relationship is interfering with the helping process. Of course once you are aware of an issue, share that awareness with the counselee, and be ready to address the problem. In order for immediacy to be therapeutic, rely on other skills such as empathy, self-disclosure, and confrontation.

The "L" refers to **Linking** your internal response to yourself. One of the main similarities between social and professional domains is that each person owns his or her own reactions and responses in any relationships (Patterson & Eisenberg, 1983). This means in part that immediacy statements are best worded beginning with the word "I" so that you own your response and reaction. For example, "I feel angry when you let yourself be mistreated" rather than "You make me feel angry when you don't stand up for yourself."

The letter "F" refers to having the **Fortitude** to address the issue and offering it in the form of **Feedback**, not criticism. Be assertive in risking the sharing of that information with the counselee. Egan (2007) points out that counselors who struggle with intimacy in their own personal lives will struggle with being immediate with their counselees. For example "Right now as I am listening to you share about this frightening memory of abuse, I feel close to you and sad that you endured such pain as a child. I also feel a sense of urgency, like I want you to see something about your cutting and its relation to how abusers have treated you. Do you see what I am seeing? I am feeling afraid for you and so sad that the abuse is now continuing at your own hand."

## THE SKILL OF SILENCE

Of all of the helping techniques, the most nondirective is silence. Silence has been defined as "the temporary absence of any overt verbal or paraverbal communication between counselor and counselee within sessions" (Feltham & Dryden, 1993, p. 117). It is in essence a pause in the counseling dialogue when neither the counselor nor counselee speaks. What exactly constitutes a silence is not clear, however. In an attempt to quantify therapeutic silence, Sharpley (1997) recommended that pauses that stretch more than five seconds define silence.

Silence is difficult to define, and it is also difficult to tolerate. Nothing may be more difficult to handle and nothing creates more anxiety for novice helpers than silence (Sharpley, Munro, & Elly, 2005). Many beginning helpers seem to think that silence indicates their incompetence (Sharpley, Munro, & Elly, 2005). After all, dialogue is what counselors are supposed to facilitate. If the professional obligation were not enough, culturally we have also been taught to fill silence with verbiage. The end result is that counselors can become uncomfortable with the absence of words.

## The Role of Silence in Helping

In social situations silence is typically unwelcomed. But in the helping process silence has a specific role to play. Actors employ the use of silent pauses in dramatic pieces to create a particular experience in the audience. In music silence or "a rest" serves three major purposes. An obvious purpose of a musical pause is that it serves the need of the musician. It provides a literal rest; time to catch a breath before proceeding with the piece. Sometimes the intensity of counseling can create a need for pause, a time to refresh and recollect one's thoughts.

Another purpose of a pause in music is to benefit the audience. A musical silence helps create a demand for the return of that singer or player. Dramatic theatrical pieces also use silence. Sometimes the phrase "pregnant pause" is used to capture the anticipation that silence can create in the hearing of a story. Think about the pregnant pause in Handel's *Messiah*, at the end of the "Hallelujah Chorus." There are a string of repetitions of the phrase "forever, and ever, hallelujah, hallelujah," followed by an abrupt two beats of sudden silence. This pause prepares the listener for the grand finale line, done slowly, "Hallelujah!" The crescendo of praise in preparation sets up the climactic moment, for the closing of the greatest choral piece in history. That moment of silence is part of the historical performance of this great anthem, causing the king of England to rise at its performance and setting a tradition for concertgoers ever since then to rise. In other words a silence or pause in music creates a hunger or anticipation for the return of the musician. Likewise silence in the helping process enables words to be heard and nonverbal communication to be read.

A third purpose of the rest in music is that it allows for changes in the "color" of music. Silence allows a composer to change the direction of the music and the role that particular instrumental sections are taking in the piece.[1] Also in the counseling context silence can allow the counselee or counselor to change directions in the dialogue.

---

[1] Special thanks to composer Don Marsh for his insights into the role of silence and music.

Some may assume that if the counselor becomes quiet in a session that nothing is happening. Yet while it might seem that counselors are passive during silent pauses in therapeutic talk, research shows they actually are active and alert to the process (Hill, Thompson, & Ladany. 2003). This fact might be the rationale behind Young's (2010) term "attentive silence." Simply because silence is nondirective does not mean that the counselor is passive.

## Kinds and Purposes of Silence

Decades of research has shown that several kinds of silence exist (Frankel, Levitt, Murray, Greenberg, & Angus, 2006; Levitt, 1998; 2001; Tindall & Robinson, 1947). After reviewing transcripts of counseling sessions Tindall and Robinson (1947) categorized silences into two types: counselor-initiated silences and counselee-initiated silences. Counselor-initiated silences have three main purposes. First, the counselor can use a pause to encourage the counselee to control the dialogue. By silence the counselor can prompt the counselee to elaborate.

A second purpose in counselor-initiated silence is for organizational purposes. For example silence allows the counselee to collect her thoughts. It gives the counselee time to reflect and become aware of her feelings.

Third, it fits the normal process of conversation by showing the natural ending of a sequence of the conversation. In general the counselor can use silences to contrast what has been occurring in the counseling dialogue.

While counselors might feel in control when they generate a therapeutic pause, often the counselee initiates the silence. Counselee-initiated silences can be generated for several different reasons. First, silence might occur because the counselee does not know how to proceed. The counselee might feel confused on what to say or where to take the conversation. He is at a loss for words, so to speak.

Second, silence might be a normal and natural ending to a discussion; as Forest Gump said, "That is all I have to say about that." Talkative counselees rarely find reason to pause in their dialogue, but most people do finish expressing their thoughts and stop speaking. When a counselee becomes silent because he has completed his thoughts, the counselor would continue the process by using another skill.

A third reason for counselee-generated silence is to enable counselees to reflect on or to collect their thoughts before elaborating on the point just made. Some people require more time for introspection before answering a question. Silence allows counselees to ponder things that the counselor has said. As a rule, the richer your statement or question, the more likely it is that you will need to give the counselee time to think before responding in an authentic and meaningful way. A related reason for silence is that the counselee is searching for more thoughts and feelings to express. Silence gives counselees space to reflect (Swain, 1995) and focus (Mearns, 1997).

Fourth, a counselee might use silence out of a need for approval, from a desire for advice or information, or to get an answer to a direct question. In other words silence is a form of conversational manipulation that some counselees have learned prompts others to do something for them. Of course you might choose not to respond as a way of challenging the counselee to wrestle with the issue.

A fifth reason for counselee silence is to withhold personal aspects that feel shameful. Some counselees might be anxious about being fully known. Thus they are reticent about disclosing aspects of themselves that they do not want the counselor to know or are not ready to let the counselor know.

Two other reasons may be added to the list offered by Tindall and Robinson (1947). Counselees might become silent because they are overwhelmed with their suffering. Consider the case of Job. Waves of tragedy found Job sitting outside the city on an ashheap (Job 2:8). So overcome with grief, Job could not speak to his friends for seven days. When people are carrying an enormous load, silence might be the only way they can express themselves.

Another reason is that silence might be a form of resistance. Some counselees have learned that silence is a passive-aggressive way to control others. In the case of counseling the message is "I dare you to help me!" Coerced counselees may enact such ploys, but even voluntary counselees have a vested interest in maintaining what is familiar.

## Benefits and Risks of Silence

Authors differ on the value of using silence in counseling. Some suggest that silence conveys empathy and concern, while others warn that silence can convey insensitivity (Gill, 1984). Whether silence helps or hinders the helping process depends on many factors. For example some research suggests that the benefits or risks of silence might depend on the timing of the silence and the counselee need (Hill, Thompson, & Ladany, 2003) and who initiates and terminates the silence. Research by Sharpley, Munro, and Elly (2005) have shown that who initiates and terminates the silence is correlated with rapport. Their research found that silences that were terminated by the counselee contributed toward rapport.

Though several factors might impact the effectiveness of silence, research has generated a number of clear positive outcomes. As Sharpley's research indicates, one benefit from therapeutic silence is an improved relationship between the counselor and the counselee. Silence can also communicate the counselor's sincere and heartfelt acceptance of the counselee (George & Cristiani, 1990). Elson (2001) referred to this as "empathic silence" (p. 357). Another benefit is that it lets counselees know that the responsibility for counseling lies on their shoulders (George & Cristiani, 1990).

The risks associated with silence involve misreading it and allowing it to continue when the counselee actually wants the counselor to take the lead. Sometimes silence can communicate that the counselor is inexperienced and potentially incompetent. However, silence, when wisely initiated and prudently responded to, can have significant positive effects. As with all techniques and strategies the counselor must use silence skillfully. We offer five guidelines to assist you in becoming competent in using silence.

## Guidelines for Using Silence

The acrostic **PAUSE** suggests ways to use silence effectively (see Table 7.7). First, "P" refers to your **Personal** comfort with silence. The most important guideline for using silence is learning to become comfortable with it, in short, learning to "cope with silence" (Burnard, 1999). Silence can be a welcomed and even necessary part of the helping process.

Table 7.7

*PAUSE: Guidelines for Using Silence*

| |
| --- |
| **P = Personal** comfort with silence |
| **A = Allow** silence |
| **U = Use** silence purposefully |
| **S = Screen** the counselee for comfort |
| **E = Encourage** the counselee in the silence |

Second, "A" refers to **Allowing** counselee-generated silences to happen. Recall the story of Job. When his friends arrived to comfort him, they were so shocked by the sight of their friend that they tore their robes and sat down next to him. For seven days and nights these friends sat in silence with their friend who could not express his grief. After Job did speak, the words of his friends would both wound Job and displease God. Nevertheless their ability to be silent for seven days was a brilliant strategy to demonstrate their love. Perhaps Job was able to be so authentic in his sharing because he felt embraced by the presence of his friends. The power of presence coupled with the value of silence can provide incredible therapeutic benefit for people who are struggling. As a rule do not interrupt silence unless you have a clear purpose in mind. Many novice counselors respond to silence with non-word sounds or a follow-up question. Such responses are typically a reflection of counselor anxiety. Try to relax and focus on your attending skills.

The "U" in PAUSE suggests you **Use** silence purposefully. Counselor-generated silences are best employed with a particular purpose in mind such as reducing the counselor's level of activity, slowing down the pace of the session, allowing the counselee time to reflect, or when the counselor is working harder than the counselee. Be sure to be fully therapeutic in your silences. A significant difference exists between a warm silence and a cold silence. One is comforting, and the other is disturbing. Also, it is important to avoid using silences when the counselee is confused, experiencing an acute crisis, or is psychotic (Sommers-Flanagan & Sommers-Flanagan, 2003).

The fourth guideline, "S," is to **Screen** the counselee during periods of silence. Young (2010) suggests that when silence occurs in the counseling, to look at the counselee to assess his level of comfort with it. If the counselee appears comfortable, allow the silence to do its work. If the counselee is looking confused or seems to be awaiting a response, then proceed with the appropriate skill for the situation.

Fifth, when seeking to use silence, **Encourage** ("E") the counselee in the process. Though it is typically prudent not to interrupt silence, particular situations might merit a well-timed and well-framed response. At times a comment might need to be interjected into a period of silence in order to let the counselee know that you are still present and actively listening. Several experts have stated that offering a process statement such as "What are you feeling at the moment?" (Culley & Bond, 2004) or "What are you thinking?" (Burnard, 1999), or "What we are talking about is bringing up some strong emotions," or "It is hard to know what to say next," or "Just tell me whatever comes to your mind."

In summary, do not become disheartened during pauses in the helping process. By being active and attentive to the counselee, guided by an understanding of how to counsel, you can come to master the art of silence. Sommers-Flanagan and Sommers-Flanagan (2003) suggest that you can become aware of how you deal with silence by listening to tape-recordings of your sessions and monitoring the number and duration of silences and who initiated them and who terminated them.

## THE SKILL OF PACING

Some use the term *pacing* to refer to mirroring or matching the counselee's behavior in the session. In this way it is a form of attending (see chap. 4, "The Person of the Counselor"). Another use of the term *pacing* refers to how the counselor manages the counseling process. In this text we use the latter definition of pacing.

An important skill in the helping process is the ability of the counselor to control the pace of the counseling sessions to ensure that things occur at the appropriate time. By pacing, the counselor attempts to work at a pace that is appropriate to where the counselee is at that time. The rationale for pacing is that issues are not to be explored too quickly or too slowly. Imagine a personal trainer attempting to get an overweight, out-of-shape person to run five miles in under 40 minutes on his first day to the gymnasium. The expectations would "outweigh" the exerciser's ability to perform. Some counselors demand that their counselees do too much too fast. Further, if the personal trainer does not encourage the exerciser to get on a treadmill and walk for a period of time at a pace that will make nominal but purposeful gains in the person's fitness, why go to the gym? Thus the personal trainer creates a workout plan that is workable for the exerciser and yet encourages fitness.

Sometimes pacing means that you keep the counselee focused on the topic at hand. For example the counselor might say to a counselee who is rambling or jumping from topic to topic, "Hold on. Let's stay with one topic at a time. Let's finish talking about your father before we go to the subject of your brother."

Pacing is not an easy task to teach nor is it an easy task to master. It seems to develop through experience. With this reality in mind, however, we offer the following mnemonic device for remembering four key guidelines to pacing the session: **PACE** (see Table 7.8).

| Table 7.8 |
| --- |
| *PACE: Guidelines for Using Pacing* |
| **P** = **Proceed** conservatively |
| **A** = **Assess** the counselee's readiness and timetable |
| **C** = emphasize **Content** less than process |
| **E** = **Encourage** but do not drive or force the counselee |

The "P" is for **Proceeding** conservatively. Egan (2007) speaks of pacing as realizing that it is possible to demand things from the counselee before he is ready. In other words counselors must time their interventions and strategies carefully. As a rule a gentle pace works best to maintain the counselee's sense of safety. Another rule is to consider the counselee's problem in pacing. For depressed counselees, for example, a slower and more deliberate approach is in order. Well-functioning counselees or counselees in crisis might benefit from a more rapid pace. In more rapid-paced sessions the counselor will be active in limiting unproductive and peripheral dialogue.

To pace the session appropriately, you will need to **Assess** ("A") the counselee's readiness to address the issues. The counselee will not look at things nor address issues before he or she is ready. As humans, we naturally resist change, and our response to someone trying to change us is to feel threatened in some way. So the counselor must consider the counselee's willingness and readiness in making those determinations. The best work on readiness is by Prochaska and DiClemente (1984). We will discuss the role of counselee readiness in the process of change in chap. 12 ("Strategies Bringing About Changes"). Continually assess the counselee's need and receptivity to addressing issues. Although the counselee might have sought help without any coercion, that does not negate the fact that motivation might still be low. Occasionally a counselee wants help and wants it immediately. While you can speed up the pace with such counselees, do not think they are willing to hear anything you have to offer. Again feedback is hard to receive, no matter how badly you are hurting. There are times, however, when the counselee needs to be slowed down by you assuring him that you will work at a pace that is likely to accomplish the greatest good without belaboring the process.

The third guideline to developing competence in pacing is to recognize that the **Content** ("C") is not as important as the process. We addressed the issue of content and process at the beginning of this chap. The focus of pacing is not to be so much on the counselee words, but on how the counselee talks about the subject. The content of communication is important, however, when you are about to address sensitive topics. Be respectful when you speak to any sensitive area such as sexual relationships and abuse. But how the counselee is relating to you and how the counselee is talking about the issues will be good indicators of whether you can speed up the process.

Fourth, it is OK to **Encourage** ("E") the counselee to move forward and progress. Do not force counselees to look at or address things before they are ready. Again a gentle pace is the best. One of the roles of personal trainers is to find ways to motivate their trainees without losing them or discouraging them. Similarly, in the counseling context you encourage the counselee to move into areas that are painful. In this vein the pacing becomes a means of developing the counselees (D'Andrea, 1984). Through pacing, the counselor is able to shape the counselee in ways that will meet the mutually agreed-on counseling goals.

Counselors need to be aware of the fact that they might want the counselee to get better more than the counselee desires change. The counselors might also want to see progress occur more quickly.

## CASE TO ILLUSTRATE THE SKILLS OF HELPING

Molly is a sixteen-year-old who was brought to counseling by her parents. She reports no recollection of her childhood prior to the age of eight. Her "intake form" reveals that she has self-mutilating behaviors, low self-esteem, and depression. Although she is intelligent, she is failing several of her classes, and her parents are concerned that this will jeopardize her opportunity to attend college. She has reluctantly come to counseling to address this issue. To simplify the process, we will assume that the intake form has been reviewed and goals established. Although the determined goals are related to her academic difficulties, the therapist suspects that there are serious underlying issues at work.

CO = Counselor
CL = Counselee

| | |
|---|---|
| **CO** | (with a smile and firm handshake) *Good morning Molly. How are you?* |
| **CL** | *Ok, I guess* (said with her head down and no eye contact). |
| **CO** | (observing her nonverbals) *You seem unhappy. What has happened to upset you?*<br><br>**Proceed conservatively:** the counselor is allowing the counselee to set the pace.<br><br>**Assessing:** with this first probe the counselor is assessing the counselee's readiness to interact. |
| **CL** | *Nothing. Life just sucks* (she looks up briefly to see how her words affected the counselor). |
| **CO** | (nonplussed) *Yes, life can certainly have its challenges. But I was wondering how it is that a smart young lady with a lot going for her finds herself talking to me about her grades.* |

**Proceed conservatively:** the counselor is allowing the counselee to set the pace.

**Assessing:** this second probe continues the assessing process.

CL      (said emphatically with her eyes raised to meet the counselor's) *You don't know anything about me! You're just doing this because it's your job!*

CO      (after a brief pause while maintaining eye contact) *Well, you're right about that. I don't know anything about what you are feeling right now, and it is my job to help you work through your feelings. Perhaps the best way for me to know "about you" is for you to tell me a little bit "about you."*

**Proceed conservatively:** the counselor is allowing the counselee to set the pace.

**Assessing:** the third probe is also part of the assessing process.

**Content:** the counselor suspects abuse based on the counselee's history, so he/she is proceeding cautiously while continuing to assess the counselee's readiness to interact. Particular attention is given to the counselee's lack of eye contact and poor posture.

CL      (after a brief pause: her head is back down again and she is not making eye contact) *Why should I?*

CO      *Molly, when you are here, you don't have to do or say anything that you don't want to. Just a moment ago, you said that this was my job. But it is much more than that to me. It is a calling, a way that I can use what I've learned from both life and school to help people. Right now, you sound like you are afraid to trust me and that is OK* (the therapist opts for silence after making this statement).

**Proceed conservatively:** the counselor is allowing the counselee to set the pace.

**Encourage:** the counselor is encouraging the counselee to pace herself and reassuring her that this is OK with her (tacitly acknowledging that it is safe to limit their conversation to the topics that she feels comfortable discussing).

*At this point, the counselee may choose to continue the conversation; otherwise the therapist may change the subject and begin discussing lighter issues.

## CHAPTER SUMMARY

Counselors can avail themselves of many different skills to help counselees. Although a number of these techniques are used in normal social life, there are particular applications and purposes in the therapeutic encounter. Knowing how to facilitate the counseling process will be a critical part of your helping efforts.

We addressed seven specific skills that can equip you with the ability to move the counseling process forward. First, knowing how to give counselees feedback is essential to offering them what you understand about their functioning and fostering greater self-awareness. Several specific feedback skills such as interpretation and confrontation offer counselees new ways of understanding their thoughts, feelings, and actions as well as those of others. Confrontation allows you to address discrepancies in what counselees are telling you and how they are behaving. Whether counselees ask you to share about your background or you believe certain personal experiences will be additive to the counseling process, know how to self-disclose. The skill of immediacy will help you handle those sessions effectively.

Though many people are uncomfortable with silence, it has a critical place in helping. Sometimes counselees need time to reflect or time to feel what they are experiencing. Regardless of the reasons for allowing silence, effective helpers know how to use it in the helping process. Counselors are responsible for the entire counseling process. You need to know how to pace the sessions, when to implement particular skills, and how to encourage counselees when they get "stuck." Together these skills become a powerful means of assisting those individuals whom you are called to serve.

The next section provides a framework for these skills, namely, an overview of the counseling process and how the skills fit into the overall work of assessment and case conceptualization. All these helping skills need to be employed in the context of a caring connection with the counselee. Every skill is actually an extension of empathic communication.

## CHAPTER 7 ACTIVITIES

1. Think of a recent time when you received feedback. How was the feedback given to you? How did you perceive the giver's attitude and agenda in giving it? Was it welcomed or not? What was your internal experience in hearing the feedback? When have you received encouraging feedback and what made it helpful (Patterson & Eisenberg, 1983)?

2. Imagine you are seeing a counselee who agrees during sessions to complete certain homework assignments, but consistently comes to sessions without doing it. Give an example of providing appropriate feedback in this situation. Specifically state what you would say.

3. List the nine guidelines given in the chap. for giving feedback and briefly discuss the importance of each. Which of these may be difficult for you and why?

4. List and describe the eight guidelines given in the chap. for effective confrontation. Describe a time when someone confronted you about something in a harsh way. Did it help or hinder you in your character growth? How might this person have given you the same feedback in a "speak the truth in love" manner? In the DVD, what did Ryan do in his self-disclosure that was poor?

5. Reflect on the following statement from a Christian perspective and relate it to the use of confrontation and counselor self-disclosure in counseling: "As a therapist and counselee sit face to face, they are both 'noble ruins' (to borrow a phrase from Pascal), which ought to call the therapist to a deep experience of empathy and understanding of the counselee's weaknesses, wounds, and vulnerabilities" (McMinn, 2008, p. 38).

6. Discuss some of the hazards of counselor self-disclosure in counseling. What are the guidelines given in the chap. for self-disclosure, and why are they important?

7. What type of information would be difficult for you to share with a counselee and why?

8. What is the skill of immediacy? Describe the three types of immediacy introduced in the chap. What important guidelines are given in the chap. for the use of immediacy? What did you like about Denise's modeling of self-disclosure?

9. What are the guidelines given in the chap. for the use of silence in counseling? Do you think you will feel comfortable using silence appropriately in counseling?

10. Describe the four guidelines given in the chap. for pacing in counseling. Why is a gentle pace best?
11. Select one of the seven specific facilitation skills introduced in this chap. and create a simulated dialog between counselor and counselee that reflects your understanding of the successful use of that skill.
12. In the DVD, you saw Denise confront Colleen. Describe how she gave that confrontation. What would you do differently?

## Vignette Questions

### Vignette 5
### Feedback

1. In the fifth vignette, you saw the counselor, Don work with Frank. Identify the skills from the previous vignettes that are utilized by Don in this session.
2. What makes feedback different from paraphrasing and summarizing?
3. What are the risks involved with using feedback with a counselee?
4. Where did Don use feedback in this session? Do you think that Don used it appropriately?
5. If you were in Frank's shoes, how would you respond to Don's feedback? Explain your response.

### Vignette 6
### Interpretation

1. In the sixth vignette you saw a continuation of the session between Frank and Don. What were you thinking as you watched the exchange between Frank and his counselor?
2. If you were in Frank's shoes, how would you feel? What was it about the session that elicited those feelings?
3. Was the use of interpretation well-timed and appropriate to the situation? Explain your response.
4. While Frank's response is not recorded, how do you anticipate he would have reacted? Why would he respond this way?
5. How would you have reacted to the counselor's interpretation and use of metaphor? Why do you think that you would respond this way?

### Vignette 7
### Confrontation

1. When you were learning about confrontation was the definition offered in the text different from your own prior to reading Chapter 7?

If so, what unique characteristics separated the book's definition from your own?

2. In what circumstances should confrontation be used? Did Denise use it appropriately? Why or why not?

3. In the seventh vignette, you saw one example of how confrontation can be used in a session. How do you think that Colleen would respond to this question? Explain your answer. How would you respond if you were in Colleen's shoes?

4. As you watched the video, did you recognize the opportunity to employ confrontation before Denise's final question? If you did, what, apart from knowing that the vignette dealt with confrontation, tipped you off?

### Vignette 8
### Self-Disclosure

1. In the eight vignette we saw our favorite counselor, Ryan attempt to use the skill of self-disclosure with Mariah. What did you observe about Ryan's interaction with Mariah? What would you do differently? Explain your rationale.

2. Compare Ryan's self-disclosure with the criteria outlined in the DISCLOSE model. Identify areas of similarity and dissimilarity between Ryan's application and the model.

3. How would you feel if you were Mariah? How would you react to Ryan if he made this statement to you in a counseling session?

4. Compare and contrast Ryan's self-disclosure with Denise's interaction with Colleen. How were they different?

5. What aspects of the DISCLOSE model did Denise incorporate into her conversation with Colleen? Identify two that stood out to you.

6. If you were Colleen, how would you react to Denise's self-disclosure? Explain your response.

### Vignette 9
### Immediacy

1. In the ninth vignette, you saw a couple of examples of immediacy. If you found yourself in each of these scenarios, would you find it easier to model immediacy with Charlie or Colleen? Explain your choice.

2. As you viewed the interaction between Colleen and Denise, what feelings did you experience? Why do you think that you felt the way that you did?

3. A common feature of observational learning is the presence of an internal dialogue or stream of thought. What were you thinking as you watched the exchange between Colleen and Denise? Reflecting upon question 2, do you find that your thoughts impacted your emotions?
4. As you followed the dialogue between Denise and Colleen, how did Denise transition from Colleen's anger about her probation to her sense that Denise viewed their relationship as a business rather than therapy?

## Recommended Reading

Derlega, V. J., & Berg, J. H. (1987). *Self-disclosure: Theory, research, and therapy*. New York City, NY: Springer.

> This book offers wonderful insights into the dynamics of self-disclosure. It discusses the neuroscience, psychology, and sociological aspects of self-disclosure in the counseling process.

# Chapter 8

# Basic Skills: Terminating the Counseling

*"Termination of services is an event of therapy that occurs with greater frequency than any other aspect of the therapeutic relationship"* (Rappleyea, Harris, White, & Simon, 2009, p. 12).

*"Then they all wept freely, and fell on Paul's neck and kissed him, sorrowing most of all for the words which he spoke, that they would see his face no more. And they accompanied him to the ship"* (Acts 20:37–38, NKJV).

## CHAPTER OBJECTIVES

» To understand the critical role that termination plays in the therapeutic journey

» To provide insight into why ending the helping relationship is difficult

» To delineate the different types of termination and their implication for practice

» To discuss the keys to understanding counselee readiness for termination

» To discuss the use of making referrals and denote guidelines for making referrals

» To foster clinical understanding of basic termination techniques and skills

## CHAPTER OUTLINE

L ike other parts of the therapeutic journey, the termination of the helping process should be considered as a separate phase rather than just a pronouncement of the completion of counseling (Kramer, 1990). In fact termination is itself an intervention strategy that helps the counselee adjust to a new life situation without reliance on a counselor. The activities associated with termination allow for gains in the counseling to be consolidated and an opportunity for the counselee to work on issues of separation and loss (Timberlake & Cutler, 2001).

The process of counseling could be likened to surgery. For the surgeon, closure signifies the end of the surgery. Without closure the body would struggle to heal itself; the raw wound would likely become infected. On closure, the surgeon relies on the patient's body to begin healing the wound. Like medical patients, counselees experience dramatic internal and external changes as a result of counseling. To terminate the counseling abruptly would be similar to a surgeon dismissing the patient from the operating room without closing the wound (Aten et al., 2009).

Yet the ending phase of counseling has received far less attention in the literature on counseling than other phases of the journey (Joyce, Piper, Ogrodniczuk, & Klein, 2006). Even in basic skills textbooks, the topic of termination is noticeably absent, leaving novice counselors forced to figure out the termination process on their own (Schlesinger, 2005). Gladding

(2009) believes that the process of termination is seldom discussed in the literature because it is associated with a sense of loss and is supposedly not directly related to the skills that facilitate the helping relationship.

On the other hand Yalom (1980) described the termination process, if properly understood and managed, as an important force in the instigation of change. We agree wholeheartedly. For that reason, we have dedicated this chap. to help equip you in finishing the journey well. We will explore the process of ending, the kinds of termination, how to make referrals, and techniques to employ in terminating counseling services.

## THE FUNCTIONS OF TERMINATION

The word *termination* can evoke a wide array of feelings in people. Consider how the word *termination* is used in common language: women terminate pregnancies (i.e., the elimination of a baby in the womb), people terminate bugs, and workers terminate contracts. While the word might not be the best to capture the end of the therapeutic journey, it does address key therapeutic functions.

Gladding (2009) offers counselors-in-training three specific reasons for having a formal termination session. First, it signals that something has ended. The ending of anything is difficult for most people (Capuzzi & Gross, 2007). Talking openly about the ending of a relationship or the cutting off of contact with someone is unpleasant at best. Life is a series of hellos and good-byes (Gladding, 2009), and we tend to handle hellos much better than good-byes. We seek to make the ultimate ending of a relationship (death) as tolerable as possible by funerals. Endings are often framed in ways to minimize the discomfort.

The same tendencies that beset human relationships outside of counseling are often brought into the counseling office. Counseling is an intense relationship that brings two strangers together around issues that are highly personal and intimate to one of the strangers. Counselors and counselees alike often ignore the fact that termination is coming, because unlike typical relationships the helping relationship is designed to end (Bertolino & O'Hanlon, 2002; Goldberg, 1986).

The loss of the helping relationship can be difficult for both. For the counselee, the ending of services might trigger issues of abandonment, reenacting a painful experience. It may evoke feelings of grief that an important relationship is ending. Some counselees may even become angry with the counselor for terminating the sessions. Counselees may resist the termination process, fearful that they may not be able to make it on their own. Counselees might insist on more sessions in order to work on their issues. At times there will be a resurgence of previously addressed issues or new issues may arise in a subconscious attempt to extend the counseling process. Some counselees end counseling abruptly as a means of taking control of the termination process.

As the counselor you too may struggle with the ending of services. Likely you have enjoyed success with the counselee and do not desire to see your time together end (Young, 2010). Some counselees give awesome encouragement and positive feedback, being very appreciative of your efforts. Because we care about our counselees, we might worry about the counselee's ability to make it on his or her own. We may also be insecure about our effectiveness, wondering if we have adequately equipped our counselee to handle life issues. If the counselee chooses to end services before we are ready, we may question our abilities and may feel inadequate or rejected. During your practicum and internship, your supervisor will help you through the process of learning how to let go.

Second, termination is a way of encouraging ongoing therapeutic changes (Gladding, 2009). The therapeutic expedition deals with moving toward health and wholeness. The changes in thinking, feeling, and behaviors that have been gained through the process need to be consolidated in this final leg of the journey, allowing the counselee to live out those changes. Along this line Gladding (1990, cited in Gladding, 2009) artfully states that the termination phase provides an "opportunity to put 'insights into actions'" (p. 130). The last leg of the journey allows for making course corrections as new behaviors are further implemented and become the counselee's new way of being.

Third, termination reminds both the counselor and the counselee that growth has occurred (Gladding, 2009). During the termination phase, changes are reviewed and reinforced, solidifying the new ways of being. Gladding sums up the role that change plays in a counselee's life: "Having achieved a successful resolution to a problem, a counselee now has new insights and abilities that are stored in memory and may be recalled and used on occasions" (p. 130).

To Gladding's (2009) three reasons for the termination phase, we would add a fourth: It serves to celebrate what God has done. In the Old Testament great victories were marked and celebrated with a concert of joy for God's marvelous works for His people. As most 12-step groups offer chips and medallions to mark the participant's success, we suggest that the counselee find some memento to symbolize the work of God. Remember to allow the termination phase of the expedition to be a time of joy.

## KINDS OF TERMINATION

Termination has been described as the planned conclusion of effective counseling, not because of circumstances of arbitrary or unavoidable interruption (Martin & Schurtman, 1985). Yet the literature seems to present many variations of the ending of counseling under the rubric of termination, including both abrupt and planned endings. Counseling can be terminated by any party for any number of reasons that might or might not signal effective help. Ideally, however, termination will be a joint decision on the part of both the counselor and the counselee. This section discusses two broad types of terminations—those initiated by the counselee and those initiated by the counselor.

### Counselee-Initiated Terminations

Ogrodniczuk, Joyce, and Piper (2005) define "counselee-initiated termination" as the counselee's choice to end the process in opposition to both the counselor's recommendation and in violation of the mutual initial agreement between the counselor and counselee. Counselee-initiated terminations are a frequent problem in counseling (Barrett, Chua, Crits-Christoph, Gibbons, & Thompson, 2008; Renk & Dinger, 2002); estimates suggest this occurs between 30 and 60 percent of the counseling sessions (Clarkin & Levy, 2004).

Learning that one's counselee is not coming back may prompt a number of troubling thoughts in many counselors: "Is the counselee dissatisfied with my services?" "Have I missed my counselee's readiness for termination?" "What should I have done differently?" The timing of the counselee's choice to end the counseling can play a pivotal role in the reason for termination and in your response to it. Those counselees who terminate before the first session or after the first interview represent a set of issues different from those who terminate well into the process (Barrett, Chua, Crits-Christoph, Gibbons, & Thompson, 2008). Often these endings are easier for counselors to accept than those that occur after the counselor and counselee have been working together for a while.

#### Kinds of counselee-initiated terminations.

All counseling ethics codes mention the fact that counselees are self-determining and have the right for autonomy. The right of the counselee to dictate counseling exists from the beginning to the end of the services. Since counselees come to counseling services of their own accord, they can also end them at their choosing.

All counselors are well acquainted with "surprise endings" to their counseling efforts; we have often been caught off guard by our counselees' announcements that they do not plan to return. Several different expressions are used to describe a counselee who ends services in this way: "unilateral termination," "discontinuing," "premature terminations," "attrition," or "therapeutic dropouts." Regardless of the words used, the result is the same; the counselee has decided no longer to attend counseling sessions.

Hatchett and Park (2003) define premature termination as occurring when a "counselee has left therapy before obtaining a requisite level of improvement or completing therapy goals" (p. 227). In short the counselee unilaterally ends the counseling before you wanted it to end. Although some suggest that counselees might end counseling without much forethought or even without notifying the counselor (Allgood, Parham, Salts, & Smith, 1995; Renk & Dinger, 2002), research shows that even one last session can be helpful (Young, 2010).

Pekarik (1992) discusses three reasons counselees terminate prematurely: (a) problem improvement, (b) dissatisfaction with treatment, and (c) environmental obstacles. Research seems to indicate that while counselors might consider the termination premature, counselees do not necessarily see their counseling as incomplete or as having failed (Hynan, 1990; Pekarik, 1992). Other reasons counselees terminate prematurely are lack of motivation (Rosenbaum & Horowitz, 1983) and resistance (Lane, 1984).

Research has shown that counselees who prematurely terminate report a higher number of depressive symptoms and had fewer sessions (Rainer & Campbell, 2001). Another predictor of premature termination involves the counselee's expectations for the duration of counseling (Pekarik, 1992); those who believe that counseling should be brief generally terminate prematurely. Research has also related premature termination to the counselee's stage of change according to the Transtheoretical Model (TTM; Prochaska & DiClemente, 1984; Prochaska, DiClemente, & Norcross, 1992; Prochaska & Velicer, 1997) (see chap. 12, "Strategies for Bringing About Changes"). According to Derisley and Reynolds (2000), those counselees who enter counseling in the precontemplation or contemplation stage have a tendency to terminate prematurely.

Most counselee-initiated terminations are premature, some of which are covert terminations and others are "doorknob" terminations.

### *Covert terminations.*

Premature termination can occur without a word being spoken by the counselee. A counselee may send the message that he is discontinuing the counseling process by either canceling or not showing up for appointments. Adding frustration for the counselor, some counselees will reschedule only to cancel or not show up again.

A counselee may use the covert type of termination for several reasons. First, he might be a fairly new counselee who is not truly committed to the counseling process (Wachtel, 2002). He is more of a customer than a counselee. An established counselee is less likely to terminate in this way, especially if the helping relationship has been a safe haven. When an established counselee uses this type of termination, the intent, often out of awareness, is to send the counselor a message (Bostic, Shadid, & Blotcky, 1996; Joyce, Piper, Ogrodniczuk, & Klein, 2006). It is likely a passive-aggressive approach to handling distressing feelings connected with the helping relationship or the counselee's normal way of distancing himself in any relationship. If a counselee fails to show or has repeated cancellations, it is important to try to determine the reason. We recommend directly asking the counselee if he plans to reschedule, and if he has rescheduled, if he believes he will keep the appointment. If the counselee states that he does not plan to return, then ask him for one more appointment to discuss the reason for termination and to tie up loose ends. This policy can be included on the Consent to Treatment form.

### *"Doorknob" terminations.*

Whereas the covert terminator ends services in silence, the doorknob terminator ends verbally. Occasionally we have encountered counselees who ambush us at the end of a session with the news that they are not returning. Often such behavior is the result of manipulative tendencies (as is common in Borderline Personality Disorder), in which the upper hand in the helping relationship is sought for various reasons. In such instances it is not wise to extend the counseling session to explore the counselee's reason for abruptly terminating the counseling. Let the counselee know that you are uncomfortable about accepting that decision without having an opportunity to discuss it. Invite the counselee to return for one more session in which you can focus on ending the counseling process. Moursund (1985) recommends saying to the counselee, "I'm sorry that you didn't tell me sooner, because I think it's important that we discuss this. I'd like you to come back one more time. Please take a couple of days to think about it; if you do decide to come in, call me and confirm your appointment. I'll hold your time open until . . ." (p. 99).

### Responding to counselee-initiated terminations.

In response to counselee-initiated termination, we offer an acrostic **DROPOUTS** that gives recommendations for mitigating against premature terminations (see Table 8.1). First, avoid **Delays** ("D") in seeing counselees (Young, 2010). The longer a counselee waits to see a counselor the greater is the chance that he will not come or return to counseling. When possible, return counselee phone calls on the same day you receive them.

When a counselee terminates counseling early in the journey, it is wise to call the counselee to process the **Reason** ("R") for ending the counseling (Young, 2010). As discussed, the counselee may terminate counseling for any of several reasons. A number of these issues might be redressed in order to help the counselee continue working on unresolved issues.

| Table 8.1 |
| --- |
| *DROPOUTS: How to Mitigate Against Premature Termination* |
| **D** = avoid **Delays** in seeing counselees |
| **R** = process the **Reasons** for termination |
| **O** = offer an **Orientation** session |
| **P** = do not **Process** the counselee through many channels |
| **O** = **Order** or contract the minimum number of sessions |
| **U** = be **Uncommon** in going the extra mile |
| **T** = use **Triggers** to motivate counselees to attend |
| **S** = consider the counselee's **Stage** of change |

Third, before initiating counseling you might consider providing an **Orientation** ("O") to counselees about counseling and offer them information about your qualifications (Young, 2010). You might give them a sheet that describes your qualifications and how you conduct counseling. We speak about role induction in chap. 9 ("Managing the Counseling Session") as a means of acquainting counselees with your expectations. We include this information in our Initial Consent form.

Young (2010) suggests that counselees not be **Processed** ("P") through several channels; in other words avoid having the counselee seen by several professionals such as an intake counselor or screened by an administrative assistant. Revealing yourself to one person is hard enough, let alone several people.

The "O" stands for **Ordering** or contracting with the counselee the number of sessions (Hatchett, 2004; Young, 2010). In settings where counselees might be expected to dropout early (e.g., because of possibly being court ordered), we have found it helpful to contract with counselees for a set number of sessions. When counselees believe they do not have much choice about coming to counseling, it is helpful to create an agreement on the minimum number of sessions to attend. Setting the number of required sessions might increase the possibility that the counselee will stick with the process. However, on the other hand this might limit your opportunity to make a greater impact.

In cases where the counselee decides to terminate the sessions before her goals are achieved, be **Uncommon** ("U") in going the extra mile (Young, 2010). Interestingly, the literature discusses the benefits of what we know to be a biblical concept, of going beyond expectations to meet a need. Young suggests making it easy for counselees to return by agreeing with their idea of interrupting counseling and by inviting them to return at a later date. You might attempt to set up a follow-up session as a means of giving counselees time to process the benefits of helping.

Young (2010) recommends that counselors motivate counselee attendance by using a **Trigger** ("T") to minimize counselee attrition. In our practices we have used our administrative assistant to call counselees one or two days before their appointment. You could also use email, texts, or other means to remind the counselee of the scheduled appointment.

Rainer and Campbell (2001) recommend considering the counselee's **Stage** ("S") of change to reduce dropouts. In chap. 12 ("Strategies for Bringing About Changes") we discuss the stages of change (Prochaska & DiClemente, 1984; Prochaska, DiClemente, & Norcross, 1992; Prochaska & Velicer, 1997) and how they provide insight into where counselees might be in their movement toward improvement. Those who are in the precontemplation and contemplation stages might be more likely to terminate counseling before achieving necessary goals. Using Motivational Interviewing (Miller & Rollnick, 2002) can help such counselees connect with the need for services.

## Counselor-Initiated Terminations

Generally speaking counselors initiate termination of services when they believe that their counselees have failed to make progress or when they believe that their counselees have achieved the mutually agreed-on therapeutic goals. Counselor-initiated terminations fall into four categories: contracted, forced, stalled, and goal-based.

### Contracted termination.

Assuming that you and the counselee have contracted for a fixed number of sessions, counseling will end when the sessions have been completed. Many counselors prefer to contract during the initial phase of counseling with counselees on how many sessions will be devoted to the helping process. In some cases this arrangement is out of necessity, such as a student who is leaving college at the end of the semester or a person who might be going to jail. It is best to acknowledge throughout the therapeutic process that these time constraints exist (Penn, 1990; Wachtel, 2002) so that counselees are well aware of how close they are to the destination.

### Forced termination.

A forced termination (Bostic, Shadid, & Blotcky, 1996) occurs when the counselor is completing her training. A forced end to the counseling process jeopardizes the therapeutic gains. Penn (1990), however, believes that forced endings may also provide opportunities for the counselee to do more work. Forced terminations may be due to counselor variables or counselee variables. One counselor variable might involve such ethical issues as counseling outside your level of competence or when there is a conflict of interest. Another counselor variable that might force termination occurs when a counselee relocates or leaves his place of employment.

Two counselee situations relate to forced termination. One situation is when a counselee is unable to pay for the sessions or other times a counselee may be uncooperative, and so the counselor must decide whether to continue when the counselee is violating the therapeutic contract.

### Stalled termination.

A stalled termination occurs when the counselee is simply not making any progress. In contrast with a forced termination in which the counselee is violating therapeutic agreements, the counselee might be giving her best effort but not seeing any benefit from the sessions. All ethical codes require that counselors refer counselees when they are no longer benefiting from counseling. Even though the counselee might want to continue, you may believe that services will not be beneficial for the counselee at this time.

### Goal-based termination.

The preferred form of termination is when the counseling has been successful, that is, when the counselee has obtained what she wanted from it. The litigious tendency of many counselees requires that counselors demonstrate that adequate services have been provided regardless of the number of contracted sessions. When the counseling goals have been met, counselor and counselee can both celebrate the accomplishments.

## TERMINATION AND READINESS

How can a counselor know when a counselee is ready for termination? Terminating services too soon can jeopardize the gains that have been made. Or waiting too long may incur needless costs for the counselee. Actually it is unethical to provide services from which the counselee cannot benefit. Knowing when a counselee is ready to finish is an essential competency that all effective counselors possess.

Sciscoe (1990, as cited in Young, 2010) offers five questions to ask when assessing counselee readiness for termination:

1. Is the presenting problem under control?
2. Has the counselee reduced the initial level of distress by developing better coping skills?
3. Has the counselee achieved greater self-awareness and better relationships?
4. Are life and work more enjoyable for the counselee?
5. Does the counselee now feel capable of living without the therapeutic relationship?

Whereas the first four questions address outcome-related issues, the last question addresses counselee self-efficacy. While you might believe a counselee is ready and able to stand on his or her own, the counselee might feel insecure about his or her ability to maintain change. This means that you must help the counselee think about her confidence to stand on her own.

Counselors generally believe that counselee self-reliance is desirable, that healthy people are not dependent on the counselor or on others (Young, 2010). Christian counselors, too, want counselees not to be dependent on them or others. Instead counselors want their counselees to develop an attitude of reliance on God. One of the most beautiful aspects of Christianity is to know that we are leaving our Christian counselees in the hands of the One who created us and whose plans are to prosper us and give us a future (Jer 29:11).

In the initial phases of counseling, counselees tend to be dependent on the counselor for help with the concern or concerns that prompted them to seek help. The work of the middle phases of counseling is to help counselees develop a dependence on God. Though a counselee might begin to develop a dependency on the counselor, the counseling relationship, no matter how intense, is designed to be temporary, and ultimate dependency needs to be placed on God. Psalm 20:7 says, "Some trust in chariots and some in horses, but we trust in the name of the LORD our God" (NIV). Our reliance is to be on God, not mankind.

When counseling goals have been met, the need for the intense relationship diminishes to the point of being unnecessary. At times the experience of ending the helping relationship is met with gratitude and satisfaction. Other times separating from such an intense relationship is not easy for the counselee or the counselor (Moursund, 1985). Both of us have felt close to particular counselees so that the parting was indeed sorrowful. The termination was like leaving a good friend. Though it might seem that a friendship is ending, we remind ourselves that counseling is based not on friendships, but on relationships rooted in choice and mutuality. Counseling is a contractual relationship, whereas friendships are a covenantal relationship. We discussed this aspect of counseling in chap. 2 ("The Fundamentals of Helping").

## MAKING REFERRALS

It is impossible to help everyone. Though Paul spoke of being all things to all people (1 Cor 9:19–22), counselors cannot be all things to all counselees. Being an effective helper with every kind of counselee is impossible. The many problems that unfold in a counselor's office means that no counselor can excel in treating every need (Leigh, 1998).

So counselors often need to make referrals. A referral involves transitioning the counselee to another resource that is equipped to help. Counselors need to learn how to refer counselees to other resources. In discussing the skill of referral Gladding (2009) considers the when, who, and how.

### When to Make a Referral

When should you make a referral? When are referrals more likely to occur? What issues are involved in the timing of a referral? Basic to making referrals is the skill of knowing when (Gladding, 2009).

Several factors suggest when a referral might be necessary. For one thing it will be ethically imperative for you to make a referral when you do not have the level of competence to be an effective helper with a particular counselee. Since no one can be skilled in dealing with every kind of problem, it becomes necessary to refer those individuals who have problems or issues that are outside your level of competence. For example counselees with significant paranoid thoughts, psychotic symptoms, or manic behavior will necessitate a referral to someone who can help the counselee with medications. It is imperative that you know your limitations and approach the work of helping with great humility. You must accept the fact that you will not always be able to help everyone, even if the counselee prefers to work with you.

Another reason for referral might be that the counselee has a problem for which a local expert would be far more effective. It is ethically responsible to connect certain counselees with those who are better trained and equipped to serve those special needs. For example you might not have some expertise in dealing with sexually abused children, whereas a colleague might have more extensive experience with that population.

Another personal limitation involves the kind of people with whom you will or will not be effective. At times you will encounter counselees with whom you will not connect. A personality clash might occur between you and the counselee, and that will hinder progress. We both have experienced such times in our counseling, and though we wanted to help, we knew that the helping relationship would not be a safe haven for the counselee. In a few cases the relationship was an unsafe place for us.

Particularly in small communities you may encounter conflicts of interest that will necessitate a referral. You might be contacted by a potential counselee who turns out to be your child's schoolteacher or a person with whom you serve on a church committee. The possibilities of conflict of interest are numerous. Regardless of the nature of the conflict, when someone with whom you have a preexisting relationship desires your services, it is unethical to work with that person. At such times make an appropriate referral to ensure that the counselee receives competent help.

Occasionally counseling becomes unproductive and the counselee fails to make any noticeable progress. When counseling has stalled, it might be necessary to make a referral to someone who has either the right expertise or right skill set to generate positive movement for the counselee. Admitting that you are not making progress can be difficult, even though the counselee too may feel "stuck." You may be tempted at such times to blame the counselee for the lack of progress. But the key to such situations is not to take it personally and to recognize that many factors might be hindering progress. Acting out of love for our counselees requires doing what is necessary to help them. Before terminating services because of stalled progress, it may be well to consult with a supervisor or colleague to ensure that you have allowed ample opportunity for progress to occur.

Also a referral might be necessary because a counselee would benefit from psychological or neuropsychological testing, medical care, a psychotropic evaluation, or hospitalization. This does not necessarily mean you are abandoning the counselee to another referral source. Instead you are arranging for adjunct or temporary services to address a specific issue. Referring a counselee to a psychiatrist for medication evaluation, for example, will require that you get a release of information so that you may inform the doctor of the reason for your referral.

## To Whom to Refer

To make appropriate referrals you will need to have a working knowledge of service providers in your area. Referrals can be made to social agencies, parachurch organizations, 12-step groups, consumer credit services, and the full range of mental-health providers. Counselors should get to know the psychiatrists in their area and how they approach the use of medications. Some psychiatrists are quick to prescribe, whereas others are more willing to wait and see if the counselee can resolve the symptoms without medication. Psychologists provide a valuable resource for assessment, especially neuropsychologists who are trained in evaluating a person's neurological functioning. You might also refer a parent to a family or marriage counselor while you are working with the child. Knowing the expertise of providers can help you connect counselees to those who can offer the most effective treatment.

## Referral Guidelines and Techniques

The acrostic **REFER** (see Table 8.2) gives five guidelines that will help facilitate effective referrals. Making sound referrals means knowing local and specialty **Referral** ("R") sources. Become well acquainted with the wide range of services in your area and with service providers.

| Table 8.2 |
|---|
| *REFER: How to Refer* |
| **R** = know **Referral** sources |
| **E** = create an **Expectation** that referrals are possible |
| **F** = **Foster** a **Full** ("F") understanding of why a referral is needed |
| **E** = **Encourage** the counselee to follow-through |
| **R** = determine the counselee's **Response** to the referral |

We have made lunch dates with local providers as a means of getting to know them. You can learn about mental-health providers from close colleagues, but getting your own impression is best. When you begin providing services, build up a sound referral resource file, and build relationships with local professionals and social agencies to facilitate better referrals.

Create an **Expectation** ("E") with informed consent that referrals are possible and in some cases likely. Chap. 9 ("Managing the Counseling Session") discusses the value of informed consent. Counselees should be aware of the fact that referrals might be recommended or required, depending on particular circumstances. It also helps to note such possibilities in your closing summary. Consider the following example:

> "Bob, you have spoken about not being able to sleep for some time, your lack of appetite, low sex drive, and loss of energy. Those are all symptoms that indicate that you might be depressed to the point where medication might be necessary. I've found that counseling does not work quite as well when someone's brain chemistry has become depleted because of depression. I think we might want to consider a referral to a psychiatrist who can evaluate you and determine if medication might be necessary. I know that you are leery of medications, so we should approach this decision with caution. Let's talk more about it next week. In the meantime pray about it to see what God might be leading you to do."

**Foster** ("F") a **Full** understanding of why you believe a referral is warranted. Take your time, and use sound listening skills to process with the counselee the reason and nature of the referral. If services are being terminated because of your inability or unwillingness to continue services, be sure that in the referral or transfer of services you are not personally rejecting or abandoning the counselee. Generally it is wise to discuss the risks with your counselee for not accepting a referral and offer at least two referral options. We recommend framing the reason in light of ensuring that the counselee obtains the best possible care. Consider the following dialogue. (CO = Counselor; CL = Counselee):

**CO:** *Sam, we have worked together for five sessions. As you might recall from our initial session we discussed how I operate as a counselor. Two expectations that I have for my counselees is that they keep appointments and do the weekly tasks that emerge out of each counseling session.*

**CL:** *Yes, I remember that, but I have been so busy with school and work that I haven't been able to get the homework done. Sometimes things happen that prevent me from keeping an appointment. I really want to continue our counseling though.*

**CO:** *It seems that you have been busy and that you have things that come up. That is something I certainly can relate to. I also appreciate your desire to continue our work together. We have spoken about this issue in previous sessions, and I'm feeling frustrated that I am not able to*

> *do my best work without your ability to follow through and keep appointments.*

**CL:** *What does that mean?*

**CO:** *As I mentioned in the Informed Consent that you read and signed at the beginning of counseling and as we have discussed in previous sessions, I will need to connect you with another counselor whose approach differs from mine. I'm disappointed about not being able to work with you, but I do appreciate the fact that you need to focus on other things right now. My approach will not work well with someone who does not have time to commit to the whole counseling process. It is important to me to get you with a person whose approach will maximize the chances that you will get what you need out of counseling.*

**CL:** *I understand, but I don't like this. I really wanted to continue with you.*

**CO:** *I'm very comfortable with you too. You and I have a good counseling relationship. I'm committed to your well-being, though I need to refer you to another professional.*

**CL:** *OK. Whom would you recommend?*

As you can see, this is not an easy conversation to have with a counselee. It is important to use active listening, to reflect feelings with empathy, and to maintain your boundary. To be sure the counselee understands the referral, coach him on what information he will need to tell the professional in order to get the proper help.

**Encourage** ("E") the counselee to follow through on the referral. How long you have been providing services might impact the counselee's willingness to accept a referral, especially when you are transferring your services to another provider. Research indicates that referrals are more likely to occur early in the process (Clarkin & Levy, 2004; Hatchett, 2004; Hynan, 1990; Leigh, 1998; Renk & Dinger, 2002). The longer counselees work with you the less likely they will be open to a referral. Once you establish a relationship with a counselee, he will be more reluctant to work with another person (Gladding, 2009).

Determine the counselee's **Response** ("R") to the referral. The overriding issue in making referrals is acting out of love or at least acting in accord with counselee welfare. Keeping your basic desire to help the counselee, follow up with him after the referral has been made. Ask questions such as, "How well did the appointment go?" "What did you think about her?"

## TERMINATION TECHNIQUES

Just as skills are necessary for the beginning and middle phases of the therapeutic expedition, they are also critical for finishing the journey. It is important to finish well. To equip you in this skill we will use an acrostic **TERMINATIONS** (see Table 8.3) to highlight twelve guidelines and techniques essential to ending counseling services effectively.

| Table 8.3 |
| --- |
| *TERMINATIONS: How to Use Termination* |
| **T** = **Talk** about **Termination** early |
| **E** = **Evaluate** progress according to the **Established** plan |
| **R** = consider the counselee's separation **Reactions** |
| **M** = **Moderate** or reduce the frequency of sessions |
| **I** = **Invite** the counselee to share his feelings about termination |
| **N** = **Notice** and **Name** your own feelings about termination |
| **A** = use **Active** listening and reflective statements to process the termination |
| **T** = review the major **Themes,** changes, and critical moments |
| **I** = be **Intentional** in affirming the counselee's changes |
| **O** = **Openly** acknowledge any unresolved areas |
| **N** = **Navigate** and **Note** any ethical issues |
| **S** = have follow-up appointments to **Sustain** change |

## Technique 1: Talk ("T") about Termination ("T") Early

Since separation is difficult, we need to help our counselees adjust and grow through life's transitions. Because of the painful process involved in terminating counseling, be proactively prepared and skilled at ending their services and discussing with the counselee that the counseling process is winding down. Make planning for termination a part of the therapeutic counseling process. Kramer (1990) argues that you need to be clear from the first contact that the intent of counseling is to help the counselee function without a counselor. In actuality the end of counseling begins with the first interview (Garfield, 1998; Hill & O'Brien, 1999; Kramer, 1990). Leslie

(2004) suggests including termination discussion on the Informed Consent. For example counselors would discuss reasons that might necessitate ending services, such as maximizing insurance coverage and the inability to come up with an alternate means of payment.

Since the destination is set by the mutually agreed-on goals, naturally the counseling ends when the goals have been met. Thus maintain awareness of the destination as you work with your counselee throughout the journey. You are ethically responsible to inform your counselees how long you will be available to work with them (Woody & Woody, 2001).

The amount of time needed to prepare a counselee for termination is generally related to the length of counseling (see Figure 8.1). Returning to the surgery analogy at the beginning of this chap., minimally invasive surgery requires little closure because the wound is small. Counseling that is brief is typically less "invasive," necessitating less preparation for termination (Pekarik, 1992; Schlesinger, 2005). A counselee who is seen for only six sessions to process an issue at one's place of employment will need far less preparation in ending the counseling than a sexual abuse survivor who has been in counseling about one year.

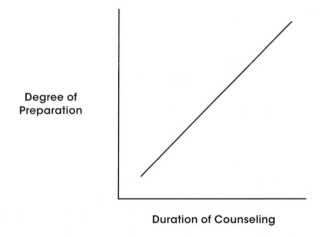

**Degree of Preparation**

**Duration of Counseling**

Figure 8.1. Relationship of preparation to the duration of counseling

## Technique 2: Evaluate ("E") Progress According to the Established ("E") Plan

Termination should be built into a well-constructed treatment plan. From the point that you and the counselee embark on the counseling journey it is important to provide accurate feedback about the counselee's improvement or lack thereof (Hatchett, 2004). Research indicates that monitoring counselee progress might encourage counselees to persist in counseling and lead to more effective outcomes (Lambert et al., 2001). Periodically revisit the map that you created together, helping the counselee to track his progress and refocus on the ultimate destination.

### Technique 3: Consider the Counselee's Separation Reactions ("R")

Consider the counselee's readiness in planning for and moving toward ending services (Gladding, 2009). Ivey and Ivey (2003) point out that the complexities of the world make it difficult to introduce new behavior into one's natural setting. An essential task then is to evaluate how well equipped the counselee is for termination. One factor to consider is the counselee's previous experiences with separation and his inner reactions to these experiences (Patterson & Eisenberg, 1983). Ending counseling is a loss for both counselees and counselors, which sometimes can revive unresolved issues from past losses (Capuzzi & Gross, 2007). If the helping relationship has been intense, expect reactions similar to those seen in the counselee in previous separations. People tend to react to attachment-related losses in similar ways. Realizing this tendency can help you cope with them effectively.

First, be clearly aware of the counselee's needs and wants (Patterson & Eisenberg, 1983). The counselor who is aware that counselees feel anxious and become resistant around the ending of helping services will be better prepared to respond appropriately. If the counselee inclines to be dependent, termination may significantly impact the counselee. Therefore explore what terminating the relationship will mean for the counselee.

Second, consider your own needs for feeling wanted, admired, or in control, and how that might affect the ending process. Nothing will provoke your feelings of inadequacy and generate insecurity reactions more than a counselee who wants to terminate prematurely. By recognizing what is going on with the counselee, you will be in a better position to understand and manage your own reactions.

### Technique 4: Moderate ("M") or Reduce the Frequency of Sessions

A useful idea in terminating counseling is to create more time between each session. Young (2010) refers to the process of reducing the frequency of counseling sessions as "fading." Young recommends spacing sessions out over one year. The dialogue below illustrates how to approach this topic with your counselee (CO = Counselor; CL = Counselee).

**CO:** *Carol, it is difficult to believe we have been working together for over nine months now.*

**CL:** *Wow, I can hardly believe that.*

**CO:** *I know. As people say, "time flies." In that time you have done a lot of hard work in facing difficulties from your past and confronting new challenges. It has been amazing what God has done in your life. Your progress has been excellent to the point where I believe we can begin to taper out our sessions to every other week and if that goes well perhaps to once a month for a couple of months. How does that sound?*

**CL:** *I think that would be great if you believe I'm ready for that.*

**CO:** *I do. I believe that will be the best method to ensure that you maintain the gains you have made and to see how well the changes generalize to other areas of your life.*

**CL:** *OK. I'm good with that, but what happens if I start struggling?*

**CO:** *That is a good question. Let's hope that doesn't happen too much, but if it does, we can reevaluate this plan and change it at any time. I'm not abandoning you, but I want to help you find that stability that has eluded you most of your life. If I'm constantly holding you up, you will not ever find it.*

**CL:** *Good. So we will get together then in two weeks.*

### Technique 5: Invite ("I") the Counselee to Share His Feelings about Termination

Invite the counselee to share how she is responding to the termination of counseling (Patterson & Eisenberg, 1983). Processing the counselee's inner experiences, thoughts, and feelings is an essential part of bringing about a healthy closure. Research indicates that counselees experience a wide range of feelings at the ending phase of counseling, including pride, self-respect, accomplishment, and loss (Baum, 2005; Hill, 2005; Wachtel, 2002). Counselees may also fear they will not be able to make it on their own. The counselee might be angry because of feeling abandoned by the counselor or because of losing an important relationship; this may especially be true in cases of forced terminations (Younggren & Gottlieb, 2008). Usually a sense of sadness is present over the ending of an important relationship.

One of the most significant aspects of the helping relationship is that the counselee can talk about and process her feelings regarding the fact that the counseling relationship is ending. Dealing explicitly with feelings about termination may give opportunity to explore new and important areas that have not been previously discussed. Many issues can be bound up in the termination process. Moursund (1985) writes, "These issues may relate directly to endings, partings, leaving, and being left; or they may involve other parts of the counselee's system which he has been reluctant to talk about but now, knowing that therapy will soon be over, he may be ready to deal with" (pp. 85–86). The goal is not to eliminate the afflicted feelings but to put them into a context that makes them tolerable. Though many painful feelings do exist around the ending of a helping relationship, the counselee might also feel joy, gratitude, and a sense of excitement about what lies ahead.

## Technique 6: Notice ("N") and Name ("N") Your Own Feelings about Termination

The counseling relationship is also intense for the counselor, and so terminating the sessions will likely generate a mix of feelings. The journey of counseling has highs and lows, laughter and sorrow, and moments of confusion and clarity. Share honestly with the counselee your response to the counseling experience (Patterson & Eisenberg, 1983). The skill of immediacy (see chap. 7, "Basic Skills: Giving Feedback") will prove useful here. Reviewing the course of counseling will help you and the counselee bring closure to the expedition.

Counselors who feel comfortable in self-reflection during the ending process serve as healthy models for their counselees (Aten et al., 2009). You can self-reflect by "thinking out loud" about your feelings in terminating the counseling venture. For example, "You know, Sharon, we have worked together for quite a while now. I've come to know you well and have enjoyed the journey we have taken together. It occurs to me just how much I'll miss meeting with you." Counselees can learn that it is normal to feel sad at the ending of counseling.

## Technique 7: Use Active ("A") Listening and Reflective Statements to Process the Termination

Chap. 5 ("Basic Skills: Creating a Connection") discussed at length how to listen actively, respond emphatically, and reflect meaningfully on the counselee's feelings. The same attending and listening skills that carried you along the journey to this point are more than capable of helping you with the counselee's kaleidoscope of feelings at this phase of the journey.

## Technique 8: Review the Major Themes ("T"), Changes, and Critical Moments

Review the major events of the counseling experience and bring the review into the present (Patterson & Eisenberg, 1983). Discuss major themes, changes, and critical moments, using focused summaries. Discuss the "before" and "after" picture of the counselee's situation. Reviewing the positive aspects of the journey helps enhance the positive changes.

## Technique 9: Be Intentional ("I") in Affirming the Counselee's Changes

Intentionally affirm and acknowledge the positive changes the counselee has accomplished (Patterson & Eisenberg, 1983). Maintaining change requires continual effort (Ivey & Ivey, 2003). In some cases changes get woven into the fabric of one's response patterns. Other times, however, intentionality is needed to keep moving forward. Recognizing and affirming the changes the counselee has made and the distress of change encourages the counselee to maintain the hard work.

## Technique 10: Openly ("O") Acknowledge Any Unresolved Areas

As human beings we are continually "under construction." We are never completely healthy and void of all unhealthy issues. Counseling cannot resolve every issue in a person's life. We would never finish with our counselees if we required them to be completely problem-free. We do not want our counselees to live under the illusion that they must be perfect and have everything together in order to function adequately in this world and to serve God faithfully and competently. We need to realize that loose ends will exist.

A helpful analogy for counseling is that of excavating at an archaeological site. An archaeologist recognizes that the purpose of digging is to unearth artifacts without destroying them. Dirt and debris is removed one layer at a time until the artifacts are exposed and laid bare. Once a treasure has been discovered, digging stops while the archaeologists painstakingly work to clear the debris and dirt away and carefully lift the finding from its tomb of soil. In a similar way counseling is a process of removing layer after layer of personality disorder or conflict. Counseling might unearth a number of significant "artifacts." However, these need not all be dealt with at the time.

Even if all the therapeutic goals have not been met in the counseling sessions, most likely progress has been made and the counselee can utilize other resources to help resolve other issues. The end of counseling does not necessarily mean the end of the counselee's personal journey toward wholeness and sanctification. If the counselee later decides that additional counseling would be beneficial, he or she can return to further excavate more personal artifacts.

## Technique 11: Navigate ("N") and Note ("N") Any Ethical Issues

Several ethical and legal issues surround the termination of services. You should record in a case file the issues related to termination (Mitchell, 2000). Failure to appropriately manage the process might result in ethical, legal, or psychological ramifications for both the counselee and the counselor. Realizing the level of risk arising from termination issues is critical to effective practice (Younggren & Gottlieb, 2008).

First, understand the difference between termination and counselee abandonment (Younggren & Gottlieb, 2008). Ethically a counselor can discontinue services if he does not believe the counselee is benefiting from the counseling or if the counselor is unable or unwilling to provide services. If the counselee has not achieved her therapeutic goals, the counselor should discuss referral and transfer of services to another professional. Abandonment occurs when the counselor abruptly ends services with little or no notice. Abandoning a counselee could be considered the equivalent of dereliction of duty; thus counselee abandonment has both ethical and legal ramifications. And consideration of one's counselees means giving them adequate time to prepare for termination. Make every effort to schedule appointments with counselees. Terminating a counselee ought not be done by a phone call or a written note without attempting to schedule a termination session (Woody & Woody, 2001). As noted in the section in this chap. on making good referrals, explain that the transfer of services does not mean that you are rejecting or abandoning the counselee. In fact we have found it useful to contact the counselee to ask how the appointment with the referral source went.

Ethical codes (e.g., AACC, 2004; ACA, 2005; see Appendixes A and B) are clear that counselors are to maintain appropriate boundaries from the initial phase of counseling through the termination phase. As the professional relationship is coming to an end, one's professionalism should not. Be clear and intentional to avoid boundary violations; maintaining professional boundaries promotes the counselee's trust. Sometimes, counselees will want to begin socializing with you once the counseling process is over. This may mean you will need to emphasize again the importance of boundaries, if they resurface at this phase of counseling.

Make it your practice to document who initiated the termination, the reasons, and the efforts you made to come to a mutual agreement regarding termination. If the counselee stops making appointments or does not show for an appointment, make an effort to contact the counselee and document your attempts (Woody & Woody, 2001). If you use a form letter, as we do, to send to counselees who fail to keep appointments or who abruptly stop services, be sure to keep a copy of the letter in your records. Mitchell (2000) recommends that you keep a written factual account of the termination process and the counselee's involvement in the process.

## Technique 12: Have Follow-up Appointments to Sustain ("S") Change

Respect and caring need not—and should not—terminate with the ending of counseling. An authentic and genuine invitation (as opposed to acting from obligation) for follow-up is a godly expression of love. Ivey and Ivey (2003) recommend having follow-up sessions in order to periodically check on the behavioral change. Many counselors fail to use follow-up as a therapeutic tool to help counselees monitor change and reinforce gains. There is no agreed-on schedule for establishing follow-up sessions, but typically such sessions may be scheduled one month to a year later.

Gladding (2009) delineated four specific methods of conducting follow-up sessions. One method is to invite the counselee to a session to discuss her progress. A less personal method is to conduct the follow-up by telephone. A third method is to send a letter asking the counselee about her progress. This method might be used when you have failed to reach the counselee by phone. For certain individuals and in particular settings, contact might be mandatory, and you may need to document your efforts to reach the counselee. A letter, especially a certified letter, provides ample documentation in most cases. A fourth method is to use a questionnaire to assess the counselee's status. Such a method can be used to also gather data on your counselee's satisfaction with services.

## CHAPTER SUMMARY

Ecclesiastes 7:8 says that "the end of a matter is better than its beginning" (NIV). However, human beings do not tend to handle endings well; people struggle to let go. Given the intimacies of the helping relationship, we believe it is wise to give as much attention to termination as to all phases of the helping process.

Helping services can end at the wish of the counselor or the counselee. Regardless of who might choose to end it, you are responsible to manage all aspects of the therapeutic expedition. An essential therapeutic task is to prepare the counselee for termination from the very beginning of the counseling sessions. Paying attention to the counselee's feelings and needs that surround termination, as well as staying in contact with your own feelings, will help you avoid unethical practice and it will help you process ending issues appropriately.

The termination phase of counseling allows you to assist counselees in maximizing therapeutic benefits. This can help counselees further the changes that have occurred through the counseling and can encourage them to develop long-range life goals.

Although many times a counselor will terminate counseling with counselees who have truly changed and benefited from counseling, sometimes the abrupt endings can plague therapeutic success. Facing the need to end a counseling relationship before goals have been achieved is unpleasant at best and may entail risk. Be able to know when services need to be ended and how ethically to handle a situation in which the counselee seeks to discontinue services before reaching the agreed-on goals. Employ sound helping skills in your terminations and maintain ethical behavior throughout the process. When referrals are necessary, especially in cases of transferring services, it is important to use sound helping skills in broaching the subject with the counselee and in processing issues surrounding it.

Hopefully the ending of each helping series will be better than the beginning. And hopefully all your counseling relationships will end because of having reached the desired goals. The joy the counselor and the counselee experience at such times will make the calling into which you are investing your life worthwhile. When God comes through and delivers therapeutic successes, counselors experience joy not only for the counselee but also joy in Him.

## CHAPTER 8 ACTIVITIES

1. Describe how and why the termination phase of counseling is a vitally important form of intervention.
2. List and describe the different forms of termination discussed in this chap.
3. Watch the DVD vignette on termination. After watching the counselor demonstrate the skills, respond to each item below.
     a. One
     b. Two
     c. Three
     d. Four
4. Based on this chap. and the DROPOUTS acronym, how would you respond to a counselee-initiated termination?
5. You accidently schedule two counselees at the same time. One of the counselees understands and asks that you call him to reschedule and the other comes into your office, closes the door, yells at you, tells you that you are incompetent, and decides that he or she wants to terminate the counseling. Write a script detailing a simulated dialog you might have with the counselee in response to this.
6. What are some questions to consider when assessing whether a counselee is ready to terminate counseling?
7. How and when should you make a referral?
8. What are some things you can do to create a referral list of colleagues in your community who are gifted and competent in diverse areas of treatment?
9. What are the 12 guidelines and techniques given in this chap. that are essential to effectively ending counseling services?
10. Write a general plan for effectively and ethically terminating treatment with your counselees.

## Vignette Questions

*Vignette 10*
*Silence*

1. In the tenth vignette you saw Don deal with Charlie over a very painful loss in Charlie's life. Place yourself in Don's shoes; would you be comfortable with silence while Charlie cried? Why or why not?
2. Now place yourself in Charlie's shoes; what would the therapist's silence communicate to you? Explain your response.

3. After reviewing the scenario, did silence move the counseling process forward? If so, in what way did this occur?

4. If you found yourself in a similar situation, would silence be a natural response to your counselee's grief? If not, how would you respond?

5. For those of you who found yourselves uncomfortable with silence, why do you think that this is so? If you were comfortable with the silence, what characteristics allow you to accept silence as a viable option when faced with a human being in pain?

### Vignette 11
### Referral

1. The eleventh vignette illustrated one means of making a referral. How well did Don utilize the REFER model? Which one of the steps had the most impact on Frank during the session? Explain your answer.

2. Why do you think that the referral process can be a source of anxiety for some counselees?

3. What can you do, as a counselor, to assist your counselees in managing their anxiety as it relates to the referral process?

4. Take a moment and consider who you might utilize as a referral source. What steps might you take to create and maintain such a list?

5. Identify the specialty areas and specific professionals in those areas who you would consider using as referral sources. How long is your list? Does it accurately represent a reasonable number of potential referral sources? Why or why not?

### Vignette 12
### Termination

1. How did you feel as you watched vignette twelve? Expound upon your emotional reaction; why do you think that you felt the way that you did after viewing this session?

2. Recall the thoughts that were going through your mind as you watched this vignette; how would you characterize them (were they positive, negative, or unrelated)? Upon examination, what did these thoughts communicate to you?

3. How did Denise integrate the four termination skills (reviewing themes, being intentional, acknowledging unresolved areas, and sustaining change) into the session? Did it feel natural to you? Why or why not?

4. Which of the four themes appeared to be the most meaningful to Shannon? Support your response.

5. Which of the four themes was the most meaningful to you? Why do you think that this was the case?

## Recommended Reading

Leigh, D. A. (1998). *Referral and termination issues for counselors: Professional skills for counselors series*. Thousand Oaks, CA: Sage.

> Leigh's book stresses the practical, ethical, and legal issues surrounding referral and termination of counseling. She addresses common reasons for referral and discusses typical mistakes made in the process. While the book is somewhat dated and might be difficult to get, it is a highly useful book to read.

# The Helping Process

The previous section focused on basic helping skills. This section focuses on the helping process itself. The intention is to help you apply the counselor skills to the tasks necessary in successful counseling.

In chap. 9 ("Managing the Counseling Session") we seek to prepare you to lead the actual journey by reviewing basic tools in the process. Beginning counselors want to know what to say or what to do in given situations. While sound counselor training prepares students with principles and decision-processes to navigate the turbulent waters of counseling, counselors must also ask what God wants to accomplish in the counselee. Ultimately counselors must learn to become sensitive to the working of the Holy Spirit in knowing which strategies to employ. That is not a skill that can be taught; it is a sensitivity that can be learned in deep communion with God. Your ability to sense God's leading is honed in your quiet time and spiritual development. All that we can provide is some general tools, strategies, and techniques that the Holy Spirit might lead you to use.

This chapter presents a model for counseling known as the AIM model. We then provide an overview of how a counseling session is sequenced and discuss the importance of giving an ethical introduction in the first counseling session. We dissect the entire counseling process into four phases and categorize the first section into four stages. Establishing goals to focus the counseling is also an early marker in the therapeutic journey. We also discuss how to devise clear counseling goals and how to set an agenda for each session.

Chap. 10 ("Conducting an Assessment") prepares you in one of the fundamental counselor tasks, namely, assessing counselees. We discuss how to explore the counselee's concerns and background, known as his psychosocial history. We present a rationale for conducting a psychosocial history and explain the structure and phases of the psychosocial interview. We explain each phase of the assessment process and educate you in how to write the information into a report. Then we suggest practical examples to help you develop your interview skills.

Chap. 11 ("Case Conceptualization and Treatment Planning") gives you tools to conceptualize the information you are gathering from your counselees. We discuss the importance of case conceptualization and show you how to dissect your counselees' remarks. We reintroduce you to the AIM model and how it fits into conceptualization and treatment planning.

People seek counseling because they want to address some specific issue in their lives. By definition they desire to change. Many people have tackled the concept of human change, but we want to focus on a specific mindset that will help you become an effective change agent. Chap. 12 ("Strategies for Bringing About Changes") is organized around questions associated with change. If you do not have a conceptualization of how people change and what people need to change into, you will flounder in your helping efforts.

There is no "approved list" of Christian counseling techniques. The traditional helping processes, skills, and techniques have reached a remarkable degree of acceptance by all kinds of Christian helpers. Be open to various strategies that might be helpful to the counselee. There are no restrictions on the possible techniques counselors can try except those that would not be for the benefit of the counselee or those that would violate ethical and biblical principles. Experimentation is an essential part of a counselor's job. The systematic testing of strategies is necessary so that the counselor can improve. Given the complexities of human nature, no one perspective will be entirely adequate to address everyone. This textbook would be unwieldingly long if we attempted to discuss every technique that addresses emotional, behavioral, cognitive, and spiritual issues.

Rather than giving a broad array of techniques, chap. 13 ("General Helping Strategies") discusses five helping techniques that will be useful in counseling including the miracle question, homework, humor, metaphor, and journaling.

Chap. 14 ("Spiritual Strategies") addresses one of the most critical areas of promoting change, namely, spirituality. This chapter explores the relationship between the physical, psychological, and spiritual dimensions. To ground you in these strategies we discuss ethical issues, the facets of spiritual assessment, and particular strategies for spiritual integration.

Chap. 15 ("Professional Issues in Helping") represents the end of our educational journey. In this chap. we deal with what it means to be a professional. We discuss issues such as professionalism, ethical and legal issues in the helping process, record keeping, diversity, and the need to develop as a counselor. We hope that your journey toward becoming an effective helper will be seen as a process, not a destination, one toward which you are always working.

## Chapter 9

# Managing the Counseling Session

*"Since helping is such a common human experience, training in both solving one's own problems and helping others solve theirs should be as common as training in reading, writing, and math. Unfortunately, this is not the case"* (Egan, 2002, p. 3).

*"Now there are varieties of gifts, but the same Spirit. And there are varieties of ministries, and the same Lord. There are varieties of effects, but the same God who works all things in all persons. But to each one is given the manifestation of the Spirit for the common good. For to one is given the word of wisdom through the Spirit, and to another the word of knowledge according to the same Spirit; to another faith by the same Spirit, and to another gifts of healing by the one Spirit, and to another the effecting of miracles, and to another prophecy, and to another the distinguishing of spirits, to another various kinds of tongues, and to another the interpretation of tongues. But one and the same Spirit works all these things, distributing to each one individually just as He wills"* (1 Cor 12:4–11, NASB).

## CHAPTER OBJECTIVES

» To give an overview of the four phases of the first intake session

» To give an overview of the four phases of the helping sessions

» To describe how to discuss ethical issues with the counselee

» To delineate how to establish appropriate goals with the counselee

» To describe how to set an agenda for counseling

264

» To introduce the Abide in Me (AIM) counseling model

» To describe the nine components of the AIM counseling model

» To present the five phases of the AIM counseling model

» To provide a case study of the AIM counseling model

## CHAPTER OUTLINE

---

**B**eginning counselors are typically concerned and uncertain as to what to do in counseling. And in fact they should be. Knowing how to manage the scope of counseling from beginning to end is foundational to being a counselor. You are the expert, and the counselee needs to feel secure in the fact that once faith is placed in you, you know what you are doing. Consider the concept of flying. When you get on an airplane, you place your confidence in the fact that the pilot is well trained. You take for granted that the pilot knows how to exit the airport, get you from your point of departure to your destination, navigate to the appropriate gate at the terminal, and respond to crisis situations. Likewise, when counselees enter your office, they presume that you know what to do each session and how to move them from their current problem to their desired state. This is what is meant by the "process" of counseling.

The word *process* means "going forward" (Adams, 1970). It refers to a series of interrelated steps that move toward a desired outcome. In our context it refers to how counseling works. It pertains to the nuts and bolts of counseling. Process captures the unfolding of a particular session and how the entire counseling proceeds. For these reasons, understanding the process of counseling is fundamental to helping your counselees.

In upcoming chaps. we will discuss in detail the basic skills of helping. But before we can proceed to those skills, we need to consider the overall picture of the process of counseling. Perhaps an analogy will show the relationship between the two. Consider the famous saying about not seeing the forest because of the trees; some people get so focused on the trees that they miss how each tree relates to the entire forest, of which they are a part. Anyone who has ever been lost in a forest can appreciate the value of having a map in order to get out of it. Other people in considering the layout of the forest might forget that it is comprised of individual trees that give shape and substance to it. The trees are the specific skills, interventions, and strategies that establish the forest. The skills and strategies of each counseling session constitute the helping process, the forest.

Our intent in this chap. is to acquaint you with the "terrain" of counseling, to give you a topographical map of the forest. First, we will present you with an aerial view of the counseling sessions from beginning to end. Second, we will discuss the sequencing that occurs from your first to last sessions. It is important to understand how you move through counseling if you are to manage the entire process. You must know where you are and where you are going. Third, we will describe the counselor's role in the helping process. Knowing what role you play will help you be clearer in your approach. Fourth, in addition to describing the course of counseling we will provide an overview of the flow that occurs in the first session and in a typical counseling session in general.

We also want to introduce you to a conceptual model to help you understand the broader perspective. In the previous chap. we discussed how counseling theories provide helpers with organized ways of understanding psychology and human development and how counseling models and interventions provide frameworks to guide helping work. In this chap. we will learn about a specific model of counseling called "Abide in Me" (AIM)" (Sosin, 2008), a Christ-centered framework grounded in biblical truth and in empirically validated counseling interventions. Because counselees come to counseling with issues and concerns that relate to their biology, psychology, social systems, and spirituality, AIM is a comprehensive "bio-psycho-social-spiritual" model (Duba, 2005). We will describe the nine components of the AIM model, present the five phases of the AIM treatment process, and present a case study to illustrate the model in action.

## AN AERIAL VIEW OF THE THERAPEUTIC PROCESS

A skilled counselor understands how to manage the entire therapeutic process from the first appointment to the achievement of the helping goals. Much as an itinerary details the various stages of a trip, an itinerary will help get your counselee through the entire course of counseling

When many people think of counseling, they think of it as one entity or as a whole. Actually the practice of counseling occurs in phases. We have chosen the concept of "phases" instead of "stages" because the activities associated with each phase are not completely distinct from each other. The overlap of one phase to the next makes the entire progression dynamic. Moreover, all phases are dynamic and can be entered into and out of based on the needs of the counselee and the judgment of the counselor.

One of the most central aspects of the helping process is the counselor's oversight of the counseling sessions. The number of stages varies from model to model, but the overall process is similar, that is, the ability to understand the big picture of what needs to happen and what is happening throughout the time you spend with the counselee. This section presents five phases of the helping process that give structure to your sessions. These phases include (a) Connection and Assessment, (b) Conceptualization and Treatment Planning, (c) Treatment, (d) Termination, and (e) Post-Treatment. These phases of the counseling journey are fluid, intersecting, and responsive to the counselee's needs (James & Gilliland, 2003; Seligman & Reichenberg, 2007). Figure 9.1 depicts the Five Phases.

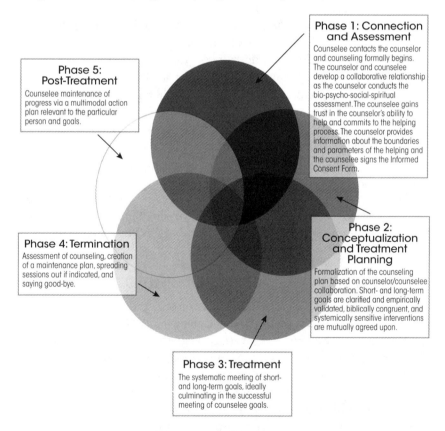

**Phase 1: Connection and Assessment**
Counselee contacts the counselor and counseling formally begins. The counselor and counselee develop a collaborative relationship as the counselor conducts the bio-psycho-social-spiritual assessment. The counselee gains trust in the counselor's ability to help and commits to the helping process. The counselor provides information about the boundaries and parameters of the helping and the counselee signs the Informed Consent Form.

**Phase 5: Post-Treatment**
Counselee maintenance of progress via a multimodal action plan relevant to the particular person and goals.

**Phase 4: Termination**
Assessment of counseling, creation of a maintenance plan, spreading sessions out if indicated, and saying good-bye.

**Phase 2: Conceptualization and Treatment Planning**
Formalization of the counseling plan based on counselor/counselee collaboration. Short- and long-term goals are clarified and empirically validated, biblically congruent, and systemically sensitive interventions are mutually agreed upon.

**Phase 3: Treatment**
The systematic meeting of short- and long-term goals, ideally culminating in the successful meeting of counselee goals.

Figure 9.1: The Five Phases of the AIM Model

## Phase 1: Connection and Assessment

If you have ever initiated counseling for yourself, you know some of the thoughts and feelings that go along with the decision; the going back and forth in your mind about it, the process of actually finding a counselor, the anxiety about finally making the call and following through with the appointment. Because of the ambivalence involved, it is important that the counselee is met with a helpful experience when she finally makes that call. Often, however, the counselee's initial contact will not be with you. It may be with the center's office manager and the first meeting may be with an "intake worker." We will assume that these workers have been properly trained to meet the counselee with grace and skill. Whatever the case, the first phase of counseling begins with the first contact with the counselee.

Sometimes the counselor's first contact with the counselee is by telephone, and at other times it is in the waiting room. From the very outset of the counseling, both the counselee and the counselor are "sizing up" one another and the surroundings, creating and receiving impressions, and assessing how the counseling might proceed. Counselees are in unfamiliar territory, for they are invited to a new experience with a stranger who will be asking them for details about their lives. In this first phase of counseling several tasks are to be accomplished. First, since neither the counselee nor the counselor has previous contact with the other, a relationship that is characterized by trust and caring must be established (Corey, 2005; Irving & Dickson, 2006; Kottler, 2004). In chap. 10, we will discuss how to make a solid connection with your counselee.

A second task that is involved in this phase of the process is setting expectations for the experience. People want to know what they are getting into before they move ahead with any experience. As the helper you must satisfy the counselee's need to know. For example people bring a host of stereotypes and fantasies about what will happen during counseling. Some counselees might think counseling is a deep, dark, mysterious undertaking. Such notions about the work of counseling need to be demystified. Your mission is to orient the counselee on what to expect, how to act, and what you, the counselor, can and cannot do. You are providing a role induction (Katz et al., 2004) for the counselee so that he or she knows what is expected. One way to prepare the counselee for his or her role is to do an ethical introduction. Because of the ethical and legal importance of this process, we have addressed this later in a separate section.

Related to this task of expectations is the need for the counselee to gain an understanding of how long it will take to be helped. Most people want quick fixes. Thus it is wise to inform all counselees that change usually does not occur after just a few sessions; it takes time to reverse the course of one's life.

Another task also connected with expectations is helping the counselee understand why you might need to ask certain questions. Many people's notions of what happens in counseling come from the media, word of mouth, or simply supposition. Depending on a person's expectations, some counselees will expect you to ask about their childhood, sexual life, or other personal matters. Some will expect you to talk little whereas others believe the counselor will give a lot of advice. Yet, other counselees might resist sharing their past because they do not believe it is relevant to their current problem. They might expect you to simply deal with the presenting concern and leave the rest of their lives out of the conversation.

Next, create and/or reinforce the notion that counseling can help. Some counselees fear that there is little hope for them, where as other individuals believe they can get better and do not need counseling. Some people might have come to the session to appease a loved one. Not only must the counselee come to see that counseling can help, but that you can help. People may doubt the process of counseling and also your expertise or credentials.

Also, you must establish a therapeutic or counseling contract that sets the agenda for the helping process. This process is addressed in more detail later in this chapter.

The central task of this first phase of counseling is hearing the counselee's story. Everyone has a story because in a sense everyone's life is a story (Allender, 1996). Each story is unique, but everyone's story has elements of other peoples stories. Most importantly our stories are interwoven into God's larger story.

A good story has several key elements that form the contours of a good novel. Our stories include characters, events, a plot, themes, settings, structure, and a style and tone that bear our identity. In fact our identity is developed throughout the story as well as being a key factor in shaping the story.

A counselor's task is to relate to another person's story with its drama, tensions, and pains. The counselor becomes part of other people's tragedies. Your role, of course, is not so much to become a main character in the story but an editor. An editor knows that the writer's story is not his story. But he desires to make the story better, while maintaining the author's own unique style. In other words he maintains the author's voice. At times the editor wears the hat of a consultant who draws out more of the story from the author, points to resources, makes suggestions, explores possibilities, and solves problems. Editors also function as motivators who support and encourage the writer along the way; so, a good editor knows when to be patient and knows when to allow the author to struggle through the process. A writer who does not like or trust her editor will fail to benefit from the editor's knowledge, skills, and ability. Perhaps most importantly, a wise editor has a vision of what the author can accomplish and knows how to draw out the writer's best talents and produce an end product that reflects excellence.

Similar to an editor a wise counselor holds forth a vision of what the counselee can become. The wise counselor knows how to call forth the counselee's story so that the story is accurately and honestly told. Some counselors may become so enamored with assessing, diagnosing, and treating that they forget that the counselee's problems are manifestations of a larger story. A problem or life event has no relevance or meaning apart from the larger context of a person's life. The wise counselor also knows how to draw out the counselee's story, to tap into the story that the counselee may be reluctant to tell (Crabb, 2003). In the hidden story are shadows that may trouble the soul and cause people to want protection.

As a counselor you are called to be an audience of one for a "storyteller" to unfold his or her journey. If you do not become enamored with the counselee's story, you will develop a weak connection with the counselee and likely fail to be of much help to the counselee.

The connection phase of counseling is most important in the first session and a few of the subsequent sessions. Yet you need to continue to reinforce the joining process throughout each phase of counseling. When you have adequately met these tasks of joining, the counselee will metaphorically make a deposit into the counseling relationship. After that, you will continue to generate more counselee deposits into the account, gain interest in what is already in the account, or do things that prompt the counselee to make withdrawals from the account. Depending on the size of the deposit, you need to have sufficient money in the relationship bank to cover the withdrawals the counselee might make from any of his mistakes (e.g., being late or forgetting an appointment), or perceptions that you have offended him. Sometimes no matter what you do, counselees will either make deposits or force withdrawals. Remember we are dealing with hurting people who know only certain ways to relate to others. Be patient and compassionate with the tasks of the connection phase.

## Phase 2: Conceptualization and Treatment Planning

People come to counseling because of issues and concerns for which they want or need help. During the conceptualization and planning phase the counselor and counselee work closely with one another to clarify these problems and express them as attainable goals. Once clarified, as the counselor you take the goals and create a written counseling plan that becomes the road map for the counseling work ahead (James & Gilliland, 2003; Jones & Butman, 1991; Seligman & Reichenberg, 2007). Because successful counseling requires the establishment of sound helping goals, we will dedicate a specific section to this process below.

## Phase 3: Treatment

The treatment phase of the helping process is the most active and emotionally intense of all the phases. It is the heart and soul of the counseling process. During this phase the counselor brings her well-stocked box of research-based and ethically sensitive, Christ-centered tools to support counselees in meeting their goals. Success during the treatment phase is related to the counselor's skill as guide and the counselee's willingness to participate vigorously in the helping process (Kuyken, Padesky, & Dudley, 2009). The wise counselor exercises great patience and provides loving encouragement as counselees often take two steps forward and one step back. Change is seldom a linear or steady process. As counselor and counselee assess they can refine the overall plan to reach the counselee's goals (Carlson & Sperry, 2000; Dinkmeyer & Sperry, 2000; McMinn, 1996; Teyber, 2006; Watts, 2000).

## Phase 4: Termination

Ideally counseling concludes when the helping goals are successfully met (Hoyt & Miller, 2000), with a tapering down of sessions and the creation of a plan to maintain the gains made in counseling. At times, because of the nurturing nature of the counseling relationship, counselees will want to continue to meet with the counselor after goals have been met. The counselor too has bonded with the counselee, and the two have developed a real, even if professional, relationship. However, one goal of counseling is for counselees to develop warm and loving relationships outside the counseling office. We do counselees a disservice when we continue to meet with them after goals have been successfully met and there is no need for further work to be done at that time. The task of counseling is to work ourselves out of a job! Knowing how to prepare and ease a counselee through this phase of helping, which signifies a loss, is both an art and a skill. This and the specific skills associated with successful termination were discussed in chap. 8 ("Basic Skills: Terminating the Counseling").

## Phase 5: Post-Treatment

This phase of counseling, often called "after-care," entails the counselee's continued use of the strategies learned in counseling in order to maintain the recovery they have worked hard to establish (James & Gilliland, 2003; Seligman & Reichenberg, 2007; Waller et al., 2007). At times it is necessary to give the counselee a formal after-care plan that succinctly summarizes the counseling process. In particular the plan provides a comprehensive listing of the biological, psychological, social, and spiritual tools that need to be utilized for successful recovery. Other times a more informal plan will do. Borrowing from Waller and associates (2007), we like to call this an after-care toolbox, which has been found to support continued recovery after counseling is complete (Bruffaerts, Sabbe, & Demyttenaere, 2004; Carter et al., 2008; Cummings, 1999; Fertman, 1991).

## THE COUNSELING HOUR

Most people are aware of the fact that counseling sessions are scheduled for one hour, but this is usually between 45 and 50 minutes and is known as the "therapeutic hour." There is nothing sacred about the therapeutic hour, and having more time with the counselee is probably warranted and beneficial to helping. However, constraints such as insurance and office protocol, prevent extending the length of the sessions.

Broadly speaking the counseling hour takes place in two distinct forms: the intake session and the helping sessions. Both sessions have four phases.

## The Intake Session

The intake session is the first formal session you have with your counselee (although at counseling centers sometimes intake workers complete this initial assessment and then assign counselees to appropriately trained counselors). Although gaining an accurate understanding of the counselee occurs over time, the intake session generally takes an hour. The actual flow of the session might be different based on your setting, but generally it occurs as follows.

### Making contact stage.

Making contact can be divided into the two stages of social chitchat and grounding. The purpose of social chitchat is to help the counselee feel comfortable and to experience the counselor as a normal human being who is friendly and wants to connect. During social chitchat you and the counselee begin the connecting process by engaging in socially appropriate talk; this stage of the process is a friendly politeness. Many counselors might inquire about such things as the drive to the office, the weather, or a significant current event. In grounding you do the role induction with the counselee, which includes the ethical introduction described in detail below.

### The purpose stage.

The counselor then transitions to this phase. There is no agreed-on comment or question to use in transitioning into this phase. A comment such as "Share with me what you are hoping to accomplish by coming to see me" allows the counselee to communicate his reason for making the appointment. The counselee's response begins a collaborative process in which the counselor seeks to better understand the basis for the appointment.

### The exploration stage.

In this stage the counselor begins to explore the themes in the counselee's life that will contribute to the counselor's understanding of the counselee as a person and help give insight into the counselee's primary concern. This stage is rarely completed in the initial interview, but it clearly takes up most of the allotted time. This stage of the intake assessment often includes completing a genogram and the use of a formal interview protocol (see chap. 10, "Conducting an Assessment").

### The wrap-up stage.

As the scheduled appointment nears a close, it is important to create a transition to signal to the counselee that time is nearing an end. Counselors usually begin this process anywhere from 5 to 10 minutes before ending the session. During the wrap-up stage the counselor gives the counselee a summary (see chap. 6 "Basic Skills: Exploring the Problem") of the session, discusses possible homework tasks to be completed before the next session, and asks the counselee about setting up another appointment. Thank the counselee for giving up his time and for allowing you the honor of peering into their lives.

## The Helping Sessions

The intake session is usually only one session, but it can take more. But I (Lisa) schedule two formal assessment sessions and a third session to review the written evaluation and collaborate on the treatment plan. Like the intake session each helping session has a general sequence that gives clear markers to the beginning and end of the allotted time.

### The social chitchat stage.

As discussed in the intake session, it is typical to chat with the counselee as you are walking to the counseling office and even after sitting down. As the relationship between you and the counselee grows, you and the counselee will both look forward to the time you have together. The counselee will especially value your presence and time as you become increasingly more integral in the helping process.

### The review stage.

The social chitchat stage ends when you transition the counselee to the purpose of your meeting. While it might be nice to talk about mundane things for a while, there is a clear need to address the counselee's issues within the limited time you have. Not all counselors follow this phase of the helping session alike. Some helpers do the review phase as a check-in process. They ask more sweeping questions to gauge where the counselee might be at the moment. For example a question like "How have things been since the last session?" or "How are you doing today with [problem]?" lets the counselor in on how the counselee has been progressing. You might also review a counselee's homework assignments to see how it went and what was learned.

### The working stage.

The counselor will transition from the review stage to the working stage by focusing on agenda-setting (discussed below). This part of the session is where the work of counseling takes place. Regardless of the counselor's theoretical orientation, activities are being implemented that support the goal of the session and the overall objectives of the counseling.

### The wrap-up stage.

The therapeutic hour can go quickly when you are actively engaged in the working stage. Often an hour does not seem sufficient to work adequately with the counselee's situation. About 5 to 10 minutes before the end of the session begin moving toward closure. You will usually use a summary statement (see chap. 6, "Basic Skills: Exploring the Problem") to capture what has occurred in the hour. At this point you might discuss a homework assignment (see chap. 13, "General Helping Strategies"). The session might begin in prayer or end in prayer, if prayer is overtly used (and consented to) at all in the session. Schedule the counselee for the next session with a clear reminder of any agreements that took place.

## ETHICAL INTRODUCTION

According to Goldberg (1986) every therapeutic encounter consists of a series of contractual obligations.

> Demands and expectations of another person are generally predicated on rules, roles, and sanctions experienced with others in previous situations approximating the emotional requirements of the present situation. Communication difficulties arise when people differ in their willingness and ability consensually to validate and comprehend the interpersonal agreements and promises they have imposed on themselves. Each of these contractual modes may be characterized by varying degrees of explicitness and informed consent. Contractual arrangements among people are, as a rule, more frequently implicit than explicit, unconscious than conscious, coercive than voluntary, unilateral than mutually endorsed. Accordingly, contractual arrangements may harmonize relations for some people, whereas they may antagonize and create tensions for others (p. 176).

An important counselor task is to address these "interpersonal agreements and promises" in the counseling situation by doing a *role induction* with all counselees. Ideally this task occurs during the connection phase of treatment and involves informing and educating the counselee on what to expect in the counseling. Role induction helps counselees understand the role they are about to adopt as a counselee in a professional counseling relationship. Many counselees come to counselors uninformed and need information to understand what counseling entails. Research indicates that counselees benefit from knowing what to expect and how to act in the counseling sessions (Nelson & Neufeldt, 1996). In a meta-analysis of role induction, Monks (1995) found that for counselees, role induction had significant positive effects on (a) treatment outcome, (b) attendance, and (c) dropout rates.

One means of doing role induction is through written forms. Putting your information, beliefs, policies, and approaches on paper is helpful for the counselee. Counselors typically have intake forms and informed consent forms for counselees to sign before the first appointment (see chap. 15, "Professional Issues in Counseling"). Informed consent refers to providing counselees with knowledge that can help them make an informed choice about the counseling in general or a particular technique (Corey, Corey, & Callanan, 2007). An Informed Consent form provides all relevant information about the counselor, counseling process, a proposed approach, a particular procedure, or type of treatment being offered.

Specifically the Informed Consent form covers the following topics: (a) the fact that the counselee is voluntarily participating in the counseling and is responsible to change; (b) the rights of the counselee; (c) the risks of counseling; (d) confidentiality and its exceptions, including whether the sessions will be recorded; (e) a brief discussion of the counseling approach or theory; (f) financial issues such as insurance reimbursement, fees, and responsibility of payment; (g) cancellation policy; (h) the credentials and professional affiliations of the counselor; (i) whether supervision or consultation will be used, including the qualifications of the supervisor/consultant; (j) if the counselor offers a Christian approach that includes prayer and other Christian techniques; and (k) the fact that ethical codes govern the counseling work (Corey, Corey, & Callanan, 2007). Clearly it would take too much time to discuss all of those issues in the counseling appointment. Also all counselees must read, understand, and affix a signature to the form, indicating that they understand their rights and the associated risks of the counseling. Because of the importance of a number of those items, the early moments of the counseling appointment should be devoted to discussing them. This process is called an "ethical introduction."

In the ethical introduction discuss these items: (a) if the session is being recorded, (b) if the counselor is receiving supervision, (c) confidentiality and its exceptions, (d) whether the counselee has had previous counseling, (e) the counselee's expectations, and (f) the counselor introducing herself to the counselee.

## Introduction of the Counselor

One important aspect of an ethical introduction is for the counselor to share about himself or herself. This includes the level of training (e.g., master's or doctoral student, practicum or internship student, under supervision, pursuing licensure) and how the counselor views counseling. Ask the counselee what would be important for him to know about you in order to make the counseling office a safe place to share and explore. This relaxes the counselee and creates a human connection, without losing the professionalism that contributes to rapport.

## Confidentiality and Exceptions

Another aspect of an ethical introduction is to discuss confidentiality. Be sure the counselee understands what confidentiality is and the conditions under which it can be broken. If you are recording the session, explain that its purpose is so that your supervisor can evaluate your work and offer input.

### Previous Counseling Experience and Expectations

Counselors often fail to explore a counselee's experience with other helpers. By inquiring about the counselee's previous experiences with counselors you can gain insight into the counselee's expectations for this encounter. Some counselees might expect to be criticized, labeled, questioned, heard, advised, healed, blamed, educated, encouraged, supported, and even to get nothing (Miller & Rollnick, 2002). If the counselee has seen a counselor before, he will have a clear sense of what to expect or at least of what he wants from the counselor. For example if a counselee says that she did not like the fact that her former counselor only talked about himself, she is saying that she does not want you to overuse self-disclosure. If a counselee says that he loved his previous counselor because the counselor shared Bible verses and prayed with him, he is informing you that he values those two activities in the helping experience. Thus it is important for you to understand what the previous helping experiences have been like. In the case of someone who has never talked with another person about personal concerns, the counselor can explore counselee expectations and clarify ambiguous expectations and concerns.

### Faith Issues

Depending on the intake form you use, it might be evident that the counselee wants a Christian approach. At other times the counselee's desire for a Christian approach needs to be discussed as a matter of informed consent. When you are sharing about your approach to counseling, include the fact that a Christian perspective is offered to those who desire such an approach. If the counselee affirms that such an approach is desirable, then you can proceed accordingly. If, however, the counselee states that a Christian approach is not welcomed, you will need to refrain from overtly approaching the counselee in a Christian manner. This does not mean that you have to abandon your values and beliefs, but do not discuss them openly. McMinn (1996) uses the term *direct censure* when a counselor's values are given higher prominence then the counselee's values. Of note is the fact that spiritual issues and concerns may be implicated in counselee problems (e.g., distorted religious beliefs may be contributing to counselee distress) and spiritual interventions may contribute to a counselee meeting his or her goal (Richards, Hardman, & Berrett, 2007).

A purposeful ethical introduction is interactive. In other words to inform the counselee of the ethical issues involved, do not simply tell him; discuss the ethical issues with him. Begin your sessions by using open-ended and indirect questions to process the details (see chap. 6 for information on these helper skills).

Below is an example of a dialogue between a counselor (CO) and a counselee (CL) that illustrates an ethical introduction in the first counseling session. Of course depending on the counselee's responses to your discussion of these items more detail and exploration may be necessary.

**CO:** *Hi, my name is Britt Pate. I'm glad to have the opportunity to work with you. Before we get into the reason for your visit, I'd like to discuss a few important details that will provide a framework for our counseling.*

**CL:** *OK. That is fine.*

**CO:** *Great! First, I want to remind you that I am required to record our sessions if I am to work with you. Because I'm still learning, my supervisor requires that I tape my sessions so he can better help me help you. I believe you signed a form giving us your permission to record our sessions.*

**CL:** *Oh, yes, I signed it. It's OK to record our sessions.*

**CO:** *Great. Thank you for your graciousness. As it stated on the form, I needed to begin the recording at the initiation of our contact. In other words we are recording right now.*

**CL:** *That's fine.*

**CO:** *Good. As I said since I am a practicum student working toward obtaining my master's degree in professional counseling, I must have my counseling supervised. The reason I record my sessions is to allow my supervisor, Dr. Thomas, to watch our sessions so that he can give me feedback to better help you. Dr. Thomas is a licensed professional counselor who has over 25 years of counseling experience.*

**CL:** *Wow. Two for the price of one.*

**CO:** (laughing) *How can you beat a deal like that! The fact that we are recording brings up an important point of discussion: confidentiality. What is your understanding of confidentiality?*

**CL:** *Well, I guess it means that you are not going to tell anyone about what we talk about.*

**CO:** *Exactly. I'm not going to share what we talk about with anyone or the fact you are coming to see me. For example, if I see you outside our counseling session, I will not acknowledge you unless you acknowledge me. I'm not being rude, but simply protecting your privacy.*

**CL:** *I appreciate that, but I'd probably say "hi."*

**CO:** *That would be great, and I would welcome that. I do want to point out, however, that there are times when counselors are required to break confidentiality. We call them exceptions to confidentiality. I imagine you can think of a couple.*

**CL:** *I guess if I was going to hurt someone or hurt myself, you would have to tell somebody.*

**CO:** *That is correct. The law says that we must protect people, including you. So if you were going to hurt yourself, hurt anyone—including a child or an older person—the law says that I have to take appropriate action to protect everyone.*

**CL:** *I'm cool with that. I'm not suicidal, and there isn't anyone I want to hurt.*

**CO:** *Good news to say the least (smiles). There are a few other times when we must break confidentiality, times most people are not aware of. One of them deals with a subpoena or court-order by a judge. Sometimes counselors are forced to testify or share notes or recollections about the counseling. Of course that rarely happens, but it is possible.*

**CL:** *OK by me. But why would a judge subpoena my records?*

**CO:** *Oh, it could be something like us talking about divorce where child custody could be an issue or something of that nature.*

**CL:** *So you're not protected against having to do that."*

**CO:** *Right. The final exception to confidentiality that I need to remind you of is if you give us permission to share what we talk about, as you did in giving me permission to record our sessions for my supervisor. I would be happy to accommodate your request to disclose elements of what we talk about with anyone you wish.*

**CL:** *I cannot think of anyone I would need you to talk with about the counseling. In fact I don't want any of my friends to know.*

**CO:** *That is understandable and is not a problem. I won't be publishing your notes with the media* (both smile). *Before we proceed to another detail, what other questions might you have about confidentiality or its limitations?*

**CL:** *I'm good; you've made it all clear.*

**CO:** *Great. I think it is important for both of us to be on the same page regarding confidentiality and its limitations; so if you did share something that required me to break confidentiality you would know the results. Now allow me to ask you about what experience you have had in talking to a counselor or another helping person.*

**CL:** *My experience? Like have I been to a counselor before?*

**CO:** *Yes.*

**CL:** *I talked to a counselor when I was in college, and I've seen my pastor a few times.*

**CO:** *So you have had a few experiences with talking to someone about personal issues. How were those experiences?*

**CL:** *The counselor I saw in college was a waste.*

**CO:** *It sounds as if that was not a good experience.*

**CL:** *He wasn't mean or anything, but just nodded his head and asked how I felt about everything. He didn't give me any help. Besides, he was not a Christian and didn't seem to value my faith.*

**CO:** *So you didn't find his interactions with you helpful at all. What about the counseling you had with the pastor?*

**CL:**    *He was fine, but didn't seem to be able to go deep enough with me. I guess I have more going on than just what biblical truth can fix.*

**CO:**    *So while you valued the strong biblical component that your pastor brought, you thought that he lacked the knowledge and skill to go beneath the surface of your situation to the heart of the matter.*

**CL:**    *Yeah, I would agree with that. I want the Bible to be part of my counseling, and I want the counselor to do more than ask how I feel. But I also need someone who can help me get to the bottom of my issues, even if it makes me uncomfortable.*

**CO:**    *It seems that you highly value the role the Bible plays in your life. Based on that, it appears that you believe counseling would serve you best if the approach was active and would go deep under the surface of your issues. Clearly, you want to know that I would be basing my work with you on God's Word. I'm glad that you are very committed to working on the things that prompted your visit.*

**CL:**    *That would sum it up.*

**CO:**    *Well I think I can help with that. Let me tell you about my background. As you know, I am a practicum student in a master of arts counseling program that believes that God's Word is the source of all truth and that God is the ultimate healer. Yet my training has also equipped me with knowledge of psychology and counseling principles to help my counselees fully explore their problems. I work with counselees to help them make the kinds of changes in their lives that will deal not just with the problems but will also enable them to know themselves better and grow in their walk with God. Of course I would never impose my values and beliefs onto everyone, but it sounds as if you have a similar faith to mine and that we can work together fully embracing those beliefs and values. What thoughts do you have about what I shared?*

**CL:** *I think that is what I've needed for a long time. It sounds great to me!*

**CO:** *Good. Since I'm going to be asking you a lot of questions, let me give you a chance to ask me a few. What else would be important for you to know about me that would help make this counseling the safest place possible to share and explore your concerns?*

**CL:** *Wow, no one has ever asked me that before. Uh, I cannot think of anything, but if I do can I ask then?*

**CO:** *You sure can. In the last couple of minutes we've discussed your permission to participate in the recording, my supervision, confidentiality and its limitations. So I think the preliminaries are covered well. Since this is your first session, it might help to share with you how I like to begin talking together.*

**CL:** *Actually, I've wondered what was going to happen.*

**CO:** *We will begin with the reason you wanted to meet with me. When you go to the doctor with the flu or something else, the nurses and doctors do all sorts of medical assessment. They weigh you, take your vitals, and check out other areas of your body far beyond the reason for your visit.*

**CL:** *That's for sure.*

**CO:** *They want to understand the symptoms you have in the context of your current medical condition. Likewise counselors want to understand your concerns in the context of your life. We don't do medical tests, of course, but we like to get to know our counselees as persons. So after the discussion of your concerns, I'll ask for you to share more about yourself, your childhood, and your family. Things of that nature.*

**CL:** *I'm fine with that. Actually I was thinking you would ask me about my childhood.*

**CO:** *Tell me about what led to your making a decision to meet with me.*

Evident throughout the dialogue is the fact that the counselor is attempting to normalize the collaborative and interactive nature of the counseling process. It would be helpful to practice this dialogue with another student or person before actually meeting with your first counselee. We suggest that your partner give you different responses so that you "think on your feet." For example your partner might ask you a lot of questions about confidentiality or question your inexperience. The more comfortable you get with going through this process, the more confidence you will carry into the actual interview portion of the session.

## THE THERAPEUTIC CONTRACT

The very nature of counseling embodies an interactive and negotiable dynamic. Herman (1997) states:

> The work of therapy is both a labor of love and a collaborative commitment. Though the therapeutic alliance partakes of the customs of every day contractual negotiations, it is not a simple business arrangement. And though it evokes all the passions of human attachment, it is not a love affair or a parent-child relationship. It is a relationship of existential engagement, in which both partners commit themselves to the task of recovery. This commitment takes the form of a therapeutic contract (pp. 147–148).

When a counselee approaches you, she is requesting help, and your response affirms or denies your desire to facilitate that help. No work in counseling can begin until you and the counselee have the same agenda. In its simplest form, that is a therapeutic contract, an agreement between you and your counselee. This agreement requires a mutual understanding of what the counselee wants from the counselor and what you are able and willing to provide in response to the request. For instance, if you hail a taxicab to take you to a particular hotel, you are assuming that the cab driver will actually take you to that hotel. You would feel angry if he stopped at another hotel, assuring you that it was a far nicer and more comfortable hotel. Even if he guaranteed that you would enjoy your stay better by changing hotels, you would likely be extremely upset—and for good reason. You got into his cab with the assumption that he was driving you to your chosen destination. While your agenda was to arrive at the hotel where you had made reservations, the cabby's agenda was to take you to a more desirable one. When a counselee seeks for you to "guide her" to a particular destination, it is her expectation that you will comply with her request. As is readily clear from the example, the therapeutic contract provides the destination for the helping efforts.

The importance of establishing a therapeutic contract has been noted for decades (Menninger, 1958; Orlinsky & Howard, 1987). On one level the therapeutic contract is tied into informed consent, which we discussed in the ethical introduction, and in the paperwork that counselees are required to complete (see chap. 15, "Professional Issues in Counseling" for more information on Informed Consent). However, the actual therapeutic contract extends to the direction the counseling process will take.

Of course a counselee's desire for a particular outcome from the counseling process does not mean that you must provide it. Returning to the taxicab analogy, simply because you want a cab driver to take you somewhere does not mean he will or can. As therapists we have both had counselees approach us for help with particular issues that we would not or could not agree to. A number of reasons might prevent a therapeutic contract from being established. You might not be willing to provide a particular service because of your values. For example, I (John) will not work with nonmarried couples who wish to work on sexual issues in their relationship. To do so would be a violation of ethical principles related to the importance of respecting a counselee's autonomy by avoiding a values conflict (see Appendixes A and B). Related to this might be a counselee who wants you to support a practice you deem psychologically unhealthy. One counselee, for instance, came to me (John) to obtain permission to have extramarital affairs because she saw her husband as harsh and abusive.

Another reason for being unable to establish a contract is that an issue might exist in your personal life that would generate a great deal of countertransference toward a counselee. A counselor we know of had recently discovered that her husband was having an affair, a revelation that left her damaged both personally and professionally. Even though she was a seasoned and effective marital counselor who had worked with many post-affair couples, she was unable to provide that service in the wake of her personal crisis.

Also, you might not agree to a therapeutic contract if you are asked to provide services for which you are not properly trained or competent. If a counselee requested family counseling or help with drug addiction and you are not trained in those treatments, you would need to decline and provide a few referral options for the counselee to consider (see chap. 8, "Basic Skills: Terminating the Counseling").

Not all complaints or statements are an invitation to explore a particular area. A counselee's comment about confusion over a parenting issue does not mean that she wants advice on that topic or even wants to address it.

Therapeutic contracts can be changed. I (John) worked with a couple who were adamant that, while they knew I provided Christian counseling, they did not wish to address any faith issues. I agreed to the contract with the understanding that they were working with a counselor who is a committed Christian and that I provide services based on God's truth. After I worked with the couple on their relationship for over six months, they stated that they had received incredible help in their marriage but believed that I was holding something back from them. I acknowledged that I was indeed doing so at their request. At the couple's urging I stated that the missing element was the Christian context and foundation to everything on which they had worked. The couple asked me to include that foundation, which required a new therapeutic contract. The couple agreed and counseling progressed. After four sessions the couple asked if they could invite Jesus Christ into their lives. I had agreed to and honored the original contract and only renegotiated the contract at the counselees' request.

To establish a therapeutic contract, you must understand the nature of the counselee's problem. Without having sufficient information on the problem and what the counselee desires, it will be impossible for you to know if you can offer services. The counselee should not feel as if counseling is done "to" them; each counselee should be a willing participant to all aspects of the therapeutic process. An example of how a therapeutic contract might be offered is given below:

> Steve, as I've been listening to you share about your recent experience, it seems that you have been through a great deal of pain. I am amazed that you have functioned so well for so long. Although you have tried a number of strategies and solutions to take control over your sexual behavior, it seems that you have continued to fall back into the same pattern. As you know, one of my specializations is working with people with sexual problems, particularly sexual compulsive behavior. It has been my experience that this problem takes a multifaceted approach and a commitment to the recovery process. As part of the counseling that I offer, I require counselees who want to deal with sexual behaviors to attend weekly counseling sessions, attend a support group, and do counseling assignments between sessions. Also as you know, I offer a Christian approach to counseling. Most approaches to addictive-like problems include a spiritual component, but I believe that basing my practice on biblical principles and truths provides a more effective treatment. What thoughts and feelings do you have about how I like to work?

Establishing a therapeutic contract is an essential and critical aspect of quality counseling. As you and your counselee arrive at a consensus on the focus of the counseling, you are in a better position to establish specific goals, which in turn will become part of the therapeutic contract.

## ESTABLISHING HELPING GOALS

Helping the counselee achieve the goals that prompted his call for help is your primary responsibility. Counselees will rarely complain about getting more than they hope from counseling, but they will not be satisfied if they do not get their needs met. The main mechanism by which counselees' needs are met is through the process of goal-setting.

Goal-setting is a key task of the Conceptualization and Treatment Planning Phase (Phase II). Goal-setting is fundamental to counseling (Corey, 2005; Cormier & Cormier, 1985; Egan, 2007; Ivey & Ivey, 2003; Young, 2010). This section discusses the benefits of goal-setting, framing the desired outcome, your role in goal-setting, three levels of goals, the characteristics of effective goals, and guidelines for establishing helping goals.

### The Benefits of Goal-Setting

Whether you recognize it or not, when you set out to counsel, you are operating from the framework of goals. It is impossible to counsel without having an idea of what needs to be done. The goals might be overt or covert, intentional or unintentional, effective or ineffective, but they are present in the interaction and activities that take place.

The value of goal-setting is recognized by virtually every writer in the helping profession (Adams, 1986; Corey, 2005; Crabb, 1977; Egan, 2007; Ivey & Ivey, 2003; Young, 2010). Cormier and Cormier (1985) describe six purposes of establishing clearly defined goals in the helping process. Goals (a) reflect the areas of the counselee's concern; (b) help the counselor determine if he has the skills, competencies, and interest in helping a particular counselee; (c) facilitate successful performance and problem resolution; (d) provide guidance for the kinds of strategies that should be used to help the counselee; (e) help determine if counseling has been successful; and (f) are reactive to the counselee's needs and counselor's responses. In short, setting goals with your counselees creates a map for you and the counselee to follow.

### The Desired Outcome

Because counselees seek out the help of a counselor to find something they lack or want, a goal represents nothing more than a desired outcome. People come to counseling when they sense that something needs to change. Behind each complaint or concern is a wish for something different.

Effective helping requires the ability to help counselees take their problems and concerns and turn them into a desired outcome. The question, as raised by Adams (1986), is "Change into what?" That is, what is the desired outcome of counseling? Adams's point is that the outcome of counseling is important because it is inextricably linked to values (Corey, 2005).

Christian counselors such as Adams (1986) and Crabb (1977) contend that the desired outcome is a level of spiritual maturity. Roberts (2001) holds that the goal of counseling is "character formation" and "character transformation." In contrast, traditional counseling writers argue that the desired outcome is to be determined not by the counselor but by the counselee (Corey, 2005; Egan, 2007). In other words the traditional helping literature argues that the desired outcome is based on what the counselee values. While you might help the counselee reach his desired outcome, you might have other ideas about what the desired outcome should be. The bottom line is that you need to have a clear idea of what to accomplish through the counseling.

Secular counseling models propose that the goals of counseling include helping counselees change behaviors (Wolpe & Lazarus, 1966), feel better (Burns, 1999), exchange faulty thinking for rational thinking (Beck, 1976; Burns, 1999; Ellis, 1957), develop skills (Stuart, 1980), eliminate symptoms (Haley, 1977), become responsible and accept reality (Glasser, 1962), acquire self-reliance (Perls, 1969), become authentic (Bugental, 1965; Jourard, 1971), increase self-awareness (Corey, 2005), or find meaning (Frankl, 1959). Christian theorists also vary considerably in their perspective on the purpose of counseling. For instance Adams (1986) advocates the need to promote godliness, Crabb (1977) believes that the goal should be to find and know God more deeply, and Collins (1980) believes that the purpose of counseling is to transform the counselee into Christlike disciples (see also McMinn & Phillips, 2001; Shields & Bredfeldt, 2001).

No approach to counseling is more clearly committed to generating Christlike behavior in counselees than nouthetic counseling (Adams, 1970). Nouthetic counseling has its central task in helping counselees to reconcile their behavior with God's eternal standards. It highlights the sufficiency and power of the Scriptures to meet the needs of modern life (Adams, 1970). Adams has stressed the importance of communicating biblical principles, giving instruction, and helping counselees understand how their patterns lead them away from trusting in God. But one need not hold to the nouthetic approach to encourage counselees to consider goals that are satisfactory to God.

While we as counselors might have our own notion about the intended end of counseling, each counselee comes to counseling to accomplish something for herself. Stated broadly, these include such things as wanting to feel better, controlling anxiety, or breaking a bad habit. In other words the counselee might want nothing more than symptom relief. The fact that the counselee is a Christian often makes little difference in what they hope to find through the help. Even though you might believe that the counselee needs to pursue far greater ends than mere relief, the counselee and not you will decide where the helping journey will end. Yet for the counselee to reach her goals you the counselor must clearly and firmly understand your role in the process.

## The Helper's Role in Goal-Setting

Though a counselee might know what he or she wants from the counseling, you have a role to play in what is ultimately accomplished. Two central factors in the process are your competence to help and your willingness to help (Brown & Brown, 1977).

No counselor is competent to help all kinds of counselees with all kinds of problems. Competence involves the counselor's knowledge, experience, ability, and skill in helping the counselee achieve the desired goals. If you are not trained in counseling children and if you are not experienced with play therapy, for instance, you will be ineffective in helping the counselee with her children's problems. In situations like these you have an ethical obligation to make a referral to a competent colleague. We will address the issue of counselor development in chap. 15 ("Professional Issues in Counseling").

Consider if you are willing to help the counselee with the stated problem and goal. At times what a counselee wants from counseling is incompatible with the counselor's values or comfort. For instance you might find the counselee's goals morally objectionable (Young, 2010). As stated earlier, I (John) have been asked by unmarried couples to assist them in working through sexual difficulties. While versed in sexual therapy my values do not permit me to work with sexual problems with an unmarried couple.

Another reason you might not be willing to help is because of interference from your own life. Every person goes through times in his life when he is struggling with some issue. Counselors are no exception. When a counselee presents a similar issue, it might make you uncomfortable. A counselor, for example, could not deal with grief cases after the sudden and unexpected death of his wife. A female counselor was unwilling to work with male sex offenders because she had been sexually abused. It is acceptable, appropriate, and ethical not to take cases when they create a level of discomfort that would interfere with your ability to be helpful.

In summary, goal-setting is a critical component in counseling. Effective helpers seek to help counselees set appropriate goals. They are able to carefully consider the purposes for which their counselees seek help and then to design together specific, clear, and realistic goals to guide the therapeutic journey. Also, consider your willingness and competence to help the counselee with his goals. If the counselee's goals are morally objectionable, uncomfortable, or if you are not competent to assist the counselee with the goal, it is important to inform the counselee early in the process.

### Three Levels of Goals

Clinton, Hart, and Ohlschlager (2005) discuss three levels of goals in counseling: (a) immediate goals, (b) intermediate goals, and (c) ultimate goals. Immediate goals are those that are the primary focus of counseling early in the process. They are short-term in duration and targeted at symptom reduction, pain control, crisis alleviation, and/or stabilization. Immediate goals deal with clear and overt behavior. But intermediate goals target more entrenched dynamics that lie beneath the surface. They address the behavior, belief patterns, and environmental conditions that underlie the immediate concerns. Ultimate goals are those that seek to orient the counselee to the person of Jesus Christ. When resolution has occurred at level one or level two, the counselee is generally satisfied with the counseling, and motivation to continue to work on more important issues decreases. At the level of ultimate goals, however, true meaning, fulfillment, and contentment are found. They provide the necessary means by which the human hunger can be truly satisfied. Ultimate goals target the spiritual vacuum that arouses the heart to pursue lesser passions and pseudo-fulfillment. Addictions, problematic habits, poor behavioral control, dysfunctional thoughts, and distressing emotions have their roots in problems of the heart. The most foundational ultimate goal is the need for salvation, by which we become reconciled with our Creator. Following that step, ultimate goals include the work of maturing in Christ (sanctification). New habits are formed that correspond with the new life a person finds in Christ. The new nature is cultivated so that the believer desires to live a righteous life (Rom 6–7; 1 Pet 4:1–2). Ultimate goals help the counselee learn to walk in the Spirit rather than in the flesh (Rom 8:1), to be conformed to the image of Christ (Rom 8:29), and to put on the "new man" (Eph 4:24; Col 3:10). Ultimate goals are those that recognize that Jesus Christ is an end in Himself; He is to be sought if the counselee desires true fulfillment.

Imagine wild onions popping up throughout your lawn. You can cut them at the ground or pull off the shoots and believe that the problem is solved. From all appearance it would seem like a job well done. But unless you get the entire root, the onion will reappear. I (Lisa) once worked with a couple who could not seem to connect with and love one another. When the usually fruitful interventions were not helping the couple reach their goals, I knew something deeper was going on. As the counseling progressed, the veil of secrecy was pulled open as the wife shared for the first time about an extremely traumatic event that occurred in her childhood that had severely wounded her "trust muscle." I told her that until this injury was dealt with, trust in the marital relationship would not be forthcoming. Fortunately with a few individual sessions, the counselee was able to work this through, and subsequently she formed a loving, emotional attachment with her husband for the first time. Sometimes counselee concerns do not reappear in the same fashion as before, but residual roots ultimately bear expression in some form.

Resolving heart issues will ultimately eliminate most of the counselees' problems and concerns. It is wise to help counselees with their presenting problem because that is what has captured their attention. However, targeting the deeper ultimate goals will yield the greatest harvest. Yet do not lose sight of the therapeutic contract you established with the counselee. If you agreed to provide a non-Christian approach to counseling, that agreement must be honored. Just as Jesus longed to have all of Jerusalem come to Him (Matt 23:7), we too long to see our counselees pursue goals that lead to spiritual transformation.

## Characteristics of Good Goals

A good goal is one that is effective in helping a person change in a meaningful way. An effective goal meets five criteria, which form the acrostic **SMART** (see Table 9.1). The "S" stands for the importance of having a **Specific** goal. Well-constructed goals are straightforward and emphasize what the counselee wants to happen as well as what you both agree will lead to a resolution of the problem. Specific goals give focus to the helping effort and clearly define what you and the counselee are working on, giving clarity to the what, why, and how. When goals are specific, they are bite-size pieces of a larger objective. Vague and ambiguous goals provide no direction. A vague goal might be phrased as "I want to feel better." A more specific goal related to feeling better might be "I want to do fun things again." In the helping process the strategy would identify what specific activities the counselee agrees to do. By creating small goals that lead toward a more global one, both you and the counselee have milestones along the way that point to the progress and the direction in which the counseling is heading. So the goal of wanting "to do fun things again" might become "I will play tennis one day each week for one hour on Tuesdays with Jennifer."

---

Table 9.1

*SMART: Characteristics of Good Goals*

**S = Specific**

**M = Measurable**

**A = Attainable**

**R = Relevant**

**T = Timetable**

---

The "M" refers to having goals that are **Measurable**. I (John) once heard a business consultant say that if you cannot measure it, you cannot manage it. The point is that measurable progress advances you toward successful completion of your goal. The specific goal above, "I will play tennis one day each week" is measurable. The counselee can note whether he or she actually played tennis that week. "I will read my Bible for 10 minutes each day" is both specific and measurable. A goal such as "I want to be happy" is specific in the sense that it speaks to a particular feeling state, but it is not measurable. How happy is happy enough? By setting specific and measurable goals both you and the counselee can mark and measure progress along the way.

The "A" captures the importance of having goals that are **Attainable**. These are goals the counselee wants to achieve and has the ability to achieve. The goal may not be easy, but it is attainable, that is, it is doable. If the counselee's goal is to never feel anxious, it is unlikely that he will ever achieve that goal. Attainable goals are ones toward which the counselee is willing and able to work. How feasible is it for the counselee to accomplish the goal? An attainable goal exerts a motivational force in the counselee's life. For example anxiety is part of the human experience. To have an anxiety level of zero is not possible; we all experience some level of anxiety. Having the counselee rate her current level of anxiety on a scale from 1 to 10, with 10 being highest and establishing a desired level of acceptable anxiety such as 3 or 4, is realistic. You might ask the counselee, "If your current level of anxiety tends to be about an 8 on a daily basis, what level of anxiety would represent an acceptable level for you?" If the counselee's goals are unrealistic, you may express doubt about the realism of the goals, confront the counselee's unrealistic goals (see chap. 7, "Basic Skills: Giving Feedback"), or encourage him to try to evaluate whether the goals are possible. To construct an attainable goal, it is better for counselees to generate their own goals because they will typically work toward something they want (Corey, 2005; Egan, 2007). Goals that a person considers too far out of reach will not generate sufficient energy to be met. Although the counselee might have the best of intentions, if he senses that the goal is unattainable, he will probably not attain it. Of course any goal should create enough stretch that it generates commitment and seems worthwhile. The counselor's task is to help the counselee figure out how to achieve the goal. What attitudes, abilities, skills, and resources does the counselee need to reach the goal? What previously overlooked opportunities will bring the counselee closer to achieving the goal? The ultimate key is helping the counselee step up to meet the goal. Young (2010, p. 234) suggests the following questions that capture the attainable and realistic dimensions of effective goal-setting:

- "How likely are you to follow through with this goal?"
- "How important is this goal to you?"
- "If you accomplished this goal, what difference would it make in your life?"
- "How likely are you to talk yourself out of trying to accomplish this goal?"
- "Is this your goal, or is it something other people want you to accomplish?"

Goals must also be **Relevant** ("R"); that is, ones that are meaningful to the counselee. It is important to establish goals that move the counselee toward his overall counseling objective. Often counselees present goals with "shoulds," "musts," or "oughts." When goals are framed this way they fail to motivate the counselee because the person is not truly invested in its success. When you as the counselor work with a counselee to develop goals, they are more likely to be motivating.

The best counseling goals have a **Timetable** ("T"). Putting an end point to the goal creates sufficient urgency to generate motivation. A target date gives accountability and helps combat procrastination. As professors, we know that deadlines for students motivate them to get their assignments completed. This boundary creates the need to plan their time appropriately in order to meet the deadline. Timetables in counseling function in the same way.

## Guidelines for Goal-Setting

Early in the counseling process begin to help your counselees turn their problem statements into goal statements. Typically these goal statements fall within the confines of immediate and intermediate levels.

An acrostic for establishing goals with the counselee is the word **GOAL** (see Table 9.2).

| Table 9.2 |
| --- |
| *GOAL: Guidelines in Establishing Goals* |
| **G** = **Ground** the counselee to the rationale for goal-setting |
| **O** = Determine the counselee's desired **Outcome** for the goal and **Operationalize** it |
| **A** = **Assess** the counselee's **Ambition** for reaching the goal |
| **L** = **Link** the goal to the counseling strategy |

The first step in establishing goals with counselees is **Grounding** ("G") them to the reason goal-setting is necessary. Describe the purpose of goal-setting and the need for the counselee and you to work together in coming up with appropriate goals that will lend themselves to helping the counselee.

Once the counselee understands the importance of goals, determine the counselee's desired **Outcome** and **Operationalize** it ("O"). Four keys are critical to obtaining an appropriate outcome. The first and most obvious is to determine what the counselee wants from coming to meet with you. The outcome is defined by the problems and concerns counselees bring to you. Your task is then to help the counselee rephrase the problem into a goal statement. For example for a counselee who feels anxious you might say something like this: "You have been talking about your struggle with anxiety, but what it sounds like is that you want to feel more peaceful during this time of uncertainty." Another means of determining the outcome is by asking probing questions. Cormier and Cormier (1985, p. 222) suggest using such questions as these:

- "Suppose a distant relative you haven't seen in years sees you after counseling. What would be different then from the way things are now?"

- "Assuming we are successful, what would you be doing or how would these situations change?"
- "What do you expect to accomplish as a result of counseling?"
- "What do you want to be doing, thinking, and feeling?"

Second, outcomes are most effective when they are worded positively (Custers & Aarts, 2005). For example if the counselee states that his desire is to "quit smoking," the outcome is framed in the negative, to stop doing something. The counselee is not considering "what to do" but is stating a prohibition of what not to do. To desire the outcome of wanting to stop smoking is logical if you are tired of smoking. Framing any goal, however, with the intention to eliminate something puts the emphasis on symptom relief and fails to motivate (Custers & Aarts, 2005). It works on the manifestation of a deeper problem but tells you nothing about what is needed. Counseling should work toward something the counselee wants to acquire in his life, not what he wishes to leave behind. Thus a goal phrased as "develop a healthy lifestyle as evidenced by smoking five fewer cigarettes per day" is positively stated, and it is specific and measurable. Obviously such a goal is more intermediate in that it does not eliminate the problem, but it initiates a process that can end in a healthy lifestyle.

Third, operationalize the outcome, that is, make the goal very specific. An operationalized goal is measurable and realistic. Vague goals that are not measurable, are unrealistic, and that do not hold the counselee to a timetable are likely to fail. For example "wanting to have fun" is specific to the point that one can make the decision if a given activity is fun. However when that goal is operationalized, it becomes simpler, concrete, and more easily measured. An operationalized version of the fun goal might be "I will play tennis at least once each week." The activity of tennis takes the concept of fun and makes it specific.

Help the counselee flesh out in detail the exact things that will take place in order to accomplish the goal. Cormier and Cormier (1985) suggest asking the counselee, "When you reach this goal, how will you explain your success, or if you don't reach it, how will you explain failure to reach it?" Young (2010, pp. 230–231) offers some questions to help the counselee take problems and make them more specific and positive:

- "I understand that you want to be 'happy,' but if you were happy, what would you be doing that you are not doing now?"
- "When you say things are not going well, specifically what things are you talking about?"

- "You say you want things to be better in your relationship with your husband. Specifically what would you like to be better?"
- "If the problem were solved, what would you be feeling, doing, or thinking that you are not now?"
- "You say that you and your husband argue constantly. If you were not arguing, what would you like to be doing?"

Fourth, when defining the counselee's desired outcome, make sure that he or she owns the goal (Cormier & Cormier, 1985). A counselee who wants to get his father to stop yelling at him does not own that goal. A human tendency is to project a desired change onto another person. You cannot help a person who is not in the counseling office. Without discounting the counselee's feelings, you need to help the counselee frame the goal into language that is positive and one that is within the counselee's power to accomplish. Cormier and Cormier (1985) suggest asking such questions as these: "How much control do you have over making this happen?" "What changes will this goal require of you?"

The ("A") refers to **Assessing** the counselee's **Ambition** in obtaining the goal. It is helpful to question the counselee about possible reasons why the goal might not be a good idea or reasons not to change. In addition, Rollnick and Miller (1995) recommend asking counselees what they get out of the current state of their situation that they like; in other words, why give it up? Even desiring to do something means that you give up something that you started doing for some "good" reason. A person who is alcohol-dependent, for example, may want to quit drinking but to do so means giving up something familiar. It also means stopping alcohol consumption which he started and continued to imbibe for a "good" reason at the time. Helping counselees look at all sides of a situation will ultimately lead to better acceptance of the goals.

The "L" in **GOAL** stands for **Linking** the goal to the counseling strategy. Goals give direction to the helping process. They illuminate possible interventions, techniques, and procedures. If a counselee wants to become a better husband by improving his communication with his wife, the choices of possible strategies become clearer. Think of it as going into a grocery store to buy a dessert. The fact that you want to purchase a dessert limits the number of aisles you must roam and it provides direction to a particular section of the store. The same is true with goals and strategy. The better the goal you establish, the smaller the number of strategic options from which the counselee can choose.

Moreover, two key factors influence the formation of goals and the treatment plan. First, certain goals take priority over others. One way priorities are determined is based on safety and outcome. Decreasing suicidal thoughts or behaviors would take precedence over improving communication skills. Another way priorities can be established is related to the way the goal is life-related. Addressing a counselee's panic attacks is more currently relevant than working with fear of flying.

Second, the goals need to be fashioned into a hierarchy. Particular issues might need to be addressed before proceeding to higher-level goals. For instance it is difficult to help a counselee with an anxiety problem or a marital issue if he or she is abusing alcohol. The need for dealing with alcohol abuse is both a priority and at a lower hierarchy level in helping the person benefit from counseling.

Not every counseling session will involve goal-setting, but every session will involve focusing on at least one goal. That leads to the next part of the counseling process, agenda-setting.

## AGENDA-SETTING

One skill that is often deficient in the work of counselors in training is setting an agenda for the session. "Agenda" refers to what will transpire during the session. When you set the agenda with the counselee, you focus the session. Agenda-setting lets everyone know what issue(s) are on the table that will be addressed during the allotted time. This prevents the session from meandering wherever the counselee's opening comments happen to take him. This is particularly the case in counselees who make efforts to focus sessions on current life crises that keep the counselor from addressing the deeper life issues.

If you are directive, you will set the agenda for what to focus on in the session. If you are more facilitative, you will likely work on the goal that your counselee desires to address. Adams (1986) believes it is the counselor's responsibility to set the agenda, whereas most professionally oriented texts view it as a collaborative effort with the counselee (Egan, 2007; Young, 2010). With the exception of the intake interview and a crisis-oriented situation we do not advocate that you set the session agenda. In the first couple of sessions your task is to understand the counselee's concerns and learn about the counselee so that the concerns can be understood in the context of the counselee's life. During this phase of the counseling process the counselor controls the agenda. Once the counselor has obtained the necessary information, however, it becomes the counselee's responsibility to set the agenda. As the counselor your job is to bring expertise to the decision and specificity to the agenda. The rule of thumb is to take the lead from the counselee. For example, asking the counselee,

"What is the most important thing you want to talk about?" puts the responsibility for the counseling on the counselee's shoulders. By agenda-setting in this manner the counselee has a greater sense of control, which often fosters his greater investment in the counseling process.

Of all the schools of counseling, none speaks more about agenda-setting than cognitive-behavioral therapy. Noted cognitive-behavioral psychiatrist David Burns (1999) has suggested the mnemonic device of *I STOP* to represent the five steps of agenda-setting. As you learn these five steps, it is important to remember that because Dr. Burns uses a cognitive-behavioral model, he is more directive and active in shaping the counseling. The exact nature of his questions might not fit your style or theory.

"I" refers to giving the counselee an **Invitation.** Do not assume that because the counselee says he wants help with a particular issue that he is ready to address it. Trying to set the agenda prematurely when the counselee is experiencing strong emotions can be unproductive. Burns (2008) recommends asking the counselee, "Would this be a good time to roll up our sleeves and begin to work on one of these problems?"

The "S" is for **Specificity**. Burns recommends that you obtain the counselee's commitment to address the issue and then specify the issue as clearly as possible. He recommends asking the counselee, "Tell me about a time when you were feeling ____ that you would like help with?" After the counselee responds, ask, "Is this something you would like to work on in today's session?"

The "T" in **STOP** refers to **Troubleshooting** with the counselee to identify the nature of the problem. For example is the counselee's problem an individual mood problem, an interpersonal problem, an addiction or habit, or some other problem?

The "O" in **Openness** is the process. Openness refers to identifying the counselee's willingness and readiness to deal with her issue. For example, "Is this a problem you want help with, or did you simply want to talk about your feeling?" "What would it be worth to you if I could show you how to deal with ____?" "Would you be willing to do assignments between sessions?" "How willing are you to work on these problems even if it is difficult, frightening, or makes things temporarily worse?"

The "P" refers to the **Plan** to use in addressing the counselee's concerns. The exact nature of the plan depends on your case conceptualization and what you have learned about the counselee's issues. As you read the script below, get a feel for the style of interaction between the counselor (CO) and counselee (CL).

| CO: | *We have discussed several different issues that you wanted to deal with in our counseling. Which one of them would you like to focus on this session?* |
|---|---|
| CL: | *I think I want to talk about whether I should break up with my girlfriend.* |
| CO: | *So you would like for us to use our time today exploring whether Julie and you should continue going together?* |
| CL: | *Yeah, she has been pressuring me to carry our relationship to the next level.* |
| CO: | *That sounds like you feel uncomfortable. Help me understand what the phrase "next level" means to you.* |
| CL: | *Well, we have been dating for six months and she is starting to talk about how much she likes kids and she points out houses that are for sale, stuff like that. It makes me feel uncomfortable because I am not sure that I am ready for that.* |
| CO: | *So you are feeling pressure from Julie to move into a more committed level of relationship than you are comfortable with.* |
| CL: | *Yeah, I guess so. I like her and all, but I am not sure that I want to settle down with anybody right now and she keeps dropping hints every time we are together. It is getting to the point where I don't look forward to being with her.* |
| CO: | *What does she say when you tell her how you feel about the "hints" that she keeps dropping?* |
| CL: | *I haven't told her* (slightly elevated tone of voice). |
| CO: | *OK, let me make certain that I understand this correctly. On the one hand you are feeling pressured by Julie to make a more serious commitment in your relationship and on the other you haven't expressed this to her yet.* |
| CL: | *Yeah, that's about it"* (slightly embarrassed). |
| CO: | *What do you think is holding you back from expressing your feelings?* |
| CL: | *I don't know . . . I guess I'm afraid that she'll break up with me.* |

CO:     *So if I am hearing you correctly, you care about Julie and you want the relationship to continue, but you are not ready to move as quickly as she is?*

CL:     *Exactly! I do care very much about her and I can see a future for us, but right now I have to pay off my student loans and find a job that will support a family. I don't want to just rush into marriage without a plan. From what I've seen, marriage is hard enough by itself!*

CO:     *It is, and it sounds like you have given this some thought. Since you have already said that you care for Julie and can see a future together, how do you propose handling this situation?*

CL:     *I don't know. I don't want to break up with her; I just want her to stop pushing me so hard right now.*

CO:     *So, how will you accomplish this?*

CL:     *Well, I guess that I will have to sit her down and tell her how I feel and go from there.*

CO:     *What will you do if she continues to push you?*

CL:     *I suppose that means that she doesn't respect my feelings about this, so I would have to either be more clear and see if she respects my feelings after that or break up with her.*

CO:     *Are you OK with that?*

CL:     *Yeah, if she won't stop.*

CO:     *Good. It sounds like you have identified how you feel about this issue and you have a plan for dealing with it.*

## THE HELPER'S ROLE

We have already spoken about the need to prepare the counselee for her role in the helping process. But the counselor has a role to fill too. As a counselor you will have a unique function in the course of the helping process. Typically early in the process you will listen more than talk, for example. The counseling literature represents a broad range of counselor roles. Although there is no agreed-on "right" role for counselors to assume in the helping process, writers use various words to express the counselor's role including facilitator, tutor, cheerleader, mediator, advocate, guide, coach, collaborator, and even parent. In short, counselors wear different hats in the counseling office. Certain counseling approaches are more geared toward a particular role. Your personality style will also influence the type of role that seems right for you. Your role will likely be fluid rather than static, changing depending on the circumstances you are facing. For example if the counselee is in crisis, you might assume the role of a troubleshooter. Or if the counselee is grieving, a pastoral role might be more fitting. The point is to match your role to the needs of the counselee and his or her situation rather than to what seems most comfortable for you.

The word *process* refers to how you relate to your counselee. In other words the role is not as evident in the types of activities you do as much as the way you position yourself with the counselee. Your role will either reinforce your authority position or seek to equalize the inherent hierarchy in the counseling relationship. The way you relate to your counselee might cause him to view himself inferior to you or to empower him as an equal. If you approach their counselees from a professional position, you create a sterile and nonauthentic role with the counselee. You are not the professional; you are a human being called to minister to the person. Interact with your counselee out of your personhood rather than out of a role. When you are infused by the power of the Holy Spirit, your interaction will give your counselees a taste of God drawing them to Christ regardless of the role you are using. The specific counselor role is far less important than the fact that you will likely be viewed as both an authority figure and a Christian. Nothing is more important than the fact that you are an ambassador for Christ, a minister of healing. We wholeheartedly agree with Crabb and Allender (1997), who stress that a Christian counselor should be more committed to representing Christ than to a particular model, style, or approach to counseling. The Christian counselor models Christ's threefold offices (see Table 9.3). Theologically Jesus is the embodiment of the perfect Prophet who revealed God the Father to the people (Luke 7:16; John 4:4; Acts 3:20–24); He is the ultimate High Priest who serves as Mediator between God and man (Ps 110:4; Heb 5:5–6; 6:19–20) and represents mankind to God; and He is the King of kings who will rule and reign for all eternity (Isa 9:6–7; John 18:33–37).

Table 9.3
*Counselor Roles*

| Role | Function | Purpose | Emphasis | Perceived As | Offers | Provides | Goal | Key Strategies |
|---|---|---|---|---|---|---|---|---|
| Prophet | Disrupts | Reveals God | Truth | Instructor | Hope | Conviction | Change | Confronting, educating |
| Priest | Connects | Represents man | Grace | Encourager | Love | Comfort | Supports | Attending, reflecting |
| King | Directs | Rules for man | Justice | Expert | Faith | Safety | Growth | Interpreting, Agenda-setting |

Based on Crabb & Allender (1997)

According to Crabb and Allender (1997) people change when they (a) are willing to wrestle with God and with other human beings about the deep matters of the heart, (b) are drawn into an intimate relationship with God and other human beings, (c) obediently walk in the path of the royal law of love based on the wonder of being forgiven.

In short, Crabb and Allender believe that for counselees to change they need to be disrupted (a) by a prophet; connected (b) through a priest, and directed (c) by a king. The counselor fulfills the role of prophet when he disrupts people's complacency and inclination to drift from God. He serves in the role of Priest when he helps people find connection with God. And the counselor is serving like a king when he provides direction for his counselees. We will briefly examine Crabb and Allender's (1997) discussion of counselor roles here, but the reader is directed to their excellent book *Hope when you're hurting: Answers to four questions hurting people ask.*

Perhaps the most uncomfortable role for most people drawn to the counseling profession is that of prophet. According to Crabb and Allender (1997) the prophet's primary function is to challenge. A prophet disrupts, troubles, and surprises. As prophet the counselor focuses on the counselee's heart that hungers for rest, joy, and reconciliation. A prophet disrupts because sin has a way of boring deep into the soul and leeching off the heart's hunger of love and wholeness. A prophet exposes and rebukes sin but, he does so in ways that hold the counselee's attention. Recall the story of Nathan, who exposed David's sin by setting the trap and seducing

David to "hang" himself (2 Sam 12:1–17). By surprising the counselee the prophet is able to create sufficient imbalance so that the door of the counselee's heart is cracked open. The counselee's hardened and idolatrous heart is exposed, and the counselee is encouraged to seek Christ. Because the prophet causes people to remember God, he offers hope. He does more than point out all the flaws in one's soul; he also points out solutions for the problems of the soul. The prophet points to a new life in the future by way of a restoring relationship with Christ. "The prophet in that case is a poet of the future—helping enter the hunger that has been denied and then seeing the path to pursue to taste the desired joy" (Crabb & Allender, 1997, p. 160). Although the prophet confronts sin, the greatest benefit comes from intensifying one's choice. Once drawn into the light, the counselee's inner passions are enlivened toward hope. The prophet offers hope through such activities as confession, repentance, and reconciliation with God through Christ.

In contrast to the prophet, the priest provides the shepherding function in the counseling. The priest is kind, tolerant, open, and engaging. As a priest the counselor provides comfort and support, and facilitates the process of healing. The priest's presence reminds the counselee of Christ who dwelt amidst our ugliness. The priest-counselor attends to the counselee and demonstrates understanding. The priest enters the counselees' struggles and seeks to deepen his faith by reminding him "in word and deed of Christ's sacrifice on our behalf" (Crabb & Allender, 1997, p. 145). As a teacher of the Scriptures, the priest orients people to truth. The priest lifts the eyes of the downfallen to the Person of Christ. As part of his intercessory work the priest "looks to God in order to remind the people of his goodness and grace" (Crabb & Allender, 1997, p. 160). Like Paul, who reminded the Corinthian readers of God's work in Israel's past, so the priest helps counselees recall the work of God. The priest enlivens a dead heart by using a well-timed word that draws "the sinful heart to God, announces the provision of redemption, and invites the forgiven to celebrate" (Crabb & Allender, 1997, p. 12). Whereas the prophet exposes sin, the priest exposes beauty and goodness.

The third role available to the counselor is that of king. The primary function of a king is to direct, lead, and guide. He creates structure and order in order to promote harmony and peace. Safety is paramount to a king, who protects by grounding people in reality. The king does not own people's problems, but he ensures that they have knowledge and access to adequate resources. "A king does not assure the resolution of a problem; he only offers to lead a person in the path of maturity" (Crabb & Allender,

1997, p. 163). Growth is the end result of people who are well nourished and who have the provisions necessary to prosper.

Crabb and Allender (1997) write, "The prophet is a poet who disturbs and arouses hope, the priest is a storyteller who comforts and deepens faith, and the king is a mentor who applies wisdom to life and leads people into war with the weapon of love" (p. 163). Counselors tend to find one role more comfortable then another. Some counselors enjoy the role of prophet by challenging counselees in areas of their lives, whereas others are drawn to the wounded and brokenhearted to offer a blanket of love and compassion. Some counselors find the role of king more befitting them; the ability to lead and direct fits well with their personality style. If we are to be like Christ, then we need to grow in each role and function. Christ functioned in all three capacities. To the woman caught in adultery He was the prophet who said "Sin no more," He was the priest who said "Neither do I condemn you," and He was the king who said "Go" (John 8:1–11). Though Christ has three distinct roles, He is one person. Likewise your counseling roles should reflect who you are.

## THE AIM MODEL

An effective counseling approach requires a person to understand, advance, and employ a conceptual philosophical framework. This structure gives shape to one's therapeutic practice. At any point in the counseling process the counselor is interfacing with thousands of bits of information (Watzlawick, Beavin, & Jackson, 1967). A philosophical framework will guide you in knowing how to handle that information. In consideration of how central therapeutic scaffolding is to helping, Corey, Corey, and Callanan (2007) wrote, "Practicing counseling without an explicit theoretical rationale is somewhat like flying a plane without a map and without instruments" (p. 102). Kurt Lewin (cited in Marrow, 1969) noted the usefulness of a clear framework this way: "There is nothing as practical as a good theory."

A framework is a model that will allow you to organize what otherwise might be an overwhelming amount of information. It gives you a means of interpreting people's communication, and it guides interventions. It will help you fit concepts together and maintain a sense of coherence in your approach.

This section gives a specific model of helping that is versatile enough to meet the particulars of different helping settings. This model is not the optimal model nor is it the only one to use. But it is biblically and psychologically sound.

The model is especially targeted to people of faith, though it is highly applicable to people who do not passionately embrace a faith. Our reason for unashamedly incorporating a biblical worldview into the model is that it is highly relevant. Research indicates that individuals of faith benefit greatly from the use of spiritual principles and interventions in counseling (Oakes & Raphael, 2008; Richards et al., 2007). In fact research has shown that for religious counselees, faith can be implicated in both the development of and recovery from symptoms (Richards & Bergin, 2000; Sosin, 2008). Our experience has confirmed this. Recall when Jesus made the incredible statement:

> Abide in Me, and I in you. As the branch cannot bear fruit of itself unless it abides in the vine, so neither can you unless you abide in Me. I am the vine, you are the branches; he who abides in Me and I in him, he bears much fruit, for apart from Me you can do nothing. If anyone does not abide in Me, he is thrown away as a branch and dries up; and they gather them, and cast them into the fire and they are burned. If you abide in Me, and My words abide in you, ask whatever you wish, and it will be done for you. My Father is glorified by this, that you bear much fruit, and so prove to be My disciples. Just as the Father has loved Me, I have also loved you; abide in My love. If you keep My commandments, you will abide in My love; just as I have kept My Father's commandments and abide in His love. These things I have spoken to you so that My joy may be in you, and that your joy may be made full (John 15:4–11, NASB).

It is to this Scripture that our model refers. Jesus said that no fruit can be born apart from Him; that apart from Him nothing of value remains; and that abiding in Him leads to our heart's desires and to God the Father's glory, love, and fullness of joy. Consider the biblical concept of fruit in reference to the concerns that bring people to counseling. Think of the marriage problems, family issues, anxiety, depression, and addictions. Counselees are desperately searching for the fruit of love, joy, peace, patience, kindness, goodness, faithfulness, gentleness, and self-control (Gal 5:22–23, NIV), fruit that is a direct gift from the Spirit of God. And so we call our model "Abide in Me" and base ourselves as Christian counselors in Jesus' love (Eph 3:18).

The words "Abide in Me" provide an acrostic for each of the components of the AIM model. AIM is a synthesis of (a) our clinical and research experience, (b) various theoretical orientations and clinical strategies, and (c) biblical truth. All these give a comprehensive bio-psycho-social-spiritual prototype for counseling. Each component of the model represents a portion of what needs to be addressed for counseling to be effective.

Figure 9.2 provides an illustration of the model. You may find using the acrostic in Table 9:4, **ABIDE IN ME**, helpful in remembering the different aspects of the model. Each component in the acrostic is described briefly and is expanded in later chaps.

## DESCRIPTION OF AIM COMPONENTS

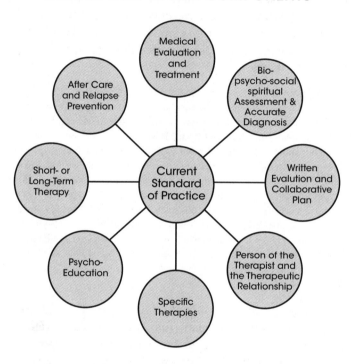

Figure 9.2: Components of the AIM Model

## Abide

The foundation of the AIM Model is Jesus Christ and a commitment to "explicitly cohere with long formulated Christian orthodoxy and orthopraxy" (Powlison, 2001, p. 40). This means that the model, first and foremost, emanates from and reflects the truths revealed in the Bible.

Because the person of the counselor and the helping relationship are the primary conduits to successful counseling (Corey, 2005; Young, 2010), the focal point of AIM is the counselor's personhood and the kind of relationship and experience he or she brings to the counselee. As such, we believe that the counselor's radical commitment to abiding in Christ and her understanding of counseling as a ministry of Jesus Christ is primary. According to Anderson (1997) "every act of ministry reveals something about God" and is "God's ministry" (p. 7). Christians are "ambassadors for Christ" (2 Cor 5:20), quite a formidable, even impossible, task apart from Him. However, with Christ, we can be His emissaries who, out of our own love and worship of Him, abide in Him and in so doing, provide what has substantial value to our counselees.

### Table 9.4

*Components of the AIM Model*

| Model Component | Description of Component |
|---|---|
| **A=Abiding in Christ** | Emphasizes the spirituality of the counselor and his or her personal relationship with Jesus Christ in the provision of an "incarnational" therapeutic relationship in counseling. |
| **B=Biblically Grounded Integration** | Utilizes empirically based and ethically sound psychological and spiritual formulations and interventions in counseling. |
| **I=Identity Work** | Focuses on solidifying of the counselee's identity (psychological differentiation), including spiritual identity, in counseling. |
| **D=Discerning Thoughts** | Utilizes the principles of cognitive-behavioral theory and therapy to encourage counselees to be "taking every thought captive to the obedience of Christ" (2 Cor 10:5). |
| **E=Emotional Wisdom** | Supports counselees as they climb up the developmental and spiritual "ladder" in managing their emotions. |
| **I=Independence of Will** | Encourages counselees to reach their goals by making decisions in keeping with personal values and faith with the help of Jesus Christ and the support of others. |
| **N=Neurobiology** | Addresses the whole person in counseling, including the need for healthy stewardship of one's body and at times psychopharmacological medication. |
| **M=Milieu** | Recognizes that counselees live in family, work, church, and community social systems and addresses/utilizes these systems, as appropriate, in counseling. |
| **E=Evil** | Attends to the reality of spiritual influences and the relationship of the world, the flesh, and the devil, to the counselee's presenting issues and concerns. |

Like your counselees, you too are on a pilgrimage. As Lewis (1950) noted every person is journeying "further up and further in" with Jesus as He encourages each person to reflect His image and likeness. Lest you run the risk of being a blind guide, keep your eyes affixed on the ultimate Guide, the Wonderful Counselor. Lest you think for a moment that you are beyond the need of a Shepherd, learn to abide in Christ.

Abiding in Christ as a counselor means living in continual fellowship with Him, receiving His grace-filled love and forgiveness, and appropriating His truth in your life by means of His power and presence. To abide in Christ as a Christian counselor means to be a person who has genuinely been liberated by the truth (John 8:31–32) and who bears the fruit of love, joy, peace, patience, kindness, goodness, faithfulness, gentleness, and self control, in and out of the counseling office (Gal 5:22–23). This communion with the mind and heart of God is gained through the use of spiritual disciplines, including the counselor's daily focus on God's glorious greatness, meditation on the Scriptures, corporate worship, talking with (praying to) God, and so forth, and is sustained by keeping the mind and body "captive" in obedience to Christ (Roberts, 2001; Shields & Bredfeldt, 2001). Once we are truly rooted and grounded in Christ, then and only then can we assist others in doing the same. This truth is aptly captured by Van Deusen Hunsinger in the following statement:

> We must acknowledge that our work of leading others through the painful process of removing illusions and making meaning from pain will be inextricably bound to our own progress on that same journey. The guide who does not keep God's back in clear view can never lead others through the wilderness (cited in McMinn and Phillips, 2001, p. 200).

Abiding in Christ, as a counselor, also means ensuring that your view of mankind is embedded in an accurate biblical theology. According to Hoekema (1986) biblical anthropology presents man as a created being, made in the image and likeness of God, dearly loved by Him, completely dependent on Him, and free to make choices. To adequately treat a person, we must address the deepest need of all humanity, namely, to be rightly related to God and free to make choices in keeping with His commands. Scripture views man as an image-bearer of God, an "unceasing, spiritual being with an eternal destiny in God's great universe" (Willard, 1997, pp. 211–212); one who, if reborn in Christ, will one day be with Him in glory (Col 3:4). You can do much to support your counselees when you help them have a biblical view of themselves and others, promoting spiritual identity while simultaneously advancing their psychological well-being

(Poll & Smith, 2003). "To be a human being in the truest sense means to love God above all, to trust him and obey him; and to live life *coram Deo*—as before the face of God" (Hoekema, 1986, p. 76).

The Bible also recognizes that mankind has been ravaged by the effects of the fall. Christian counselors therefore deeply understand the heinous reality of pervasive depravity and its link to the presenting concerns of our counselees. As part of the treatment of symptoms, you can emphasize the radical pursuit of holiness, instead of merely focusing on secular strategies that may ultimately "weaken our devotion to Christ and replace the kingdom of God in the hearts of his people with such aims as individuation, self-esteem, feeling good, congruence and satisfaction with life" (Roberts, 2001, p. 134). As Christian counselors we must proficiently treat disorders, relational disturbances, and the like within the context of a spirituality that promotes the renewal of the image of God and ultimate healing. While "insights" can be gleaned from psychology (Poll & Smith, 2003), we must never lose a sense of the importance of putting Christ first in one's life.

## Biblically Grounded Integration

Spiritual integration refers to the use of a combination of spiritual and psychological principles and interventions in counseling. AIM is a biblically integrative counseling model that stems from the research-based knowledge that faith significantly supports mental, physical, and social health (Harris, Schoneman, & Carrera, 2002) and that faith in and reliance on God has the potential to decrease anxiety, depression, and character pathology (Laurencelle, Abell, & Schwartz, 2002).

Christian counselors carefully assess both psychological and spiritual treatment protocols for their compatibility with biblical truth (Garzon, 2005; Jones & Butman, 1991; Powlison, 2001) and provide services with the utmost legal, ethical, and professional integrity (AACC, 2004; APA, 2002; Collins, 1991; Ohlschlager, 2004; Sanders, 1997). The AIM model draws on empirically validated treatments; interventions widely recognized and recommended by experienced clinicians; excellence in assessment, diagnosis, and treatment planning; and ethically sound clinical principles (Chambless & Ollendick, 2001; Groth-Marnat, 2003; James & Gilliland, 2003; Nathan & Gorman, 2002; Seligman & Reichenberg, 2007) from both secular and spiritual sources. This makes Christian counseling both complex and exciting.

## Identity Work

Establishing and solidifying one's identity is considered by many to be the primary developmental task of the adolescent period (Burch, 1985;

Hayes, 1982; Piaget, 1955). Individuals with a diffuse or unformed identity are unable to enjoy the peace and stability of a strong and central sense of self. It is imperative to address identity in counseling because symptoms that counselees present (e.g., anxiety and depression), are often related to a lack of self-awareness and solid psychological boundaries (Cloud & Townsend, 1992). At times attachment failure is at the root of such disturbances in self-formation (Cichetti & Toth, 1995; Clinton & Sibcy, 2002). The counseling relationship provides an avenue for identity formation and the addressing of faulty identity patterns that result from failed attachment (Levenkron, 2000).

Identity development includes acquiring meaningful moral standards, values, and belief systems; establishing of an authentic sense of individuality along with the ability to connect deeply with others; and joy in the use of one's gifts, talents, and uniquely fashioned personhood (Grotevant, 1998; Predo, 2005; Simpson, 2001). A stable identity is imperative to psychological health and maturity. The Christian counselor assesses psychological identity (Boman, 2007; Erikson & Erikson, 1997), and also spiritual identity. Helping counselees be sure their view of God and themselves is in keeping with biblical truth is a key component in the AIM model.

## Differentiating Thoughts

The Bible and contemporary psychology concur on the importance of accurate perceiving, feeling, and behaving. The AIM model integrates the Scriptures with empirically validated cognitive-behavioral interventions in an endeavor to help counselees "demolish arguments and every high-minded thing that is raised up against the knowledge of God, taking every thought captive to the obedience of Christ" (2 Cor 10:5). Christian counselors utilize traditional cognitive-behavioral interventions with an integration of Scripture and Christian perspectives (Sosin, 2008; Tan, 2003).

In addition to traditional cognitive tools (Beck & Weishaar, 1995; Safran, 1990), skilled helpers recognize that dysfunctional cognitions are often rooted in trauma and attachment failure (McGinn, Young, & Sanderson, 1995; Young, Klosko, & Weishaar, 2003). By using biblical perspectives, Christian counselors have the added benefit of applying spiritual factors in dysfunctional thinking (Roberts, 2001; Shields & Bredfeldt, 2001; Sperry, 2001) that develops from failed attachment. Using cognitive theory and cognitive-behavioral techniques in the AIM model does not mean that insights from neurobiological, psychodynamic, interpersonal, and other theories are not relevant to case conceptualization and treatment. Skilled counselors work integratively, drawing from available empirically based protocols and best practice guidelines in their treatment planning and treatment.

## Emotional Wisdom

The AIM model incorporates a biblical understanding of emotion and a focus on healthy emotional management. Maturation of emotionality is a developmental task (Simpson, 2001), as indicated in the biblical mandate to grow in Christlikeness (1 Cor 13:11) and the exhortation to bear the fruit of the Spirit (Gal 5:22–23). When a child has temper tantrums, the parents sigh, "I can't wait to get past the terrible twos." The same behavior, however, exhibited by a grown man or woman who is still a "vacuum of self concern" at age 27 is not so tolerable. Many of the problems with couples and families that we encounter require the fostering of mature emotional functioning and the capacity to love others.

Our experiences are that individuals who have not climbed up the developmental ladder in terms of emotion have often experienced trauma and/or attachment failure in their history. Research indicates that interpersonal and environmental trauma sensitizes the nervous system and leads to unbearably painful emotional states (Allen, 2001; Cichetti & Toth, 1995; Sroufe, 1997). An integral part of the AIM model is "fostering the capacity for containing emotions through a stable treatment structure, self-regulation, secure attachment, and the construction of a coherent trauma narrative" (Allen, 2001, p. 19). Much destructive behavior, cognition, and emotions are rooted in the undeveloped self and the triggering of the biological processes behind past trauma. Although the wounded we serve may not bear all the responsibility for the psychological outcomes of their traumatic histories, if they are Christians, they are still responsible to manage their behavior, cognition, emotions in keeping with the Word of God. Figure 9.3 illustrates Allen's trauma model (2001, p. 18) with a biblical adaptation. Knowledge of unresolved grief and trauma and its impact on affect, developmental pathways, and behavioral choices and emotions goes a long way in helping counselees understand and ultimately control their emotional reactions (Allen, 2001; Allen, Kelly, & Glodich, 1997). The mature handling of anger, fear, guilt, loneliness, sadness, and shame is essential to healthy functioning. Emotions that are met with grace and truth in the helping relationship can be utilized in counseling as an opportunity for developmental growth and healing (Hendlin, 1987; Teyber, 2006).

## Independence of Will

The AIM model encourages counselees to take responsibility for their emotional needs, behavioral choices, and treatment goals. AIM embraces the attitude that it is the counselee's right and responsibility to make choices in keeping with personal values and goals (James & Gilliland,

2003; Wubbolding & Brickell, 1998). As Joshua exhorted, "Choose for yourselves today the one you will worship. . . . As for me and my family, we will worship the LORD" (Josh 24:15, HCSB). To have the freedom and will to make choices that follow God's commands, to be able to enjoy the power that comes from abiding in Christ, and to understand the dire consequences (not punishments, but natural consequences) of walking outside His commands, is the zenith of independence and maturity.

A critical skill in assessing counselee independence of will is the ability to discern the counselee's readiness for change (Geller, Cassin, Brown, & Srikameswaran, 2009; Lewis et al., 2009). Along with the responsibility to make one's own choices goes ownership of those choices. The Bible teaches and illustrates the principle that we reap what we sow (Gal 6:7). The counselor can use motivational techniques to help bring about readiness and to encourage the counselee to take ownership (Miller & Rollnick, 2002); however, it is not the counselor's responsibility to force a counselee to make the "right" choice. A counselor can clearly and convincingly present truth to counselees, but he must recognize where his own responsibility ends. Facilitating counselee motivation and freedom is a key focus in the AIM model and is further elaborated on in chap. 12 ("Strategies for Bringing About Changes").

## Neurobiology

The field of biopsychiatry has demonstrated that certain disorders have a neurobiological component (Gabbard & Atkinson, 1996; Nathan & Gorman, 2002). Thus counselors must discern when a referral for medical, psychiatric, and/or psychological assessment is indicated. Also, comprehensive treatment of brain biology may require medication along with responsible body stewardship, relaxation, emotional expression, and a positive outlook, which have been shown to effect neurobiology (Bourne, 1995). How to assess medical factors is discussed in chap. 10 ("Conducting an Assessment").

## Milieu

Mental-health difficulties are often based on interpersonal dynamics and not merely intrapersonal struggles (Gladding, 2002). The AIM model incorporates an evaluation of the counselee's family, faith, occupation, and other social environments to determine which relationships may need to be addressed in counseling. Family counseling, couple counseling, group therapy, church-based small-group participation, community groups, professional counseling, and pastoral counseling are among the options for intervening in the counselee's world.

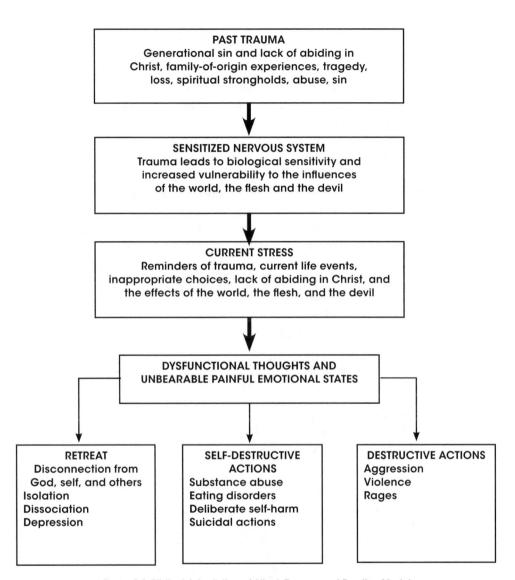

Figure 9.3: Biblical Adaptation of Allen's Trauma and Emotion Model

## Evil

Evil is real and an ever-present foe in our society. A theological understanding of human struggles and suffering involves recognizing the multiple agents of human affliction. Thomas and Habermas (2008) suggest that there are four sources of human suffering. First, we *encounter suffering because we live in a broken and fallen world.* Philosophers say this pain and suffering results from natural or physical laws. Because this world is not what God designed it to be, natural disasters, diseases, disorders, disillusionment, and despair are experienced. Second, we *encounter suffering because of supernatural causes.* Job's suffering was the result of Satan's evil imagination and intervention. Satanic forces can create great discomfort in a human life. Although Satan's accusations may have led in some sense to Job's suffering, God allowed and permitted it. The truth of the matter is that when we face tragedy, God knows that we hurt and cares that we hurt. Third, we *encounter suffering because of other people's choices.* Suffering may result from the choices and behavior of both Christians and non-Christians alike. We may be hurt intentionally or unintentionally by what others choose. Also people's choices can be intermingled with evil forces to create even more destruction. Fourth, we *encounter suffering because of the choices we make.* Even as we face the consequences of our own actions, all too often we point our finger at Satan, others, and even God, blaming everyone else for our pain. But the truth is, the choice to defy God's will, defy common sense, or defy God's calling will inevitably lead to suffering. Considering the powerful role that the sin nature and the flesh plays in suffering, Erickson (1998) wrote,

> From an evangelical perspective, the problem lies in the fact that human beings are sinful by nature and live in a world in which powerful forces seek to induce them to sin. The cure for sin will come through a supernaturally produced alteration of one's human nature and also through divine help in countering the power of temptation. It is individual conversion and regeneration that will alter the person and bring him or her into a relationship with God that will make successful Christian living possible (p. 617).

Erickson further clarifies that the fall has affected the entire creation.

> Not only are the individual human members of creation now separated and alienated from God, but so also are the powers that organize and influence them. . . . Behind the visible structures and institutions of society and culture, evil forces are at work using these invisible powers to enslave and bind believers, to attack them and do them harm. . . . Any of the patterns of a society can be used by the forces of evil to influence the thoughts and actions of the members of that society. . . . To the extent that they control or at least influence humans, they are powers. The term *structures* is appropriate, for the patterns utilized by the forces of evil form and constitute the very framework within which a person functions. They make their impact before or at a level below conscious influence and choice. Characteristically, the individual is not really conscious of their influence. There may be no awareness that other viable options exist (pp. 666–667).

The good news we bring to our counselees is that Christ has disarmed these powers (Col 2:13–15) and is available to help us "fight the good fight" against tenacious symptoms, well-established maladaptive patterns, and evil influences.

In summary the AIM model is an example of problems to be addressed in counseling. Counseling the whole person in a Spirit-led and ethically sound manner will reap the most profound harvest in the heart, mind, body, family, and community of our counselees.

## CASE STUDY UTILIZING THE AIM MODEL

The following case study is an example of the use of AIM in counseling. Although the counselee in this case study is not an actual person either of us has treated, he does represent countless counselees we have worked with over our combined 50-plus years of counseling experience. As you read the case of Sean Martina, take note of the components and phases of the AIM model that are being focused on. You will be asked to label the different elements and stages of the model in the exercises at the end of the chap.

Sean Martina, age 21, grew up in a loving, connected family, one that exhibited all the qualities that healthy families should (Gladding, 2002). The family members were committed to and appreciated each other, they spent a good amount of time together, they communicated well, handled difficulties in a positive manner, had clear rules and boundaries, and had a faith in Jesus Christ that was the center of their lives. They were not a perfect family, of course, but they knew how to love and forgive (Parrott, 1996).

Presently Sean attended college about a hundred miles from where his family lived. He had a dual major in art and literature and was hoping to become a writer and illustrator. He was doing exceptionally well in school, was a gifted artist, and had a fulfilling social life, including a girlfriend named Nancy. In short, Sean was flourishing in every way. He and his roommate Simon lived in a small, yellow house about a mile from the college campus. A narrow stream rambled through a meadow just across the street and there was a lovely view of the mountains in the distance. Sean and Simon were a good match because they both loved Jesus, art, being with friends, and keeping the house tidy. In fact they had just spent three months in producing a wall mural that included some of their favorite Scripture verses and scenes from the life of Christ. They were looking forward to hosting their fellowship group the next weekend so they could show the mural to their friends.

That weekend Simon was away on a retreat, so when Sean arrived home at about 11:30 p.m. he expected an empty house. As he walked up the steps, he began to feel uneasy and something inside of him told him to go no farther; in fact he sensed he should turn around and run. But he ignored his feelings and proceeded inside. After Sean entered the front door, one of two thieves grabbed him, beat him profusely until he was unconscious, and then joined his partner as they finished destroying Sean's and Simon's belongings, including their beautiful wall mural, and left him bloody and broken on the living-room floor. Sean was not found until the next afternoon when Nancy came over for their usual Saturday afternoon get-together. He was still unconscious.

Nancy, Sean's family and extended family, and special friends spent the next nine days at the hospital praying and hoping for Sean's recovery. After Sean was in intensive care for nine days, he was cognizant enough to speak and two weeks later was able to leave the hospital. He took with him a broken arm, two incompletely healed knife wounds, a couple of painfully swollen body parts, and a deeply troubled mind and heart.

Sean and his family were absolutely shaken up. Nothing like this had ever happened to him or anyone they knew. For several weeks after his release from the hospital, Sean stayed at his parents' house trying to recover. However, when it was time to return to school and get back into the swing of things, he told his parents he could not go back. He said he felt scared all the time, that his mind would not stop replaying the incident, that he could not understand why God had abandoned him, and that everything felt so overwhelming. He did not want to read his Bible, talk to God, see his friends, or even spend time with Nancy. He could not focus on his writing or artwork. When he told his mother he wished he had died the night of the crime, they decided to contact their pastor for some additional prayer and help.

Sean's church family had been praying for and ministering to Sean and his family since the incident occurred, so Pastor Clark was well aware of the problem. When Sean and his parents met with him, he explained why he thought it would be helpful for Sean to see Dr. West, a Christian counselor who specialized in helping people recover from complicated grief and trauma. He also asked Sean if he would get together with him and a couple of elders for prayer and if he would consider meeting weekly for prayer and encouragement with one of the shepherding elders until he felt like himself again. Although angry at God, Sean agreed.

After discussing things with his school advisor, Sean decided to take one semester off of school to pursue recovery. He then called Dr. West, who, with Sean's consent, also planned to collaborate with Sean's parents, Pastor Clark, Sean's school advisor, and Sean's medical doctor to obtain as much information as possible so as to best serve him. Because Sean was becoming more and more anxious, Dr. West scheduled to see him right away. As was his custom, Dr. West, who was committed to providing his counselees with an "incarnational" therapeutic relationship (Eberly, 2005; Wall, 2003), began praying that God would Himself lead the counseling, provide healing for Sean, and give him wisdom, discernment, and power during all the sessions with Sean. The initial phone conversation brought to light that Sean was questioning God's goodness and power. So Dr. West knew he would need to start with an implicit approach to spiritual integration (e.g., praying privately for Sean before, during, and after sessions, being Christlike himself, carefully following the leading of God's Spirit in his work with Sean). And he hoped to be able to use more explicit approaches, including praying with Sean, referring to the Bible during the sessions, helping Sean develop an accurate theodicy or understanding of the problem of evil, assigning readings that address the nature of God's goodness and greatness, and so forth (McMinn, 1996; Sperry, 2003).

The following afternoon Sean was nervously waiting to meet Dr. West in his quiet, well-lit, and comfortable waiting room. His mind was racing, nervously questioning himself about why he had come and what value it could possibly have. However, when Dr. West came to get him, right on time, Sean found that his friendly, kind, and genuinely caring manner immediately put him at ease. After the first session Sean felt that Dr. West truly understood his problems and that he had the resources to help him. For the first time since the crime occurred, Sean felt a glimmer of hope.

Dr. West and Sean completed a thorough bio-psycho-social-spiritual assessment during the first two appointments. This enabled Dr. West to know Sean fairly well (Lukas, 1993). Dr. West and Sean then worked together to create a counseling plan that addressed Sean's goals and needs. When Dr. West asked Sean what would be different if he were feeling better, Sean immediately said, "I wouldn't be haunted day and night by the replaying of that night. I would feel like myself again, be able to sleep at night, go places without feeling afraid, and enjoy the things I have always enjoyed. I'm tired of being "on" all the time. It's like I am a racing car and I can't get off the track, if that makes sense. Also I have always trusted God, talked with Him throughout the day, read the Bible a few times a day, you know, trusted Him. But now it's like He's disappeared. I go to pick up the Bible and I start thinking, I just don't know about any of this anymore; it just doesn't make sense. I guess I just do not trust Him anymore. I don't feel I can count on Him for protection. I mean, how could He let this happen to me if He's good, if He's real?"

Dr. West knew that for recovery to occur Sean needed to come to understand the normal effects of trauma and talk through the traumatic event. It was his hope to facilitate Sean's ability to work through the trauma-derived emotions by providing a consistent treatment structure and articulating a clear trauma narrative (Allen, 2001). Through the use of the therapeutic relationship, psycho-education, cognitive-behavioral, psychodynamic, and spiritual interventions, Dr. West hypothesized that Sean could come to understand and change how he thought about what happened to him. As Sean worked through the traumatic experience and recognized the painful emotions associated with it, Dr. West believed that Sean's symptoms of hopelessness about the future, detachment and lack of concern for significant others, difficulty concentrating and making decisions, hyperarousal, flashbacks, disturbing dreams, inability to focus, inability to eat, difficulty sleeping, racing heart, sweating, sadness, anxiety, anger, irritability, avoidance, and crisis of faith would dissipate. Indeed this was his experience with countless others as he "walked through the fire" with them.

Based on what Sean expressed and Dr. West's knowledge of treatments for post-traumatic stress syndromes (Briere & Scott, 2006), he and Dr. West came up with goals that were specific, measurable, attainable, and straightforward (Seligman, 1998; Seligman & Reichenberg, 2007; Young, 2010). Written from Sean's perspective these were from: (1) I will talk through and work through the traumatic event with Dr. West and focus on identifying the particular thoughts and images that make me feel afraid and upset. (2) I will replace these thoughts and images with ones that are less disturbing and based on the truth. (3) I will change the way I react to the disturbing memories by developing a bio-psycho-social-spiritual "toolbox" that will help me cope with painful thoughts, feelings, and images that are a normal reaction to my traumatic experience. (4) I will resume normal functioning, including regaining the ability to trust God and focus on and enjoy reading, artwork, relationships, and social experiences.

Dr. West completed a written evaluation right after the second session and subsequently reviewed it with Sean, who then worked with him to create the treatment plan (see chap. 11, "Case Conceptualization and Treatment Planning," for another case study that includes the report, diagnosis, and treatment plan and additional information about the initial interview, full bio-psycho-social-spiritual diagnostic/assessment evaluation, and treatment planning).

Sean and Dr. West met for eight sessions after the assessment and treatment planning were complete. After processing the trauma by utilizing relaxation and imagery techniques in two sessions, Sean's symptoms significantly subsided. By the third session Sean felt like he wanted to pray and ask God to give him additional healing, especially wanting God to help him trust Him again. Sean asked God to help him understand what happened and where God was in the process. This brought Sean an immediate and deep sense of peace and relief. Although he did not hear or see anything in particular, he did experience a palpable sense of God's loving presence and a peace that went beyond his mind and body. He said it was as if "a blanket of love was gently wrapped around me and I immediately felt safe, wanted, chosen, and loved." Later Sean reported that this was a turning point in his relationship with God because "I had never wrestled with the problem of evil before. It brought me face to face with the cross, both the need for it and an understanding of what God Himself was willing to endure in this fallen world in order to secure an eternal relationship with us."

Together Sean and Dr. West created a "toolbox" with several helpful means of dealing with trauma-related symptoms. Dr. West taught Sean about trauma and its effect on the mind, body, and spirit. He helped Sean learn how to track his thoughts and counter ones that were harmful with truthful, helpful thinking. He helped Sean learn how to systematically relax his body and, as Dr. West referred to it, to "speak peace to the winds and waves of his thoughts and emotions." He helped Sean develop spiritual disciplines that would bring him closer to God and support him in times of stress and fear. Working diligently from session to session, Sean and Dr. West addressed and met each of Sean's counseling goals.

Once all of Sean's goals were met, he and Dr. West reviewed the treatment and created an after-care plan that included subsequent follow-up visits two, four, and six weeks later. With Sean's permission Dr. West also contacted the counseling center on Sean's college campus and collaborated with a counselor there, if Sean should need more support once he was back in school.

In the end Sean felt that the terrible event, as difficult and as troubling as it was, had brought him to a much deeper understanding of God, a desire to ask Him for protection daily, and an ability to "guard his mind and heart" with diligence and prayerful concentration. Family, friends, art, indeed all of life had great purpose and meaning to him again, and he knew that he would never be the same.

## CHAPTER SUMMARY

This chap. gave you a bird's-eye view of the counseling process. Whether you are sitting with a counselee in a session or foreseeing the entire process, you are the guide responsible for the entire journey. The Christian helper represents the three earthly offices of Christ: the prophet who disturbs but offers hope, the priest who shepherds and offers a taste of Christ, and the king who leads his counselee into battle and provides order.

The chap. has also discussed how to do an ethical introduction, establishing both a therapeutic contract and helping goals with the counselee, and how to set an agenda for a session. Counselors hold the sacred trust of stories of trauma and travail that are personified in flesh. Christ did more than hear our sinful stories; He identified with them. You too can enter in to counselees' problems as you care deeply and take risks as necessary.

The "Abide in Me" (AIM) model is a Christ-centered template for counseling that integrates empirically validated treatments and biblical theology. As an integrative bio-psycho-social-spiritual approach, AIM involves the four domains of biology, psychology, social systems, and spirituality. Components of the model were described and a case study was included.

The nine-component, five-phase AIM counseling model provides an effective way of understanding the elements of effective, Christ-centered counseling. We hope that you will find it helpful as you grow as a counselor and begin formulating a model that both glorifies God and successfully serves the counselees He sends your way.

## CHAPTER 9 ACTIVITIES

1. Describe the five phases of the AIM model. Which phases do you think you are most prepared for and in which phases do you need the most training? Why?
2. According to this chap. how is a counselor like an editor?
3. Describe the stages of the initial intake session and a typical helping session.
4. Create your own simulated ethical introduction dialogue between you and a new counselee that includes an introduction of you as a counselor, confidentiality (including exceptions to confidentiality), asking about previous counseling experiences and expectations, and faith issues.
5. What are some of the differences between Christian and secular counselors' views on appropriate goals in counseling? What are your

thoughts on this important topic? Who, counselor or counselee, needs to decide where the counseling journey will end?

6. What morally objectionable or uncomfortable counselee goals would cause you to refer a counselee?
7. Describe the three levels of goals presented in this chap.
8. Describe each of the five characteristics of good goals presented in this chap.
9. Consider a goal you are presently working on in your own life. Answer the following questions about that goal:

   - "How likely are you to follow through with this goal?"
   - "How important is this goal to you?"
   - "If you accomplished this goal, what difference would it make in your life?"
   - "How likely are you to talk yourself out of trying to accomplish this goal?"
   - "Is this your goal, or is it something other people want you to accomplish?" (Young, 2005, p. 234)
   - Why is it important to establish goals that are meaningful to the counselee?

10. What guidelines for establishing goals are presented in this chap.? Discuss the importance of each one.
11. How does a Christian counselor model the threefold role of Jesus Christ in counseling? Assess yourself in each of these roles and functions? What can you do that will help you grow in each of these areas?
12. What are the components of the AIM model? Why is each part important to address in counseling?
13. Briefly describe when each of the phases and aspects of the AIM model are depicted in the case study given in this chap.

## Vignette Questions

*Vignette 13*
*Ethical Introduction*

1. Vignette thirteen showed a skill of counseling that is needed in the first session. What key ethical issues did Denise cover in her ethical introduction?
2. Why is it important to cover these issues in the first counseling session?

3. How does talking about forms that have already been filled out build the therapeutic relationship?
4. How did you feel as you watched this vignette? Explain your response. What caused you to feel this way?
5. What made the most impression upon you as you watched the video? Why do you think that this made such an impression?

*Vignette 14*
*Goal Setting*

### Ryan

1. In vignette fourteen, how did you feel when you watched Ryan work with Mariah? How do you think Mariah felt? Explain your response.
2. What could Ryan have done differently to improve the outcome of his goal-setting session?
3. What do you think might be behind Ryan's counseling approach? Do you see any similarities between your perspective and Ryan's perspective?

### Don

1. How did you feel when you watched Don? How do you think Charlie felt? Explain your response
2. When you recall the goal-setting styles of Ryan and Don, which one appeared to be more effective? Why do you think this was the case?
3. What did you appreciate most about Don's approach? Why do you think that this was meaningful to you?

*Vignette 15*
*Assessment*

1. Review vignette fifteen; did this vignette fit your mental picture of a counselee assessment? Why or why not?
2. What mental picture of the counseling session do you think Colleen had prior to the start of the therapy? Why do you think she felt this way?
3. Describe your perception of Coleen's experience during this portion of the assessment. What emotions might she have been feeling?
4. How was Denise able to overcome Coleen's initial resistance to counseling? How do you think this impacted the outcome of the counseling session?

5. Do you believe that the information that Denise obtained from Colleen was important to the assessment process? Explain your response.

## Recommended Reading

Fine, S. F., & Glasser, P. (1996). *The first helping interview: Engaging the client and building trust.* Thousand Oaks, CA: Sage.

> The benefits of this book apply to several different chaps. of this text. These authors provide a clear case for why the first contact with the counselee is critical. They address the topics of scheduling appointments, creating safety, establishing clear boundaries, and interviewing the counselee.

Strachan, D., & Pitters, M. (2008). *Managing facilitated processes: A guide for consultants, facilitators, managers, trainers, even planners, and educators.* San Francisco, CA: Jossey-Bass.

> Though not a counseling book, this is an excellent resource in the art of managing processes similar to counseling. It includes a wealth of information, especially for those who plan to provide training and consultation.

## Chapter 10

# Conducting an Assessment

*"Assessment in counseling should be viewed not as a
one-time prediction activity but rather as continuous
throughout the counseling process"* (Vacc, 1982, p. 40).

*"Test me, O Lord, and try me, examine my
heart and my mind"* (Ps 26:2, NIV).

## CHAPTER OBJECTIVES

» To present a rationale for conducting a psychosocial history

» To explain the structure and phases of the psychosocial interview

» To provide skills for conducting the interview through each phrase

» To detail information related to the key areas necessary for assessment

» To explain how to write a report

» To provide practical examples to help you develop your interview skills

## CHAPTER OUTLINE

THE ROLE OF THE PSYCHOSOCIAL HISTORY

THE NUTS AND BOLTS OF THE INTERVIEW
    Counseling Interview Phases

KEY AREAS TO EXPLORE IN THE PSYCHOSOCIAL REPORT

---

**B**asic to the counseling enterprise is an accurate and thorough understanding of the person you are trying to help. Since people are complex, it is imperative that the counselor obtain information about how the counselee is doing in the major domains of life. In some cases counselors are assessing the counselee's symptoms while at other times they are gathering a general life history. It is helpful to view these life domains in four primary areas: (a) biological functioning, (b) psychological functioning, (c) social functioning, and (d) spiritual functioning. In the secular literature these domains are referred to as the "bio-psychosocial" model. Of course the secular model does not include the spiritual domain as a separate entity. To better capture the four domains, we use the term "bio-psycho-soc-spiritual" model (Cumella, 2002) or what Miller and Kurtz (1994) referred to as the "spirit-bio-psycho-social"model. The more comprehensive the exploration of these areas, the more likely the counselor can formulate a plan to address the counselee's presenting issues. In a more comprehensive fashion Hawkins (n.d.) conceptualizes this process in terms of concentric circles (see Figure 10.1).

The previous chap. focused on the major phases of the counseling process. The first phase, Initiation and Assessment, is conducting an assessment on the counselee. To accomplish that task you need a framework for conducting the assessment. This chap. discusses what is widely called the "psychosocial interview." We begin by discussing the role this interview plays in the helping process, and then we discuss the major components of the interview.

## THE ROLE OF THE PSYCHOSOCIAL HISTORY

All counseling work is built on the foundation of an interview. In a casual conversation with a friend no set agenda or purpose to the interaction is generally present. The dialogue often ambles about at a leisurely pace from one topic to another, based on each party's interests and whims. A counseling interview, in contrast, has an objective. It is a conversation with a purpose. The overarching purpose of a counseling interview is to help the counselee with his presenting concerns. The interview is specifically geared at gathering the counselee's relevant life information, assessing his or her interpersonal style and skills, and uncovering those areas in the counselee's life that need to be addressed in order to help with the presenting concern. The information obtained through the interview allows you to put the counselee's presenting concerns in context.

Your role in the psychosocial history process is to be an interviewer. Some novice counselors may easily be seduced into the role of a detective. Both detectives and interviewers attempt to gain access to information, but for different purposes and with different mindsets. Particular populations of counselees such as those with addictions or who are court-ordered seem more than others to evoke our inner tendency to be like sleuth. We know that counselees hide, distort, deny, and lie. Your role, however, is not to be the detective assigned to the case, and you are neither judge nor jury to the counselee. By mastering counseling skills you can obtain more accurate information, but you will never know the complete truth. Especially in the interview process, accept the counselee's stories and information as a matter of course. Over time certain information will bear out the truth or falsehood of what is said, and more data will come to light.

Sommers-Flanagan and Sommers-Flanagan (2003) state that a counseling interview should include the following: (a) a professional relationship between counselor and counselee; (b) the counselee has some level of motivation to accomplish something; (c) the counselor and counselee work together to establish and achieve mutually agree on goals for the counselee; (d) a verbal and nonverbal interaction between the counselor and counselee in which the helper applies a variety of active listening skills and psychological techniques to evaluate, understand, and help the counselee accomplish the goals; and (e) the quality and quantity of interactions between the helper and counselee are influenced by many factors such as the counselor and counselee's personality, attitudes, and mutually agreed on goals (pp. 17–18).

The focus of the psychosocial interview, like all aspects of counseling, is on the life and needs of the counselee; it is never about the needs of the counselor. No one likes talking with a friend who dominates the conversation with facts about himself. In fact a technique employed in interpersonal relations is to talk about other people's favorite topic, themselves. Such a strategy helps you win friends and influence people (Carnegie, 1981). The first counseling session in particular should be completely focused on gleaning information about the counselee's life.

## THE NUTS AND BOLTS OF THE INTERVIEW

The structure of the interview depends on the specific purpose. If you are working in a setting that requires a diagnosis by the end of the first session, your interview might need to be at least semi-structured to ensure that you gather the information necessary for a diagnosis. In contrast, if diagnosing is not the driving force in the interview, then a more relaxed, conversational structure can be used. This does not mean that you abandon control of the process to the counselee. Rather, you can gather the information necessary for the counselee's psychosocial history in a less-structured way. In general, however, counselors typically develop their own style of interviewing. Some will feel more comfortable with a more directive style, and others will prefer a more nondirective approach to the interview process.

### Counseling Interview Phases

It is helpful to think about the counseling interview as occurring in sequences, each one associated with a task. The acrostic **INTAKE** suggests these steps (see Table 10.1).

Table 10.1

*INTAKE: Phases of the Interview Process*

**I** = **Invite** the counselee to the interview
**N** = **Normalize** the interview process
**T** = **Target** the interview
**A** = **Assess** the counselee's functioning
**K** = **Know** the counselee's history
**E** = **End** the interview

### "I": Invite the counselee to the interview.

Inviting the counselee means seeing yourself as a hospitable host (Nouwen, 1975) by welcoming the counselee to the helping process. "Inviting the counselee puts him at ease and helps you connect with him." The skills associated with connecting were discussed in chap. 5 ("Basic Skills: Creating a Connection"). This section highlights the importance of putting counselees at ease by sharing personal information with a stranger. The task of connecting occurs from the initial contact about the interview. The interview actually begins with the first contact with the counselee. At times that might be on the phone after receiving a call. The questions you ask and the counselee's voice and words on the phone can generate useful information for the very first appointment. Many times the first contact with a counselee is in the waiting room. Be sure to greet the counselee with your name. Remember that the process of building rapport starts with the first contact. From the phone contact to greeting the counselee in the waiting area you are working to establish a connection with the counselee that will form the basis of your helping process. Typically, as you and the counselee enter into the counseling room you are engaged in social conversation on such topics as finding the office and the weather. Like all appointments, the interview or session begins with social conversation to highlight the human factor of the meeting. As you and the counselee strengthen the connection, you are inviting a greater depth to sharing and journeying with the counselee further into his life.

### "N": Normalize the counseling process.

As you are working to connect with the counselee, you are also engaging in the process of "normalizing" the helping process. Normalizing refers to explaining and establishing the rules and guidelines that will govern the helping process. From the chitchat phase of inviting the counselee to the interview, you transition to the ethical introduction (chap. 9, "Managing the Counseling Session"). You will also inform the counselee of the time allotted for the interview (whether 45, 60, or 90 minutes).

### "T": Target the interview.

Most counselors develop their own structure for the psychosocial interview. Once the preliminaries are covered, the counselor moves to the reason for the counselee's appointment. Any one of several "session starter" responses can be used, including the following: "What are your goals in coming to see me?" "What is it that prompted you to make an appointment with me?" "With those details covered, I can put the ball into your court. Share with me what led to your deciding to see a counselor." "On the phone you mentioned that you wanted to see me because you were struggling with some significant decisions that must be made."

## "A": Assess the counselee's functioning.

The main goal of the intake interview is to assess the counselee's functioning. In the interview, aspects of the counselee's personality will be evident. Your job is not to read meaning into everything the counselee says. Rather you are to begin developing a comprehensive and holistic view of the counselee. Of course an all-encompassing portrait of the counselee is not possible in one or two interviews. One of my (John's) professors once said that the initial interview was a series of snapshots that will eventually evolve into a video throughout the counseling process. Assessment of a counselee's functioning occurs through three primary modalities: observation, assessing the counselee, and questioning symptoms.

### Assessment through observation.

One of the most overlooked counseling skills is the ability to observe. First, observation gives you the initial building blocks of rapport. Second, through observation we collect information relevant to our counselee's functioning, diagnosis, and problems.

Before discussing observation further, we need to note the difference between *signs* and *symptoms*. Signs refer to those things you observe. Signs include such behaviors as laughing, crying, posture, appearance, eye contact, agitation, restlessness, and the like. Though signs are objective in nature, their meaning is not always clear. For example if a counselee is crying, she might be doing so because she is sad, happy, or afraid. Symptoms, on the other hand, are subjective. Thus you rely on the counselee to tell you her symptoms. Symptoms include such subjective experiences as feelings, thought content, and other internal experiences. In this section we discuss the nature of observing signs, which comprise the mental status exam (MSE).

One of the most important principles in making use of observations is not contaminating your interpretation of the behavior by unsupported assumptions. Keeping your mind open to alternative explanations lessens the likelihood of jumping to the wrong conclusions. For example if an overweight teenage male is experiencing difficulty maintaining focus during the intake session, it would be very easy to assume that he is disinterested or unmotivated. The reality, however, may be far different; he may need to be evaluated for sleep apnea by a pulmonologist, since such symptoms are also consistent with this disorder. Helpers should pay attention to the following nonverbal cues.

*1. Observe general nonverbal cues.* If a picture is worth a thousand words, then what we see in our counselees' behavior is worth far more than what is said. The counselee's culture will impact the meaning of nonverbal behavior. Observing nonverbal cues includes noting appearance, clothing, grooming, posture, eye contact, gestures, and mannerisms.

*2. Observe appearance.* A person's appearance is one of the first things people notice. Concluding someone's sex, race, relative age, concern for appearance, and attractiveness are easily discernible in most people. Take note of the counselee's complexion, weight, height, posture, and obvious physical disabilities (walker, cane, oxygen tank, glasses, hearing aid, etc.).

*3. Observe the counselee's clothing.* In the old adage "clothing makes the man" the idea is that clothing can reveal subcultures, social status, occupation, and concern for self-care. People associated with certain parts of society dress in ways to demarcate their affiliation with certain groups. Through the kinds of clothing a counselee wears you can get a sense of the person's income status, a sense of his self-preoccupation, and potentially a means of managing a poor image. We have had counselees come in clothing associated with manual labor, work uniforms, and military garb.

*4. Observe the counselee's grooming.* Grooming can show you how careful a person is about her appearance and dress. A person can come to an appointment from work and not have time to change or shower. Some people who are dressed in less than desirable clothing can be well groomed but a person in a suit that is stained, wrinkled, and misbuttoned shows that he has little concern for self-care. Such a person might be poorly clothed and groomed as a manner of course or because of something interfering with her motivation to maintain self-care.

*5. Observe the counselee's facial expressions.* People reveal aspects of what they are thinking and feeling through their faces. Blank stares, frowns, grimaces, and smiles convey different thinking and feeling states. Of course some counselees have "poker faces" behind which they are hiding their true feelings, whereas others wear their feelings "on their sleeves." One of the things an experienced counselor notices is when the counselee's conversation does not seem to match one's facial expression. In other words, is the nonverbal congruent or incongruent with the conversation? A person displaying no facial expression when sharing about the death of a spouse is incongruent because it is normal to express some sense of sadness when talking about the death of a loved one.

**Assessing the counselee himself.**

Because people usually enter counseling because of relational difficulties, such problems will manifest themselves in the counseling relationship.

When interviewing or counseling, your body can act as a thermometer. As you are aware of your own body and its reactions to different types of people and to particular kinds of interactions, you can gain a sense of the counselee's functioning. I (John) have learned that I internally react a certain way to people who are controlling. Learning what those visceral body reactions mean provides insight into a counselee when the content of the messages might be conveying a different message.

### Assess a counselee's functioning by asking questions about symptoms.

This task in the interview includes the Mental Status Exam (MSE), which is discussed in a later section. The purpose of this phase of the interview is to obtain information related to the counselee's target. If the counselee is requesting help for depression, it is important to find when the depression occurs, how often, how intense, how it interferes with life, and so forth. Key questions related to assessing symptoms include these: (a) When did the symptoms start? (b) How frequently do they occur? (c) How long do they last? (d) How would you rate the severity of the symptoms? (e) How do these symptoms interfere with your life? (f) When are the symptoms worse? (g) When have the symptoms not occurred, or when have they been the easiest to manage? (h) Are there any exceptions to these symptoms? (i) Who is most concerned about your symptoms?

### "K": Knowledge of the counselee's history.

The fifth phase of the interview is to obtain information relevant to the counselee's history. After the counselee's target has been identified and you have assessed his overall functioning, it is time to turn attention to the larger context of the presenting concerns and issues. The specific areas to explore are discussed in a section below.

### "E": End the interview.

The final phase of the interview is to terminate or close it. The time can pass quickly when you are exploring a counselee's life. Whether the session is 45, 60, or 90 minutes, there is rarely enough time to cover everything. As suggested earlier, it is recommended that you begin closing the interview about 5 to 10 minutes before the agreed-on concluding time. Sommers-Flanagan and Sommers-Flanagan (2003) stress the importance of intentionally following guidelines when closing the interview.

First, reassure and support the counselee. For example "We have covered lots of ground today" or "I appreciate your efforts in telling me about yourself" or "Thanks for being so open and sharing so much about yourself with me" (pp. 157–158). For those who were ambivalent about coming to counseling, the following can be stated: "I want to congratulate you for coming here today. Coming to someone for help can be difficult. I know some people think otherwise, but I believe that getting help for yourself is a sign of strength" (p. 158). Your goal is to reassure counselees that you were not overwhelmed with the information nor do you hold a negative view of them.

Second, in closure cover key themes and issues. You can increase the likelihood of the counselee returning by clearly identifying why the counselee has come, summarizing the key issues covered, and reviewing the goals the counselee has set for herself. Sommers-Flanagan and Sommers-Flanagan (2003) offer the following example.

> "Based on what you've said today, it seems you're here because you want to feel less self-conscious about yourself. I think you said 'I want to believe in myself,' and you also talked about how you want to figure out what you're feeling inside and how to share your emotions with others you care about" (p. 158).

The closure can also instill hope. After all, because of the power and work of Christ there is always hope. Sommers-Flanagan and Sommers-Flanagan (2003) offer the following example.

> "You've said you want to feel better, and I think therapy can help you move in that direction. Of course, not everyone who comes for therapy reaps great benefits. But most people who use therapy to improve their lives are successful, and I believe that you're the type of person who is very likely to get good results from this process" (p. 159).

You can also ask the counselee if she has any questions for you, ask whether the session met her expectations, or ask if any areas were missed (Sommers-Flanagan and Sommers-Flanagan, 2003). The counselee can then tie up any lose ends such as scheduling additional appointments, discussing fees, signing any forms, and the like. Sommers-Flanagan and Sommers-Flanagan (2003) refer to "doorknob statements" as comments that counselees make as the session is ending. They provide a few examples that include a counselee (a) saying thank you while shaking your hand or giving you a hug, (b) stating that they would like to get together for coffee during the week, (c) saying that they feel a lot better, or (d) asking when they might begin to feel better. These statements can be important cues in understanding your counselees' motives, hidden agenda, or diagnosis.

Remember that you are in control of the counseling process. Counselees are often watching the clock as much as you are during the appointment.

Oftentimes a counselee will reveal an important piece of information just when you are ready to close. We have had counselees report, in the closing minutes of a session, having been raped, abused, fired, and that they were suicidal. Use your judgment to determine whether additional time is truly warranted, whether another appointment needs to be scheduled sooner, or whether the issue can wait until the next appointment.

In summary, remember that the counseling interview occurs in phases. It is these phases that you are tasked with maintaining.

## KEY AREAS TO EXPLORE IN THE PSYCHOSOCIAL HISTORY

What information does the counselor want to know? This section discusses assessing the counselee's functioning and obtaining knowledge about the counselee. Sommers-Flanagan and Sommers-Flanagan (2003) provide a helpful list of questions to use in conducting a psychosocial history (see Table 10.2).

Table 10.2

*Psychosocial Questions*

| Content Areas | Questions |
| --- | --- |
| 1. First Memories | What is your first memory?<br>How old were you then?<br>Do you have any very positive (or negative) early memories? |
| 2. Descriptions and memories of parents | Give me three words to describe your mother (or father).<br>Whom did you spend more time with, Mom or Dad?<br>What methods of discipline did your parents use with you?<br>What recreational or home activities did you do with your parents? |
| 3. Descriptions and memories of siblings | Did you have any brothers or sisters? (If so, how many?)<br>What memories do you have of time spent with your siblings?<br>Who was your closest sibling and why?<br>Who were you most similar to in your family?<br>Who were you most dissimilar to in your family? |

Table 10.2 (cont.)

*Psychosocial Questions*

| Content Areas | Questions |
|---|---|
| 4. Elementary school experiences | Do you remember your first day of school?<br>How was school for you? (Did you like school?)<br>What was your favorite (or best) subject in school?<br>What subject did you like least (or were you worst at)?<br>Do you have any vivid school memories?<br>Who was your favorite (or least favorite) teacher?<br>What made you like (or dislike) this teacher so much?<br>Were you ever suspended or expelled from school?<br>Describe the worst trouble you were ever in when in school.<br>Were you in any special or remedial classes in school? |
| 5. Peer relationships (in and out of school) | Do you remember having many friends in school?<br>What kinds of things did you do for fun with your friends?<br>Did you get along better with boys or girls?<br>What positive (or negative) memories do you have from relationships you had with your friends in elementary school? |
| 6. Middle school, high school, and college experiences | Do you remember having many friends in high school?<br>What kinds of things did you do for fun with your friends?<br>Did you get along better with boys or girls?<br>What positive (or negative) memories do you have from high school?<br>Do you remember your first day of high school?<br>How was high school for you? (Did you like high school?)<br>What was your favorite (or best) subject in high school?<br>What subject did you like least (or were you worst at)?<br>Do you have any vivid high school memories?<br>Who was your favorite (or least favorite) high school teacher?<br>What made you like (or dislike) this teacher so much?<br>Were you ever suspended or expelled from high school?<br>Describe the worst trouble you were ever in when in high school.<br>What was your greatest high school achievement (or award)?<br>Did you go to college?<br>What were your reasons for going (or not going) to college?<br>What was your major field of study in college?<br>What is the highest degree you obtained? |

| Table 10.2 (cont.) | |
| --- | --- |
| *Psychosocial Questions* | |
| **Content Areas** | **Questions** |
| 7. First employment and work experience | What was your first job or the first way you ever earned money? How did you get along with your coworkers? What kinds of positive and negative job memories do you have? Have you ever been fired from a job? What is your ultimate career goal? How much money would you like to make annually? |
| 8. Military history and experiences | Were you ever in the military? Did you volunteer, or were you drafted? Tell me about your most positive (or most negative) experiences in the military. What was your final rank? Were you ever disciplined? What was your offense? |
| 9. Romantic relationship history | Have you ever had romantic feelings for someone? Do you remember your first date? What do you think makes a good romantic or loving relationship? What do you look for in a romantic (or marital) partner? What first attracted you to your spouse (or significant other)? |
| 10. Sexual history (including first sexual experience) | What did you learn about sex from your parents (or school, siblings, peers, television, or movies)? What do you think is most important in a sexual relationship? Have you had any traumatic sexual experiences (e.g., rape or incest)? |
| 11. Aggressive history | What is the most angry you have ever been? Have you ever been in a fight? Have you ever been hit or punched by someone else? What did you learn about anger and how to deal with it from your parents (or siblings, friends, or television)? What do you usually do when you get angry? Tell me about a time when you got too angry and regretted it later. When was your last fight? Have you ever used a weapon (or had one used against you) in a fight? What is the worst you have ever hurt someone physically? |

Table 10.2 (cont.)

*Psychosocial Questions*

| Content Areas | Questions |
|---|---|
| 12. Medical and health history | Did you have any childhood diseases?<br>Any medical hospitalizations? Any surgeries?<br>Do you have any current medical concerns or problems?<br>Are you taking any prescription medications?<br>When was your last physical examination?<br>Do you have any problems with eating or sleeping or weight loss or gain?<br>Have you ever been unconscious?<br>Are there any major diseases that seem to run in your family (e.g., heart disease or cancer)?<br>Tell me about your usual diet.<br>What kinds of foods do you eat most often?<br>Do you have any allergies to foods, medicines, or anything else?<br>What are your exercise patterns?<br>How often do you engage in aerobic exercise? |
| 13. Psychiatric or counseling history | Have you ever been in counseling before?<br>If so, with whom and for what problems, and how long did the counseling last?<br>Do you remember anything your previous counselor did that would be particularly helpful (or particularly unhelpful)?<br>Did counseling help with the problem? If not, what did help?<br>Why did you end counseling?<br>Have you ever been hospitalized for psychological reasons?<br>What was the problem then?<br>Have you ever taken medication for psychiatric problems?<br>Has anyone in your family been hospitalized for psychological reasons?<br>Has anyone in your family had significant mental disturbances?<br>Can you remember that person's problem or diagnosis? |
| 14. Alcohol and drug history | When did you have your first drink of alcohol (or pot, etc.)?<br>About how much alcohol do you consume each day (or week, month)?<br>What is your "drink/drug of choice"?<br>Have you ever had any medical, legal, familial, or work problems related to alcohol?<br>Under what circumstances are you most likely to drink?<br>What benefits do you believe you get from drinking? |

Table 10.2 (cont.)

*Psychosocial Questions*

| Content Areas | Questions |
|---|---|
| 15. Legal history | Have you ever been arrested or ticketed for an illegal activity?<br>Have you been issued any tickets for driving under the influence?<br>Have you been given any tickets for speeding?<br>How many and how often?<br>Have you ever declared bankruptcy? |
| 16. Recreational history | What is your favorite recreational activity?<br>What recreational activities do you hate or avoid?<br>What sport, hobby or leisure time pursuit are you best at?<br>How often do you engage in your favorite (or best) activity?<br>What prevents you from engaging in this activity more often?<br>Whom do you do this activity with?<br>Are there any recreational activities that you'd like to do, but you've never had the time or opportunity to try? |
| 17. Developmental history | Do you know the circumstance surrounding your conception?<br>Was your mother's pregnancy normal?<br>What was your birth weight?<br>Do you know whether you were nursed or bottle-fed?<br>When did you sit, stand, and walk?<br>When did your menses begin? (for females) |
| 18. Spiritual or religious history | What is your religious background?<br>What are your current religious or spiritual beliefs?<br>Do you have a religious affiliation?<br>Do you attend church, pray, meditate, or otherwise participate in religious activities?<br>What other spiritual activities have you been involved in previously? |

Taken from Sommers-Flanagan, J., & Sommers-Flanagan, R. (2003). Clinical interviewing (3rd ed.). New York City, NY: Wiley.

## Demographic and Identifying Information

The demographic and identifying information about the counselee is initially obtained over the phone. Additional information is gathered through the intake form the counselor uses and through observation. This information includes the counselee's name, date of birth, age, sex, racial/ethnic information, marital status, occupation, and referral source.

## Reason for the Referral

This section and the next focus on the phase of the interview that deals with the target of the counseling (i.e., the "T" of the INTAKE acrostic). One aspect of the target can be obtained in the reason for the counselee being sent to you. If someone referred the counselee, the name and contact information of the referral source should be noted in the report. Sometimes this information is obtained through an intake form, and at other times it is learned in the process of the interview.

The most important information is the reason for the referral and what is typically labeled as the "referral question." First, what is the reason for the referral—an evaluation, counseling, or consultation? Second, in making a referral what question is the referral source seeking to have answered?

## Presenting Complaint or Problem

People seek help because they have a problem or concern they have not been able to resolve on their own. At the time of the initial interview the problem or concern is at the forefront of the counselee's mind. Some counselees are anxious to jump into sharing their problems, while others are more reticent. Also the counselee will normally share the problem or concern in a broad manner, which is to be fleshed out through use of the basic helping skills. At first the counselee usually reveals only the tip of the iceberg rather than what is the real problem or root to the problem.

Pay attention to the counselee's wording of the presenting problem. For example if the counselee says, "My wife is impossible to live with. She has berated me for years," tells a different story from "My wife and I have been having problems. We do not get along well anymore." The first disclosure presents a persecutor-victim dynamic, drips with profound bitterness and resentment, and puts the responsibility of changing the situation on the wife. By contrast the second presentation of the concern is a factual and straightforward depiction of the problem without blaming.

This part of the interview is critical because it makes you aware of the problem that the counselee has chosen to focus on, how he or she views it, and how it is interfering with life functioning. Even the tip of the iceberg gives you some idea about the iceberg, though it is still significantly incomplete. A useful model that can help you understand a counselee's functioning is referred to as "Concentric Circles" (Hawkins, n.d.). According to Hawkins these circles capture the forces of personality (see Figure 10.1).

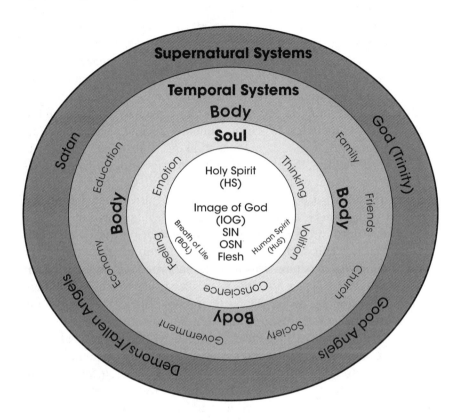

Figure 10.1: Hawkin's (n.d.) Theory of Concentric Circles

The innermost circle is called the "core" (Hawkins, n.d.), which includes the Holy Spirit, the image of God, and sin. These are all aspects that are inherent in human nature. As discussed in chap. 1, we are made in the image of God. As a result of bearing God's image, we have the ability to recognize God. Since the fall of Adam and Eve, sin is at our core. The inner core is now corrupted by our sin nature, the flesh, the human spirit, and the breath of life. The situation, however, is not the same for the regenerate and the unregenerate individual. The unregenerate person has a self-centered nature because he or she is not filled with the Holy Spirit. The regenerate individual is continually going through the spiritual process to become spiritually mature because he or she is indwelt by the Holy Spirit. Because Jesus died on the cross, His sacrifice makes it possible for the Holy Spirit to reside within believers. This core nature of the individual then affects the other outer circles. While believers can fall into sin—and many times that is the source of their dysfunction—they also have the capability to recognize that sin through the presence of the Holy Spirit. These two distinct natures that reside inside believers cause many conflicts in the choices they make.

Hawkins's second circle is the human soul. This circle includes how we think, and feel, and our volitions. Many times dysfunction begins at this level. Everything in the soul's circle (especially thoughts) influences the next two circles. When our thinking becomes warped, we act out in self-defeating ways. Many times thinking is distorted by irrational beliefs. In order to heal, the person must become aware of the faulty thinking and then replace it with the truth of God's Word. Other times feelings lead us astray. We act on how we feel, and that drives our personality. Many counseling interventions are aimed at this level of the soul.

Hawkins's third circle continues the movement outward and represents the "body." This factor of the human makeup encompasses every aspect of our physical nature. This includes inherited factors, physiological processes, and diseases, to name a few. Because of the holistic nature of human functioning, our physical functioning affects the functioning of our soul and vice versa. For example emotional issues such as anxiety might manifest themselves physically and cause illness such as ulcers.

The next circle is the "temporal systems." Everyone we come in contact with affects our personality. Friends, family, church, government personnel, and other interactions profoundly influence how we develop. Individuals often learn to become who they are through the family system.

The fifth circle includes the supernatural systems we encounter. The Godhead (i.e., God the Father, God the Son, God the Holy Spirit), Satan, fallen angels, demonic forces, and heavenly angels are all included. When we think supernaturally about how our personality develops, we realize that our belief in God or lack of it affects our development. Satanic influence can cause Christians to follow the lust of the flesh. These elements all shape our personality.

Essentially Hawkins's model of Concentric Circles demonstrates how everything surrounding the core affects the core and then the soul too, and vice versa. What a person thinks affects who he or she is. If their thoughts come into alignment with God's Word, so too will their feelings, will, and body. The Spirit will help guide them to live a spiritual life in which they are living in dependence on God.

## Behavioral Observations

Another aspect of the interview involves assessing the counselee's functioning, including his appearance (hygiene, eye contact, body posture, and facial expressions), quality and quantity of speech and responsivity to questioning, mood, primary thought content (including the presence or absence of suicidal ideation), and level of cooperation. This observational part of the interview is based primarily on signs, those things that can be observed in the counselee.

## Current Situation and Functioning

Relevant to the counselee's presenting problem is how he or she is functioning at the time of the interview. A person's functioning can range from being unimpaired to being severely impaired on any number of life issues. Often a person seeks counseling when he is functioning fairly normally. At these times the person might be experiencing normal life problems that mean he does not have a mental disorder. To have a mental disorder, as defined by the DSM-IV-TR (APA, 2000) a person must have impairment in social and/or occupational functioning. One means of gauging the counselee's level of impairment is to learn about their typical daily activities. Simply ask the person to tell you about his normal day. How does he spend his time? Does the counselee spend much time alone? How much time does the counselee spend with family members? Are the person's activities purposeful and meaningful? What does the counselee do that brings enjoyment?

When a counselee is doing poorly, counselors will often assess the counselee's ability to adequately maintain activities of daily living (ADLs). In other words you need to determine how well the person is taking care of herself. Can the person work, do homemaking, maintain hygiene, dress, groom, feed herself, engage in leisurely activities?

One significant aspect of a person's functioning is the quality and usefulness of coping skills. Coping skills are characteristic ways of dealing with life's difficulties. They influence how we identify and try to solve problems. Successful coping skills help one develop realistic views of situations that have an effect on one's personality and relationships. Some coping strategies are defensive coping, and others are direct coping. Defensive coping involves strategies that are designed to protect the person from feeling afflicted. These strategies include denial, fantasy, acting out, displacement, suppression, regression, undoing, compensation, reaction formation, projection, rationalization, intellectualization, and passive aggression, to name a few (Bovey & Hede, 2001; Franco,

2006; Tashlykov & Vale, 1997). In contrast, direct coping strategies are ones that are aimed at facing the reality of the circumstances. These include humor, prayer, praise, surrender, acceptance, grief, confession, and repentance. When evaluating a counselee's coping style, consider the situation in which the counselee is attempting to cope. For example humor might be a defensive strategy if it is used to insulate the person from facing reality. Such humor tends to be sarcastic, negative, excessive, and inappropriate. Gall and associates (2005) offer four spiritual coping styles: (a) self-directing that involves acting independently of God; (b) deferring coping, that is, passively waiting on God to intervene; (c) collaborative coping, which involves working with God to solve problems; and (d) surrender coping, which means releasing control of the situation over to God. These authors state that collaborative and surrender coping are the most spiritually healthy because they are solution-oriented and engage God in the process. While it is helpful to ask counselees how they cope with difficulties, we have found that a person's real coping strategies are uncovered by asking how they deal with situations.

Ask the counselee why he or she chose to come to counseling now can be helpful. In other words ask the counselee what specifically triggered the desire for the counselee to follow through in seeing a counselor now.

## History of the Present Problem(s)

The counselor needs to understand the counselee's presenting problem or problems. This is particularly true if the counselee voluntarily sought the counselor because of some undesirable levels of distress. Since the problem is the primary reason the counselee wants help, it is best to show your level of concern from the counselee by giving it some attention.

The part of the interview details how the problem or concern has interfered with the counselee's life. An exploration of the presenting problem would include (a) the genesis of the problem(s), (b) the course or development of the problem(s), (c) signs and symptoms, (d) frequency and duration, (e) level of impairment, (f) stressors that have occurred over the past several years, and (g) the environmental/social context of the problem.

One of the significant aspects of this part of the interview is to flesh out the counselee's concerns and to note the counselee's responses. For example if the counselee states that he has been "very sad over the last several months," ask the counselee to define what "very sad" means, to discuss what it feels like.

In general you are trying to answer the following questions: (a) What is the specific problem? (b) When did the problem begin? (c) What was going on in the counselee's life when it started? In other words did something trigger it? (d) How is life different since the problem began? (e) Why did the counselee decide to come to counseling now? (f) Who in the counselee's life is concerned about the problem? (g) How has the counselee tried to resolve the problem before coming to see you? (h) What other concerns does the counselee want to address? A few questions the counselor may ask are these:

- "Where were you and what was happening when the problem first occurred?"
- "How did it impact you?"
- "In what ways has it interfered with work or school, relationships, leisurely activities, and faith?"
- "Who else was affected by it?"
- "How have you tried to cope with it or eliminate it?"
- "What thoughts or images are associated with the problem?"
- "When has the problem been worse?"
- "When has the problem been absent or barely noticeable?"
- "Tell me the first thing you think you would notice if the problem disappeared."

Of course, the questions to ask depend on the actual problem. Problems with mood or anxiety, for example, often require questions that focus on the counselee's level of distress. That is, the questions have a more internal focus. Problems that deal with relationships focus more interpersonally. The bottom line is that you seek to "flesh" out" the concerns as much as possible. Think about what it would be like for you to have the problem and what facets of your life would be affected by it and how. That level of cognitive empathy will help you determine which questions to ask.

Where appropriate or relevant to the presenting problems, the counselor would note that the counselee denied particular issues. For example, "The counselee denied any history of manic episodes" or "The counselee denied any thoughts of suicide."

## Psychiatric History and Family History

The other area to be discussed deals with obtaining knowledge of the counselee's history. The counselor needs to assess any previous clinical problems or episodes that are not part of the counselee's presenting problem(s). For example if the counselee is presenting a problem of clinical anxiety, the counselor might want to determine if there have been any other clinical issues such as a substance abuse problem or treatment for an eating disorder. The counselor also seeks to ascertain if the counselee has had any previous treatments, including inpatient hospitalizations, medications, outpatient psychotherapy or counseling, or case management. If the counselee has had previous counseling, it might be helpful to obtain a release of information from the counselee so you can contact the former helpers. The perspectives of these previous helpers can provide critical data in helping you understand the counselee. At times counselees will refuse to give you permission to speak with their previous counselors. They might believe that the past counseling was poor, inadequate, or unrelated to the current concern. Though the benefits outweigh the risks, it is not wise to push the counselee into signing a release.

Often counselees will fail to disclose particular issues because of shame, fear, or perceived negative consequences for doing so. Moreover, research indicates that a large number of disorders are genetic. So the counselor is wise to assess the counselee's family history of substance abuse and psychological problems. And he should inquire about any and all blood relatives, such as parents, siblings, grandparents, children, aunts, uncles, and cousins. If the counselee's family history is full of substance abuse, it is likely though not indicative that the counselee might have a substance abuse problem. If time permits, you might want to learn about any significant major medical disorders in blood relatives (e.g., cancer, diabetes, seizure disorders, thyroid disease).

One powerful method by which to assess the counselee's family is the genogram (McGoldrick, Gerson, & Shellenberger, 2008). A genogram is an invaluable tool that provides a multigenerational diagram of family relations and patterns. In creating the genogram counselees often gain insight about their presenting concerns. You will receive further instruction about constructing genograms in the chap. activities. We strongly encourage you to complete a genogram with all the counselees you work with. In doing so you will quickly come to learn that even the most uncanny passions, addictions, relational patterns, and incidents tend to repeat themselves in families. When coupled with a life map and an attachment survey (see end-of-chap. activities), an immense amount of vital information for accurate case conceptualization is engendered.

Many psychological factors can impact a counselee's functioning. One significant factor to assess is the counselee's *emotional regulation*

(Eisenberg & Spinrad, 2004; Fogel, 1982; Fox, 1994; Greenspan & Greenspan, 2003). Emotional regulation deals with the processes by which a person copes with heightened levels of desired emotions such as happiness and joy, and heightened levels of distressed emotions, such as sadness, distress, anger, and fear (Fox, 1994; Kopp, 1989). Each of us attempts to regulate our emotions in some way. In conjunction with our coping strategies, people attempt to deny, weaken, curtail, mask, intensify, or completely change their emotions. Some people's feelings escalate quickly, and they experience emotions they can neither understand nor explain. Some people cannot talk about their emotional responses or connect an emotion to an event. Healthy functioning requires people to keep their emotions at an appropriate level of control.

An important clinical distinction is between emotions and feelings. Although many people use the words interchangeably, they are different. Emotions are in the background. They are an intrinsically private, subjective aspect of our lives (Clore, 1994). According to Roseman and Smith (2001) emotions provide value information because they are elicited from a person's appraisal of events and situations. Emotions also provide a forensic to a person's past since they are stored in memory. By contrast, feelings are in the foreground. They are a conscious subjective experience of an emotion (Tsuchiya & Adolphs, 2007). One analogy is the difference between climate and the weather. A region's climate might reflect a mild winter, but the current weather may or may not align with the climate. We all know of days that were unseasonably cold or hot. Emotions are similar to the climate, and feelings are similar to the weather. A person may generally have a depressed emotion (mood), but at the moment he may feel happy.

Everyone has emotions and feelings, and everyone has the tendency to focus on getting away from his feelings or having them validated. Both emotions and feelings can be very intense, give a sense of being out of control, and demand expression. Problems in emotional regulation can be manifested in a wide array of problems and disorders (Izard, Fine, Mostow, Trentacosta, & Campbell, 2002). Poor emotional regulation has been linked to such forms of psychopathology as mood and anxiety disorders; schizophrenia; personality disorders such as borderline, histrionic, and obsessive-compulsive; and eating disorders (Schore, 2003). Excessive guilt, shame, lust, hatred, and apathy are also manifestations of poor emotional regulation (Johnson, 2007). Problems with regulating emotions might stem from deregulation problems in the frontal lobes of the brain (Damasio, 1994, 1999), failure to establish a secure attachment with one's parents (Laurent & Powers, 2007) a history of child abuse (Bolen, 2005), poor modeling from caregivers (Lunkenheimer, Shields, & Cortina, 2007), or traumatic brain injury (Henry, Phillips, Crawford, Ietswaart, & Summers, 2006).

The first step in understanding a counselee's emotional regulation is to assess the counselee's ability to identify her *feelings*. Evaluate the counselee's ability to control and monitor emotions. For example does the counselee struggle with being impulsive or volatile? Counselors who work with children and adolescents may notice that the counselee's feelings can escalate quickly and intensely. Typically they are unable to understand or clearly explain their strong feelings. How well someone can acknowledge emotions, soothe his painful emotions, receive comfort from others, or appropriately express his feelings is a significant indicator of emotional and spiritual health.

Similarly in your evaluation assess psychological *adjustment*. Determine how well the counselee is able to adjust to life circumstances. This area can tap into basic mental-health issues such as stress, anxiety, chronic sadness, unresolved grief, and pessimism, to name a few.

Closely tied into the above concepts is the counselee's level of *risk-taking*. Risk-taking can encompass many different activities including deviancy, addictions, extreme sports, achievement, and many others. Some people are naturally predisposed to sensation-seeking and the pursuit of novel, intense, or risky experiences. Knowing how adventuresome a counselee can be in various settings may give insight into his behavioral tendencies and problems.

Evaluate the counselee's sense of s*elf-efficacy*. A person who is self-efficacious has a sense of control over his own life rather than feeling buffeted by chance or controlled by other people or circumstances.

Also, determine whether a counselee's *locus of control* is internal or external (cf. Rotter, 1966). Locus of control refers to a person's perception about the root causes of his life events. According to Zimbardo (1985) locus of control is "a belief about whether the outcomes of our actions are contingent on what we do (internal control orientation) or on events outside our personal control (external control orientation)" (p. 275). Perception of control is a powerful concept, impacting any endeavor (Lefcourt, 1991). People who operate from an internal perspective are individuals who accept responsibility for their lives. They own their feelings because they believe they have control over their lives. They believe they can influence outcomes through their own abilities, skills, efforts, and characteristics. Research indicates that internally oriented people are healthier (Rao & Murthy, 1984), though not every situation is best perceived from an internal perspective. In contrast, people who are external believe that outcomes are contingent on luck, chance, fate, powerful others, environmental factors, and supernatural factors. Externally oriented people acknowledge that events can be unpredictable because of the many complexities in the environment. And they are more prone to mood and anxiety disorders. Actually, people fall along a spectrum of very internal to very external, and one's orientation can change depending on the particular issue.

## Relevant Medical History and Substance Use

A clear connection exists between our psychological functioning and our physical functioning. Our emotional life can affect our physical health and vice versa. Some physical diseases are associated with particular disorders, and psychological functioning can trigger episodes of certain disorders. Because psychological symptoms may actually be derived from physiological problems, it is necessary that before beginning the work of counseling, all counselees have a physical examination if they have not had one in the last year. Clinical depression or anxiety that is caused by medical issues or medication will not be alleviated via counseling. Table 10.3 provides a brief assessment of the physical realm (see also "Symptoms Survey" in Appendix I). For a more thorough discussion of the mind-body connection we recommend you read *The mind and the brain: Neuroplasticity and the power of mental force,* by Jeffrey M. Schwartz and Sharon Begley (2002).

Assessing the counselee's physical habits (including smoking, caffeine consumption, substances, hours and patterns of sleep, eating patterns, and exercise) are all relevant to understanding the counselee. Any medications, dosages, and frequencies should be noted. Hospitalizations can be both telling and traumatic. Probe for any medical illnesses associated with either the counselee or the counselee's family of origin. Some of the counselee's physical and medical information can be obtained through an intake form or through a specific form requesting this information. Obtaining information before the visit allows the counselor to scan the form for any issues that need follow-up.

Table 10.3

*Brief Assessment of Physical Health*

1. When and where have you had your last full medical examination?
2. Have laboratory examinations been done in which electrolytes, thyroid function (full screen), liver enzymes, and hematological indexes were determined to be within normal limits?
3. Are you currently taking any medications? What is the name of the medication, the dosage, the purpose for taking it, and how long have you used it?
4. Do you have a family history that includes family members with any of the symptoms you are currently experiencing, or any other mental-health problems?
5. For how long have you had these symptoms?
6. Have you had any previous treatment (including counseling of any kind) for these or any other symptoms that were medical or psychological? If yes, please explain. Include any diagnosis or treatment process you received.

7. General health: _____

   Physician's name:_____

   Date of last physical or doctor's visit_____

Any recent changes in the following (please explain):

- sleeping patterns (over or under sleeping, hardly sleeping for three or more consecutive days)
- eating habits:
- behavior:
- mood swings:
- energy level:
- weight:
- tension level:
- Describe any significant medical problems/conditions/symptoms:

8. Do you have a history of substance use? Do you currently use alcohol or drugs? If yes, please describe your daily, weekly, and monthly use.
9. Do you exercise regularly? If yes, how, how often, how much?

Ask about the counselee's use of caffeine, nicotine, alcohol, and other drugs. It is best to normalize these questions in how they are worded. For example, "It is common for people to have used alcohol at some point in their lives. When was the first time you tasted alcohol?"

When writing the assessment report, include the counselee's physician information, including phone numbers and address. Be sure to obtain permission to contact the counselor's physician in order to coordinate all care; in fact some managed-care companies require that the counselor and physician collaborate.

## Developmental History

Another significant area for exploration is the counselee's developmental history. Some counselees might think their childhood history is irrelevant to their present concerns. But one's developmental history helps give a well-rounded picture of the counselee. It can help determine a particular diagnosis, the nature of current problems, or the root of the counselee's problems.

Developmental areas to assess include the following: (a) the situation surrounding the counselee's mother's pregnancy; (b) information pertaining to the counselee's birth; (c) social, behavioral, and cognitive milestones; (d) educational history including school performance; (e) information pertaining to interactions with peers and people in authority; (f) extracurricular activities such as participating in sports or clubs. Asking these questions about the counselee's developmental history can become tedious and can prolong the interview. But obtaining much of the relevant information through intake forms can greatly reduce the time in this part of the interview (see Appendix C for a sample intake form).

## Social and Family History

We are social beings and made for relationships; thus understanding a counselee's relationships is central to understanding what motivates or hinders the counselee. Research strongly indicates that a person's social support is vital to physical and emotional health (Bonanno et al., 2008; Button, 2008; Robinson et al., 2008). David Seamands (1991), in his book *Healing for damaged emotions,* makes the point that there is a dynamic interplay between interpersonal relationships and one's knowledge and experience of God. In that regard family relationships are by far the most influential. Thus when it comes to knowing who God is, what we have experienced in our most intimate relationships has a critical impact.

Horney (1945) observed that relationships are never static. They are always dynamic and are always in an active state of either "moving toward," "moving against," or "moving away." That process holds true in all human relationships. We are always in some mode of moving closer to one another, moving away from one another, or in conflict with one another. In the course of normal relationships all three states will occur in time and over time.

Key to understanding the quality of the counselee's social support is the mutuality of the friendships and the level of openness that exists. Counselees who can give to their friends and who also receive from their friends function better (Ryan, 2006). The counselor does well to ask about how the counselee has related to others in the past and the present, and what disappointments he or she has experienced.

Get the counselee to talk about her parents, siblings, grandparents, and any other significant relationships in the counselee's development. Ask about the counselee's romantic relationships and sexual history. Also inquire about abuse or traumas. How was anger expressed in the home? Does the counselee have a history of aggression, violence, or victimization?

Also ask counselees to share their earliest memories. Research indicates that memories can point to life themes that relate to a counselee's current level of functioning (Lehman, 2004; Mosak, 1989; Sakaki, 2007). Memories, however, are highly subject to distortion and deletions. When we pull from our memory banks, we reconstruct the memory, and it is constructed through our current lens of seeing the world. For that reason memories can reveal a counselee's level of functioning.

When asked about early memories, some counselees will express uncertainty about responding. Simply have them think about their life as far back as possible and tell you the first incident that comes to mind. You can ask counselees to share memories associated with their mother, father, sibling, school, friends, and others. As they share their memories and you respond with appropriate helping skills, the memory will often become more vivid and specific.

A number of key factors are related to a counselee's interpersonal functioning. The first facet of interpersonal functioning is one's level of *sociability*. The concept of sociability resembles introversion-extroversion in that highly sociable people like contact and interaction. A second interpersonal facet to ascertain is the counselee's *social confidence*. How comfortable a person feels in various social situations may reflect various disorders (e.g., avoidant personality), issues (e.g., insecurity), and unmet needs (e.g., acceptance). Another interpersonal characteristic is the counselee's *social poise*, which describes characteristics that relate to changing, influencing, and leading others. Some people are naturally outgoing and influential in their interactions with others. Others, who lack social poise, may struggle with codependency, dependent personality, victim mentality, or various other issues. Also, assess the counselee's level of *social conformity*, which speaks to how well someone bends with or opposes social norms. For example strongly nonconforming people may enjoy being oppositional for its own sake.

## Employment History

Another significant aspect of the counselee's social history is her employment, and military history if applicable. What kind of work is the counselee currently engaged in and what kinds(s) of work in the past? How many jobs has the counselee held and in what time frame? Is the counselee working a prepared career? What is the counselee's level of performance in her current job (any performance issues)? What does the counselee like most and least about her job?

A counselee's military history can provide insight into how well he or she functions in a controlled and structured setting. If the counselee is in the military, how does he or she view her experience? Did the counselee have an honorable discharge?

## Religious Background and Affiliation

A quality bio-psycho-social-spiritual assessment includes an evaluation of the counselee's religious functioning. For Christian counselors this is no surprise. But a number of issues need to be explored, issues that most counselors do not naturally consider. Evaluating the counselee's spiritual history can include the following: (a) past and present religious experiences and training; (b) past and present religious affiliations; (c) faith commitment (e.g., church, spirituality, the Bible) and how it influences daily living; (d) family members' faith and its impact on the counselee; (e) battle with spiritual warfare; (f) values and significant religious beliefs; and (g) relationship with God, Jesus Christ, and the Holy Spirit. We have found that assessing a counselee's relationship with God is more helpful than knowing about his church background.

The relationship of one's spirituality and personal functioning is well documented and supported in the literature. Spiritual practices and spiritual healing are being actively sought out as means for coping with daily stress and illness, whether minor or chronic conditions (Graham, Furr, Flowers, & Burke, 2001; Rowe & Allen, 2004). Spirituality profoundly impacts health, mental stability, and overall quality of life.

O'Grady and Richards (2007) have developed a set of questions which assess a counselee's experience of God and spiritual identity. These include the following:

<u>Experience of God:</u>

1. Is God there for me? How do I know?
2. Do I believe that my image of God corresponds to a being who actually exists?

3. Am I good enough for God's love?
4. How much can God control me and I control God?
5. Do I believe God wants to have a relationship with me and will help me develop a relationship with Him?
6. Do I believe God will comfort me in times of trial?
7. Do I believe God will help me heal emotionally?
8. Am I afraid to surrender control to God?
9. What does God's love feel like in my life?
10. What can I do to foster a relationship with God? (p. 195)

<u>Sense of Spiritual Identity:</u>

1. Do you believe you are a child of God?
2. Do you believe you have divine worth and potential?
3. Do you feel God loves you?
4. Do you feel that you are of divine spiritual worth?
5. Do you believe there is any special purpose to your life?
6. Do you believe God knows you as an individual?
7. Do you believe you play a role in God's plan for humankind?
8. Do you have a personal relationship with God?
9. Do you believe you are a valued creation of God?
10. Do you believe your spiritual identity is eternal? (p. 196 )

## Strengths and Weaknesses

When people are going through difficult times, they tend to forget about their strengths. Yet strengths can be the vehicle to help counselees arrive at their destination. Research clearly links strengths with interviewing and counseling (Duncan, Miller, & Sparks, 2004; Peterson & Seligman, 2004; Sweeney & Myers, 2005). Counselors are wise to directly ask counselees their perceived strengths and weaknesses. Listening in on how counselees share their stories can also give you insight into possible unrecognized strengths.

## Diagnostic Impressions

In the interview or appointment it might be premature to discuss your diagnostic impressions, even at the end of the session. If, however, you are required to produce a psychosocial report, you will need to address this area. A significant purpose of the interview is to gather information so that you can determine the diagnosis. Although a diagnosis is valuable, it is a bit like the law that affirms the existence of sin, but cannot remove it. Counseling, in particular problem-solving, is a bit like grace that removes sin (Trozer, personal communication, October 17, 2009). Just as the law identifies and labels sin, so diagnosis provides a means of identification and labeling of dysfunction.

When creating a psychosocial report, write it so that all the previous information builds up to the diagnosis. All the preceding information culminates in a five-axis diagnosis. The counselor provides a brief discussion of the diagnostic issues obtained from the psychosocial history. Often it is difficult to finalize a diagnosis based on one session. When writing the actual report, you can use a descriptor—either Rule-Out (R/O), Provisional, or Defer—as a means of communicating your level of confidence in the diagnosis.

## Case Formulation and Treatment Plan

Another significant area of the psychosocial report that proceeds from the information and diagnostic impressions is the case formulation and treatment plan. Since you have spent a good bit of time with the counselee, you will have ideas about root issues and recommendations for treatment.

In summary, the counseling interview should cover the major life domains associated with the bio-psycho-social-spiritual. All the information obtained through the interview should be culled and synthesized together in the psychosocial report.

## WRITING THE PSYCHOSOCIAL REPORT

A psychosocial history report can be organized in several key areas related to the areas of exploration addressed above. The report can be organized as follows: (a) identifying information, (b) reason for the referral, (c) behavioral observations, (d) current situation and functioning, (e) history of the presenting problem, (f) psychiatric history and family history, (g) relevant medical history, (h) developmental history, (i) social and family history, (j) employment history, (k) religious background and affiliation, (l) strengths and weaknesses, (m) diagnostic impressions, and (n) case formulation and treatment recommendations.

When writing your report, bear in mind the purpose of the report and who will be reading it. A report that is for the case file and only available to the counselor can be written with more professional language than if it is for the counselee, referral source, or some nonprofessional recipient.

Sommers-Flanagan and Sommers-Flanagan (2003) offer the following recommendations to bear in mind when writing a report: (a) write the report as soon as possible (immediately following the session is ideal because it is difficult to reconstruct the session later); (b) write an immediate draft without worrying about making it perfect—you can edit it later; (c) carefully follow an outline; (d) get clear information from your supervisor or employer about what is expected; (e) look over any sample reports to help you in creating your own; and (f) remember that writing is a skill that takes time to develop—the more you practice the more competent you will become. We want to recommend, whether or not it is required in the setting of your practice, that you write a formal and thorough psychosocial report, including multiaxial diagnosis, case conceptualization, and treatment plan for each counselee you are working with. In the process of doing so, you will find that your understanding of the individual, couple, or family will deepen significantly and thus enable you to provide more comprehensive, effective, and ethical counseling services (MacLean, 2005).

## CHAPTER SUMMARY

Conducting a psychosocial interview is the most basic and foundational skill in counseling. Like any counseling session, it occurs in phases. It is difficult to cover all the necessary areas in one session without being rushed or overly directive. If your setting requires you to obtain information in the first session, be sure to inform the counselee of your limitations. When writing your report, bear in mind for whom you are writing it, and allow yourself time to become a competent report writer. By the time you get through your internship, you will have seen numerous counselees and will have conducted the numerous intake interviews. Although conducting the interview will become more natural and comfortable, try to avoid falling into a rut of always doing it the same way. Remember that each counselee is uniquely created in the image of God and deserves an individualized approach.

## CHAPTER 10 ACTIVITIES

1. Identify the areas that are most likely to interest you when conducting an assessment: the presenting problem, history of the presenting problem, stressors, future goals, social history, family of origin, relationship history (including marriage), sexual life, substance use, health issues (eating, sleeping, conditions, ailments, hospitalizations, etc.), spiritual life, educational background, strengths, or some other area. Write out why you believe those areas are of interest to you. Do you believe you have a healthy interest in those areas? If not, what can you do to address your issues?
2. Why is appropriate bio-psycho-social-spiritual assessment foundational to providing ethical and effective counseling?

3. Name and describe the phases of the counseling interview, as introduced in this chap.
4. What are the key areas that are important to explore in the psychosocial history?
5. Complete O'Grady and Richard's (2007) Experience of God and Sense of Spiritual Identity questions that are found in this chap. about your own spiritual experience. What have you learned from this activity?
6. DVD: Watch vignette 15 in which the counselor demonstrates an assessment with an involuntary counselee. What skills does Denise use to engage Colleen in the work of counseling? How effective was it?
7. DVD: Watch vignette 16 in which the counselor demonstrates how to acquire a history of a counselee's presenting problem. What types of questions and counselor responses does the counselor, Don use in carrying out the assessment? How effective was it?
8. Imagine that you are a counselee seeking counseling at a community-counseling center. Create a simulated psychosocial report on yourself that covers the following areas: (a) identifying information, (b) reason for the referral, (c) behavioral observations, (d) current situation and functioning, (e) history of the presenting problem, (f) psychiatric history and family history, (g) relevant medical history, (i) developmental history, (j) social and family history, (k) employment history, (l) religious background and affiliation, (m) strengths and weaknesses, (n) diagnostic impressions, and (o) case formulation and treatment recommendations.
9. Imagine someone you know seeking counseling at the community-counseling center where you work. Create a simulated psychosocial report on this person that covers all the areas listed above in item 5.

## Vignette Questions

*Vignette 16*
*Advanced Assessment*

1. Based upon vignette 16, what information is Don seeking to elicit from Frank? Be specific.
2. When does assessment occur? Explain your answer.
3. What are the two models of assessment identified in the textbook? Which one do you prefer? Why?
4. How do you feel when you hear the word *assessment*? Take a moment to explore why you feel that way.

5. What does your emotional response to the word *assessment* tell you about yourself? Are you comfortable with what you discovered? Why or why not?

## Recommended Reading

Morrison, J. (2007). *The first interview* (3rd ed.). New York City, NY: Guildford Press.

> Dr. Morrison provides a practical "do-it-yourself" manual to help young practitioners learn how to successfully conduct a first interview. As a psychiatrist Morrison discusses sound diagnostic techniques to help anyone assess a counselee from a clinical perspective. Its easy-to-read format and practicality make it a wonderful resource.

Seligman, L. (2004). *Diagnosis and treatment planning in counseling* (3rd ed.). New York City, NY: Plenum.

> Dr. Seligman has produced a number of solid resources in the field of counseling. This book provides an excellent resource to help novice counselors diagnose and intervene with counselees. She synthesizes the latest developments in counseling. Her practical "DO A CLIENT MAP" helps counselors structure the most efficacious approach possible. She also addresses how to work with specific populations such as families, couples, and groups.

## Chapter 11

# Case Conceptualization and Treatment Planning

*"Interviewing the counselee and having the counselee engage in other assessment procedures are only part of the overall assessment process in counseling and therapy. Equally important is the therapist's own mental, or covert, activity that goes on during the process. . . . Unless the therapist can integrate and synthesize the data, they are of little value and use"* (Cormier & Cormier, 1985, p. 147).

*"A plan in the heart of a man is like deep water, but a man of understanding draws it out"* (Prov 20:5, NASB).

## CHAPTER OBJECTIVES

» To understand the importance of case conceptualization

» To learn how to interpret counselee statements by analyzing them for generalizations, deletions, and distortions

» To relate the AIM model to case conceptualization

» To provide a sample psychosocial report

» To discuss how treatment planning naturally follows accurate case conceptualization

» To provide a sample treatment plan

## CHAPTER OUTLINE

In the last chap. we presented salient issues related to effective bio-psycho-social-spiritual assessment. In this chap., we describe how a counselor carefully and systematically analyzes the data collected from the assessment and formulates an in-depth understanding of the counselee's issues and concerns. This is called *case conceptualization*, and it is the foundation of treatment planning and all the therapeutic work ahead. Of all the skills in the counselor's toolbox, case conceptualization and treatment planning are among the most important and the most difficult to learn. This is because without ethical and effective assessment and case formulation, counseling will likely fail to focus on the core issues underlying a counselee's presenting problems and concerns, leading to a nebulous treatment course and an unsuccessful outcome.

As related in earlier chaps., counseling is much like an expedition. Imagine you are a guide on such an excursion, but you do not know the terrain, or the safest route to the destination, and you do not have an itinerary or map. The explorers are ready, willing, and able (hopefully), but if you do not know the way and do not have knowledge about the course, then you have little hope for a successful journey. In fact, in counseling nothing is more important to successful "journeying" than your becoming an expert guide who grasps the "course and terrain" of counseling in general and of each counselee in particular.

A successful journey requires a specialized set of skills. The skilled guide knows how to read the terrain and link that knowledge to the best way to take the journey. The wise guide creates a journey that accounts for the abilities of the trekkers. Likewise the counselor must effectively link a counselee's presenting concerns to an effective treatment plan. Treatment is tailored to the counselee's needs and expectations.

To accomplish these tasks you need to understand the many kinds of counselees. According to Carlson, Sperry, and Lewis (2005),

> Case conceptualization is a method and process of summarizing seemingly diverse case information into a brief, coherent statement or "map" that elucidates the counselee's basic pattern of behavior. The purpose of a well-articulated case conceptualization is to better understand and more effectively treat a counselee or counselee-system, that is, a couple or family (p. 190).

How you describe a counselee's problem will reveal what you truly believe about human nature. That perspective will ultimately drive what you want to do to help. Thus case conceptualization is your map to the way the counselee functions and the map to determining the root of the counselee's difficulty. It includes your working hypotheses of the therapeutic needs, which are to be met for counseling to be successful. Case conceptualization is the infrastructure of the counseling because it enables you to know what needs to be addressed and how best to accomplish it. Case conceptualization is where theory and practice intersect.

As foundational as case conceptualization skills are to successful counseling, developing them is no small task (Caspar, Berger, & Hautle, 2004). It takes much experience and practice to hone the skills necessary to make sense of counselee problems. Effective helpers have moment-to-moment awareness of their thought processes during a session (Borders & Brown, 2005) and a framework to organize the pieces of the counselee's puzzle.

## COMMUNICATION PATTERNS: UNDERSTANDING MENTAL MAPS

Case conceptualization refers to the construction of a comprehensive explanation of a counselee and his issues. It involves observation and assessing what is happening, what is needed, options for responding and intervening, and evaluating progress (Borders & Brown, 2005). One part of case conceptualization skills is built on the recognition of themes and patterns. Being able to dissect a counselee's verbalizations is fundamental to making sense of what is happening with the counselee.

## The Role of the Counselee's Mental Maps

God custom-designed our brains to handle incredible amounts of information. Nevertheless the brain cannot possibly attend to the billions and billions of incoming stimuli it encounters daily. The brain is bombarded by stimuli that seek to formally enter its inner sanctum. In order to process the mass of incoming stimuli, the brain filters out stimuli it considers unnecessary.

The fact that two people can perceive the same event or stimulus and have two different experiences is due, in significant part, to the brain's filtering ability. The brain's filtering of experience also helps explain why there are so many different denominations or interpretations of passages of Scripture. Though God's Word is absolute, no one person perfectly understands it all. Our humanness simply prevents us from completely understanding all there is in Scripture. Our digestion of Scripture is filtered through our subjective and fallen internal world. This is referred to as perception, the process whereby we use our senses to become aware of our environment.

One model for describing how the brain filters stimuli is offered by psychologist Bandler and linguist Grinder (1975). Known as the "meta-model of language," these theorists identified three processes or patterns that seem to play a role in helping the brain make sense of the world: (a) deletions, (b) distortions, and (c) generalizations. The conclusions drawn from our perception that is ultimately filtered by these processes creates the mental maps that navigate us through life. As Bandler and Grinder point out, the "map is not the territory"; it only represents the territory it depicts. In other words, a person's view of an event is only a view of reality; it is not reality itself.

When working with counselees, it is important to remember that (a) their perception is flawed, (b) your perception of their perceptions is flawed, (c) some people's perceptions are more accurate representations of reality than other people's representations of reality, and (d) perceptions rarely include information that suggests that they are wrong. Counselees' stories are based on their internal maps of how the stories fit together. An example illustrates this concept. If a counselee seeks counseling because of depression, one counselee might begin his story by talking about his childhood. Another counselee might begin talking about her overwhelming sadness or inability to sleep. In general, the way a counselee chooses to communicate her story is not typically a conscious decision. Rather the story tends to be shared in a way that fits with the counselee's mental map, which operates according to the counselee's set of rules of which she may not even be aware. The rules interact with the counselee's needs, concerns, expectations, and priorities , all of which work to frame the story.

A thorough discussion of Bandler and Grinder's (1975) material is beyond the scope of this text. The reader is encouraged to read *The structure of magic* in order to more fully grasp the material. However, these processes are discussed briefly below.

The basic principle behind mental maps is that we create them in order to guide our behavior. Put another way, we do not operate directly on the world in which we live. The difference between the map and the actual territory is based on the extent that deletions, distortions, and generalizations are used. We will examine each one below.

## Deletions

According to Bandler and Grinder (1975) we begin developing our personal map of reality through the process of deleting. This communication process refers to leaving out or ignoring aspects of reality. In psychology, deletion is often described as "selective abstraction" (Beck, 1976). This is a form of mental bias whereby a person selects one piece of information from a context and "mentally deletes" the rest of the information. Simply put, we pay attention to certain aspects of an experience and not others. We may overlook certain information and omit other information. Since it is impossible for our brains to handle all the stimuli it receives, it filters out some sensory input in order to function. Deletion is one means by which the brain can attend to particular pieces of information that the person finds most relevant.

The process of deletion further occurs as individuals seek to recall their experiences and even more when they seek to relay their experiences to others. Throughout the entire process what is actually deleted depends on context, sensory relevance, beliefs and values, consistency with what is already believed, and appraised importance.

From a human functioning perspective, deletion is God's way of protecting our conscious minds from the plethora of information we are faced with at any given moment. But our fallen nature leads us to use deletion in a way that changes reality. A good example of deletion is found in Gen 3 where Satan the serpent deleted information from the original context. In chap. 2, God said that Adam and Eve could freely eat from any tree in the garden except the tree of the knowledge of good and evil. Satan omitted a significant piece of information from his comment when he said, "Did God really, say, 'You can't eat from any tree in the garden'?" He left out the fact that God told them to eat freely from any tree except one.

The concept of deletion is relevant to helpers because often people come to counseling because they block themselves from seeing options open to them. According to their maps other options do not exist. In order to enrich the counselee's map, the counselor probes the story for missing information. To fill in the gaps created by deletions, counselors need to ask for the missing pieces.

Bandler and Grinder (1975) describe three particular classes of deletions. Class 1 is referred to as "Real compared to what?" This class involves comparatives and superlatives such as "She is more difficult," "He is better for me," "I resent happier people," "She always leaves the harder job for me," and "She is the most interesting." What is deleted in the comparative deletion is "compared to what?" For example "More happier compared to what?" or "Harder compared to what?" Superlative deletions can be clarified by asking questions such as, "With respect to what?" If the counselee states, "I've had too many problems in my life," a number of deletions could be queried. You might ask, "Too many compared to what?" or "What kinds of problems?"

The second class of deletions Bandler and Grinder (1975) mention are referred to as "clearly and obviously." For example "Obviously my parents dislike me." Class 2 deletions omit the qualifiers such as "Obvious to whom?"

Class 3 deletions are referred to as "modal operators" (Bandler & Grinder, 1975). These deletions involve rules or generalizations that counselees have developed in their models of the world. For example, "I have to take other people's feelings into account" or "Other people must like me." These statements make the claim that something must occur, which often deletes the words "or what?" In other words what will or would happen if that does not occur? You can ask for the deleted material by using the phrase, "What would happen if . . ."

Thus deletion is a powerful process that allows us to focus on certain aspects of reality to help our brains make sense of the world, while at the same time limiting our experience by ignoring other aspects of reality that could change the meaning. In your work with counselees you might need to assist them in enriching their map by obtaining pieces that are missing, and thus have a more accurate sense of their world.

### Distortions

Whereas deletion limits information, distortion shifts the information. Distortions arise, at least in part, out of the flawed perception people have of their world. People misinterpret reality because the human race is fallen. More cynically, however, people distort reality to support their preconceived notions of how things are. Referring back to the example from the garden of Eden, Satan and Eve both distorted key information from the original event. Eve's distortion was likely not motivated by intentional deception. God told them not to "eat" of the tree, but Eve told Satan that God said that they were not even to "touch it." To the degree that reality gets distorted is the degree to which the person will likely limit their perspective and choices. Eve failed to view God's words as freedom to enjoy the garden; she focused instead on the one thing He had forbidden.

Several terms and phrases discussed in the psychological literature capture the process of distortion. One of these is called "cognitive dissonance" (Festinger, 1957) in which people have to reckon the dissonance created by conflicting realities. To reduce the anxiety associated with the conflicting realities, the person attempts to reduce the dissonance by distorting some aspect of one of the realities. Typically what is retained is what one previously has believed to be true. In essence, cognitive dissonance operates by filtering any information that conflicts with what is already believed to be true. As a result, it prevents the person from considering or accepting new ideas, perspectives, or interpretations.

Perhaps the most significant form of distortion is "nominalization," in which the counselee turns a process into an event or a thing. Nominalizations are nouns that cannot be physically touched or carried. If a counselee says that he or she "regrets the decision to return home" the event word "decision" is a nominalization because decision is often a process (Grinder & Bandler, 1976a). In other words a nonnominalization form of that statement would be, "I regret that I'm deciding to return home." Nominalizations can be challenged by focusing on the process: "What prevents you from changing your decision?" or "What would happen if you reconsidered and decided not to return home?"

Grinder and Bandler (1976a) state that reversing normalizations helps a counselee to see that "what he had considered an event, finished and beyond his control, is an ongoing process which can be changed" (p. 74). For example if a counselee states, "Communication in our family is poor," a reversal of that distortion would be "How would you like for your family to communicate?" or "How would you like to communicate more effectively?"

The first step in helping to better understand what is happening in the counselee's life is to determine to what degree the counselee's map is based on reality. If the counselee seems to be distorting information, you can attempt to clarify the counselee's mental map by probing for process. For example if a counselee says, "She is trying to hurt me," you could respond, "How do you know she is trying to hurt you?" Or perhaps a husband might say, "I know that my wife is cheating on me"; you could help clarify the map by asking, "How do you know she is cheating on you?" Surprisingly counselees often cannot articulate a solid rationale for their perception. Their map is often based on a feeling that something is the way it appears or that they sense it is true but without any facts.

In working with counselees, pay attention to what they say and how they report it to you. Look for distortions in their communication process and help them clarify their stories so that it better represents reality.

## Generalizations

The third communication pattern that makes up our internal filter, according to Bandler and Grinder (1975), is what they call *generalizations*. Everyone is aware of the human tendency to draw conclusions based on limited information. Generalizations are a way of learning, for they allow us to take information and draw conclusions about the world based on our experiences. Unfortunately, however, we often take a single event and transform it into an overall, generalized experience. Generalizations keep us from making distinctions that would create a fuller set of choices in coping with life (Bandler & Grinder, 1976a). Thus generalizations can lead to wrong decisions and judgments.

One type of generalization is referred to as "referential indexes" (Bandler & Grinder, 1975; Grinder & Bandler, 1976a). They offer the example, "People push me around," in which case the word "people" has no specific referential index. In contrast the statement "My father pushes me around" has two clear referential indexes (father and me). Asking the counselee, "Who specifically?" or "What specifically?" can help the counselee focus on the original experience that ultimately led to the generalization. For example suppose a counselee said, "No one cares about me." Responding to the generalization you might ask, "Who does not care about you?" If a counselee said, "I couldn't do that," responding to the generalization you might inquire, "What would happen if you did do that?"

Grinder and Bandler (1976a) also describe complex generalizations in which the counselee equivocates two claims. For example, "My husband never appreciates me . . . my husband doesn't smile at me." In this case the counselee is making the assumption that her husband's not appreciating her is shown by his not smiling at her. One response is to ask the counselee, "Does your husband's not smiling at you always mean that he doesn't appreciate you?"

A final category of generalizations is referred to as "incompletely specified verbs" (Bandler & Grinder, 1975). If a counselee says, "My mother hurt me" or "My children disobey me," the mental map has been generalized from a specific situation or a series of situations to a universal claim. In such cases it is wise to request the particular situation or situations from which the counselee has generalized. If, however, the counselee provides more specific clarity by saying, "My mother hurt me when she refused to come to my play," there is more completeness. The counselee has linked the hurt to a specific event. Yet, that statement is still not complete. For instance it does not include "how" the mother refused. Refusing could have been concluded by the counselee when the mother said that she had to work and could not get time off. Or the mother might have refused by ignoring the counselee's request. Regardless of the reason, knowing how the mother communicated that message is important.

Grinder and Bandler's works (1975, 1976a) help the counselor find ways to expand their counselee's view of the world. Their books are rich with examples and guidelines for learning how to address counselee deletions, distortions, and generalizations. The main objective, however, is that you seek to gain as complete an understanding of the counselee's model of the world as possible. Probing and exploring will help you in your assessment and diagnosis, and it will also help the counselee see that an impoverished model of the world will result in more distress.

## THE AIM MODEL AND CASE CONCEPTUALIZATION

I (Lisa) like to conduct phenomenological research, which involves collecting qualitative (often interview, document, and/or observation) data and analyzing it for meaningful themes that relate to the phenomenon studied. It is an arduous and time-consuming endeavor, which reveals its true value during the process of heuristic explication, that is, via writing. Like a researcher, the counselor collects and then delves into the assessment "data," mining it for meaningful themes related to the counselee's presenting issues and concerns. He reviews the biological, cognitive, affective, developmental, interpersonal, social, and spiritual factors relating to the counselee's symptoms. One way of forming a holistic view of the person is by using the AIM model as a framework for assessment and treatment planning. By carefully assessing each of the nine areas introduced in the model, counselors can gain a clear, even if preliminary, understanding of counselee bio-psycho-social-spiritual functioning and use this information for writing the report and treatment plan. The goal is formulating a deep and thorough written conceptualization of the counselee from which the treatment plan emerges. Table 11.1 presents a summary of the AIM components in the form of a chart you can use for case conceptualization.

To develop an accurate conceptualization you need to make a comprehensive assessment during the first couple of sessions and throughout the counseling process (Beck, 1995). Conceptualization is "the counselor's

intentional, focused, and ongoing effort to understand a particular counselee case. It precedes and makes possible individualized treatment planning" (Osborn, Dean, & Petruzzi, 2004, p. 122). The more you know about
a counselee, the more likely you can construct an individualized treatment
plan (Radwin, 1995). Gaining an understanding of the bio-psycho-social-
spiritual issues related to the counselee's presenting concerns is a challenge.

The psychosocial report, discussed in chap. 10 ("Conducting an Assessment"), provides an effective template for elucidating and organizing your
conceptualizations, while the AIM model covers the areas that must be
accurately conceptualized. In the following sample report, data collected
from two clinical interviews, a mental status exam, a three-generational
Genogram, an abbreviated attachment survey, a life map, demographic,
history, symptom surveys, a family assessment, and physician consultation give ample data for case conceptualization to begin.

## Table 11.1
### Case Conceptualization and the AIM Model

| AIM COMPONENT | Functioning: 1–10 | Counselee Comments | Counselor Notes | Prelimi- nary Goal |
|---|---|---|---|---|
| A: Level of Spiritual Functioning | | | | |
| B: Biblical and Psycho- logical Functioning (General) | | | | |
| I: Level of Identity Differentiation | | | | |
| D: Level of Cognitive Functioning | | | | |
| E: Level of Emotional Functioning | | | | |
| I: Level of Self- Regulation | | | | |
| N: Level of Biologi- cal/Physiological Functioning | | | | |
| M: Level of Interpersonal Functioning | | | | |
| E: Level of Awareness: World, Flesh, and the Devil | | | | |

## Sample Psychosocial Report

### Identifying information.

James, age 39, has been married for 10 years to Georgia, and they have two children, Robbie (4) and Stephanie (6). James is a successful accountant and lives with his family in Huntington, Pennsylvania.

### Reason for referral.

James was referred to counseling by his physician, Dr. Schmidt, because he was experiencing "unbearable anxiety for the last three months," causing marked disruption in his ability to function well.

### Behavioral observations.

James was well groomed and neatly dressed in professional clothing. He discussed emotional material in a matter-of-fact manner with expressions of anxiety apparent in nonverbal behaviors (e.g., muscle tightness, shaking leg, holding his breath). He maintained good eye contact and spoke well. No unusual mannerisms or abnormalities of motion were detected. His thought process was goal-directed, and he responded clearly to questions of information.

During the family assessment, James was tense and self-focused. Although his children intermittently sat on his lap, he gave them little attention, something his wife reported as very uncharacteristic of him before about three months ago. A picture Stephanie drew of the family revealed daddy at a distance. Mom, Stephanie, and Robbie all had arms and hands with colorful dress; dad had no arms and no color. James's mental status exam revealed no physical problems.

### Current situation and functioning.

"I love my family so much, but everything is strained by my craziness. I just can't relax anymore. I don't know what is happening to me." James shared that he used to enjoy playing baseball for fun and going on family outings, but lately he has not been able to do these things because he is consumed with trying to figure out what medical condition he has. He said he "feels so strongly that something bad is happening, and I have to do something about it before it gets so bad that I can't do anything at all."

James is obsessed with his health status (he rated his anxiety about illness at the highest level). He reports going to work and functioning fairly well there. "It is as if I am ultra-focused at work, consumed with keeping order there, making everything work out right for my clients, so much so that I become distracted from this other quest for a while." "Everything seems OK while I am working. But once I come home, I must find out what my condition is and catch it before it is too late. I have no choice but to protect my family from losing me."

Ethnic or cultural issues of note relate to James's fear of God and his guilt about sexuality (for three months he has been masturbating several times a day). He has been avoiding going to church with his family. James reports a very small social network of friends and family. For leisure he used to attend movies, go out to dinner, and travel. James denies any legal issues of significance or military history.

### History of the presenting problem.

James shared that in the last couple of months the problem "slowly inched up on me and then took over." The problem started out "like a little nothing and has blossomed into taking up every moment of my free time trying to figure out what is going on."

In an individual session with Georgia, she reported that James no longer engages in cuddling, sexual activity, or daily intimate conversation as of four months ago. "I just don't know who he is anymore or where he has gone. You'd think he was having an affair, but he fears God's wrath too much to ever do that." She is finding that she is distancing herself emotionally. "It just hurts so much." One threat to the marriage is that an old boyfriend of Georgia's recently e-mailed her. She has not responded but finds her mind "going there" a lot.

### Psychiatric history and family history.

James did not know much about his father's family, but my consultation with his mother, which James consented to, revealed that his father was an alcoholic, as was his father's father. His paternal grandparents were German and came to the United States at the turn of the century. Although not very religious, his father's family was Catholic, and she thought they attended church regularly while James was growing up. She believes that James's grandfather was abusive both to his father's mother and to him and his siblings. James's father had two older brothers, one who was killed in a car accident when his father was six, and the other brother, like their father, was a "mean alcoholic." He also had four sisters, who she remembers as "fairly friendly." She thinks that James's mother was anxious and depressed.

James's maternal grandparents were both born in England and came to the United States before the First World War. James's mom was an only child whose parents met in the military before the Second World War. Early in their marriage her father was killed (James's mother was two years old) in a civilian accident (he was an auditor of some kind for the military and she was a clerk), and her mother remarried when James's mother was seven. They did not have any other children. James's mother and her family attended a Methodist church "somewhat regularly" growing up, but she had never really had any understanding of or connection to God. She thought, and she reported this in a sarcastic tone, that "maybe it had something to do with the fact that my stepfather's brother had intermittently molested me from the ages of 8 to 11 (once her mom found out there was no further contact with that uncle) and even though I called out to God, I guess He did not see me as someone worthy of helping out." James's mother shared that she is very confused and anxious about God and wants to sort all that out if she can. About 10 years ago her doctor prescribed Prozac "because I just got to feeling so down and anxious. James doesn't know about this." Although her physician had recommended psychotherapy as well, she has not opted for personal counseling herself.

James's parents met at a community dance and, to the chagrin of his mother's parents who "disapproved of anyone who was not Methodist," they eloped, at the urging of James's father, four and half months later. Regarding this choice his mother said, "My parent's practically disowned me, and it really wasn't until the last 10 years or so that we have begun to really connect again."

James's father was an airplane mechanic whose work led them to move to Pennsylvania (from North Carolina), causing feelings of isolation and loneliness for James's mother. James was three and his brother, Jason, was born that same year. Over the next four years James's dad's drinking increased, and with it episodes of aggression and violence toward his mother and a few times toward him and Jason as well. He reported becoming very protective of his mother and brother during this period. Right before James's father abandoned the family, when James was nine, he remembers his father locking him and his brother in the bathroom while he took his mother upstairs. They could hear his mother screaming, but could not do anything about it. No one ever discussed this event, and soon afterward James's father disappeared. When asked about what he felt at this time, James shared only what he thought at the time, "I'm the man around here now." His mother told him this as well.

Reviewing James's genogram and extended family history revealed that the types of interactions and relational experiences that promote secure attachment and emotional development in children were not adequately met in James's family line for several generations. Not surprisingly, an attachment survey revealed that James had an anxious attachment style with some traits of disorganization (we will elaborate on the importance of understanding attachment, emotional and cognitive development, constitutional factors, and trauma shortly). He had no memories of feeling close with his dad or his mom. When he described how he felt in relation to his dad while growing up, he unemotionally replied, "Scared, never knowing when the shoe was going to drop, alone, disinterested, gone," and in relation to his mom he said she was "overwhelmed, downtrodden, loving, busy, sad." I had to provide him with a list of feeling words in order for him to answer this question. James reported that he never really felt safe or intimately connected with anyone in his childhood home. "I felt responsible but not really close; in fact not ever close with anyone except Jason, but it was more of me taking care of him."

James reported that he thought that both his mother and his mother's mother had a history of depression and that "maybe my dad had some kind of problems that he turned to alcohol to deal with." Although his father and grandfather were alcoholics, James reported that he himself "never drank a drop, ever."

Of particular relevance is the fact that 10 months before initiating counseling, James's younger brother Jason called James on the phone because he did not feel well. James went over to Jason's house to comfort and take care of him and then left him to rest. Then later that night Jason died of an aneurism. When asked how he felt about this, James said, "I have been in a daze since then." When asked how he has dealt with his grief over such a substantial loss, James looked up with a blank stare, shrugged his shoulders, and said, "Grief?" James shared that he hasn't talked to anyone about his feelings and thoughts about the incident. He said, "It's just too hard."

### Relevant medical history.

James presently reveals severe anxiety symptoms (fear of dying). He reports that his mother suffers with depression and his father (with whom he has very little contact) had a major social disorder, "very nervous." James is of normal height and weight, and reports that he eats well and exercises regularly. He denies any history of major medical problems. Sleep, eating, energy, and tension level were reported to be abnormal at present with significant decreases in the first three and increase in the last.

James reported a history of intermittent gastrointestinal problems, sleep disturbance, nightmares, and bedwetting ("until I was 12") since he was five.

James currently believes that he has a terminal illness and spends all his free time trying to figure out what it is. Consultation with the referring physician revealed that a full medical evaluation ruled out any biologic, organic, or medical (including medication) issues and concerns. According to the doctor, "James is in radiant health." Knowledge of these facts has not influenced James's continued fear that he will soon die because of some terminal illness.

James reported feeling anxious and hopeless most of the time, as corroborated by the Beck Anxiety Scale. Also he reported that most of the time he is disinterested in many of the activities that once gave him pleasure, including sexuality. He also reported sleep disturbance (waking about 3 a.m. and unable to get back to sleep), decreased energy and fatigue, loss of appetite, feeling sad, and having negative thoughts. He experiences these thoughts as intrusive, but stated, "I can't make them stop." The Beck Depression Inventory reflected a high degree of depression. James shared that he has always had a need for keeping things ordered and arranged, having some difficulty with change, and liking things "just so." He believes that these traits have made him "a success in the accounting business but now, it is as if my mind has turned against me." The intrusive fearful thoughts center around sickness, getting old, death, and God's wrath; compulsive actions include relentless Internet searching and daily masturbating, without pornography use, sometimes three or four times a day.

James reported that anxiety emerged about six months ago ("and has become worse and worse") when he became convinced that he had contracted Lou Gehrig's disease. He then feared Parkinson's disease, brain cancer, and a series of other illnesses that the referring doctor had ruled out. Recognizing his symptoms as anxiety, the referring doctor started a regimen of 30 mgs of Cymbalta and Xanax one week before the evaluation and referred him for counseling. James reported that as of yet "the medication hasn't done a thing."

James complained of being inundated with constant catastrophic thoughts and fears that appear to reflect underlying feelings of grief, fear, guilt, and shame, but James does not articulate these feelings as such. Although he reported experiencing some attention problems, it is likely that these are due to excessive levels of anxiety because attention issues did not manifest themselves when James was a child. The presence of a long-term, low-grade depression was denied. Manic symptoms were denied. Dissociative processes will need to be further explored. James denied having thoughts of suicide or homicide, any present or past substance use, and any previous psychiatric treatment or counseling.

### Developmental history.

James reported that his mother told him he was really "quite a carefree kid, before my dad left," but James does not remember this. He shared that he "knows he is smart because of all the testing they did all through school; I always came up in the upper 96th percent." "I worked hard at school, but at the same time it came pretty easy. I wasn't Mr. Popular, but I always got along well with classmates and baseball teammates. James shared that he needed to take care of his mother and brother. "It just lived strongly in my heart that that was what I needed and wanted to do. I shared my work earnings from the farm and then the bank with my mom, who did some editing work from home."

James's lifemap revealed that he spent most of his time when he was not working or at school doing things around his house for his mother and brother. He shared that he had not felt as if he was really missing out on anything. He enjoyed being home with them, playing games, doing odd jobs around the house, keeping the house in order. "We didn't live close to my mom's parents and she was an only child, so it was basically just us."

James's mother reported that ever since she could remember James liked things organized, clean, and put away. "When his daddy left us, he never cried or even asked after him. He just took his little brother by the hand and sort of took off where Justin (his father) left off. I know it wasn't right, but I was so destroyed myself that I didn't take the time to explain things better, you know, about why and about how it wasn't about anything he did. All of a sudden, he got so serious. At age nine he used to make lists about what needed to be done around the house, and he'd do them. He never teased or fought with Jason anymore; he just sort of became the dad around the house. He watched over that little guy like a hawk. I was too much involved in my own world to see that as a red flag." Regarding Jason's death, his mother said, "I wonder if this whole thing is related to that, but you'd think it would have popped up sooner and been over with by now. I mean that was 10 months ago."

### Social history.

Severe parental conflict, divorce, and alcoholism were present in James's childhood home.

James reported a history of primarily attending to the needs of his mother and brother. His lifemap revealed that he got along well with and enjoyed his peers in the baseball team in junior high and senior high. James said he "didn't attend extracurricular events, parties, dances, or the like, because I was too busy working at the farm (he worked for a neighbor on their farm), helping my little brother keep up with his homework, keeping things around the house in order."

James lacked a social network of family with no grandparents, aunts, uncles, and cousins for emotional or demographic connection. Church attendance was intermittent, as previously mentioned. "After not being reciprocated after attempting to form relationships, school and neighborhood friends stopped initiating." James reported having "two long-term buddies from baseball and I still get together with them from time to time." He shared, "My social life was my brother and mom; and Georgia, after we met in high school."

James is very grateful for his baseball coach "whom I had for five years. We still keep in touch, and he took a very fatherly interest in me."

James shared that he recalls family traditions they enjoyed at holiday times with "just the three of us."

James met Georgia during his senior year in high school when her family transferred to the area from Kentucky. "It was love at first sight." Georgia had come with some girlfriends to one of James's baseball games, and she "was the first person I ever pursued. She was so beautiful and full of life and faith and joy." Georgia and James dated through college; they had both stayed local, and then had a small beach wedding with friends and family. "We have totally devoted ourselves to our kids and our family and until recently that was all fine."

Georgia's parents moved to Florida several years ago, and her one brother now lives in Manhattan. "We all get together once a year at Christmas in Florida."

James shared that he thinks that his marriage is threatened because recently Georgia, "who has always been such a joy and support," told him that she "just doesn't think she can take much more of this anymore."

### Employment history.

James currently works as an accountant and has been with his current company since 1992. He reported that it is, "OK work, but nothing I am passionate about." James has worked steadily since he was nine years old when he found his first paying "job" as a local farmhand. He did that three days a week until he was 17. When he started his accounting training, he found a job at a local bank as a clerk and stayed with the bank all through college. When he graduated, he worked at a local accounting firm and then became a partner at his current firm where he "makes an excellent living but is pretty bored with it all." When asked what he wishes he could be doing he smiled and said, "I wish I could get back on that farm."

### Religious background and affiliation.

"We went to church when I was little, but after my dad left something happened and we stopped going. My mom said that God does not approve of divorce, so I guess we did not go for that reason. My mom prayed for us at night and at meals and sometimes would light candles and do some kind of reading. She seemed to be hounded by guilt about my dad and maybe other things too. Her parents were devoutly religious, and she always felt that my dad's leaving may have been some kind of punishment for something she did or didn't do. I think there may have been some kind of sexual thing that happened with her uncle, I don't know, we didn't really talk about sexual types of things." (James's legs began to bounce as he relayed this information.)

A spiritual assessment revealed that when James thinks about God, he believes that God is "totally disgusted with me." It seems that he has experienced intermittent terror of God since he was a child, and he believes that his brother's death may have been "a judgment against me because I didn't go and check on him that night. I know I should have gone, but I didn't."

James reported that there is a significant amount of tension between him and Georgia about church attendance. They are members of Belmont Church, a nondenominational church, but he finds it difficult to attend. "There is something overwhelming and uncomfortable about going, although I don't think I always felt this bad about it. Georgia worries that I have lost faith in God. But that's not it at all. I know God is, and I just want to run and hide from Him. I hadn't thought of this before, but I get this feeling that He is just waiting to slam me, to give me what I deserve for what I've done. Really, I get no comfort from God or church or reading the Bible. I hadn't thought of this, but I guess reading the Bible makes me even more scared. Georgia goes to church and enjoys it. She sings, and dresses up the kids and laughs and talks to people. I just want to get out of there as fast as I can."

### Strengths and weaknesses.

James is a hardworking man, deeply devoted to his wife and family. Although his faith is presently functioning in a maladaptive manner, he believes in God and wants to do what is right and good. James is intelligent, motivated to work in counseling, and has interests that once gave him joy and pleasure.

James's recent and past history is replete with loss and trauma, much of which he has yet to resolve. Probably the recent death of his brother, Jason, has triggered a complicated array of emotions related to both the past and the present losses. Also, James's compromised developmental history may have led to a failure to develop secure attachment and the subsequent biological, psychological, social, and interpersonal developmental components that are grounded in secure attachment (including adaptive internal working models of self, others, the world, and God; the ability to regulate the self, the development of initiative; and the ability to differentiate, label, communicate, and regulate one's emotions in an increasingly mature manner). These compromises to James's development have likely led to successive inability "to distinguish inner from outer reality, physical experience from mind, and intrapersonal mental and emotional processes from interpersonal communications" (Skarderud, 2007, p. 325). James's emotional life is therefore being communicated through the body rather than through words. Counseling will need to focus on the development of the ability to reflect on, experience, put words to, and bring to relationship his internal experience, with an emphasis on how his body is presently acting out the unbearable terror, grief, guilt, and shame within him.

## Diagnostic Impressions

The following is an example of multiaxial diagnosing, using the DSM system. (We trust that you will learn about ethical diagnosing and its relation to treatment planning from other courses and resources.)

> Axis I: 309.81 Post Traumatic Stress Disorder; no code: Complicated Grief; V61.1 Partner Relational Problem
> Axis II: V71.09 No Diagnosis on Axis II
> Axis III: None
> Axis IV: Death of brother; waning commitment of spouse; lack of social support; compromised intrapsychic development
> Axis V: 42

James's symptoms reveal a compromised developmental history or a "development that has gone awry" (Cichetti & Toth, 1995). Normal development includes passing through a succession of stages that involve "the securing of attachment; the development of initiative; the ability to move from dependency, pleasure, excitement, assertiveness, curiosity, anger, rage, fears, loss and separation, empathy, and mature forms of love, to verbal representation of these; and increased initiative and expressions of self in healthy, loving relationships and in the world in general" (Greenspan, 1997). James is currently functioning at a very young level of affective development, which makes sense based on his history, with symptoms unconsciously expressing his internal experiences.

James's developmental history is filled with experiences of feeling terrified and alone, the very definition of trauma (Allen, 2001). These have had a significantly debilitating effect on his bio-psycho-social-spiritual development and the development of his identity and personhood. In particular, insecure and disorganized attachment, continual affective arousal, constitutional factors, and trauma have impaired his ability to mentalize (i.e., to reflect on his affective experience, accurately verbalize his experience, bring his experience into relationship for soothing, and learn how to self-soothe). And these have led to intolerable emotional states related to maladaptive internal working models of self, others, the world, and God. Without the ability to discern and speak his internal experience James's physical symptoms can be deciphered as expressions of his emotional experience. In short, although James does not have what he needs to feel secure or to express his terror and sadness, his symptoms are busy relaying the truth. Just as these skills emerge out of bio-psycho-social-spiritual processes that occur during normal development from infancy to adulthood, counseling will need to focus on these vital developmental tasks.

James's brother's death was the "last straw" in an already compromised and challenged system. We can surmise that this incident not only triggered previous maladaptive attachment and schema mechanisms, but it is at the very heart of the intolerable guilt, shame, and terror he is currently experiencing. James needs help "unpacking," sorting through, and grieving this terrible loss. His loss has been stuffed away and symbolized in behavioral symptoms. James's belief in his own impending death is a direct transference to himself of what he can never undo, namely, the failure to keep his brother Jason alive and safe.

The loss of Jason has also activated James's false image of God, which is causing significant existential turmoil as well. Once his relationship with God is addressed in counseling, first implicitly (in the person of the counselor) and then, with consent, explicitly (use of Scripture, reading of Christian literature, prayer, clergy collaboration, etc.), his Christian faith may become a great resource in his recovery.

Most probably James's current masturbation habit has become a way of coping with intolerable emotional states. As the orgasm produces a rush of chemicals (dopamine) similar to those released when snorting cocaine, James has found a way to "self-medicate" his unbearably painful emotional states.

The good news is that in the context of a meaningful relationship with his counselor—in which the counselor has a thorough knowledge of the normal developmental processes that are likely to have gone awry in

James's case and has skill in facilitating cognitive and emotional development—compromised and/or missed phases can be redressed, and recovery promoted (Gabbard, 2009). What is exciting is that God has "pre-wired" humans to naturally go through the developmental process. When the right ingredients are present, the appropriate balance of grace (secure attachment) and truth (counselor expertise), one can learn how to trust (bond), to know and communicate authentically about oneself, experience a wide spectrum of emotional experiences, and love and be loved. James needs to learn how to speak his pain with a caring person who will not move away from it. In this way he will no longer be alone in his shame, terror, loss of control, and grief. While James's developmental experiences and traumatic losses impaired his ability to effectively mentalize, the counseling relationship will provide a "secure base" (Bowlby, 1988) from which mentalization can emerge and grief work can be accomplished. Then James's body and behavior will no longer need to convey the intolerable terror that lies within him.

Table 11.2

*James's Functioning on the AIM Chart*

| AIM COMPONENT | Symptoms | Counselee Comments | Counselor Notes | Preliminary Goal |
|---|---|---|---|---|
| A: Level of Spiritual Functioning | Terrified of God; Disconnected from God | "God is totally disgusted with me." | Insecure / disorganized God-attachment; "toxic" faith contributing to symptoms. | Understand God image development and begin to develop spiritual security. |
| B: Biblical and Psychological Functioning (General) | Deeply confused theologically and psychologically | "Jason's death was God's judgment against me." | Core existential schema: "You do one thing wrong and bam . . ." | Understand the nature of bio-psycho-social-spiritual disturbance. |
| I: Level of Identity Differentiation | Low level of identity differentiation | No memories of feeling close to anyone. | Insecure/disorganized attachment style leading to developmental psychopathology | Get back on developmental track: work to attain secure attachment, initiation, and increased levels of mentalization. |

Table 11.2 (cont.)

*James's Functioning on the AIM Chart*

| AIM COMPONENT | Symptoms | Counselee Comments | Counselor Notes | Preliminary Goal |
|---|---|---|---|---|
| D: Level of Cognitive Functioning | Low insight level | "I am totally obsessed with figuring out what disease I have." | Pre-representational thought processes (concrete level of development related to grief, terror, dependency, shame). | Learn to recognize and put words to disorganized cognitive content. |
| E: Level of Emotional Functioning | Low insight level | "Grief?" | Intolerable emotional states related to maladaptive models of self, others, and God. | Learn to recognize and put words to disorganized affective content. |
| I: Level of Self-Regulation | Low level of self-regulation | "Everything is totally out of control." | Intolerable emotional states with the inability to self-soothe or find comfort from others or God | Build upon the above goals; learn to regulate self by bringing intolerable affective experience into relationship. |
| N: Level of Biological/ Physiological Functioning | Hyper-aroused system | "I am incredibly anxious all the time." | Concretization; traumatized; Constitution: need for order; possibly compromised visual-spatial processing disability. | Move from concretization to verbal representation. Develop internal object constancy (ability to "see" and experience loved ones mentally as needed). |
| M: Level of Interpersonal Functioning | Discon-nected | "I have never been really close to anyone." | Promote secure attachment in the therapeutic relationship; have collateral couple sessions as needed. | Develop a circle of intimate relationships as attachment issues resolve. |
| E: Level of Awareness: the World, the Flesh, and the Devil | Low level of aware-ness | | Currently identifies with these maladaptive "voices" | Facilitate differentiation from these "voices." |

## TREATMENT PLANNING BASED ON ACCURATE CASE CONCEPTUALIZATION

Once you have developed a clear conceptualization of your counselee's dynamics you can relate these to the goals he or she has for counseling. James came to counseling desperate to get relief from his fear of impending death. He had no insight on how his fears related to his feelings of guilt, fear, and shame about his brother's death or how these feelings triggered core schemas from earlier development. On some level, James knew that the medical tests had ruled out any serious illness, but without the internal resources to draw on to regulate his emotions, these facts did not impact his feelings. He strongly felt terror, he emotionally reasoned that something terrifying was therefore happening, and he transferred this terror to a belief in a terminal condition and impending death.

Treatment planning begins with the counselor relating the case conceptualization to the counselee's goals and formulating those goals into a plan of action. The primary question the counselor asks himself is, "What needs to happen in counseling for this person to reach his goals? What are the empirically based bio-psycho-social-spiritual formulations, strategies, and tools that I can bring to the plan to support this person's recovery?" No matter how many years you are practicing as a counselor, you will never outgrow the need to collaborate with colleagues and go to the current literature and research to determine how best to intervene.

Once the case conceptualization is written, the counselor then creates the written treatment plan or roadmap for counseling. The written report and the treatment plan are then fully discussed with the counselee so that consent for treatment can be ascertained (Corey, Corey, & Callanan, 2007). I (Lisa) usually take two full sessions for assessment, several hours of exploring and reviewing the data, consulting with relevant others, praying for wisdom and discernment, and then writing the report and treatment plan. Then in one session I discuss the written report and treatment recommendation/plan with the counselee. The final plan is always a collaborative effort based on the counselee's goals. Once I am sure the counselee fully understands and consents to the plan (the counselee would have already signed a general Consent to Treatment form; this is an additional "consent to assessment and treatment plan" form), the therapeutic work can begin.

Table 11.3 on the next page is an example of a treatment plan based on James's goals and our case conceptualization. You can see that the treatment plan is divided into three sections. The first column provides a summary of James's "Identified Problems." We used the DSM-IV-TR (APA, 2000) criteria for Post-Traumatic Stress Disorder (the primary diagnosis) to succinctly summarize James's presenting issues and concerns. In the second column are James's goals, as determined in the assessment and through a collaborative (counselee and counselor) "boiling down" process (Young, 2010). Notice how the goal has been operationally defined through the use of SUDS (Significant Units of Distress/Disturbance Scale). By providing an assessment measure, we will be able to track James's progress toward recovery. Column three presents the Treatment Plan to address the identified problems and goals. In order to come up with an effective plan of action that addresses the counselee's problems and will likely facilitate reaching of the counselee's goals, search the literature relative to the diagnosis and/ or presenting concerns and clearly document the bio-psycho-social-spiritual treatment interventions that will be utilized to promote change and recovery.

## Table 11.3
### James's Treatment Plan

| IDENTIFIED PROBLEMS | THE COUNSELEE'S GOALS | THE TREATMENT PLAN |
|---|---|---|
| Debilitating fear, helplessness, and horror. Recurrent and intrusive images and thoughts related to contracting a terminal illness, including nightmares. Physiologic reactivity on exposure to internal or external cues that symbolize or resemble an aspect of a contracting illness. Significantly diminished interest or participation in significant activities. Feelings of detachment or estrangement from others. Restricted range of emotions (e.g., unable to have loving feelings). | Decreases in all PTSD (Post-Traumatic Stress Disorder ) symptoms (under column 1, Identified Problems) as measured by SUDS (Significant Units of Distress/Disturbance) from the present 10 (on a scale of 1–10) to 4 or less. | **Biological Components:** -Continue with medication as prescribed by referring physician and work collaboratively to ensure patient care on the physiological level. -Utilize behavioral strategies (e.g., systematic relaxation, mindfulness training, safe place, imaginal exposure to traumatic events, experiential activities) to facilitate decreases in hyperarousal. -As recovery progresses, encourage returning to previously enjoyed exercise, nutrition, and recreational activities. |

Table 11.3 (cont.)

*James's Treatment Plan*

| IDENTIFIED PROBLEMS | THE COUNSELEE'S GOALS | THE TREATMENT PLAN |
|---|---|---|
| Sense of foreshortened future.<br>Persistent symptoms of increasing arousal, including difficulty falling or staying asleep.<br>Irritability or outbursts of anger.<br>Difficulty concentrating.<br>Hyper-vigilance.<br>Duration of more than one month.<br>The disturbance causes clinically significant distress or impairment in social, occupational, or other important areas of functioning. | | **Psychological Components:**<br>-Utilize psycho-education (grief, trauma, hyperarousal/ stress cycle, normal development, etc.) to promote understanding.<br>-Utilize cognitive-behavioral and developmentally based therapy strategies to facilitate increased mentalization capacities and general growth up the developmental ladder.<br>-Address concretization by focusing on increasing ability to differentiate, experience, and represent with words the wide range of emotional themes to decrease the need for concretization (transfer and expression of feelings onto the body).<br>-Facilitate resolution of complicated grief by means of verbal and experiential activities.<br><br>**Social Components:**<br>-Joint sessions to educate his spouse and facilitate reconciliation.<br>-Encourage the development of a social network, including a grief-support group. |

| Table 11.3 (cont.) *James's Treatment Plan* | | |
|---|---|---|
| IDENTIFIED PROBLEMS | THE COUNSELEE'S GOALS | THE TREATMENT PLAN |
| | | **Spiritual Components:** Utilize implicit and then explicit empirically supported spiritual interventions to address his image of God and the establishment of "nontoxic" faith experience. |

We have had the privilege of witnessing the fruit of accurate case conceptualization and treatment planning. We have also seen the unfortunate ravages of inaccurate conceptualization and treatments. As counselee care is at stake, and your ethics codes require, please do your best to learn these vital skills and work closely with supervisors and colleagues throughout your career to insure that your counselees receive care that is effective and God-glorifying.

## CHAPTER SUMMARY

Accurate case conceptualization and treatment planning are critical skills that you will develop over time. Because effective counseling is founded on this "journey map," counselors have an enormous ethical obligation to become experts in this area of the counseling process. We say this to encourage you to seek out continual supervision and consultation with expert colleagues, to immerse yourself in the literature and research, and to walk humbly and closely to our God so you will have wisdom for these essential tasks. Having others further along in the field to walk beside you will comfort you and provide a "safety net" for your counselee's well-being.

## CHAPTER 11 ACTIVITIES

1. What is case conceptualization, and why is it vitally important?
2. Describe Bandler and Grindler's (1975) threefold principle of mental maps. With each of the three, describe one way to help enrich a counselee's "mental map."
3. Evaluate each of the statements below and identify whether the state-

ment is a deletion, distortion, or generalization. Explain the reason for your answer. Then include your response to the counselee's statement.

> a. "I cannot trust people."
> b. "My wife makes me mad."
> c. "My client is difficult."
> d. "My husband doesn't love me."
> e. "I am scared."
> f. "My teacher is out to get me."
> g. "My mother was angry."
> h. "I'm mad."
> i. "These chap. activities are boring."
> j. "God will not answer my prayer."

4. Using Figure 11.1, rate your own functioning in each of the nine areas described in the AIM model.
5. Carefully read again the report on James. Share some of your thoughts and feelings in response to this.
6. Describe how treatment planning flows from accurate case conceptualization.
7. Carefully explore Table 11.3, James's Treatment Plan. Discuss your thoughts and feelings in response to each section depicted (Identified Problems, The Counselee's Goals, and The Treatment Plan). Imagine that you were going to see a counselor for a particular personal goal (not a disorder, just a personal goal). Based on your current knowledge, what would you write in your Treatment Plan in each of these areas?

## Recommended Reading

Clinton, T., & Ohlschlager, G. (Eds.) (2002a). *Competent Christian counseling: Foundations & practice of compassionate soul care* (Vol. 1). Colorado Springs, CO: Waterbrook Press.

> This book is filled with chapters on virtually every aspect of the counseling process. Several chapters are dedicated to topics relevant to case conceptualization.

Crabb, L. (1988). *Inside out*. Colorado Springs, CO: NavPress.

> Crabb is one of the major pioneers in integrating psychology and theology. This particular work provides a type of psychodynamic view into human functioning. This book should be required reading for all who desire to understand the human heart.

# Chapter 12

# Strategies for Bringing About Changes

*"One of the paradoxes of psychotherapy is that no matter how strongly patients want to overcome their problems, and no matter how much time and money they invest in therapy, they also persistently engage in efforts to fight the treatment, to avoid facing their pain, to resist growth and to hang on to their maladaptive patterns"* (Narramore, 1994, p. 306).

*"More is involved in changing us on the inside than increased diligence on the outside"* (Crabb, 1988, p. 46).

*"First clean the inside of the cup, so the outside of it may also become clean"* (Matt 23:26, HCSB).

## CHAPTER OBJECTIVES

» To discuss the nature of change from a secular and biblical worldview

» To present the transtheoretical model of change

» To help students understand the difference between reluctance and resistance

» To provide strategies for dealing with resistance

» To give students opportunities to apply the chap. material

## CHAPTER OUTLINE

THE NATURE OF CHANGE
   Transtheoretical Model of Change

QUESTION 1: DO I NEED TO CHANGE, AND DO I WANT TO GET WELL?

As stated throughout this text, counseling involves movement and journey. The foundation of counseling, whether Christian or not, is built on the process and content of change, that is, helping people move from one place to another. People seek the help of a counselor in order to be different in some meaningful way. The most central role of the helper, then, is being a change agent. The counselor guides the counselee on a journey from his present location to a new destination, to a place that represents true life.

Each expedition is unique; no two trekkers are the same. Though the points of origin and destination might be similar in ways, how each one came to where he is reflects a number of related factors. Regardless of the journey they took to where they are, the unifying factor of all counselees is the realization that they are dissatisfied with where they are and want to be somewhere else. Erickson (cited in Watzlawick, Weakland, & Fisch, 1974), the famed psychiatrist, said, "Psychotherapy is sought not primarily for enlightenment about the unchangeable past but because of dissatisfaction with the present and a desire to better the future" (p. ix).

Getting from one place to another captures the essence of change. The concept of change is one that has been debated for years by those in both psychology and theology. Everyone seems to have an opinion on change and how it is accomplished through counseling. The opinions are as diverse as those who hold them. While we do not assume we have a corner on therapeutic change, we do wish to equip you for the task of being a helper to those who seek it.

To equip you for being a change guide, this chap. addresses the totality of the therapeutic expedition. Specifically we want to help you get your counselee from point A to point B. We hope to answer several questions through this chapter. What is change? How do people change? What blocks people from being able to change? How do you guide a counselee on a journey of change?

In this chapter we respond to three central questions about the change process. Effective counselors understand the issues of motivation and readiness for change, the objective of change, and how to help a counselee make the journey.

## THE NATURE OF CHANGE

One of the best gifts God has given us is the capacity to change. We possess the inherent ability to change in positive ways and to change in less desirable ways. Each of us can make movement toward God and away from God. We can adapt to good circumstances far too easily and to bad circumstances far too naturally. Once we have adapted, we prefer the status quo. Innately we want routine and predictability, thus the prospect of something different, no matter how much it is needed or even desired, is threatening.

Most people are willing to change not because they see the need to change or know that God wants them to change, but because they feel pain. Anxiety, sadness, grief, rejection, and the like are the great equalizers of life. No one comes to our offices to express gratitude. Rather they come out of grief over the way things are in their lives. They come with the hope that we have answers or an ability to help them be different. Each counselee desires to move away from his miserable condition. They want to take a therapeutic expedition.

An expedition of any kind consists of three fundamental questions. And when speaking about change in the context of the helping profession, three fundamental questions need to be answered before undertaking the journey (see Table 12.1). The answer to these questions will shape and influence the entire experience of an expedition.

Table 12.1

*Fundamental Questions of Change*

| Expedition Questions | Change Questions | Processes |
|---|---|---|
| Do I want to journey? | Do I need to change? | Need |
|  | Do I want to get well? | Motivation, readiness |
| Where do I want to go? | Change into what? | Goal, outcome |
| How will I get there? | How do I change? | Process, methods |

The first expedition question is, "Do I need to or want to go somewhere else?" It is a question about the need to move, to step out, and to get out from under our present status. Not all journeys need to be made. Many journeys are needed, but people cling to that in which they find escape, no matter how harmful. At times some people might wonder whether change is necessary. For a host of reasons the idea is dismissed. The foundational question has two parts: "Do I need to change?" and "Do I want to change?" The journey toward change will only commence at the point of need, desire, willingness, and readiness to commit to the journey. It encompasses motivation and the therapeutic topics of reluctance and resistance. Question one asks "if" I need to go on this journey.

The second question each explorer asks is, "Where do I want to go?" It is one thing to consider taking a journey and another to know where you are going. Nearly all counselors would agree that the goal of helping is to facilitate change in the lives of counselees. But "change people—into what?" (Adams, 1986, p. 59). The "what" or object of change specifically addresses the goal of counseling. As discussed in chap. 9, the goals of counseling are established by the counselee. Yet what the counselor desires to see happen as a result of the counseling is also equally important. That is, what you believe is the primary objective of counseling will be influence how you work. As discussed in chap. 9, the task of counselors is not to impose their goals on counselees. Yet this does not mean that the counselor's perspective on people's situations and what ultimately will help them have no merit.

Change and the desired "destination" can take on many forms, depending on the starting point of the counselee. Some are lost in unhealthy behaviors and need to journey toward understanding the cause of their problems so that they can be replaced with healthier behaviors. For some counselees ignorance or a deficit in essential life skills calls for learning new skills. Others are overly enmeshed or disengaged from other people and need to learn how to have intimate and authentically loving relationships. Others need to get "unstuck" so they can move forward in their lives. Many counselees need to experience change from spiritual deadness or lethargy to spiritual vitality. Regardless of where they are, the point is that they are unhappy and want to find a different place to be. Virtually all counselees simply want relief, and this is an understandable goal when one is hurting. As guides who have studied life's terrain, we know that ultimately all counselees, regardless of the nature and maturity of their spiritual lives, need to grow in loving God and loving others more deeply and with more purity. Addressing the purpose and goal of change is essential to making the journey. The questions "Where do I *want* to go?" and "Where do I *need* to go?," however, are not always the same. More will be said about this later.

The fundamental question each person who undertakes a therapeutic expedition needs to ask is: "How am I going to get there?" Explorers determine whether the journey can be made on foot, if the hikers have the capacity to make it, and how to get to the destination. Counselees too wonder "how." They want to find the answer to the question, "How do I change?" This basic question is not easily answered. The question, "How do I do it?" gets to the heart of the therapeutic expedition. If counselees knew how, they would not seek our services. Counselors are to be guides, who know how to make the journey. One of the most fundamental tools needed for helping is a map. A good map provides direction for an expedition. The counselor's therapeutic map must provide clear directions on how to work with the counselee. The counselor needs to know the destination but also how to get there. For counselors a therapeutic map includes your theoretical orientation, how you conceptualize the counselee's problem (see chap. 11, "Case Conceptualization and Treatment Planning," and what you believe needs to occur to get where the counselor needs to go.

The first tool is a model of change, that is, a "change map" to help you understand the internal processes and actions that counselees must undergo in order to change. This will help you locate the counselee's current condition so that you can devise the strategies appropriate for that situation. The following section explains a well-known model of change known as the Transtheoretical Model of Change. This model shows how people move from where they are to where they need to be. Some of the stages in the model correspond to the three fundamental questions we will explore in detail.

## Transtheoretical Model of Change

Based on years of research (Prochaska & DiClemente, 1984; Prochaska, DiClemente, & Norcross, 1992; Prochaska & Velicer, 1997) Prochaska and DiClemente developed an integrative model of change known as the Transtheoretical Model (TTM). Their model incorporated constructs from other theories and weaved them into a model to describe how people modify a problem and acquire change. The TTM has become one of the leading intervention models for behavioral change (O'Donnell, 1997).

The cornerstone of the model is the identification of stages through which each person must progress in moving toward change. Other models view change as an event, but the TTM views change as occurring through a series of five progressive stages (see Figure 12.1 and Table 12.2) that occur over time: (a) precontemplation, (b) contemplation, (c) preparation, (d) action, and (e) maintenance. Each stage is demarcated by a person's relative closeness to making the needed change. The stages involve the role that the counselee's emotions, cognitions, and behaviors play in the change process. One of the strengths of the model is that it highlights the importance of counselee decision-making.

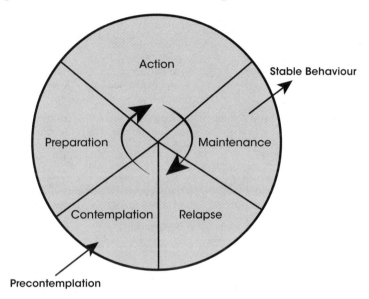

Figure 12.1: Stages of Change Model

The developers and researchers of the model sought to identify the needed tasks in each stage that would move the person to the following stage and closer to making the necessary change.

### Precontemplation.

The stage that is farthest from making a change is the Precontemplation stage. At this stage the individual has not given much thought to change, if any at all. Precontemplators ask questions such as "Do I need to change?" or "Why can't I stay the same?"

| Table 12.2 | | | |
| --- | --- | --- | --- |
| *Transtheoretical Model of Change* | | | |
| **Stage** | **Concern** | **Issues** | **Tasks** |
| Precontemplation | Need to change | • Denial<br>• Reluctance<br>• Resistance | • Increase awareness of need to change<br>• Increase concern<br>• Envision possibility of change |
| Contemplation | • Willingness<br>• Readiness<br>• Ability | • More cons than pros<br>• Ambivalence<br>• Fear consequences of change | • Maintain optimum level of anxiety<br>• Patience<br>• Analyze pros and cons |
| Preparation | What will it take? | • Hope for change<br>• Commitment<br>• Plan | • Instill hope<br>• Reinforce commitment<br>• Develop plan |
| Action | How will it work? | • Success mindset<br>• Efficacy | • Implement strategies<br>• Revise plan<br>• Sustain commitment |
| Maintenance | Will it continue? | • Sustainability | • Relapse plan<br>• Sustain commitment |

Denial, reluctance, or resistance to change prevents and limits a person from seeing the need to change. He might be unaware of the repercussions of his behaviors or believe they are insignificant or have given up on changing. Perhaps the person has not connected the problem to his behavior, thoughts, feelings, or relationships. Being unaware or under aware that a problem exists prohibits change. If a person does not see a problem or want to see a problem, he is content with where he is. Ignorance and denial are bliss. Problems can often cripple a person's ability to see reality. Even those who see a problem often have no intention of changing in the foreseeable future. People who are blind to a problem or do not wish to give up a behavior will not seek help. If these individuals do appear in your office, it will be because someone has persuaded or coerced them. Others who choose to see a counselor might do so because their lives have deteriorated to the point of being in a state of crisis. They might be entangled in a legal problem, threatened with the loss of a significant other, be in danger of losing their job, or facing some emotional trauma.

For those in the precontemplation stage the therapeutic tasks are to increase awareness of the need to change, increase concern about the current pattern of behavior, and envision the possibility of change. The wise helper does not preach or persuade the counselee to change. Rather he listens to the counselee's side of the issue and helps the counselee explore the benefits of change. If a counselee wants genuine change in the "fruits" of his life, he first clears out the "weeds" of deception, loosens the "soil" with honesty, and then sows "seeds" of truth (Wilson, 2001).

### Contemplation.

People who are in the contemplation stage of the process are wrestling with the question of whether they want to change and whether they have the ability to change. Contemplators recognize more of the pros of changing than Precontemplators, but they overestimate the difficulties. The result of weighing the pros and cons of change leads to ambivalence. Their ambivalence is evident in "Yes, but" or "I don't know." Ambivalence might stem from wanting to change but being unsure if it is worth the time, energy, or effort to achieve it. They might wish to change to please others but fear the consequences of what being different represents. The counselor seeks to help the counselee be willing for and ready to change.

Change exacts a price and raises questions as to the repercussions. To change often requires discomfort. No one will make significant behavioral change unless the behavior patterns they want to give up are not working well. Still the unpredictability of a change that may be filled with unexpected twists and ironic turns makes the prospect of changing threatening. Kovaks (1976) addressed the struggle of helping someone to change. "It is only when the familiar, the ordinary, repetitive, the predictable is made impossible by the therapist . . . that the counselee is forced, kicking and screaming in terror—to give birth to something new" (pp. 324–25). The "kicking and screaming in terror" might be an exaggeration, but the analogy aptly fits the natural reluctance people have to give up something they have been doing for some time. Throughout the change process, counselors will note waves of intense and fluctuating feelings. Anxiety, threat, guilt, shame, hostility, sadness, confusion, fear, and lostness often mark the pathway of change. Counselees will loosen and tighten their grip on entrenched beliefs and assumptions as they move toward something different. Change involves a deconstruction and construction, often simultaneously. Framed this way, a counselee's discomfort and protests at the work of counseling is not a problem; they are part of the process in the journey of change.

Getting through the contemplation stage can take some time. You may never get through the stage, however, if you are focusing on a problem that is not the counselee's problem. A key question in the change process is, Who owns the problem? When the problem is solely or largely owned by someone else, the counselee might not be able to do much about the problem. You can help the counselee at such times to focus on how he responds and reacts to the problem.

During the contemplation stage one of the tasks of helping is holding anxiety and discomfort at an optimum level in order to motivate the counselee to change. Helping a counselee feel better quickly may be sentencing him to feel worse in the long run. Provide a climate where the counselee can consider changing without any pressures such as guilt, blame, and/or reasoning. Pressure is usually not effective at this point. It is wise to go along with the ambivalence, which can be accomplished by helping the counselee analyze the pros and cons of his current behavior and consider the costs and benefits of change. One of your tasks is to help the counselee make a decision that hopefully will tip the balance in favor of change.

### Preparation.

Once the counselee has made the decision to change, the next question is, What will it take to change? The Preparation stage deals with "how to." The counselee needs to identify (a) those things he has to *do*, (b) those things he has to *stop doing*, (c) those things he needs to *continue to do,* and (d) those things he needs to *accept* (Burnard, 1999).

At this stage the counselee's work involves making a commitment to take action to change the behavior and to develop a plan to bring about the desired and necessary change. Those in this stage should decide to take action within the next 30 days, perhaps even taking small steps toward that goal. For change to occur, the counselee needs to see how it feels and looks to be different. Your helping task during this stage is to increase the counselee's commitment and help him create a change plan. Explore possibilities together but allow the counselee to choose the method and plan that seems to resonate best with them.

### Action.

Individuals in the Action stage are overtly engaged in modifying their problems and behaviors. Change does not occur until the counselee actually implements the plan. At this point the counselee takes steps to change his current behavior pattern and begins creating a new behavior pattern. Change does not mean that the counselee moves completely from A to Z. Rather change is moving from A to B and then to C. In order words, true change is incremental, and even the smallest change can have a great impact.

Your task during the Action stage is to help the counselee implement strategies for change, to revise the plan as needed, and to help him sustain commitment in face of difficulties. For a person to change he has to make new choices along with consistent practice (Wilson, 2001). The hope is that the plan will be successful and lead to permanent changes. To establish a new pattern of behavior it takes a significant period of time, usually three to six months.

### Maintenance.

Over time the changes begin to take root in the counselee's life. At the Maintenance stage individuals work on sustaining the action. They develop contingency plans to prevent slips, slides, and relapses. Change is not static; it is dynamic. It does not stop once the action has been taken and has been incorporated into the counselee's lifestyle. Change continues as the counselee matures and progresses. New thoughts and behaviors are to be sustained for an extended period of time across a wide range of different situations. Some problems require an active plan. The plan should be realistic, reliable, and responsive. *Realistic* plans are those in which the counselee sees the components of the plan as practical and doable. A good plan is one that works, one the counselee can *rely* on to reinforce the changes. A good plan is *responsive*, that is, it is flexible and can be adapted to new situations. Circumstances change in our lives and components of our plan that once worked may stop being helpful. That is simply life. A flexible plan is one that can be reshaped as necessary so that it can continue to be sustained.

### Summary.

Prochaska and DiClemente (1986) argue that for most people change is not linear but spiral, with several slips, slides, and relapses to earlier stages. The value of the TTM is illustrated by a study at a northeastern university that surveyed approximately 1,500 freshmen and sophomores on alcohol abuse. Findings indicated that 70 percent of those surveyed were in the Precontemplation stage and less than 10 percent were in the Preparation stage for addressing their alcohol abuse (Laforge, 2001, cited in Prochaska et al., 2004). With only 10 percent of the participants interested in taking action, it is not surprising that many of the university's organizational change initiatives failed. Precontemplators and Contemplators are likely to see change as imposed rather than intended, thereby resulting in defensiveness and resistance. By applying the principles of TTM, effective strategies can be implemented to maximize impact for counselees.

## QUESTION 1: DO I NEED TO CHANGE, AND DO I WANT TO GET WELL?

To begin a therapeutic expedition each person determines if he has a need and if he wants to undertake a journey. The most fundamental obstacle to change is recognizing the need to change and then deciding if change is desired. The first two stages of the TTM deal with these questions. At some point each person must evaluate his life situation and determine if a problem exists. If so, then he decides whether he wants to address the problem.

### Do I Need to Change?

Not everyone recognizes a problem when one exists, or at least does not recognize the severity of the problem. You will find it difficult to convince a person that he has a problem when you are the only one observing it. If other people in the counselee's life have seen the problem, they have likely pointed it out. But many counselees cannot see their problem or do not want to. Often they will rationalize their situation and explain why it is not a problem.

A wiser approach is to help the person explore the reasons for remaining the same and also to consider what value there would be in making a change. The overarching goal is to create a moment of lucidity for the counselee in which he can recognize his need.

### Do I Want to Get Well?

Perhaps one of the most important concepts in spirituality and counseling is the will to change. One biblical story aptly reports the will to change. On one occasion, Jesus met a man who had been paralyzed for 38 years (John 5). Throughout his life he lay beside the pool of Bethesda, which was believed to have healing properties. When Jesus came face to face with the sick man, He asked him a rather strange question: "Do you want to get well?" As the master Counselor and Healer, Jesus' question exposed the man's heart. Rather than answering Jesus' question, the lame man replied, "Lord, I don't have anyone to put me in the pool when the water is stirred up. I try to get in, but someone else always gets there first" (John 5:7, CEV). The sick man's heart was bitter and defeated. His focus was on the unkindness of those around him, rather than on his inability to walk. In his heart he saw the mistreatment of others as his most pressing problem. In contrast Jesus saw that the problem was his lack of desire for a change more than his inability to walk.

Many people who come for counseling believe their inability to change is the fault of other people's. In their mind, change hinges on what others need to do or on what has prevented them from being well. The man at Bethesda saw himself as a victim; he was completely dependent on the efforts of others to be well. Life had so beaten this man down that he lived as a perpetual victim. What must happen, of course, is for the counselee to have a will to change. No amount of counseling will make a difference if the counselee does not want to change. What the lame man failed to realize is that helplessness was the best estate when intersected with the power of Christ. Victims often blame others, but people can be helped when they reach out.

Nothing is more empowering than realizing you have the ability to make changes. A person can start a new behavior, and he can stop being unproductive, unwise, and ungodly. The process to do both might be difficult, but having the ability to respond in ways that make dramatic differences is freeing. Counselees need to distinguish between those things within their power to act on and those things they cannot; change and, therefore, must accept. The Serenity Prayer is built on those two truths: serenity to accept what cannot be changed and the courage to change the things that can be changed.

The fundamental reality of being willing and ready to change is felt pain. Pain is but one of the signposts of reality. The saying, "If you keep doing what you've done you will keep getting what you've got," speaks about the pain that results from the consequences of one's behavior. At one level of pain some people state that they need to make a change, but they lack the drive and energy to do so. One reason for the inability to change is that the individual has not reached the point of abandoned willingness. The person's life may not have deteriorated to the point of being desperate for change; the person simply has not come to the place where the level of pain outweighs the prospect of having to change. The degree of pain becomes a key factor in engaging the will. From this vantage point pain is actually a friend, not a foe. It is a tool of God to bring about needed change in someone's life.

A formula that we use to understand change is: $C = n \, x \, P/t$. Written out, the formula means that Change (c) is the result of the Need (n) to change times feeling Pain (P) over Time (t). The time factor is critical because most people muddle around in their unhealthy, unproductive, and ungodly behavior for some time before arriving at the "right" threshold of pain that compels them to cross over the doorstep and choose change.

Two reasons many people refuse to change are reluctance and resistance. Before moving to the second question on the expedition of change, we want to explore these two significant factors.

## Counselee Reluctance and Resistance

Typically helpers are trained and oriented to working with counselees who voluntarily seek help, those who are motivated to change (Larrabee, 1982). But helpers are often called to work with involuntary counselees, and in some settings (e.g., hospitals, prisons, clinics) these counselees might represent the majority. Perhaps one of the ironic aspects of counseling is that while counselees seek our services they are reluctant or resistant to receive help.

Reluctance and resistance are two terms that might be used interchangeably, yet they represent two different issues (Egan, 2007). Reluctant counselees are those who were coerced or at least are involuntarily seeking our services; they are not self-referred (Egan, 2007), and if given the choice they would prefer not to talk about themselves (Patterson & Eisenberg, 1983). In many cases the reluctance might be reasonable (Riordan, Matheny, & Harris, 1978), given the condition that forced their participation. Reasonable or not, research indicates that counselee reluctance is associated with poor satisfaction, poor outcome, and premature termination from services (Paradise & Wilder, 1979).

Resistance, on the other hand is the experience of some people who do not adequately give themselves to the helping process (Egan, 2007). Whereas reluctance deals with being an involuntary counselee, resistance can describe all counselees to some degree. Bischoff and Tracey (1995) define resistance as "any counselee behavior that exhibits a reluctance, on the part of the counselee, to participate in the tasks of therapy as set forward by the therapist . . . any behavior that indicates covert or overt opposition to the therapist, the counseling process, or the therapist's agenda" (p. 488). Resistance then is any attitude or behavior that *opposes* change. Redl (1966) characterizes resistance as a natural part of our make-up: "Resistance is an unavoidable process in every effective treatment, for that part of the personality that has an interest in the survival of the pathology actively protests each time therapy comes close to inducing a successful change" (p. 216). In this light resistance is to be expected because it is part of human nature. People enter counseling with an orientation to be self-protective (Crabb, 1988). Therefore attempts to change the counselee are perceived as a threat. The threat of change might be so great that staying the same is saner. The curse might be viewed as worse than the disease; thus learning to live with it is more desirable.

Resistance occurs in varying degrees and for personal reasons. Counselees may be viewed as being on a continuum of compliance to defiance (see Figure 12.2). Typically counselors consider a good counselee to be compliant—someone who is polite and does what the counselor requests. Actually, however, both compliance and defiance can be forms of resistance.

Figure 12.2: Resistance Continuum

### Expressions of reluctance and resistance.

Both reluctance and resistance are complex phenomena. The faces of both are manifold, but there are some clearly identifiable characteristics in the way they manifest themselves in counselee emotions and beliefs. Key emotions that play a role in reluctance and resistance include (a) frustration (e.g., *"This is going too slow"*), (b) anger (e.g., *"You are not helping me,"* (c) fear (e.g., of failing, of getting hurt, mistrust), (d) pride (e.g., *"I won't do that"*), and (e) shame (e.g., *"I'm not good enough"*). Emotions are typically the byproduct of belief. At least four beliefs are linked with reluctance and resistance, which express themselves in four negatively framed statements: (a) not being biblical or godly (e.g., *"Christian people don't get angry"*), (b) not being me (e.g., *"I'm not that kind of person"*), (c) not being like them (e.g., *"She would never come to counseling"*), and (d) not able (e.g., no time, no money, no permission).

These emotions and beliefs can manifest themselves in varies behaviors; (a) passive-aggressive behavior (e.g., silence, delaying tactics, coming late for appointments, issues with the fees and parameters of counseling); (b) denial (e.g., not being ready yet, *"What good will it do me,"* *"Nothing is wrong with me"*), (c) hostile-aggressive behavior (e.g., blaming, intimidating, threats), (d) placing unrealistic demands on you (e.g., extending sessions, giving full sessions when they have come very late for their appointment, reducing fees), (e) distancing behavior (e.g., suspiciousness, talking too little, humor to keep you at arm's length), (f) rationalizations (e.g., intellectualizing, excuses) and justifications (e.g., *"It won't do any good anyway," "My wife won't change," "No one else has to do it"*).

### Factors that produce reluctance and resistance.

The face of reluctance and resistance can come from different and diverse factors. We have categorized these factors into three distinct facets of the therapeutic expedition: counselee factors, counselor factors, and therapeutic factors.

#### *Counselee factors.*

Some counselees might be reluctant because they do not believe in counseling. Others harbor suspicions about counseling (Egan, 2007) or fear that it will cause them to give up their faith. Some counselees may feel stigmatized and fear that others will belittle them for going to a professional counselor. Still other counselees might doubt your ability, credibility, and competence. For such counselees you will earn your fees in attempting to establish trust.

A second factor is when counselees do not believe they have a problem. In other words they are in denial. Closely related to denial is ambivalence about changing (Miller & Rollnick, 2002). All counselees have a level of ambivalence about change; being different is unfamiliar and unknown territory. For some, denial has become such a way of life that it seems to define them.

A third factor is when the counselee does not want to change. Counselees might resist because they have fear about uncovering something they would prefer is left buried. Like all defensive coping strategies, resistance is learned early in life and is activated when certain levels of fear or anxiety are present (Sommers-Flanagan & Sommers-Flanagan, 2003).

#### *Counselor factors.*

You may find it relatively easy to label the counselee as reluctant or resistant, but it may be more difficult to know how to deal with rude counselees. Counselors, both consciously and unconsciously, contribute to counselee resistance. The literature suggests a number of possible counselor factors that contribute to the problem. First, some counselees might become reluctant to see you or resistant to change when the counselor has a bad reputation (Egan, 2007). Proverbs 22:1 says that a good reputation is a precious treasure ("A good name is to be chosen over great wealth," HCSB). How you have treated previous counselees and how competent you have been in your work will go before you. Your reputation might be deserved or not, but how you have been described by others will impact your rapport with future counselees.

Counselors do not cause reluctance, but they can make reluctant counselees more resistant. If a counselor has higher expectations than the counselee, the latter may exhibit resistance. Perhaps the counselor wants more for the counselee than the counselee wants for himself. A counselor may have misguided expectations of counselee behavior and counselee roles. The counselor may expect the counselee to respond in a particular way, and when they do not respond accordingly they assume the counselee is being resistant.

Another factor related to resistance involves how well the counselor respects a counselee's rights. Sometimes a seemingly innocuous comment or nonverbal behavior can provoke resistance. I (John) remembered a woman who came to see me for counseling. When I reached out my hand to shake hers, she immediately recoiled. A normal social gesture produced fear in a heightened and vigilant counselee.

Poor skill or poorly implemented techniques can also produce resistance. Competence and timing are critical. Experience will improve your ability to use skills and know when to use them.

Your race, gender, appearance, office décor, and the like can also generate resistance. Many of these factors are beyond your ability to do anything about them, though some, like décor, can be addressed. Counselors use satisfaction surveys to learn about their services so that they can continue to improve.

### *Therapeutic factors.*

First, resistance can occur because of the lack of rapport (Golden, 1983). If the counselee does not feel safe, change will be hindered. A strong helping relationship will facilitate cooperation and be a leverage for change far better than your abilities or knowledge base.

The strategies and techniques used by counselors also may contribute to resistance. Be cognizant of your strategies, making sure they are appropriate for the counselee in the given moment. Similarly assign only homework assignments that are relevant to the issue at hand and that are not too time-consuming.

Resistance can occur when the counselor is moving at a pace faster than the counselee is ready to experience. Change is not easy, and people will proceed at a pace that feels safe and appropriate to them. Do not be overly eager to help the counselee. Remember that while our Lord does not want anyone to perish (2 Pet 3:9), He is willing to stand at the door and knock (Rev 3:20). That is, He is willing to wait patiently for us to return to Him.

Resistance might develop when the counselor fails to make culturally or developmentally sensitive modifications in the approach (Sommers-Flanagan & Sommers-Flanagan, 2003). Counselors need to be sensitive to the fact that people are different and that uniqueness requires carefully considering their behavior. Most counselor education programs have a course in multicultural issues in counseling in order to raise awareness of how diversity can impact the therapeutic expedition.

Egan (2007) points out that having different helping goals can create resistance. Sometimes the counselor's goals and the counselee's goals are not in alignment. When you believe that the counselee is not going anywhere, ask yourself where he is supposed to be going. The literature consistently notes that the counselor and counselee need to have mutually agreed-on goals for counseling to be successful.

## Guidelines for Dealing with Reluctance

Reluctant counselees will always pose a challenge for counselors, especially helpers who are strong in caring. The eight guidelines that follow may assist you in being more effective with involuntary counselees. Each guideline is associated with one letter of the acrostic **RELUCTANT** (see Table 12.3).

---

Table 12.3

*RELUCTANT: Guidelines for Dealing with Reluctance*

**R** = know the **Reason** for the **Referral**

**E** = **Empathize** with the counselee's concerns about participating in counseling

**L** = **Learn** and **Limit** your own anger and resistance to the counselee

**U** = establish a joint **Understanding** of your role and parameters of the helping

**C** = establish a **Contract** with the counselee

**T** = **Temper** your emotions

**A** = **Affirm** and **Accept** the counselee

**N** = seek to maintain **Neutrality** with the counselee

**T** = **Terminate** sessions if appropriate

---

The "R" speaks to considering the **Reason** for the **Referral**. Be sensitive to what the counselee might have experienced that led to the referral. Some counselees may have been through an arrest and incurred the hassle, force, punitive measures, and expense of the legal system. Others might be seeing you rather than being terminated from their job. Or a family member may be urging the counselee to see you. Whatever the system that prompted their referral, a number of our counselees have had some very different experiences (sometimes warranted and at other times not) before arriving at our offices. Be sensitive to their complaints. Sometimes they need to vent "system rage" in order to move forward.

**Empathize** ("E") with the counselee's concerns about participating in counseling. Give the counselee the right to be reluctant; that is, the right to want to use your services. Do not take it personally. If you have had your arm twisted to do something you did not want to do, you can certainly understand a counselee who was forced against his will to see you. Use reflective listening as discussed in chap. 5 ("Basic Skills: Creating a Connection") to establish a solid connection with the counselee.

**Learn** and **Limit** ("L") your own resistance to the counselee. The nature of the counseling relationship has the potential to fire up issues in yourself (see chap. 3, "The Hazards of Helping," and chap. 4, "The Person of the Counselor"). Fremont and Anderson (1986) found that counselors reported four forms of resistance that triggered their own anger: (a) the counselee not showing up for agreed appointments, (b) the counselee blaming others for his problems or being unwilling to recognize how he contributes to the problems, (c) the counselee refusing to work on problems to the counselor's satisfaction, and (d) the counselee refusing help from the counselor. Counselees might attack the counselor, impose on the counselor's time, question the counselor's competence, or even threaten the counselor. If you know your own sources of resistance, you will be in a much better position to respond appropriately.

Establish a joint **Understanding** ("U") of your role in helping and the parameters of the helping. One important task is for you to help your counselee understand your role. Some counselees expect the counselor to be an advice-giver, disciplinarian, interrogator, or extension of the legal system. At the initial session make sure that you clearly establish the parameters of the helping process (see chap. 9, "Managing the Counseling Session"). Be sure to fully cover issues of confidentiality, its limitations and exceptions, and informed consent. By understanding these issues you can assuage the initial fear and foster a safe haven. By making your role and the helping parameters less ambiguous, you reduce reluctance.

The "C" is for **Contracting** with the counselee. A contract plays a pivotal role with reluctant counselees. The bottom line is what the counselee must do in order to successfully complete counseling. Egan (2007) speaks of tapping into incentives to encourage counselee participation. If necessary, use other resources such as the legal system, parents, peers, teachers, employers, and others to help the counselee stay focused on achieving the helping goals.

The "T" stands for **Tempering** your emotions. Though you might feel the urge at times, avoid becoming sarcastic, frustrated, angry, hostile toward the counselee. Be patient and longsuffering, demonstrating self-control (see Gal 5:22–23; 1 Cor 13:4–8). By the same token, avoid placating the counselee. You might think that if you become nicer and more accepting you will win the counselee over, but such a strategy will fail.

The "A" is to **Affirm** and **Accept** the counselee, even if he is angry at being there or is angry at you (Larrabee, 1982). Difficult and involuntary counselees are not used to being accepted and affirmed, nor are they used to having their complaints truly heard. The goal is to create an atmosphere that will promote openly exploring both the positive and negative aspects of their lives. Using open-ended statements such as "Tell me about . . ." or "Let's talk about . . ." encourage the counselee to explore without your challenging them.

Though it is difficult to see your counselee doing things you know are harmful or unhealthy, maintain **Neutrality** ("N"). A counselor should not want the counselee to change more than he wants to change. If you find yourself in a power struggle with the counselee, you are likely not neutral with regard to change. We often tell resistant counselees that we will go on with our lives whether or not they change, though it will sadden us that they have chosen to live in pain and misery.

**Terminate** ("T") the session if appropriate. Be prepared to end the session when anger blocks receptivity, disclosure, and dialogue, or if the counselee is threatening you. Do not allow yourself to be continually abused and scapegoated for the counselee's problems. Establish appropriate boundaries with counselees that are neither too rigid nor too lax. The wisest decision is to tell a counselee, "Come back when you are willing to work."

Dealing with reluctant and involuntary counselees is not one of the delightful aspects of helping people. You will encounter reluctant counselees; this simply cannot be avoided. By employing these guidelines you will augment the possibility of making a difference in the life of the reluctant counselee.

### Guidelines for Dealing with Resistance

We offer 14 guidelines to work effectively with counselee resistance; these guidelines are formed into the mnemonic device **LESS RESISTANCE** (see Table 12.4). The "L" in the word **LESS** is to remind you not to give in to your desire to be **Liked** by your counselees. Do not put a premium on getting the counselee to like you. Instead work on building rapport through sound use of skills.

| Table 12.4 |
| --- |
| *LESS RESISTANCE: Guidelines for Dealing with Resistance* |
| **L** = deal with your need to be **Liked** by counselees |
| **E** = **Expect** resistance |
| **S** = you must have a solid degree of **Self-assurance** |
| **S** = avoid being too **Suspicious** and gullible |
| **R** = remember that your best friend is **Rapport** |
| **E** = **Evaluate** the reasons for the resistance |
| **S** = determine what **Secondary** gains might be maintaining problem behavior |
| **I** = seek to **Influence**, not control |
| **S** = have the counselee **Speak** to the resistance |
| **T** = **Take** the resistance and go with it |
| **A** = **Agree** with the counselee |
| **N** = **Normalize** the counselee's resistance |
| **C** = **Challenge** your counselee |
| **E** = if necessary, **End** or terminate the session |

**Expect** ("E") resistance because it is part of human nature. Watzlawick (1978) suggests anticipating resistance, especially with reluctant counselees. One method to diffuse the resistance is by predicting that it will happen. For example you might say, "I think this will really help you, but you're probably not ready to do it yet," or "You are probably going to think this is too difficult for you to do right now." By predicting the resistance, you lessen it. The predictions force the counselee to oppose you and do the assignment or to reinforce your credibility by not accepting it. Either way it is a win for the therapeutic expedition. Consider another example: "You know, I was going to suggest something to you, but it is probably not going to work anyway." Just as curiosity got the cat, many counselees cannot help but request the directive. As a homework assignment you might ask the counselee to list possible reasons for not carrying out the agreed-on task. Also you can caution the counselee not to get better too quickly. Remember that all counselees are resistant or involuntary to some degree.

The counselee might have voluntarily chosen to come to counseling as opposed to jail, but emphasize that you view them as having chosen to be with you. At the same time, however, be careful that your expectation does not lead to a self-fulfilling prophecy.

Third, you will be well served by having a solid degree of **Self-assurance** ("S"). Sometimes the resistance will challenge your competence. Counselors might project their own resistance or insecurities onto their counselees. We are affected by our environments (e.g., overworked, difficult place to work), life issues (e.g., level of personal stressors, adequacy of our coping abilities), physical and psychological limitations (e.g., tiredness, burnout, rigidity, unwillingness to learn or grow), and professional limitations (e.g., inadequate training, poor supervision). Consider whether you are projecting your own issues onto the counselee. If the counselee is overtly resistant by challenging you, consider the following suggestions: (a) empathize about the difficulty in working with someone like yourself, (b) probe the counselee's concern, (c) answer appropriate questions directly and with no more information than was requested, (d) explain how people benefit from counseling, (e) suggest a trial run, (e.g., "Let's give it a try for three or four sessions and see if it is working with you"), (f) use humor if appropriate, (g) explore the issue of a referral, and (h) consult with your supervisor or obtain clinical consultation. Do not lower your expectations, and do not proceed in a halfhearted manner (Egan, 2007)

The second "S" in the acrostic LESS represents the need to avoid **Suspiciousness** and gullibility. One extreme reaction to avoid is being too gullible and accepting everything the counselee has to say. The opposite extreme involves being so suspicious and cynical that you discount everything the counselee has to say.

The "R" in the word RESISTANT stands for the need to establish a solid basis of **Rapport** with all counselees, especially the resistant ones. Work to create an atmosphere as nonthreatening as possible. Because resistance is so common, its presence in the session does not mean you have a bad counselee.

**Evaluate** ("E") the reason for the resistance. As already seen, resistance can be generated from the counselee, the counselor, or therapeutic factors. It is often easier to assess and label counselee factors than to examine your own. Be willing to explore what role you might be playing in the resistance. Consider your techniques, your sensitivity to the counselee's plight, and what personal issues are being provoked inside you.

Related to the evaluation of the reasons for resistance, ascertain if there is a **Secondary** gain ("S") for the counselee in maintaining the problem behavior. What factors might diminish the counselee's motivation to change? For example the attention received from friends for having the problem might outweigh the benefits to be free of it. Counselees initially engage in behavior for "good" reasons that seem appropriate at the time.

The "I" is to remind you to work on **Influencing**, not controlling or coercing, your counselee. The tendency is to try to force change on a resistant counselee. After all, what you offer is a healthy or a more godly alternative. But as noted, counselees have reasons for their resistance and often gain benefit from their problems. Thus it is best to use an approach that seeks to influence the counselee without controlling him. If you determine that confrontation is necessary, be direct and firm without being provocative.

A technique that requires a level of motivation from the counselee is to have the counselee **Speak** ("S") to the resistance. One method of helping the counselee talk to the resistance is by using the empty-chair technique, in which the counselee addresses the resistance in a monologue, as if the resistance were a person seated in the chair.

A method of dealing with resistance is **Taking** ("T") it and going with it. In martial arts, which I (John) have studied, one method of dealing with an attack is to take the power of the attacker and use it against him. In the counseling context this means encouraging the counselee to exhibit resisting behavior (Haley, 1973, 1976; Watzlawick, Beavin, & Jackson, 1967; Watzlawick, Weakland, & Fisch, 1974). When a counselee is invited to resist, he has one of two choices, either to comply with the request, thus behaving in a cooperative way, or to refuse to comply with the request, which means acting in a nonresistant way. The bottom line is to do your best to avoid power struggles with the counselee.

Another technique is to **Agree** ("A") with the counselee. If the counselee says, "Yes, but" to your suggestions, you can say, *"You are right. Nothing really can be done about your situation."* This might sound as if it is violating every facet of Scripture, but recall the question Jesus posed to the infirmed man at the pool of Bethesda: "Do you want to get well?" (John 5:1–15). Self-pity can lead to adopting the role of a victim, where living with despair is easier than hoping for hope.

A helpful technique is to **Normalize** ("N") the counselee's resistance. You might tell a counselee that it is normal to resist change and that you are skeptical of any change that does not involve a level of protest. The very nature of change requires us to do things that are neither familiar nor natural.

You can also **Comment** on and **Challenge** ("C") resistance. Sommers-Flanagan and Sommers-Flanagan (2003) address the importance of naming the resistance and discussing what makes it necessary. For example you might say, "Obviously, you don't want to talk about your father's death. So instead, let's just talk briefly about what makes it so hard to talk about." Or "What might happen if you did start talking about your father's death?" (p. 123).

If necessary, you might need to **End** ("E") or terminate the session, if the counselee's resistance prevents improvement. Ethically counselors need not continue with helping services if the counselee is not benefiting (see the ACA Code of Ethics in Appendix A and the AACC Code of Ethics in Appendix B). If you terminate the counseling, then either recommend a referral or tell the counselee that when he is ready to change he can contact you.

In summary, working with resistance is a necessary part of helping someone. Your success at moving through and around the resistance will be linked to your ability to accept it, work with it, and employ the guidelines described above as skillfully as possible. As with most counseling issues, there is no substitute for experience.

## QUESTION 2: CHANGE INTO WHAT?

The second question of the expedition speaks to where you want to go, and this will determine who can help you get there. Not all guides can take you to where you want to go; some are not familiar with the destinations and do not know the terrain that must be traversed. If you wanted to explore the Grand Canyon, you would not hire a guide who is familiar with only Yellowstone National Park. Imagine a guide telling you that while you want to see the Grand Canyon, she will take you to Yellowstone. It is ultimately the explorer's decision, not the guide's, to determine where he wants to go.

Whether a person is conscious of it or not, thoughts and actions are moving toward a distinct goal. People are teleological beings; controlled by purposes (Crabb & Allender, 1997). When an individual reaches the point of needing to change and wanting to change, he then must decide where he needs to be.

Where are we trying to take our counselees relates to how we counsel. As Christian helpers we truly believe our greatest human need is to be reconciled and restored to God and to live in right relationship with Jesus Christ. Not all Christians, and certainly not unbelievers, who come to us for counseling have those spiritual goals in mind. Though our primary counseling goal might be to see the counselee experience spiritual transformation and growth, counselees' goals are usually for cognitive, emotional, or behavioral improvement.

However, real problems do not lie in people's cognitive distortions, emotional disturbances, or poor impulse control. As important as those issues are, they are not the real problem. The Bible clearly identifies sin as the foundational root of human struggles; from the seeds of sin sprout all kinds of human maladies. That is not to say, however, that every problem is a direct cause of sin. A woman who is raped will experience incredible aftermath from the violation and act of violence. Yet the woman may allow the sin of hatred and rebellion to be born in her heart. In this broken and fallen world we will experience injustices that we neither invited nor deserved.

Sin manifests itself in biological malfunctions or abnormalities, in what we think, in our emotions, and in our behavior. Sin contaminates and pollutes the entire person. The Christian helper seeks to probe the depths of the counselee's inner world to find the entanglements of sin in the counselee's personality. Sin becomes twisted around the networks of needs, cognitions, and emotions much as a tumor entwines neurons. You cannot address sin issues without bringing into light the internal network of psychological systems anymore than a neurosurgeon can remove a tumor without carefully handling the fettered neurons. Often our struggles might look as if they are primarily problems of cognition or emotion, but it is never that simple. Because we are spiritual beings infused with the virus of sin, there is always a spiritual component to each struggle. Romans 6–8 depict the battle between a believer's old nature characterized by sin and his new nature rooted in Christ.

True and lasting change is possible in and through Christ (1 Cor 6:9–11). The Christian life is about all things becoming new (2 Cor 5:17). In that verse two freedoms are implied: *freedom from* and *freedom to*. The believer is freed *from* enslavement and freed *to* live for Christ. Like the children of Israel enslaved in Egypt, our desire is to be free from unpleasant circumstances. The demand in our hearts is for things to be different and for us to feel different. The children of Israel were *freed from* Egypt to be *freed to* possess the promised land. When we accept Christ as our personal Savior, we are freed from our old nature in order to be freed to possess a new identity. Change embodies the dual nature of freedom: freedom from condemnation, trauma, and other problems, and freedom to live as a follower of Christ. Putting off harmful and unhealthy attitudes and behavior, as Eph 4:20–27 points out, is not an event or a destination, but a process of making correct decisions. It is not a journey we make on our own but one in which God walks with us each step of the way.

The process of biblical change is transformation; a change in the way of being (what Watzlawick, Weakland, & Fisch, 1974, call second-order change). Sometimes we change in ways that do not make us different. Leaving your cozy home in the cold of winter requires putting on a coat so that your body temperature will remain relatively the same. This is first-order change. You have made a change by putting on a coat, but the change maintains the status quo—your body temperature. True change, however, is second-order change. From a biblical point of view second-order change comes from conversion and from exercising ourselves toward godliness (1 Tim 4:7). Trying to change by our own initiative will be futile and leave us frustrated. But the one who seeks to be mature in Christ will be healthier in mind and body.

God's redemptive power is operative in those who from a human standpoint seem beyond hope. Johnson (2007) puts it this way: "The worse a believer's biopsychosocial damage and even ethnical problems, and the more barriers a believer has for accomplishing much in this world, the greater the overall glory-potential in that person's Godward story" (p. 554).

In the previous chap. we delineated the importance of creating a connection with your counselee. We spoke of the need to create a safe haven and to come alongside and empathically attend to the counselee's story. To a person-centered counselor, that would be enough. This means unconditionally caring for your counselee, being authentic, accepting what the counselee says, and being reflective in your responses. Biblically, we believe that the counseling relationship and empathy are but the platform from which you can dive into a counselee's heart. The helping relationship is a safety net as you explore the ugliness of counselees' inner stories without fear of their being shamed.

As people gain freedom from their problems, they increasingly experience the freedom to walk intimately with God, to serve Him, and to love others. One task, as the helper, is to remove obstacles in the path of change. Perhaps the most important task is creating a hunger in the counselee to desire what is good and satisfying. We cannot push our agendas on our counselees, but we can creatively whet their appetites for what God provides.

## QUESTION 3: HOW DO I CHANGE?

At some point counselees may become open to the possibility that hope and healing can enter their lives. When a counselee becomes willing to change, then the question becomes "How do I do it?" The process of how to change correlates with the Preparation and Action stages in the TTM, which involve gradual steps toward change.

One significant means of changing is having access to resources. Crabb and Allender (1997) have identified four resources in the change process (see Table 12.5). First, the individual is a resource for himself. The burden of change rests solely and squarely on the counselee's shoulders. Like the lame man at the pool of Bethesda, one cannot avoid his personal responsibility to make needed changes. One means of helping counselees change, then is by having them take ownership of their lives.

| Table 12.5. | |
|---|---|
| *Four Resources for Change** | |
| **Resource** | **Description** |
| The Individual | Responsibility for change is largely on the person's shoulders. |
| Natural Community | Support from family, friends, and minister may be useful. |
| God | I must tap into God's sufficient power. He is all I need. |
| Professional Help | Trained specialists may be necessary. |

*From Crabb & Allender (1997)

A second resource for change is the counselee's natural community. Each one of us needs others to be successful. The recovery movement has highlighted the importance of other people in giving up addictive behaviors. Long before the recovery movement the Bible focuses on the power of community and fellowship (John 13:34–35; 1 Cor 12:26–27; Eph 4:15–16). Counselors should help counselees connect to significant others and to people who can support them in their change process.

The third resource is God. Those who are believers and possess a faith in God have a means outside themselves by whom to succeed in making change. He works to change people from the inside out. The recovery movement wisely understands that change from an addiction requires acknowledging unmanageability (pain), powerlessness (desperation), and then surrender to put an addict on the road of recovery. God is not a magic wand to produce change in our lives mystically and miraculously. God's plans almost always seem to go through problems, not around them, so that we learn to depend on Him. One way that dependency is evident is through a conscious contact with God in prayer.

Fourth, a professional helper can also be a significant resource. One way counselors, as change agents, can be a resource is by helping the counselee access and tap into the other three resources, which can work together to help the counselee accomplish his change goal(s). As a helper you can promote change by (a) instilling hope, (b) establishing a meaningful counseling relationship, (c) modeling healthy behavior, (d) crafting change plans, and (e) teaching the counselee new skills.

Hope is critical at all stages of the change process. As counselors, especially Christian counselors, we offer hope—not wishful thinking or fantasy, but hope that is based on the gospel of Christ. Jesus Christ's promise of eternal life offers a foundation that can instill hope in the most demoralized of counselees.

In chap. 5 ("Basic Skills: Creating a Connection") we spoke of the critical importance of the helping relationship. A secure counseling relationship creates favorable conditions for change. The counselee must encounter a person "with skin on," who provides the kind of nurture and security that is found in the nature of God and the person of Jesus Christ. When God's love is internalized, it responds to the unmet needs behind the counselee's problem(s) while also "mending" his faith.

As a reflection of Christ, a Christian counselor models what is true, proper, righteous, and healthy. A counselor's character and behavior can help the counselee change. The apostle Paul acknowledged that he was a model to his young follower, Timothy. The apostle also encouraged Timothy to follow the examples of his mother and grandmother (2 Tim 1:5). In a counseling relationship the counselor models how to relate.

Research by Carey and associates (2007) has shown that counselees' descriptions of how change occurred in their counseling could be categorized into six themes: (a) motivation and readiness (e.g., "I was desperate to get back to my old self"), (b) tools and strategies (e.g., "It's the changes in my behavior that I learned"), (c) interaction with the counselor (e.g., "They don't judge your character or think they know you"), (d) perceived aspects of self (e.g., "I am a strong person mentally"), (e) learning (e.g., "I would take a lot of stuff home to read"), and (f) relief in talking (e.g., "Let me get everything out, let me relieve myself of everything").

It is not enough that you and your counselee understand his or her old patterns or even that the counselee understands them. Insight is highly valuable, but alone it does not often move someone forward into new ways of behaving. For real and lasting change to occur at this level, the counselee must discover new patterns. A counselee who talks about how her father hurt her needs to go beyond simply talking about the past wounds and present-day hurts. Otherwise she will not make lasting changes. Somehow she must experience that relationship differently, especially at an emotional level so that she can learn how to cognitively, emotionally, and behaviorally respond to her father in a healthier way. The hope is that once those past wounds have been transformed she can take the new learning into the world of her present-day relationships.

Crafting an effective treatment plan is also necessary to facilitate change. Cormier and Cormier (1985) distilled 11 criteria that identify effective helping strategies. In devising a strategy and plan for the counselee counselors must consider whether it (a) is easy to carry out, (b) creates additional problems for the counselee or significant others, (c) overburdens the counselee or significant others, (d) matches the counselee's unique characteristics and preferences, (e) matches the characteristics of the problem and related factors, (f) is positive, not punitive, (g) encourages the development of self-management skills, (h) strengthens the counselee's self-efficacy, (i) is supported by the literature, (j) is within the counselor's ability to manage and (k) repeats or builds on previous unsuccessful solutions.

Choosing the proper intervention strategies that match the counselee's current stage in the change model can help the counselee move toward change. Thompson (2003) states that effective change strategies follow three guidelines. First, employ key change strategies first. Research often points to the most effective strategies to use with particular problems; these techniques are to be used as the first line of offense. Second, use the "shifting-change strategy." That is, begin with the most efficacious change strategy first before switching to other strategies. Third, use the "maximum-impact strategy," that is, with more complex cases work with several patterns simultaneously.

In the following chaps. we will examine general helping strategies and spiritual strategies to facilitate change in the counselee. Research has found that particular techniques and interventions seem to be more beneficial at particular stages of the change process. Cognitive and experiential strategies seem to be more important in the earlier stage of the TTM, and behavioral strategies seem to be more beneficial later in the process (Perz, DiClemente, & Carbonari, 1996). Not surprisingly, spiritual techniques have not been included in the research.

## CHAPTER SUMMARY

Many people enjoy the hobby of shopping for old pieces of furniture, antiques. Once found the antiquer can restore the piece to its original condition and beauty. Though counselors do not shop for counselees, therapeutic change does involve restoring souls not to their original condition but to the beautiful being God has called them to be. The Bible is a love story, but included in the drama is how God seeks to remake us. The Scriptures highlight our need for transformation and the fact that true and meaningful change happens in concert with our spiritual walk.

Research has conveyed a clear sense of how people change. Changing an undesirable thought, feeling, or behavior is not an event; it is a gradual process in which people move through incremental changes toward a desired end. Guiding the counselee on the journey requires that we know where counselees are in the process of change.

The level of your competence will be linked to your ability to assess the counselee's level of recognition for change, readiness for change, and willingness to change. You will also be well served by the ability to work with counselees who do not see the need to change, who are unwilling to change, and who do not know how to make the necessary changes. A skilled helper customizes the counseling strategies based on whether the counselee is in the precontemplation, contemplation, preparation, action, or maintenance stage of change. The strategies generate insight, explore and validate emotional and cognitive processes, and promote behavioral change.

Real and lasting change rarely if ever occurs instantaneously. Even people who have had radical conversions find that while some behaviors might cease on the very day they accepted Christ, other behaviors or beliefs continue to plague them for years.

The following chaps. discuss specific helping strategies.. No one can become competent in all the techniques to the same level of skill. Supervised experience will refine your skill development and help you learn when and how to apply techniques. As you continue on your counselor education training program, be willing to experiment and fail so that you can expand your repertoire of therapeutic skills in order to guide as many explorers of change possible.

## CHAPTER 12 ACTIVITIES

1. Identify the domain that you are more likely to focus on when helping a counselee change: thoughts, feelings, or actions. Explain why you believe that should be a focus.
2. Describe the Transtheoretical Model (TTM) of change.
3. Select a personal goal that you have in any area of your life (bio-psycho-social-spiritual). In the TM in which stage are you in as you seek to reach this goal? How would you know that you have met

this goal? What would it take to get you through each stage of the model and to reach this goal?

4. What counselee and counselor factors relate to reluctance and resistance to change?
5. Based on the contents of this chap., what are some guidelines for dealing with reluctance and resistance in counseling?
6. What does this statement mean: "The [therapeutic] relationship provides a safety net to explore the ugliness of our inner story without fear of being shamed"? How does a secure counseling relationship "create favorable conditions for change"?
7. Think of a time in your life when you had a goal or wanted to make a change. What did you do to make that happen?
8. What 11 criteria do Cormier and Cormier (1985) offer as effective helping strategies?
9. According to Carey and associates (2007), change occurring in counseling can be categorized into what six themes?
10. Thompson (2003) encourages counselors to follow what three change-strategy guidelines?
11. Select some Scriptures that reflect what persons must do to change their thoughts, actions, or lives. Write out the references, the Scriptures, and a sentence that captures the thought of each verse.

## Recommended Reading

Engle, D., & Arkowitz, H. (2006). *Ambivalence in psychotherapy: Facilitating readiness to change.* New York City, NY: Guilford Press.

As noted in this chapter, counselors will encounter resistance. Engle and Arkowitz provide insights into resistance and change. The book provides useful and practical clinical guidelines toward producing change in people's lives.

O'Hanlon, W. H., & Weiner-Davis, M. (2003). *In search of solutions: A new direction in psychotherapy.* Rev. ed. New York City, NY: W. W. Norton.

This work is a revised edition of a classic book in the solution-focused field. It provides brief and solution-focused training by two experts and pioneers in the field.

Ortberg, J., Pederson, L., & Poling, J. (2000). *Growth: Training vs. trying (pursuing spiritual transformation).* Grand Rapids, MI: Zondervan Publishing House.

Ortberg and his colleagues tackle the issue of spiritual growth. The book is filled with wonderful insights into how we can experience new life in Christ.

Rosenthal, H. G. (Ed.). (1998). *Favorite counseling techniques: 51 therapists share their most creative strategies.* New York City, NY: Brunner-Routledge.

This is an excellent catalog of techniques to use in counseling.

Watzlawick, P., Weakland, J., & Fisch, R. (1974). *Change: Principles of problem formation and problem resolution.* New York City, NY: W. W. Norton.

These authors unpack the concept of change from a logical perspective. This book should be read several times. In fact it is so deep that it takes more than one read to grasp the concepts fully. Once understood, the book gives an excellent platform on which to build change interventions upon.

# Chapter 13

# General Helping Strategies

*"To focus on technique is like cramming your way through school. You sometimes get by, perhaps get good grades, but if you don't pay the price day in and day out, you'll never achieve true mastery of the subjects you study or develop an educated mind"* (Covey, 1989, pp. 21–22).

*"The purposes of a man's heart are deep waters, but a man of understanding draws them out"* (Prov 20:5, NIV).

## CHAPTER OBJECTIVES

» To equip students with specific techniques that are valuable to promoting counselee change

» To describe the use of the miracle question and its role in the counseling process

» To describe the use of therapeutic homework and give the student clear guidelines on how to use it effectively

» To help students learn how humor can be an effective strategy in helping

» To discuss the role of metaphor in promoting counselee insight and change

» To teach students how journaling can be a valuable tool for counselee change

## CHAPTER OUTLINE

THE MIRACLE QUESTION

THE USE OF HOMEWORK IN THE HELPING PROCESS
  Benefits in Using Homework
  Kind of Homework Assignments
  Factors That Influence Homework Compliance
  Guidelines to Using Homework Effectively

THE THERAPEUTIC USE OF HUMOR
  The Therapeutic Benefits of Humor
  Guidelines for Using Humor

THE THERAPEUTIC USE OF METAPHOR
  Therapeutic Benefits of Metaphor
  The Source of Metaphors
  The Forms of Metaphors
  Guidelines for Using Metaphors

JOURNALING

CHAPTER SUMMARY

CHAPTER 13 ACTIVITIES

As we have embarked on this journey of learning how to conduct a therapeutic expedition, we have explored the skills of establishing a working relationship with the counselee and the skills and strategies to promote change. Most importantly we have suggested spiritual interventions that encourage counselees toward spiritual maturity. This chap. discusses five techniques to employ as you guide your counselee on the journey.

## THE MIRACLE QUESTION

The miracle question is a fantasy or imaginary exercise that seeks to inquire what life would be like if things were different for the counselee (De Shazer, 1988). Some counselors we know begin with a relaxation technique, but the technique requires only the following question: "Imagine that after you went to bed this evening, while you were sleeping God performed a miracle in your life. When you awoke, you would find that all your problems have been solved by the miracle. You no longer feel troubled by [presenting problem]. Now, what things would you notice first that would tell you that the miracle occurred?" We then follow up with, "What would your best friend notice that would tell him a miracle had occurred?" As the counselee is considering the question and responding, do not interrupt. If the counselee gives some seemingly unreasonable response to the question, you can remain silent in order to encourage the counselee to consider her response further.

You may respond to the counselee's answer with a question that seeks to focus the counselee's attention on the exceptions to the rule. The counselor might ask, "When was the most recent time (perhaps days, hours, weeks) that you can remember when things were sort of like this day after the miracle?" The purpose of this question is to help the counselee see that the problem was not *always* a problem. Sometimes the counselee does not get anxious, become angry, drink, or do whatever it is that they desire to change. By redirecting the counselee's focus to the times when they did not experience the problem, you can discover what was occurring and who was present (context) and what the counselee was doing or not doing (content) that seemed to inhibit the problem behavior or thought.

## THE USE OF HOMEWORK IN THE HELPING PROCESS

You can greatly enhance your counselees' ability to change by assigning homework (Kazantzis & Ronan, 2006). No uniform definition of what constitutes "homework" in counseling has been agreed on (Kazantzis & Ronan, 2006). But homework is nothing more than assigning tasks for the counselee to complete outside the counseling sessions.

The value of homework in the helping process has been noted by many practitioners (Kazantzis & Ronan, 2006; Young, 2010). In fact a recent survey demonstrated that 98 percent of practicing psychologists use homework in their clinical practice (Kazantzis & Lampropoulos, 2002). To avoid the negative connotation associated with the word "homework" some authors suggest using phrases such as "self-help assignments" (Burns, 1999), "extratherapy assignments" (Kornblith, Rehm, O'Hara, & Lamparski, 1983), "empowering assignments," and "between-session tasks" (Hay & Kinnier, 1998; Kazantzis & Ronan, 2006).

Some counselors we know will not see counselees if they do not agree to doing homework when it is given. They make it part of their informed consent. A few counselors we know will not see counselees if they show up for their session but did not do the homework. While we do not advocate that approach, we do strongly encourage our counselees to complete the agreed-upon tasks.

## Benefits in Using Homework

Assigning counselees various kinds of homework assignments has a number of benefits. One of the best benefits is that it can increase the effectiveness of the counseling (Hay & Kinnier, 1998; Kazantzis & Ronan, 2006). Suinn (1990, cited in Hay & Kinnier, 1998) offers a number of specific benefits to the use of homework in counseling. The list includes: the following: (a) it helps ensure counseling compliance, integrating counseling into the counselee's daily routines; (b) it provides personal meaning for the counselee in the helping process; (c) it is a means of obtaining information about progress for treatment planning; and (d) it is a way to transfer learning or generalize gains into one's life. Weekly counseling sessions without any homework to do between sessions will produce the same results as a person who takes weekly piano lessons without practicing (Jacobs, 1992). Just as piano competence will suffer as a result of not using the time between lessons to implement the skills, so too will counseling effectiveness.

Cummings (1999) states that using homework sends the message to counselees that the responsibility of changing is on them. Homework is also an opportunity for the counselee to practice new behavior (Ackerman, 1974). Homework can offer options for targeting certain goals that are restricted to particular times and locations, such as helping couples with sexual disorders (Charlton & Brigel, 1997). Engle, Beutler, and Daldrup (1991, cited in Hay & Kinnier, 1998) state that homework (a) enhances the work of the session, (b) keeps the counselee aware of incomplete work in the counseling, and (c) offers a means of celebrating breakthroughs.

Also homework can provide a surrogate role during counselor absences. At times counselors are unavailable to their counselees because of vacation, illness, or professional training.

## Kinds of Homework Assignments

Hay and Kinnier (1998) describe several kinds of homework assignments, some of which are active (e.g., talking to strangers) and others passive (e.g., listening to an audiotape), or both. Another kind is "paradoxical assignments," in which the counselor requests what is the opposite of the counselee's desired goals. For example for a counselee who wants to lose weight, the counselor might ask him to eat as much as possible until the next session and to write down what he ate. The hope is that the counselee's self-monitoring and being given permission to eat anything will result in his eating less. Obviously a counselor needs to know what he is doing before using these kinds of homework assignments. We recommend close supervision and additional reading. Two excellent resources are Haley (1984), *Ordeal thera-*

*py,* and Weeks and L'Abate (1982), *Paradoxical psychotherapy: Theory and practice with individuals, couples, and families.*

Another kind of homework identified by Hay and Kinnier (1998) is experiential/behavioral assignments. Experiential and behavioral tasks can promote awareness, regulation, and transformation of emotion (Greenberg & Warwar, 2006). Tasks in this category call for the counselee to take specific actions such as engaging in pleasurable activities if he is depressed or doing things his spouse desires. Risk-taking and shame-attacking assignments encourage counselees to take risks that are associated with their problem. For example an individual who fears leaving home (i.e., agoraphobia) might be asked to walk to the mailbox each day. These tasks typically involve exposure to a feared stimulus.

Hay and Kinnier (1998) also discuss writing assignments, such as journaling, writing letters, and documenting their thoughts, feelings, or actions.

At times counselors will ask counselees to read books, listen to something, or watch a particular show (Hay & Kinnier, 1998). Reading has been called "bibliotherapy" and can be used to augment what is happening in the counseling. If a person is diagnosed with heart disease, a doctor may recommend literature on heart disease, medicines, and a heart-healthy lifestyle. Likewise counselors can recommend books or other literature that provide more nsight into the issue(s). We have also recommended that counselees watch videotapes or particular movies. Movies and television programs can offer insight into dynamics, offer information, and assist the counselee to work through his or her issues. Some videotapes or audiotapes are educational in nature and are another means of informing the counselee. We have prescribed sermons for counselees to view or listen to along with other visual media.

Another category offered by Hay and Kinnier (1998) are solution-focused assignments. These tasks require counselees to seek solutions to their problems. They include specific activities such as looking for exceptions to the problem and changing what she is doing.

Another kind of homework offered by Hay and Kinnier (1998) is captured by the title "Don't-do-anything assignments." The idea here is that counselees are to take a vacation from a certain behavior, even from working on their problem. A counselee may also be told not to read anything related to his problem. This approach might be useful with someone overly immersed in self-help.

## Factors That Influence Homework Compliance

Three factors may contribute to homework compliance: task factors, helper factors, and counselee factors. Task factors concern particular features of homework assignments that increase the likelihood that the counselee can carry them out, such as whether the homework assignment is described clearly and concretely and is doable according to the counselee's given level of functioning (Tompkins, 2002). Easier homework tasks are more likely to be carried out than more difficult ones (Helbig & Fehm, 2004).

Counselees are more likely to carry out a homework assignment, if the helper can develop and maintain a positive relationship. According to Dattilio (2002) the counselor's behavior in reviewing assigned homework tasks is the strongest predictor of homework compliance. Researchers found that there was no relationship between homework compliance and counselees' ratings of helpers' empathy. Counselees were more likely to comply when they perceived the helper as highly self-confident and if the helper sent written notices to remind the counselee (Helbig & Fehm, 2004). We have had counselees who failed to complete tasks because we failed to make the assignments clear and specific.

A third group of factors that relate to homework compliance involves certain counselee variables. One psychological counselee factor that seems to impact homework compliance is the severity of the counselee's problem. (Edelman and Chambless, (1993). Also males are less likely to comply with homework assignments (Helbig & Fehm, 2004). Another factor to consider is the counselee's level of motivation. Some counselees do not want to take responsibility or do the work needed to change or report that they lack the time and energy to do so (Hay & Kinnier, 1998). The higher the counselee's level of motivation, the greater the level of compliance. Thus counselees who do not voluntarily seek counseling are more likely not to follow through than are those who made the personal choice to begin counseling (Hay & Kinnier, 1998).

## Guidelines to Using Homework Effectively

The mnemonic device for using homework assignments in counseling is **ASSIGN** (see Table 13.1).

Table 13.1

*ASSIGN: Guidelines for Using Homework*

**A** = make the homework **Applicable** to the goal

**S** = **State** how the assignment will help

**S** = **Specify** the details of the assignment

**I** = determine what might **Interfere**

**G** = **Gain** the counselee's commitment

**N** = ask the counselee the **News** of how it went

The first guideline is to make the assignment **Applicable** to the goal that is being addressed (Greenberg & Warwar, 2006; Hay & Kinnier, 1998). Homework is most helpful when the therapist and counselee not only tie the activity closely to the counselee's target complaints and goals but also when it relates to a theme covered during the current session (Coon & Thompson, 2002).

**State** the actual assignment you believe will help the counselee. This guideline means that you share what you would like the counselee to do. For example you might say something like this:

> "We have been discussing how the loss of your father has opened up old wounds for you. You have expressed your desire to forgive him for all of the hurt you experienced while growing up. I have found that it is often helpful if the counselee expresses her thoughts by writing a letter to a deceased person. The letter is obviously not something that can be sent to your father, but it will allow you to pour out your heart to him and help you to begin to work through your pent-up feelings. What thoughts do you have about doing that type of an assignment?"

**Specify** the details of the assignment. If possible, you and the counselee should design the homework together. This means it will have the greatest chance of success (Dunn, Morrison, & Bentall, 2002). The details include when the task is to be done, how the assignment is done, where it is to be done, and how often the counselee is to do the assignment. Cox, Tisdelle, and Culbert (1988) recommend writing down the details to enhance compliance.

After you and the counselee have discussed the task in detail, it is important to determine what might hinder the counselee from successfully carrying out the assignment. Many things can **Interfere** with homework being completed, including time, resources, lack of understanding, and even others who might prevent it from occurring. For example you might say, "What things might prevent you or hinder you from being able to carry out this activity?"

After the assignment has been examined from different angles, **Gain** agreement and commitment from the counselee to do the assignment as discussed. Kazantzis and Lampropoulos (2002) state that the effectiveness of any given homework assignment depends on the extent to which the counselee actually engages in the task. If you sense that the counselee is not committed to the task, you can share that you sense that he or she seems reluctant about it. You might say:

> "We have discussed the benefit of writing a letter to your father to address your feelings and your sense of loss over what you didn't have

> with him. We have discussed how that can be carried out and we have
> looked at a few potential obstacles to your being able to write such a
> letter. On a scale from 1 to 10, how committed are you with 10 being
> absolutely committed, to writing that letter before our next session?"

Counselees can become demotivated if you assign a task and then do not follow up on it in the next session. Write down the assignment that was agreed to in your note, and at the beginning of the next session ask the counselee for the **News** on how it went. It is as simple as saying, "Last week you agreed to writing a letter to your dad. How did that go?"

The use of homework in counseling is a very effective way to help the counselee address his concerns and to transfer any key learning into other aspects of life. Your ability to engage the counselee in the process effectively will enhance the likelihood that the counselee will follow through. Kazantzis and L'Abate (2007) have edited an excellent resource on homework assignments in counseling (*Handbook of homework assignments in psychotherapy*). It provides much more than a laundry list of ideas and might be a useful reference tool to include in your library. Another resource is *The therapist's notebook for integrating spirituality in counseling,* edited by Helmeke and Sori (2006), on homework, handouts, and activities that help incorporate spirituality into counseling.

## THE THERAPEUTIC USE OF HUMOR

Humor can be an effective communication tool for both counselors and counselees. The use of humor is one means of infusing our personalities into the helping relationship (Dewane, 2006), and it can be a positive part of the counseling experience (Gladding, 2009). The Association for Applied and Therapeutic Humor (AATH) defines humor as:

> any intervention that promotes health and wellness by stimulating a
> playful discovery, expression or appreciation of the absurdity or in-
> congruity of life's situations. This intervention may enhance health or
> be used as a complementary treatment of illness to facilitate healing
> or coping, whether physical, emotional, cognitive, social or spiritual.
> (http://www.aath.org/

Because humor has cultural and personal significance, what constitutes humor can range from harsh and sarcastic comments, which cuts down another person, to light jovial comments, which enjoys another. In other words humor can be either a way of connecting to others or disassociating from others.

Counselors ought to avoid harsh and sarcastic comments that are pejorative in nature, including humor related to sarcasm, gender putdowns, racist or sexual issues, religious faith smashing, or physical handicaps. The inappropriate use of humor can diminish the importance of the counselee's issue(s) and can create distance in the helping relationship. However, the use of positive, uplifting humor in counseling carries with it a number of therapeutic benefits.

## The Therapeutic Benefits of Humor

### General benefits of humor.

One significant benefit of humor is that it is associated with psychological and physical well-being. The AATH highlights several psychological and physical benefits of humor: (a) triggering endorphins, the body's natural painkillers; (b) stimulating the cardiovascular system; (c) relieving stress and preventing negative tension; and (d) helping people creatively face life's challenges.

### Benefits to the counseling relationship.

Humor in the counseling relationship can reflect the bond between the counselor and the counselee (Nelson, 2008) because humor can both enhance and assess the level of rapport.

### Humor can soften a message.

Humor can be used to deliver emotionally charged information that might otherwise be interpreted as unacceptable in a conversation (Herring & Meggert, 1994).

### Humor can benefit the counselee's emotional state.

The counselor can use humor to help put the counselee at ease and minimize anxiety associated with the beginning stages of counseling (Bedi, Davis, & Williams, 2005). Humor can help counselees shift from viewing their circumstances negatively. It also has the power to provide a fresh perspective on a difficult situation (e.g., seeing positive points that might emerge from the situation, looking at life less seriously), helping the counselee learn to regulate himself emotionally, normalizing an experience, reducing stress in general, lightening an overly tense situation during a session, overcoming counselee resistance, and facilitating counselee learning of coping skills. The power of humor is in the fact that life-changing messages can be embedded in the humor.

### Humor can aid in assessment and diagnosis.

Humor can be especially valuable in understanding your counselees. One factor in evaluating a counselee's humor is to determine the role it plays. Counselees may use humor to condemn themselves, to defend against feeling the emotional impact of a situation and to hide true feelings by masking them. Thus a counselee's humor can assist you in making an accurate diagnosis. For example humor can be used to assess the degree of a counselee's mood reactivity (i.e., the counselee has the ability to laugh in an appropriate context) or to assess if the counselee's mood is appropriate to the context (e.g., does the counselee laugh at inappropriate times).

## Guidelines for Using Humor

The following mnemonic device **HUMOR** highlights five guidelines in using humor in counseling (see Table 13.2). The "H" reminds us that humor has an impact on the **Helping** relationship. Humor can either contribute or diminish rapport. If appropriate, using humor can help establish and maintain the bond in the therapeutic relationship.

Table 13.2

*HUMOR: Guidelines for Using Humor*

**H** = mind the **Helping** relationship

**U** = be sure that you **Understand** the counselee first

**M** = it is **Merited**

**O** = have a clear and specific **Outcome** in mind

**R** = choose the best **Routine** to deliver the humor

The "U" refers to making sure you **Understand** the counselee before using humor. As with all techniques and interventions, humor is to be used in the interest of the counselee. Gladding (2009) emphasizes that humor must be used with great care because the results can sometimes backfire. Be sure the counselee would not be offended, distracted, or put down by humorous statements. Some people are simply more serious in temperament and personality than others.

The third guideline is to determine if the humor is **Merited** ("M"). Whether humor is merited or not means that you need to ask yourself several questions. First, is the counselee's personality appropriate for the use of humor (Gladding, 2009)? Some counselees would not find value in the counselor's use of humor. For example a counselee might be distracted by the inappropriate timing of humor and confused by the counselor's effort to communicate in that fashion. Would the use of humor minimize or mock the counselee's situation (Gladding)? Some counselees may think you are making light of their situation, or that you misunderstand their cultural and individual views (cf. Dupey, Garrett, Maples, Phan, Torres-Rivera, & Vereen, 2001). Others may think humor is unprofessional. You need to ask, is this the right time to use humor (Bordan & Goldin, 1999)? For example in a crisis situation the use of humor would be inappropriate.

The "O" is somewhat related to the question of whether the humor is merited or not: do you have a clear **Outcome** in mind. Know the purpose for using humor. Everything a counselor does should be intentional. The benefits of using humor were noted. Possible outcomes include (a) building rapport, (b) reframing a counselee's situation, (c) softening a message, (d) normalizing, (e) reducing tension, and (f) reducing counselee resistance.

The fifth point, "R," refers to choosing the best **Routine** for delivering the humor. The work of counseling is not a place to practice a stand-up comedy routine. Humor can be used in different ways. For example one means of using humor is to exaggerate a situation in order to put it into perspective. Young (2010) shares an example of a woman who was concerned about what people would think when they learned about her divorce. Believing that the counselee was making a mountain out of a molehill, the counselor responded, "I can see it now, news headlines 'Woman Divorced, Friends Abandon Her.' The evening news will certainly carry the astounding story." The counselor was not mocking the counselee; he was helping her see that she was blowing the problem out of portion. Other humor routines might involve a humorous story, joke, irony, wit, wordplays, or caricature, to name a few.

For more information on the therapeutic use of humor we recommend the following two resources. Buckman (1994) and Fry and Salameh (1987) are two books that explore the use of therapeutic humor when counseling children, couples, groups, individuals, the elderly, and cancer patients.

## THE THERAPEUTIC USE OF METAPHOR

The use of metaphor in human conversation is a charter member of early civilization. In fact the OT and NT are replete with the use of metaphor. Even the forbidden tree in the garden of Eden had a metaphorical aspect in that part of the death caused by eating it was spiritual, not physical (Gen 3).

Traditionally metaphor has been more closely associated with poetry and literary thought (Sims, 2003). One reason metaphor has a noted place in literary and conversational communication is that it allows new knowledge and ideas to be transmitted by relating it to things familiar to the learner.

The word *metaphor* comes from the Latin *metaphora* and the Greek *metapherein*, which mean "to transfer" (Peeks, 1989). It carried the idea of transferring or carrying a meaning across from one domain to another. Kopp (1971) defined a metaphor as "a way of speaking in which one thing is expressed in terms of another, whereby this bringing together throws new light on the character of what is being described" (p. 269). For example "he is a lion in battle," "there is more than one way to skin a cat," or "making a mountain out of a molehill" illustrate the various domains that can be bridged by the use of metaphor.

In the counseling context Bryant, Katz, Becvar, and Becvar (1988) defined metaphor as "any verbal or concrete illustration, description or reference designed to bring about perceptual and/or behavioral change" (p. 113). Perhaps the broad appeal of metaphor is that it allows people to link emotions to past events (Campbell, 1988). The best known use of therapeutic metaphor is by famed psychiatrist Dr. Milton Erickson. He had an uncanny ability to create analogous stories and jokes that were structurally similar to counselees' situations but that made no direct mention of the counselees or their descriptions of their problems (Haley, 1973).

Speaking the counselee's language has long been recognized as a means to establish a connection with counselees and bring about conditions for change. Metaphors offer a facilitative role in counseling through stories, anecdotes, objects, and music. Metaphors are a rich means for conveying new ideas. Counselors have incorporated metaphors into various theoretical orientations and approaches to the point where they have become fairly common practice (Barker, 1985; Gordon, 1978; Sims, 2003). For example Bryant and associates (1988) surveyed clinical members of the American Association of Marriage and Family Therapists (AAMFT) and found that 95 percent of those who responded used metaphor in their counseling.

## Therapeutic Benefits of Metaphor

Barker (1985) discusses eight of the benefits associated with using metaphor in counseling. First, metaphors convey information in a more interesting manner. Well-thought-out and well-narrated stories can "capture imagination, and inspire people to undertake tasks or think about things they would not have considered before" (p. 17). Second, through the use of metaphor information is presented indirectly, has meanings that are veiled in varying degrees, and are less threatening than more direct statements. It is a way to bypass counselee defenses. A third benefit is that it allows counselees to find their own applications. Fourth, metaphors speak more to the unconscious, and thus evading the possibility that a rational point of view can override the embedded messages. Because metaphors bypass one's conscious thought processes located in the left side of the brain and speak to the right cerebral hemisphere, they are a powerful way to bring truth to life. Fifth, metaphors offer a flexible approach to communicating different types of information. Metaphors can suggest solutions, offer opinions, illustrate points, increase motivation, and enable counselees to see things differently. Sixth, metaphors can help communicate a message to the counselee "in quotes." For example you can tell a story in which one character says to another, *"That was a foolish decision."* The counselee is not directly threatened by the remark even though the comment in the story is constructed so that it is relevant to the counselee. A seventh benefit is that metaphor can facilitate rapport in the helping relationship. Telling stories is so embedded in many cultures and in our own heritage that it creates a bond. Eighth, using metaphors in the counseling process can model for the counselee another way of communicating. For example Dr. Gary Smalley and Dr. John Trent (1992) popularized the use of metaphors for relationships in their book *The language of love: How to be instantly understood by those you love.* Metaphors are a powerful way to communicate truths, which is why Jesus made frequent use of them.

In addition to Barker's (1985) eight benefits, Lyddon, Clay, and Sparks (2001) discuss four more. First, metaphors can access and symbolize counselee emotions. Through metaphors counselees become more aware of their emotions, and it can help them symbolize personal experiences in meaningful ways. Second, metaphor's can uncover and challenge counselee assumptions. Third, metaphors can minimize counselee resistance. Because they can lower defensiveness (Barker, 1985), they are effective in dealing with resistance. Fourth, metaphors can introduce new frames of reference. Metaphors are not intended to change a counselee's problem but to change the counselee's perception of the problem, thus allowing for new solutions.

We would also add to the list of 12 benefits the fact that embedding messages in stories makes the truths easier to grasp and remember. A gifted speaker makes regular use of stories because he or she knows that an audience will most likely remember a story. In fact one of the reasons Jesus' teachings stick in our minds is that He used so many illustrations, metaphors, analogies, and stories (Adams, 1986). So to be an effective communicator, use stories.

## The Source of Metaphors

In the counseling context there are two major sources of metaphors. They are generated by either the counselee or the counselor. Counselee-generated metaphors manifest themselves in the counselee's communication. A competent helper pays attention to what the counselee says and how the counselee frames it. Counselee-generated metaphors can become an integral part of the helping process.

## The Forms of Metaphors

Barker (1985) describes six forms that metaphors may take. First, metaphors can take the form of long stories. The characteristics of a good story include (a) a single, clear theme or message, (b) an interesting plot, (c) good characterization, (d) dramatic appeal, (e) vivid and pleasing style of delivery, and (f) a link to the counselee's personal story. When using this form of metaphor, carefully construct the story to accomplish major therapeutic goals. Have a clear objective in mind and a clear understanding of the counselee's situation. These stories usually come later in the counseling process since they require an in-depth understanding of the counselee's case. Gordon's (1978) book *Therapeutic metaphors* explains how to use long stories.

Another form metaphors can take is anecdotes and short stories. Unlike long stories, anecdotes do not require the degree of development, elaboration, and careful attention to details. This form of metaphor comes closest to the way Jesus used parables. In this form particular points can be illustrated or emphasized.

A third form of metaphor described by Barker (1985) involves analogies, similes, and other brief metaphorical statements. Analogies and similes are a normal part of English conversation. We speak about "putting money in the bank" when we are referring to storing away something important for later use. Almost any activity is available as a subject for metaphorical allusion such as sports, money, children, theater, movies, marriage, politics, medicine, science, and the like.

A fourth form of metaphors is putting them in the context of relationship. The Bible compares the relationship of Christ and the church to the relationship between a husband and wife (Eph 5) and the relationships in a church to the way the body works (1 Cor 12). Metaphors can also be used to address any number of family issues as well as other interpersonal relationships.

The use of metaphorical objects is another form. I (John) have referred to a rock to represent casting the first stone and a door mat and dirty boots to represent an abusive relationship. One therapeutic metaphorical task could be to ask counselees to find an object that represents their current feelings and how they want things to be. One counselee brought in a piece of junk mail to represent her current state of feeling and a vase that was a treasured family heirloom to represent how she wanted to see herself. Throughout our work together we would refer to both items as a means of capturing the meaning attached to them.

A sixth form is the use of artistic metaphors. Counselees can build things with Lego's or wooden blocks, draw pictures, bring in photographs, write or share music, create sculptures, or creatively express things through the use of sand tray. Each creation is a metaphorical message of some experience. For example you can have counselees draw their pain and what it looks like when the pain is better.

Regardless of the form that metaphors take, they offer a powerful means of communicating truths. Typically, counselors find particular forms that fit their style better than other forms, but the more tools you carry in your therapeutic bag the more versatile you can be.

## Guidelines for Using Metaphors

To effectively employ metaphors in counseling, we offer the following mnemonic device, **METAPHOR** (see Table 13.3) to guide your use of them. The "M" is to remind you to know the **Message** you want to deliver. One of the main points of using metaphors is offering specific information in a disguised form. The objective is speaking to the "right brain," not the logical, digital language of the left brain (Barker, 1985).

Table 13.3

*METAPHOR: Guidelines for Using Metaphor*

**M** = know the **Message** you want to deliver

**E** = **Equate** the message with the counselee's view of the world

**T** = **Timing** is critical in delivery

**A** = decide on the **Appearance** to deliver the metaphor

**P** = remember to consider the **Plot** and take time for **Preparation**

**H** = **Highlight** key phrases or passages in your delivery

**O** = keep the desired **Outcome** the focus of the metaphor

**R** = **Read** the counselee's **Response**

"E" suggests that you **Equate** the message with the counselee's view of the world. Each person develops specific ideas as to what constitutes the experiences of love, hate, generosity, happiness, interest, spirituality, and so forth. As noted in an earlier chap., it is essential that you consider the counselee's view of the world. Since metaphors are an important part of the information-gathering process in shaping our perspective on life, they must fit into the counselee's model of the world. According to Gordon (1978) meeting the counselee at his model of the world means that the metaphor preserves the structure of the counselee's problematic situation. For example I (John) worked with an older couple who had experienced problems in their marriage from early on. Although manageable before they had children, their problems were heightened because of behavioral issues associated with their children. The husband blamed his wife for everything, especially the problems with the children. A traditional and conventional man, he believed that the man was the head of his home and that his wife's job was to carry out his biddings. I learned that the husband used to coach football, having a very successful record that he held in high regard. I mentioned my own love of football and told him about my favorite professional team that was experiencing significant problems manifested in playing poorly. Coaches were blaming one another and the players, while the players were blaming coaches and other players for their inability to win. I asked him his assessment of the situation to which he adamantly stated that everything begins and ends with the head coach. He argued that it was the head coach's job to manage the entire team and to bring order. *"The buck starts and stops with the head coach. He is responsible for the playing on the field and what happens in the locker room. If things don't change, it is the head coach's job that should be in jeopardy!"* As he resolutely gleamed in his appraisal of the situation, I then asked him, *"Well, aren't you the head coach of your family?"* The man's mouth dropped open as his head turned on a swivel between his wife and myself. After a period of many seconds he looked at his wife and sincerely apologized for blaming her. The metaphor worked because it had a clear message, and it was one that fit with his model of the world.

Consider carefully the **Timing** ("T") of the metaphor. Timing refers to when the technique is best employed in the counseling work. By using simpler metaphors early in the process, the tone is set for using more complex metaphors later. As a rule of thumb more involved metaphors should occur later in the counseling process.

Decide on the **Appearance** ("A") of the metaphor. Appearance refers to the form and tone of the metaphor. Will the metaphor be an involved story, analogy, or something else? The tone of the metaphor includes the style and flavor of the metaphor. Is it fun? Serious? Realistic? Fictional? For example Jesus' parables were often fictional stories that involved situations common to His hearers.

Remember to consider the **Plot** and take time for **Preparation** ("P"). If you like using stories it is wise to spend time thinking about the situation you want to address and the story you will construct. In constructing a story consider the look, feel, and sound. In considering the plot determine if the story is: (a) a truth to learn, (b) a treasure to find, (c) a change to make, (d) an obstacle to overcome, (e) a conflict to resolve, (f) a problem to solve, (g) a mystery to unravel, or (h) a lesson to learn.

Context is also important to consider in developing the metaphor. The right context, according to Barker (1985), is one in which stories are told, tasks are given, and points are illustrated by the use of similes and analogies. Also think about the setting for the story. Should it happen in a distant country; be set in the past, present, or future; indoors or outdoors; real people or fictional people; children, adults, animals, objects, entities (e.g., spirits, aliens, monsters), or plants? Select traits (e.g., kind, compassionate, outgoing, impulsive, greedy, lustful, dependable, steadfast, prideful) for the characters that match the life situation of the counselee. The last part of the preparation involves how the story will conclude. In other words what is the moral of the story that you desire the counselee to take away?

**Highlight** ("H") or emphasize key phrases or themes in your delivery. In printed form metaphors are less impactful and lifelike (Barker, 1985). Putting emphasis on different words and phrases can increase their effectiveness.

One of the most important steps in using metaphors is having the desired **Outcome** ("O") clearly in view. As noted above, metaphors contain opportunities to offer counselees new choices, new perspectives, and new opportunities to tap into unused resources. Goals are clearly defined because a metaphor is a strategic method aimed at targeting a specific objective. Have a clear and precise picture of the desired state before using a metaphor (Barker, 1985).

The final guideline, "R," refers to **Reading** the counselee's **Response**. An aspect of all counseling interventions is to evaluate its impact on the counselee. Some metaphors might be intended to confuse the counselee in order to force him or her to wrestle with some truth. Other metaphors might take time for the counselee to process before grasping the various embedded meanings. Thus how a counselee responds might depend in part on the intended outcome.

## JOURNALING

Journaling is a technique in which a counselee can put his innermost thoughts, feelings, and beliefs on paper. Whether the feelings are fearful, anger, painful, or tender and whether the thoughts are biblical or not, the journal can become a means of objectifying what the counselee is thinking and feeling. Some people prefer to think of this assignment like a diary, but the purpose is the same: to write down what is going on inside of the counselee without censoring or editing.

One of the great paradoxes of journaling is that what a person writes is permanent but at the same time it is only a snapshot of one moment in time. It is a station between the past and the future. Young (cited in Adams, 1993) writes, "Each entry is a record of a dynamic adventure punctuated by our testament to learning, growth, courage, and healing" (p. vii).

Using journaling in your counseling is one of the simplest homework assignments you can request of a counselee. Different methods can be used in journal writing, and how you use it is limited only by your creativity. Perhaps the most widely used method of journaling encourages free writing in which the counselee writes his feelings in open-ended, unstructured, and nondirected ways. Adams (1993) advocates that structured journaling is often the method of choice, particularly with counselees suffering from post-traumatic syndrome. Her workbook provides a structured method of journaling designed to move the counselee toward healing. You can also ask the counselee to respond to particular questions such as: what makes you worthwhile, what is the purpose of your life, what do you fear or what makes you most scared, what has hurt you the most? and the like.

Some people have written notes in their journals as prayers to God. At times people get lost in the complex web of their internal thoughts and feelings, especially when they are having a difficult time. Some people are even unable to pray during times of suffering. Writing the journal as a "Dear God" letter can help people connect with the One who can provide the greatest resource for change, as well as allow them to lament what they are experiencing.

## CHAPTER SUMMARY

Each counselor is his or her own unique person. The personality style and gifts will predispose you toward the kinds of techniques you naturally and comfortably employ in counseling. Some counselors, for instance, find the use of humor easy, but they find using metaphors difficult. We encourage you to develop skills that will stretch you. The miracle question, humor, metaphor, and journaling are highly valuable techniques that can help make the therapeutic journey successful.

## CHAPTER 13 ACTIVITIES

1. Answer the "Miracle Question" in a goal area you have for yourself. Be specific and detailed in your answer.
2. Discuss the importance and benefits of using homework assignments in counseling.
3. Review the DVD about recommending the use of homework to a counselee. What skills did you see presented by the counselor? What do you think made the counselee who was initially reluctant to doing homework more willing?
4. Create a biblical homework assignment for a counselee that addresses the problem of anger.
5. What is a behavioral task that might be a good homework assignment for someone who feels depressed? Why?
6. What guidelines for effectively using homework, humor, and meta-phors in counseling are provided in this chap.? Provide a brief description of each guideline.
7. Watch and review the DVD vignette on the use of metaphor. Then respond to each item below:

   a. How did the counselor structure the metaphor to meet the counselee's needs?
   b. Two _____

8. Describe a time when Jesus used metaphor(s) to teach something to His followers.
9. How might a counselor *creatively* express a metaphor for the way a spouse's angry emotional abandonment relates to the fear and depression of his spouse?
10. For 15 minutes write down what you are thinking and feeling without censoring yourself (this will not be handed in). Reflect on how this type of journaling might be helpful for persons trying to regulate their anger or intervene with negative internal self-talk.
11. Write a letter to someone who has hurt you (you will not give this letter to them). Be detailed about what this person did and its influence on you. Tell this person what you feel about what he or she did to you. Write it all out, everything you want to say. When this is complete, write a letter to God, asking Him to heal the hurt caused by this person and to help you see yourself the way He does. Also, take the time you

need to share with God any other thoughts and feelings that come up in response to this activity. If you want or need to, share this activity with a family member or friend who cares about you.

## Vignette Questions

*Vignette 17*
*Assigning Homework*

1. Based upon vignette 17, what was your initial reaction at the mention of the word "homework" within the counseling session? Why do you think that you felt this way?
2. What is one of the main purposes behind giving homework? Why is this important?
3. How does Denise use homework to move Shannon toward her goal? Was she successful in accomplishing her task? Why or why not?
4. Did Denise follow the ASSIGN model? Explain your answer.
5. When should a counselor assign homework? Support your response.

## Recommended Reading

Adams, K. (1998). *The way of the journal: A journal therapy workbook for healing* (2nd ed.). Lutherville, MD: Sidran Press.

> This is a practical book on how to use journaling in counseling those who need healing. The author suggests an easy-to-learn 10-step process.

Gordon, D. (1978). *Therapeutic metaphors: Helping others through the looking glass.* Cupertino, CA: Meta.

> This book is an excellent resource to learn how to share stories as a means of promoting change. Jesus Christ was a powerfully effective communicator who used stories to lead people to Himself. As counselors we should become skilled and proficient at using stories with clients. Gordon's work is one of the best resources to learn more about using metaphors in counseling.

# Chapter 14

# Spiritual Strategies

*"Psychological difficulties are pervasive and influence multiple domains of life, including the religious and spiritual domains. People who identify with a theistic perspective and are encountering emotional difficulties often experience conflict in their personal experience of God. They intellectually understand the theological components of their faith, but have difficulty emotionally grasping them"* (Moriarty & Hoffman, 2007, p. 1).

*"We are born broken. We live by mending.*
*The grace of God is the glue"*
(Eugene O'Neill cited in Anderson, 1997, p. 213).

*"And he will be called Wonderful Counselor, Mighty God,*
*Everlasting Father, Prince of Peace"* (Isa 9:6b, NIV).

## CHAPTER OBJECTIVES

» To understand the relationship between psychological and spiritual functioning

» To learn about ethical issues related to spiritual integration in counseling

» To develop skills in spiritual assessment

» To be exposed to spiritual integration tools

## CHAPTER OUTLINE

THE RELATIONSHIP BETWEEN PSYCHOLOGICAL AND SPIRITUAL FUNCTIONING

ETHICAL ISSUES IN SPIRITUALLY INTEGRATED COUNSELING

SPIRITUAL ASSESSMENT IN COUNSELING

W hat a privilege to serve as guides for healing expeditions in which we lead under the direction, protection, leadership, and power of the One who is the "Wonderful Counselor, Mighty God, Everlasting Father, [and] Prince of Peace" (Isa 9:6, NIV). We are not travailing through the wilderness of symptoms, grief, and trauma alone; we are joining God in what He is accomplishing in this world. And what is God busy doing? Consider these words from Isaiah (61:1–4, NIV), part of which Jesus quoted Himself (Luke 4:18–19).

> The Spirit of the Sovereign LORD is on me, because the LORD has anointed me to preach good news to the poor.
>
> He has sent me to bind up the brokenhearted, to proclaim freedom for the captives, and release from darkness for the prisoners; to proclaim the year of the LORD's favor and the day of vengeance of our God, to comfort all who mourn, and provide for those who grieve in Zion— to bestow on them a crown of beauty instead of ashes, the oil of gladness instead of mourning, and a garment of praise instead of a spirit of despair. They will be called oaks of righteousness, a planting of the LORD for the display of his splendor.
>
> They will rebuild the ancient ruins and restore the places long devastated; they will renew the ruined cities that have been devastated for generations.

We are called to join Jesus Christ as encouragers, providers, healers, freedom-seekers, warriors, comforters, mourners, and rebuilders. Can you think of anything more meaningful and important to do? And where do we get the power for such a formidable task? Contemplate this remarkable statement from the Word of God:

> I pray also that the eyes of your heart may be enlightened in order that you may know the hope to which he has called you, the riches of his glorious inheritance in the saints, and his incomparably great power for us who believe. That power is like the working of his mighty strength, which he exerted in Christ when he raised him from the dead and seated him at his right hand in the heavenly realms, far above all rule and authority, power and dominion, and every title that can be given, not only in the present age but also in the one to come. And God placed all things under his feet and appointed him to be head over everything for the church, which is his body, the fullness of him who fills everything in every way (Eph 1:18–23, NIV).

Isn't that incredible? The power that raised Jesus Christ from the dead, the power that is above everything in this fallen world, is available to us as we join Him in "setting captives free." Abiding in Jesus and bringing His grace, truth, and power into the counseling process is the focus of this chap.

This chap. covers the logistics of bringing the spiritual dimension into counseling, which is called spiritual integration. This is not as widely accepted as one might think, especially when the spirituality is evangelical-fundamental in nature. According to Worthington and Scott (1983), Christian counselees may avoid seeing secular counselors for a variety of reasons including fears that their spirituality and spiritual issues will be ignored, mishandled, or seen as abnormal and that treatment may include interventions that they consider morally wrong. Several researchers suggest that religious counselees with negative concepts about counselors are resistant to therapy and have high rates of premature termination (Lovinger, 1979, 1984; Worthington, 1986).

According to Vande Kemp (1984), the integration of psychotherapy with religion and spiritual matters has been an active enterprise since the establishment of psychology as an independent discipline during the nineteenth century. But in the past century the integration of psychology and theology shifted to the position that such integration is problematic. Ellis (1974), for example, considered personality problems equivalent to pathological religiosity, small-mindedness, fanaticism, and unscientific thinking.

In considering how integration occurs, Moon (1997) discusses the importance of the personal character of the counselor. Thomas and French (1999) state that because of the influence that values have in counseling, each counselor must understand his own attitudes toward Christian topics, moral issues, key doctrinal beliefs, and relevant theological issues (suffering, the nature of God, and so forth).

## THE RELATIONSHIP BETWEEN PSYCHOLOGICAL AND SPIRITUAL FUNCTIONING

Bringing the spiritual element into counseling is more complex than one might think. This is because a person's experience of God entails both conscious and unconscious elements and neurological, psychological, and spiritual components. An extensive body of research suggests that there is much more to faith than meets the eye. Underneath a counselee's knowledge of his faith experiences are psychological and neurological processes that influence how he relates to and experiences God (Noffke & Hall, 2007). Research reveals that what a person experiences internally or feels in relationships with significant people (i.e., "attachment figures") he or she is likely to experience in relationship with God. This is particularly relevant in the dimensions of security and lovability, our two most primary developmental needs (Firestone, 1996).

Human development is an internalization process in which representations of the self, others, and God develop around the themes of felt security and love. These representations are stored in the limbic system of the brain as neurological processes and events (Gabbard, 2000; Garzon, 2005). Internal representations or "working models," as Bowlby (1980) referred to them, develop into a general "attachment style" and reflect a person's early attachment experiences with primary caregivers. Attachment style forms around early interpersonal experiences in conjunction with individual temperament, constitution, and processing styles (Greenspan, 1997). If a person is constitutionally fearful and tends to become easily overwhelmed by circumstances, security is more difficult to experience, no matter how sensitive the parenting. In other words internalized models are not precise representations of actual attachment history, but are subjective reflections resulting from a combination of bio-psycho-social-spiritual factors. Although working models of reality are formulated throughout one's life span, much of what we "know" viscerally (deep down, intuitively, in the body) is based on internalizations that were conceived during preverbal phases of development (Bucci, 1997; Greenspan, 1997), encoded as neurobiological data in the limbic areas of the brain (Noffke & Hall, 2007), and elaborated on or solidified throughout later development (Young, Klosko, & Weishaar, 2003). The attachment system is the lens from which a person's interpersonal reality is viewed.

The literature on attachment reveals much about these fundamental developmental processes (Bowlby, 1988; Clinton & Sibcy, 2002). To summarize, people who acquire a secure attachment style generally reflect trust in oneself, others, and God. Securely attached individuals generally experience life through the lens, "I am safe, wanted, and loved." Insecurely attached people (and more severely, individuals with a disorganized attachment style), generally mistrust themselves, others and God. Their internal experience involves the intermittent triggering of viscerally felt anxiety and terror. They experience life through the lens, "I am unsafe, alone, unwanted, unloved." Attachment style and related schemas are biologically primed and when triggered they are experienced at an affective, experiential, and not cognitive, level (Ainsworth, Blehar, Waters, & Wall, 1978; Hill & Hall, 2002).

Research findings indicate that although maladaptive schemas may develop in times of trauma, deprivation, and neglect, they emerge intermittently in subsequent developmental phases (Sroufe, 2005). Most counselees are unaware that their present symptoms relate to their attachment system and related "maladaptive schemas" (Young, Klosko, & Weishaar, 2003) and that their coping mechanisms and addictive behaviors place distance between them and their intolerable emotional experiences (Allen, 2001).

In conjunction with the development of insecure/disorganized attachment style and maladaptive schemas, it is common for harsh, internal "voices" to emerge, based on complex developmental processes involving "splitting defenses" and the subjective experience of the caregiver's voice (Firestone, 1996). This internal, abusive dialog with the self is difficult to extinguish because it reflects a biologically based, internalization of attachment to the caregiver, and thus a "fantasy bond" with security and love (Firestone, 1996).

The development and maintenance of maladaptive attachment systems, schemas, and internal dialog is not only related to attachment experiences, genetics, temperament, and processing styles, but also the fundamental and powerful generational dynamics and fallen matrices in which we live (the world, the flesh, and the devil; Satan (Shields & Bredfeldt, 2001). As unconscious processes, altering these mechanisms is obviously no easy task.

So how does a person's attachment history, neurobiology, schemas, and coping behaviors relate to his experience of God? As previously stated, brain research reveals that circuits and patterns of neuronal activation associated with attachment experiences are reinforced and stored biologically, formed into a sense of security and lovability, and later generalized to other relationships (Moriarty & Hoffman, 2007). What this means is that people experience their relationship with themselves, others, and God, at least in part, from the template of these unconscious, internal working models.

To sum, when security is threatened, an individual's attachment system is activated, and that person experiences himself or herself in relation to significant others as safe, wanted, and loved or unsafe, unwanted, and unloved. The Christian person, like all other people, has developed an attachment system and related schemas, voices, and worldviews that are generally functioning below the level of conscious awareness. A Christian who has acquired a secure attachment system is able to trust others, and more importantly he is able to turn to his relationship with God and find love, protection, and support as needed ("Let us then approach the throne of grace with confidence, so that we may receive mercy and find grace to help us in our time of need" [Heb 4:16, NIV]). However, the Christian whose attachment style is insecure or disorganized has a completely different experience when her attachment system is triggered. That person may intellectually know that she can turn to God when afraid and she can quote verses about her security with Him ("I sought the Lord, and he answered me; he delivered me from all my fears" [Ps 34:4, NIV]), but she is unable to ascertain that on an experiential level. Therefore when she feels threatened, she will unconsciously rely on certain rules, behaviors, mechanisms, or relationships, what Firestone (1996) calls "fantasy bonds" (e.g., pleasing others; never saying no) instead of going to the true and living God to soothe and comfort her through her fears. Although these believing counselees have learned theological truths by explicit instruction, these objective truths about God and spiritual reality

> are reshaped according to individuals' implicit relational representations. The perception of self and others and the interactional patterns infants develop to maintain felt security are represented in self-perpetuating neural networks that are automatically and nonconsciously elicited by attachment related stimuli with God (Noffke & Hall, 2007, p. 62).

In other words what a person "knows" about God cannot readily supersede what he or she experiences and feels on the inside.

Christian counselees are often mystified by their intermittent feelings of terror, guilt, anger, shame, and worry that their "lack of faith" displeases God. But counselee symptoms and schemas make perfect sense when seen in light of the bio-psycho-social-spiritual ramifications of early developmental experiences, trauma history, temperament, constitution, processing styles, and the influences of the fallen world. Counselors do a great service for the Lord when they use psycho-education to help these believers understand their internal experience and provide hope for healing in the therapeutic relationship and ultimately through God's unfailing love. Research has begun to evaluate how the therapeutic relationship and psychotherapy affects the attachment system and God-image, and the good news is that God is doing wonderful things through counselors who understand these dynamics and are able to provide a therapeutic experience that facilitates what the research calls "earned attachment" (Roisman, Padron, Sroufe, & Egeland, 2002).

"Individuals with histories of insecure attachment tend to perceive God as controlling, less accepting, nurturing and distant," and these "gut level experiences of God are unconscious" (Noffke & Hall, 2007, p. 63). This is why spiritual integration in counseling is not simply a matter of assigning Scriptures and citing theological truths to counselees. In order for one's image of God to be healed, the very mechanisms of the attachment system (indeed the neurological mechanisms and brain pathways underlying the attachment structure) must be assessed, addressed, and reworked. How this occurs will be presented in the section on spiritual integration tools, later on in this chap.

## ETHICAL ISSUES IN SPIRITUALLY INTEGRATED COUNSELING

Although only briefly summarized here, the importance of following guidelines for the proper handling of ethical issues in counseling cannot be understated. As representatives of Christ to individuals of diverse faiths and backgrounds, counselors must move cautiously and respectfully in the realm of the spiritual. In addition to the following guidelines for spiritual integration, readers are encouraged to consult other resources for further elaboration including Clinton and Ohlschlager, 2002a; Corey, Corey, and Callanan, 2007; Diller, 2007; Entwistle, 2004b; and Gladding, 2009.

As a counselor you are free to utilize spiritual integration under the following conditions: (a) you have completed a full bio-psycho-social-spiritual assessment, determined the counselee's diagnosis, if any, and developed a written treatment plan that appropriately addresses the counselee's medical, psychological, interpersonal, and spiritual needs; (b) your counselee has expressed a desire to utilize his faith as part of the multimodal treatment plan; (c) your counselee fully understands the particular interventions to be utilized, along with the rationale for them, and has provided written, informed consent for them; (d) the interventions are congruent with your counselee's religious/spiritual belief system; (e) you have had adequate training in cultural, ethnic, and religious/spiritual diversity and integration in general and in the particular interventions to be utilized; (f) you and your counselee have developed a trusting and empathic relationship; (g) you have determined that your counselee is not psychotic or delusional; and (h) you and your counselee believe that the interventions have relevancy to your counselee's issues, concerns, and goals (Collins, 1991; Garzon, 2005; Gubi, 2001; Hardman, Berrett, & Richards, 2004; Kelly, 1995; McMinn, 1996; Miller & Thoresen, 1999; Ohlschlager, 2004; Richards & Bergin, 2000; Sperry, 2001; Sperry, 2003).

The need for a spiritual assessment as part of the full bio-psycho-social-spiritual evaluation is the focus of the next section.

## SPIRITUAL ASSESSMENT IN COUNSELING

When a person tells us he is Christian or Jewish or Muslim, what does this actually mean? If we are not careful, we will make the mistake of thinking it means for our counselee what it means to us. But it is safe to assume that it does not. The lack of information on this matter can be dangerous. This is why we have emphasized the importance of thorough examination. Know your counselee medically and be able to answer the question, Does this counselee's diagnosis and symptoms relate to a medical problem (Morrison, 2007)? Psychological assessment is no less critical. Be able to recognize the presence of mental disorders and be prepared to treat them effectively. Also, evaluate the counselee interpersonally and systemically to gain information the counselee might not know or share (spouse, parents, friends, teachers, pastor, medical doctors, and others) and to involve these people in the treatment when indicated. Also seek to understand the spiritual experience and history of the counselee. Determine if spiritual issues and concerns are related to their presenting problems and determine if spiritual integration is likely to support them in reaching their goals.

Begin to assess spirituality at intake in order to facilitate its inclusion in the treatment planning (Tisdale, 2003). Only when you accurately understand your counselees' unique experience of God can you ethically and effectively address any God-related problems (Tisdale et al., 1997; Cheston, Piedmont, Eanes, & Patrice, 2003) and properly integrate spiritual interventions in counseling.

Because a counselee's experience of God is a complex matter, it is not easy to appraise. As you probably know about yourself, there is often a vast difference between what we intellectually know about God and what we experience. For example right now as you sit reading this, can you say that you are genuinely feeling like you are "holy and dearly loved" (Col 3:12, NIV) and hemmed in "behind and before" with God's thoughts toward you as numerous as "the grains of sand" (Ps 139:5,18)? Grimes (2007) captures this well in his differentiation between the "God image" and the "God construct."

> The God image as a psychological construct is concerned with how an individual feels toward God, and how they feel God feels about them. The God image is primarily an unconscious phenomenon, as compared to the God concept. The God concept, as a distinct construct, refers to an individual's cognitive understanding of God.
>
> Hoffman (2005) summarizes the God concept as being largely conscious and rational, based upon what a person is taught about God, and influenced by such things as religious teachings of parents, spiritual leaders, and religious texts. Comparatively, Hoffman notes that the God image is more complex and is emotional, experiential, and unconscious in nature (Grimes, 2007, p.12).

As with assessment in general, spiritual assessment actually occurs over time as trust in the therapeutic relationship grows and the counselee reveals more about himself. We find it helpful to utilize different strategies to elicit information about counselees' spiritual experiences. This section briefly introduces a few spiritual assessment tools we have found helpful (we encourage you to explore the literature to gather more).

## Questions during the Intake Evaluation

Spiritual assessment can begin with a few simple questions during the intake interview. According to Sperry (2003), a useful beginning question is, "Can you tell me a little about your religious beliefs and feelings?" This can be followed up with questions that elicit the individual's specific experience of God, prayer, etc. and might include the counselees' "religious upbringing, their images of God, their basic values and beliefs, their involvement in a spiritual community, and the place of prayer and other spiritual practices in their lives" (p. 7). As your counselee responds to your questions, simply listen and utilize basic counseling skills (invitational skills, open-ended questions, reflection skills) to encourage deep and rich expression.

Surveys have been developed specifically for the purpose of spiritual assessment. Two examples of these are the Attachment to God Inventory (AGI) and the Remuda Spiritual Assessment Questionnaire (RSAQ). You can find a copy of the AGI and research related to it in Beck and McDonald (2004) and the RSAQ and related research in Wall, Cumella, and Darden

(2003) and Darden (2005). You will have an opportunity to take both of these surveys as part of the end-of-this-chap. exercises.

## The Spiritual Life Map

A Spiritual Life Map is a chronological, illustrated account of a person's relationship with God from her birth, through her entire life, and into eternity. An excellent example of a life map can be found in Hodge (2005). You can learn more about spiritual assessment and find other assessments of this sort in Hodge (2003).

## Letter to God

A *Letter to God* can be assigned for homework or dictated to the counselor during a session. The counselee is instructed to share her true thoughts, feelings, questions, concerns, requests, etc., in relation to God. The counselee should be told that there is no right or wrong way to do this, but simply to "look" into her own heart and sincerely, genuinely, and candidly express to God what is there.

## Attachment with God Experiential Survey

This survey taps into the counselee's internal experience of God. The following is an example of how it may be done.

> *Close your eyes and begin focusing on your breath. Take a deep breath into your abdomen, hold it, and then let it go. Take several breaths like this and as you do, allow your body to become more and more relaxed. With each inhale, imagine yourself feeling more and more peaceful and with each exhale imagine yourself letting go of all fear and worries. If you notice thoughts coming into your mind, imagine them passing by like little clouds. Don't follow the thoughts and begin contemplating their contents; just let them pass. Imagine that you are becoming even more and more relaxed, with no place you have to go, and nothing you have to do; your body is free from all tension and fear. Imagine yourself feeling more and more peaceful, more and more relaxed, more and more free from thoughts and fears.*
>
> *Now I want you to begin to become mindful of your relationship with God and what your relationship with God feels like. Don't go into your head on this or look for it in your mind, instead let what your relationship with God feels like emerge into your awareness. Right now, as you begin to meditate on your relationship with God, what words come to mind to describe what it feels like for you with God. If you feel comfortable doing so, you can even ask Him to reveal to you what your relationship with Him is presently like. Keep breathing and keep focusing inward. There is no right or wrong answers here, only what you really feel and notice.*

> *When you are ready, see if you can describe what your relationship*
> *with God feels like in response to this experience. Especially become*
> *aware of how your relationship feels in terms of eternal security and*
> *unconditional love. What does your relationship with God feel like in*
> *terms of security and what does it feel like in terms of love? When*
> *you are ready, open your eyes and write some notes down about this*
> *experience and then describe this experience to me as fully as you can.*

An alternative to having counselees write down their descriptions is having them draw or color what they felt during the experience. Be sure to tell them that it does not matter what their depiction looks like because they are using art as a means of expression and not as a fine arts project.

Over time you will likely come up with your own means of assessing counselee spirituality. Perhaps more important than how you assess spirituality is the person you are in the process. According to Miller and Thoresen (1999) competent counselors engaging in spiritual assessment and integration have a

> nonjudgmental, accepting, and empathic relationship with the coun-
> selee, an openness and willingness to take time to understand the
> counselee's spirituality as it may relate to health-related issues, some
> familiarity with culturally related values, beliefs, and practices that are
> common among the counselee populations likely to be served, com-
> fort in asking and talking about spiritual issues with counselees, and
> a willingness to seek information from appropriate professionals and
> coordinate care concerning counselees' spiritual traditions (p. 10).

## SPIRITUAL INTEGRATION TOOLS

### "Incarnational" Counseling

When Jesus Christ came to earth, He perfectly represented and revealed God the Father (Heb 1:3). As a result man "met" God and found in Him an irresistible force of grace, truth, and power. Like Jesus, we are also called to represent and reflect God the Father, and we can do this *if we truly abide in Christ.*

Incarnational counseling means the counselor stays so close to Jesus that he or she implicitly (i.e., without words) brings Jesus into the counseling as God's Spirit is working in and through her during each session. As discussed earlier, the nurturing therapeutic relationship becomes internalized and then works change in the counselee's internal working models (Cumella, 2002; Jones, 2007). The integration literature presents the character and person of the therapist as one of the primary healing factors of spiritual dysfunction and mental and emotional disorder (e.g., Anderson,

1997; Anderson, 2007; Benner, 1983; Cheong & DiBlasio, 2007; Hardy, 2000; Langberg, 2006; White, 1984).

Grace (in the form of patience, kindness, and interest) and truth (in the form of consistent limits, boundaries, and rules) are emotional and developmental needs that many individuals have never experienced. Those who are Christians and who have been deprived of this nurturing tend to project this neglect and disinterest onto their image of God and either cower from Him or make little use of their relationship with Him. As counselors abide in Christ, reflect His likeness, and draw on His power in counseling, without reference to spiritual language at all, shifts in counselee working models occur and experiences of self, others, and God, and the biological processes in the brain actually reformat.

### Exploring Counselee Beliefs and Experiences

As you work with people, you will discover that many have harmful religious/spiritual beliefs (often incongruent with the tenets of their faith but present at the experiential level). Many times these beliefs are directly related to the counselee's presenting issues and concerns (Richards & Bergin, 1997). Exploring and discussing a counselee's spiritual and religious beliefs is a means of increasing awareness of and addressing this incongruity. It brings the counselee's internal process in relation to God out into the light. In the context of a safe and trusting relationship counselees can be encouraged to explore their spiritual beliefs without fear of judgment or condemnation. The ultimate goal of this process is not correction by the counselor but increased self-understanding for the counselee. Although you may be tempted to correct your counselee's faulty beliefs, a much more powerful means of promoting change is turning the counselee inward to feel their internal experiences in relation to God and spiritual matters. This process promotes developmental health, including spiritual health (Gabbard, 2009).

Sometimes it is not easy to sit with people who vent rage, fear, guilt, and shame in relation to God, but doing so is vitally important. As you provide a peaceful, listening ear, you become like an anchor for your counselee to hold onto as he or she explores and experiences the nuances of his internal world. Your peace is a safe place or haven from which the counselee can discover the truth of his experience. By being an anchor, you are providing a space for your counselee to solidify both psychologically and spiritually. This provision of an "anchor" is a crucial and important form of spiritual intervention.

### Spiritual Disciplines

The Christian faith contains a long history of spiritual "interventions" that for centuries have promoted mental, physical, social, and spiritual health (McMinn & Phillips, 2001; Sperry, 2001; Sperry, 2003). This section focuses on five disciplines: prayer, meditation, spiritual reading and memorization, confession and reconciliation, and forgiveness.

### Prayer.

Many varieties and forms of prayer can be utilized in counseling (McCullough & Larson, 1999, McMinn, 2001; Entwistle, 2004b; Garzon, 2005), and the effective and ethical use of prayer in treatment is addressed well in the writings of many others (Ashby & Lenhart, 1994; Entwistle, 2004b; Gubi, 2001; Hardman & Berrett, 2005; Hurding, 1995; Matthews, 2000; McCullough, 1995; McCullough & Larson, 1999; Miller et al., 1999; Poloma & Pendleton, 1991; Richards, 1991; Sperry, 2001; Sperry, 2003; Tan, 2003; Walker, Tonigan, Miller, Comer, & Kahlich, 1997; Weld & Eriksen, 2007). We encourage you to review this literature. Counselors can personally pray for their counselees, encourage counselees to pray in a manner congruent with their beliefs and in keeping with their comfort level, pray directly with counselees during sessions, and/or encourage counselees to request prayer from supportive others. The key is to help the counselee find in God the unconditional love and security he needs and to develop that relationship with God by means of prayer. Prayer themes may relate to goals and symptoms and/or any of the patient's other life issues.

A multimodal intervention that is grounded in prayer involves meditation, relaxation training, and imagery, all of which are commonly used in spiritually integrated counseling (Carlson, Bacaseta, & Simanton, 1988; Elkins, Anchor, & Sandler, 1979; Garzon, 2005; Marlatt & Kristeller, 1999). An example of such a tool is called inner healing prayer, developed by Tan (1996a):

> A seven-step model I have developed includes the following steps: (1) Begin with prayer for God's healing and protection. (2) Conduct brief relaxation training to help the counselee relax as deeply as possible. (3) Ask the counselee to go back to the painful memory or event in imagery (if possible) and relive it. (4) After some time, pray for God to minister his healing grace and love to the counselee in whatever way is appropriate or needed, without making too many specific suggestions. Jesus imagery or other guided imagery may or may not be used at this time. (5) Have a period of quiet waiting in contemplative prayer and letting go, being receptive to whatever God wants the counselee to experience in terms of inner healing. The counselor will periodically ask the counselee, "What are you experiencing or feeling now? What's happening?" to track with the counselee. (6) Close the inner-healing session with prayer, often including thanksgiving. (7) Have a time of debriefing (pp. 372–473).

With spiritual imagery and meditation in counseling counselees often experience "powerful affirmations and flashes of insight into their spiritual identity and worth" (Richards & Bergin, 1997, p. 272). The use of visualization and meditation, for example, may involve revisiting traumatic experiences that relate to the development of the counselee's symptoms and visualizing God bringing comfort and healing to those memories.

Examples of the use of spiritual imagery in the literature will help you understand the process (Cecero, 2002; Garzon & Burkett, 2002; Garzon, 2005; Hurding, 1995; Smith, 1999). It is important to note that there is some controversy about the use of such interventions in treatment, so careful attention to ethical issues is imperative (see Entwistle, 2004b, and Garzon, 2005, for further information).

### Meditation

Meditation simply means to focus one's mind on God. Combining systematic relaxation and deep breathing while concentrating the mind on "whatever is true, whatever is noble, whatever is right, whatever is pure, whatever is lovely, whatever is admirable" (Phil 4:8, NIV) is central to meditation. You can help counselees learn to allow the thoughts that are prevalent in their minds to recede as they focus instead on their breathing and the presence of God in the here-and-now moment. You may want to instruct the counselee to "breathe in" God's peace ("Peace I leave with you; my peace I give you. I do not give to you as the world gives. Do not let your hearts be troubled and do not be afraid" (John 14:27, NIV) and "breathe out" their concerns and fears. Meditation and mindfulness exercises can ease one's emotion and decrease his tensions (Dimeff & Koerner, 2007). "Practicing the presence of God" (Jones, 2010), that is, being mindful of His unconditional love and provision of security by repeating Scripture, by thinking of a loving parent, and considering the simple miracle of His life and Spirit within us is a habit from which all Christians can benefit.

### Spiritual reading and memorization.

Spiritual reading and memorization are common in spiritually integrated counseling (Azhar, Varma, & Dharap, 1994; Bearon & Koenig, 1990; Byrd, 1988; Finney & Malony, 1985; Miller & Thoresen, 1999; Sperry, 2001; 2003; Tan, 1996b and 2003). Appropriate readings can correct misunderstandings, inspire, teach, comfort, strengthen, provide meaning, support relief from symptoms, and aid in the development of an authentic and solid personal identity (Hardman & Berrett, 2000; Hardman, Berrett, and Richards, 2004; Richards & Bergin, 2000; Tan, 1996a).

In addition to recommending spiritual readings relevant to the counselee's struggles, counselors can encourage counselees to find and memorize Scripture verses related to their issues and concerns and to utilize these in "fighting the good fight" against problematic symptoms and behaviors. Our ultimate Counselor and Guide, Jesus, said, "My sheep listen to my voice; I know them, and they follow me" (John 10:27, NIV). There is a peace that comes from trusting God and coming under the authority of His Word (Prov 3:4–5). According to Tan (2007), "problems in thought and behavior may often (not always, because of other factors, eg., organic, or biological) underlie problem feelings (Prov 23:7; Rom 12:1–2; Phil 4:8; Eph 4:22–24) and [Christian Counseling] will use biblical truth (John 8:32), not relativistic values, to conduct cognitive restructuring and behavioral change interventions" (p. 102). We have seen that the correct use of Scripture in counseling (with Christians who believe in the authority of the Bible and want to incorporate it into their counseling) is powerful.

Tan has spent the last 25 years adding to the empirical research on spiritual integration in counseling (see Tan, 2007, for a summary of this research and case studies of inner healing prayer and the use of Scripture in counseling). He recommends utilizing Scripture for the following purpose and in the following ways:

> to comfort, clarify (guide), correct (cognitively restructure), change character, cleanse, convict (convert), and cure (or heal) (e.g., see 2 Tim 3:16; Jn 15:3; Ps 119:9,11; Heb 4:12; 1 Pet 2:2; Ps 119:105; Ps 119:97–100; 1 Pet 1:2–3; Rom 10:17; Jn 8:32). It can be used in the following ways: indirectly by alluding to biblical truth or directly by generally referring to teachings or examples in the Bible or specifically citing biblical texts by chap. and verse; by reading, meditating, memorizing, hearing, or studying Scripture (see Tan & Gregg, 1997); or assigning it for reading, study, memorization, or meditation in between therapy sessions (2007, p. 108).

### Confession and reconciliation.

Christians who utilize confession and accept the unconditional love and forgiveness of God (reconciliation) report experiencing deep joy, freedom, and security (Davis, 2001). Confession and reconciliation in counseling involves sharing personal experiences and issues related to problematic symptoms and addictions, including the underlying thoughts, feelings, and needs behind them. Confession allows counselees to face their shame and to let go of the painful belief that God could not and would not love them because of their symptoms and addictive behaviors (Wall, Eberly, & Cumella, 2005).

According to Wall and associates (2002; 2005), when Christian counselees come to understand, through the use of Scripture and experiencing grace-filled therapeutic relationships, that God loves them completely
no matter what their behavior, they can begin the work of recovery, not
because of condemnation and fear but "because we are loved and have
been granted infinite worth by God" (Wall et al., 2005, p. 9). Confession
to others about the reality of one's disorder denotes coming out of denial,
being motivated to recover, being interested in utilizing spirituality as a
resource in treatment, and desiring to engage directly with God as part
of the recovery process (Cooper, 2006; Rogers, 2004). Other clinicians,
researchers, and theorists writing about the Christian process of confession in counseling in general include Allender, 1995; Braem, 2004; Foster,
1988; Monroe, 2001; Smith, 1999.

### Forgiveness.

Many counselees are confused about what forgiveness does and does not
mean. Clarifying this important biblical concept (and command) is often
very helpful for counselees. According to Sanderson and Linehan (1999),
"forgiveness means to give up or give away anger and the actions associated
with it [namely], retribution and revenge" (p. 207). Richards and associates
(1997) encourage therapists to help counselees consider forgiveness as a gift
they can choose to give to themselves, others, and God.

> Forgiveness work is considered a process that is not to be hurried as
> intense feelings of hurt, disappointment, anger, and rage must often
> be acknowledged, re-experienced, and worked through before patients
> are ready to forgive. To foreclose on these emotions and prematurely
> forgive often gets many patients into trouble emotionally, as they must
> deny their feelings of hurt, disappointment, resentment, and anger over
> what they have suffered (p. 274).

Forgiveness from a Christian perspective is rooted in the Christian's
belief in God's immeasurable love for mankind, as demonstrated by the
forgiveness He has provided through Jesus Christ. Here the focus is on
God's forgiveness and love toward man as the motivator for forgiveness
and love for oneself and others. Of particular importance to therapeutic
work with counselees who are often laden with guilt and shame, is forgiveness as a manifestation of God's acceptance, compassion, understanding,
and love. Seibold (2001) captures this thought in this way:

> When we have been deeply wounded, someone has acted unlovingly
> toward us. The antidote is to be bathed in love until we are so filled up
> with love that we can begin to imagine letting some love flow out into

forgiveness. Forgiving must flow from love, and forgiving is a form of loving. When we are sufficiently full of love—love that we are receiving and love that we are giving—we will naturally be drawn to offer forgiveness. However, we start not by loving the offender, but by loving people and receiving love from people who will rebuild the broken self, people who are safe and trustworthy. There is no need to force love toward the offender or to will forgiveness. The love, and hence the forgiving, will come with time, gently, the way winter melts into spring. This love flows from the soul (p. 307).

For the counselee who is a Christian and yet feels disconnected, unloved, unwanted, shameful, and alone, understanding God's love and forgiveness provides a foundation of lasting and unchanging security, attachment, and identity that can be the basis of true and lasting recovery (Cooper, 2006; Cumella, 2002; Eberly & Cumella, 2003; Eberly, 2005; Wall, Eberly, & Cumella, 2005).

Much has been written on the topic of forgiveness in counseling (e.g., Al-Mabuk, Enright, & Cardis, 1995; Cheong et al., 2007; Freedman & Enright, 1996; Hebl & Enright, 1993; McCullough, Worthington, & Rachal, 1997; Sartor, 2003; Seibold, 2001; Worthington et al., 1996; Worthington, 1998), and we encourage you to explore this literature to help you best guide your counselees in the forgiveness process.

## COLLABORATION WITH RELIGIOUS LEADERS

One of the things we have emphasized throughout this text is the importance of collaborating with other professionals in providing ethical and effective care. We may consult with medical doctors, psychiatrists, and nutritionists to address the counselee's biological needs; psycho-diagnosticians, supervisors, and colleagues for the counselee's psychological needs; and family members, teachers, and friends for the counselee's social needs. Also, we can, and sometimes should, consult with the counselee's spiritual leaders to best facilitate spiritual health and goals.

When counselees' spiritual leaders are healthy people who are available to support them in recovery, a resource of caring, support, wisdom, guidance, and comfort can emerge as the therapist and the spiritual leader work together with the counselees (Hardman & Berrett, 2005; Richards et al., 1997). Additional relevant information about such collaboration can be found in Berrett, 2003; Evans, 2005; Gorsuch and Maylink, 1998; Sperry, 2003; Tan, 2003; Weaver, Koenig, and Larson, 1997; Weaver et al., 1997; and Winger and Hunsberger, 1988.

Involvement with a healthy religious community has also been shown to promote health and well-being (Arteburn & Felton, 2001; Berrett, 2003;

Eberly, 2005; Griffith & Griggs, 2001; Vorhees et al., 1996). Individuals with mental illness are often extremely isolated people. Counselors utilizing spiritual integration can promote involvement with their counselee's spiritual community once they are ready for healthy participation and connection.

Counselees who wish to participate in their spiritual community may need help moving from being extrinsically oriented, that is, concerned about outward appearance and pleasing others, to a more intrinsic orientation, which involves being more "internal, devout, service, and worship oriented" (Richards et al., 1997, p. 276). When ready, such involvement offers opportunities for healthy interpersonal experiences that can help counselees mature and more fully recover.

Figures 14.1 and 14.2 depict a step care approach and a decision tree for utilizing spiritual integration in counseling.

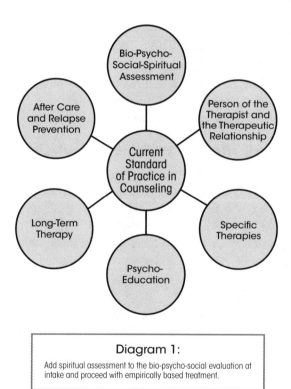

### Diagram 1:
Add spiritual assessment to the bio-psycho-social evaluation at intake and proceed with empirically based treatment.

Figure 14.1: Step Care Approach to Spiritual
Integration in Counseling

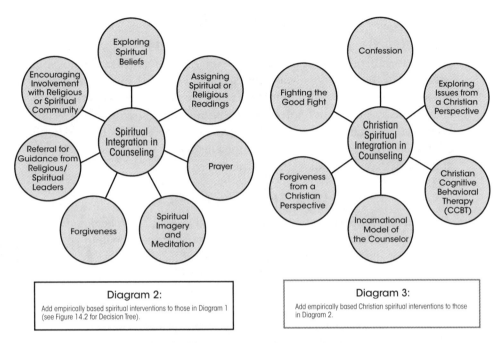

Diagram 2:
Add empirically based spiritual interventions to those in Diagram 1 (see Figure 14.2 for Decision Tree).

Diagram 3:
Add empirically based Christian spiritual interventions to those in Diagram 2.

Figure 14.1: Step Care Approach to Spiritual Integration in Counseling

Figure 14.1: Step Care Approach to Spiritual Integration in Counseling

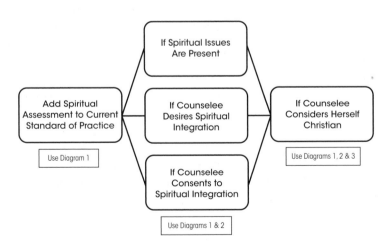

Figure 14.2: Spiritual Integration: Decison Tree

## CHAPTER SUMMARY

Only God has the power to heal counselees and bring them into bio-psycho-social-spiritual wholeness. This chap. explored the relationship between the psychological and the spiritual, focused on ethical issues related to spiritual integration in counseling, reviewed the skills related to spiritual assessment, and noted some spiritual integration tools. It is our hope that as you utilize empirically based interventions in your work with counselees, that you will not neglect the One who has the power, wisdom, and ability to make crooked paths straight.

## CHAPTER 14 ACTIVITIES

1. Find several Scriptures that speak to God as comforter, healer, refuge, deliverer, etc. Write these out and discuss what they mean to you personally and how they relate to your work as a counselor.
2. What do you want to remember from Eph 1:18–22 as you deal with your own brokenness and the brokenness of your counselees?
3. How does a person's attachment history, neurobiology, schemas, and coping behaviors relate to their experience of God?
4. Why is internal, abusive dialog with oneself often very difficult to extinguish?
5. Why do counselee symptoms and schemas make perfect sense in light of the bio-psycho-social-spiritual ramifications of early developmental experiences, trauma history, temperament, constitution, processing styles, and the elements of the fallen world with its influences from the world, the flesh, and the devil?
6. How do you plan to address the ethical issues related to integrating spirituality into your practice?
7. How might you assess a person's spirituality during your initial evaluation?
8. Create a spiritual life map on yourself. What did you learn from doing this project?
9. Write a personal letter to God. How did this activity impact you?
10. Describe three of the spiritual integration "tools" discussed in the chap. Which tools do you personally use in your life? Which ones do you think you will incorporate into your practice?

## Recommended Reading

McMinn, M. R. (1996). *Psychology, theology, and spirituality in Christian counseling*. Wheaton, IL: Tyndale House.

> We love the work of McMinn. This book is absolutely essential for Christian counselors. It covers the theoretical and practical aspects of prayer, confession, and the use of the Scriptures in counseling.

Worthington, E. (2006). *Forgiveness and reconciliation: Theory and application*. New York City,: NY: Routledge.

> As a prominent researcher, author, and speaker, Dr. Worthington shares his work on the nature of forgiveness and reconciliation, two highly relevant topics in the field of counseling. Based on his research and personal experience, Worthington helps practitioners apply theoretical concepts in a pragmatic way in order to promote change and healing.

# Professional Issues
# in Counseling

*"Christ is the One who holds the profession of Christian
counseling together, like a sun that holds otherwise chaotic
planets in a firm and stable gravitational grip. Christ
is the head of the practice and profession of Christian
counseling"* (Clinton & Ohlschlager, 2002a, p. 89).

*"Then I observed that most people are motivated to
success because they envy their neighbors. But this, too, is
meaningless—like chasing the wind"* (Eccl 4:4, NLT).

## CHAPTER OBJECTIVES

»   To place helping skills and techniques into a professional
    context

»   To define how professional counseling differs from other
    occupations

»   To discuss the difference between ethical guidelines and
    legal standards

»   To discuss the role of ethical and legal issues as they relate to
    skills and techniques

»   To relate ethics and legal issues to a biblical worldview

»   To discuss the importance of keeping clinical records with
    regard to the counselee and the counselor

»   To review the various types of documents that comprise a
    professional record

»   To offer professional guidelines for maintaining clinical
    records

»   To highlight the need to be culturally competent

» To relate diversity to a biblical worldview

» To encourage you to understand that you will always be a student

» To discuss the levels of professional counselor development

» To encourage you to strive to grow personally, in particular spiritually

## CHAPTER OUTLINE

PROFESSIONALISM

ETHICS AND LEGAL STANDARDS IN COUNSELING

RECORD-KEEPING IN THE COUNSELING PROCESS
  The Importance and Purposes of Record-Keeping
  The Kinds of Forms
  Guidelines for Record-Keeping

DIVERSITY IN COUNSELING

DEVELOPING AS A COUNSELOR
  The Process of Counselor Development
  The Benefits of Experience
  Commitment to Growing Professionally
  Commitment to Growing Personally and Spiritually

CHAPTER SUMMARY

CHAPTER 15 ACTIVITIES

Throughout this text we have described counseling as a journey. But counseling, unlike most expeditions has a beginning but no real end (Young, 2010). We have also emphasized the need to build your counseling on a biblical foundation and to view your work through a biblical worldview lens. The Word of God and the work of the Holy Spirit in the process are the ultimate factors in your counseling work and the penultimum in the counseling process is you. Chap. 3 ("The Hazards of Helping") and chap. 4 ("The Person of the Counselor") encouraged you to consider the personal role you play in the helping process. To help you develop competence in the knowledge and skills of your work we have discussed numerous aspects of the helping profession. We have laid out the necessary skills for being effective in addressing soul needs. This final chap. focuses on the professional aspect of the therapeutic journey.

## PROFESSIONALISM

In sports there are clear demarcations between amateur sports, semi-professional sports, and professional sports. Most participants of a sport have a desire to become pro; to make their living by the sport they love. But because of the demands of sports few will realize their dream.

Unlike the field of sports, becoming a professional in the helping profession is attainable for each one of you. Much as athletes begin playing their sport in backyards, streets, and neighborhood courts, you too likely began helping people in a social setting, dorm room, or over a cup of coffee. Somewhere along the way you made the decision to pursue the helping profession full-time. You desired to learn the most effective ways to engage and help solve human problems. As a student seeking a degree in counseling, you are preparing yourself for your chosen profession just as student athletes ready themselves to be selected into the professional ranks. If you stay focused and determined, eventually you will obtain your degree and enter into the society of professional counselors.

Bernard and Goodyear (2004) highlight three distinctives of professional helpers from those who work in other occupations. They state that professional counselors (a) have significantly more autonomy than those in other occupations, (b) are required to make judgments under conditions of uncertainty, and (c) rely on a knowledge base that is sufficiently unique and specialized.

Though the bottom line of professionalism is receiving tangible reward for your labor, it is more than having a paying job in the field. It is more than wearing a uniform or suit and joining a professional organization. It is more than serving your counselee. Although pay, dress, memberships, and serving are aspects of professionalism, they are but the expression of it. Professionalism is how you "carry" yourself; it is an expression of your inner self. Professionalism is seen in how you approach your work, counselees colleagues, employer, customers, and community. It is your character as expressed in all aspects of your helping. Professionalism arises from inside of you. The point is not to *act* like a professional, but to *be* a professional.

## ETHICS AND LEGAL STANDARDS IN COUNSELING

Ethical and legal standards play an important role in the helping profession. Ethical and legal issues are gaining a higher prominence in the professional literature (Bernard & Goodyear, 2004). Even though ethical and legal issues are often linked together, each serves a unique purpose. Ethical issues are related to professional conduct, and ethical codes are a means of regulating conduct. The existence of and adherence to a code of ethics is a distinguishing characteristic of professionalism (Corey, Corey, & Callanan, 2007; Ponton & Duba, 2009). According to Clinton and Ohlschlager (2002a), "a code of ethics is a systematic statement of ethical standards that represent the moral convictions and guide the practice behavior of" (p. 245) counselors. Ethical codes are a call to excellence in counseling activities.

Legal standards, on the other hand, are introduced when a particular act or series of acts has been determined to have endangered or harmed those whom the profession serves (Bernard & Goodyear, 2004). The law is not aimed at producing excellence, but in holding people to minimal standards of practice. For a counselor to be considered liable of violating a particular legal standard, the implied allegation is that the counselor has acted outside the realm of accepted practice. Ethical codes are often used by the legal system to determine if the professional had a duty to the counselee and if that duty was not met in some manner.

At the most basic level both ethical and legal standards are protective mechanisms. Simply put, the ultimate aim of ethical codes and legal standards is to ensure that the person you are helping is not harmed in the process (Corey, Corey, & Calanan, 2007). Ponton and Duba (2009) point out that professions are inextricably linked to society, and ethical standards are the implicit and explicit understanding of the relationship that exists between a profession and society. Ponton and Duba speak of professional ethics as a covenant, a concept that should resonate with those who ascribe to a biblical worldview. The welfare of society in general and counselees in particular are placed above the welfare of the counselors. The fact that the counselee needs the counselor more and the counselor has permission to comment on the counselee gives the counselee less power. As such, the counselee is more vulnerable to being exploited. From a legal standpoint, because trust is placed in the counselor to serve a counselee's best interests, the legal system regards counseling as a contract (Corey, Corey, & Callanan, 2007). Technically speaking, the counseling relationship is viewed as a "fiduciary" relationship, because the power is entrusted for the benefit of the counselee.

One of the means by which professions self-regulate is through the establishment of a professional code of ethics, which provides a common standard, minimizes interpersonal strife, protects the profession from legal intrusion, and guides professionals through common pitfalls of practice (Ponton & Duba, 2009).

Biblically speaking you are a steward of your counselee's well-being (cf. Heb 13:1–3). How you treat your counselee is a reflection of your faith. For the Christian counselor the desire to be ethical and legal in practice should be a byproduct of our personal relationship with Jesus Christ. Because of our relationship with Christ, we look to the Bible to find direction on how to live as virtuous people; our morals are rooted in the absolute standard of the Word of God. Clinton and Ohlschlager (2002a) discuss seven virtues that are basic to ethical behavior: (a) accountability to truth-telling, (b) responsibility to love one another, (c) fidelity to integrity, (d) trustworthiness in keeping confidentiality, (e) competent beneficence, (f) humility in justice, and (g) sufferability. Chap. 11 in Clinton and Ohlschlager's (2002a) book *Competent Christian counseling* has a more thorough examination of ethics from a biblical worldview perspective.

Our ethical practice is to be an expression of our personal relationship with Christ and the absolutes found in the Bible. But also our ethical behavior is linked to the One whose image we bear. God never has to urge Himself to be good, because He is good (Erickson, 2001). His nature is always inclined irresistibly toward righteous living. God is a God of truth (Exod 34:6; Ps 31:5; Isa 65:16), who is committed to our well-being (Pss 48:9; 51:1; John 3:16; Rom 5:8; 6:22; 2 Cor 4:15; Eph 2:4), and who has no intention to harm us (Gen 50:20; Deut 7:12; Rom 8:28). Because God is virtuous, we are to be virtuous. Our ethical practice must proceed from the very character and nature of God. For Christian counselors adherence to ethical and legal standards is a *spiritual* issue.

At times counselors commit ethical and legal violations out of ignorance. Whether a "sin" of commission or omission, an act of ignorance still puts you in jeopardy of having your license or practice sanctioned, or your being sued for malpractice, and worst of all, your seriously wounding those you have been called to help. You are responsible to be fully acquainted with the code of ethics of each organization to which you belong. Two major ethical standards are included in Appendixes A and B: the American Counseling Association's Code of Ethics (ACA, 2005) and the American Association of Christian Counselors' Code of Ethics (AACC, 2001). When counselors are members of multiple organizations, the possibility exists that at some point the code of ethics of one organization might conflict with that of another organization. In such cases adhere to the one with the highest standard. Remember that ethical codes are guiding principles, and so they cannot give specific directions for dealing with all ethical and legal quandaries. The more familiar you are with the codes, however, the more likely you will be able to make wise decisions. A wise move is to have a lawyer on retainer who is familiar with laws relating to the mental-health profession. An informed attorney can save you much time, grief, and even money.

Professional codes and legal standards for counseling recognize that counselees have rights that must be safeguarded in order for them to receive the maximum benefit from our services. In other words if you fail to meet an ethical standard, the counselee's rights are violated. As a Christian, when you fail to live up to ethical and legal mandates, you have violated the law of love (cf. Matt 5:38–44; 22:35–40; 1 John 3:17–18) and bear the added guilt of tarnishing the name of Christ.

Counselors are responsible to know what is required and what is forbidden. Thus familiarize yourself with the laws of your state since each has its own laws, policies, and protocol related to such clinical issues as involuntary commitment. As the saying goes, "There is no excuse for ignorance of the law," and, we would add, "for ignorance of the ethical code."

## RECORD-KEEPING IN THE COUNSELING PROCESS

Since counselors focus on people, the idea of completing paperwork does not excite many in the helping professions. Yet the maintenance of counselee records is the mark of a professional. In fact it is an ethical responsibility to keep adequate records of your professional services to your counselees, and it has become a standard of care (Moline, Williams, & Austin, 1998) and a wise defense against litigation (Brantley, 2000).

A professional counselee record or case record should provide an accurate and clear record of the counselee. Luepker and Norton (2003) state that a record "contains a series of sketches that depict moments in time as well as historical processes, such as counselees' history, needs, and the work they engage in during treatment to solve their problems" (p. 16). Although some counselors do not keep any records out of fear of having them subpoenaed, most counselors keep records for different purposes. Some counselors tape record their notes with their perceptions, hunches, and reactions that might be misleading if they were read (Earle & Barnes, 1999). Other counselors choose to maintain their records on computer, and others file written notes.

Many counselors in the helping profession have said, "If it is not documented, it did not happen." Record-keeping will either help you or hurt you. It will either protect you or convict you (Brantley, 2000; Munson, 2002). Failure to keep records might hurt you and convict you in court proceedings.

## The Importance and Purposes of Record-Keeping

Maintaining appropriate records is consistent with ethical codes and legal standards for counseling (Mitchell, 2000). Though you may not like keeping records, you simply must do it.

Record-keeping is also mandatory if you will be working in a setting that bills a third party for counselee services such as Medicaid, Medicare, or an insurance carrier. The government agencies and insurance agencies often have their own forms, requirements, and penalties if counselors do not maintain proper records accordingly.

Beyond the obligation, however, record-keeping serves a valuable role in serving the counselee. If multiple service providers (e.g., other counselors, physicians, psychiatrists, or lawyers) are involved in assisting the counselee, record-keeping enhances the communication between them. Also, record-keeping can better facilitate the possibility of continuity of care. Records provide a history and current status of the counselee in the event that another professional needs to work with the counselee. For example if you end up leaving your work setting or if you need to pass the counselee onto another counselor, the case record facilitates others in knowing where you have been with the counselee and where you were going.

Although record-keeping clearly benefits the counselee, it can also benefit the counselor in several critical ways (Mitchell, 2000). What is included in the counselee's records can form the basis of assessing, diagnosing, and treating the counselee. The case record can help you plan and implement an appropriate course of services, help you monitor your work, and remind you of what has transpired in previous sessions, especially if there has been a significant lapse of time between sessions. As already noted, well-documented records might also protect you from professional liability, if you become the subject of legal or ethical proceedings. In malpractice suits good record-keeping can serve as credible evidence of responsible conduct.

A realistic concern for many practitioners is the possibility that a counselee record will be required to be disclosed against the wishes of the counselee or the counselor. Further, the record might be open to people unqualified and ill-equipped to interpret the records. I (John) have had to release records to members of a union who would then be privy to intimate details of the counselee. One piece of legislation that has impacted the helping professions is the Health Insurance Portability and Accountability Act (HIPAA). Among other things, HIPAA established a privacy rule that considers all health-care information as confidential and regulates the disclosure of it. Known as Protected Health Information (PHI), a counselee's health-care information must be guarded and not be released without the counselee's consent. The act has raised the level of consciousness of helping professionals in their record-keeping and billing practices. HIPAA, however, does not prevent a record from being subpoenaed or keep the counselee from requesting that you give it to another party. Actually no record is exempt from disclosure, and your maintaining records should bear that fact in mind at all times.

## The Kinds of Forms

No standard exists for a counselee record. Agencies and practitioners generally develop their own set of guidelines or practices. What is actually contained in a case record can vary significantly. For that reason, you can only offer the following pieces of information as worthy considerations for your case records. The actual number of forms may vary depending on the counselor or agency who organizes the information.

### Intake form.

Everyone has been to see a medical health professional who has required a form to be completed before the visit. In counseling that form is what we refer to as the intake form, which can record the counselee's demographic information, emergency contact information, general concerns, and any number of other items. Appendix C includes an intake form we have used in our own work. Most agencies have their own intake form that will be maintained in the counselee's case record. As services are delivered over a period of time, it is occasionally helpful to ask the counselee to review the contact information for any changes that might have occurred since the initial form was completed.

### Informed consent form.

People have a right to know what they are getting into when they come for counseling. Informing counselees of what to expect in counseling is part of the role induction process that we wrote about in chap. 2 ("The Fundamentals of Helping") along with the types of information included in an informed consent. Informed consent is probably one of the most central ethical and legal processes in counseling because it refers to providing access to knowledge that can help a counselee make a prudent choice. Counseling is a voluntary relationship in which the counselee has the freedom to choose whether he wishes to begin or continue with the services. Even counselees who are considered "involuntary" choose to come to counseling in order to avoid a more adverse consequence.

An informed consent form is a practical means of honoring the more abstract principles of the rights and dignity of the counselee. It is a way to ensure that the counselee's welfare is of utmost importance in your work. It safeguards a counselee's autonomy or right to choose. This form can help you protect your counselees' dignity, well-being, and free will.

To be sure the counselee is well informed, informed consent is generally given in writing before the first visit, and verbally at the beginning of the first session, and as needed throughout the services. In other words informed consent is an ongoing practice throughout the helping process. The written form is sometimes called a disclosure statement; it begins the role induction process. Counselees are typically required to sign the disclosure statement in order to meet with the counselor. We have included a sample disclosure statement or written informed consent form in Appendix D, and one that can be used when recording your sessions in Appendix E.

At the beginning of your first session with a counselee you will also need to attain verbal informed consent on particular issues that you want to highlight. In chap. 9 ("Managing the Counseling Session") we referred to this dialogue as an ethical introduction.

The ACA Code of Ethics (2005) details the elements of an ethically sound consent in Standard A.2.b (see Appendix A). Although the ethical codes specify pieces of information that must be included, we believe that additional disclosure statements are important to successful counseling. An ideal informed consent should include but not be limited to the following items of information: (a) the nature of counseling; (b) the goals and purposes of particular techniques and procedures; (c) the fact that counseling is voluntary and the counselee has the right to refuse or terminate services; (d) the fact that counselee involvement is expected for it to be successful; (e) your credentials, qualifications, role, obligations, and level of involvement in the process; (f) confidentiality and its exceptions; (g) your counseling approach described in lay language; (h) financial requirements including fees, insurance billing, co-pays, how unpaid balances are handled; (i) your cancellation policy; (j) what happens with the counselee's record following termination of services; (k) how emergencies are handled such as the counselor being unavailable through death or injury or the counselee being in a state of crisis between sessions; (l) logistics of counseling such as length and frequency of sessions; (m) alternatives to counseling such as support groups and medicine and alternatives to particular techniques or strategies; (n) the determined diagnosis in simple language, (o) the intended use of tests and reports, (p) what the counselee should do if dissatisfied with your services; and (q) obtaining permission to make a visual or audio recording of the session and/or permission that the session(s) will be shared with a supervisor or consultant. Clearly the counselee needs much information in order to make the best use of your services.

In their book *Issues and ethics in the helping professions* Corey and associates (2007) do an excellent job of covering all aspects of informed consent.

### Counseling authorization form.

The counseling authorization form requires that the counselee provide consent for you to offer your services. It generally includes items such as the nature of counseling, your background and credentials, your approach to counseling, the fact that your help is fee for service, and the like. An example of a counseling authorization form is in Appendix F.

### Emergency instructions form.

An emergency instructions form specifies whom the counselee should contact in case of an emergency, each contact's phone numbers, and what to do if they cannot reach the contacts. A separate emergency instructions form might not be ethically or legally required, but we value its inclusion in the file for two reasons. First, it provides the emergency contact information on one sheet for the counselee to quickly obtain the necessary protocol. Second, it can protect you in case of liability. We make a copy of the signed form; the original is placed in the counselee file and the copy is given to the counselee. Having a signed original form that verifies you have educated the counselee on your emergency protocol gives you protection in case of a suit for malpractice.

### Release-of-information form.

If a counselee has been referred to you from another source such as a pastor, physician, lawyer, teacher, employer, parent, probation officer, or some other person, you might need to have the counselee sign a form that permits you to break confidentiality. What you share with the third party depends on what is needed and specified in the actual release form. As a rule, the disclosed information should be as limited as possible. Often it suffices to inform the party that the counselee is keeping appointments, participating in the session, and is making progress. Other times what is released might include a more detailed account of what is being discussed in the counseling services. A sample release form is in Appendix G.

### Progress notes and process notes.

Note-taking is nothing more than writing down what happens in the counseling session and the counselee's progress toward the treatment goals.

Counselors should document information about what occurred in the session, the types of help offered, reasons for your professional decisions and actions, and mutually agreed-on goals (Soisson, VandeCreek, & Knapp, 1987).

In discussing note-taking Corey and associates (2007) distinguish between progress notes and process notes. They define progress notes as behavioral in nature and addressing what is said and done. Progress notes include diagnosis, functional states, symptoms, treatment plan, consequences, alternative treatments, and counselee progress. Progress notes, which are required by law to be included in the counselee record, deal with "counselee reactions such as transference and the therapist's subjective impressions of a counselee . . . intimate details about the counselee; details of dreams or fantasies; sensitive information about a counselee's personal life; and a therapist's own thoughts, feelings, and reactions to counselees" (p. 169).

Process notes, on the other hand, are for the practitioner; they exclude items such as diagnosis and symptoms found in the progress notes. This set of notes does not need to be included in the main file (Corey, Corey, & Callahan, 2007). The focus is on writing progress notes, though having process notes at your disposal, especially when working with challenging counselees, is often wise.

Two frequently asked questions about note-taking are these: (a) "Should I take notes during the session?" and (b) "How should I keep notes?"

*"Should I take notes during the session?"* In our counseling careers we have taken notes during sessions and also have waited until after the session to write our notes. If you do take notes during the session, you will still need to write formal notes following the session. You simply cannot take time to write the notes well enough while you are connecting with the counselee. It is helpful to develop a shorthand with abbreviations and symbols that allow you to maintain appropriate attending skills (SOLER as in chap. 5) while documenting the session. These notes are not the final copy to be maintained in the counselee's case record, but these notes can help you create a more accurate representation of the session, especially if you are not able to write your notes following the session. During your practicum and internship you might try to wait until after the session before taking notes. You will likely be recording those sessions and will not be required to recall the session. We have noticed that beginning counselors tend to focus too much on their note-taking during the session, which diminishes rapport.

*"How should I keep notes?"* Typically your notes should be written in narrative form. The most widely used system of writing notes is referred to as **SOAP** notes (see Table 15.1). In the progress notes each aspect of SOAP is addressed in either separate paragraphs or as one large paragraph. The

"S" in the acrostic stands for **Subjective**, which addresses the counselee's current condition. This subjective aspect of the notes is from the counselee's point of view. You might write how the counselee presented herself in the session (e.g., emotions, thoughts, behavior, concerns, symptoms), the counselee's reported symptoms, history of the symptoms or problem, your reaction to the counselee, and issues related to the counseling relationship. It is appropriate to quote the counselee if you want to highlight the way the counselee phrased something. Remember that this section should not include your interpretation of the counselee or counselee's situation.

| Table 15.1 |
| --- |
| *SOAP Notes: Structure for Note-Taking* |
| **S** = **Subjective**, which are things from the counselee's point of view |
| **O** = **Objective**, which are things related to your observation; factual |
| **A** = **Assessment**, which pulls together the information from S and O |
| **P** = **Plan**, which captures your future intentions |

The "O" stands for **Objective**, which includes specific and factual information on the counselee's behavior and progress and about the session itself. This section focuses on your professional observations. Note various aspects of the MSE, such as hygiene, posture, eye contact, appearance, manner of speaking, expressions, and mood states. Include the strategies or approach you used during the session. Mention what you said in the session and what the counselee said or did. As in the subjective section you should not include your interpretations in this section. The section is focused strictly on objective findings.

The "A" for **Assessment** provides a synthesis of the material you obtained in the subjective and objective sections. In this section you form hypotheses and interpretations. You note skills that the counselee has developed, new insights, and the counselee's overall progress toward the treatment goals. The assessment section also provides a quick summary of the counselee's issues including the diagnosis. This is a good place to write out issues that have not yet been noted. For example if you assess that the counselee has suicidal or hostile intentions, record whether the counselee endorsed or denied having harmful intentions. Documenting specific items such as these can protect you in the event of legal proceedings.

The "P" is to include your **Plan** on how you intend to help the counselee. This addresses the issues noted in the assessment section. Also include in this section the homework assignments you give the counselee, what you plan to address or do in the next session, potential referrals that need to be made, the frequency of contacts with the counselee, and when you plan to see the counselee next. Two sample SOAP notes are included in Tables 15.2 and 15.3.

---

Table 15.2

*Sample 1 SOAP Notes*

**September 15, 2011 10 a.m.**

(S) Client reports that he does not believe that counseling will help him to "get his wife back," but argues that he will do what is necessary. He contends that he has done everything possible to show her that he has changed. Client revealed six symptoms of depression and six symptoms of PTSD. Client reports a history of domestic violence, but denies any physical aggression since their separation. Client reports being placed in six different foster care placements between the ages of 5 to 18.

(O) Client vacillated by agitation and tearfulness. Client seemed guarded, but was cooperative.

(A) Major depression, post-traumatic stress disorder, ruled out borderline personality disorder, narcissistic personality disorder.

(P) Client will make appointment with psychiatrist Dr. David Smith to be evaluated for medication. Recommended clinic's male violence group. Scheduled appointment for 9/20/2011.

---

Table 15.3

*Sample 2 SOAP Notes*

**October 14, 2011 2 p.m.**

(S) Client reported not doing recommended homework assignment from previous session. Client reported feeling hopeless about change; stated, "I just can't please my parents no matter what I do." Client changed the subject when asked about anger toward her mother. Client denied any suicidal ideation, homicidal ideation, self-destructive behavior, or desire to run away.

(O) Client was dressed casually and age appropriate. Hygiene and grooming were normal. Displayed both sad and angry emotions. Client talked slowly and softly with infrequent pauses. Client raised her voice when discussing parental expectations and avoided eye contact with counselor during this discussion.

(A) Client endorsed four symptoms of depression; appears mildly depressed. Client seems to be threatened by suggestion that she might feel anger toward her parents.

(P) Helped client connect emotions to feelings of abandonment. Explored hostile dependency on parents. Continue to monitor suicidal tendencies, aggression, self-destruction, and desires to escape.

### Testing reports and professional evaluation reports.

At times counselors give tests or receive them from other mental-health providers. All tests, regardless of who administered them, should be included in the record. Sometimes counselors receive reports or letters from professional colleagues such as a physician, psychiatrist, minister, teacher, or employer. These reports and letters should also be included in the file.

If the counselee record is subpoenaed or if you are asked to make a copy of the record, however, you would send only test reports that you personally have written. Any reports or correspondence received from another source would not be copied and mailed. It is the responsibility of the party wanting a copy to obtain those pieces of information from the originator.

### Financial form.

The financial form includes the counselee's insurance information and authorization to bill a third party. It informs the counselee of the consequences of failing to pay balances and authorizes release of information to the billing party. Most practitioners make a copy of the counselee's insurance card in order to document the point that insurance exists. Many practitioners keep their counselees' financial balances and payments on their computer, and do not keep hard copies in the case file. An example is included in Appendix H.

### Contact sheet.

We recommend that you consider keeping a contact sheet in your records. This is to record each contact and attempted contact with a counselee. Include the type of contact, the date of the contact, the time (including the beginning and ending time), and a one- or two-sentence summary of what transpired. This contact sheet can help you in resolving conflicts on billing, and gives you documentation of contacts with a counselee in case your records are disclosed in court.

A case record on a counselee can be constructed in a number of ways. During your practicum and internship pay attention to what you like about an agency's or facility's record-keeping procedures. Ask more seasoned colleagues how they keep records; determine what works best for them and what they have learned through their years of experience.

## Guidelines for Record-Keeping

This section includes guidelines to assist you in becoming proficient in creating and maintaining records. The acrostic **RECORDS** (see Table 15.4) outlines seven guidelines for this skill.

Table 15.4

*RECORDS: Guidelines for Record-Keeping*

**R** = do not let your record-keeping interfere with your **Rapport**

**E** = **Ensure** that the records are protected

**C** = document; the **Court** might subpoena them or the **Counselee** may want to view them

**O** = be **Open** about your records and notes

**R** = **Record** what is necessary and prudent

**D** = if in **Doubt Document**

**S** = develop a consistent **Structure** to write your notes

The question of whether you should take notes in the sessions is a highly personal one. Some practitioners believe that it interferes with their ability to attend to the counselee while others find it useful in documenting accurately what occurred and recalling the events and nuances of the session. The main guideline to keep in mind is to not allow anything to diminish your **Rapport** ("R") with the counselee. In addition do not allow the flow of the session to become hindered by your record-keeping practices. As you gain experience in working with counselees, you will develop and refine your record-keeping and note-taking procedures that fit your personal preferences, setting, and needs.

The "E" stands for the importance of **Ensuring** that your records are kept in a secure location and that only authorized persons have access to them. If you leave your office, do not leave your records or notes on your desk. And do not take a file out of the office because this opens up the possibility that you might accidently leave it somewhere. The counselee and his file are your responsibility; you are the steward of them and no one should have more concern over their handling than yourself.

The "C" means that your records should be kept in view of the possibility that they could be subpoenaed by the **Court** or viewed by the **Counselee**. Document what occurs in the counseling process with the idea that you and your records might be examined or cross-examined during legal proceedings. Do not record anything that you do not want to be revealed in court or for the counselee to view.

The letter "O" refers to being **Open** about your records and your taking of notes. Explain the purposes of your records and note-taking. Do not be secretive about what you are writing in your notes. If a counselee wants to see what is in your notes, explore their request and show it to them.

The "R" stands for **Recording** what is necessary and prudent. Your record, especially your notes, is a legal document. You might wonder if it is possible to document too much. The answer is yes. Be sensible and honor your institutional guidelines, but consider if what is in the record could hurt your counselee. Some information might be misleading if the person does not have the context in which to make sense of it. Choose your wording carefully and consider how someone else might interpret what you have written. By all means be honest, but follow the simple rule to not record more than is necessary.

The "D" is to remind you that if you are in **Doubt, Document**. If you are unsure whether you should write it down, it is generally best to record it. As the popular saying goes, It is better to be safe than sorry.

The "S" is to develop a **Structure** for writing your progress notes. Although a number of different structures exist, the most widely used structure, as noted earlier, especially for medical professionals is referred to as SOAP.

Technology has changed the way mental-health practitioners keep their records. Many helpers maintain electronic notes, bill insurance companies electronically, and use computer software for treatment planning. As in maintaining records in a file cabinet, ensure the privacy of electronic ecords and keep a backup in case of technology problems.

## DIVERSITY IN COUNSELING

The United States is becoming more and more diverse by the decade (Erwin, Huang, & Lin, 2002). Given the diversity of the population, it is impossible to engage in the work of counseling without dealing with cross-cultural issues. In fact Bergin and Jensen (1990) carry the idea of cross-cultural counseling further by advocating that every relationship between a counselor and counselee is a cross-cultural experience. In other words in one sense all counseling is multicultural in nature (Speight, Myers, Cox, & Highlen, 1991).

Although the populations that counselors confront are becoming more diverse, many counselors have failed to respond to the need to become culturally competent. In fact May and Albee (1992) propose that counselors are culturally insensitive. Emphasis on the importance of sensitivity to the cultural, ethnic, and diversity background of counselees is well supported in the professional literature, in continuing education programs, in professional ethical codes, and in counselor education accreditation standards (Chandras, Eddy, & Spaulding, 2000).

Counseling without respect for differences of diversity will likely fail (Erwin, Huang, & Lin, 2002; McKenzie, 1986; Romero, 1985; Sue, 1998; Sue & Zane, 1987). Sue (1998) contends that counselors should be multiculturally competent by developing cultural skills. To assist with that need, Ivey and Ivey (2003) developed a model to teach counseling skills and techniques that are rooted in multicultural awareness.

The apostle Paul recognized how vital it is to be able to respond to diversity of needs. "I have become all things to all men so that by all possible means I might save some" (1 Cor 9:22, NIV). Paul's outlook that embraced diversity was influenced by a heart that was passionate about seeing people come to Christ. He was willing to remove any unnecessary impediment to the gospel and was committed to breaking down cultural barriers. Counselors should have the same outlook and passion.

Five key skill-based areas relate to being culturally competent. First, in order to be effective with diverse populations, have personal awareness (McKenzie, 1986). Understand your own cultural heritage and worldview before you seek to understand other cultures (Speight, Myers, Cox, & Highlen, 1991). Each person has his own philosophy of life, his own prejudices and biases. Begin the process of becoming culturally competent by recognizing that your frames of reference are based on your own backgrounds. Acknowledge your own tendencies, the way you perceive other cultures, and how your own experience limits your ability to comprehend other cultures.

Second, develop personal characteristics that allow for working with diverse populations. Unless you value and respect people who are different from you in characteristics, behaviors, and beliefs, you will not be able to express empathy. The point is that effective counselors are tolerant. Clearly the word *tolerant* has been abused and used as a bludgeon against conservative Christians. Tolerance is less of a problem when one considers people's characteristics and behaviors, that is, the fact that people look different and are different. Cultural customs, rituals, and ethnic appearances are neither good or bad nor right or wrong (LaFromboise, 1985). They are simply a reflection of the groups' preferences and traditions. Tolerance does not mean accepting other beliefs as having equal value or being equally true; tolerance is recognizing peoples' right to those beliefs.

In no way do we wish to diminish the centrality of truth or underline the value of accurate doctrine. At the same time, however, Christian counselors will encounter nonbelievers in the course of their work; thus counselors need to be *religiously sensitive*, and to be able to work with people of different faiths. Counselors need to be aware that each counselee uniquely integrates a religious and spiritual perspective into a life worldview. Christian counselors need to realize that not every counselee wants a Christian approach. Moreover, many counselees who desire a Christian approach to counseling would not necessarily be in agreement with the counselor on issues relevant to therapy. Richards and Bergin (1997) discuss the importance of adopting one's approach to people who are from different religious orientations or even from different denominations. Though you cannot adopt another person's ethnicity and cultural heritage, it is possible to develop a cultural sensitivity to counselee expectations, attributions, values, roles, beliefs, and themes of coping (LaFromboise, 1985).

Third, develop knowledge and understanding of other cultures. Lack of understanding may hinder effective intervention (McKenzie, 1986). In fact historically cultural differences have been viewed as deficits (Romero, 1985). How much knowledge you have about other cultures is vital in thinking culturally. Sue and Zane (1987) wrote that:

> The most important explanation for the problem in the services delivery involves the inability of therapists to provide culturally responsive forms of treatment. The assumption, and a good one, is that most therapists are not familiar with the cultural background and styles of the various ethnic-minority groups and have received training primarily developed for Anglo, or mainstream, Americans (p. 37).

Become knowledgeable about people from diverse backgrounds. What is considered accepted in one culture might be viewed as rude in another. Erwin, Huang, and Lin (2002) offer Christian counselors specific guidelines for counseling people of diverse backgrounds.

Fourth, seek to understand and express your awareness of diverse populations. The ability to understand another requires each of the three previous skill areas (i.e., self-awareness, personal characteristics that allow for connecting with diverse people groups, and cultural knowledge). In chap. 5 ("Basic Skills: Creating a Connection") we examined how a safe haven can be created and how a working relationship with a counselee can be established. Empathy requires the ability to see the world through the eyes of another; the more diverse the other person, the greater the energy required to establish a connection.

Fifth, counselors need to use approaches and techniques that fit the presumed characteristics of counselees (Sue & Sue, 1990). Every theory and every technique has its own inherent cultural biases. For example if you are working with a young Asian, it would be inappropriate to suggest that he be assertive with his parents. To do so in that culture is simply not appropriate. You would need to collaborate with your counselee to determine the best method or approach to working with his family issues without violating cultural norms.

Although it is impossible for you to divest yourself of your background, it is still possible to have self-awareness, to avoid stereotyping and false expectations by having knowledge of cultures, and to develop the skills to understand people who are different. Increase your cultural sensitivity and cultural competence and seek to use counseling methods that suit each counselee's needs.

## DEVELOPING AS A COUNSELOR

Becoming a professional counselor is a lifelong process (Gladding, 2002; Skovholt & Ronnestad, 1992). Clinton, Hart, and Ohlschlager (2005) believe that counselors should be diligent about their level of competence, ability, stability, and spirituality, to name a few.

### The Process of Counselor Development

A number of theorists have developed models to explain the process of counselor development (Blocher, 1983; Daniels, Rigazio-Digilio, & Ivey, 1997; Littrell, Lee-Borden, & Lorenz; 1979; Loganbill, Hardy, & Delworth, 1982; Rodenhauser, 1994; Ronnestad & Skovholt, 2003; Stoltenberg & Delworth, 1987; Watkins, 1995). Counselors grow through developmental levels as they progress toward greater expertise in their work. The acrostic "ASK" suggests the counselor's development along the continuum of (a) awareness, (b) skill, and (c) knowledge.

Stoltenberg, McNeill, and Delworth (1998) suggest that counselor development should occur in three areas: (a) self-awareness and "other awareness," which addresses the counselor's self-preoccupation, awareness of the counselee's world, and self-awareness; (b) motivation, which relates to the counselor's interests, investment, and effort in pursuing excellence; and (c) autonomy, which reflects the counselor's degree of independence.

Stoltenberg, McNeill, and Delworth (1998) suggest that counselor development occurs in four stages. Level one is characterized by high motivation, high anxiety, commitment to learning how to correctly apply skills, higher dependency on supervision, the need for positive feedback, less likelihood to confront counselees, a high level of self-focus, limited self-awareness, and apprehension about being evaluated. Counselors at level one tend to be characterized by black-and-white thinking and broad, somewhat simplistic understanding of counselees. The counselor's thinking and behavior might be fairly rigid.

The second level involves making transitions on issues associated with the three major areas of development. First, the counselee may fluctuate between depending on supervision to showing more autonomy and independence. The counselor might alternate between feeling confident and assured to feeling unconfident and confused. Positively he may tend to show a greater ability to empathize; yet the possibility of enmeshment is sometimes evident. The ability to conceptualize each counselee's unique issues is developing, as is the counselor's ability to be flexible. In this second level the counselor is showing greater confidence and more self-awareness.

At level three he focuses on developing a personal approach to helping. Motivation seems to be more consistent. The counselor is developing a solid belief in his professional judgment. Awareness is also high, as he gravitates toward self-focus in observing his role in the helping process.

Level four is characterized by an integration of all aspects of the helping process across the three major domains. At this level the counselor is enjoying working with a greater diversity of counselees and is increasingly comfortable with more difficult cases. He has a greater ability to understand and analyze counselees in a more robust manner. And he tends to be more creative in his interventions and employs more clinically sound strategies.

Bernard and Goodyear (2004) point out that the developmental process may not be consistent in all stages of the therapeutic process. In other words you might master some aspects of the helping process while still faltering with others.

You might be thinking that you will never arrive at level three, let alone level four. Commitment, dedication to excellence, and time will bring you to greater levels of development. The pace at which you proceed through the four stages might depend on a number of factors; but regardless of your pace be patient. The greatest level of growth still awaits you. In fact some evidence indicates that counselors grow more after their formal education (Skovholt and Ronnestad, 1992). Be assured that your counselees will survive your limitations and inadequacies.

## The Benefits of Experience

Of course nothing can replace experience. The more you counsel, the more you can learn and develop into an effective helper. As you work, you will come to the place where certain skills are second nature. You will learn how to differentiate among and manipulate a wide range and large number of important facts and casual factors. In time you will develop clearer hypotheses about what might be going on with a counselee. Your ability to integrate and synthesize your knowledge and experience will help you arrive at a more accurate picture of the psychological and spiritual realities inside your counselees.

Do not assume that other counselors never doubt what they are doing. Even the most seasoned counselors face roadblocks in their counseling. You will never develop into a "super counselor" who can leap toward counselee problems in a single bound and who is faster than even managed care demands. Growth as a counselor, like growth in life, is a process. Experience can take you far, but it can never make you perfect. Simply accept the fact that you can become a better counselor next year and even a better one in five years.

As you grow personally, psychologically, and spiritually, and through your counseling experience, you will come to see things in your counseling that you previously missed. You will also learn how to work with multiple perspectives. Regardless of people's worldviews, problems, or sins you will develop the ability to be empathic. We have all had certain kinds of counselees with whom we struggled. Whether the person had been arrested for a sexual offense, or abused substances, or was court-ordered, or had a differing sexual orientation, or posed a challenge to us in another way, we learned that we could grow into helping. Our Redeemer, Jesus Christ, ministered to all kinds of people with a kaleidoscope of problems. His ministry was not limited by His perception of the person. He adapted Himself to minister to each one in a way that fit his or her unique needs and circumstances.

Our limitations to helping people often stem from within us, not in the counselee. Our limitations might result from our lack of training in a particular area or with a specific population. Or perhaps our limitations will arise out of our own unresolved issues or present circumstances. As we allow God to do His work in us, as we stay true to Him and our calling, and as we allow God to work through us, the possibilities of helping people are exciting.

## Commitment to Growing Professionally

To be truly equipped to counsel, counselors need to be knowledgeable about a wide range of topics and issues (Clinton, Hart, & Ohlschlager, 2005). Become educated toward understanding the issues that are prevalent in society today, how to view them from a biblical worldview, and how to address those issues. You can never know everything, however, and we can never know enough. Fresh insights and new knowledge always await us.

Unless you have a good deal of experience in counseling, when you finish with your degree you are still a learner. A counseling degree gives you knowledge, but you have not learned all you need to know. Professional organizations and state legislative bodies often require that members or licensees obtain ongoing education, known as continuing education units (CEUs). Staying up to date in our field is not an easy task, given the amount of information and knowledge being generated today. Do not choose trainings that reinforce what you already think or know. Instead make choices that will expand your knowledge base and help you develop expertise in other areas.

Another means of developing as a counselor is to obtain supervision or request a consultation from a colleague. Supervision is typically an ongoing relationship in which a more seasoned professional person helps a less-experienced learner improve (Bernard & Goodyear, 2004). Consultation involves an egalitarian relationship that employs a problem-solving process for a specific purpose (Brown, Pryzwansky, & Schulte, 2006); often in the counseling context it involves the consultee going to a consultant to get help with a difficult or challenging case.

Research confirms that practice alone does not result in becoming a better counselor (Wiley & Ray, 1986). Your knowledge (i.e., the science of helping) and skill (i.e., the art of helping) cannot be shaped solely by experience (Bradley & Olson, 1980). As Bernard and Goodyear (2004) state, "Clinical supervision provides the crucible in which supervisees can blend these two knowledge types and begin to incorporate them as their own working knowledge" (p. 4). Make wise use of your supervision time. Although there is an evaluative aspect to supervision (Bernard & Goodyear, 2004), the purpose of it is to accelerate your progress toward being a professional. Allowing fear of scrutiny, performance anxiety, or pride to interfere with your ability to benefit from your experiences is self-defeating. Take ownership of your supervision, and approach it as a treasured gift from a seasoned professional.

Moreover, believing you are competent does not make it true. Yes, one should have confidence in his abilities, but research indicates that counselors are not necessarily an accurate measure of their own competence (Bernard & Goodyear, 2004). The feedback of a trained professional can provide a more accurate appraisal of your developmental progress.

Though no one person can know everything, strive toward excellence and have a plan to help you grow. Ongoing learning should not be a burden;

when learning is no longer fun, you are bogged down in the mire of life and need a break. You may need to take a vacation!

### Commitment to Growing Personally and Spiritually

Because you are the tool that creatively seeks to help people, it is necessary to personally improve if you desire your counseling work to improve (recall chap. 4, "The Person of the Counselor"). If honoring God through your work is your desire, then you will not become satisfied where you are; rather you will continue to press toward excellence (Col 3:23).

Be committed to lifelong growth. Your past is your blueprint for your present and future. If issues from your past are weighing you down, face them and deal with them. As stated in chap. 4, obtaining counseling for yourself will make you a better counselor. If counseling seems like overkill, then develop a discipleship plan that can help you grow in the areas where you are lacking.

One of the most salient means of growing personally is your marriage. In fact being married can be the best therapy you will ever obtain. When two sinners come together and seek to live in an intimate relationship, there is bound to be friction. The friction comes from the fallen parts of our lives and our "unfinished areas." Rather than being committed to changing your spouse, use your spouse to sharpen you personally.

The most powerful means of growing comes from the indwelling work of the Holy Spirit (John 16:8; Rom 8:9–11; 1 Cor 6:19; Eph 1:13–14; 3:16). The gospel is about transformation; God's plan is for each one of us to be conformed into the image of His Son (Rom 8:29; 12:1–2). That is no short order for anyone.

The best insurance plan for making it through difficult times is a strong relationship with the Lord during the good times. As Jeremiah wrote,

> But blessed is the man who trusts in the LORD, whose confidence is in him. He will be like a tree planted by the water that sends out its roots by the stream. It does not fear when heat comes; its leaves are always green. It has no worries in a year of drought and never fails to bear fruit (17:7–8, NIV).

Christian counselors are called to be "rooted" in the Lord (Col 2:7). When you operate from a root system that is based in the character and person of God, you will develop into a person who can make an impact in this world. Your mission is to serve the Lord, not yourself. As a Christian, morals should flow out of commitment to honor the Lord. Your methods should never violate the clear teachings of the Scriptures.

Doing the work of Christian counseling is not easy. You are on a battlefield engaged in warfare that comes from the flesh and from spiritual beings (Rom 6:12–13; Eph 6:11–12). Reflecting on the attacks we receive from those in the flesh, Clinton and Ohlschlager (2002a) state that "an aggressive assault against the validity and operation of competent Christian Counseling . . . is coming from both within the church (Bobgan & Bobgan, 1987; Hunt, 1987) and outside it (Ellis, 1971; Santa Rita, 1996)" (p. 694). The Word of God is the most reliable source to understand the roots of behavior and the hope we have in Christ. Never become so intelligent or academic that you view the Bible as an inferior source or as peripheral to your work of counseling. It is our centerpiece.

To those who disagree with our commitment to integrating psychology and theology, we do not hide the fact that we view the world through a biblical lens and operate in ways designed to help people grow into the image of Christ. Every approach to counseling is built on a philosophical understanding of people. The philosophy on which every traditional counseling approach rests has no more "proof" than the philosophical/theological foundations of the Scriptures. We of course could argue that the Scriptures are highly verifiable and have a more solid basis than philosophies developed by others. We believe that every Christian counselor would benefit from courses in apologetics, systematic theology, and hermeneutics in order to better grasp the foundation on which our helping ministry rests.

## CHAPTER SUMMARY

Our thoughts about how people operate are subject to biases stemming from limitations of our own cognitive abilities, biblical hermeneutics, motives, and experience. This does not mean that we do a poor job of making sense of our counselees. We actually do surprisingly well given the complexity of God's human creation and the huge amounts of information provided by actions, words, appearances, and so forth. Singer (1965) wrote:

> The question then is never how many or how much of life's problems the therapist has solved already but much more how much he continually strives toward increased understanding and subtle solutions of issues in his life, how much he cherishes his own struggle for freedom and active involvement; or conversely, how much he has given up this effort, how defeated and resigned he is, how much he despairs about his own life and rejects the value of growth (p. 118).

Few careers offer this sort of challenge and this sort of opportunity. There is much at risk and so much we do not know. Our dependency cannot be on what we can learn from the next workshop, book, supervisor, or minister. Healthy reliance rests on God, the giver of life, rest, hope, and faith.

We have attempted to characterize the existing practical, theoretical, empirical, and biblical literature related to helping skills. Our goal has been to equip you with skills necessary to take counselees on a therapeutic expedition, as you make the Word of God central in your counseling.

We close with a metaphor that we introduced in chap. 2 ("The Fundamentals of Helping"). We spoke about the fact that counseling is both a science and an art, that blending the two creates the "science-practitioner" approach to counseling. Although artistry is a highly individualistic and creative process, artists are trained in basic methods of art. The aim is for the student to take the science of a particular art discipline and express it in a very personalized way. This textbook has discussed the methods and science of helping, with the hope that you will make it your own and create artistry in your helping.

Counseling means using the skills and techniques of establishing a working relationship with a counselee and learning how to bring about meaningful change in the counselee's life. Patience is required in learning these skills and even more patience is called for in walking with a counselee in the path of his expedition. May the Lord bless you as you continue on your journey.

## CHAPTER 15 ACTIVITIES

1. Describe the critical role that ethical and legal standards play in the helping profession.
2. How is adherence to ethical and legal standards a spiritual issue?
3. Read the ACA and AACC code of ethics found in Appendixes A and B of this text. How are the two codes similar? How do they differ?
4. Discuss your plans for knowing and honoring the ethical codes established for the field of counseling.
5. Describe the importance and purposes of record-keeping.
6. Create a thorough, ideal consent form.
7. What is the difference between progress notes and process notes? Do you think it is important to keep both? Why or why not?
8. What elements should be covered in progress notes?
9. Describe the five key skill areas relative to cultural competency discussed in this chap. and your plan to insure cultural competency in your clinical work.
10. How do you plan on remaining committed to ongoing personal, professional, and personal growth?

## Recommended Reading

Corey, G., Corey, M. S., & Callanan, P. (2007). *Issues and ethics in the helping professions* (7th ed.). Monterey, CA: Brooks/Cole.

> This is a classic in the field of counseling. There is no better book on ethical and legal issues in counseling. It covers every aspect of such issues you must be familiar with in order to provide safe counseling.

Mitchell, R. W. (2000). *Documentation in counseling records: The ACA legal series* (2nd. ed.). Alexandria, VA: American Counseling Association Press.

> This is a detailed look at documentation, addressing the benefits and the potential results of documentation.

# References

Abercrombie, M. L. J. (1989). *The anatomy of judgment: An investigation into the processes of perception and reasoning.* London, UK: Free Association Books.

Ackerman, N. (1974). *Treating the troubled family.* New York City, NY: Basic Books.

Adams, J. (1970). *Competent to counsel.* Phillipsburg, NJ: Presbyterian and Reformed.

Adams, J. (1979). *A theology of Christian counseling.* Grand Rapids, MI: Zondervan Publishing House.

Adams, J. (1986). *A theology of Christian counseling* (2nd ed). Grand Rapids, MI: Zondervan Publishing House.

Adams, K. (1993). *The way of the journal: A journal therapy workbook for healing.* Lutherville, MD: Sidran Press.

Adams, K. (1998). *The way of the journal: A journal therapy workbook for healing* (2nd ed.). Lutherville, MD: Sidran Press.

Adler, A. (1958). *What life should mean to you.* New York City, NY: Capricorn.

Ainsworth, M. D. S., Blehar, M. C., Waters, E., & Wall, S. (1978). *Patterns of attachment: A psychological study of the strange situation.* Hillsdale, NJ: Erlbaum.

Albee, G. W. (1968). Conceptual models for manpower requirements in psychology. *American Psychologist, 23*, 317–320.

Alexander, I. (n.d.). *Integration in the practice of Christian counselors: Behaviors, beliefs, and being.* Retrieved on October 2009 from http://www.ccaa.net.au/documents/CCAA CounsellingIntegration.pdf.

Allen, J. G. (2001). *Traumatic relationships and serious mental disorders.* New York City, NY: Wiley.

Allen, J. G., Kelly, K. A., & Glodich, A. (1997). A psychoeducational program for patients with trauma-related disorders. *Bulletin of the Menninger Clinic, 61*, 222–239.

Allender, D. B. (1995). *The wounded heart: Hope for adult victims of childhood sexual abuse.* Colorado Springs, CO: NavPress.

Allender, D. B. (1996). *To be told: Know your story, shape your future.* Colorado Springs, CO: Waterbrook Press.

Allgood, S. M., Parham, K. B., Salts, C. J., & Smith, T. A. (1995). The association between pretreatment change and unplanned termination in family therapy. *The American Journal of Family Therapy, 23*(3), 195–202.

Al-Mabuk, R. H., Enright, R. D., & Cardis, P. A. (1995). Forgiveness education with parentally love-deprived late adolescents. *Journal of Moral Education, 24*, 427–444.

Alvarez, A. N., & Piper, R. E. (2005). Integrating theory and practice: A racial-cultural counseling model. In R. T. Carter (Ed.), *Handbook of racial-cultural psychology and counseling* (Vol. 2, pp. 235–248). Hoboken, NJ: John Wiley & Sons.

American Association of Christian Counselors, AACC code of ethics (2004). Retrieved October 13, 2008, from http://www.aacc.net/about-us/code-of-ethics/

American Association of Christian Counselors (2001). *AACC Christian Counseling Code of Ethics*. Forest, VA: AACC.

American Counseling Association (2005). *Code of ethics and standards of practice*. Alexandria, VA: Author.

American Counseling Association. ACA code of ethics (2005). Retrieved October 13, 2008, from http://www.counseling.org/Resources/CodeOfEthics/TP/Home/CT2.aspx.

American Psychological Association, APA code of ethics (2002). Retrieved October 13, 2008, from http://www.apa.org/ethics/code2002.html#principle_a

American Psychological Association (2000). *Diagnostic and statistical manual of mental disorders: DSM-IV-TR* (4th ed.). Washington, DC: Author.

Anderson, K. (2007, October 18). *Overview of Remuda Ranch programs for eating disorders*. Presentation given at Remuda Ranch: Programs for eating disorders. Wickenburg, AZ.

Anderson, R. S. (1997). *The soul of ministry*. Louisville, KY: Westminster John Knox Press.

Anderson, S. K., & Kitchener, K. S. (1996). Nonromantic, nonsexual posttherapy relationships between psychologists and former clients: An exploratory study of critical incidence. *Professional Psychology: Research and Practice, 27*, 59–66.

Anderson, W., & Andersen, B. (1985). Counselor self-disclosure. Paper presented at the Annual Convention of the American Psychological Association (93rd, Los Angeles, CA, August 23–27, 1985).

Andreas, S. (1991). *Virginia satir*. Palo Alto, CA: Science and Behavior Books.

Andrews, G., Hall, W., Teesson, M., & Henderson, S. (1999). National survey of mental health and well-being report 2: The mental health of Australians. Canberra, AU: Commonwealth of Australia.

Aponte, H. J. (1994). How personal can training get? *Journal of Marital and Family Therapy, 20*, 3–15.

Aponte, H. J., & Winter, J. E. (1987). The person and practice of the therapist: Treatment and training. *Journal of Psychotherapy and the Family, 3*, 85–111.

Arbuckle, D. S. (1965). *Counseling: Philosophy, theory, and practice*. Boston, MA: Allyn & Bacon.

Arizmendi, T. G. (2008). *Psychoanalytic Psychology, 25*(3), 443–457.

Arteburn, S., & Felton, J. (2001). *Toxic faith: Experiencing healing from painful spiritual abuse*. Colorado Springs, CO: Waterbrook Press.

Asay, T. P., & Lambert, M. J. (1999). The empirical case for the common factors in therapy: Quantitative findings. In M. A. Hubble, B. L. Duncan, & S. D. Miller (Eds.), *The heart and soul of change: What works in therapy* (pp. 23–55). Washington, DC: American Psychological Association Press.

Ashby, J. S., & Lenhart, R. S. (1994). Prayer as a coping strategy for chronic pain patients. *Rehabilitation Psychology, 39*, 205–209.

Astington, J. W. (1996). What is theoretical about the child's theory of mind? A Vygotskian view of its development. In P. Carruthers & P. K. Smith (Eds.),

*Theories of theories of mind* (pp. 184–199). Cambridge, UK: Cambridge University Press.

Aten, J. D., Mangis, M. W., Campbell, C., Tucker, B. T., Kobeisy, A. N., & Halberda, R. (2009). Spirituality in therapy termination. In J. Aten & M. Leach (Eds.), *Spirituality and the therapeutic process: A comprehensive resource from intake through termination.* Washington, DC: American Psychological Association Press.

Augsburger, D. (1973). *Caring enough to confront: How to understand and express your deepest feelings toward others.* Scottdale, PA: Herald Press.

Azhar, M. Z., Varma, S. L., & Dharap, A. S. (1994). Religious psychotherapy in anxiety disorder patients. *Acta Psychiatrica Scandinavica, 90,* 1–3.

Bandler, R., & Grinder, J. (1975). *The structure of magic I: A book about language and therapy.* Palo Alto, CA: Science & Behavior Books.

Banks, G. (1971). The effects of race on one-to-one helping interviews. *Social Service Review, 45,* 137–146.

Barker, P. (1985). *Using metaphors in psychotherapy.* New York City, NY: Brunner/Mazel.

Baron-Cohen, S. (2003). *The essential difference: male and female brains and the truth about autism.* New York City, NY: Basic Books.

Baron-Cohen, S. (2005). The empathizing system: A revision of the 1994 model of the mindreading system, in origins of the social mind. In B. J. Ellis & D. F. Bjorklund (Eds.), *Evolutionary psychology and child development* (pp. 468–492). New York City, NY: Guilford Press.

Barrett, M. S., Chua, W. J., Crits-Christoph, P., Gibbons, M. B., & Thompson, D. (2008). Early withdrawal from mental health treatment: Implications for psychotherapy practice. *Psychotherapy: Theory, Research, Practice, Training, 45,* 247–267.

Baruth, L. G., & Huber, C. H. (1985). *Counseling and psychotherapy: Theoretical, analyses, and skills applications.* Columbus, OH: Charles E. Merrill.

Baruth, L. G., & Manning, M. L. (1999). *Multicultural counseling and psychotherapy: A lifespan perspective* (2nd ed.). Upper Saddle River, NJ: Merrill/Prentice Hall.

Baruth, L. G., & Manning, M. L. (2003). *Multicultural counseling and psychotherapy: A lifespan perspective* (3rd ed.) Upper Saddles River, NJ: Merrill Prentice-Hall.

Bauer, W. A., Arndt, W. F., & Gingrich, F. W. (1979). *A Greek-English lexicon of the New Testament and other early Christian literature* (2nd ed.). Chicago, IL: University of Chicago Press.

Baum, N. (2005). Correlates of clients' emotional and behavioral responses to treatment termination. *Clinical Social Work Journal, 33* (3), 309–326.

Bearon, L. B., & Koenig, H. G. (1990). Religious cognitions and use of prayer in health and illness. *The Gerontologist, 30,* 249–253.

Beck, A. T. (1972). *Depression: Causes and treatment.* Philadelphia, PA: University of Pennsylvania Press.

Beck, A. T. (1976). *Cognitive therapy and emotional disorders.* New York City, NY: International Universities Press.

Beck, A. T., & Weishaar, M. E. (1995). Cognitive therapy. In R. J. Corsini & D. Wedding (Eds.), *Current psychotherapies* (5th ed., pp. 229–261). Itasca, IL: F. E. Peacock.

Beck, J. S. (1995). *Cognitive therapy: Basics and beyond.* New York City, NY: Guilford Press.

Beck, R., & McDonald, A. (2004). Attachment to God: The attachment to God inventory, tests of working model correspondence, and an exploration of faith group differences. *Journal of Psychology and Theology, 32*(2), 92–103.

Bedi, R. P., Davis, M. D., & Williams, M. (2005). Critical incidents in the formation of the therapeutic alliance from the client's perspective. *Psychotherapy: Theory, Research, Practice, Training, 42*(3), 311–323.

Benner, D. G. (1983). The incarnation as a metaphor for psychotherapy. *Journal of Psychology and Theology, 11*, 287–294.

Berenson, B. G., & Mitchell, K. M. (1974). *Confrontation!: For better or worse.* Amherst, MA: Human Resources Development Press.

Bergin, A. E., & Jensen, J. P. (1990). Religiosity of psychotherapists: A national survey. *Psychotherapy, 27*(1), 3–7.

Bermak, G. (1977). Do psychiatrists have special emotional problems? *The American Journal of Psychoanalysis, 37*, 141–146.

Bernard, J. M., & Goodyear, R. K. (2004). *Fundamentals of clinical supervision* (3rd ed.). New York City, NY: Pearson.

Bernstein, B. L., & Figioli, S. W. (1983). Gender and credibility introduction effects on perceived counselor characteristics. *Journal of Counseling Psychology,* 30, 506–513.

Berrett, M. E. (2003). *Social support: The cradle in which growth and recovery take place.* Orem, UT: Center for Change.

Bertolino, B., & O'Hanlon, B. (2002). Collaborative, competency-based counseling and therapy. Needham Heights, MA: Allyn & Bacon.

Beutler, L. E. (1991). Have all won and must all have prizes? Revisiting Luborsky et al.'s verdict. *Journal of Counseling and Clinical Psychology, 59*, 226–232.

Beutler, L. E., Crago, M., & Arizmendi, T. G. (1986). Therapist variables in psychotherapy process and outcome. In S. L. Garfield & A. E. Bergin (Eds.), *Handbook of psychotherapy and behavior change* (3rd ed., pp. 257–310). New York City, NY: Wiley.

Beutler, L. E., Machado, P. P., & Neufeldt, S. A. (1994). Therapist variables. In A. E. Bergin & S. L. Garfield (Eds.), *Handbook of psychotherapy and behavior change* (4th ed., pp. 229–269). New York City, NY: Wiley.

Bianco, J. A. (2007). *Therapists' willingness to self-disclose as a function of theoretical orientation and client diagnosis.* Unpublished doctoral dissertation, Columbia University, New York City, NY.

Bischoff, M. M., & Tracey, T. J. G. (1995). Client resistance as predicted by therapist behavior: A study of sequential dependence. *Journal of Counseling Psychology, 42*(4), 487–495.

Blocher, D. H. (1983). Toward a cognitive developmental approach to counseling supervision. *The Counseling Psychologist, 11*(1), 27–34.

Bobgan, M., & Bobgan, D. (1987). *Psychoheresy: The psychological seduction of Christianity.* Santa Barbara, CA: Eastgate.

Bohart, A. C. (2001, August). *The therapist as improvisational artist.* Paper presented at the annual meeting of the American Psychological Association, San Francisco, CA.

Bohart, A., & Greenberg, L. (Eds.). (1997). *Empathy reconsidered.* Washington, DC: American Psychological Association Press.

Boisvert, C. M., & Faust, D. (2003). Iatrogenic symptoms in psychotherapy: A theoretical exploration of the potential impact of labels, language, and belief system. *American Journal of Psychotherapy, 546,* 244–259.

Bolen, R. M. (2005). Attachment and family violence: Complexities in knowing. *Child Abuse & Neglect, 29*(8), 845–852.

Bolton, R. (1979). *People skills: How to assert yourself, listen to others and resolve conflicts.* New York City, NY: Simon and Schuster.

Boman, K. K. (2007). Assessing psychological and health-related quality of life (HRQL) late effects after childhood cancer. *Acta Paediatrica, 96*(9), 1265–1268.

Bonanno, G. A., Ho, S. M. Y., Chan, J. C. K., Kwong, R. S. Y., Cheung, C. K. Y., Wong, C. P. Y. et al. (2008). Psychological resilience and dysfunction among hospitalized survivors of the SARS epidemic in Hong Kong: A latent class approach. *Health Psychology, 27*(5), 659–667.

Bonham, T. D. (1988). *Humor: God's gift.* Nashville, TN: Broadman Press.

Bordan, T., & Goldin, E. (1999). The use of humor in counseling: The laughing cure [Electronic version]. *Journal of Counseling and Development, 77*(4), 405–410.

Borders, L. D., & Brown, L. L. (2005). *The new handbook of counseling supervision.* Mahwah, NJ: Lawrence Erlbaum Associates.

Bostic, J. Q., Shadid, L. G., & Blotcky, M. J. (1996). Our time is up: Forced terminations during psychotherapy training. *American Journal of Psychotherapy, 50*(3), 347–359.

Bourne, E. J. (1995). *The anxiety and phobia workbook* (2nd ed.). Oakland, CA: New Harbinger.

Bovey, W. H. & Hede, A. (2001). Resistance to organizational change: The role of defense mechanisms. *Journal of Managerial Psychology, 16*(7), 534–548.

Bowen, M. (1966). The use of family theory in clinical practice. *Comprehensive Psychiatry, 7,* 345–374.

Bowlby, J. (1940). The influence of early environment in the development of neurosis and neurotic character. *International Journal of Psycho-Analysis, 21,* 154–178.

Bowlby, J. (1969). *Attachment and loss, Vol. 1: Attachment.* New York City, NY: Basic Books.

Bowlby, J. (1973). *Attachment and loss, Vol. 2: Separation.* New York City, NY: Basic Books.

Bowlby, J. (1980). *Loss, sadness, and depression.* New York City, NY: Basic Books.

Bowlby, J. (1988). *A secure base: Parent-child attachment and healthy human development.* New York City, NY: Basic Books.

Bradley, J. R., & Olson, J. K. (1980). Training factors influencing felt psychotherapeutic competence of psychology trainees. *Professional Psychology, 11*, 930–934.

Brady, J. L, Healy, F. L., Norcross, J. C., & Guy, J. D. (1995). Stress in counselors: An integrative research review. In W. Dryden (Ed.), *Stress in counseling in action* (pp. 1–27). Newbury Park, CA: Sage.

Braem, G. (2004). Christian family therapy with eating disorders. *The Remuda Review, 3*, 20–23.

Brammer, L. M. (1973). *The helping relationship: Process and skills.* Englewood, NJ: Prentice-Hall.

Brammer, L. M., & Shostrom, E. L. (1982). *Therapeutic psychology: Fundamentals of counseling and psychotherapy* (4th ed.). Englewood Cliffs, NJ: Prentice-Hall.

Brammer, L. M., Shostrom, E. L., & Abrego, P. J. (1989). *Therapeutic psychology: Fundamentals of counseling and psychotherapy* (5th ed.). Englewood Cliffs, NJ: Prentice-Hall.

Brantley, A. P. (2000). A clinical supervision documentation form. In L. VandeCreek & T. L. Jackson (Eds.), *Innovations in clinical practice: A sourcebook* (Vol. 18, pp. 301–307). Sarasota, FL: Professional Resource Press.

Brems, C. (1993). *A comprehensive guide to child psychotherapy.* Needham Heights, MA: Allyn & Bacon.

Briere, J. & Scott, C. (2006). *Principles of trauma therapy: A guide to symptoms, evaluation, and treatment.* Thousand Oaks, CA: Sage.

Brockman, W. P. (1980). *Empathy revisited: The effects of representational system matching on certain counseling process and outcome variables.* Unpublished doctoral dissertation, College of William and Mary, Williamsburg, VA.

Brown, D., Pryzwansky, W. B., & Schulte, A. C. (2006). *Psychological consultation and collaboration: Introduction to theory and practice* (6th ed.). New York City, NY: Pearson.

Brown, J. H., & Brown, S. (1977). *Systematic counseling: A guide for the practitioner.* Champaign, IL: Research Press.

Bruffaerts, R., Sabbe, M., & Demyttenaere, K. (2004). Effects of patient and health-system characteristics on community tenure of discharged psychiatric inpatients. *Psychiatric Services, 55*(6), 685–690.

Bryant, B. H., & Krause, M. S. (1998). *John: The College Press NIV commentary.* Joplin, MO: College Press.

Bryant, L., Katz, B., Becvar, R., & Becvar, D. (1988). The use of therapeutic metaphor among members of the AAMFT. *The American Journal of Family Therapy, 16*, 112–120.

Buber, M. (1970). *I and thou.* New York City, NY: Scribner and Sons.

Bucci, W. (1997). *Psychoanalysis and cognitive science: A multiple code theory.* New York City, NY: Guilford Press.

Buckman, E. S. (Ed.). (1994). *The handbook of humor: Clinical applications in psychotherapy.* Malabar, FL: Krieger.

Bufford, R. K. (2007). Consecrated counseling: Reflections on the distinctives of Christian counseling. In D. H. Stevenson, B. E. Eck, and P. C. Hill Eds, *Psychology and Christianity integration: Seminal works that shaped the move-*

*ment* (pp. 253–263). Batavia, IL: Christian Association for Psychological Studies International.

Bugental, J. F. T. (1965). *The search for authenticity: An existential analytic approach to psychotherapy.* New York City, NY: Holt, Rinehart, and Winston.

Burch, C. A. (1985). Identity foreclosure in early adolescence: A problem of narcissistic equilibrium. *Adolescent Psychiatry, 12,* 145–161.

Burnard, P. (1999). *Counseling skills for health professionals* (3rd ed.). Cheltenham, UK: Stanley Thomas.

Burns, D. D. (1999). *The feeling good handbook.* New York City, NY: William Morrow.

Burns, D. D. (March 2008). Paper presented at conference, *Scared Straight.*

Burton, Arthur (Ed.). (1976). *What makes behavior change possible?* New York City, NY: Brunner/Mazel.

Button, L. A. (2008). Effect of social support and coping strategies on the relationship between health care-related occupational stress and health. *Journal of Research in Nursing, 13*(6), 498–524.

Byrd, R. C. (1988). Positive therapeutic effects of intercessory prayer in a coronary care unit population. *Southern Medical Journal, 81,* 826–829.

Campbell, J. (1988). *The power of myth.* New York City, NY: Doubleday.

Candill, O. B. (2003). Twelve pitfalls for psychotherapists. *Clinical Update, 33*(2), 10–12.

Capuzzi, D., & Gross, D. (2007). *Counseling and psychotherapy: Theories and interventions* (4th ed.). Upper Saddle River, NJ: Pearson Prentice Hall.

Carey, T. A., Carey, M., Stalker, K., Mullan, R. J., Murray, L. K., & Spratt, M. B. (2007). Psychological change from the inside looking out: A qualitative investigation. *Counselling and Psychotherapy Research, 7,* 178–187.

Carkhuff, R. R. (1969a). *Helping and human relations: Vol 1. Selection and training.* New York City, NY: Holt, Rinehart, & Winston.

Carkhuff, R. R. (1969b). *Helping and human relations: Vol 2. Practice and research.* New York City, NY: Holt, Rinehart, & Winston.

Carkhuff, R. R., & Berenson, B. G. (1967). *Beyond counseling and therapy.* New York City, NY: Holt, Rinehart, and Winston.

Carkhuff, R. R., & Pierce, R. M. (1977). *The art of helping-III: Trainer's guide.* Amherst, MA: Human Resource Development Press.

Carlozzi, A. F., Bull, K. S., Eells, G. T., & Hurlburt, J. D. (1995). Empathy as related to creativity, dogmatism, and expressiveness. *Journal of Psychology, 29,* 365–373.

Carlozzi, A. F., Gaa, J. P., & Liberman, D. B. (1983). Empathy and ego development. *Journal of Counseling Psychology, 30,* 13–116.

Carlson, C. R., Bacaseta, P. E., & Simanton, D. A. (1988). A controlled evaluation of devotional meditation and progressive relaxation. *Journal of Psychology and Theology, 16,* 362–368.

Carlson, D. E. (1976). Jesus' style of relating: The search for a biblical view of counseling. *Journal of Psychology and Theology, 4*(3), 181–188.

Carlson, J. & Sperry, L. (Eds.). (2000). *Brief therapy with individuals and couples.* Phoenix, AZ: Zeig, Tucker, & Theisen.

Carlson, J., Sperry, L., & Lewis, J. A. (2005). *Family therapy techniques: Integrating and tailoring treatment*. New York City, NY: Routledge.

Carnegie, D. (1981). *How to win friends and influence people*. New York City, NY: Pocket Books.

Carnes, P. J. (2001). *Facing the shadow: Starting sexual and relationship recovery: A gentle path to beginning recovery from sexual addiction*. Carefree, AZ: Gentle Path Press.

Carter, J. D., & Narramore, B. (1979). *The interaction of psychology and theology*. Grand Rapids, MI: Zondervan Publishing House.

Carter, R. E., Haynes, L. F., Back, S. E., Herrin, A. E., Brady, K. T., Leimberger, J. D. et al. (2008). Improving the transition from residential to outpatient addiction treatment: Gender differences in response to supportive telephone calls. *American Journal of Drug and Alcohol Abuse, 34*(1), 47–59.

Caspar, F., Berger, T., & Hautle, I. (2004). The right view of your patient: A computer-assisted, individualized module for psychotherapy training. *Psychotherapy: Theory, Research, Practice, Training, 41*(2), 125–135.

Cecero, J. J. (2002). *Praying through our lifetraps: A psychospiritual path to freedom*. Totowa, NJ: Resurrection Press.

Cepeda-Benito, A., & Short, P. (1998). Self-concealment, avoidance of psychological services, and perceived likelihood of seeking professional help. *Journal of Counseling Psychology, 45*, 273–279.

Chae, M. H. (2001). White racial identity attitudes and white counselor awareness. *The Journal of the Pennsylvania Counseling Association, 4*(1), 7–15.

Chambless, D. L., & Ollendick, T. H. (2001). Empirically supported psychological interventions: Controversies and evidence. *Annual Review of Psychology, 52*, 685–716.

Chandras, K. V., Eddy, J. P., & Spaulding, D. J. (Winter, 2000). Counseling Asian Americans: Implications for Training. *Education, 12*(2), 239–246.

Chaos Theory (n.d.). In *Wikipedia*. Retrieved from http://en.wikipedia.org/wiki/Chaos_theory.

Charlton, R. S., & Brigel, F. W. (1997). Treatment of arousal and orgasmic disorders. In R. S. Charlton & I. D. Yalom (Eds.), *Treating sexual disorders* (pp. 237–280). San Francisco, CA: Jossey-Bass.

Cheong, R. K., & DiBlasio, F. A. (2007). Christ-like love and forgiveness: A biblical foundation for counseling practice. *Journal of Psychology & Christianity, 26*, 14–25.

Cheston, S. E., Piedmont, R. L., Eanes, B., & Patrice, L. (2003). Changes in client's images of God over the course of outpatient therapy. *Counseling and Values, 47*, 96–108.

Chittick, E. V., & Himelstein, P. (1967). The manipulation of self-disclosure. *The Journal of Psychology, 65*, 117–121.

Cichetti, D., & Toth, S. (1995). A developmental psychopathology perspective on child abuse and neglect. *Journal of the American Academy of Child and Adolescent Psychiatry, 42*, 541–565.

Claiborn, C. D. (1982). Interpretation and change in counseling. *Journal of Counseling Psychology, 29*, 439–453.

Clarkin, J. F., & Levy, K. N. (2004). Influence of client variables on psychothera-py. In M. J. Lambert (Ed.), *Handbook of psychotherapy and behavior change* (5th ed.). New York City, NY: Wiley.

Clarkson, P. (2009). *The therapeutic relationship* (2nd ed.). Philadelphia, PA: Whurr.

Clinton, T., Hart, A., & Ohlschlager, G. (Eds.). (2005). *Caring for people God's way: Personal and emotional issues, addictions, grief, and trauma.* Nashville, TN: Thomas Nelson.

Clinton, T., & Ohlschlager, G. (Eds.) (2002a). *Competent Christian counseling: Foundations & practice of compassionate soul care* (Vol. 1). Colorado Springs, CO: Waterbrook Press.

Clinton, T., & Ohlschlager, G. (2002b). Christian counseling and compassionate soul care: The case for twenty-first-century practice. In T. Clinton & G. Ohlschlager (Eds.), *Competent Christian counseling* (Vol. 1, pp. 11–35). Colorado Springs, CO: WaterBrook Press.

Clinton, T. & Ohlschlager, G. (2002c). Competent Christian counseling: Definitions and dynamics. In T. Clinton & G. Ohlschlager (Eds.), *Competent Christian counseling: Foundations & practice of compassionate soul care* (Vol. 1, pp. 36–68). Colorado Springs, CO: Waterbrook Press.

Clinton, T., & Sibcy, G. (2002). *Attachments: Why you love, feel, and act the way you do.* Brentwood, TN: Integrity.

Cloud, H., & Townsend, J. (1994). *Boundaries: When to say yes and when to say no to take control of your life.* Grand Rapids, MI: Zondervan.

Colby, K. (1951). *A primer for psychotherapists.* New York City, NY: Roland Press.

Clore, G. C. (1994). Why emotions are felt. In P. Ekman & R. J. Davidson (Eds.), *The nature of emotion: Fundamental questions* (pp. 103–111). New York City, NY: Oxford University Press.

Coleman, E., & Schaefer, S. (1986). Boundaries of sex and intimacy between client and counselor. *Journal of Counseling and Development, 64,* 341–344.

Collins, G. R. (1972). *The rebuilding of psychology.* Wheaton, IL: Tyndale House.

Collins, G. R. (1980). *Christian counseling: A comprehensive guide.* Waco, TX: Word Books.

Collins, G. R. (1991). *Excellence and ethics in Christian counseling.* Dallas, TX: Word Books.

Colson, C., & Pearcey, N. (1999). *How shall we live?* Carol Stream, IL: Tyndale House.

Combs, D., Avila, D., & Purkey, W. (1971). *Helping relationships: Basic concepts for the helping professions.* Boston, MA: Allyn and Bacon.

Coon, D. & Thompson, D. (2002). Encouraging homework completion among older adults in therapy. *Journal of Clinical Psychology, 58*(5), 549–563.

Cooper, D. M. (2006). *Behind the broken image.* Nashville, TN: Remuda Ranch.

Corey, G., (2005). *Theory and practice of counseling and psychotherapy* (7th ed.). Monterey, CA: Brooks/Cole.

Corey, G., Corey, M. S., & Callanan, P. (2007). *Issues and ethics in the helping professions* (7th ed.). Monterey, CA: Brooks/Cole.

Cormier, W. H., & Cormier, L. S. (1985). *Interviewing strategies for helpers: Fundamental skills and cognitive behavioral interventions* (2nd ed.). Pacific Grove, CA: Brooks/Cole.

Cormier, L. S., & Hackney, H. (2008). Counseling strategies and interventions (7th ed.). Boston, MA: Pearson/Allyn & Bacon.

Corsini, R., & Wedding, D. (Eds.). (1995). *Current psychotherapies* (5th ed.). Itasca, IL: Peacock.

Council for Accreditation of Counseling and Related Educational Programs. (2001). *CACREP accreditation standards and procedures manual.* Alexandria, VA: Author.

Covey, S. (1989). *7 habits of highly effective people.* New York City, NY: Simon and Schuster.

Cox, D. J., Tisdelle, D. A., & Culbert, J. P. (1988). Increasing adherence to behavioral homework assignments. *Journal of Behavioral Medicine, 11*, 519–522.

Crabb, L. (1977). *Effective biblical counseling.* Grand Rapids, MI: Zondervan Publishing House.

Crabb, L. (1988). *Inside out.* Colorado Springs, CO: NavPress.

Crabb, L. (2003). *Soultalk: The language God longs for us to speak.* Brentwood, TN: Integrity.

Crabb, L. J., & Allender, D. B. (1997). *Hope when you're hurting: Answers to four questions hurting people ask.* Grand Rapids, MI: Zondervan Publishing House.

Craigie, E., Jr. (1994). Problem-solving, discipleship, and the process of change in Christian counseling. *Journal of Psychology and Christianity, 13*(3), 205–216.

Crews, J., Smith, M., Smaby, M., Maddux, C., Torres-Rivera, E., Urbani, S. et al. (2005). Self-monitoring and counseling skills: Skills-based versus interpersonal process recall training. *Journal of Counseling and Development, 83*, 78–85.

Culley, S., & Bond, T. (2004). *Integrative counseling skills in action.* London, UK: Sage.

Cumella, E. (2002). Bio-psycho-social-spiritual: Completing the model. *The Remuda Review: The Christian Journal of Eating disorders, 1*(1), 1–5.

Cummings, S. M. (1999). Adequacy of discharge plans and rehospitalization among hospitalized dementia patients. *Health & Social Work, 24* (4), 249–259.

Curtis, J. M. (1982). Principles and techniques of non-disclosure by the therapist during psychotherapy. *Psychological Reports, 51*, 907–914.

Cushway, D., Tyler, P. A., & Nolan, P. (1996). Development of a stress scale for mental health professionals. *British Journal of Clinical Psychology, 35*, 279–295.

Custers, R., & Aarts, H. (2005). Positive affect as implicit motivator: On the nonconscious operation of behavioral goals. *Journal of Personality and Social Psychology, 89*(2), 12–142.

Damasio, A. (1994). *Descartes' error: Emotion, reason and the human brain.* New York: Grosset.

Damasio, A. (1999). *The feeling of what happens.* London: Random House.

D'Andrea, M. (1984). The counselor as pacer: A model for the revitalization of the counseling profession. *Counseling and Human Development, 16*(6), 1–15.

D'Andrea, M., & Daniels, J. (1992). *Do the leaders of counselor education programs think graduate students should be required to participate in personal counseling: The results of a national survey.* (ERIC Document Reproduction Service No. ED349508).

Daniels, T., Rigazio-Digilio, S., & Ivey, A. (1997). Microcounseling: A training and supervision paradigm. In E. Watkins (Ed.), *Handbook of psychotherapy supervision.* New York City, NY: Wiley.

Darden, R. A. (2005). Spiritual assessment and treatment strategies. *The Remuda Review, 4* (2), Retrieved on January 2010 from http://www.remudaranch.com/articles/26-remuda-review/145-spiritual-assessment-and-treatment-of-eating-disorders

Dattilio, F. (2002, May). Homework assignments in couple and family therapy. *Journal of Clinical Psychology, 58*(5), 535–547.

Davis, C. (2001). Joy. In W. A. Elwell (Ed.), *Evangelical dictionary of theology* (2nd ed., pp. 636–637). Grand Rapids, MI: Baker Academic.

Deacon, S. A. (1996). Using experiential activities in the training of the person of the therapist. *Family Therapy, 23,* 171–187.

DeForest, C., & Stone, G. L. (1980). Effects of sex and intimacy level on self-disclosure. *Journal of Counseling Psychology, 20,* 344–348.

Demetri, P. (2007). Facilitating analysis with implicit and explicit self-disclosures. *The American Journal of Psychoanalysis, 67*(2), 197–199.

Derlega, V. J., & Berg, J. H. (1987). *Self-disclosure: Theory, research, and therapy.* New York City, NY: Springer Publishing Co.

Derisley, J., & Reynolds, S. (2000). The transtheoretical stages of change as a predictor of premature termination, attendance and alliance in psychotherapy. *British Journal of Clinical Psychology, 39,* 371–382.

De Shazer, S. (1988). *Clues: Investigating solutions in brief therapy.* New York City, NY: Norton & Co.

Dewane, C. J. (2006). Use of self: A primer revisited. *Clinical Social Work Journal, 34*(4), 543–558.

Deutsch, C. (1985). A survey of therapists' personal problems and treatment. *Professional Psychology: Research and Practice, 16*(2), 305–315.

Diller, J. V. (2007). *Cultural diversity* (3rd ed.). Belmont, CA: Thomson Learning.

Dimeff, L. A., & Koerner, K. (2007). *Dialectical behavior therapy in clinical practice.* New York City, NY: Guilford Press.

Dinkmeyer, D., Dinkmeyer, K., & Sperry, L. (1987). *Adlerian counseling and psychotherapy.* Columbus, OH: Merrill.

Dinkmeyer, D. Jr., & Sperry, L. (2000). *Counseling and psychotherapy: An integrated, individual psychology approach.* Upper Saddle River, NJ: Prentice-Hall.

Dobson, D., & Dobson, K. S. (2009). *Evidence-based practice of cognitive-behavioral therapy.* New York City, NY: Guilford Press.

Donat, D. C., & Neal, B. (1991). Situational sources of stress for direct care staff in a public psychiatric hospital. *Psychosocial Rehabilitation Journal, 14,* 76–82.

Duan, C., & Hill, C. E. (1996). The current status of empathy research. *Journal of Counseling Psychology, 43*(3), 261–274.

Duba, J. D. (2005). Integrative and biopsychosocial therapy: An interview with Len Sperry. *The Family Journal: Counseling and Therapy for Couples and Families, 13*(1), 101–108.

Duddle, M., & Boughton, M. (2009). Development and psychometric testing of the nursing workplace relational environment scale (NWRES). *Journal of Clinical Nursing, 18*(6), 902–909.

Duncan, B. L., Miller, S. D., & Sparks, J. A. (2004). *The heroic client: A revolutionary way to improve effectiveness through client-directed outcome-informed therapy.* New York City, NY: Jossey-Bass/Wiley.

Dunkle, J. H., & Friedlander, M. L. (1996). Contributions of therapist experience and personal characteristics to the working alliance. *Journal of Counseling Psychology, 43*(4), 456–460.

Dunn, H., Morrison, A., & Bentall, R. (2002). Patients experience of homework tasks in cognitive behavioral therapy for psychosis: A qualitative study. *Clinical Psychology and Psychotherapy, 9*(5), 361–369.

Dupey, P., Garrett, M., Maples, M., Phan, L., Torres-Rivera, E., & Vereen, L. (2001). Ethnic diversity and the use of humor in counseling: Appropriate or inappropriate? [Electronic version]. *Journal of Counseling & Development, 79*(1), 53–60.

Earle, R. H., & Barnes, D. J. (1999). *Independent practice for the mental health professional: Growing a private practice for the 21st century.* Philadelphia, PA: Brunner/Mazel.

Eberly, M. (2005). Bringing the spiritual into treatment. *The Remuda Review, 4,* 2–5.

Eberly, M., & Cumella, E. J. (2003). Cognitive-behavioral therapy: Applications and skills. *The Remuda Review, 2,* 1–7.

Edelman, R. E., & Chambless, D. L. (1993). Compliance during sessions and homework in exposure-based treatment of agoraphobia. *Behaviour Research and Therapy, 31*(8), 767–773.

Edwards, C. E., & Murdock, N. L. (1994). Characteristics of therapist self-disclosure in the counseling process. *Journal of Counseling & Development, 72,* 384–389.

Edwards, N., Peterson, W. E., & Davies, B. L. (2006). Evaluation of a multiple component intervention to support the implementation of a "Therapeutic Relationships" best practice guidelines on nurses' communication skills. *Patient Education and Counseling, 63*(1–2), 3–11.

Egan, G. (2002). *The skilled helper: A problem-management and opportunity-development approach to helping* (7th ed.). Pacific Grove, CA: Brooks/Cole-Thomson.

Egan, G. (2007). *The skilled helper: A problem-management and opportunity-development approach to helping* (8th ed.). Pacific Grove, CA: Brooks/Cole-Thomson.

Eisenberg, N. & Spinrad, T. (2004). Emotion-related regulation: Sharpening the definition. *Child Development. 75*(2), 334–339.

Elich, M., Thompson, R. W., & Miller, L. (1985). Mental imagery as revealed by eye movements and spoken predicates: A test of neurolinguistic programming. *Journal of Counseling Psychology, 32*(4), 622–625.

Elkins, E., Anchor, K., & Sandler, H. (1979). Relaxation training and prayer behavior as tension reduction techniques. *Behavioral Engineering, 5*, 81–87.

Ellerton, R. (2005). *Live your dreams . . . let reality catch up: NLP and common sense of coaches, managers and you.* Victoria, BC, Canada: Trafford.

Elliott, K. S., Di Minno, M., Lam, D., & Tu, A. M. (1996). Working with Chinese families in the context of dementia. In G. Yeo & D. Gallagher-Thompson (Eds.), *Ethnicity and dementia* (pp. 89–100). New York City, NY: Taylor and Francis.

Ellis, A. (1957). *How to live with a neurotic.* Oxford, UK: Crow.

Ellis, A. (1971). *The case against religion: A psychotherapist's view.* New York City, NY: Institute for Rational Living.

Ellis, A. (1974). Experience and rationality: The making of a rational-emotive therapist. *Psychotherapy: Theory, Research, and Practice, 11*, 194–198.

Ellis, P. J. (1997). *A qualitative and quantitative analysis of counselor-client verbal interactions with adolescents receiving counseling services in the school setting.* Unpublished doctoral dissertation, University of Houston, Houston, TX.

Elson, M. (2001). Silence, its use and abuse: A view from self-psychology. *Clinical Social Work Journal, 29*(4), 351–360.

Eng, T. C., & Kuiken, D. (2006). Cultural fusion, conflict and preservation: Expressive styles among Chinese Canadians. *Journal of Cultural and Evolutionary Psychology, 4*(1), 51–76.

Engle, D., & Arkowitz, H. (2006). *Ambivalence in psychotherapy: Facilitating readiness to change.* New York City, NY: Guilford Press.

Entwistle, D. N. (2004a). *Integrative approaches to psychology and Christianity.* Eugene, OR: Wipf and Stock.

Entwistle, D. N. (2004b). Shedding light on Theophostic Ministry 2: Ethical and legal issues. *Journal of Psychology and Theology, 32*, 35–42.

Erikson, E. H. (1950). *Childhood and society.* New York City, NY: W. W. Norton.

Erikson, E. H., & Erikson, J. (1997). *The life cycle completed.* New York City, NY: W. W. Norton.

Erickson, M. J. (1998). *Christian Theology* (2nd ed.). Grand Rapids, MI: Baker Book House.

Erickson, M. J. (2001). *Introducing Christian doctrine* (2nd ed.). Grand Rapids, MI: Baker Academia.

Erwin, K. T., Huang, W. J., & Lin, S. L. S. (2002). The world at our doorstep: Multicultural counseling and special populations (pp. 615–637). In T. Clinton & G. Ohlschlager (Eds.), *Competent Christian counseling.* Colorado Springs, CO: WaterBrook.

Evans, B. A. (2005). Ancient and classical pastoral counsel: Approaches to anxiety, doubt, and guilt. *Journal of Psychology & Christianity, 24*, 80–88.

Evans, C. S. (1986). The blessings of mental anguish. *Christianity Today, 30*(1), 26–29.

Fauth, J., & Hayes, J. A. (2006). Counselors' stress appraisal as predictors of countertransference behavior with male clients. *Journal of Counseling and Development, 84*, 430–439.

Feltham, C., & Dryden, W. (1993). *Dictionary of counseling.* London, UK: Whurr.

Fertman, C. I. (1991). Aftercare for teenagers: Matching services and needs. *Journal of Alcohol and Drug Education, 36*(2), 1–11.

Festinger, L. (1957). *A theory of cognitive dissonance.* Stanford, CA: Stanford University Press.

Figley, C. R. (Ed.). (1995). *Compassion fatigue: Coping with secondary traumatic stress disorder in those who treat the traumatized.* New York City, NY: Routledge.

Fine, S. F., & Glasser, P. (1996). *The first helping interview: Engaging the client and building trust.* Thousand Oaks, CA: Sage.

Finney, J. R., & Malony, H. N. (1985). An empirical study of contemplative prayer as an adjunct to psychotherapy. *Journal of Psychology and Theology, 13*, 284–290.

Finney, J. W. (2004, August). *Assessing treatment and treatment processes.* Retrieved November 2007 from the National Institute on Alcohol Abuse and Alcoholism. Available at http://pubs.niaaa.nih.gov/publications/Assesing%20Alcohol/finney.pdf.

Firestone, R. W. (1996). *Voice therapy: Combating destructive thought processes.* Newbury Park, CA: Sage.

Fitzpatrick, M. R., & Irannejad, S. (2008). Adolescent readiness for change and the working alliance in counseling. *Journal of Counseling & Development, 86* (4), 438–445.

Fogel, A. (1982). Affect dynamics in early infancy: Affect tolerance. In T. Field & A. Fogel (Eds.), *Emotion and early interaction* (pp. 26–56). Hillsdale, NJ: Erlbaum.

Foster, R. J. (1988). *Celebration of discipline: The path to spiritual growth.* New York City, NY: HarperCollins.

Fox, N. A. (Ed.). (1994). The development of emotion regulation: Biological and behavioral considerations. *Monographs of the Society for Research in Child Development, Serial 59* (2–3, Serial no. 240).

Franco, D. (2006). Action as ejection. *Journal of the American Psychoanalytic Association, 54*(1), 88–107.

Frankl, V. (1959). *Man's search for meaning.* New York City, NY: Washington Square Press.

Frankel, Z., Levitt, H., Murray, D., Greenberg, L., & Angus, L. (2006). Assessing silent processes in psychotherapy: An empirically derived categorization system and sampling strategy. *Psychotherapy Research, 16*(5), 627–638.

Freedman, S .R., & Enright, R. D. (1996). Forgiveness as an intervention goal with incest survivors. *Journal of Consulting and Clinical Psychology, 64*, 983–992.

Freeman, S. M. (2004). *Cognitive behavior therapy in nursing practice.* New York City, NY: Springer.

Fremont, S., & Anderson, W. (1986). What client behaviors make counselors angry? An exploratory study. *Journal of Counseling and Development, 65*, 67–70.

Freud, S. (1895). Project for a scientific psychology (1954 [1895]). In M. Bonaparte, A. Freud, & E. Kris (Eds.), In *The origins of psycho-analysis* (J. Strachey, trans.) (pp. 347–445). New York City, NY: Basic Books.

Freudenberger, H. J. (1974). Staff burnout. *Journal of Social Issues, 30*(1), 159–165.

Fry, W. F., & Salameh, W. A. (Eds.). (1987). Handbook of humor and psychotherapy: Advances in the clinical use of humor. Sarasota, FL: Professional Resource Exchange.

Fussell, F., & Bonney, W. (1990). A comparative study of childhood experiences of psychotherapists and physicists: Implications for clinical practice. *Psychotherapy, 27*, 505–512.

Gabbard, G. O. (2000). A neurologically informed perspective on psychotherapy. *British Journal of Psychiatry, 177*, 117–122.

Gabbard, G. O. (2009). *Textbook of psychotherapeutic treatments.* Arlington, VA: American Psychiatric Publishing.

Gabbard, G. O., & Atkinson, S. (1996). *Synopsis of treatments of psychiatric disorders* (2nd ed.). Washington, DC: American Psychiatric Press.

Gall, T., Charbonneau, C., Clarke, N. H., Grant, K., Joseph, A., & Shouldice, L. (2005). Understanding the nature and role of spirituality in relation to coping and health: A conceptual framework. *Canadian Psychology, 46*, 88–104.

Garfield, S. L. (1983). Effectiveness of psychotherapy: The perennial controversy. *Professional Psychology: Theory, Research, and Practice, 14*, 35–43.

Garfield, S. L. (1998). *The practice of brief psychotherapy* (2nd ed.). New York City, NY: Wiley.

Garfield, S. L., & Bergin, A. E. (1986). Introduction and historical overview. In S. L. Garfield & A. E. Bergin (Eds.), *Handbook of psychotherapy and behavior change* (pp. 3–22). New York City, NY: Wiley.

Garzon, F. (2005). Interventions that apply scripture in psychotherapy. *Journal of Psychology and Theology, 33*, 113–121.

Garzon, F. & Burkett, L. (2002). Healing of memories: models, research, future directions. *Journal of Psychology and Christianity, 21*(2), 42–49.

Geisler, N. L., & Watkins, W. D. (2003). *Worlds apart: A handbook on world views* (2nd ed.). Eugene, OR: Wipf & Stock.

Geller, J., Cassin, S. E., Brown, K. E., & Srikameswaran, S. (2009). Factors associated with improvements in readiness for change: Low vs. normal BMI eating disorders. *International Journal of Eating Disorders, 42*(1), 40–46.

Gelso, C. J., Latts, M. G., Gomez, M. J., & Fassinger, R. E. (2002). Countertransference management and therapy outcome: An initial evaluation. *Journal of Clinical Psychology, 58*, 861–867.

George, R. L., & Cristiani, T. S. (1981). *Theory, methods, and processes of counseling and psychotherapy.* Englewood Cliffs, NJ: Prentice-Hall.

George, R. L., & Cristiani, T. S. (1990). *Counseling: Theory and practice* (3rd ed.). Upper Saddle River, NJ: Prentice Hall.

Gill, M. M. (1984). Psychoanalysis and psychotherapy: A revision. *International Review of Psychoanalysis, 11,* 161–179.

Gilliland, B. E., & James, R. K. (1988). *Crisis intervention strategies.* Pacific Grove, CA: Brooks/Cole.

Gladding, S. T. (1990). Coming full cycle: Reentry after the group. *Journal for Specialists in Group Work, 15,* 130–131.

Gladding, S. T. (2002). *Becoming a counselor: The light, the bright, and the serious.* Alexandria, VA: American Counseling Association.

Gladding, S. T. (2009). *Counseling: A comprehensive profession* (updated 6th ed.). Upper Saddle River, NJ: Prentice Hall.

Gladstein, G. A. (1983). Understanding empathy: Integrating counselling, developmental, and social psychology perspectives. *Journal of Counselling Psychology, 30,* 467–482.

Glass, C. R., Arnkoff, D. B., & Shapiro, S. J. (2001). Expectations and preferences. *Psychotherapy, 38*(4), 455–461.

Glass, L. (2003). The gray areas of boundary crossings and violations. *American Journal of Psychotherapy, 57*(4), 429–444.

Glasser, W. (1962). *Reality therapy.* New York City, NY: HarperCollins.

Goldberg, C. (1986). *On being a psychotherapist.* Northvale, NJ: Jason Aronson.

Golden, W. (1983). Resistance in cognitive-behavior therapy. *British Journal of Cognitive Psychotherapy, 1*(2), 33–42.

Goldman, A. I. (2006). *Simulating minds: The philosophy, psychology and neuroscience of mindreading.* New York City, NY: Oxford University Press.

Goodman, C. C. (2007). Family dynamics in three-generation grandfamilies. *Journal of Family Issues, 28*(3), 355–379.

Gorsuch, R. L., & Maylink, W. D. (1988). Toward a co-professional model of clergy-psychologist referral. *Journal of Psychology and Christianity, 7,* 22–31.

Gordon, D. (1978). *Therapeutic metaphors: Helping others through the looking glass.* Cupertino, CA: Meta Publications.

Graham, S., Furr, S., Flowers, C., & Burke, M. T. (2001). Religion and spirituality in coping with stress. *Counseling and Values, 46*(1), 2–5.

Grant, B. (1985). The moral nature of psychotherapy. *Counseling and Values, 29,* 141–150.

Gratton, C. (1992). *The art of spiritual guidance.* New York City, NY: Crossroad.

Greenberg, L. S., & Warwar, S. H. (2006). Special issue: Integration of between-session (homework) activities into psychotherapy. *Journal of Psychotherapy Integration, 16*(2), 178–200.

Greenspan, S. I. (1997). *Developmentally based psychotherapy.* Madison, WI: International Universities Press.

Greenspan, S. I., & Greenspan, N. K. (2003). *The clinical interview of the child.* Washington, DC: American Psychiatric.

Griffith, B. A., & Griggs, J. C. (2001). Religious identity status as a model to understand, assess, and interact with client spirituality. *Counseling and Values, 44,* 213–222.

Grimes, C. (2007). God-image research: A literature review. *Journal of Spirituality in Mental Health, 9,* 11–32.

Grimmer, A., & Tribe, R. (2001). Counselling psychologists' perceptions of the impact of mandatory personal therapy on professional development—an exploratory study. *Counselling Psychology Quarterly, 14*(4), 287–301.

Grinder, J., & Bandler, R. (1976a). *The structure of magic II.* Palo Alto, CA: Science & Behavior.

Grinder, J., & Bandler, R. (1976b). *Patterns of the hypnotic techniques of Milton H. Erickson, M.D. Volume I.* Cupertino, CA: Meta.

Grinder, J., & Bostic St. Clair, C. (2001). *Whispering in the wind.* Scotts Valley, CA: J & C Enterprises.

Groothuis, D. (2000). *Truth decay.* Downers Grove, IL: InterVarsity Press.

Grotevant, H. D. (1998). Adolescent development in family contexts. In W. Darnon and N. Eisenberg (Eds.), *Handbook of child psychology: Social, emotional, and personality development* (5th ed., pp 1097–1149). New York City, NY: Wiley.

Groth-Marnat, G. (2003). *Handbook of psychological assessment* (4th ed.). New York City, NY: John Wiley & Sons.

Grounds, V. (1976). *Emotional problems and the gospel.* Grand Rapids, MI: Zondervan Publishing House.

Gubi, P. M. (2001). An exploration of the use of Christian prayer in mainstream counseling [Electronic version]. *British Journal of Guidance & Counselling, 29*(4), 425–434. Retrieved September 21, 2008, from EbscoHost database.

Guerin, P. J., & Hubbard, I. M. (1987). Impact of therapist's personal family system on clinical work. *Journal of Psychotherapy and the Family, 3*(2), 47–60.

Guttman, J., & Daniels, S. (2001). What do school counselors gain from their role as psychotherapists? *Educational Psychology, 21,* 203–218.

Guy, J. D. (1987). *The personal life of the psychotherapist.* New York City, NY: Wiley.

Guy, J. D., & Brown, C. F. (1992). How to benefit emotionally from private practice. *Psychotherapy in Private Practice, 10*(4), 27–39.

Guy, J. D., Brown, C. K., & Poelstra, P. L. (1990). Psychotherapists as victim: A discussion of patient violence. *The California Psychologist, 22,* 20–22.

Guy, J. D., & Liaboe, G. (1986). The impact of conducting psychotherapy on psychotherapists' interpersonal functioning. *Professional Psychology, 17,* 111–114.

Haber, R. (1996). *Dimensions of psychotherapy supervision: Maps and means.* New York City, NY: W. W. Norton.

Haferkamp, H. (1989). *Social structure and culture.* New York City, NY: Walter De Gruyter.

Haley, J. (1973). *Uncommon therapy: The psychiatric techniques of Milton H. Erickson M.D.* New York City, NY: W. W. Norton.

Haley, J. (1976). *Problem-solving therapy.* San Francisco, CA: Jossey-Bass.

Haley, J. (1977). *Problem-solving therapy.* San Francisco, CA: Jossey-Bass.

Haley, J. (1984). *Ordeal therapy.* San Francisco, CA: Jossey-Bass.

Hall, E. T. (1966). *The hidden dimension.* New York City, NY: Doubleday.

Hall, J., Guterman, D., Lee, H., & Little, S. (2002). Counselor-client matching on ethnicity, gender, and language: Implications for counseling school-aged children. *North American Journal of Psychology, 4*(3), 367–380.

Halverson, S., & Miars, R. (2005). The helping relationship. In D. Capuzzi & D. Gross (Eds.), *Introduction to the counseling profession* (4th ed., pp. 56–74). Boston, MA: Allyn & Bacon.

Hansen, J. A. (2008). *Therapist self-disclosure: Who and when.* Unpublished doctoral dissertation, Alliant International University, Fresno, CA.

Hansen, J. C., Stevic, R. R., & Warner, R. W. (1982). *Counseling: Theory and process* (3rd ed.). Boston, MA: Allyn & Bacon.

Hardaway, T. T. (1976). The effects of short-term, personal counseling on prospective counselors. *Dissertation Abstracts International, 37*(7), A4133. (UMI NO. 760398).

Hardman, R. K., & Berrett, M. E. (2000). *Eating disorder recovery: A spiritual perspective.* Orem, UT: Center for Change.

Hardman, R. K., & Berrett, M. E. (2005). *Therapeutic guidelines and experiential interventions for the treatment of eating disorders.* Orem, UT: Center for Change.

Hardman, R. K., Berrett, M. E., & Richards, P. S. (2003). Spirituality and ten false pursuits of eating disorders: Implications for counselors. *Counseling and Values, 48,* 67–77.

Hardman, R. K., Berrett, M. E., & Richards, P. S. (2004). A theistic inpatient treatment approach for eating disorder patients: A case report. In S. Richards & A. Bergin (Eds.), *Casebook for a spiritual strategy in counseling and psychotherapy* (pp. 55–73). Washington, DC: American Psychological Association.

Hardy, D. (2000). A Winnicottian redescription of Christian spiritual direction relationships: Illustrating the potential contribution of psychology of religion to Christian spiritual practice. *Journal of Psychology and Theology, 28,* 263–275.

Harper, J. (1996). Interpersonal issues in counseling a resistant child: A case study. *British Journal of Guidance & Counseling, 24*(1), 129–140.

Harrington, J. A. (2001, October 27). *Self-disclosure: Temptations and alternatives.* Paper presented at SACES conference, Athens, GA. (judithharrington@worldnet.att.net)

Harris, I. J., Schoneman, S. W., & Carrera, S. R. (2002). Approaches to religiosity related to anxiety among college students. *Mental Health, Religion & Culture, 5*(3), 253–265.

Hartley, G. D. (1995). Empathy in the counseling process: The role of counselor understanding in client change. *Journal of Humanistic Education and Development, 34,* 13–23.

Hatchett, G. T. (2004). Reducing premature termination in university counseling centers. *Journal of College Student Psychotherapy, 19*(2), 13–27.

Hatchett, G. T., & Park, H. L. (2003). Comparison of four operational definitions of premature termination. *Psychotherapy: Theory, Research, Practice, Training, 40,* 226–231.

Hathaway, W. L. (2005). Scripture and psychological science: Integrative challenges & callings. *Journal of Psychology & Theology, 33*(2), 89–97.

Hawkins, R. (n.d.). *Concentric circles.* COUN 507 Counseling and Theology PowerPoint Slides.

Hay, C. E., & Kinnier, R. T. (1998). Homework in counseling. *Journal of Mental Health Counseling, 20*(2), 122–132.

Hayes, R. L. (1982). A re-view of adolescent identity formation: Implications for education. *Adolescence, 17*(65), 153–165.

Hazler, R., & Barwick, N. (2001). *The therapeutic environment: Core conditions for facilitating therapy.* London, UK: Open University Press.

Heap, M. (1988). Neuro-linguistic programming. In M. Heap (Ed.), *Hypnosis: Current clinical, experimental and forensic practices.* London, UK: Croom Helm.

Hebl, J. H., & Enright, R. D. (1993). Forgiveness as a psychotherapeutic goal with elderly females. *Psychotherapy: Theory, Research, Practice, Training, 30,* 658–667.

Helbig, S., & Fehm, L. (2004). Problems with homework in CBT: Rare exception or rather frequent? *Journal Behavioral and Cognitive Psychology, 32*(3), 291–301.

Helmeke, K. B., & Sori, C. F. (Eds.). (2006). *The therapist's notebook for integrating spirituality in counseling: Homework, handouts, and activities.* New York City, NY: Haworth Press.

Hemmings, A. (2000). Counselling in primary care: A review of the practice evidence. *British Journal of Guidance and Counseling, 28*(2), 234–254.

Herman, J. (1997). *Trauma and recovery: The aftermath of violence—from domestic abuse to political terror.* New York City, NY: Basic Books.

Hendlin, S. J. (1987). Gestalt therapy: Aspects of evolving theory and practice. *Humanistic Psychologist, 15,* 184–196.

Henry, J. D., Phillips, L. H., Crawford, J. R., Ietswaart, M., & Summers, F. (2006). Theory of mind following traumatic brain injury: The role of emotion recognition and executive dysfunction. *Neuropsychologia, 44*(10), 1623–1628.

Herring, R., & Meggert, S. (1994). The use of humor as a counselor strategy with Native American Indian children [Electronic version]. *Elementary School Guidance & Counseling, 29*(1), 67–76.

Hill, C. (2005). Therapist techniques, client involvement, and the therapeutic relationship: Inextricably intertwined in the therapy process. *Psychotherapy Theory, Research, Practice, Training, 42*(4), 431–442.

Hill, C. E., Helms, J. E., Spiegal, S. B., & Tichenor, V. (1988). Development of a system for categorizing client reactions to counselor interventions. *Journal of Counseling Psychology, 33,* pp. 3–22.

Hill, C. E., & O'Brien, K. M. (1999). *Helping skills: Facilitating exploration, insight, and action.* Washington, DC: American Psychological Association Press.

Hill, C. E., & O'Grady, K. (1985). List of therapeutic intentions illustrated in a case study with therapists of varying theoretical orientations. *Journal of Counseling Psychology, 35,* 257–306.

Hill, C. E., Thompson, B. J., & Ladany, N. (2003). Therapist use of silence in therapy: A survey. *Journal of Clinical Psychology, 59,* 513–524.

Hill, P. C., & Hall, T. W. (2002). Relational schemas in processing one's image of God and self. *Journal of Psychology and Christianity, 21*(4), 365–373.

Hodge, D. R. (2003). *Spiritual assessment: Handbook for helping professionals.* Botsford, CT: North American Association of Christians in Social Work.

Hodge, D. R. (2005). Developing a spiritual assessment toolbox: A discussion of the strengths and limitations of five different assessment methods. *Health & Social Work, 30*(4), 314–324.

Hoekema, A. A. (1986). *Created in God's image.* Grand Rapids, MI: William B. Eerdmans.

Holloway, E. L., & Wampold, B. E. (1986). Relation between conceptual level and counseling related tasks: A meta-analysis. *Journal of Counseling Psychology, 33*(3), 310–319.

Holmes, J. (2001). *The search for the secure base: Attachment theory and psychotherapy.* New York City, NY: Brunner-Routledge.

Horney, K. (1945). *Our inner conflicts.* New York City, NY: W. W. Norton.

Howard, K. I., Kopta, S. M., Krause, M. S., & Orlinsky, D. E. (1986). The dose-effect relationship in psychotherapy. *American Psychologist, 41,* 159–164.

Hoyt, M. F., & Miller, S. D. (2000). Stage appropriate change-oriented brief therapy. In J. Carlson & L. Sperry (Eds.), *Brief therapy with individuals and couples* (pp. 289–330). Phoenix, AZ: Zeig, Tucker, & Theisen.

Hunt, D. (1987). *Beyond seduction.* Eugene, OR: Harvest House.

Hurding, R. F. (1995). Pathways to wholeness: Christian journeying in a postmodern age. *Journal of Psychology and Christianity, 14,* 293–305.

Hynan, D. J. (1990). *Ending therapy: The meaning of termination.* New York City, NY: New York University Press.

Icenogle, G. W. (1994). *Biblical foundations for small group ministry: An integrational approach.* Downers Grove, IL: InterVarsity Press.

Irving, P., & Dickson, D. (2006). A re-conceptualization of Rogers' core conditions: Implications for research, practice and training. *International Journal for the Advancement of Counselling, 28*(2), 183–194.

Ivey, A. E., & Ivey, M. B. (2003). *Intentional interviewing and counseling* (5th ed.). Pacific Grove, CA: Brooks/Cole.

Ivey, A. E., Ivey, M. B., Zalaquett, C. P. (2010). *Intentional interviewing and counseling: Facilitating client development in a multicultural society* (7th ed.). Pacific Grove, CA: Brooks/Cole.

Ivey, A. E., & Simek-Downing, L. (1980). *Counseling and psychotherapy: Skills, theories, and practice.* Englewood Cliffs, NJ: Prentice-Hall.

Izard, C. E., Fine, S. Mostow, A., Trentacosta, C., & Campbell, J. (2002). Emotion processes in normal and abnormal development and prevention intervention. *Development and Psychopathology, 14,* 761–787.

Jacobs, E. (1992). *Creative counseling techniques: An illustrated guide.* Lutz, FL: Psychological Assessment Resources.

James, R. K. & Gilliland, B. E. (2003). *Theories and strategies in counseling and psychotherapy.* New York City, NY: Pearson Education.

Johns, H. (1996). *Personal development in counselor training.* London, UK: Cassell.

Johnson, E. (2007). *Foundations for soul care: A Christian psychology proposal.* Downers Grove, IL: InterVarsity Academic Press.

Jones, J. W. (2007). Psychodynamic theories of the evolution of the God image. In G. L. Moriarty and L. Hoffman (Eds.), *God image handbook for spiritual counseling and psychotherapy: Research, theory, and practice* (pp. 33–56). Binghamton, NY: Hawthorne.

Jones, S. L., & Butman, R. E. (1991). *Modern psychotherapies.* Downers Grove, IL: InterVarsity Press.

Jones, T. (2010). *Practicing the presence of God: Learn to live moment-by-moment – Brother Lawrence of the Resurrection.* Brewster, MA: Paraclete.

Jourard, S. (1971). *The transparent self* (Rev. ed.). New York City, NY: Van-Nostrand Reinhold.

Joyce, A. S., Piper, W. E., Ogrodniczuk, J. S., & Klein, R. H. (2006). *Termination in psychotherapy: A psychodynamic model of processes and outcomes.* Washington, DC: American Psychological Association Press.

Jung, C. G. (1954a). Two essays on analytical psychology. In H. Read, M. Fordham, & G. Adler (Eds.), *The Collected Works of C. G. Jung* (Vol. 7). New York City, NY: Pantheon.

Jung, C. G. (1954b). Psychology and religion: West and east. In H. Read, M. Fordham, & G. Adler (Eds.), *The Collected Works of C. G. Jung* (Vol. 11). New York City, NY: Pantheon.

Jurkovic, G. (1997). *Lost childhoods: The plight of the parentified child.* New York City, NY: Brunner/Mazel.

Kaslow, F., & Schulman, N. (1987). How to be sane and happy as a family therapist or the reciprocal impact of family therapy and practice and therapists' personal lives and mental health. *Journal of Psychotherapy and the Family, 3*(2), 79–96.

Katz, E. C., Brown, B. S., Schwartz, R. P., Weintraub, E., Barksdale, W., & Robinson, R. (2004). Role induction: A method for enhancing early retention in outpatient drug-free treatment. *Journal of Consulting and Clinical Psychology, 72*(2), 227–234.

Kazantzis, N., & L'Abate, L. (Eds.). (2007). *Handbook of homework assignments in psychotherapy: Research, practice, and prevention.* New York City, NY: Springer.

Kazantzis, N., & Lampropoulos, G. (2002, May). Reflecting on homework in psychotherapy: What can we conclude from research and experience? *Journal of Clinical Psychology, 58*(5), 576–585.

Kazantzis, N., & Ronan, K. R. (2006). Can between-session (homework) activities be considered a common factor in psychotherapy? *Journal of Psychotherapy, 16*, 115–217.

Keijsers, G. P. J., Schaap, C. P. D. R., & Hoogduin, C. A. L. (2000). The impact of interpersonal patient and therapist behavior on outcome in cognitive-behavioral therapy: A review of empirical studies. *Behavior Modifications, 24*, 264–297.

Kelly, A. E., & Rodriguez, R. R. (2007). Do therapists self-disclose more to clients with greater symptomatology? *Psychotherapy: Theory, Research, Practice, Training, 44*, pp. 470–475.

Kelly, E. W. (1995). *Religion and spirituality in counseling and psychotherapy.* Alexandria, VA: American Counseling Association.

Kernberg, O. (1976). *Object relations theory and clinical psychoanalysis.* Northvale, NJ: Jason Aronson.

Kiesler, D. (1996). *Contemporary interpersonal theory*. New York City, NY: Wiley.

Kim, B. S. K., Ng, G. F., & Ahn, A. J. (2005). Effects of client expectation for counseling success, client-counselor worldview match, and client adherence to Asian and European American cultural values on counseling process with Asian Americans. *Journal of Counseling Psychology, 52*(1), 67–76.

King, R. R., Jr. (1978). Evangelical Christians and professional counseling: A conflict of values? *Journal of Psychology and Theology, 6*(4), 276–281.

Kivlighan, D. M., Jr. (2007). Where is the relationship in research on the alliance? Two methods for analyzing dyadic data. *Journal of Counseling Psychology, 54*(4), 423–433.

Kopp, C. B. (1989). Regulation of distress and negative emotions: A developmental view. *Developmental Psychology, 25*, 343–354.

Kopp, S. B. (1971). *Guru: Metaphors from a psychotherapist*. Palo Alto, CA: Science & Behavior Books.

Kornblith, S. J., Rehm, L. P., O'Hara, M. W., & Lamparski, D. M. (1983). The contribution of self-reinforcement training and behavioral assignments to the efficacy of self-control therapy for depression. *Cognitive Therapy and Research, 7*, 499–528.

Kottler, J. A. (1994). *Advanced group leadership*. Pacific Grove, CA: Brooks/Cole.

Kottler, J. (2004). *Introduction to therapeutic counseling: Voices from the field* (5th ed.). Pacific Grove, CA: Thompson.

Kottler, J., & Brown, R. (1992). *Introduction to therapeutic counseling* (2nd ed.). Pacific Grove, CA: Brooks/Cole.

Kovaks, A. L. (1976). The emotional hazards of teaching psychotherapy, *Psychotherapy: Theory, Research and Practice, 13*, 321–334.

Kramer, S. (1990). *Positive endings in psychotherapy: Bringing meaningful closure to therapeutic relationships*. San Francisco, CA: Jossey-Bass.

Kuyken, W., Padesky, C. A., & Dudley, R. (2009). *Collaborative case conceptualization: Working effectively with clients in cognitive-behavioral therapy*. New York City, NY: Guilford Press.

Lackie, B. (1983). The families of origin of social workers. *Clinical Social Work Journal, 11*(4), 309–322.

LaFromboise, T. D. (1985). The role of cultural diversity in counseling psychology. *The Counseling Psychologist, 13*, 649–655.

Lambert, M. J., & Cattani-Thompson, K. (1996). Current findings regarding the effectiveness of counseling: Implications for practice. *Journal of Counseling and Development, 74*(6), 601–608.

Lambert, M. J., & Miller, M. J. (2001). Helping prospective patients avoid harmful psychotherapies. *Contemporary Psychology, 46*, 386–388.

Lambert, M. J., Shapiro, D. A., Bergin, A. E. (1986). The effectiveness of psychotherapy. In S. L. Garfield & A. E. Bergin (Eds.), *Handbook of psychotherapy and behavior change* (pp. 157–211). New York City, NY: John Wiley & Sons.

Lambert, M. J., Whipple, J. L., Smart, D. W., Vermeersch, D. A., Nielsen, S. L., & Hawkins, E. J. (2001). The effects of providing therapists with feedback on patient progress during psychotherapy: Are outcomes enhanced? *Psychotherapy Research, 11*, 49–68.

Lane, R. C. (1984). The difficult patient, resistance, and the negative therapeutic reaction: A review of the literature. *Current Issues in Psychoanalytic Practice, 1*(4), 83–106.

Langberg, D. (1996, September). *Garbage city*. Paper presented at the meeting of the AACC World Conference, Nashville, TN.

Langberg, D. (2006). The spiritual life of the therapist: We become what we habitually reflect. *Journal of Psychology & Christianity, 25*, 258–266.

Lankton, S. R. (1980). *Practical magic: A translation of basic neurolinguistic programming into clinical psychotherapy*. Cupertino, CA: Meta.

Larrabee, M. J. (1982). Working with reluctant clients through affirmation techniques. *Personnel and Guidance Journal, 61*, 105–109.

Laurencelle, R. M., Abell, S. C., & Schwartz, D. J. (2002). The relation between intrinsic religious faith and psychological well-being. *International Journal for the Psychology of Religion, 12*(2), 109–123.

Laurent, H. & Powers, S. (2007). Emotion regulation in emerging adult couples: Temperament, attachment, and HPA response to conflict. *Biological Psychology, 76*(1–2), 61–71.

Leaper, C., Carson, M., Baker, C., Holiday, H., & Myers, S. (1995). Self-disclosure and listener verbal support in same-gender and cross-gender friends' conversation. *Sex Roles, 33,* 387–403.

Leech, K. (1989). *Spirituality and pastoral care*. Cambridge, MA: Cowley.

Lefcourt, H. M. (1991). Locus of control. In J. P. Robinson, P. R. Shaver, & L. S. Wrightsman (Eds.), *Measures of personality and social psychological attitudes* (pp. 413–499). San Diego, CA: Academic Press.

Lehman, K. (2004). *The real you: Becoming the person you want to be*. Grand Rapids, MI: Fleming H. Revell.

Leigh, D. A. (1998). *Referral and termination issues for counselors: Professional skills for counselors series*. Thousand Oaks, CA: Sage.

Leitner, L. M. (2006). Therapeutic artistry: Evoking experiential and relational truths. In P. Caputi, H. Foster, & L. Viney (Eds.), *Personal construct psychology: New ideas* (pp. 83–98). Sydney, AU: Wiley.

Leitner, L. M. (2007). Theory, technique, and person: Technical integration in experiential constructivist psychotherapy. *Journal of Psychotherapy Integration, 17*(1), 33–49.

Leong, F. T. L. (Ed.). (2008). *Encyclopedia of counseling*. Thousand Oaks, CA: Sage.

Leslie, R. S. (2004, May/June). Termination of treatment. *Family Therapy Magazine, 3*(3), 46–48.

Levenkron, S. (2000). *Anatomy of anorexia*. New York City, NY: W. W. Norton.

Levitt, H. M. (1998). *Silence in psychotherapy: The meaning and functions of pauses*. Unpublished doctoral dissertation, York University, Toronto, Canada.

Levitt, H. M. (2001). The sounds of silence in psychotherapy: Clients' experiences of pausing. *Psychotherapy Research, 11*, 295–309.

Lewis, C. C., Simons, A. D., Silva, S. G., Rohde, P., Small, D. M., Murakami, J. L. et al. (2009). The role of readiness to change in response to treatment of adolescent depression. *Journal of Consulting and Clinical Psychology, 77*(3), 422–428.

Lewis, C. S. (1950). *The lion, the witch, and the wardrobe.* London, UK: Geoffrey Bles.

Lewis, G. R., & Demarest, B. A. (1996). *Integrative theology.* Grand Rapids, MI: Zondervan Publishing House.

Lightner, R. P. (1997). *A biblical case for total inerrancy: How Jesus viewed the Old Testament.* Grand Rapids, MI: Kregel Academic & Professional.

Likowski, K. U. Mühlberger, A., Seibt, B., Pauli, P., & Weyers, P. (2008). Modulation of facial mimicry by attitudes. *Journal of Experimental Social Psychology, 44*(4), 1065–1072.

Lilienfeld, S. O. (2007). Psychological treatments that cause harm. *Perspectives on Psychological Science, 2*, 53–70.

Lin, Y. (2002). Taiwanese university students' conceptions of counseling. *Journal of Contemporary Psychotherapy, 31,* 199–211.

Lints, R. (1993). *The fabric of theology.* Grand Rapids, MI: William B. Eerdmans.

Littrell, J. M., Lee-Borden, N., & Lorenz, J. A. (1979). A developmental framework for counseling supervision. *Counselor Education and Supervision, 19*, 119–136.

Loganbill, C., Hardy, E., & Delworth, U. (1982). Supervision: A conceptual model. *Counseling Psychologist, 10*(1), 3–42.

Lovinger, R. J. (1979). Therapeutic strategies with "religious" resistances. *Psychotherapy: Theory, Research and Practice, 16*, 419–427.

Lovinger, R. J. (1984). *Working with religious issues in therapy.* New York City, NY: Jason Aronson.

Luepker, E. T., & Norton, L. (2003). *Record keeping in psychotherapy and counseling: Protecting confidentiality and the professional relationship.* New York City, NY: Brunner-Routledge.

Lukas, S. (1993). *Where to start and what to ask.* New York City, NY: W. W. Norton.

Lunkenheimer, E. S., Shields, A. M., & Cortina, K. S. (2007). Family stressors, emotional competence, and adolescent risky behavior. *Social Development, 16*(2), 232–248.

Lutwak, N., & Hennessy, J. (1982). Conceptual systems functioning as a mediating factor in the development of counseling skills. *Journal of Counseling Psychology, 29*, 265–260.

Lyddon, W. J., Clay, A. L., & Sparks, C. L. (2001). Metaphor and change in counseling. *Journal of Counseling & Development, 79*, 269–274.

MacLean, A. P. (2005). A problem well stated is a problem half solved. In M. Cierpka, V. Thomas, & D. H. Sprenkle (Eds.), *Family assessment: Integrating multiple perspectives* (pp. 53–80). Ashland, OH: Hogrefe & Huber.

Madell, T. O. (1982). The relationship between values and attitudes toward three therapy methods. *Counseling and Values, 27*, 52–60.

Malle, J. D. (2005). Three puzzles of mindreading. In B. F. Malle & S. D. Hodges (Eds.), *Other minds: How humans bridge the divide between self and others* (pp. 26–43). New York City, NY: Guilford Press.

Manser, M. (2001). *Westminster collection of Christian quotations.* Louisville, KY: Westminster John Knox Press.

Marcus, E. R. (2007). Transference and countertransference to medication and its implications for ego function. *Journal of the American Academy of Psychoanalysis and Dynamic Psychiatry, 35*(2), 211–218.

Marlatt, G. A., & Kristeller, J. L. (1999). Mindfulness and meditation. In W. R. Miller (Ed.), *Integrating spirituality into treatment: resources for practitioners* (pp. 67–84). Washington, DC: American Psychological Association Press.

Marrow, A. J. (1969). *The practical theorist: The life and work of Kurt Lewin.* New York City, NY: Basic Books.

Martin, D. (1999). *Counseling and therapy skills.* Prospect Heights, IL: Waveland Press.

Martin, E. S., & Schurtman, R. (1985). Termination anxiety as it affects the therapist. *Psychotherapy, 22*(1), 92–96.

Matthews, S. (2000). Prayer and spirituality. *Rheumatic Disorder Clinic, 26*, 177.

May, V. M., & Albee, G. W. (1992). Psychotherapy and ethnic minorities. In D. K. Freedheim (Ed.), *History of psychotherapy* (pp. 552–570). Washington, DC: American Psychological Association Press.

Mayer, J. D., Salovey, P., Caruso, D. R., & Sitarenios, G. (2001) Emotional intelligence as a standard intelligence. *Emotion, 1*(3), 232–242.

McCann, L., & Pearlman, L. (1990). Vicarious traumatization: A framework for understanding psychological effects of working with victims. *Journal of Traumatic Stress, 3*(1), 131–149.

McCullough, M. E. (1995). Prayer and health: Conceptual issues, research review, and research agenda. *Journal of Psychology and Theology, 25*, 15–29.

McCullough, M. E., & Larson, D. B. (1999). Prayer. In W. R. Miller (Ed.), *Integrating spirituality into treatment: resources from practitioners,* (pp. 85–110). Washington, DC: American Psychological Association Press.

McCullough, M. E., Worthington, E. L., Jr., & Rachal, K. C. (1997). Interpersonal forgiving in close relationships. *Journal of Personality and Social Psychology, 73*, 321–336.

McGinn, L., Young, J., & Sanderson, W. (1995). When and how to do longer term therapy without feeling guilty. *Cognitive and Behavioral Practice, 2*, 187–212.

McGoldrick, M., Gerson, R., & Shellenberger, S. (2008). *Genograms: Assessment and intervention* (3rd ed.). New York City, NY: W. W. Norton.

McKenzie, V. M. (1986). Ethnographic findings on West Indian-American clients. *Journal of Counseling & Development, 65*, 40–44.

McMinn, M. R. (1996). *Psychology, theology, and spirituality in Christian counseling.* Wheaton, IL: Tyndale House.

McMinn, M. R. (2001). Psychology, theology, and care for the soul. In M. R. McMinn & T. R. Phillips (Eds.), *Care for the soul: Exploring the intersection of psychology and theology* (pp. 9–22). Downers Grove, IL: InterVarsity Press.

McMinn, M. R. (2008). *Sin and grace in Christian counseling: An integrative paradigm.* Downers Grove, IL: IVP Academic.

McMinn, M. R., & Campbell, C. D. (2007). *Integrative psychotherapy: Toward a comprehensive Christian approach.* Downers Grove, IL: InterVarsity Press.

McMinn, M. R., & McRay, B. W. (1997). Spiritual disciplines and the practice of integration: Possibilities and challenges for Christian psychologists. *Journal of Psychology and Theology, 25*(1), 101–109.

McMinn, M. R., & Phillips, T. R. (Eds.). (2001). *Care for the soul: Exploring the intersection of psychology and theology.* Downers Grove, IL: InterVarsity Press.

McMinn, M. R., Ruiz, J. N., Marx, D., Wright, J. B., & Gilbert, N. B. (2006). Professional psychology and the doctrines of sin and grace: Christian leaders' perspective. *Professional psychology: Research and practice, 37*(3), 295–302.

Mearns, D. (1997). *Person-centered counseling training.* London, UK: Sage.

Meichenbaum, D. (1977). *Cognitive-behavior modification: An integrative approach.* New York City, NY: Plenum.

Meier, S. T. (1989). *The elements of counseling.* Pacific Grove, CA: Brooks/Cole.

Meldrum, L., King, R., & Spooner, D. (2002). Secondary traumatic stress in case managers working in community mental health services. In C. R. Figley (Ed.), *Treating compassion fatigue* (pp. 85–106). New York City, NY: Brunner Mazel.

Menninger, K. A. (1958). *Theory of psychoanalytic technique.* New York City, NY: Harper & Row.

Miller, A. (1990). *The drama of the gifted child.* (Rev. ed.) (R. Ward, trans.). New York: Basic Books. (Original work was published in 1979.)

Miller, W. R., Benefield, R. G., & Tonigan, J. S. (1993). Enhancing motivation for change in problem drinking: A controlled comparison of two therapist styles. *Journal of Consulting and Clinical Psychology, 61*(3), 455–461.

Miller, W. R., & Rollnick, S. (2002). *Motivational interviewing: Preparing people for change* (2nd ed.). New York City, NY: Guilford Press.

Miller, W. R., & Thoresen, C. E. (Eds.). (1999). *Integrating spirituality into treatment: Resources for practitioners.* Washington, DC: American Psychological Association Press.

Minirth, F. B. (1977). *Christian psychiatry.* Old Tappan, NJ: Fleming H. Revell.

Mitchell, R. (2000). *Documentation in counseling records* (2nd ed.). Alexandria, VA: American Counseling Association.

Mohr, D. C. (1995). Negative outcome in psychotherapy: A critical review. *Clinical Psychology: Science and Practice, 2,* 1–27.

Moline, M. E., Williams, G. T., & Austin, K. M. (1998). *Documenting psychotherapy: Essentials for mental health practitioners.* Thousand Oaks, CA: Sage.

Monks, G. M. (1995). *A meta-analysis of role induction studies.* Unpublished doctoral dissertation, University of Hartford, West Hartford, CT.

Monroe, P. G. (2001). Exploring clients' personal sin in the therapeutic context: Theological perspectives on a case study of self-deceit. In M. McMinn & T. Phillips, *Care for the soul: Exploring the intersection of psychology and theology* (pp. 202–217). Downers Grove, IL: InterVarsity Press.

Moon, G. W. (1997). Training tomorrow's integrators in today's busy intersection: Better look four ways before crossing. *Journal of Psychology and Theology, 25,* 284–293.

Moreland, J. P., & Craig, W. L. (2003). *Philosophical foundations for a Christian worldview.* Downers Grove, IL: InterVarsity Press.

Moriarty, G. L., & Hoffman, L. (2007). *God image handbook for spiritual counseling and psychotherapy: Research, theory, and practice.* Binghamton, NY: Hawthorn Press.

Morrison, J. (1995). *The first interview: Revised for DSM-IV.* New York City, NY: Guilford Press.

Morrison, J. (2007). *The first interview* (3rd ed.). New York City, NY: Guilford Press.

Morrison, J. (2007). *Diagnosis made easier: Principles and techniques for mental health clinicians.* New York City NY: Guilford Press.

Morrissette, P. J. (2002). *Self-supervision: A primer for counselors and helping professionals.* New York City, NY: Brunner-Routledge.

Mortensen, C. D. (2008). *Optimal human relations: The search for a good life.* New Brunswick, NJ: Transaction.

Mosak, H. H. (1989). Adlerian psychotherapy. In R. J. Corsini & D. Wedding (Eds.), *Current psychotherapies* (4th ed., pp. 64–116). Itasca, IL: Peacock.

Mosak, H. H., & Maniacci, M. (1999). *A primer of adlerian psychology: The analytic behavioural-cognitive psychology of Alfred Adler.* Philadelphia, PA: Brunner/Mazel.

Moursund, J. (1985). *The process of counseling and therapy.* Englewood Cliffs, NJ: Prentice-Hall.

Moursund, J., & Kenny, M. C. (2002). *The process of counseling and therapy* (4th ed.). Upper Saddle River, NJ: Prentice Hall.

Mueller, W. J., & Keel, B. L. (1972). *Coping with conflict: Supervising counselors and psychotherapists.* New York City, NY: Appleton-Century-Crofts.

Munson, C. E. (2002). *Handbook of clinical social work supervision* (3rd ed.). New York City, NY: Haworth Press.

Murphy, K. C., & Strong, S. R. (1972). Some effects of similarity self-disclosure. *Journal of Counseling Psychology, 19,* 121–124.

Murray, A. (1908). *The full blessing of Pentecost: The one thing needful.* London, UK: James Nisbet & Co., Ltd.

Najavits, L. M., & Weiss, R. D. (1994). Variations in therapist effectiveness in the treatment of patients with substance use disorders: An empirical review. *Addiction, 89,* 679–688.

Narramore, B. (1994). Dealing with religious resistance in psychotherapy. In D. H. Stevenson (Ed.), *Psychology and Christianity integration: Seminal works that shaped the movement* (pp. 306–314). Batavia, IL: Christian Association for Psychological Studies.

Nash, R. H. (1992). *Worldviews in conflict: Choosing Christianity in a world of ideas.* Grand Rapids, MI: Zondervan Publishing House.

Nathan, P. E., & Gorman, J. M. (2002). *A guide to treatments that work* (2nd ed.). New York City, NY: Oxford University Press.

Nelson, J. K. (2008). Laugh and the world laughs with you: An attachment perspective on the meaning of laughter in psychotherapy. *Clinical Social Work Journal, 36,* 41–49.

Nelson, M. L., & Neufeldt, S. A. (1996). Building on an empirical foundation: Strategies to enhance good practice. *Journal of Counseling & Development, 74*, 609–615.

Newmark, G. R. (2001). Spirituality in eating disorder treatment. *Healthy Weight Journal, 15,* 76–78.

Nichols, M. (2009). *The lost art of listening.* New York City, NY: Guilford Press.

Noffke, J. L., & Hall, T. W. (2007). Attachment psychotherapy and the God image. *Journal of Spirituality in Mental Health, 9,* 57–78.

Norcross, J. C. (1986). Special section: Training integrative/eclectic psychotherapists. *Journal of Integrative & Eclectic Psychotherapy, 5*(1), 71–94.

Norcross, J. C. (2005). The psychotherapist's own psychotherapy: Educating and developing psychologists. *American Psychologist, 60*(8), 840–850.

Nouwen, H. J. M. (1975). *Reaching out: The three movements of the spiritual life.* New York City, NY: Image Books.

Nouwen, H. J. M. (1979). *The wounded healer: Ministry in the contemporary society.* New York City, NY: Image Books.

Oakes, K. E., & Raphael, M. M. (2008). Spiritual assessment in counseling: Methods and practice. *Counseling and Values, 52*(3), 240–252.

O'Connor, J., & Seymour, J. (2002). *Introducing NLP.* London, UK: HarperCollins.

O'Donnell, M. P. (1997). Editorial: The anatomy of stages of change. *American Journal of Health Promotion, 12,* 8–10.

O'Grady, K. A., & Richards, P. S. (2007). Theistic psychotherapy and God image. In G. L. Moriarty & L. Hoffman (Eds.), *God image handbook for spiritual counseling and psychotherapy* (pp. 183–209). New York City, NY: Haworth Press.

O'Hanlon, W. H., & Weiner-Davis, M. (2003). *In search of solutions: A new direction in psychotherapy (*Rev. ed.) New York City, NY: W. W. Norton.

Ohlschlager, G. (2004). More on Christian counseling regulation. *Christian Counseling Connection, 1,* 8–9.

Ogrodniczuk, J. S., Joyce, A. S., & Piper, W. E. (2005). Strategies for reducing patient-initiated premature termination of psychotherapy. *Harvard Review of Psychiatry, 13*(2), 57–70.

Olthuis, J. (1989). On worldviews. In P. A. Marshall, S. Griffioen, & R. J. Mouw (Eds.), *Stained glass: Worldviews and social science* (pp. 24–40). Lanham, MD: University Press of America.

Orlinsky, D.E., & Howard, K. I. (1987) A generic model of psychotherapy. *J Integrative Eclectic Psychotherapy* 6, 6–27.

Orlinsky, D. E., Norcross, J. C., Rønnestad, M. H., & Wiseman, H. (2005). Outcomes and impacts of psychotherapists' own psychotherapy. In J. D. Geller, J. C. Norcross, & D. E. Orlinksy (Eds.), *The psychotherapist's own psychotherapy: Patient and clinician perspectives* (pp. 214–230). New York City, NY: Oxford University Press.

Ortega, A. N., & Rosenheck, R. (2002). Hispanic client-case manager matching: Differences in outcomes and service use in a program for homeless persons with severe mental illness. *Journal of Nervous and Mental Disease, 190*(5), 315–323.

Osborn, C. J., Dean, E. P., & Petruzzi, M. I. (2004). Use of simulated multi-disciplinary treatment teams and client actors to teach case conceptualization and treatment planning skills. *Counselor Education and Supervision, 44,* 121–134.

Paradise, L. V., & Wilder, D. H. (1979). The relationship between client reluctance and counseling effectiveness. *Counselor Education and Supervision,19,* 35–41

Parrott, L. (1996). *Once upon a family: Building a healthy home when your family isn't a fairy tale.* Kansas City, MO: Beacon Hill.

Pascal, Blaise (1662). *Pensees.* Translated by A. J. Krailsheimer (1966). New York City, NY: Penguin. Cited from *Devotional classics*, R. Foster (Ed.), 1993. New York City, NY: Revovare Press.

Patterson, C. H. (1986). *Theories of counseling and psychotherapy* (4th ed.). New York: Harper & Row.

Patterson, G. R., & Forgatch, M. S. (1985). Therapist behavior as a determinant for client noncompliance: A paradox for the behavior modifier. *Journal of Consulting and Clinical Psychology, 53,* 846–851.

Patterson, L. E., & Eisenberg, S. (1983). *The counseling process.* Boston, MA: Houghton Mifflin.

Pattison, C. (2007). The growth and shaping of a relationship. *Infant Observation, 10*(2), 155–164.

Peeks, B. (1989). Strategies for solving children's problems understood as behavioral metaphors. *Journal of Strategic and Systemic Therapies, 8,* 22–25.

Pekarik, G. (1992). Relationship of clients' reasons for dropping out of treatment to outcome and satisfaction. *Journal of Clinical Psychology, 48*(1), 91–98.

Penn, L. S. (1990). When the therapist must leave: Forced termination of psychodynamic psychotherapy. *Professional Psychology: Research and Practice, 21*(5), 379–384.

Perls, F. S. (1969). *Gestalt therapy verbatim.* Moab, UT: Real People.

Peterson, C., & Seligman, M. (Eds.) (2004). *Character strengths and virtues.* Oxford, UK: Oxford University Press.

Perz, C. A., DiClemente, C. C., & Carbonari, J. P. (1996). Doing the right thing at the right time? The interaction of stages and processes of change in successful smoking cessation. *Health Psychology, 15*(6), 462–468.

Piaget, J. (1955). *The language and thought of the child.* New York City, NY: Meridian Books.

Pinchot, N., Riccio, A. C., & Peters, H. J. (1975). Elementary school students' and their parents' preferences for counselors. *Counselor Education and Supervision, 15,* 28–33.

Poll, J. B., & Smith, T. B. (2003). The spiritual self: toward a conceptualization of spiritual identity development. *Journal of Psychology and Theology, 31*(2), 120–142.

Poloma, M. M., & Pendleton, B. F. (1991). The effects of prayer and prayer experiences on measures of general well-being. *Journal of Psychology and Theology, 19,* 71–83.

Ponton, R. F., & Duba, J. D. (2009). The ACA code of ethics: Articulating counseling's professional covenant. *Journal of Counseling & Development, 87,* 117–121.

Postema, D. (1983). *Space for God.* Grand Rapids, MI: Board of Publications of the Christian Reformed Church.

Powlison, D. (2001). Questions at the crossroads: The care of souls and modern psychotherapies. In M. R. McMinn & T. R. Phillips (Eds.), *Care for the soul: Exploring the intersection of psychology and theology.* Downers Grove, IL: InterVarsity Press.

Predo, N. G. (2005). Transformation of the family system during adolescence. In B. Carter & M. McGoldrick (Eds.), *The expanded family life cycle: individual, family and social perspectives* (3rd ed.) (pp. 241–248). Boston, MA: Pearson Education.

Prochaska, J. M., Prochaska, J. O., Cohen, F. C., Gomes, S. O., Laforge, R. G., & Eastwood, A. L. (2004). The Transtheoretical model of change for multilevel interventions for alcohol abuse on campus. *Journal of Alcohol and Drug Education, 47*(3), 34–50.

Prochaska, J. O., & DiClemente, C. C. (1984). *The transtheoretical approach: Crossing traditional boundaries of therapy.* Homewood, IL: Dow Jones/Irwin.

Prochaska, J. O., & DiClemente, C. C. (1986). The transtheoretical approach. In J. Norcross (Ed.), *Handbook of eclectic psychotherapy* (pp. 163–200). New York City, NY: Brunner/Mazel.

Prochaska, J. O., DiClemente, C. C., & Norcross, J. C. (1992). In search of how people change. *American Psychologist, 47,* 1102–1114.

Prochaska, J. O., & Velicer, W. F. (1997). The Transtheoretical Model of health behavior change. *American Journal of Health Promotion, 12,* 38–48.

Prosser, D., Johnson, S., Kuipers, E., & Szumukler, G. (1997). Perceived sources of work stress and satisfaction among hospital and community mental health staff and their relation to mental health, burnout, and job satisfaction. *Journal of Psychosomatic Research, 43,* 51–59.

Radwin, L. (1995). Knowing the patient: a process model for individualized interventions. *Nursing Research, 44,* 364–370.

Rainer, J. P., & Campbell, L. F. (2001). Premature termination in psychotherapy: Identification and intervention. *Journal of Psychotherapy in Independent Practice, 2*(3), 19–41.

Raines, C., & Ewing, L. (2006). *The art of connecting: How to overcome differences, build rapport, and communicate effectively with anyone.* New York City, NY: AMACOM.

Raines, J. (1996). Self-disclosure in clinical social work. *Clinical Social Work Journal, 24*(4), 357–375.

Rao, S., & Murthy, V. N. (1984). Psychosocial correlates of locus of control among college students. *Psychological Studies, 29*(1), 51–56.

Rappleyea, D. L., Harris, S. M., White, M., & Simon, K. (2009). Termination: Legal and ethical considerations for marriage and family therapists. *The American Journal of Family Therapy, 37,* 12–27.

Redl, F. (1966). *When we deal with children.* New York City, NY: Free Press.

Reis, B. F., & Brown, L. G. (1999). Reducing psychotherapy dropouts: Maximizing perspective convergence in the psychotherapy dyad. *Psychotherapy, 36,* 123–136.

Renk, K., & Dinger, T. M. (2002). Reasons for therapy termination in a university psychology clinic. *Journal of Clinical Psychology, 58,* 1173–1181.

Rhule, D. M. (2005). Take care to do no harm: Harmful interventions for youth problem behavior. *Professional Psychology: Research and Practice, 36,* 618–625.

Richards, D. G. (1991). The phenomenology and psychological correlates of verbal prayer. *Journal of Psychology and Theology, 19,* 354–363.

Richards, P. S., & Bergin, A. E. (1997). *A spiritual strategy for counseling and psychotherapy.* Washington, DC: American Psychological Association Press.

Richards, P. S., & Bergin, A. E. (2000). Toward religious and spiritual competency for mental health professionals. In P. S. Richards and A. E. Bergin (Eds.), *Handbook of psychotherapy and religious diversity* (pp. 3–26). Washington, DC: American Psychological Association Press.

Richards, P., Hardman, R., & Berrett, M. (2000). *Spiritual renewal: A journey of healing and growth.* Orem, UT: Center for Change.

Richards, P., Hardman, R., & Berrett, M. (2001, August). *Evaluating the efficacy of spiritual interventions in the treatment of eating disorder patients: An outcome study.* Paper presented at the annual convention of the American Psychological Association, San Francisco, CA.

Richards, P., Hardman, R., & Berrett, M. (2007). *Spiritual approaches in the treatment of women with eating disorders.* Washington, DC: American Psychological Association.

Richards, P. S., Hardman, R. K., Frost, H., Clark-Sly, J. B., & Anderson, D. K. (1997). Spiritual Issues and interventions in the treatment of patients with eating disorders. *Eating Disorders: The Journal of Treatment & Prevention, 5,* 262–276.

Rigazio-DiGilio, S. A., Daniels, T. G., & Ivey, A. E. (1997). Systemic-cognitive developmental supervision: A developmental-integrative approach to psychotherapy supervision. In C. E. Watkins, Jr. (Ed.), *Handbook of psychotherapy supervision.* New York City, NY: John Wiley & Sons.

Riordan, R. J., Matheny, K. B., & Harris, C. (1978). Helping counselors minimize client reluctance. *Counselor Education and Supervision, 18,* 6–13.

Robbins, A. (2008). A healing space for mental health professionals. *Psychoanalytic Review, 95*(1), 17–44.

Roberts, R. C. (2001). Outline of Pauline Psychotherapy. In M. R. McMinn & T. R. Phillips (Eds.). *Care for the soul: Exploring the intersection of psychology and counseling.* Downers Grove, IL: InterVarsity Press.

Robinson, E., DiIorio, C., DePadilla, L., McCarty, F., Yeager, K., Henry, T. et al. (2008). Psychosocial predictors of lifestyle management in adults with epilepsy. *Epilepsy & Behavior, 13*(3), 523–528.

Robinson, T. L. (1993). The intersections of gender, class, race, and culture: On seeing clients whole. *Journal of Multicultural Counseling and Development, 21,* 50–58.

Robinson, T. L. (1999). The intersections of dominant discourses across race, gender, and other identities. *Journal of Counseling & Development, 77*, 79–85.

Robinson, T. L., & Howard-Hamilton, M. F. (2000). *The intersections of race, ethnicity, and gender: Multiple identities in counseling.* New Jersey City, NJ: Merrill Prentice Hall.

Rodenhauser, P. (1994). Toward a multidimensional model for psychotherapy supervision based on developmental stages. *Journal of Psychotherapy Practice and Research, 3*, 1–15.

Roisman, G. I., Padron, E., Sroufe, L. A., & Egeland, B. (2002). Earned secure attachment status in retrospect and prospect. *Child Development, 73*(4), 1204–1219.

Rogers, C. (1951) *Client-centered Therapy: Its current practice, implications and theory.* Boston, MA: Houghton Mifflin.

Rogers, C. (1961). *On becoming a person.* Boston, MA: Houghton Mifflin.

Rogers, D. J. (2004). The demise and restoration of intimacy: Eating disorders and recovery. *The Remuda Review, 3*, 30–35.

Rollnick, S., & Miller, W. R. (1995). What is motivational interviewing? *Behavioral and Cognitive Psychotherapy, 23*, 325–334.

Romero, D. (1985). Cross-cultural counseling: Brief reactions for the practitioner. *The Counseling Psychologist, 13*, 665–671.

Rønnestad, M. H., & Skovholt, T. M. (2003). The journey of the counselor and therapist: Research findings and perspectives on professional development. *Journal of Career Development, 30*, 5–44.

Roseman, I. J., & Smith, G. A. (2001). Appraisal theory: Assumptions, varieties, controversies. In K. Scherer, A. Schorr, & T. Johnstone (Eds.), *Handbook of emotions* (2nd ed.) (pp. 397–416). New York City, NY: Guilford Press.

Rosengren, D. B. (2009). *Building motivational interviewing skills: A practitioner workbook.* New York City, NY: Guilford Press.

Rosenbaum, R., & Horowitz, M. (1983). Motivation for psychotherapy. *Psychotherapy: Theory, Research and Practice, 20*, 346–354.

Rosenthal, H. G. (Ed.). (1998). *Favorite counseling techniques: 51 therapists share their most creative strategies.* New York City, NY: Brunner-Routledge.

Rosenthal, H. G. (Ed.) (2001). *Favorite counseling and therapy homework assignments: Leading therapists share their most creative strategies.* Philadelphia, PA: Brunner-Routledge.

Ross, R. R., Altmaier, E. M., & Russell, D. W. (1989). Job stress, social support, and burnout among counseling center staff. *Journal of Counseling Psychology, 36*, 464–470.

Rothschild, B. (2000). *The body remembers.* New York City, NY: W. W. Norton.

Rotter, J. (1966). Generalized expectancies for internal versus external control of reinforcement. *Psychological Monographs, 80*, Whole No. 609.

Rowe, M. M., & Allen, R. G. (2004). Spirituality as a means of coping with chronic illness. *American Journal of Health Studies, 19*(1), 62–74.

Ryan, K. C. (2006). *Attachment style, centrality of groups membership, reported emotional intelligence, and friendships in children and adolescents.* Unpublished doctoral dissertation, Adelphi University, Garden City, NY.

Ryle, A. (1998). Transferences and countertransferences: The cognitive analytic perspective. *British Journal of Psychotherapy, 14*, 303–309.

Safran, J. D. (1990). Towards a refinement of cognitive therapy in light of interpersonal theory I: Theory. *Clinical Psychology Review, 10*, 87–105.

Sakaki, M. (2007). Organization of emotional autobiographical memories: How is emotional knowledge of personal events represented in one's autobiographical knowledge base? *Japanese Journal of Educational Psychology, 55*(2), 184–196.

Samler, J. (1960). Changes in values: A goal in counseling. *Journal of Counseling Psychology, 7*, 32–39.

Sanders, R. K. (Ed.). (1997). *Christian counseling ethics: A handbook for therapists, pastors, and counselors*. Downers Grove, IL: InterVarsity Press.

Sanderson, C., & Linehan, M. M. (1999). Acceptance and forgiveness. In W. R. Miller (Ed.), *Integrating spirituality into treatment: Resources for practitioners* (pp. 199–216). Washington, DC: American Psychological Association Press.

Santa Rita, E. (1996). Filipino families. In M. McGoldrick, J. Pearce, & J. Giordano (Eds.), *Ethnicity and family therapy*. New York City, NY: Guilford Press.

Sartor, D. C. (2003). Psychotherapy, contemplative spirituality, and the experience of divine mercy. *Journal of Psychology & Christianity, 22*, 250–254.

Schlesinger, H. J. (2005). *Ending and beginnings. On termination psychotherapy and psychoanalysis*. Hillsdale, NJ: Analytic Press.

Schore, A. (2003). *Affect dysregulation and disorders of the self*. New York City, NY: W. W. Norton.

Schwartz, J. M., & Begley, S. (2002). *The mind and the brain: Neuroplasicity and the power of mental force*. New York City, NY: HarperCollins.

Schwebel, M., & Coster, J. (1998). Well-functioning in professional psychologists: As program heads see it. *Professional Psychology: Research and Practice, 29*, 284–292.

Seamands, D. (1991). *Healing for damaged emotions*. Elgin, IL: David C. Cook.

Segal, J. (1993). Against self-disclosure. In W. Dryden (Ed.), *Questions and answers on counseling in action* (pp. 11–18). London, UK: Sage.

Seibold, M. (2001). When the wounding runs deep: Encouragement for those on the road to forgiveness. In M. R. McMinn & T. R. Phillips, *Care for the soul: Exploring the intersection of psychology and theology* (pp. 294–308). Downers Grove, IL: InterVarsity Press.

Seligman, L. (1998). *Selecting effective treatments: A comprehensive systematic guide to treating mental disorders*. San Francisco: Jossey-Bass.

Seligman, L. (2004). *Diagnosis and treatment planning in counseling* (3rd ed.). New York City, NY: Plenum.

Seligman, L., & Reichenberg, L. W. (2007). *Selecting effective treatments: A comprehensive systematic guide to treating mental disorders* (3rd ed.). San Francisco, CA: Jossey-Bass.

Seligman, M. (1995). The effectiveness of psychotherapy: The consumer reports study. *American Psychologist, 22*, 6–78.

Shapiro, D. A., & Shapiro, D. (1982). Meta-analysis of comparative therapy outcome studies: A replication and refinement. *Psychological Bulletin, 92,* 581–604.

Sharpley, C. F. (1987). Research findings on neuro-linguistic programming: Non-supportive data or an untestable theory? *Journal of Counseling Psychology, 34*(1), 103–107.

Sharpley, C. F. (1997). The influence of silence upon client-perceived rapport. *Counseling Psychology Quarterly, 10*(3), 237–246.

Sharpley, C. F., Munro, D. M., & Elly, M. J. (2005). Silence and rapport during initial interviews. *Counseling Psychology Quarterly, 18*(2), 149–159.

Shepard, M. (1975). *Fritz: An intimate portrait of Fritz Pearls and Gestalt therapy.* Oxford, UK: Saturday Review Press.

Shertzer, B., & Stone, S. C. (1974). *Fundamentals of counseling.* Boston, MA: Houghton Mifflin.

Shields, H., & Bredfeldt, G. (2001). *Caring for souls: Counseling under the authority of Scripture.* Chicago, IL: Moody Press.

Shulman, L. (2009). *The skills of helping individuals, families, groups and communities* (6th ed.). Belmont, CA: Wadsworth-Thomson Learning.

Simpson, A. R. (2001). *Raising teens: A synthesis of research and a foundation for action.* Boston: Center for Health Communication, Harvard School of Public Health.

Simone, D. H., McCarthy, P., & Skay, C. L. (1998). An investigation of client and counselor variables that influence the likelihood of counselor self-disclosure. *Journal of Counseling and Development, 76,* 174–182.

Sims, P. A. (2003). Working with metaphor. *American Journal of Psychotherapy, 57*(4), 528–536.

Singer, E. (1965). *Key concepts in psychotherapy.* New York City, NY: Random House.

Sire, J. W. (2009). *The universe next door: A basic worldview catalog.* Downers Grove, IL: InterVarsity Press.

Skarderud, F. (2007). Eating one's words: Part III. Mentalization-based psychotherapy for anorexia nervosa—an outline for a treatment and training manual. *European Eating Disorder Reviews, 15,* 323–339.

Skinner, B. F. (1938). *The behavior of organisms. An experimental analysis.* New York City, NY: D. Appleton-Century.

Skinner, B. F. (1974). *About behaviorism.* New York City, NY: A. A. Knopf.

Skovholt, T. M., & Jennings, L. (Eds.) (2004 ). *Master therapists: Exploring expertise in therapy and counseling.* Boston, MA: Allyn & Bacon.

Skovholt, T. M., & Ronnestad, M. H. (1992). Themes in therapist and counselor development. *Journal of Counseling and Development, 70,* 505–515.

Sloane, R. B., Staples, F. R., Cristol, A. H., Yorkston, N. J., & Whipple, K. (1975). *Psychotherapy versus behavior therapy.* Cambridge, MA: Harvard University Press.

Smalley, G., & Trent, J. (1992). *The language of love.* New York City, NY: Pocket.

Smith, A. J., Kleijn, W. C., & Hutschemekers, G. J. M. (2007). Therapist reactions in self-experienced difficult situations: An exploration. *Counseling and Psychotherapy Research, 7,* 34–41.

Smith, E. (1999). *Beyond tolerable recovery: Moving beyond tolerable existence into biblical maintenance free victory*. Cambellsville, KY: Family Care.

Smith, F., Richards, P., Fischer, L., & Hardman, R. (2003). Intrinsic religiousness and spiritual well-being as predictors of treatment outcome among women with eating disorders. *Eating Disorders: Journal of Treatment and Prevention, 11*, 15–26.

Smith, M. H., Richards, P. S., & Maglio, C. J. (2004). Examining the relationship between religious orientation and eating disturbances. *Eating Behaviors, 5*, 171–180.

Smith, M. L., Glass, G. V., & Miller, T. I. (1980). *The benefits of psychotherapy*. Baltimore, MD: Johns Hopkins University Press.

Smith, M. R. (2003) The relationship between personality traits and trainee effectiveness in counseling sessions: Cognitive flexibility, spirituality, and self-actualization. *Dissertation Abstracts International Section A: Humanities and Social Sciences, 63*(7-A), 2469.

Smith, M. W. (1993). Friends are friends forever [Recorded by Michael W. Smith]. On *Change your world* [CD]. Nashville, TN: Reunion.

Soisson, E. L., VandeCreek, L. & Knapp, S. (1987). Thorough record keeping: A good defense in a litigious era. *Professional Psychology: Research and Practice, 18*, 498–502.

Sommers-Flanagan, J., & Sommers-Flanagan, R. (2003). *Clinical interviewing* (3rd ed.). New York City, NY: Wiley.

Sosin, L. (2008). *The cell keys are turning*. Unpublished doctoral dissertation, Liberty University, Lynchburg, VA.

Speight, S. L., Myers, L. J., Cox, C. L., & Highlen, R. S. (1991). A redefinition of multicultural counseling. *Journal of Counseling & Development, 70*, 29–36.

Sperry, L. (2001). *Spirituality in clinical practice: Incorporating the spiritual dimension in psychotherapy and counseling*. Philadelphia, PA: Taylor & Francis.

Sperry, L. (2003). Integrating spiritual direction functions in the practice of psychotherapy. *Journal of Psychology and Theology, 31*(1), 3–13.

Sperry, L., & Shafranske, E. P. (Ed.). (2005). Spiritually oriented psychotherapy. Washington, DC: American Psychological Association Press.

Sroufe, L. A. (1997). Psychopathology as an outcome of development. *Development and Psychopathology, 9*, 251–268.

Sroufe, L. A. (2005). Attachment and development: A prospective, longitudinal study from birth to adulthood. *Attachment and Human Development, 7*(4), 349–367.

Stadler, H. A., & Willing, K. L. (1988). Impaired counselors. *Counseling and Human Development, 21*(2), 1–8.

Stein, D. M., & Lambert, M. J. (1995). Graduate training in psychotherapy: Are therapy outcomes enhanced? *Journal of Counseling Psychology, 63*, 182–196.

Stevens, H. B., Dinoof, B. L., & Donnenworth, E. E. (1998). Psychotherapy training and theoretical orientation in clinical psychology programs: A national survey. *Journal of Clinical Psychology, 54*, 91–96.

Stewart, M. J. (2008). *A phenomenological study: Local churches providing community service with diminishing membership and increasing expenses.* Unpublished doctoral dissertation, University of Phoenix, Phoenix, AZ.

Stoltenberg, C. D., & Delworth, U. (1987). *Supervising counselors and therapists.* San Francisco, CA: Jossey & Bass.

Stoltenberg, C. D., McNeil, B., & Delworth, U. (1998). *IDM supervision: An integrated developmental model for supervising counselors and therapists.* San Francisco, CA: Jossey-Bass.

Stone, S. C., & Shertzer, B. (1963). The militant counselor. *Personnel Guidance Journal, 42,* 342–347.

Strachan, D., & Pitters, M. (2008). *Managing facilitated processes: A guide for consultants, facilitators, managers, trainers, even planners, and educators.* San Francisco, CA: Jossey-Bass.

Strain, E. C. (1999). Psychosocial treatment for cocaine dependence: Rethinking lessons learned. *Archives of General Psychiatry, 56*(6), 503–504.

Stricker, G., & Fisher, M. (Eds.). (1990). *Self-disclosure in the therapeutic relationship.* New York City, NY: Plenum Press.

Strong, S. R. (1968). Counseling: An interpersonal influence process. *Journal of Counseling Psychology, 15*(3), 215–224.

Strong, S. R., & Claiborn, C. D. (1982). *Change through interaction: Social psychological processes of counseling and psychotherapy.* New York City, NY: Wiley.

Strong, T., & Zeman, D. (2010). Dialogic considerations of confrontation as a counseling activity: An examination of Allen Ivey's use of confronting as a microskill. *Journal of Counseling & Development, 88,* 332–339.

Strupp, H. H. (1980a). Success and failure in time-limited psychotherapy: A systematic comparison of two cases—comparison 1. *Archives of General Psychiatry, 37,* 595–603.

Strupp, H. H. (1980b). Success and failure in time-limited psychotherapy: A systematic comparison of two cases—comparison 2. *Archives of General Psychiatry, 37,* 708–716.

Strupp, H. H. (1980c). Success and failure in time-limited psychotherapy: With special reference to the performance of a lay counselor. *Archives of General Psychiatry, 37,* 831–841.

Strupp, H. H. (1980d). Success and failure in time-limited psychotherapy: A systematic comparison of two cases—comparison 4. *Archives of General Psychiatry, 37,* 947–954.

Strupp, H. H., Hadley, S. W., & Gomez-Schwartz, B. (1977). *Psychotherapy for better or worse: The problem of negative effects.* New York City, NY: Aronson.

Stuart, R. B. (1980). *Helping couples change.* New York City, NY: Guilford Press.

Sue, D. W., & Sue, D. (1990). *Counseling the culturally different: Theory and practice* (2nd ed.). New York City, NY: Wiley.

Sue, S. (1998). In search of cultural competence in psychotherapy and counseling. *American Psychologist, 53*(4), 440–448.

Sue, S., & Zane, N. (1987). The role of culture and cultural techniques in psychotherapy. *American Psychologist, 42,* 37–45.

Sullivan, H. S. (1947). *Conceptions of modern psychiatry*. Washington, DC: William Alanson White Psychiatric Foundation.

Sullivan, H. S. (1953). *The interpersonal theory of psychiatry*. New York City, NY: W. W. Norton.

Sussman M. B. (1992). *A curious calling: Unconscious motivations for practicing psychotherapy*. New York City, NY: Jason Aronson.

Swain, J. (1995). *A guide for therapists*. Oxford, UK: Butterworth Heinemann.

Sweeney, T. J., & Myers, J. E. (2005). Optimizing human development: A new paradigm for helping. In A. Ivey, M. B. Ivey, J. E. Myers, & T. J. Sweeney (Eds.), *Developmental counseling and therapy* (2nd ed., pp. 39–68). Boston, MA: Lahaska/Houghton Mifflin.

Talan, J. (2005). Half are mentally ill. *Scientific American Mind, 16*(3), 9.

Tan, S.-Y. (1996a). Religion in clinical practice: Implicit and explicit integration. In E. P Shafranske (Ed.), *Religion and the clinical practice of psychology* (pp. 365–387), Washington, DC: American Psychological Association Press.

Tan, S. -Y. (1996b). Practicing the presence of God: The work of Richard J. Foster and its applications to psychotherapeutic practice. *Journal of Psychology and Christianity,15,* 17–28.

Tan, S.-Y. (2003). Integrating spiritual direction into psychotherapy: Ethical issues and guidelines. *Journal of Psychology and Theology. 31*(1), 14–23.

Tan, S.-Y. (2007). Use of prayer and Scripture in cognitive-behavioral therapy. *Journal of Psychology and Christianity, 26,* 101–111.

Tan, S.-Y. (2010). *Counseling and psychotherapy*. Grand Rapids, MI: Baker Book House.

Tashlykov, V. A. & Vale, M. (1997). Coping behavior in the temporal evolution of the mental systems accompanying neurosis. *International Journal of Mental Health, 26*(2), 42–45.

Teyber, E. (2006). *Interpersonal processes in psychotherapy* (5th ed.). Belmont, CA: Wadsworth.

Thomas, J. C., & French, L. L. (1999). Counseling Christian clients. *Directions, 9*(15), 189–208.

Thomas, J. C., & Habermas, G. (2008) *What's good about feeling bad?: Finding purpose and a path through your pain*. Carol Stream, IL: Tyndale House.

Thompson, R. A. (2003). *Counseling techniques: Improving relationships with others, ourselves, our families and our environment* (2nd ed.). New York City, NY: Brunner-Routledge.

Thoreson, R. W., Budd, F. C., & Krauskopf, C. J. (1986). Perceptions of alcohol misuse and work behavior among professionals: Identification and intervention. *Professional Psychology: Research & Practice, 17,* 210–216.

Timberlake, E., & Cutler, M. (2001). *Developmental play therapy in clinical social work*. Boston, MA: Allyn & Bacon.

Tindall, R., & Robinson, F. (1947). The use of silence as a technique in counseling. *Journal of Clinical Psychology, 3,* 136–141.

Tinsley, H. E. A., Bowman, S. L., & Ray, S. B. (1988). Manipulation of expectancies about counseling and psychotherapy: Review and analysis of expectancy manipulation strategies and results. *Journal of Counseling Psychology, 35,* 99–108.

Tisdale, T. C. (2003). Listening and responding to spiritual issues in psychotherapy: an interdisciplinary perspective. *Journal of Psychology and Christianity, 22*(3), 262–272.

Tisdale, T. C, Key, T. L., Edwards, K. J., Brokaw, B. F., Kemperman, S. R., & Cloud, H. (1997). Impact of God image and personal adjustment, and correlations of the God image to personal adjustment and object relations development. *Journal of Psychology and Theology, 25,* 227–239.

Tompkins, M. (2002). Guidelines for enhancing homework compliance. *Journal of Clinical Psychology, 58*(5), 565–576.

Tozer, A. W. (1996). *Man: The dwelling place of God.* Camp Hill, PA: Wing-Spread.

Tracey, T. J., Hays, K. A., Malone, J., & Herman, B. (1988). Changes in counselor responses as a function of experience. *Journal of Counseling Psychology, 35,* 119–126.

Truax, C. B., & Carkhuff, R. R. (1965). Client and therapist transparency in the psychotherapeutic encounter. *Journal of Counseling Psychology, 12,* 3–9.

Truax, C. B., & Carkhuff, R. R. (1967). *Toward effective counseling and psychotherapy: Training and practice.* Chicago, IL: Aldine.

Truax, C. B., & Mitchell, K. M. (1971). Research on certain therapist interpersonal skills in relation to process and outcome. In A. E. Bergin & S. Garfield (Eds.), *Handbook of psychotherapy and behavior change* (pp. 299–344). New York City, NY: Wiley.

Tsuchiya, N., & Adolphs, R. (2007) Emotion and consciousness. *Trends in Cognitive Sciences, 11*(4), 158–167.

Tudor, K., & Worrall, M. (1994). Congruence reconsidered. *British Journal of Guidance & Counseling, 22*(2), 197–206.

Turock, A. (1980). Immediacy in counseling: Recognizing client's unspoken messages. *Personnel and Guidance Journal, 59,* 168–172.

Urbani, S., Smith, M. R., Maddux, C. D., Smaby, M. H., Torres-Rivera, E., & Crews, J. (2002). Skills-based training and counseling self-efficacy. *Counselor Education and Supervision, 42,* 93–106.

Vacc, N. A. (1982). A conceptual framework for continuous assessment of clients. *Measurement and Evaluation in Guidance, 15*(1), 40–47.

VandeCreek, L., & Angstadt, L. (1985). Client preferences and anticipations about counselor self-disclosure. *Journal of Counseling Psychology, 32,* 206–214.

Vande Kemp, H. (1984). *Psychology and theology in Western thought, 1672–1965.* White Plains, NY: Kraus.

Van Deusen Hunsinger, D. (1995). *Theology and pastoral counseling: A new interdisciplinary approach.* Grand Rapids, MI: William B. Eerdmans.

Van Deusen Hunsinger, D. (2001). An interdisciplinary map for Christian counselors. In M. R. McMinn & T. R. Phillips (Eds.), *Care for the soul: Exploring the intersection of psychology and theology* (pp. 218–240). Downers Grove, IL: InterVarsity Press.

Vorhees, C. C., Stillman, F. A., Swank, R. T., Heagerty, P. J., Levine, D. M., & Becker, D. M. (1996). Heart, body, and soul: Impact of church-based smoking cessation interventions on readiness to quit. *Preventive Medicine, 25,* 277–285.

Wachtel, P. (2002). Termination of therapy: An effort at integration. *Journal of Psychotherapy Integration, 12*(3), 373–383.

Waehler, C. A., Lenox, R. A. (1994). A concurrent (versus stage) model for conceptualizing and representing the counseling process. *Journal of Counseling and Development, 73*(1), *17–22*.

Walker, D. E., (1956). Carl Rodgers and the nature of man. *Journal of Counseling Psychology, 3*, 89.

Walker, S. R., Tonigan, J. S., Miller, W. R., Comer, S., & Kahlich, L. (1997). Intercessory prayer in the treatment of alcohol abuse and dependence: A pilot investigation. *Alternative Therapies, 3*, 79–86.

Wall, A. D., Cumella, E. J., & Darden, R. A. (2003). Remuda Spiritual Assessment Questionnaire Version 1.0. Wickenburg, AZ : Remuda Ranch Center for Anorexia and Bulimia.

Wall, D. (2003). Cognitive-behavioral therapy with eating disorders: A Christian Perspective. *The Remuda Review, 2, 1–7*.

Wall, D., & Eberly, M. (2002). Five biblical factors in eating disorder development. *The Remuda Review, 1*, 6–10.

Wall, D., Eberly, M., & Cumella, E. J. (2005). Spiritual development: Growing in God's love. *The Remuda Review, 4*, 6–11.

Waller, G., Cordery, H., Corstorphine, E., Hinrichsen, H., Lawson, R., Mountford, V. et al. (2007). *Cognitive behavioral therapy for eating disorders: A comprehensive treatment guide*. New York City, NY: Cambridge University Press.

Wallin, D. J. (2007). *Attachment in psychotherapy*. New York City, NY: Guilford Press.

Wampold, B. E. (2001). *The great psychotherapy debate: Models, methods, and findings*. Mahwah, NJ: Erlbaum.

Warren, R. (2002). *The purpose driven life: What on earth am I here for?* Grand Rapids, MI: Zondervan Publishing House.

Watkins, C. E. (1985). Countertransference: Its impact on the counseling situation. *Journal of Counseling & Development, 63*(6), 356–359.

Watkins, C. E. (1995). Psychotherapy supervision in the 1990s: Some observations and reflections. *American Journal of Psychotherapy, 49*, 568–581.

Watts, R. (2000). Biblically based Christian spirituality and Adlerian psychotherapy. *Individual Psychology, 56*(3), 316–328.

Watzlawick, P. (1978). *The language of change*. New York City, NY: Basic Books.

Watzlawick, P., Beavin, J. H., & Jackson, D. D. (1967). *Pragmatics of human communication: A study of interactional patterns, pathologies, and paradoxes*. New York City, NY: W. W. Norton.

Watzlawick, P., Weakland, J., & Fisch, R. (1974). *Change: Principles of problem formation and problem resolution*. New York City, NY: W. W. Norton.

Weaver, A. J., Koenig, H. G., & Larson, D. B. (1997). Marriage and family therapy and the clergy. *Journal of Marital & Family Therapy, 23*, 13–25.

Weaver, A. J., Sanford, J. A., Kline, A. E., Lucus, L. A., Larson, D. B., & Koenig, H. G. (1997). What do psychologists know about working with the clergy? An analysis of eight APA journals: 1991–1994. *Professional Psychology, 28*, 471–474.

Weeks, G., & L'Abate, L. (1982). *Paradoxical psychotherapy: Theory and practice with individuals, couples, and families*. New York City, NY: Brunner/Mazel.

Weld, C., & Eriksen, K. (2007). The ethics of prayer in counseling. *Counseling and Values, 51,* 125–138.

Wheeler, C. D., & D'Andrea, L. M. (2004). Teaching counseling students to understand and use immediacy. *Journal of Humanistic Counseling, Education, and Development, 43,* 117–128.

White, P. E., & Franzoni, J. B. (1990). A multidimensional analysis of the mental health of graduate counselors in training. *Counselor Education and Supervision, 29,* 258–267.

White, S. A. (1984). Imago Dei and object relations theory: Implications for a model of human development. *Journal of Psychology and Theology, 12,* 286–293.

Wiley, M., Ray, P. (1986). Counseling supervision by developmental level. *Journal of Counseling Psychology, 33,* 439–445.

Willard, D. (1988). *The spirit of the disciplines.* New York City, NY: HarperCollins.

Willard, D. (1997). *The Divine conspiracy: Rediscovering our hidden life in God.* New York City, NY: HarperCollins.

Willard, D. (2002). *Renovation of the heart: Putting on the character of Christ.* Colorado Springs, CO: NavPress.

Williamson, E. G. (1962). The counselor as technique. *Personnel and Guidance Journal, 41,* 108–111.

Wilson, S. (1990, October). *ACOA families.* Paper presented at the meeting of the International Congress on Christian Counseling Conference, Atlanta, GA.

Wilson, S. D. (2001). *Hurt people hurt people: Hope and healing for yourself and your relationships.* Grand Rapids, MI: Discovery House.

Winger, D., & Hunsberger, B. (1988). Clergy counseling practices, Christian orthodoxy and problem solving styles. *Journal of Psychology and Theology, 16,* 41–48.

Winter, R. (2008). A framework for Christian counseling – Applied to perfectionism. *Edification: Journal of the Society for Christian Psychology, 2*(2), 31–38.

Wintersteen, M. B., Mensinger, J. L., & Diamond, G. S. (2005). Do gender and racial differences between patient and therapist affect therapeutic alliance and treatment retention in adolescents? *Professional Psychology: Research and Practice, 36*(4), 400–408.

Wolpe, J., & Lazarus, A. A. (1966). *Behavior therapy techniques.* New York City, NY: Pergamon Press.

Woody, J. D., & Woody, R. H. (2001). Protecting and benefiting the client: The therapeutic alliance, informed consent, and confidentiality. In J. D. Woody (Ed.), *Ethics in marriage and family therapy* (pp. 13–42). Washington, DC: American Association for Marriage and Family Therapy.

Woody, S. R., Detweiler-Bedell, J., Teachman, B. A., & O'Hearn, T. (2004). *Treatment planning in psychotherapy.* New York City, NY: Guilford Press.

Workman, E. A., & Williams, R. L. (1979). A brief method for determining the effect of selected counselor characteristics on clients' expectations of counseling success. *Journal of Behavior Therapy and Experimental Psychiatry, 10*(1), 41–45.

Worthington, E. L., Jr. (1986). Religious counseling: A review of published empirical research. *Journal for Counseling and Development, 64,* 421–431.

Worthington, E. L., Jr. (1998). *Dimensions of forgiveness.* Philadelphia, PA: Templeton Foundation Press.

Worthington, E. L., Jr. (2006). *Forgiveness and reconciliation: Theory and application.* New York City, NY: Routledge.

Worthington, E. L., Jr., Kuruse, T. A., McCullough, M. E., & Sanders, S. J. (1996). Empirical research on religion and psychotherapeutic processes and outcomes: A 10-year review and research prospectus. *Psychological Bulletin, 119,* 448–487.

Worthington, E. L., Jr., & Scott, G. G. (1983). Goal selection for counseling with potentially religious clients by professional and student counselors in explicitly Christian or secular settings. *Journal of Psychology and Theology, 11,* 318–329.

Wrenn, C. G. (1957). The status and role of the school counselor. *Personnel Guidance Journal, 36,* 182.

Wrong, D. H. (1961). The oversocialized conception of man in modern sociology. *Sociological Review, 26,* 183–193.

Wubbolding, R. E., & Brickell, J. (1998). Qualities of the reality therapist. *International Journal of Reality Therapy, 17*(2), 47–49.

Yahav, R., & Oz, S. (2006). The relevance of psychodynamic psychotherapy to understanding therapist-patient sexual abuse and treatment of survivors. *Journal of the American Academy of Psychoanalysis and Dynamic Psychiatry, 34*(2), 303–331.

Yalom, I. D. (1980). *Existential psychotherapy.* New York City, NY: Basic Books.

Yalom, I. D. (2002). *The gift of therapy: An open letter to a new generation of therapist and patients* New York City, NY: HarperRow.

Yalom, I. D., & Leszcz, M. (2005). *Theory and practice of group psychotherapy* (5th ed.). New York City, NY: Basic Books.

Young, J. E., Klosko, J. S., & Weishaar, M. E. (2003). *Schema therapy: A practitioner's guide.* New York City, NY: Guilford Press.

Young, M. E. (1992). *Counseling methods and techniques: An eclectic approach.* New York City, NY: Merrill.

Young, M. E. (2005). *Learning the art of helping: Building blocks and techniques* (3rd ed.). Upper Saddle River, NJ: Pearson.

Young, M. E. (2010). *Learning the art of helping: Building blocks and techniques* (4th ed.). Upper Saddle River, NJ: Pearson.

Younggren, J. N., & Gottlieb, M. C. (2008). Termination and abandonment: History, risk, and risk management. *Professional Psychology: Research and Practice, 39*(5), 498–504.

Zargar, F., & Neshat-Doost, H. T. (2008). Divorce incidence factors in Falavarjan township. *Journal of Family Research, 3*(3), 737–749.

Zimbardo, P. G. (1985). *Psychology and life.* Glenview, IL: Scott Foreman.

Zimmick, R., Smaby, M. H., & Maddux, C. (2000). Improving the use of a group counseling scale and related model to teach theory and skills integration. *Counselor Education and Supervision, 39,* 284–295.

# Appendixes

# Appendix A
# ACA (American Counseling Association) Code of Ethics

## Mission

*The mission of the American Counseling Association is to enhance the quality of life in society by promoting the development of professional counselors, advancing the counseling profession, and using the profession and practice of counseling to promote respect for human dignity and diversity.*

## Contents

# *ACA Code of Ethics* Preamble

The American Counseling Association is an educational, scientific, and professional organization whose members work in a variety of settings and serve in multiple capacities. ACA members are dedicated to the enhancement of human development throughout the life span. Association members recognize diversity and embrace a cross-cultural approach in support of the worth, dignity, potential, and uniqueness of people within their social and cultural contexts.

Professional values are an important way of living out an ethical commitment. Values inform principles. Inherently held values that guide our behaviors or exceed prescribed behaviors are deeply ingrained in the counselor and developed out of personal dedication, rather than the mandatory requirement of an external organization.

# *ACA Code of Ethics* Purpose

The *ACA Code of Ethics* serves five main purposes:

1. The *Code* enables the association to clarify to current and future members, and to those served by members, the nature of the ethical responsibilities held in common by its members.
2. The *Code* helps support the mission of the association.
3. The *Code* establishes principles that define ethical behavior and best practices of association members.
4. The *Code* serves as an ethical guide designed to assist members in constructing a professional course of action that best serves those utilizing counseling services and best promotes the values of the counseling profession.
5. The *Code* serves as the basis for processing of ethical complaints and inquiries initiated against members of the association.

The *ACA Code of Ethics* contains eight main sections that address the following areas:

Section A: The Counseling Relationship
Section B: Confidentiality, Privileged Communication, and Privacy
Section C: Professional Responsibility
Section D: Relationships With Other Professionals
Section E: Evaluation, Assessment, and Interpretation
Section F: Supervision, Training, and Teaching
Section G: Research and Publication
Section H: Resolving Ethical Issues

Each section of the *ACA Code of Ethics* begins with an Introduction. The introductions to each section discuss what counselors should aspire to with regard to ethical behavior and responsibility. The Introduction helps set the tone for that particular section and provides a starting point for its members that invites reflection on the ethical mandates contained in each part of the *ACA Code of Ethics*.

When counselors are faced with ethical dilemmas that are difficult to resolve, they are expected to engage in a carefully considered ethical decision-making process. Reasonable differences of opinion can and do exist among counselors with respect to the ways in which values, ethical principles, and ethical standards would be applied when they conflict. While there is no specific ethical decision-making model that is most effective, counselors are expected to be familiar with a credible model of decision making that can bear public scrutiny and its application.

Through a chosen ethical decision-making process and evaluation of the context of the situation, counselors are empowered to make decisions that help expand the capacity of people to grow and develop.

A brief glossary is given to provide readers with a concise description of some of the terms used in the *ACA Code of Ethics*.

# Section A

## The Counseling Relationship

## Introduction

Counselors encourage client growth and development in ways that foster the interest and welfare of clients and promote formation of healthy relationships. Counselors actively attempt to understand the diverse cultural backgrounds of the clients they serve. Counselors also explore their own cultural identities and how these affect their values and beliefs about the counseling process.

Counselors are encouraged to contribute to society by devoting a portion of their professional activity to services for which there is little or no financial return (pro bono publico).

## A.1. Welfare of Those Served by Counselors

### A.1.a. Primary Responsibility

The primary responsibility of counselors is to respect the dignity and to promote the welfare of clients.

### A.1.b. Records

Counselors maintain records necessary for rendering professional services to their clients and as required by laws, regulations, or agency or institution procedures. Counselors include sufficient and timely documentation in their client records to facilitate the delivery and continuity of needed services. Counselors take reasonable steps to ensure that documentation in records accurately reflects client progress and services provided. If errors are made in client records, counselors take steps to properly note the correction of such errors according to agency or institutional policies.
*(See A.12.g.7., B.6., B.6.g., G.2.j.)*

### A.1.c. Counseling Plans

Counselors and their clients work jointly in devising integrated counseling plans that offer reasonable promise of success and are consistent with abilities and circumstances of clients. Counselors and clients regularly review counseling plans to assess their continued viability and effectiveness, respecting the freedom of choice of clients.
*(See A.2.a., A.2.d., A.12.g.)*

### A.1.d. Support Network Involvement

Counselors recognize that support networks hold various meanings in the lives of clients and consider enlisting the support, understanding, and involvement of others (e.g., religious/spiritual/community leaders, family members, friends) as positive resources, when appropriate, with client consent.

### A.1.e. Employment Needs

Counselors work with their clients considering employment in jobs that are consistent with the overall abilities, vocational limitations, physical restrictions, general temperament, interest and aptitude patterns, social skills, education, general qualifications, and other relevant characteristics and needs of clients. When appropriate, counselors appropriately trained in career development will assist in the placement of clients in positions that are consistent with the interest, culture, and the welfare of clients, employers, and/or the public.

## A.2. Informed Consent in the Counseling Relationship

*(See A.12.g., B.5., B.6.b., E.3., E.13.b., F.1.c., G.2.a.)*

### A.2.a. Informed Consent

Clients have the freedom to choose whether to enter into or remain in a counseling relationship and need adequate information about the counseling process and the counselor. Counselors have an obligation to review in writing and verbally with clients the rights and responsibilities of both the counselor and the client. Informed consent is an ongoing part of the counseling process, and counselors appropriately document discussions of informed consent throughout the counseling relationship.

### A.2.b. Types of Information Needed

Counselors explicitly explain to clients the nature of all services provided. They inform clients about issues such as, but not limited to, the following: the purposes, goals, techniques, procedures, limitations, potential risks, and benefits of services; the counselor's qualifications, credentials, and relevant experience; continuation of services upon the incapacitation or death of a counselor; and other pertinent information. Counselors take steps to ensure that clients understand the implications of diagnosis, the intended use of tests and reports, fees, and billing arrangements.

Clients have the right to confidentiality and to be provided with an explanation of its limitations (including how supervisors and/or treatment team professionals are involved); to obtain clear information about their records; to participate in the ongoing counseling plans; and to refuse any services or modality change and to be advised of the consequences of such refusal.

### A.2.c. Developmental and Cultural Sensitivity

Counselors communicate information in ways that are both developmentally and culturally appropriate. Counselors use clear and understandable language when discussing issues related to informed consent. When clients have difficulty understanding the language used by counselors, they provide necessary services (e.g., arranging for a qualified interpreter or translator) to ensure comprehension by clients. In collaboration with clients, counselors consider cultural implications of informed consent procedures and, where possible, counselors adjust their practices accordingly.

### A.2.d. Inability to Give Consent

When counseling minors or persons are unable to give voluntary consent, counselors seek the assent of clients to services, and include them in decision making as appropriate. Counselors recognize the need to balance the ethical rights of clients to make choices, their capacity to give consent or assent to receive services, and parental or familial legal rights and responsibilities to protect these clients and make decisions on their behalf.

## A.3. Clients Served by Others

When counselors learn that their clients are in a professional relationship with another mental health professional, they request release from clients to inform the other professionals and strive to establish positive and collaborative professional relationships.

## A.4. Avoiding Harm and Imposing Values

### A.4.a. Avoiding Harm

Counselors act to avoid harming their clients, trainees, and research participants and to minimize or to remedy unavoidable or unanticipated harm.

### A.4.b. Personal Values

Counselors are aware of their own values, attitudes, beliefs, and behaviors and avoid imposing values that are inconsistent with counseling goals. Counselors respect the diversity of clients, trainees, and research participants.

## A.5. Roles and Relationships With Clients

*(See F.3., F.10., G.3.)*

### A.5.a. Current Clients

Sexual or romantic counselor–client interactions or relationships with current clients, their romantic partners, or their family members are prohibited.

### A.5.b. Former Clients

Sexual or romantic counselor–client interactions or relationships with former clients, their romantic partners, or their family members are prohibited for a period of 5 years following the last professional contact. Counselors, before engaging in sexual or romantic interactions or relation-

ships with clients, their romantic partners, or client family members after 5 years following the last professional contact, demonstrate forethought and document (in written form) whether the interactions or relationship can be viewed as exploitive in some way and/or whether there is still potential to harm the former client; in cases of potential exploitation and/or harm, the counselor avoids entering such an interaction or relationship.

### A.5.c. Nonprofessional Interactions or Relationships (Other Than Sexual or Romantic Interactions or Relationships)

Counselor–client nonprofessional relationships with clients, former clients, their romantic partners, or their family members should be avoided, except when the interaction is potentially beneficial to the client. *(See A.5.d.)*

### A.5.d. Potentially Beneficial Interactions

When a counselor–client nonprofessional interaction with a client or former client may be potentially beneficial to the client or former client, the counselor must document in case records, prior to the interaction (when feasible), the rationale for such an interaction, the potential benefit, and anticipated consequences for the client or former client and other individuals significantly involved with the client or former client. Such interactions should be initiated with appropriate client consent. Where unintentional harm occurs to the client or former client, or to an individual significantly involved with the client or former client, due to the nonprofessional interaction, the counselor must show evidence of an attempt to remedy such harm. Examples of potentially beneficial interactions include, but are not limited to, attending a formal ceremony (e.g., a wedding/commitment ceremony or graduation); purchasing a service or product provided by a client or former client (excepting

unrestricted bartering); hospital visits to an ill family member; mutual membership in a professional association, organization, or community. *(See A.5.c.)*

### A.5.e. Role Changes in the Professional Relationship

When a counselor changes a role from the original or most recent contracted relationship, he or she obtains informed consent from the client and explains the right of the client to refuse services related to the change. Examples of role changes include

1. changing from individual to relationship or family counseling, or vice versa;
2. changing from a nonforensic evaluative role to a therapeutic role, or vice versa;
3. changing from a counselor to a researcher role (i.e., enlisting clients as research participants), or vice versa; and
4. changing from a counselor to a mediator role, or vice versa. Clients must be fully informed of any anticipated consequences (e.g., financial, legal, personal, or therapeutic) of counselor role changes.

## A.6. Roles and Relationships at Individual, Group, Institutional, and Societal Levels

### A.6.a. Advocacy

When appropriate, counselors advocate at individual, group, institutional, and societal levels to examine potential barriers and obstacles that inhibit access and/or the growth and development of clients.

### A.6.b. Confidentiality and Advocacy

Counselors obtain client consent prior to engaging in advocacy efforts on behalf of an identifiable client to improve the provision of services and to work toward removal of systemic barriers or obstacles that inhibit client access, growth, and development.

## A.7. Multiple Clients

When a counselor agrees to provide counseling services to

two or more persons who have a relationship, the counselor clarifies at the outset which person or persons are clients and the nature of the relationships the counselor will have with each involved person. If it becomes apparent that the counselor may be called upon to perform potentially conflicting roles, the counselor will clarify, adjust, or withdraw from roles appropriately. *(See A.8.a., B.4.)*

## A.8. Group Work
*(See B.4.a.)*

### A.8.a. Screening
Counselors screen prospective group counseling/therapy participants. To the extent possible, counselors select members whose needs and goals are compatible with goals of the group, who will not impede the group process, and whose well-being will not be jeopardized by the group experience.

### A.8.b. Protecting Clients
In a group setting, counselors take reasonable precautions to protect clients from physical, emotional, or psychological trauma.

## A.9. End-of-Life Care for Terminally Ill Clients

### A.9.a. Quality of Care
Counselors strive to take measures that enable clients

1. to obtain high quality end-of-life care for their physical, emotional, social, and spiritual needs;
2. to exercise the highest degree of self-determination possible;
3. to be given every opportunity possible to engage in informed decision making regarding their end-of-life care; and
4. to receive complete and adequate assessment regarding their ability to make competent, rational decisions on their own behalf from a mental health professional who is experienced in end-of-life care practice.

### A.9.b. Counselor Competence, Choice, and Referral
Recognizing the personal, moral, and competence issues related to end-of-life decisions, counselors may choose to work or not work with terminally ill clients who wish to explore their end-of-life options. Counselors provide appropriate referral information to ensure that clients receive the necessary help.

### A.9.c. Confidentiality
Counselors who provide services to terminally ill individuals who are considering hastening their own deaths have the option of breaking or not breaking confidentiality, depending on applicable laws and the specific circumstances of the situation and after seeking consultation or supervision from appropriate professional and legal parties. *(See B.5.c., B.7.c.)*

## A.10. Fees and Bartering

### A.10.a. Accepting Fees From Agency Clients
Counselors refuse a private fee or other remuneration for rendering services to persons who are entitled to such services through the counselor's employing agency or institution. The policies of a particular agency may make explicit provisions for agency clients to receive counseling services from members of its staff in private practice. In such instances, the clients must be informed of other options open to them should they seek private counseling services.

### A.10.b. Establishing Fees
In establishing fees for professional counseling services, counselors consider the financial status of clients and locality. In the event that the established fee structure is inappropriate for a client, counselors assist clients in attempting to find comparable services of acceptable cost.

### A.10.c. Nonpayment of Fees
If counselors intend to use collection agencies or take legal measures to collect fees from clients who do not pay for services as agreed upon, they first inform clients of intended actions and offer clients the opportunity to make payment.

### A.10.d. Bartering
Counselors may barter only if the relationship is not exploitive or harmful and does not place the counselor in an unfair advantage, if the client requests it, and if such arrangements are an accepted practice among professionals in the community. Counselors consider the cultural implications of bartering and discuss relevant concerns with clients and document such agreements in a clear written contract.

### A.10.e. Receiving Gifts
Counselors understand the challenges of accepting gifts from clients and recognize that in some cultures, small gifts are a token of respect and showing gratitude. When determining whether or not to accept a gift from clients, counselors take into account the therapeutic relationship, the monetary value of the gift, a client's motivation for giving the gift, and the counselor's motivation for wanting or declining the gift.

## A.11. Termination and Referral

### A.11.a. Abandonment Prohibited
Counselors do not abandon or neglect clients in counseling. Counselors assist in making appropriate arrangements for the continuation of treatment, when necessary, during interruptions such as vacations, illness, and following termination.

### A.11.b. Inability to Assist Clients
If counselors determine an inability to be of professional assistance to clients, they avoid entering or continuing counseling relationships. Counselors are knowledgeable about culturally and clinically appropriate referral resources and suggest these alternatives. If clients decline the

suggested referrals, counselors should discontinue the relationship.

### A.11.c. Appropriate Termination

Counselors terminate a counseling relationship when it becomes reasonably apparent that the client no longer needs assistance, is not likely to benefit, or is being harmed by continued counseling. Counselors may terminate counseling when in jeopardy of harm by the client, or another person with whom the client has a relationship, or when clients do not pay fees as agreed upon. Counselors provide pretermination counseling and recommend other service providers when necessary.

### A.11.d. Appropriate Transfer of Services

When counselors transfer or refer clients to other practitioners, they ensure that appropriate clinical and administrative processes are completed and open communication is maintained with both clients and practitioners.

## A.12. Technology Applications

### A.12.a. Benefits and Limitations

Counselors inform clients of the benefits and limitations of using information technology applications in the counseling process and in business/billing procedures. Such technologies include but are not limited to computer hardware and software, telephones, the World Wide Web, the Internet, online assessment instruments and other communication devices.

### A.12.b. Technology-Assisted Services

When providing technology-assisted distance counseling services, counselors determine that clients are intellectually, emotionally, and physically capable of using the application and that the application is appropriate for the needs of clients.

### A.12.c. Inappropriate Services

When technology-assisted distance counseling services are deemed inappropriate by the counselor or client, counselors consider delivering services face to face.

### A.12.d. Access

Counselors provide reasonable access to computer applications when providing technology-assisted distance counseling services.

### A.12.e. Laws and Statutes

Counselors ensure that the use of technology does not violate the laws of any local, state, national, or international entity and observe all relevant statutes.

### A.12.f. Assistance

Counselors seek business, legal, and technical assistance when using technology applications, particularly when the use of such applications crosses state or national boundaries.

### A.12.g. Technology and Informed Consent

As part of the process of establishing informed consent, counselors do the following:

1. Address issues related to the difficulty of maintaining the confidentiality of electronically transmitted communications.
2. Inform clients of all colleagues, supervisors, and employees, such as Informational Technology (IT) administrators, who might have authorized or unauthorized access to electronic transmissions.
3. Urge clients to be aware of all authorized or unauthorized users including family members and fellow employees who have access to any technology clients may use in the counseling process.
4. Inform clients of pertinent legal rights and limitations governing the practice of a profession over state lines or international boundaries.
5. Use encrypted Web sites and e-mail communications to help ensure confidentiality when possible.
6. When the use of encryption is not possible, counselors notify clients of this fact and limit electronic transmissions to general communications that are not client specific.
7. Inform clients if and for how long archival storage of transaction records are maintained.
8. Discuss the possibility of technology failure and alternate methods of service delivery.
9. Inform clients of emergency procedures, such as calling 911 or a local crisis hotline, when the counselor is not available.
10. Discuss time zone differences, local customs, and cultural or language differences that might impact service delivery.
11. Inform clients when technology-assisted distance counseling services are not covered by insurance.

*(See A.2.)*

### A.12.h. Sites on the World Wide Web

Counselors maintaining sites on the World Wide Web (the Internet) do the following:

1. Regularly check that electronic links are working and professionally appropriate.
2. Establish ways clients can contact the counselor in case of technology failure.
3. Provide electronic links to relevant state licensure and professional certification boards to protect consumer rights and facilitate addressing ethical concerns.
4. Establish a method for verifying client identity.
5. Obtain the written consent of the legal guardian or other authorized legal representative prior to rendering services in the event the client is a minor child, an adult who is legally incompetent, or an adult incapable of giving informed consent.

6. Strive to provide a site that is accessible to persons with disabilities.

7. Strive to provide translation capabilities for clients who have a different primary language while also addressing the imperfect nature of such translations.

8. Assist clients in determining the validity and reliability of information found on the World Wide Web and other technology applications.

# Section B

## Confidentiality, Privileged Communication, and Privacy

### Introduction

Counselors recognize that trust is a cornerstone of the counseling relationship. Counselors aspire to earn the trust of clients by creating an ongoing partnership, establishing and upholding appropriate boundaries, and maintaining confidentiality. Counselors communicate the parameters of confidentiality in a culturally competent manner.

### B.1. Respecting Client Rights

#### B.1.a. Multicultural/Diversity Considerations

Counselors maintain awareness and sensitivity regarding cultural meanings of confidentiality and privacy. Counselors respect differing views toward disclosure of information. Counselors hold ongoing discussions with clients as to how, when, and with whom information is to be shared.

#### B.1.b. Respect for Privacy

Counselors respect client rights to privacy. Counselors solicit private information from clients only when it is beneficial to the counseling process.

#### B.1.c. Respect for Confidentiality

Counselors do not share confidential information without client consent or without sound legal or ethical justification.

#### B.1.d. Explanation of Limitations

At initiation and throughout the counseling process, counselors inform clients of the limitations of confidentiality and seek to identify foreseeable situations in which confidentiality must be breached. *(See A.2.b.)*

### B.2. Exceptions

#### B.2.a. Danger and Legal Requirements

The general requirement that counselors keep information confidential does not apply when disclosure is required to protect clients or identified others from serious and foreseeable harm or when legal requirements demand that confidential information must be revealed. Counselors consult with other professionals when in doubt as to the validity of an exception. Additional considerations apply when addressing end-of-life issues. *(See A.9.c.)*

#### B.2.b. Contagious, Life-Threatening Diseases

When clients disclose that they have a disease commonly known to be both communicable and life threatening, counselors may be justified in disclosing information to identifiable third parties, if they are known to be at demonstrable and high risk of contracting the disease. Prior to making a disclosure, counselors confirm that there is such a diagnosis and assess the intent of clients to inform the third parties about their disease or to engage in any behaviors that may be harmful to an identifiable third party.

#### B.2.c. Court-Ordered Disclosure

When subpoenaed to release confidential or privileged information without a client's permission, counselors obtain written, informed consent from the client or take steps to prohibit the disclosure or have it limited as narrowly as possible due to

potential harm to the client or counseling relationship.

#### B.2.d. Minimal Disclosure

To the extent possible, clients are informed before confidential information is disclosed and are involved in the disclosure decision-making process. When circumstances require the disclosure of confidential information, only essential information is revealed.

### B.3. Information Shared With Others

#### B.3.a. Subordinates

Counselors make every effort to ensure that privacy and confidentiality of clients are maintained by subordinates, including employees, supervisees, students, clerical assistants, and volunteers. *(See F.1.c.)*

#### B.3.b. Treatment Teams

When client treatment involves a continued review or participation by a treatment team, the client will be informed of the team's existence and composition, information being shared, and the purposes of sharing such information.

#### B.3.c. Confidential Settings

Counselors discuss confidential information only in settings in which they can reasonably ensure client privacy.

#### B.3.d. Third-Party Payers

Counselors disclose information to third-party payers only when clients have authorized such disclosure.

#### B.3.e. Transmitting Confidential Information

Counselors take precautions to ensure the confidentiality of information transmitted through the use of computers, electronic mail, facsimile machines, telephones, voicemail, answering machines, and other electronic or computer technology. *(See A.12.g.)*

#### B.3.f. Deceased Clients

Counselors protect the confidentiality of deceased clients, consistent with legal requirements and agency or setting policies.

## B.4. Groups and Families

### B.4.a. Group Work

In group work, counselors clearly explain the importance and parameters of confidentiality for the specific group being entered.

### B.4.b. Couples and Family Counseling

In couples and family counseling, counselors clearly define who is considered "the client" and discuss expectations and limitations of confidentiality. Counselors seek agreement and document in writing such agreement among all involved parties having capacity to give consent concerning each individual's right to confidentiality and any obligation to preserve the confidentiality of information known.

## B.5. Clients Lacking Capacity to Give Informed Consent

### B.5.a. Responsibility to Clients

When counseling minor clients or adult clients who lack the capacity to give voluntary, informed consent, counselors protect the confidentiality of information received in the counseling relationship as specified by federal and state laws, written policies, and applicable ethical standards.

### B.5.b. Responsibility to Parents and Legal Guardians

Counselors inform parents and legal guardians about the role of counselors and the confidential nature of the counseling relationship. Counselors are sensitive to the cultural diversity of families and respect the inherent rights and responsibilities of parents/guardians over the welfare of their children/charges according to law. Counselors work to establish, as appropriate, collaborative relationships with parents/guardians to best serve clients.

### B.5.c. Release of Confidential Information

When counseling minor clients or adult clients who lack the capacity to give voluntary consent to release confidential information, counselors seek permission from an appropriate third party to disclose information. In such instances, counselors inform clients consistent with their level of understanding and take culturally appropriate measures to safeguard client confidentiality.

## B.6. Records

### B.6.a. Confidentiality of Records

Counselors ensure that records are kept in a secure location and that only authorized persons have access to records.

### B.6.b. Permission to Record

Counselors obtain permission from clients prior to recording sessions through electronic or other means.

### B.6.c. Permission to Observe

Counselors obtain permission from clients prior to observing counseling sessions, reviewing session transcripts, or viewing recordings of sessions with supervisors, faculty, peers, or others within the training environment.

### B.6.d. Client Access

Counselors provide reasonable access to records and copies of records when requested by competent clients. Counselors limit the access of clients to their records, or portions of their records, only when there is compelling evidence that such access would cause harm to the client. Counselors document the request of clients and the rationale for withholding some or all of the record in the files of clients. In situations involving multiple clients, counselors provide individual clients with only those parts of records that related directly to them and do not include confidential information related to any other client.

### B.6.e. Assistance With Records

When clients request access to their records, counselors provide assistance and consultation in interpreting counseling records.

### B.6.f. Disclosure or Transfer

Unless exceptions to confidentiality exist, counselors obtain written permission from clients to disclose or transfer records to legitimate third parties. Steps are taken to ensure that receivers of counseling records are sensitive to their confidential nature. *(See A.3., E.4.)*

### B.6.g. Storage and Disposal After Termination

Counselors store records following termination of services to ensure reasonable future access, maintain records in accordance with state and federal statutes governing records, and dispose of client records and other sensitive materials in a manner that protects client confidentiality. When records are of an artistic nature, counselors obtain client (or guardian) consent with regards to handling of such records or documents. *(See A.1.b.)*

### B.6.h. Reasonable Precautions

Counselors take reasonable precautions to protect client confidentiality in the event of the counselor's termination of practice, incapacity, or death. *(See C.2.h.)*

## B.7. Research and Training

### B.7.a. Institutional Approval

When institutional approval is required, counselors provide accurate information about their research proposals and obtain approval prior to conducting their research. They conduct research in accordance with the approved research protocol.

### B.7.b. Adherence to Guidelines

Counselors are responsible for understanding and adhering to state, federal, agency, or institutional policies or applicable guidelines regarding confidentiality in their research practices.

### B.7.c. Confidentiality of Information Obtained in Research

Violations of participant privacy and confidentiality are risks of participation in research involving human participants. Investigators maintain all research records in a secure manner.

They explain to participants the risks of violations of privacy and confidentiality and disclose to participants any limits of confidentiality that reasonably can be expected. Regardless of the degree to which confidentiality will be maintained, investigators must disclose to participants any limits of confidentiality that reasonably can be expected. *(See G.2.e.)*

### B.7.d. Disclosure of Research Information

Counselors do not disclose confidential information that reasonably could lead to the identification of a research participant unless they have obtained the prior consent of the person. Use of data derived from counseling relationships for purposes of training, research, or publication is confined to content that is disguised to ensure the anonymity of the individuals involved. *(See G.2.a., G.2.d.)*

### B.7.e. Agreement for Identification

Identification of clients, students, or supervisees in a presentation or publication is permissible only when they have reviewed the material and agreed to its presentation or publication. *(See G.4.d.)*

### B.8. Consultation

### B.8.a. Agreements

When acting as consultants, counselors seek agreements among all parties involved concerning each individual's rights to confidentiality, the obligation of each individual to preserve confidential information, and the limits of confidentiality of information shared by others.

### B.8.b. Respect for Privacy

Information obtained in a consulting relationship is discussed for professional purposes only with persons directly involved with the case. Written and oral reports present only data germane to the purposes of the consultation, and every effort is made to protect client identity and to avoid undue invasion of privacy.

### B.8.c. Disclosure of Confidential Information

When consulting with colleagues, counselors do not disclose confidential information that reasonably could lead to the identification of a client or other person or organization with whom they have a confidential relationship unless they have obtained the prior consent of the person or organization or the disclosure cannot be avoided. They disclose information only to the extent necessary to achieve the purposes of the consultation. *(See D.2.d.)*

# Section C

## Professional Responsibility

## Introduction

Counselors aspire to open, honest, and accurate communication in dealing with the public and other professionals. They practice in a nondiscriminatory manner within the boundaries of professional and personal competence and have a responsibility to abide by the *ACA Code of Ethics.* Counselors actively participate in local, state, and national associations that foster the development and improvement of counseling. Counselors advocate to promote change at the individual, group, institutional, and societal levels that improve the quality of life for individuals and groups and remove potential barriers to the provision or access of appropriate services being offered. Counselors have a responsibility to the public to engage in counseling practices that are based on rigorous research methodologies. In addition, counselors engage in self-care activities to maintain and promote their emotional, physical, mental, and spiritual well-being to best meet their professional responsibilities.

## C.1. Knowledge of Standards

Counselors have a responsibility to read, understand, and follow the *ACA Code of Ethics* and adhere to applicable laws and regulations.

## C.2. Professional Competence

### C.2.a. Boundaries of Competence

Counselors practice only within the boundaries of their competence, based on their education, training, supervised experience, state and national professional credentials, and appropriate professional experience. Counselors gain knowledge, personal awareness, sensitivity, and skills pertinent to working with a diverse client population. *(See A.9.b., C.4.e., E.2., F.2., F.11.b.)*

### C.2.b. New Specialty Areas of Practice

Counselors practice in specialty areas new to them only after appropriate education, training, and supervised experience. While developing skills in new specialty areas, counselors take steps to ensure the competence of their work and to protect others from possible harm. *(See F.6.f.)*

### C.2.c. Qualified for Employment

Counselors accept employment only for positions for which they are qualified by education, training, supervised experience, state and national professional credentials, and appropriate professional experience. Counselors hire for professional counseling positions only individuals who are qualified and competent for those positions.

### C.2.d. Monitor Effectiveness

Counselors continually monitor their effectiveness as

professionals and take steps to improve when necessary. Counselors in private practice take reasonable steps to seek peer supervision as needed to evaluate their efficacy as counselors.

### C.2.e. Consultation on Ethical Obligations

Counselors take reasonable steps to consult with other counselors or related professionals when they have questions regarding their ethical obligations or professional practice.

### C.2.f. Continuing Education

Counselors recognize the need for continuing education to acquire and maintain a reasonable level of awareness of current scientific and professional information in their fields of activity. They take steps to maintain competence in the skills they use, are open to new procedures, and keep current with the diverse populations and specific populations with whom they work.

### C.2.g. Impairment

Counselors are alert to the signs of impairment from their own physical, mental, or emotional problems and refrain from offering or providing professional services when such impairment is likely to harm a client or others. They seek assistance for problems that reach the level of professional impairment, and, if necessary, they limit, suspend, or terminate their professional responsibilities until such time it is determined that they may safely resume their work. Counselors assist colleagues or supervisors in recognizing their own professional impairment and provide consultation and assistance when warranted with colleagues or supervisors showing signs of impairment and intervene as appropriate to prevent imminent harm to clients. *(See A.11.b., F.8.b.)*

### C.2.h. Counselor Incapacitation or Termination of Practice

When counselors leave a practice, they follow a prepared plan for transfer of clients and files.

Counselors prepare and disseminate to an identified colleague or "records custodian" a plan for the transfer of clients and files in the case of their incapacitation, death, or termination of practice.

## C.3. Advertising and Soliciting Clients

### C.3.a. Accurate Advertising

When advertising or otherwise representing their services to the public, counselors identify their credentials in an accurate manner that is not false, misleading, deceptive, or fraudulent.

### C.3.b. Testimonials

Counselors who use testimonials do not solicit them from current clients nor former clients nor any other persons who may be vulnerable to undue influence.

### C.3.c. Statements by Others

Counselors make reasonable efforts to ensure that statements made by others about them or the profession of counseling are accurate.

### C.3.d. Recruiting Through Employment

Counselors do not use their places of employment or institutional affiliation to recruit or gain clients, supervisees, or consultees for their private practices.

### C.3.e. Products and Training Advertisements

Counselors who develop products related to their profession or conduct workshops or training events ensure that the advertisements concerning these products or events are accurate and disclose adequate information for consumers to make informed choices. *(See C.6.d.)*

### C.3.f. Promoting to Those Served

Counselors do not use counseling, teaching, training, or supervisory relationships to promote their products or training events in a manner that is deceptive or would exert undue influence on individuals who may be vulnerable. However, counselor educators may adopt textbooks they

have authored for instructional purposes.

## C.4. Professional Qualifications

### C.4.a. Accurate Representation

Counselors claim or imply only professional qualifications actually completed and correct any known misrepresentations of their qualifications by others. Counselors truthfully represent the qualifications of their professional colleagues. Counselors clearly distinguish between paid and volunteer work experience and accurately describe their continuing education and specialized training. *(See C.2.a.)*

### C.4.b. Credentials

Counselors claim only licenses or certifications that are current and in good standing.

### C.4.c. Educational Degrees

Counselors clearly differentiate between earned and honorary degrees.

### C.4.d. Implying Doctoral-Level Competence

Counselors clearly state their highest earned degree in counseling or closely related field. Counselors do not imply doctoral-level competence when only possessing a master's degree in counseling or a related field by referring to themselves as "Dr." in a counseling context when their doctorate is not in counseling or related field.

### C.4.e. Program Accreditation Status

Counselors clearly state the accreditation status of their degree programs at the time the degree was earned.

### C.4.f. Professional Membership

Counselors clearly differentiate between current, active memberships and former memberships in associations. Members of the American Counseling Association must clearly differentiate between professional membership, which implies the possession of at least a master's degree in counseling, and regular membership, which is open to individuals whose interests and activities are consistent with those of ACA but are not qualified for professional membership.

## C.5. Nondiscrimination

Counselors do not condone or engage in discrimination based on age, culture, disability, ethnicity, race, religion/ spirituality, gender, gender identity, sexual orientation, marital status/partnership, language preference, socioeconomic status, or any basis proscribed by law. Counselors do not discriminate against clients, students, employees, supervisees, or research participants in a manner that has a negative impact on these persons.

## C.6 . Public Responsibility

### C.6.a. Sexual Harassment

Counselors do not engage in or condone sexual harassment. Sexual harassment is defined as sexual solicitation, physical advances, or verbal or nonverbal conduct that is sexual in nature, that occurs in connection with professional activities or roles, and that either

1. is unwelcome, is offensive, or creates a hostile workplace or learning environment, and counselors know or are told this; or
2. is sufficiently severe or intense to be perceived as harassment to a reasonable person in the context in which the behavior occurred.

Sexual harassment can consist of a single intense or severe act or multiple persistent or pervasive acts.

### C.6.b. Reports to Third Parties

Counselors are accurate, honest, and objective in reporting their professional activities and judgments to appropriate third parties, including courts, health insurance companies, those who are the recipients of evaluation reports, and others. *(See B.3., E.4.)*

### C.6.c. Media Presentations

When counselors provide advice or comment by means of public lectures, demonstrations, radio or television programs, prerecorded tapes, technology-based applications, printed articles, mailed material, or other media, they take reasonable precautions to ensure that

1. the statements are based on appropriate professional counseling literature and practice,
2. the statements are otherwise consistent with the *ACA Code of Ethics,* and
3. the recipients of the information are not encouraged to infer that a professional counseling relationship has been established.

### C.6.d. Exploitation of Others

Counselors do not exploit others in their professional relationships. *(See C.3.e.)*

### C.6.e. Scientific Bases for Treatment Modalities

Counselors use techniques/ procedures/modalities that are grounded in theory and/or have an empirical or scientific foundation. Counselors who do not must define the techniques/ procedures as "unproven" or "developing" and explain the potential risks and ethical considerations of using such techniques/procedures and take steps to protect clients from possible harm. *(See A.4.a., E.5.c., E.5.d.)*

## C.7. Responsibility to Other Professionals

### C.7.a. Personal Public Statements

When making personal statements in a public context, counselors clarify that they are speaking from their personal perspectives and that they are not speaking on behalf of all counselors or the profession.

# Section D

## Relationships With Other Professionals

## Introduction

Professional counselors recognize that the quality of their interactions with colleagues can influence the quality of services provided to clients. They work to become knowledgeable about colleagues within and outside the field of counseling. Counselors develop positive working relationships and systems of communication with colleagues to enhance services to clients.

## D.1. Relationships With Colleagues, Employers, and Employees

### D.1.a. Different Approaches

Counselors are respectful of approaches to counseling services that differ from their own. Counselors are respectful of traditions and practices of other professional groups with which they work.

### D.1.b. Forming Relationships

Counselors work to develop and strengthen interdisciplinary relations with colleagues from other disciplines to best serve clients.

### D.1.c. Interdisciplinary Teamwork

Counselors who are members of interdisciplinary teams delivering multifaceted services to clients, keep the focus on how to best serve the clients.

They participate in and contribute to expose inappropriate employer decisions that affect the well-being of policies or practices. clients by drawing on the perspectives, values, and experiences of the counseling profession and those of colleagues from other disciplines. *(See A.1.a.)*

### D.1.d. Confidentiality

When counselors are required by law, institutional policy, or extraordinary circumstances to serve in more than one role in judicial or administrative proceedings, they clarify role expectations and the parameters of confidentiality with their colleagues. *(See B.1.c., B.1.d., B.2.c., B.2.d., B.3.b.)*

### D.1.e. Establishing Professional and Ethical Obligations

Counselors who are members of interdisciplinary teams clarify professional and ethical obligations of the team as a whole and of its individual members. When a team decision raises ethical concerns, counselors first attempt to resolve the concern within the team. If they cannot reach resolution among team members, counselors pursue other avenues to address their concerns consistent with client well-being.

### D.1.f. Personnel Selection and Assignment

Counselors select competent staff and assign responsibilities compatible with their skills and experiences.

### D.1.g. Employer Policies

The acceptance of employment in an agency or institution implies that counselors are in agreement with its general policies and principles. Counselors strive to reach agreement with employers as to acceptable standards of conduct that allow for changes in institutional policy conducive to the growth and development of clients.

### D.1.h. Negative Conditions

Counselors alert their employers of inappropriate policies and practices. They attempt to effect changes in such policies or procedures through constructive action within the organization. When such policies are potentially disruptive or damaging to clients or may limit the effectiveness of services provided and change cannot be effected, counselors take appropriate further action. Such action may include referral to appropriate certification, accreditation, or state licensure organizations, or voluntary termination of employment.

### D.1.i. Protection From Punitive Action

Counselors take care not to harass or dismiss an employee who has acted in a responsible and ethical manner

## D.2. Consultation

### D.2.a. Consultant Competency

Counselors take reasonable steps to ensure that they have the appropriate resources and competencies when providing consultation services. Counselors provide appropriate referral resources when requested or needed. *(See C.2.a.)*

### D.2.b. Understanding Consultees

When providing consultation, counselors attempt to develop with their consultees a clear understanding of problem definition, goals for change, and predicted consequences of interventions selected.

### D.2.c. Consultant Goals

The consulting relationship is one in which consultee adaptability and growth toward self-direction are consistently encouraged and cultivated.

### D.2.d. Informed Consent in Consultation

When providing consultation, counselors have an obligation to review, in writing and verbally, the rights and responsibilities of both counselors and consultees. Counselors use clear and understandable language to inform all parties involved about the purpose of the services to be provided, relevant costs, potential risks and benefits, and the limits of confidentiality. Working in conjunction with the consultee, counselors attempt to develop a clear definition of the problem, goals for change, and predicted consequences of interventions that are culturally responsive and appropriate to the needs of consultees. *(See A.2.a., A.2.b.)*

# Section E
## Evaluation, Assessment, and Interpretation

### Introduction

Counselors use assessment instruments as one component of the counseling process, taking into account the client personal and cultural context. Counselors promote the well-being of individual clients or groups of clients by developing and using appropriate educational, psychological, and career assessment instruments.

### E.1. General

**E.1.a. Assessment** The primary purpose of educational, psychological, and career assessment is to provide measurements that are valid and reliable in either comparative or absolute terms. These include, but are not limited to, measurements of ability, personality, interest, intelligence, achievement, and performance. Counselors recognize the need to interpret the statements in this section as applying to both quantitative and qualitative assessments.

### E.1.b. Client Welfare

Counselors do not misuse assessment results and interpretations, and they take reasonable steps to prevent others from misusing the information these techniques provide. They respect the client's right to know the results, the interpretations made, and the bases for counselors' conclusions and recommendations.

### E.2. Competence to Use and Interpret Assessment Instruments

**E.2.a. Limits of Competence**

Counselors utilize only those testing and assessment services for which they have been trained and are competent. Counselors using technology-assisted test interpretations are trained in the construct being measured and the specific instrument being used prior to using its technology based application. Counselors take reasonable measures to ensure the proper use of psychological and career assessment techniques by persons under their supervision. *(See A.12.)*

### E.2.b. Appropriate Use

Counselors are responsible for the appropriate application, scoring, interpretation, and use of assessment instruments relevant to the needs of the client, whether they score and interpret such assessments themselves or use technology or other services.

### E.2.c. Decisions Based on Results

Counselors responsible for decisions involving individuals or policies that are based on assessment results have a thorough understanding of educational, psychological, and career measurement, including validation criteria, assessment research, and guidelines for assessment development and use.

### E.3. Informed Consent in Assessment

### E.3.a. Explanation to Clients

Prior to assessment, counselors explain the nature and purposes of assessment and the specific use of results by potential recipients. The explanation will be given in the language of the client (or other legally authorized person on behalf of the client), unless an explicit exception has been agreed upon in advance. Counselors consider the client's personal or cultural context, the level of the client's understanding of the results, and the impact of the results on the client. *(See A.2., A.12.g., F.1.c.)*

### E.3.b. Recipients of Results

Counselors consider the examinee's welfare, explicit understandings, and prior agreements in determining who receives the assessment

results. Counselors include accurate and appropriate interpretations with any release of individual or group assessment results. *(See B.2.c., B.5.)*

### E.4. Release of Data to Qualified Professionals

Counselors release assessment data in which the client is identified only with the consent of the client or the client's legal representative. Such data are released only to persons recognized by counselors as qualified to interpret the data. *(See B.1., B.3., B.6.b.)*

### E.5. Diagnosis of Mental Disorders

### E.5.a. Proper Diagnosis

Counselors take special care to provide proper diagnosis of mental disorders. Assessment techniques (including personal interview) used to determine client care (e.g., locus of treatment, type of treatment, or recommended follow-up) are carefully selected and appropriately used.

### E.5.b. Cultural Sensitivity

Counselors recognize that culture affects the manner in which clients' problems are defined. Clients' socioeconomic and cultural experiences are considered when diagnosing mental disorders. *(See A.2.c.)*

### E.5.c. Historical and Social Prejudices in the Diagnosis of Pathology

Counselors recognize historical and social prejudices in the misdiagnosis and pathologizing of certain individuals and groups and the role of mental health professionals in perpetuating these prejudices through diagnosis and treatment.

### E.5.d. Refraining From Diagnosis

Counselors may refrain from making and/or reporting a diagnosis if they believe it would

cause harm to the client or others.

### E.6. Instrument Selection

### E.6.a. Appropriateness of Instruments

Counselors carefully consider the validity, reliability, psychometric limitations, and appropriateness of instruments when selecting assessments.

### E.6.b. Referral Information

If a client is referred to a third party for assessment, the counselor provides specific referral questions and sufficient objective data about the client to ensure that appropriate assessment instruments are utilized. *(See A.9.b., B.3.)*

### E.6.c. Culturally Diverse Populations

Counselors are cautious when selecting assessments for culturally diverse populations to avoid the use of instruments that lack appropriate psychometric properties for the client population. *(See A.2.c., E.5.b.)*

### E.7. Conditions of Assessment Administration

*(See A.12.b., A.12.d.)*

### E.7.a. Administration Conditions

Counselors administer assessments under the same conditions that were established in their standardization. When assessments are not administered under standard conditions, as may be necessary to accommodate clients with disabilities, or when unusual behavior or irregularities occur during the administration, those conditions are noted in interpretation, and the results may be designated as invalid or of questionable validity.

### E.7.b. Technological Administration

Counselors ensure that administration programs function properly and provide clients with accurate results when technological or other electronic methods are used for assessment administration.

### E.7.c. Unsupervised Assessments

Unless the assessment instrument is designed, intended, and validated for self-administration and/or scoring, counselors do not permit inadequately supervised use.

### E.7.d. Disclosure of Favorable Conditions

Prior to administration of assessments, conditions that produce most favorable assessment results are made known to the examinee.

## E.8. Multicultural Issues/ Diversity in Assessment

Counselors use with caution assessment techniques that were normed on populations other than that of the client. Counselors recognize the effects of age, color, culture, disability, ethnic group, gender, race, language preference, religion, spirituality, sexual orientation, and socioeconomic status on test administration and interpretation, and place test results in proper perspective with other relevant factors. *(See A.2.c., E.5.b.)*

## E.9. Scoring and Interpretation of Assessments

### E.9.a. Reporting

In reporting assessment results, counselors indicate reservations that exist regarding validity or reliability due to circumstances of the assessment or the inappropriateness of the norms for the person tested.

### E.9.b. Research Instruments

Counselors exercise caution when interpreting the results of research instruments not having sufficient technical data to support respondent results. The specific purposes for the use of such instruments are stated explicitly to the examinee.

### E.9.c. Assessment Services

Counselors who provide assessment scoring and interpretation services to support the assessment process confirm the validity of such interpretations. They accurately describe the purpose, norms, validity, reliability, and applications of the procedures and any special qualifications applicable to their use. The public offering of an automated test interpretations service is considered a professional-to-professional consultation. The formal responsibility of the consultant is to the consultee, but the ultimate and overriding responsibility is to the client. *(See D.2.)*

## E.10. Assessment Security

Counselors maintain the integrity and security of tests and other assessment techniques consistent with legal and contractual obligations. Counselors do not appropriate, reproduce, or modify published assessments or parts thereof without acknowledgment and permission from the publisher.

### E.11. Obsolete Assessments and Outdated Results

Counselors do not use data or results from assessments that are obsolete or outdated for the current purpose. Counselors make every effort to prevent the misuse of obsolete measures and assessment data by others.

## E.12. Assessment Construction

Counselors use established scientific procedures, relevant standards, and current professional knowledge for assessment design in the development, publication, and utilization of educational and psychological assessment techniques.

## E.13. Forensic Evaluation: Evaluation for Legal Proceedings

### E.13.a. Primary Obligations

When providing forensic evaluations, the primary obligation of counselors is to produce objective findings that can be substantiated based on information and techniques appropriate to the evaluation, which may include examination of the individual and/ or review of records. Counselors are entitled to form professional opinions based on their professional knowledge and expertise that can be supported by the data gathered in evaluations. Counselors will define the limits of their reports or testimony, especially when an examination of the individual has not been conducted.

### E.13.b. Consent for Evaluation

Individuals being evaluated are informed in writing that the relationship is for the purposes of an evaluation and is not counseling in nature, and entities or individuals who will receive the evaluation report are identified. Written consent to be evaluated is obtained from those being evaluated unless a court orders evaluations to be conducted without the written consent of individuals being evaluated. When children or vulnerable adults are being evaluated, informed written consent is obtained from a parent or guardian.

### E.13.c. Client Evaluation Prohibited

Counselors do not evaluate individuals for forensic purposes they currently counsel or individuals they have counseled in the past. Counselors do not accept as counseling clients individuals they are evaluating or individuals they have evaluated in the past for forensic purposes.

### E.13.d. Avoid Potentially Harmful Relationships

Counselors who provide forensic evaluations avoid potentially harmful professional or personal relationships with family members, romantic partners, and close friends of individuals they are evaluating or have evaluated in the past.

# Section F

## Supervision, Training, and Teaching

### Introduction

Counselors aspire to foster meaningful and respectful professional relationships and to maintain appropriate boundaries with supervisees and students. Counselors have theoretical and pedagogical foundations for their work and aim to be fair, accurate, and honest in their assessments of counselors-in-training.

### F.1. Counselor Supervision and Client Welfare

#### F.1.a. Client Welfare

A primary obligation of counseling supervisors is to monitor the services provided by other counselors or counselors-in-training. Counseling supervisors monitor client welfare and supervisee clinical performance and professional development. To fulfill these obligations, supervisors meet regularly with supervisees to review case notes, samples of clinical work, or live observations. Supervisees have a responsibility to understand and follow the *ACA Code of Ethics*.

#### F.1.b. Counselor Credentials

Counseling supervisors work to ensure that clients are aware of the qualifications of the supervisees who render services to the clients. *(See A.2.b.)*

#### F.1.c. Informed Consent and Client Rights

Supervisors make supervisees aware of client rights including the protection of client privacy and confidentiality in the counseling relationship. Supervisees provide clients with professional disclosure information and inform them of how the supervision process influences the limits of confidentiality. Supervisees make clients aware of who will have access to records of the counseling relationship and how these records will be used. *(See A.2.b., B.1.d.)*

### F.2. Counselor Supervision Competence

#### F.2.a. Supervisor Preparation

Prior to offering clinical supervision services, counselors are trained in supervision methods and techniques. Counselors who offer clinical supervision services regularly pursue continuing education activities including both counseling and supervision topics and skills. *(See C.2.a., C.2.f.)*

#### F.2.b. Multicultural Issues/Diversity in Supervision

Counseling supervisors are aware of and address the role of multiculturalism/diversity in the supervisory relationship.

### F.3. Supervisory Relationships

#### F.3.a. Relationship Boundaries With Supervisees

Counseling supervisors clearly define and maintain ethical professional, personal, and social relationships with their supervisees. Counseling supervisors avoid nonprofessional relationships with current supervisees. If supervisors must assume other professional roles (e.g., clinical and administrative supervisor, instructor) with supervisees, they work to minimize potential conflicts and explain to supervisees the expectations and responsibilities associated with each role. They do not engage in any form of nonprofessional interaction that may compromise the supervisory relationship.

#### F.3.b. Sexual Relationships

Sexual or romantic interactions or relationships with current supervisees are prohibited.

#### F.3.c. Sexual Harassment

Counseling supervisors do not condone or subject supervisees to sexual harassment. *(See C.6.a.)*

#### F.3.d. Close Relatives and Friends

Counseling supervisors avoid accepting close relatives, romantic partners, or friends as supervisees.

#### F.3.e. Potentially Beneficial Relationships

Counseling supervisors are aware of the power differential in their relationships with supervisees. If they believe nonprofessional relationships with a supervisee may be potentially beneficial to the supervisee, they take precautions similar to those taken by counselors when working with clients. Examples of potentially beneficial interactions or relationships include attending a formal ceremony; hospital visits; providing support during a stressful event; or mutual membership in a professional association, organization, or community. Counseling supervisors engage in open discussions with supervisees when they consider entering into relationships with them outside of their roles as clinical and/or administrative supervisors. Before engaging in nonprofessional relationships, supervisors discuss with supervisees and document the rationale for such interactions, potential benefits or drawbacks, and anticipated consequences for the supervisee. Supervisors clarify the specific nature and limitations of the additional role(s) they will have with the supervisee.

### F.4. Supervisor Responsibilities

#### F.4.a. Informed Consent for Supervision

Supervisors are responsible for incorporating into their supervision the principles of informed consent and participation. Supervisors inform supervisees of the policies and procedures to which they are to adhere and the mechanisms for due process appeal of individual supervisory actions.

### F.4.b. Emergencies and Absences

Supervisors establish and communicate to supervisees procedures for contacting them or, in their absence, alternative on-call supervisors to assist in handling crises.

### F.4.c. Standards for Supervisees

Supervisors make their supervisees aware of professional and ethical standards and legal responsibilities. Supervisors of postdegree counselors encourage these counselors to adhere to professional standards of practice. *(See C.1.)*

### F.4.d. Termination of the Supervisory Relationship

Supervisors or supervisees have the right to terminate the supervisory relationship with adequate notice. Reasons for withdrawal are provided to the other party. When cultural, clinical, or professional issues are crucial to the viability of the supervisory relationship, both parties make efforts to resolve differences. When termination is warranted, supervisors make appropriate referrals to possible alternative supervisors.

## F.5. Counseling Supervision Evaluation, Remediation, and Endorsement

### F.5.a. Evaluation

Supervisors document and provide supervisees with ongoing performance appraisal and evaluation feedback and schedule periodic formal evaluative sessions throughout the supervisory relationship.

### F.5.b. Limitations

Through ongoing evaluation and appraisal, supervisors are aware of the limitations of supervisees that might impede performance. Supervisors assist supervisees in securing remedial assistance when needed. They recommend dismissal from training programs, applied counseling settings, or state or voluntary professional credentialing processes when those supervisees are unable to provide competent professional services. Supervisors seek consultation and document their decisions to dismiss or refer supervisees for assistance. They ensure that supervisees are aware of options available to them to address such decisions. *(See C.2.g.)*

### F.5.c. Counseling for Supervisees

If supervisees request counseling, supervisors provide them with acceptable referrals. Counselors do not provide counseling services to supervisees. Supervisors address interpersonal competencies in terms of the impact of these issues on clients, the supervisory relationship, and professional functioning. *(See F.3.a.)*

### F.5.d. Endorsement

Supervisors endorse supervisees for certification, licensure, employment, or completion of an academic or training program only when they believe supervisees are qualified for the endorsement. Regardless of qualifications, supervisors do not endorse supervisees whom they believe to be impaired in any way that would interfere with the performance of the duties associated with the endorsement.

## F.6. Responsibilities of Counselor Educators

### F.6.a. Counselor Educators

Counselor educators who are responsible for developing, implementing, and supervising educational programs are skilled as teachers and practitioners. They are knowledgeable regarding the ethical, legal, and regulatory aspects of the profession, are skilled in applying that knowledge, and make students and supervisees aware of their responsibilities. Counselor educators conduct counselor education and training programs in an ethical manner and serve as role models for professional behavior. *(See C.1., C.2.a., C.2.c.)*

### F.6.b. Infusing Multicultural Issues/ Diversity

Counselor educators infuse material related to multiculturalism/diversity into all courses and workshops for the development of professional counselors.

### F.6.c. Integration of Study and Practice

Counselor educators establish education and training programs that integrate academic study and supervised practice.

### F.6.d. Teaching Ethics

Counselor educators make students and supervisees aware of the ethical responsibilities and standards of the profession and the ethical responsibilities of students to the profession. Counselor educators infuse ethical considerations throughout the curriculum. *(See C.1.)*

### F.6.e. Peer Relationships

Counselor educators make every effort to ensure that the rights of peers are not compromised when students or supervisees lead counseling groups or provide clinical supervision. Counselor educators take steps to ensure that students and supervisees understand they have the same ethical obligations as counselor educators, trainers, and supervisors.

### F.6.f. Innovative Theories and Techniques

When counselor educators teach counseling techniques/procedures that are innovative, without an empirical foundation, or without a well-grounded theoretical foundation, they define the counseling techniques/procedures as "unproven" or "developing" and explain to students the potential risks and ethical considerations of using such techniques/procedures.

### F.6.g. Field Placements

Counselor educators develop clear policies within their training programs regarding field placement and other clinical experiences. Counselor educators provide clearly stated roles and responsibilities for the student or supervisee, the site supervisor, and the program supervisor.

They confirm that site supervisors are qualified to provide supervision and inform site supervisors of their professional and ethical responsibilities in this role.

### F.6.h. Professional Disclosure

Before initiating counseling services, counselors-in-training disclose their status as students and explain how this status affects the limits of confidentiality. Counselor educators ensure that the clients at field placements are aware of the services rendered and the qualifications of the students and supervisees rendering those services. Students and supervisees obtain client permission before they use any information concerning the counseling relationship in the training process. *(See A.2.b.)*

## F.7. Student Welfare

### F.7.a. Orientation

Counselor educators recognize that orientation is a developmental process that continues throughout the educational and clinical training of students. Counseling faculty provide prospective students with information about the counselor education program's expectations:

1. the type and level of skill and knowledge acquisition required for successful completion of the training;
2. program training goals, objectives, and mission, and subject matter to be covered;
3. bases for evaluation;
4. training components that encourage self-growth or self-disclosure as part of the training process;
5. the type of supervision settings and requirements of the sites for required clinical field experiences;
6. student and supervisee evaluation and dismissal policies and procedures; and
7. up-to-date employment prospects for graduates.

### F.7.b. Self-Growth Experiences

Counselor education programs delineate requirements for self-disclosure or self-growth experiences in their admission and program materials. Counselor educators use professional judgment when designing training experiences they conduct that require student and supervisee self-growth or self-disclosure. Students and supervisees are made aware of the ramifications their self-disclosure may have when counselors whose primary role as teacher, trainer, or supervisor requires acting on ethical obligations to the profession. Evaluative components of experiential training experiences explicitly delineate predetermined academic standards that are separate and do not depend on the student's level of self-disclosure. Counselor educators may require trainees to seek professional help to address any personal concerns that may be affecting their competency.

## F.8. Student Responsibilities

### F.8.a. Standards for Students

Counselors-in-training have a responsibility to understand and follow the *ACA Code of Ethics* and adhere to applicable laws, regulatory policies, and rules and policies governing professional staff behavior at the agency or placement setting. Students have the same obligation to clients as those required of professional counselors. *(See C.1., H.1.)*

### F.8.b. Impairment

Counselors-in-training refrain from offering or providing counseling services when their physical, mental, or emotional problems are likely to harm a client or others. They are alert to the signs of impairment, seek assistance for problems, and notify their program supervisors when they are aware that they are unable to effectively provide services. In addition, they seek appropriate professional services for themselves to remediate the problems that are interfering with their ability to provide services to others. *(See A.1., C.2.d., C.2.g.)*

## F.9. Evaluation and Remediation of Students

### F.9.a. Evaluation

Counselors clearly state to students, prior to and throughout the training program, the levels of competency expected, appraisal methods, and timing of evaluations for both didactic and clinical competencies. Counselor educators provide students with ongoing performance appraisal and evaluation feedback throughout the training program.

### F.9.b. Limitations

Counselor educators, throughout ongoing evaluation and appraisal, are aware of and address the inability of some students to achieve counseling competencies that might impede performance. Counselor educators

1. assist students in securing remedial assistance when needed,
2. seek professional consultation and document their decision to dismiss or refer students for assistance, and
3. ensure that students have recourse in a timely manner to address decisions to require them to seek assistance or to dismiss them and provide students with due process according to institutional policies and procedures.

*(See C.2.g.)*

### F.9.c. Counseling for Students

If students request counseling or if counseling services are required as part of a remediation process, counselor educators provide acceptable referrals.

## F.10. Roles and Relationships Between Counselor Educators and Students

### F.10.a. Sexual or Romantic Relationships

Sexual or romantic interactions or relationships with current students are prohibited.

### F.10.b. Sexual Harassment

Counselor educators do not condone or subject students to sexual harassment. *(See C.6.a.)*

### F.10.c. Relationships With Former Students

Counselor educators are aware of the power differential in the relationship between faculty and students. Faculty members foster open discussions with former students when considering engaging in a social, sexual, or other intimate relationship. Faculty members discuss with the former student how their former relationship may affect the change in relationship.

### F.10.d. Nonprofessional Relationships

Counselor educators avoid nonprofessional or ongoing professional relationships with students in which there is a risk of potential harm to the student or that may compromise the training experience or grades assigned. In addition, counselor educators do not accept any form of professional services, fees, commissions, reimbursement, or remuneration from a site for student or supervisee placement.

### F.10.e. Counseling Services

Counselor educators do not serve as counselors to current students unless this is a brief role associated with a training experience.

### F.10.f. Potentially Beneficial Relationships

Counselor educators are aware of the power differential in the relationship between faculty and students. If they believe a nonprofessional relationship with a student may be potentially beneficial to the student, they take precautions similar to those taken by counselors when working with clients. Examples of potentially beneficial interactions or relationships include, but are not limited to, attending a formal ceremony; hospital visits; providing support during a stressful event; or mutual membership in a professional association, organization, or community. Counselor educators engage in open discussions with students when they consider entering into relationships with students outside of their roles as teachers and supervisors. They discuss with students the rationale for such interactions, the potential benefits and drawbacks, and the anticipated consequences for the student. Educators clarify the specific nature and limitations of the additional role(s) they will have with the student prior to engaging in a nonprofessional relationship. Nonprofessional relationships with students should be time-limited and initiated with student consent.

## F.11. Multicultural/ Diversity

### Competence in Counselor Education and Training Programs

### F.11.a. Faculty Diversity

Counselor educators are committed to recruiting and retaining a diverse faculty.

### F.11.b. Student Diversity

Counselor educators actively attempt to recruit and retain a diverse student body. Counselor educators demonstrate commitment to multicultural/diversity competence by recognizing and valuing diverse cultures and types of abilities students bring to the training experience. Counselor educators provide appropriate accommodations that enhance and support diverse student well-being and academic performance.

### F.11.c. Multicultural/ Diversity Competence

Counselor educators actively infuse multicultural/diversity competency in their training and supervision practices. They actively train students to gain awareness, knowledge, and skills in the competencies of multicultural practice. Counselor educators include case examples, role-plays, discussion questions, and other classroom activities that promote and represent various cultural perspectives.

# Section G
## Research and Publication

## Introduction

Counselors who conduct research are encouraged to contribute to the knowledge base of the profession and promote a clearer understanding of the conditions that lead to a healthy and more just society. Counselors support efforts of researchers by participating fully and willingly whenever possible. Counselors minimize bias and respect diversity in designing and implementing research programs.

## G.1. Research Responsibilities

### G.1.a. Use of Human Research Participants

Counselors plan, design, conduct, and report research in a manner that is consistent with pertinent ethical principles, federal and state laws, host institutional regulations, and scientific standards governing research with human research participants.

### G.1.b. Deviation From Standard Practice

Counselors seek consultation and observe stringent safeguards to protect the rights of research participants when a research problem suggests a deviation from standard or acceptable practices.

### G.1.c. Independent Researchers

When independent researchers do not have access to an Institutional Review Board (IRB), they should consult with researchers who are familiar with IRB procedures to provide appropriate safeguards.

### G.1.d. Precautions to Avoid Injury

Counselors who conduct research with human participants are responsible for the welfare of participants throughout the research process and should take reasonable precautions to avoid causing injurious psychological, emotional, physical, or social effects to participants.

### G.1.e. Principal Researcher Responsibility

The ultimate responsibility for ethical research practice lies with the principal researcher. All others involved in the research activities share ethical obligations and responsibility for their own actions.

### G.1.f. Minimal Interference

Counselors take reasonable precautions to avoid causing disruptions in the lives of research participants that could be caused by their involvement in research.

### G.1.g. Multicultural/Diversity Considerations in Research

When appropriate to research goals, counselors are sensitive to incorporating research procedures that take into account cultural considerations. They seek consultation when appropriate.

## G.2. Rights of Research Participants

*(See A.2, A.7.)*

### G.2.a. Informed Consent in Research

Individuals have the right to consent to become research participants. In seeking consent, counselors use language that

1. accurately explains the purpose and procedures to be followed,
2. identifies any procedures that are experimental or relatively untried,
3. describes any attendant discomforts and risks,
4. describes any benefits or changes in individuals or organizations that might be reasonably expected,
5. discloses appropriate alternative procedures that would be advantageous for participants,
6. offers to answer any inquiries concerning the procedures,
7. describes any limitations on confidentiality,
8. describes the format and potential target audiences for

the dissemination of research findings, and
9. instructs participants that they are free to withdraw their consent and to discontinue participation in the project at any time without penalty.

### G.2.b. Deception

Counselors do not conduct research involving deception unless alternative procedures are not feasible and the prospective value of the research justifies the deception. If such deception has the potential to cause physical or emotional harm to research participants, the research is not conducted, regardless of prospective value. When the methodological requirements of a study necessitate concealment or deception, the investigator explains the reasons for this action as soon as possible during the debriefing.

### G.2.c. Student/Supervisee Participation

Researchers who involve students or supervisees in research make clear to them that the decision regarding whether or not to participate in research activities does not affect one's academic standing or supervisory relationship. Students or supervisees who choose not to participate in educational research are provided with an appropriate alternative to fulfill their academic or clinical requirements.

### G.2.d. Client Participation

Counselors conducting research involving clients make clear in the informed consent process that clients are free to choose whether or not to participate in research activities. Counselors take necessary precautions to protect clients from adverse consequences of declining or withdrawing from participation.

### G.2.e. Confidentiality of Information

Information obtained about research participants during the course of an investigation is confidential. When the possibility exists that others may obtain access to such information, ethical research practice requires that

the possibility, together with the plans for protecting confidentiality, be explained to participants as a part of the procedure for obtaining informed consent.

### G.2.f. Persons Not Capable of Giving Informed Consent

When a person is not capable of giving informed consent, counselors provide an appropriate explanation to, obtain agreement for participation from, and obtain the appropriate consent of a legally authorized person.

### G.2.g. Commitments to Participants

Counselors take reasonable measures to honor all commitments to research participants. *(See A.2.c.)*

### G.2.h. Explanations After Data Collection

After data are collected, counselors provide participants with full clarification of the nature of the study to remove any misconceptions participants might have regarding the research. Where scientific or human values justify delaying or withholding information, counselors take reasonable measures to avoid causing harm.

### G.2.i. Informing Sponsors

Counselors inform sponsors, institutions, and publication channels regarding research procedures and outcomes. Counselors ensure that appropriate bodies and authorities are given pertinent information and acknowledgment.

### G.2.j. Disposal of Research Documents and Records

Within a reasonable period of time following the completion of a research project or study, counselors take steps to destroy records or documents (audio, video, digital, and written) containing confidential data or information that identifies research participants. When records are of an artistic nature, researchers obtain participant consent with regard to handling of such records or documents. *(See B.4.a, B.4.g.)*

## G.3. Relationships With Research Participants (When Research Involves Intensive or Extended Interactions)

### G.3.a. Nonprofessional Relationships

Nonprofessional relationships with research participants should be avoided.

### G.3.b. Relationships With Research Participants

Sexual or romantic counselor–research participant interactions or relationships with current research participants are prohibited.

### G.3.c. Sexual Harassment and Research Participants

Researchers do not condone or subject research participants to sexual harassment.

### G.3.d. Potentially Beneficial Interactions

When a nonprofessional interaction between the researcher and the research participant may be potentially beneficial, the researcher must document, prior to the interaction (when feasible), the rationale for such an interaction, the potential benefit, and anticipated consequences for the research participant. Such interactions should be initiated with appropriate consent of the research participant. Where unintentional harm occurs to the research participant due to the nonprofessional interaction, the researcher must show evidence of an attempt to remedy such harm.

## G.4. Reporting Results

### G.4.a. Accurate Results

Counselors plan, conduct, and report research accurately. They provide thorough discussions of the limitations of their data and alternative hypotheses. Counselors do not engage in misleading or fraudulent research, distort data, misrepresent data, or deliberately bias their results. They explicitly mention all variables and conditions known to the investigator that may have affected the outcome of a study or the interpretation of data. They describe the extent to which results are applicable for diverse populations.

### G.4.b. Obligation to Report Unfavorable Results

Counselors report the results of any research of professional value. Results that reflect unfavorably on institutions, programs, services, prevailing opinions, or vested interests are not withheld.

### G.4.c. Reporting Errors

If counselors discover significant errors in their published research, they take reasonable steps to correct such errors in a correction erratum, or through other appropriate publication means.

### G.4.d. Identity of Participants

Counselors who supply data, aid in the research of another person, report research results, or make original data available take due care to disguise the identity of respective participants in the absence of specific authorization from the participants to do otherwise. In situations where participants self-identify their involvement in research studies, researchers take active steps to ensure that data is adapted/changed to protect the identity and welfare of all parties and that discussion of results does not cause harm to participants.

### G.4.e. Replication Studies

Counselors are obligated to make available sufficient original research data to qualified professionals who may wish to replicate the study.

## G.5. Publication

### G.5.a. Recognizing Contributions

When conducting and reporting research, counselors are familiar with and give recognition to previous work on the topic, observe copyright laws, and give full credit to those to whom credit is due.

### G.5.b. Plagiarism

Counselors do not plagiarize, that is, they do not present another person's work as their own work.

### G.5.c. Review/Republication of Data or Ideas

Counselors fully acknowledge and make editorial reviewers aware of prior publication of ideas or data where such ideas or data are submitted for review or publication.

### G.5.d. Contributors

Counselors give credit through joint authorship, acknowledgment, footnote statements, or other appropriate means to those who have contributed significantly to research or concept development in accordance with such contributions. The principal contributor is listed first and minor technical or professional contributions are acknowledged in notes or introductory statements.

### G.5.e. Agreement of Contributors

Counselors who conduct joint research with colleagues or students/supervisees establish agreements in advance regarding allocation of tasks, publication credit, and types of acknowledgment that will be received.

### G.5.f. Student Research

For articles that are substantially based on students course papers, projects, dissertations or theses, and on which students have been the primary contributors, they are listed as principal authors.

### G.5.g. Duplicate Submission

Counselors submit manuscripts for consideration to only one journal at a time. Manuscripts that are published in whole or in substantial part in another journal or published work are not submitted for publication without acknowledgment and permission from the previous publication.

### G.5.h. Professional Review

Counselors who review material submitted for publication, research, or other scholarly purposes respect the confidentiality and proprietary rights of those who submitted it. Counselors use care to make publication decisions based on valid and defensible standards. Counselors review article submissions in a timely manner and based on their scope and competency in research methodologies. Counselors who serve as reviewers at the request of editors or publishers make every effort to only review materials that are within their scope of competency and use care to avoid personal biases.

# Section H

## Resolving Ethical Issues

## Introduction

Counselors behave in a legal, ethical, and moral manner in the conduct of their professional work. They are aware that client protection and trust in the profession depend on a high level of professional conduct. They hold other counselors to the same standards and are willing to take appropriate action to ensure that these standards are upheld. Counselors strive to resolve ethical dilemmas with direct and open communication among all parties involved and seek consultation with colleagues and supervisors when necessary. Counselors incorporate ethical practice into their daily professional work. They engage in ongoing professional development regarding current topics in ethical and legal issues in counseling.

## H.1. Standards and the Law

*(See F.9.a.)*

### H.1.a. Knowledge

Counselors understand the *ACA Code of Ethics* and other applicable ethics codes from other professional organizations or from certification and licensure bodies of which they are members. Lack of knowledge or misunderstanding of an ethical responsibility is not a defense against a charge of unethical conduct.

### H.1.b. Conflicts Between Ethics and Laws

If ethical responsibilities conflict with law, regulations, or other governing legal authority, counselors make known their com-

mitment to the *ACA Code of Ethics* and take steps to resolve the conflict. If the conflict cannot be resolved by such means, counselors may adhere to the requirements of law, regulations, or other governing legal authority.

## H.2. Suspected Violations

### H.2.a. Ethical Behavior Expected

Counselors expect colleagues to adhere to the *ACA Code of Ethics*. When counselors possess knowledge that raises doubts as to whether another counselor is acting in an ethical manner, they take appropriate action. *(See H.2.b., H.2.c.)*

### H.2.b. Informal Resolution

When counselors have reason to believe that another counselor is violating or has violated an ethical standard, they attempt first to resolve the issue informally with the other counselor if feasible, provided such action does not violate confidentiality rights that may be involved.

### H.2.c. Reporting Ethical Violations

If an apparent violation has substantially harmed, or is likely to substantially harm a person or organization and is not appropriate for informal resolution or is not resolved properly, counselors take further action appropriate to the situation. Such action might include referral to state or national committees on professional ethics, voluntary national certification bodies, state licensing boards, or to the appropriate institutional authorities. This standard does not apply when an intervention would violate confidentiality rights or when counselors have been retained to review the work of another counselor whose professional conduct is in question.

### H.2.d. Consultation

When uncertain as to whether a particular situation or course of action may be in violation of the *ACA Code of Ethics,* counselors consult with other counselors who are knowledgeable about

ethics and the *ACA Code of Ethics,* with colleagues, or with appropriate authorities

### H.2.e. Organizational Conflicts

If the demands of an organization with which counselors are affiliated pose a conflict with the *ACA Code of Ethics,* counselors specify the nature of such conflicts and express to their supervisors or other responsible officials their commitment to the *ACA Code of Ethics.* When possible, counselors work toward change within the organization to allow full adherence to the *ACA Code of Ethics.* In doing so, they address any confidentiality issues.

### H.2.f. Unwarranted Complaints

Counselors do not initiate, participate in, or encourage the filing of ethics complaints that are made with reckless disregard or willful ignorance of facts that would disprove the allegation.

### H.2.g. Unfair Discrimination Against Complainants and Respondents

Counselors do not deny persons employment, advancement, admission to academic or other programs, tenure, or promotion based solely upon their having made or their being the subject of an ethics complaint. This does not preclude taking action based upon the outcome of such proceedings or considering other appropriate information.

## H.3. Cooperation With Ethics Committees

Counselors assist in the process of enforcing the *ACA Code of Ethics.* Counselors cooperate with investigations, proceedings, and requirements of the ACA Ethics Committee or ethics committees of other duly constituted associations or boards having jurisdiction over those charged with a violation. Counselors are familiar with the *ACA Policy and Procedures for Processing Complains of Ethical Violations* and use it as a reference for assisting in the enforcement of the *ACA Code of Ethics.*

# Glossary of Terms

**Advocacy** – promotion of the well-being of individuals and groups, and the counseling profession within systems and organizations. Advocacy seeks to remove barriers and obstacles that inhibit access, growth, and development.

**Assent** – to demonstrate agreement, when a person is otherwise not capable or competent to give formal consent (e.g., informed consent) to a counseling service or plan.

**Client** – an individual seeking or referred to the professional services of a counselor for help with problem resolution or decision making.

**Counselor** – a professional (or a student who is a counselor-in-training) engaged in a counseling practice or other counseling-related services. Counselors fulfill many roles and responsibilities such as counselor educators, researchers, supervisors, practitioners, and consultants.

**Counselor Educator** – a professional counselor engaged primarily in developing, implementing, and supervising the educational preparation of counselors-in-training.

**Counselor Supervisor** – a professional counselor who engages in a formal relationship with a practicing counselor or counselor-in-training for the purpose of overseeing that individual's counseling work or clinical skill development.

**Culture** – membership in a socially constructed way of living, which incorporates collective values, beliefs, norms, boundaries, and lifestyles that are cocreated with others who share similar worldviews comprising biological, psychosocial, historical, psychological, and other factors.

**Diversity** – the similarities and differences that occur within and across cultures, and the intersection of cultural and social identities.

**Documents** – any written, digital, audio, visual, or artistic recording of the work within the counseling relationship between counselor and client.

**Examinee** – a recipient of any professional counseling service that includes educational, psychological, and career appraisal utilizing qualitative or quantitative techniques.

**Forensic Evaluation** – any formal assessment conducted for court or other legal proceedings.

**Multicultural/Diversity Competence** – a capacity whereby counselors possess cultural and diversity awareness and knowledge about self and others, and how this awareness and knowledge is applied effectively in practice with clients and client groups.

**Multicultural/Diversity Counseling** – counseling that recognizes diversity and embraces approaches that support the worth, dignity, potential, and uniqueness of individuals within their historical, cultural, economic, political, and psychosocial contexts.

**Student** – an individual engaged in formal educational preparation as a counselor-in-training.

**Supervisee** – a professional counselor or counselor-in-training whose counseling work or clinical skill development is being overseen in a formal supervisory relationship by a qualified trained professional.

**Supervisor** – counselors who are trained to oversee the professional clinical work of counselors and counselors-in-training.

**Teaching** – all activities engaged in as part of a formal educational program designed to lead to a graduate degree in counseling.

**Training** – the instruction and practice of skills related to the counseling profession. Training contributes to the ongoing proficiency of students and professional counselors.

# Appendix B

# AACC (American Association of Christian Counselors) Code of Ethics

## The Y2004 Final Code

Developed and Drafted by the

### AACC Law and Ethics Committee
George Ohlschlager, Chairman

## CONTENTS

# PREFACE TO THE Y2004 FINAL CODE

Welcome to the Y2004 final revision of the AACC Christian Counseling Code of Ethics (Code). This edition of the Code revises the 1998, 2000, 2001, and 2003 Provisional Codes, and supercedes those versions of the Code in their entirety. This is the Final Code version—the Code, with "Procedural Rules," in its completed form—which was first presented to the AACC membership at the 2003 AACC World Conference in Nashville, Tennessee.

With the publication of this Code on our website—www.aacc.net—we publicly present our ethics to our over 50,000 members in all 50 states and 50 other nations (as of Summer 2003). We also respectfully submit this document to the church and the helping professions, to the courts, legislatures, and licensure boards of America, to mental health and health-care organizations everywhere, and to the world-at-large.

This Code has already been adopted, in whole or in part, in nearly two dozen countries on every continent. It has been translated into Spanish, German, French, and Dutch languages. We at the AACC anticipate this Code becoming the basis of a worldwide statement of Christian counseling ethics and, as it spreads further internationally, the foundation of a 21st-century, global standard of Christian counseling care.

Work on this Code has been continuous for 10 years—since AACC created the Law and Ethics Committee in 1993. The primary mission given this group a decade ago was to construct and manage a new, Christ-centered, interdisciplinary code of ethics for Christian counseling as it matures into the 21st century. This code begins to fulfill this mission.

Committee members, AACC leaders, and other colleagues who helped me develop, draft, and survive this project through 18 evolving drafts over 10 years included: AACC President Tim Clinton, EdD; former president Gary Collins, PhD; Mark McMinn, PhD; Rosemarie Hughes, PhD; the late David Gatewood, MS; Peter Mosgofian, MA; W. L. Ryder, MD; Elizabeth York, MEd; Siang-Yang Tan, PhD; Chris Thurman, PhD; Ev Worthington, PhD; Tom Whiteman, PhD; Norm Wright, MA; Leigh Bishop, MD; Freda Crews, DMin, PhD; Gary Oliver, PhD; Bill Secor, PhD; Ron Hawkins, DMin, EdD; Diane Langberg, PhD; Michael Lyles, MD; and Archibald Hart, PhD.

The Holy Scriptures and the AACC Doctrinal Statement are foundational to this Code. Other ethics codes, in alphabetical order, that were consulted as we drafted this statement included those from the:

- American Association of Marriage and Family Therapists (AAMFT), including portions of the California Association of Marriage and Family Therapists (CAMFT)
- American Association of Pastoral Counselors (AAPC)
- American Counseling Association (ACA), including the Association for Counselor Education and Supervision (ACES—ACA related), and the Association for Spiritual, Ethical, and Religious Values in Counseling (ASERVIC—also ACA related)
- American Psychiatric Association (APiA)
- American Psychological Association (APoA), including APoA General Guidelines for Providers of Psychological Services
- Christian Association for Psychological Studies (CAPS)
- National Association of Social Workers (NASW), including NASW Standards for the Private Practice of Clinical Social Work
- The Society of Professionals in Dispute Resolution (SPDR)

Furthermore, many writings influenced this Code, especially by Alister McGrath, on "Doctrine and Ethics," and Alan Tjeltveit, on "Psychotherapy and Christian Ethics." Some rules for procedure, for resolution of conflicted values, and the detail in this document was suggested by the legal profession's Code of Professional Responsibility, and by selected court cases, mental health license statutes, and licensure board administrative rules from California, Virginia, Texas, Colorado, Florida, Minnesota, Washington, and New York.

This Code may be downloaded from the AACC web site, or purchased in paper form from AACC at a nominal cost. We continue to invite your feedback about this code (to George@AACC.net)—ideas and suggestions that will be considered for inclusion into future Code revisions. Also, we are developing a new section on the ethics of remote counseling—using the phone, the Internet, and doing in-home counseling—and a code specifically for lay helping ministry in the church. Your thoughts and comments here are also welcome. Thank you and may God bless your study and use of this new Code of Ethics

Sincerely,

George Ohlschlager, JD, LCSW
Chairman, AACC Law & Ethics Committee

# APPLICABILITY OF THE CODE

All members of the AACC, the IACC (International Association of Christian Counselors), and Christian counselors everywhere are invited to fully adopt this *AACC Code of Ethics* (Code) in their work as Christian counselors, ministers, and helpers as soon as they are able. This Code may inform and enlighten all Christian counselors and ministers, but is not strictly enforceable toward non-AACC persons, nor upon AACC members in their private lives apart from professional-ministerial roles.

The Code will become a mandatory ethic for all AACC/IACC members who elect to become credential holders or members of either the American Board of Christian Counselors (ABCC) or the Christian Care Network (CCN). *

# INTRODUCTION AND MISSION

The Code is designed to assist AACC members to better serve their counselees and congregants and to improve the work of Christian counseling worldwide. It will help achieve the primary goals of the AACC—to bring honor to Jesus Christ and his church, promote excellence in Christian counseling, and bring unity to Christian counselors.

## *A New Code for an Emerging Profession*

The Code is a comprehensive, detailed, and integrative synthesis of biblical, clinical, systemic, ethical, and legal information. It was created this way because vaguely worded, content limited, and overly generalized codes are insufficient for the complexities of the modern, 21st-century counseling environment. A more comprehensive and behavior-specific ethical code is needed for Christian counselors (and all mental health and ministerial professions, we believe) because of:

(1) the mounting evidence of questionable and incompetent practices among Christian counselors, including increasing complaints of counselee-parishioner harm;
(2) the largely unprotected legal status of Christian counseling, including the increasing state scrutiny, excessive litigation, and unrelenting legalization of professional ethics; and more positively
(3) the vitality and growing maturity of Christian counseling—including its many theories and controversies—indicating the need for an overarching ethical-legal template to guide the development of biblical and empirically sound Christian counseling models.

This Code—beyond defining the boundaries of unethical practice—affirmatively educates counselors in the direction of becoming helpers of ethical excellence, capable of more consistently securing the best counseling outcomes. This Code shows four streams of influence. These include (1) the Bible (both Old and New Testaments) and historic orthodox Christian theology; ** (2) accepted standards of counseling and clinical practice from Christian counseling and the established mental health disciplines; (3) codes of ethics from other Christian and mental health professions; and (4) current and developing standards derived from mental health and ministry-related law.

---

* NOTE 1. This code is adopted in its entirety by AACC affiliate organizations, the ABCC and the CCN. All ABCC and CCN members will be required to mandatory adherence to this code.

** NOTE 2. Although rooted primarily in an orthodox evangelical biblical theology, this Code is also influenced (according to the paradigm offered by Richard Foster) by the social justice, charismatic-pentecostal, pietistic-holiness, liturgical, and contemplative traditions of Christian theology and church history.

## *Mission, Uses, and Limits of the Code*

The mission of this Code is to

(1) help advance the central mission of the AACC—to bring honor to Jesus Christ and promote excellence and unity in Christian counseling;

(2) promote the welfare and protect the dignity and fundamental rights of all individuals, families, groups, churches, schools, agencies, ministries, and other organizations with whom Christian counselors work;

(3) provide standards of ethical conduct in Christian counseling that are to be advocated and applied by the AACC (and ABCC and CCN) and that can be respected by other professionals and institutions.

This Code defines biblically based values and universal behavioral standards for ethical Christian counseling. We intend this Code to become a core document by which Christian counselors, counselees, and the church oversee and evaluate Christian counselors and counseling values, goals, process, and effectiveness. Furthermore, the Code asserts a Christian counseling standard of care that invites respect and application by the courts, the regulatory bodies of church and state, insurance and managed care groups, other professions, and by society.

This Code should be seen as normative but non-exhaustive. It provides a common definition of practice, but does not presume to be a complete picture of Christian counseling nor does it necessarily cover all ethical issues. This Code outlines a foundation of preferred values and agreed professional behavior upon which Christian counselors can shape their identity and build their work. It defines standards upon which practice diversity is acknowledged and encouraged as well as the limits beyond which practice deviance is not allowed.

The Code is aspirational throughout the AACC and enforceable in ABCC and CCN. It consists of four major parts—Introduction and Mission, Biblical-Ethical Foundations, Ethical Standards, and Procedural Rules (which are being developed). It aspires to define, in the mission and the biblical-ethical foundations statements, the best ideals and goals of Christian counseling. The ethical standards and procedural rules are the codes of individual practice and organizational behavior that are to guide the membership of the AACC. The mission and foundations statements are to be consulted in working out the problems and dilemmas of ethics application and procedural rules interpretation.

Concerning language, we have endeavored to avoid pedantic, legalese, and sexist language, but we also avoid a radical inclusivism that de-sexes the name of God. Unless denoted, we use the term "counselee" to refer to counselees, patients, congregants, parishioners, or helpees. "Counseling" is usually a generic reference to clinical, psychiatric, pastoral, and lay helping.

### *Grace for the Task Ahead*

This is a dynamic Code, one that will anchor the mission of the AACC and retain some elements without change, but one that will also live and grow with the life and growth of the Association and its membership. The Code calls us to a life-long commitment to ethical and excellent service; it challenges us to encourage ethical behavior in our colleagues, churches, organizations, and communities. May God give us the grace to own it professionally, the strength to live it honorably, and the hope to see it as a foundation of common identity and corporate unity.

# Biblical-Ethical Foundations of the AACC Ethics Code +

| | |
|---|---|
| 1st FOUNDATION: | *Jesus Christ—and His revelation in the Old and New Testaments of the Bible—is the pre-eminent model for Christian counseling practice, ethics, and caregiving activities.* |
| 2nd FOUNDATION: | *Christian counseling maintains a committed, intimate, and dedicated relationship with the worldwide church, and individual counselors with a local body of believers.* |
| 3rd FOUNDATION: | *Christian counseling, at its best, is a Spirit-led process of change and growth, geared to help others mature in Christ by the skillful synthesis of counselor-assisted spiritual, psycho-social, familial, bio-medical, and environmental interventions.* |
| 4th FOUNDATION: | *Christian counselors are dedicated to Jesus Christ as their "first love," to excellence in counselee service, to ethical integrity in practice, and to respect for everyone encountered.* |
| 5th FOUNDATION: | *Christian counselors accord the highest respect to the Biblical revelation regarding the defense of human life, the dignity of human personhood, and the sanctity of marriage and family life.* |
| 6th FOUNDATION: | *The biblical and constitutional rights to Religious Freedom, Free Speech, and Free Association protects Christian counselor public identity, and the explicit incorporation of spiritual practices into all forms of counseling and intervention.* |
| 7th FOUNDATION: | *Christian counselors are mindful of their representation of Christ and his church and are dedicated to honor their commitments and obligations in all social and professional relations.* |

---

+ NOTE 4. This statement of "biblical-ethical foundations" is not a doctrinal statement, nor is it intended to substitute for one. The AACC Doctrinal Statement is a separate standard that reflects the baseline religious beliefs and biblical commitments of AACC members. However, it is true that these seven foundation statements are implicitly rooted in the AACC doctrinal statement. Furthermore, combined with the Scriptures, the AACC doctrinal statement, and the statement of "Introduction and Mission" to this code, this section stands as the baseline ethics policy that will ground this code, assist the search for clear meaning and common interpretation, and guide the resolution of disputed applications of ethical standards and procedural rules.

# Ethical Standards

## I. Ethical Standards for Christian Counselors

### *ES1–100 First, Do No Harm*

Christian counselors acknowledge that the first rule of professional-ministerial ethical conduct is: *do no harm* to those served.

### *1–101 Affirming the God-given Dignity of All Persons*

Affirmatively, Christian counselors recognize and uphold the inherent, God-given dignity of every human person, from the pre-born to those on death's bed. Human beings are God's creation—in fact, the crown of His creation—and are therefore due all the rights and respect and ordered logic that this fact of creation entails.

Therefore, regardless of how we respond to and challenge harmful attitudes and actions, Christian counselors will express a loving care to any counselee, service-inquiring person, or anyone encountered in the course of practice or ministry, without regard to race, ethnicity, gender, sexual behavior or orientation, socio-economic status, education, denomination, belief system, values, or political affiliation. God's love is unconditional and, at this level of concern, so must be that of the Christian counselor.

### *1–102 No Harm or Exploitation Allowed*

Prohibitively, then, Christian counselors avoid every manner of harm, exploitation, and unjust discrimination in all counselee-congregant relations. Christian counselors are also aware of their psychosocial and spiritual influence and the inherent power imbalance of helping relationships—power dynamics that can harm others even without harmful intent.

### *1–110 Avoidance of Counselee Harm, Intended or Not*

Christian counselors strictly avoid all behavior or suggestion of practice that harms or reasonably could harm counselees, counselee families, counselee social systems and representatives, students, trainees, supervisees, employees, colleagues, and third-party payors and authorizers.

### *1–111 Managing Counselee Conflicts*

Christian counselors acknowledge that counselee conflicts are unavoidable. In fact, conflict and resistance are often a central dynamic of the helping process. We will attempt to resolve all counseling conflicts in the counselee's best interest. Counselors tempted to respond in harmful ways to counselees shall seek out consultative and restorative help. If self-control is not accomplished—and counselee harm is not avoided—counselors shall terminate counseling relations and make referral in the counselee's best interest.

### *1–112 Action Regarding Counselees Harmed by Other Helpers*

Christian counselors take proper action against the harmful behavior of other counselors and pastors. We will act assertively to challenge or expose those who exploit others, and protect counselees against harm wherever it is found, taking care to honor and support counselee decision-making regarding curative action against violators.

### *1–113 Managing Problems with Managed Care*

Managed care has greatly expanded its influence in health and mental health service delivery. Widespread problems in counselee-provider-managed care relations are now being reported: breach of confidentiality, counselee abandonment, failure to maintain continuity of care, incompetent care, restriction of therapist choice and access, and even infliction of emotional distress. Christian counselors acknowledge these legal-ethical problems, and will avoid and work to correct any unethical entanglement and unintended counselee harm due to managed care relations.

### 1–120 Refusal to Participate in the Harmful Actions of Counselees

Christian counselors refuse to condone, advocate for, or assist the harmful actions of counselees, especially those that imperil human life from conception to death. We agree that the protection of human life is always a priority value in any professional or ministerial intervention. We will not abandon counselees who do or intend harm, will terminate helping relations only in the most compelling circumstances, and will continue to serve counselees in these troubles so far as it is humanly possible.

#### 1–121 Application to Deadly and Threatening Behavior

Christian counselors refuse to condone, advocate for, or assist the suicidal, homicidal, or assaultive/abusive harm done to self or others by counselees, including that which is threatened by verbal or other means. In fact, we are under an affirmative ethical duty to prudently intervene for the sake of protecting life, and under certain conditions, to report deadly threats to the proper authorities and those threatened by counselees (see Code sections 1–430ff).

#### 1–122 Application to Substance Abuse and Other Addictions

Christian counselors refuse to condone, advocate for, or assist substance abuse or other addictions and addictive behaviors by counselees. We recognize and accept the distinction between drug dependence and addiction, and may support or assist counselees in the use of necessary drugs—even those from which dependencies may develop for limited periods of time—when medically justified and under a physician's supervision.

#### 1–123 Application to Abortion

Christian counselors refuse to condone or advocate for abortion and the abortion-related activities of counselees. All counselors will consider and inform counselees of alternative means to abortion and, as far as it is possible, will continue to serve counselees and work compassionately with them through the abortion crisis.

#### 1–124 Application to Divorce

Christian counselors refuse to assume the decision for counselee divorce. We may assist counselees in analyzing and making the decision to divorce, insofar as it is biblically permissible, as God does allow for divorce in some cases. Therefore, we may assist counselees through the divorce process without being a divorce advocate, as that divorce decision must always reside in and be owned by the counselee.

Christian counselors working in divorce mediation will be careful to communicate that such work is not an endorsement of divorce, but rather a decision to offer a better choice than adversarial litigation and its destructive family impact when divorce is inevitable.

#### 1–125 Application to Premarital and Extramarital Sexual Behavior

Christian counselors refuse to condone or advocate for the pursuit of or active involvement in pre-marital and extra-marital sexual behavior by counselees—promoting an affair is never proper counsel as a solution to marital problems. We acknowledge that sex is God's good creation and a delightful gift when confined to one man and one woman in marriage. We may agree to and support the wish to work out issues of sexual behavior, identity, and attractions, but will encourage sexual celibacy or biblically proscribed sexual behavior while such issues are being addressed.

#### 1–126 Application to Homosexual and Transgendered Behavior

Christian counselors refuse to condone or advocate for the pursuit of or active involvement in homosexual, transgendered, and cross-dressing behavior, and in the adoption gay & lesbian & transgendered lifestyles by counselees. We may agree to and support the wish to work out issues of homosexual and transgendered identity and attractions, but will refuse to describe or reduce human identity and nature to sexual reference or orientation, and will encourage sexual celibacy or biblically proscribed sexual behavior while such issues are being addressed.

Christian counselors differ, on biblical, ethical, and legal grounds, with groups who abhor and condemn reparative therapy, willingly offering it to those who come into counseling with a genuine desire to be set free of homosexual attractions and leave homosexual behavior and lifestyles behind. Either goal of heterosexual relations and marriage or life-long sexual celibacy is legitimate and a function of counselee choice in reparative therapy.

It is acknowledged that some persons engaged in same-sex change or reparative therapy will be able to change and become free of all homo-erotic behavior and attraction, some will change but will still struggle with homosexual attraction from time to time, and some will not change away from homosexual practices.

### 1–127 Application to Euthanasia and Assisted Suicide

Christian counselors refuse to condone or advocate for active forms of euthanasia and assisted suicide. We may agree to and support the wish not to prolong life by artificial means, and will often advocate for hospice care, more effective application of medicine, and other reasonable means to reduce pain and suffering.

Regarding patients or counselees who wish to die, we will not deliver, nor advocate for, nor support the use of drugs or devices to be utilized for the purpose of ending a patient's life. We recognize that the death of a patient may occur as the unintended and secondary result of aggressive action to alleviate a terminally ill patient's extreme pain and suffering.

So long as there are no other reasonable methods to alleviate such pain and suffering, the Christian counselor is free to support, advocate for, and participate in such aggressive pain management in accordance with sound medical practice, and with the informed consent of the patient or the patient's authorized representative.

### 1–130 Sexual Misconduct Forbidden

All forms of sexual misconduct in pastoral, professional, or lay relationships are unethical. This includes every kind of sexual exploitation, deception, manipulation, abuse, harassment, relations where the sexual involvement is invited, and relations where informed consent presumably exists. Due to the inherent power imbalance of helping relationships and the immoral nature of sexual behavior outside of marriage, such apparent consent is illusory and illegitimate.

Forbidden sexual activities and deceptions include, but are not limited to, direct sexual touch or contact; seductive sexual speech or non-verbal behavior; solicitation of sexual or romantic relations; erotic contact or behavior as a response to the sexual invitation or seductive behavior of counselees; unnecessary questioning and/or excessive probing into the counselee's sexual history and practices; inappropriate counselor disclosures of counselee attractiveness, sexual opinions, or sexual humor; advocacy of the healing value of counselor-counselee sexual relations; secretive sexual communications and anonymous virtual interaction via the Internet or other electronic and informational means; sexual harassment by comments, touch, or promises/threats of special action; and sexual misconduct as defined by all applicable laws, ethics, and church, organizational, or practice policies.

### 1–131 Sexual Relations with Former Counselees Forbidden

All sexual relations as defined in 1–130 above with former counselees are unethical. Furthermore, we do not terminate and refer counselees or parishioners, even at first contact, in order to pursue sexual or romantic relations.

### 1–132 Counseling with Marital/Sexual Partners

Christian counselors do not counsel, but make appropriate referral, with current or former sexual and/or marital partners.

### 1–133 Marriage with Former Counselees/Patients

Since marriage is honorable before God, the lone exception to this rule against marriage to a former counselee, is a case anticipating marriage, so long as (1) counseling relations were properly terminated, and not for the purpose of pursuing marriage or romantic relations, (2) the counselee is fully informed that any further counseling must be done by another, (3) there is no harm or exploitation of the counselee or the counselee's family as a result of different relations with the counselor, and (4) the marriage takes place two years or more after the conclusion of a counseling or helping relationship.

### 1–140 Dual and Multiple Relationships

Dual relationships involve the breakdown of proper professional or ministerial *boundaries*. A dual relationship is where two or more roles are mixed in a manner that can harm the counseling relationship. Examples include counseling plus personal, fraternal, business, financial, or sexual and romantic relations.

Some dual relationships are not unethical—it is counselee exploitation that is wrong, not the dual relationship itself. Based on an absolute application that harms membership bonds in the Body of Christ, we oppose the ethical-legal view that all dual relationships are per se harmful and therefore invalid on their face. Many dual relations are wrong and indefensible, but some dual relationships are worthwhile and defensible (per section 1–142 below).

### 1–141 The Rule of Dual Relationships

While in therapy, or when counseling relations are imminent, or for an appropriate time after termination of counseling, Christian counselors do not engage in dual relations with counselees. Some dual relationships are always avoided—sexual or romantic relations, and counseling close friends, family members, employees, or supervisees. Other dual relationships should be presumed troublesome and avoided wherever possible.

### 1–142 Proving an Exception to the Rule

The Christian counselor has the burden of proving a justified dual relationship by showing (1) informed consent, including discussion of how the counseling relationship might be harmed as other relations proceed, and (2) lack of harm or exploitation to the counselee.

As a general rule, all close relations are unethical if they become counselor-counselee or formal lay helping relations. Dual relations may be allowable, requiring justification by the foregoing rule, if the counselee is an arms-length acquaintance—if the relationship is not a close one. This distinction is crucial in the applications below.

### 1–143 Counseling with Family, Friends, and Acquaintances

Christian counselors do not provide counseling to close family or friends. We presume that dual relations with other family members, acquaintances, and fraternal, club, association, or group members are potentially troublesome and best avoided, otherwise requiring justification.

### 1–144 Business and Economic Relations

Christian counselors avoid partnerships, employment relations, and close business associations with counselees. Barter relations are normally avoided as potentially troublesome, and require justification; therefore if done, barter is a rare and not a common occurrence. Unless justified by compelling necessity, customer relations with counselees are normally avoided.

### 1–145 Counseling with Fellow Church Members

Christian counselors do not provide counseling to fellow church members with whom they have close personal, business, or shared ministry relations. We presume that dual relations with any other church members who are counselees are potentially troublesome and best avoided, otherwise requiring justification. Pastors and church staff helpers will take all reasonable precautions to limit the adverse impact of any dual relationships.

### 1–146 Termination to Engage in Dual Relations Prohibited

Christian counselors do not terminate counseling to engage in dual relationships of any kind. Some counselors and their former counselees will agree that any future counseling will be done by someone else if, after legitimate termination, they decide to pursue another form of relationship.

## ES1–200 Competence in Christian Counseling

### 1–210 Honoring the Call to Competent Christian Counseling

Christian counselors maintain the highest standards of competence with integrity. We know and respect the boundaries of competence in ourselves and others, especially those under our supervision. We make only truthful, realistic statements about our identity, education, experience, credentials, and about counseling goals and process, avoiding exaggerated and sensational claims. We do not offer services or work beyond the limits of our competence and do not aid or abet the work of Christian counseling by untrained, unqualified, or unethical helpers.

### 1–220 Duties to Consult and/or Refer

Christian counselors consult with and/or refer to more competent colleagues or supervisors when these limits of counseling competence are reached: (1) when facing issues not dealt with before or not experienced in handling, (2) when counselees need further help outside the scope of our training and practice, (3) when either counselor or counselees are feeling stuck or confused about counseling and neither is clear what to do about it, or (4) when counselees are deteriorating or making no realistic gain over a number of sessions. Christian counselors shall honor the counselee's goals and confidential privacy interests in all consultations and referrals.

### 1–221 Consultation Practice

When counseling help is needed, and with counselee consent, consultation may be attempted first, when in the counselee's best interest and to improve helper's knowledge and skill where some competence exists. Counselors shall take all reasonable action to apply consultative help to the case in order to gain/maintain ground toward counselee objectives. The consultant shall maintain a balanced concern for the counselee discussed and the practice/education needs of the consultee, directing the counselor-consultee to further training or special resources, if needed.

### 1–222 Referral Practice

Referral shall be made in situations where counselee need is beyond the counselor's ability or scope of practice or when consultation is inappropriate, unavailable, or unsuccessful. Referrals should be done only after the counselee is provided with informed choices among referral sources. As much as possible, counselors referred to shall honor prior commitments between counselee and referring counselor or church.

### 1–223 Seek Christian Help, If Available

When consulting or referring, Christian counselors seek out the best Christian help at a higher level of knowledge, skill, and expertise. If Christian help is not available, or when professional skill is more important than the professional's beliefs, Christian counselors shall use the entire network of professional services available.

### 1–224 Avoid Counsel Against Professional Treatment

Christian counselors do not counsel or advice against professional counseling, medical or psychiatric treatment, the use of medications, legal counsel, or other forms of professional service merely because we believe such practice is per se wrong or because the provider may not be a Christian.

### 1–230 Duties to Study and Maintain Expertise

Christian counselors keep abreast of and, whenever possible, contribute to new knowledge, issues, and resources in Christian counseling and our respective fields. We maintain an active program of study, continuing education, and personal/professional growth to improve helping effectiveness and ethical practice. We seek out specialized training, supervision, and/or advanced certification if we choose to gain expertise and before we practice and advertise in recognized specialty areas of counseling and clinical practice.

### 1–240 Maintaining Integrity in Work, Reports, and Relationships

Christian counselors maintain the highest standards of integrity in all their work, in professional reports, and in all professional relationships. We delegate to employees, supervisees, and other subordinates only that work these persons can competently perform, meeting the counselee's best interest and done with appropriate supervision.

### 1–250 Protective Action When Personal Problems Interfere

Christian counselors acknowledge that sin, illnesses, mental disorders, interpersonal crises, distress, and self-deception still influence us personally—and that these problems can adversely affect our counselees and parishioners. When personal problems flare to a level that harm to one's counselees is realized or is highly likely, the Christian counselor will refrain from or reduce those particular professional-ministerial activities that are or could be harmful. During such times, the counselor will seek out and use those reparative resources that will allow for problem resolution and a return to a fully functioning ministry, if possible.

## ES1–300 Informed Consent in Christian Counseling

### 1–310 Securing Informed Consent

Christian counselors secure counselee consent for all counseling and related services. This includes the video/audio-taping of counselee sessions, the use of supervisory and consultative help, the application of special procedures and evaluations, and the communication of counselee data with other professionals and institutions.

Christian counselors take care that (1) the counselee has the *capacity* to give consent; (2) we have discussed counseling together and the counselee *reasonably understands* the nature and process of counseling; the costs, time, and work required; the limits of counseling; and any appropriate alternatives; and (3) the counselee *freely gives consent* to counseling, without coercion or undue influence.

### 1–320 Consent for the Structure and Process of Counseling

Christian counselors respect the need for informed consent regarding the structure and process of counseling. Early in counseling, counselor and counselee should discuss and agree upon these issues: the nature of and course of therapy; counselee issues and goals; potential problems and reasonable alternatives to counseling; counselor status and credentials; confidentiality and its limits; fees and financial procedures; limitations about time and access to the counselor, including directions in emergency situations; and procedures for resolution of disputes and misunderstandings. If the counselor is supervised, that fact shall be disclosed and the supervisor's name and role indicated to the counselee.

### 1–321 Consent from Parent or Counselee Representative

Christian counselors obtain consent from parents or the counselee's legally authorized representative when counselees are minors or adults who are legally incapable of giving consent.

### 1–322 Documentation of Consent

Christian counselors will document counselee consent in writing by professional service contract or consent form, the standard now required in most professional therapy relations, or by case note at the very least.

### 1–330 Consent for Biblical-Spiritual Practices in Counseling

Christian counselors do not presume that all counselees want or will be receptive to explicit spiritual interventions in counseling. We obtain consent that honors counselee choice, receptivity to these practices, and the timing and manner in which these things are introduced: prayer for and with counselees, Bible reading and reference, spiritual meditation, the use of biblical and religious imagery, assistance with spiritual formation and discipline, and other common spiritual practices.

### 1–331 Special Consent for More Difficult Interventions

Close or special consent is obtained for more difficult and controversial practices. These include, but are not limited to: deliverance and spiritual warfare activities; cult deprogramming work; recovering memories and treatment of past abuse or trauma; use of hypnosis and any kind of induction of altered states; authorizing (by MDs) medications, electro-convulsive therapy, or patient restraints; use of aversive, involuntary, or experimental therapies; engaging in reparative therapy with homosexual persons; and counseling around abortion and end-of-life issues. These interventions require a more detailed discussion with patient-counselees or counselee representatives of the procedures, risks, and treatment alternatives, and we secure detailed written agreement for the procedure.

## ES1–400 Confidentiality, Privacy, and Privileged Communication

### 1–410 Maintaining Counselee Confidentiality

Christian counselors maintain counselee confidentiality to the fullest extent allowed by law, professional ethics, and church or organizational rules. Confidential counselee communications include all verbal, written, telephonic, audio or videotaped, or electronic communications arising within the helping relationship. Apart from the exceptions below, Christian counselors shall not disclose confidential counselee communications without first discussing the intended disclosure and securing written consent from the counselee or counselee representative.

### 1–411 Discussing the Limits of Confidentiality and Privilege

Counselees should be informed about both the counselor's commitment to confidentiality and its limits before engaging in counseling. Christian counselors avoid stating or implying that confidentiality is guaranteed or absolute. We will discuss the limits of confidentiality and privacy with counselees at the outset of counseling.

### 1–420 Asserting Confidentiality or Privilege Following Demands for Disclosure

Protecting confidential communications, including the assertion of privilege in the face of legal or court demands, shall be the first response of counselors to demands or requests for counselee communications and records.

### 1–421 Disclosure of Confidential Counselee Communications

Christian counselors disclose only that counselee information they have written permission from the counselee to disclose or that which is required by legal or ethical mandates. The counselor shall maintain confidentiality of counselee information outside the bounds of that narrowly required to fulfill the disclosure and shall limit disclosures only to those people having a direct professional interest in the case. In the face of a subpoena, counselors shall neither deny nor immediately comply with disclosure demands, but will assert privilege in order to give the counselee time to consult with a lawyer to direct disclosures.

### 1–430 Protecting Persons from Deadly Harm: The Rule of Mandatory Disclosure

Christian counselors accept the limits of confidentiality when human life is imperiled or abused. We will take appropriate action, including necessary disclosures of confidential information, to protect life in the face of counselee threats of suicide, homicide, and/or the abuse of children, elders, and dependent persons.

### 1–431 The Duty to Protect Others

The duty to take protective action is triggered when the counselor (1) has reasonable suspicion, as stated in your state statute, that a minor child (under 18 years), elder person (65 years and older), or dependent adult (regardless of age) has been harmed by the counselee; or (2) has direct counselee admissions of serious and imminent suicidal threats; or (3) has direct counselee admissions of harmful acts or threatened action that is serious, imminent, and attainable against a clearly identified third person or group of persons.

### 1–432 Guidelines to Ethical Disclosure and Protective Action

Action to protect life, whether you're a counselee or a third-person, shall be that which is reasonably necessary to stop or forestall deadly or harmful action in the present situation. This could involve hospitalizing the counselee, intensifying clinical intervention to the degree necessary to reasonably protect against harmful action, consultation and referral with other professionals, or disclosure of harm or threats to law enforcement, protective services, identifiable third-persons, and/or family members able to help with protective action.

### 1–433 Special Guidelines When Violence Is Threatened Against Others

Action to protect third persons from counselee violence may involve or, in states that have a third-person protection *(Tarasoff)* duty, require disclosure of imminent harm to the intended victim, to their family or close friends, and to law enforcement. When child abuse or elder abuse or abuse of dependent adults exists, as defined by state law, Christian counselors shall report to child or elder protective services, or to any designated agency established for protective services. We shall also attempt to defuse the situation and/or take preventive action by whatever means are available and appropriate.

When counselees threaten serious and imminent homicide or violence against an identifiable third-person, the Christian counselor shall inform appropriate law enforcement, and/or medical-crisis personnel, and the at-risk person or close family member of the threat, except when precluded by compelling circumstances or by state law.

When the counselee threat is serious but not imminent, the Christian counselor shall take preventive clinical action that seeks to forestall any further escalation of threat toward violent behavior.

### 1–440 Disclosures in Cases of Third-Party Payment and Managed Care

Christian counselors are diligent to protect counselee confidences in relations with insurance and third party payors, employee assistance programs, and managed care groups. We are cautious about demands for confidential counselee information that exceed the need for validation of services rendered or continued care. We do not disclose or submit session notes and details of counselee admissions solely on demand of third-party payors. We will narrowly disclose information that the counselee has given written authorization only after we have discussed and are assured that the counselee understands the full implications of authorizations signed or contemplated to sign.

*1–450 Disclosures for Supervision, Consultation, Teaching, Preaching, and Publication*
Christian counselors do not disclose confidential counselee communications in any supervisory, consultation, teaching, preaching, publishing, or other activity without written or other legal authorization by the counselee. Counselors under supervision will disclose that fact to their counselees. We will adequately disguise counselee identifiers by various means when presenting cases in group or in public forums. We will not presume that disguise alone is sufficient counselee protection, but will consider seeking counselee authorization when counselee identity is hard to conceal.

## 1–460 Maintaining Privacy and Preserving Written Records
Christian counselors will preserve, store, and transfer written records of counselee communications in a way that protects counselee confidentiality and privacy rights. This requires, at minimum, keeping records files in locked storage with access given only to those persons with a direct professional interest in the materials.

### 1–461 Maintaining Privacy in Electronic Databases
Christian counselors take special precautions to protect counselee privacy rights with records stored and transferred by electronic means. This requires, at minimum, use of password entry into all electronic counselee files and/or coded files that do not use counselee names or easy identifiers. Counselee information transferred electronically—FAX, E-mail, or other computerized network transfer—shall be done only after the counselor determines that the process of transmission and reception of data is reasonably protected from interception and unauthorized disclosures.

## 1–470 Advocacy for Privacy Rights Against Intrusive Powers
Christian counselors hear the most private and sensitive details of counselee lives—information that must be zealously guarded from public disclosure. Rapidly expanding and interlocking electronic information networks are increasingly threatening counselee privacy rights. Though federal and state laws exist to protect counselee privacy, these laws are weak, are routinely violated at many levels, and the record of privacy right enforcement is dismal. Accordingly, Christian counselors are called to wisely protect and assertively advocate for privacy protection on behalf of our counselees against the pervasive intrusion of personal, corporate, governmental, even religious powers.

# ES1–500 Ethical Practice in Christian Counseling and Evaluation

## 1–510 Fees and Financial Relationships in Christian Counseling
Professional Christian counselors will set fees for services that are fair and reasonable, according to the services contracted and time performed, and with due regard for the counselee's ability to pay. We avoid all deception, confusion, and misrepresentation about fees and in our financial relationships with counselees and counselee systems.

### 1–511 Disclosure of Fees and Payment History
Fee schedules and rules for payment shall be outlined clearly for counselee review at the outset of counseling. Moreover, agreement about fees and payment schedules will be made as early as possible in the course of professional relations. We will provide counselees or their representatives with a full and accurate account of previous and current charges upon request.

### 1–512 Sliding Fee Scales Encouraged
Christian counselors are free, within the bounds of biblical, professional, and community standards, to set their own fees. Clinicians are encouraged, however, to use sliding fee schedules, scaled to counselee's ability to pay, and other reduced payment methods to increase counseling accessibility to those of lesser financial means.

### 1–513 Pro Bono Work

Christian counselors are encouraged, beyond their fee schedule, to make a portion of their time and services available without cost or at a greatly reduced fee to those unable to pay.

### 1–514 Avoiding Self-Serving Financial Relations

Christian counselors avoid financial practices that result or appear to result in greedy and self-serving outcomes. We do not select counselees or prolong therapy based on their ability to pay high fees, nor do we quickly terminate counseling with low-fee counselees. When making referrals, we do not divide fees with other professionals nor accept or give anything of value for making the referral. We do not exaggerate problems nor refer exclusively for specialized services to get counselees into special programs or institutions in which we have a proprietary interest.

### 1–515 Financial Integrity with Insurance and Third-Party Payors

Christian counselors maintain financial integrity with counselee insurers and other third-party payors. We do not charge third-party payors for services not rendered, nor for missed or cancelled appointments, unless specially authorized to do so. We do not distort or change diagnoses to fit restricted reimbursement categories. Any special benefits or reductions in counselee fees must also be extended in full to third-party payors.

## 1–520 Case Notes and Proper Record-Keeping

Christian counselors maintain appropriate documentation of their counseling activities, adequate for competent recall of prior sessions and the provision of later services by oneself or others. Records used in legal and other official capacities will show the quality, detail, objectivity, and timeliness of production expected by professionals who practice in these arenas.

### 1–521 Records Maintenance and Ownership

Records of professional activities will be created, maintained, stored, and disposed of in accordance with the law and the ethical duties of the counselor, especially maintaining counselee confidentiality. Ordinarily, counselee records belong to the employing organization or to the therapist in a private or group practice. However, in view of the expanding right of counselee record access and the ethic of continuity of care, counselees' records should follow the counselee. Therefore, in any dispute about record access or ownership at the termination of professional employment, the records will stay with the employer if the therapist is leaving the area and his or her counselees, or they should go with the therapist if he or she is staying in the area and the counselees are staying with the therapist.

## 1–530 Ethics in Testing, Assessment, and Clinical Evaluation

Christian counselors do clinical evaluations of counselees only in the context of professional relations, in the best interests of counselees, and with the proper training and supervision. Christian counselors avoid (1) incompetent and inaccurate evaluations, (2) clinically unnecessary and excessively expensive testing, and (3) unauthorized practice of testing and evaluation that is the province of another clinical or counseling discipline. Referral and consultation are used when evaluation is desired or necessary beyond the competence and/or role of the counselor.

### 1–531 Use of Appropriate Assessments

Christian counselors use tests and assessment techniques that are appropriate to the needs, resources, capabilities, and understanding of the counselee. We apply tests skillfully and administer tests properly and safely. We substantiate our findings, with knowledge of the reliability, validity, outcome results, and limits of the tests used. We avoid both the misuse of testing procedures and the creation of confusion or misunderstanding by counselees about testing purposes, procedures, and findings.

*1–532 Reporting and Interpreting Assessment Results*

Christian counselors report testing results in a fair, understandable, and objective manner. We avoid undue testing bias and honor the limits of test results, ensuring verifiable means to substantiate conclusions and recommendations. We recognize the limits of test interpretation, and avoid exaggeration and absolute statements about the certainty of counselee diagnoses, behavior predictions, clinical judgments, and recommendations. Due regard is given to the unique history, values, family dynamics, sociocultural influences, economic realities, and spiritual maturity of the counselee. Christian counselors will state any and all reservations about the validity of test results and present reports and recommendations in tentative language and with alternative possibilities.

*1–540 Working with Couples, Families, and Groups*

Christian counselors often work with multiple persons in session—marriage couples, families or parts of families, and small groups—and should know when these forms of counseling are preferred over or used as an adjunct to individual counseling. In these relationships we will identify a primary counselee—the group as a unit or the individual members—and will discuss with our counselee(s) how our differing roles, counseling goals, and confidentiality and consent issues are affected by these dynamics.

*1–541 Safety and Integrity in Family and Group Counseling*

Christian counselors will maintain their role as fair, unbiased, and effective helpers in all marital, family, and group work. We will remain accessible to all persons, avoiding enmeshed alliances and taking sides unjustly. As group or family counseling leaders, Christian counselors respect the boundary between constructive confrontation and verbal abuse, and will take reasonable precautions to protect counselee members from any physical, psychological, or verbal abuse from other members of a family or group.

*1–542 Confidentiality in Family and Group Counseling (see also ES1–400)*

Christian counselors do not promise or guarantee confidentiality in family and group counseling, but rather explain the problems and limits of keeping confidences in these modes of therapy. We communicate the importance of confidentiality and encourage family or group members to honor it, including discussion of consequences for its breach. Christian counselors do not share confidences by one family or group member to others without permission or prior agreement, unless maintaining the secret will likely lead to grave and serious harm to a family member or someone else.

*1–543 Avoiding and Resolving Role Conflicts*

If/when Christian counselors are asked to perform conflicting roles with possible unethical consequences (i.e.: pressure to keep "secrets" or called to testify as an adverse witness in a counselee's divorce), we will clarify our therapeutic, neutral, and mediative role and/or decline to serve in a conflicted capacity, if possible. Some counselors will contract for professional neutrality at the beginning of professional relations, securing counselee agreement not to have oneself or one's records subpoenaed or deposed in any legal proceeding.

*1–550 Working with Persons of Different Faiths, Religions, and Values*

Christian counselors do not withhold services to anyone of a different faith, religion, denomination, or value system. We work to understand the counselee's belief system and always maintain respect for the counselee. We strive to understand when faith and values issues are important to the counselee and foster values-informed counselee decision-making in counseling. We share our own faith only as a function of legitimate self-disclosure and when appropriate to counselee need, always maintaining a humility that exposes and never imposes the way of Christ.

### 1–551 Action if Value Differences Interfere with Counseling

Christian counselors work to resolve problems—always in the counselee's best interest—when differences between counselor and counselee values becomes too great, adversely affecting counseling. This may include discussion of the issue as a therapeutic matter, renegotiation of the counseling agreement, consultation with a supervisor or trusted colleague or, as a last resort, referral to another counselor if the differences cannot be reduced or bridged.

### 1–560 Continuity of Care and Service Interruption

Christian counselors maintain continuity of care for all patients and counselees. We avoid interruptions in service to counselees that are too lengthy or disruptive. Care is taken to refer counselees and network to provide emergency services when faced with counselor vacations, illnesses, job changes, financial hardships, or any other reason services are interrupted or limited.

### 1–570 Avoiding Abandonment and Improper Counseling Termination

Christian counselors do not abandon counselees. To the extent the counselor is able, counselee services are never abruptly cut-off or ended without giving notice and adequately preparing the counselee for termination or referral.

### 1–571 Ethical Termination of Counseling

Discussion and action toward counseling termination and/or referral is indicated when (1) counseling goals have been achieved; (2) when the counselee no longer wants or does not return to counseling; (3) when the counselee is no longer benefiting from counseling; or (4) when counseling is harmful to the counselee. Christian counselors shall discuss termination and/or referral with counselees, offer referral if wanted or appropriate, and facilitate termination in the counselee's best interest. If crisis events alter, even end counseling prematurely, the counselor, if it is safe and proper, should follow-through with the counselee to ensure proper termination and referral.

## ES1–600 Ethical Relations in the Professional Workplace

### 1–610 Honorable Relations Between Professional and Ministerial Colleagues

Christian counselors respect professional and ministerial colleagues, both within and outside the church. We strive to understand and, wherever able, respect differing approaches to counseling. We strive to maintain collaborative and constructive relations with other professionals serving our counselee, in the counselee's best interest.

### 1–611 Solicitation of Counselees Under Another's Care

Christian counselors do not solicit counselees nor do we knowingly offer professional services to those under the care of another mental health professional or pastor, except with that provider's knowledge, or when someone is in crisis. When approached by counselees being served by other counselors, due regard will be given that relationship with a commitment to encourage counselee resolution with the other counselor before starting professional relations.

### 1–612 Maintaining Honor Toward Others When in Conflict

If a counselor learns that a current counselee is receiving therapy from another pastor or mental health professional, reasonable steps will be taken to inform the other helper and resolve the situation. Professional relations in this case are to be maintained, as much as is possible, with a priority of Christian love and peace.

Any action to challenge or confront the wrongdoing of other service providers will be done with accuracy, humility, and protecting the dignity and reputation of others. Behavior that slanders, libels, or gossips about colleagues, or uncritically accepts these things from others about other service providers, will be strictly avoided.

### 1–620 Maintaining Honorable Professional and Employment Relations

Christian counselors create and preserve honorable relations in the professional workplace, whether church, counseling agency, or other setting. We maintain the utmost honesty, respect, and integrity in all employment and collegial relations. We shall contract relations that balance the best interests of counselees, colleagues, and our organizations, and will honor all contractual obligations, even if it is costly for us to do so. We will avoid all actions and appearances of greed, fraud, manipulation, and self-serving action in all collegial and employment relations, and will disclose and discuss all reasonably foreseen problems to our colleagues before they enter into relations with us.

### 1–621 Toward Clear Role Boundaries and Work Definitions

All professional/employment relations should be mutually understood and described in sufficient detail by work agreement. Administrators and staff should reasonably understand (1) required work behavior, expectations, and limits; (2) lines of authority and responsibility; (3) bases for and boundaries of accountability; and (4) procedures for voicing and curing disagreements and substandard work performance. When such guidelines do not exist, Christian counselors encourage development of sound collegial and employer-employee rules and relations.

### 1–630 Christian Counselors as Employers

Employers of Christian counselors shall provide a personnel program that honors the dignity and promotes the welfare of employees. Information will be given about the mission, goals, programs, policies, and procedures of the employing person or organization. Employers should deliver regular programs of in-service training, supervision of staff, and evaluation and review of employee work performance. Employers do not coerce, manipulate, threaten, or exploit employees or colleagues.

### 1–631 Employers Avoid Discrimination and Promote Meritoriously

Employers hire, evaluate, and promote staff meritoriously—based on staff training, experience, credentials, competence, responsibility, integrity, and ethical excellence. We do not discriminate in hiring or promotion practices on the basis of age, race, ethnicity, gender, disability, medical status, socioeconomic status, or special relationship with employer or other staff.

### 1–640 Christian Counselors as Employees

Counselors accept employment only when they are qualified for the position—by education, supervised training, credentials, skill, and experience. We will honor and advance the mission, goals, and policies of employing organizations. Employees have duties to both employers and counselees and, in the event of conflict between these duties, shall strive to resolve them in ways that harmonize the best interests of both.

### 1–641 Employees Serve with Integrity and Dedication

Employees serve with dedication, diligence, and honesty, maintaining high professional and ethical standards. We do not abuse our employment positions, nor presume excessive demands or rights against an employer.

### 1–642 Moving from an Agency to Private Practice

While employed in a counseling agency, and for a reasonable time after employment, we do not take counselees from an employing organization to develop a private or group practice of a competing kind. Any part-time practice while employed must be kept strictly separate from the counselees and resources of the employing agency. If we develop a full-time private practice with intent to resign employment and take current counselees, each counselee shall be apprised of their right to choose to stay with the employing organization or go with the therapist.

## ES1–700 Ethics in Advertising and Public Relations

All advertising and public communications by Christian counselors shall be done with accuracy and humility, with a primary goal of assisting counselees to make informed choices about counseling services.

### 1–710 Unethical Statements in Public Communications

Christian counselors make only factual and straightforward public communications and avoid statements that: (1) are false, inaccurate, exaggerated or sensational; (2) are likely to deceive or mislead others because it is partial or taken out of context; (3) are testimonials by current counselees; (4) exploit other's fears or distressing emotions; (5) note the inferiority or negative characteristics of another counselor; and (6) express unique or unusual helping abilities outside the range of accepted Christian counseling practices.

### 1–720 Communication of Association with the AACC and Other Groups

Public communication of AACC or other professional membership should adhere to all the requirements of this section and should not express or imply that such membership confers special status, expertise, or extraordinary competence in counseling.

### 1–721 Communication About Professional Status and Credentials

Christian counselors do not state that professional credentials—state licenses, graduate degrees, specialized training, church, professional, or governmental certifications, or any other credentials—confer greater status or power than the credentials actually represent. Advanced credentials shall be communicated with accuracy and humility, adhering to the guidelines of the credential itself.

### 1–722 Communication of Unaccredited and Unrelated Credentials

Christian counselors avoid public communication of degrees or credentials received from schools and organizations (1) not holding or maintaining a reputable and widely-known national stature, (2) not accredited by state, regional, or national authorities, or that (3) are not substantially related to counseling, pastoral counseling, or mental health services. Holders of a religious license or credential for church ministry only shall not state or imply that they are counseling professionals, or that they hold a mental health practice license.

### 1–730 Communication of Work Products and Training Materials

Christian counselors ensure that advertisements about work products and training events adhere to these ethics. We take care to avoid undue influence and respect informed consumer choice in promoting our work to anyone under our professional influence or authority.

### 1–740 Ethical Guidelines in Public Statements by Others

Christian counselors ensure adherence to these ethics by third parties we engage to create and make public statements about our work—employers, publishers, producers, sponsors, marketers, organizational counselees, and representatives of the media. We do not pay for or compensate the news media for news items about our work. We are responsible to correct, in timely fashion, any misinformation by third parties regarding our work.

## ES1–800 Ethical Relations with the State and Other Social Systems

Christian counselors, as individual members and as an Association, will strive to maintain ethical relations with the world-wide and the local church, with the state in its various forms, with the mental health professions and associations to which some of us belong, with other professions and organizations, and with society-at-large.

*1–810 Ethical Relations to Other Professions and Institutions*

Christian counselors recognize and respect that we are part of larger networks of Christian ministry and of mental health care. To borrow a metaphor, we envision church-based ministry and professional mental health care as the two tracks on which runs the Christian counseling train—tracks with different rather than opposing objectives.

Within the AACC are representatives of many different mental health and ministerial disciplines—we invite and welcome them all in the name of Christ. We will honor and preserve these relations, will challenge value differences with respect, and will build the best relations we can with all these professions and institutions that intersect with us as Christian counselors.

*1–820 Working for a Caring Church, a Just Government, and a Better Society*

Christian counselors are dedicated to build a more caring church, a more just government, and a better society in which to live. We will honor the laws and customs of our culture, and will challenge them when they threaten or abuse our freedoms, dishonor our God, or deny the rights of those most powerless. When critical, we will strive to offer a better alternative—model programs to govern our ecclesiastical, socio-cultural, and governmental life.

We will support the cause of Christ and advocate for Christian counseling in the church, in our ministries and professions, and in society. We will work to shape laws and policies that encourage the acceptance and growth of Christian ministry generally and Christian counseling in particular. We will facilitate harmonious relations between church and state and will serve and advocate the best interests of our counselees in church, community, and governmental relations.

*1–830 Being Salt and Light in a Post-Christian Culture*

Christian counselors acknowledge that we live in a post-Christian and pluralistic culture that no longer shares a common Judeo-Christian value base. We are called by Christ to be "salt and light" throughout our culture, a call of engagement with our culture and the world-at-large. Hence, the AACC will be and our members are encouraged to engage in active and honorable relations with the world around us—relations in which the world can see the light and taste the salt of Christ.

*1–831 Christ and Culture: Diversity over Conformity*

We accept that there are differing views within our Association on the proper relationship of the Christian life to a modern culture that no longer substantially honors Christ. Our association includes those who are largely apolitical—acknowledging a receding religious-cultural status as Christians but dedicated to building up the church and our profession. There are also those who believe it is necessary to retain a vibrant Christian value base in society and seek to return our culture to these roots, including by political and legal action. We wish to support this diversity and encourage this ongoing debate, respecting the validity of these different views as the healthy evidence of a living church and a vibrant and growing profession.

## II. ETHICAL STANDARDS FOR SUPERVISORS, EDUCATORS, RESEARCHERS, AND WRITERS

### The Ministry of Christian Counseling Leaders

Some Christian counselors serve in senior professional roles—as administrators, supervisors, teachers, consultants, researchers, and writers. They are recognized for their counseling expertise, their dedication to Christ and the ministry or profession to which they belong, and for their exemplary ethics. These leaders are responsible for the development and maturation of the Christian counseling profession, for serving as active and ethical role models, and for raising up the next generation of Christian counselors and leaders.

## ES2–100 Base Standards for Supervisors and Educators

### 2–110 Ethics and Excellence in Supervision and Teaching

Christian counseling supervisors and educators maintain the highest levels of clinical knowledge, professional skill, and ethical excellence in all supervision and teaching. They are knowledgeable about the latest professional and ministerial developments and responsibly transmit this knowledge to students and supervisees.

### 2–111 Preparation for Teaching and Supervision

Christian counseling supervisors and educators have received adequate training and experience in teaching and supervision methods before they deliver these services. Supervisors and educators are encouraged to maintain and enhance their skills through continued clinical practice, advanced training, and continuing education.

### 2–120 Supervisors and Educators Do Not Exploit Students and Trainees

Christian counseling supervisors and educators avoid exploitation, appearances of exploitation, and harmful dual relations with students and trainees. Students and trainees are taught by example and by explanation, with the mentor responsible to define and maintain clear, proper, and ethical professional and social boundaries.

### 2–121 Sexual and Romantic Relations Forbidden with Students and Supervisees

Christian counseling supervisors and educators (1) shall not engage in any form of sexual or romantic relations with their students and trainees, (2) nor subject them, by relations with others, to any form of sexual exploitation, abuse, or harassment, (3) nor pressure them to engage in any questionable social relationships. The standards of sections 1–130ff, "Sexual Misconduct Forbidden," shall apply fully here.

### 2–122 Dual Relationships Cautioned

Integrity and caution shall be the hallmark of dual relationships between supervisors and supervisees and between teacher and student. Those relations that harm or are likely to harm students and trainees, or that impair or are likely to distort the professional judgment of supervisors and teachers shall be avoided. The standards of sections 1–140ff, "Dual and Multiple Relationships," and those stated below shall apply here.

### 2–123 Supervisors and Educators Do Not Provide Psychotherapy

Christian counseling supervisors and educators do not engage in psychotherapeutic relations with supervisees or students. Personal issues can be addressed in supervision and teaching only insofar as they adversely impact counselor supervision and training. Students and supervisees needing or wanting counseling or psychotherapy shall be referred to appropriate resources.

### 2–124 Acknowledgement of Professional Contributions

Christian counseling supervisors and educators shall fully acknowledge the contributions of students and trainees in any creative professional activity, scholarly work, research, or published material. This shall be done by coauthorship, assistance in speaking or project presentation, or other accepted forms of public acknowledgement.

## ES2–200 Ethical Standards for Christian Counseling Supervisors

### 2–210 Counselor Supervision Programs

Christian counseling supervisors ensure that supervision programs integrate theory and practice and train counselors to respect counselee rights, promote counselee welfare, and assist counselees in the acquisition of mutually agreed goals in the counseling process.

Supervision programs in Christian counseling shall adhere to these ethics, to those of other applicable professional groups, and to all applicable state and federal laws.

### 2–211 Baseline Program Standards

Counseling programs shall only accept supervisees who are capable of professional practice, are fully informed about the program, and are committed to engage in counselor training following (1) mutual agreement that the supervisee meets base standards of education and experience; (2) disclosure of the training goals, supervisory site policies and procedures, and theoretical orientations to be used; (3) understanding of program relationship to national accreditation and credentialing organizations; (4) understanding of the standards, procedures, and time of evaluations of supervisee skill, professional-ethical awareness, and clinical effectiveness; and (5) disclosure of the manner and expectations regarding remediation of professional deficiencies and substandard performance.

### 2–220 Supervisors to Provide a Varied Experience

Christian counseling supervisors will provide a varied counseling experience, exposing the trainee to different counselee populations, clinical activities, and theoretical approaches to counseling. Supervisees should gain experience in direct counseling practice, clinical evaluation, treatment planning, record keeping, case management and consultative presentation, legal and ethical decision-making, and the development of professional identity.

### 2–221 Supervisors Are Responsible for Services to Counselees

Christian counselor supervisors ensure that supervisee work with counselees maintains accepted professional and ministerial standards. Supervisors do not allow supervisees to work with counselees or in situations where they are not adequately prepared. Supervisors retain full professional-clinical responsibility for all supervisee cases.

### 2–230 Supervision Evaluation and Feedback

Christian counseling supervisors meet frequently and regularly with supervisees and give timely, informative feedback about counselor performance and effectiveness. These evaluations shall minimally require supervisor review of case notes and discussion or brief check of each counselee case. Evaluative feedback is given in both verbal and written forms, covering counseling content, process, and ethical-legal issues of counselor training.

### 2–231 Supervisors Are Aware of Licensure and Certification Requirements

Christian counseling supervisors are aware of and honor the legal, ethical, and professional requirements of supervisees who are pursuing state licensure and specialized certification standards.

## ES2–300 Ethical Standards for Christian Counseling Educators

### 2–310 Counselor Education and Training Programs

Counselor education programs are dedicated to train students as competent practitioners using current theories, techniques, and ethical-legal knowledge. Christian counseling educators ensure that prospective students and trainees are fully informed, able to make responsible decisions about program involvement.

### 2–311 Baseline Program Standards

Christian counseling educators accept students on the basis of their educational background, professional promise, ethical integrity, and ability to reasonably complete the program. Program information should clearly disclose (1) the subject matter and coursework to be covered; (2) program relationship to national accreditation and credentialing organizations; (3) the kinds and level of counseling skills necessary to learn; (4) personal and professional growth requirements and opportunities; (5) the requirements and kinds of supervised clinical practicums and field placements offered; (6) the kinds and quality of research opportunities, including thesis/dissertation possibilities and requirements; (7) the basis for student evaluation, including appeal and dismissal policies and procedures; and (8) the latest employment prospects and program placement figures.

### 2–312 Student and Faculty Diversity

Christian counseling educators ensure that their programs seek and attempt to retain students and faculty of a diverse background, including representation by women, minorities, and people with special needs.

### 2–320 Student and Trainee Evaluation

Christian counseling educators provide students and trainees with periodic and ongoing evaluation of their progress in classroom, practice, and experimental learning settings. Policies and procedures for student evaluation, remedial training requirements, and program dismissal and appeal shall be clearly stated and delivered to student-trainees. Both the method and timing of evaluations are disclosed to students in advance of program involvement.

### 2–321 Overcoming Student Limitations

Educators help students overcome limitations and deficiencies that might impede performance as Christian counselors. Student-trainees will be assisted and encouraged to secure remedial help to improve substandard professional development. Honoring student due process, supervisors and educators will retain and fairly exercise their duty to dismiss from programs student-trainees who are unable to overcome substandard performance.

### 2–322 Student-Trainee Endorsement

Educators and field supervisors endorse the competence of student-trainees for graduation, admission to other degree programs, employment, certification, or licensure only when they have adequate knowledge to judge that the student-trainee is qualified.

### 2–330 Integration Study and Training

Christian counseling educators ensure that programs include both academic and practice dimensions in counselor training and integrate biblical-theological study with learning in the bio-psycho-social sciences, however these are emphasized. Students, if not producing research, should learn to be effective research consumers.

### 2–331 Exposure to Various Counseling Theories Encouraged

Educators develop programs that expose students to various accepted theoretical models for counseling, including data on their relative efficacy, and will give students opportunities to develop their own practice orientations. If a program adheres to or emphasizes one particular theoretical model, that fact should be clearly stated in all public communications without asserting that the model is superior to all others.

### 2–332 Teaching Law, Ethics, and the Business of Practice

Training programs should teach students about the legal, ethical, and business dimensions of Christian counseling. This includes study of these issues throughout didactic and clinical training. Students should be able to make competent ethical judgments and assess their own practice limitations, learning how to analyze and resolve ethical-legal conflicts and do consultation and referral competently.

### 2–340 Field Placement, Practicum, and Intern Training

Educators develop clear policies and procedures for all field experience, practicum, and intern training experiences. Roles and responsibilities are clearly delineated for student-trainees, site supervisors, and academic supervisors. Training sites shall meet required training standards, including national accreditation standards if applicable. Field supervisors shall be competent and ethical in their clinical and supervisory work.

Educators do not solicit and will not accept any form of fee, service, or remuneration for the field placement of a student-trainee.

### 2–341 Counselees of Student-Trainees

Academic and field supervisors ensure that counselees of student-trainees are fully informed of trainee status, and the trainees' duty to honor all professional obligations. Trainees shall secure counselee permission to use, within the bounds of confidential duties, information from the counseling work to advance their counseling education.

## ES2–400 Ethical Standards for Christian Counseling Researchers

### 2–410 Respecting Standards of Science and Research

Christian counseling researchers honor accepted scientific standards and research protocol in all research activities. Research is ethically planned and competently conducted. Researchers do not undertake nor do they let subordinates conduct research activities they are not adequately trained for or prepared to conduct.

### 2–420 Protecting Human Research Participants and Human Rights

Researchers maintain the highest care for human participants and respect human rights in all bio-psycho-social-spiritual research activities. Researchers plan, design, conduct, and report research projects according to all applicable state and federal laws, ethical mandates, and institutional regulations regarding human participants.

### 2–421 Special Precautions to Protect Persons

Researchers take special precautions and observe stringent standards when (1) a research design suggests deviation from accepted protocol, or (2) when there is any risk of pain or injury to participants, whether of a physical, psychosocial, spiritual, reputational, or financial nature. In all such cases, we will obtain appropriate consultation that apprises participants of these risks and secures informed consent.

### 2–422 Minimizing Undesirable Consequences

Researchers reasonably anticipate and diligently work to minimize any adverse or undesirable consequences of the research on human participants. This includes a commitment to minimize any possible long-term research effects, including those on the participants' person, family and family life, spiritual beliefs, moral values, reputation, relationships, vocation, finances, or cultural system.

### 2–430 Informed Consent and Confidentiality in Research

Researchers obtain informed consent from research participants using language that the participant can understand. This consent shall disclose (1) a clear explanation of research purposes and procedures; (2) any risk of harm, injury, or discomfort that the participant might experience; (3) any benefits that the participant might experience; (4) any limitations on confidentiality; (5) a commitment to discuss all concerns of the participant about the research; and (6) instructions on the right and the way to honorably withdraw from the research project. Researchers shall honor all commitments made to research participants. Data and results shall be explained to participants in ways that are understandable and that clarify any confusion or misconceptions.

### 2–431 Consent from Those Legally Incapable

Researchers obtain consent from parents or a participant's legal representative when the research participants are minors or adults incapable of giving consent. Researchers inform all participants about the research in understandable language, seeking the participant's understanding and assent.

### 2–432 Concealment and Deception in Research

When a research design requires concealment or deception, the researcher shall apply these methods most narrowly and will inform participants as soon as possible after the procedure. The research value of a deceptive practice must clearly outweigh any reasonably foreseen consequences, especially how such deception may reflect adversely on Christ and the church. Normally, we do not use methods of deception and concealment when alternative research procedures are available to accomplish the project objectives.

### 2–433 Protecting Confidentiality and Voluntary Participation

Researchers ensure participant confidentiality and privacy, and that subjects are participating voluntarily in the project. Any deviation from these ethics shall (1) be necessary to the project and justifiable upon panel review, (2) shall not harm the participants, and (3) shall be disclosed to the participants, ensuring their consent.

## 2–440 Reporting Research Results

Researchers report research results fully, accurately, and without alteration or distortion of data. Data and conclusions are reported clearly and simply, with any problems with the research design fully discussed. Researchers do not conduct fraudulent research, distort or misrepresent data, manipulate results, or bias conclusions to conform to preferred agendas or desired outcomes.

### 2–441 Protecting Participant Identity

Researchers are diligent to protect the identity of research participants in all research reports. Due care will be taken to disguise participant identity in the absence of consent by participants.

### 2–442 Reporting Challenging or Unfavorable Data

Outcomes that challenge accepted policies, programs, donor/sponsor priorities, and prevailing theory shall be reported and all variables known to have affected the outcomes shall be disclosed. Upon formal request, researchers shall provide sufficient original data to qualified others who wish to replicate the study.

## ES2–500 Writing and Publication Ethics in Christian Counseling

### 2–510 Integrity in Writing and Publication

Christian counselors maintain honesty and integrity in all writing and publication ventures, giving full credit to whom credit is due. Christian counselors recognize the work of others on all projects, avoid plagiarism of other's work, share credit by joint authorship or acknowledgement with others who have directly and substantially contributed to the work published, and honor all copyright and other laws applicable to the work.

### 2–520 Submission of Manuscripts

Christian counselors honor all publication deadlines, rules of submission of manuscripts, and rules of format when submitting manuscripts or agreeing to write invited works. Articles published whole or in major part in other works shall be done only with the acknowledgement and the permission of the previous publisher.

### 2–521 Review of Manuscripts

Christian counselors and editors who review manuscripts for publication shall consider the work strictly on its merits, avoiding prejudice for or against a particular author. Reviewers will diligently protect the confidential, reputational, and proprietary rights of all persons submitting materials for publication.

*2–522 Encouragement to New Authors*
Christian counseling editors and publishers will be diligent to call forth, encourage, and help develop new writers and materials from among the growing community of Christian counselors.

*2–530 Avoiding Ghost Writers*
Christian counselors shall resist use of ghostwriters, where the name of a prominent leader-author is attached to work substantially or wholly written by someone else. Instead, in accordance with section 2–510 above, Christian counseling authors will give due authorship credit to anyone who has substantially contributed to the published text. Order of authorship should reflect the level of substantive contribution to a work.

## III. Standards & Exemptions for Ordained Pastors and Pastoral Counselors

### *ES3–100 Definitions and Roles of Pastors and Pastoral Counselor*

*3–110 The Pastor and Pastoral Counselor: Ordained Ministers of the Gospel*
Pastors and pastoral counselors have central roles in the counseling and care ministry of the church. They are normally ordained ministers, recognized by a reputable church denomination as called of God, set apart for special church ministry, and have fulfilled the education and preparatory tasks the church requires for that ministry.

*3–111 The Specialized Pastoral Counselor*
Pastoral counselors and psychotherapists have received advanced training in counseling and psychotherapy and often counsel in a church or a specialized counseling setting. Pastoral counselors often have advanced degrees in counseling, have undergone counseling practicum training under supervision, and may be certified by national associations as a pastoral counselor or pastoral psychotherapist.

### *ES3–200 Rules of Ethics Code Application and Exemption*

*3–210 General Rule of Ethical Code Application and Exemption*
Pastors and pastoral counselors shall honor this Code in it entirety, except for those code sections (1) not applicable due to their clinical professional nature, or (2) because a higher duty to church or ministry rules require a narrow exemption from this Code. Anyone claiming exemption to the Code has the burden of proving it, and the duty to draw that exemption as narrowly as possible, honoring all other Code requirements.

*3–220 The Call of Christian Counseling to Gospel Fidelity*
Pastors and pastoral counselors have a special call as intermediaries between Christian counseling and the church. They can challenge Christian counselors to hold faith to the Gospel and to apply counseling ministry to the mission and work of the church. They can mediate, explain, and refer parishioners to Christian counselors. They can also encourage involvement for those who need help, and communicate and explain the guidelines of the Code so that parishioners can better judge the value and safety of the Christian counseling work.

# IV. Standards & Exemptions for Lay Helpers And Other Ministers

## *ES4–100 Definitions and Roles of Lay Helpers and Non-ordained Ministers*

Lay helpers or non-ordained ministers have a significant role in the counseling and care ministry of the church. They are not professional clinicians nor ordained ministers, but may work as salaried staff or as volunteers in designated helping roles. These helpers often function in one-to-one helping roles and are increasingly involved in developing and leading the many small support and recovery group ministries of the contemporary church.

## *ES4–200 Rules of Ethics Code Application and Exemption*

### *4–210 General Rule of Ethical Code Application and Exemption*

Lay helpers and non-ordained ministers shall honor the Code in it entirety, except for those code sections (1) not applicable due to their manifestly professional or pastoral nature, or (2) because a higher duty to church or ministry rules require a narrow exemption. Anyone claiming exemption to the Code has the burden of proving it, and the duty to draw that exemption as narrowly as possible, honoring all other Code requirements.

### *4–220 Lay Helping Under Supervision of the Church*

Lay helpers minister only under the supervision of the church or a Christian counseling organization. Lay helpers seek out and secure supervision and spiritual-ethical covering by pastors and professional clinicians. Independent, unsupervised, and solo practice or ministry by lay and unlicensed helpers and non-ordained staff shall be avoided due to its excessive risk for legal, ethical, spiritual, interpersonal, and ecclesiastical trouble.

### *4–221 Lay Helpers Do Not Accept Fees or Communicate False Roles*

Lay helpers shall not seek or accept fees or other remuneration for ministry. Lay helpers do not state or allow helpees to believe that they are professional or pastoral counselors. Some lay or non-ordained helpers may receive a salary as a church or ministry employee, income that should not be confused with fees for services.

### *4–222 Aiding and Abetting Unauthorized Practice*

Pastors and professional Christian counselors do not aid and abet the practice of unlicensed, untrained, unqualified, or unethical counseling or lay helping by anyone. In counseling situations requiring help clearly beyond the scope, training, experience, or license required of the helper, supervising pastors and clinicians will require and assist appropriate consultation and/or referral.

# V. Standards for Resolving Ethical-Legal Conflicts

## *ES5–100 Base Standards for Ethical Conflict Resolution*

### *5–110 Base Rule for Resolving Ethical-Legal Conflicts*

Christian counselors acknowledge the sometimes conflicting responsibilities to counselees, to colleagues and employing organizations, to professional ethics, to the law, and to Christ. If a higher obligation to Christ or to the counselee's best interest suggests or requires action against legal, ethical, or organizational rules, we will act peaceably and humbly in its outworking, in a way that honors God and our role as Christian counselors.

*5–111 First, Attempt to Harmonize Conflicting Interests*
When caught between legal-ethical demands and the way of Christ or the best interests of the counselee, we will first attempt to harmonize biblical, clinical, legal, ethical, and counselee interests, if possible. We will secure proper consultation and take action that defines and offers a better and harmonious standard of professional conduct.

*5–112 When Conflicts Cannot Be Harmonized*
Christian counselors' fidelity to Christ sometimes calls us to respectfully decline adherence to non-Christian values and behavior. When such conflicts cannot be harmonized, some counselors will stand firm or act on Christian principle against the law of the state, the ethics of one's profession, or the rules of one's employing organization. Such action should be (1) defensible biblically and ethically, (2) according to the counselee's best interest, (3) done without self-seeking purposes, (4) done with sober consideration after consulting with informed colleagues and Christian counseling leaders, and (5) done with a willingness to pay any adverse consequences. Such action must never be done to hide wrongdoing or to justify an obscure or self-promoting position.

The AACC suggests that priority values in the resolution of these conflicts be (a) integrity to Christ and the revelation of Scripture, then (b) the counselee's best interests, then (c) fulfilling our legal, ethical, and organizational obligations in a way that is least harmful to Christ or our counselee's interest.

## ES5–200 Resolving Conflicts with Employers and Colleagues

*5–210 Ethical and Value Differences with Employers and Colleagues*
If values and other differences with employers or colleagues become a source of conflict or influence counselee injustice, Christian counselors shall take appropriate action to resolve these problems in a way that honors Christ while also serving the counselee's best interest.

*5–211 Christian Counselors Working in Public Agencies*
Christian counselors working in public agencies will respect fair and circumspect rules against counselee evangelism or communicating Christian values without counselee consent. However, we may also challenge unjust prohibitions against the free expression of our beliefs, grounded in our biblical and constitutional right to religious freedom. These legitimate expressions of Christian beliefs include, but are not limited to: (1) serving Christian counselees from a Christian value base; (2) sharing Christian values as a legitimate part of counselor self-disclosure; (3) responding to spiritual needs expressed by counselees from a Christian frame of reference; and (4) displaying Christian symbols and literature in our office or place of work.

*5–212 Conflict Resolution Process with Employers and Colleagues*
Resolution of conflicts with employers or colleagues shall honor this process: (1) first attempt direct negotiations, (2) then mediation, and (3) then arbitration and/or binding arbitration. Litigation (4), when considered at all, shall be only as a last resort and only in cases of gross injustice where the offending party refuses or disdains all reasonable offers of non-litigated dispute resolution.

*5–220 Law and Ethics Violations by Colleagues and Employers*
Christian counselors with credible knowledge of legal or ethical violations by colleagues and employers shall take appropriate action to cure this problem, in the best interests of counselees, and according to the requirements of applicable law-ethics. Curative action might include (1) confidential consultations (usually the first step), (2) direct communications with the violator, (3) report to one's own or the violator's supervisor, (4) assisting violated counselees to take action, (5) report/complaint to the appropriate state agency or professional association, or (6) any other action appropriate to the matter.

## ES5–300 Resolving Professional and Organizational Conflicts

### 5–310 The Higher Ethics of Jesus Christ

Christian counselors are bound to honor the ethics and rules of one's profession, church, or employing organization in every way possible. However, when these ethics and rules are in direct opposition to God, and if unable to harmonize the mandates of Scripture with these rules, we declare and support the right of Christian counselors to elect non-adherence to those ethics and rules that offend the way of Christ.

### 5–311 First, Act to Resolve Conflict with Church or Profession

Christian counselors always first seek peaceable and biblically defensible resolution of disputes. After proper consultation with colleagues and Christian counseling leaders, we will define and advocate for a new ethical standard as an alternative to the offensive rule—one that honors Christ, protects the counselee's interest, and attempts to fulfill the policy behind the ethical rule.

### 5–312 When Ethical Harmony Is Not Reached

If ethical harmony is not possible, and after all attempts at resolution have been exhausted, Christian counselors may elect to violate the offending rule for the sake of Christ or the counselee. The violative action should be defensible biblically, logically, and clinically and, if possible, in accordance with the ethics intent.

Counselors shall (1) define the rule that cannot be respected in the narrowest form possible, (2) declare to honor all other ethical mandates, (3) consult with other colleagues and soberly count the cost of such action and (4) be prepared to face any consequences for breach of ethics or rules.

## ES5–400 Resolving Conflicts with the State and Its Laws

### 5–410 The Higher Law of Jesus Christ

Christian counselors are bound to honor the law in every way possible. However, when the law is in direct opposition to God, and if unable to harmonize the mandates of Scripture and the law, we declare and support the right of Christian counselors to elect non-adherence to those laws that offend the way of Christ.

### 5–411 First, Act to Resolve Legal Conflict

Christian counselors always seek first the peaceable and biblically-defensible resolution of disputes with the state and its laws. After proper consultation, including consulting with an attorney and with Christian counseling colleagues and leaders, we will attempt to define and advocate for a new and harmonious legal standard as an alternative to the law-offending rule at issue. This newly proposed standard will honor Christ, protects the counselee's best interest, and shows how the action of the new rule fulfills the intent or policy behind the law.

### 5–412 When Legal Harmony Is Not Reached

If harmony is not possible with the state and its laws, and after all attempts to resolve the issue have been exhausted, Christian counselor may elect action that violates the law for the sake of Christ or the counselee. The violative action should be defensible biblically, logically, clinically and, if possible, by the law's intent or policy.

Counselors shall (1) define the law that cannot be respected in the narrowest form possible; (2) declare to honor all other legal mandates; (3) consult with other colleagues, including lawyers, and soberly count the cost of such action; and (4) be prepared to face any consequences that may be imposed for violation of the law.

# PROCEDURAL RULES

In order to fulfill its professional and ethical mission the AACC adopts these procedural rules for accurate assessment and the fair hearing and resolution of ethical complaints against its members. These rules purpose to (1) show society, the church, our related professions, and our multitude of counselees and parishioners that *the AACC has a serious commitment to live by and enforce these ethics*, and (2) show our members that *we are serious about protecting their ministries and reputations by honoring their right to justice and due process*. In any action under these rules, the AACC shall consider this ethics code, its corporate bylaws, and the mandates of Scripture in the resolution of any problems in rule interpretation.

## VI. AUTHORITY, JURISDICTION, AND OPERATION OF THE AACC LAW AND ETHICS COMMITTEE (LEC)

### *PR6–100 Mission, Authority, and Jurisdiction of LEC*

*6–110 LEC Mission*

The mission of the AACC Law and Ethics Committee is to educate, encourage, and help maintain the highest levels of ethical conduct, practice excellence, and ministerial integrity among Christian counselors. This includes protecting counselees and society-at-large from unethical conduct, educating and advocating this code to the AACC and the larger church and society, and to aid the AACC in its mission to bring unity and excellence to the Christian counseling field.

*6–120 LEC Authority*

LEC is authorized to formulate and promulgate ethical standards for Christian counseling that are to be honored by AACC members particularly, and the church and larger society more generally. LEC, or any committee it shall designate, shall investigate, hear, and act to justly resolve ethical complaints against AACC members. LEC shall also have authority to adopt rules and procedures, as needed, to govern the conduct of LEC and any person or matter within its jurisdiction. LEC shall also have authority to publish and publicly communicate its official actions, including disciplinary actions toward its members.

*6–130 LEC Jurisdiction*

LEC has personal jurisdiction with any member of the AACC. LEC also has subject matter jurisdiction regarding the ethical behavior and rules defined in this Code. LEC may, by the AACC's direction, address any issue or matter that affects the Association's integrity and ethical achievement of its mission.

### *6–200 General Orientation to Ethical Enforcement*

*6–210 Attitude and Action Toward Ethical Complaints*

Neither LEC nor any member of the AACC shall refuse to hear nor uncritically accept a complaint against another member of the Association. Any LEC or Association member hearing a complaint individually shall take whatever action deemed appropriate to address and resolve the matter. When appropriate and feasible, this shall be done by direct consultation with violators or by working through local or regional collegial networks, taking care to honor the confidential and reputational rights of all those concerned in the matter.

### 6–211 Reporting Violations to LEC

If resolution attempts were unsuccessful by the member, or if the matter is more serious, or cannot be resolved by personal intervention, the member may direct the complainant to LEC.

### 6–220 Respecting Fundamental Rights of All Parties Involved

When LEC must act against an AACC member, it shall take care to maintain respect for the member's rights and reputation. The entire membership shall support LEC in this process, both to honor its ruling and to check and warn it when it might begin to stray from these values and purposes. Whenever possible, LEC shall balance and protect the multiple interests of counselee and community protection, Association integrity, and the legal and ethical rights and professional reputations of both complainants and complainees.

### 6–230 LEC Duties Toward the Complainant

Toward the complainant, LEC will honor his or her concerns, invite a full hearing of the complaint if needed, will seek to separate fact from rumor, and will take appropriate action to resolve the matter to the best of its ability to honor Christ and the complainant.

### 6–240 LEC Duties Toward the Complainee

Toward the complainee, LEC will honor his or her right to be heard and defend against allegations, will protect the complainee's professional reputation and due process rights, will invite and give reasonable time to fairly respond to a complaint, and will narrow the issue(s) to that which is reasonably beyond dispute. LEC will always pursue the most just result, avoiding the extremes of minimized justice or excessive sanction.

## PR6–300 Membership Response to LEC Action

### 6–310 Commitment to Cooperate with Ethics Process

AACC members assist the Association to honor and help enforce these ethical standards and rules. All members of the AACC shall cooperate fully and in a timely way with LEC and the entire ethics mission to assure the best achievement of our core commitment to excellence and unity in Christian counseling.

### 6–311 Failure to Cooperate with Ethics Process

Failure to cooperate with LEC or the ethics process in any manner shall not stop LEC from executing its duty. Failure to cooperate is itself a code violation and can result in ethical sanction.

# VII. PROCEDURES FOR THE ADJUDICATION OF COMPLAINTS AGAINST AACC MEMBERS

## PR7–100 General Rules of LEC Operation

### 7–110 Making and Amending Rules and Procedures

LEC may adopt and amend rules and procedures to govern the conduct of any matter within its jurisdiction. Any new or amended rule must be approved by a two-thirds vote of the Committee and also be ratified by a majority of the National Advisory Board. No new or amended rule shall adversely affect the rights of a member under investigation by LEC at the time of the rules adoption.

*7–111 Choice of Procedures and Action*
Except as otherwise denoted in these ethics and rules, LEC reserves the right to choose the appropriate procedures to resolve matters justly and efficiently, balancing the interests of the general public, affected counselees, the AACC, and its members.

## 7–120 LEC Meetings and Officers

*7–121 Frequency of Meeting and Quorum*
LEC shall meet at regular intervals, as needed. Conference calls can substitute for face-to-face meetings. A quorum shall consist of the majority of LEC members and official actions may be authorized by LEC when its members respond in person, by phone, by fax, by letter, or any other agreed means of action.

*7–122 Selection of Officers and Sub-committees*
Officers and Sub-committees may be appointed by LEC and/or AACC executive leadership action to serve terms and engage issues as are agreed among LEC members and AACC executive leadership.

*7–123 Duties of the Chairperson and the Vice-chair*
The Chairperson of LEC is responsible for the executive leadership of the Committee. He or she shall direct, in person or through appropriate designees, the work and process of LEC in all its responsibilities to the AACC. The Vice-chair shall be empowered to perform all the duties of Chair when s/he is not able to perform them, and shall perform other duties as are assigned by the Chair.

*7–124 Majority Rule*
Unless otherwise directed by these rules (see section 7–110 above), all official actions of LEC shall be authorized by a majority vote of its members present, or by any other authorized means of voting (see 7–121).

## 7–130 Open vs. Confidential LEC Process

LEC meetings and activities shall be either open to the membership or closed and confidential, with access in closed meetings given only to those designated parties with an interest in the particular matter. Closed meetings shall be done in ethical adjudications where the privacy interests of members or others deserve confidential process. All other LEC meetings may be open to any interested member.

*7–131 Access to Closed Meetings*
LEC and the AACC reserve the right to invite AACC executives or other desired personnel, experts, or consultants into confidential meetings, as may be necessary or desired to assist the adjudicatory process.

*7–132 Open vs. Confidential Records*
Except to inform the membership of final official disposition of a formal case and to assist the information/disclosure needs of the Association and the parties to the matter, all information and records of ethical adjudication against a member shall held in confidence by LEC. This may be further accepted in cases where counselee-parishioner risk or risk to the public welfare is judged by LEC to be significant. All other proceedings and records of LEC action shall be open to the membership.

## *PR7–200 Ethical Complaint Procedures*

*7–210 Reception of a Complaint*
Proceedings against a member are initiated by the reception of a formal complaint, in verbal and written form, by LEC. Complaints may be received from members or non-members of AACC.

### 7–211 LEC (Sua Sponte) Action

LEC may initiate proceedings on its own when it has sufficient evidence to do so, or as a response against a member who files a frivolous complaint, or if the complainant has a primary intention to harm another member.

### 7–220 Procedure for Making a Complaint

Members shall contact LEC or Association offices to present their complaint. The complaint should be outlined in writing, in no more than one page initially, and note both the alleged violation of AACC ethics or rules, and any direct and other evidence the complainant has to support it.

### 7–221 Unacceptable Complaints

LEC will not initiate proceedings in situations of anonymous complaints, complaints against nonmembers, or in counter complaints. In the latter case, LEC may consider whether a counter complaint has cause to proceed further only after the initial complaint is fully resolved.

### 7–222 Multiple Complaints

When numerous complaints against a member are received simultaneously, LEC may elect to combine them into one action or deal with them separately. When consecutive complaints are heard, LEC may elect to consider the disposition of any previous case against the member in its resolution of a current complaint.

### 7–230 Warning Against Frivolous and Vindictive Complaints

AACC members shall not make frivolous reports, without substantiation, or that are primarily motivated by anger or vindictiveness, or with an intent to harm the alleged violator. The primary motivations in reporting ethical misconduct are to protect counselees and parishioners, to maintain the honor of Christ and the church, the honor of our professions, and to assist the cure and restoration of violators to ethical and effective ministry, if possible.

## PR7–300 Complaint Assessment and Initial Action by LEC

### 7–310 Inability to Take Further Action

Failure of any one of the following standards shall render LEC unable to take further action against an AACC member. If it is dismissed, LEC shall so rule, the complainant notified of LEC's decision, and the matter closed.

### 7–311 Lack of Jurisdiction

LEC shall first determine whether it has jurisdiction. Personal jurisdiction is met if the complaint is directed toward a member in good standing of the AACC. Subject matter jurisdiction is met when the alleged wrongdoing of a member, acting in a professional-ministerial capacity, intersects the standards of this code.

### 7–312 Insufficient Information to Act Further

LEC shall then determine whether it has sufficient information to take further action. There must be (a) a clear violation of the Association's ethics, policies, or procedural rules, and (b) the information supporting the violation must be of sufficient weight and quality that, in LEC's judgment, it cannot be dismissed.

### 7–313 Failure of Procedure or Time Limits

Finally, LEC shall determine that proper procedures and time limits have been honored in the complaint process, as defined by this code.

### 7–320 Cause for Further Action

If, in LEC's judgment, the standard of section 7–310 and following are satisfied, then it shall rule that cause for further action exists. It shall then review and decide the steps necessary to seek the most just, restorative, and least costly resolution. It shall gather the most reputable evidence that applies to the matter at hand, rejecting evidence that is speculative, incredible, and unsupportable.

#### 7–321 LEC May Seek Informal Resolution of the Matter

LEC may empower the Chair or a committee to address the matter directly with the complainee to seek a just resolution. The intervener may then recommend to LEC whether or not to close the matter at this stage and the reasons for its recommendation, and LEC may elect whether or not to accept the recommendation of the committee or pursue further action.

### 7–330 Initial Notification to Complainee

If informal resolution is not elected or does not work, the violations and evidence supporting it shall be simply and clearly outlined in a query letter signed by the Chair and Vice-chair of LEC. This letter and a copy of the applicable ethics and rules shall be delivered to the complainee by mail or in person by LEC.

#### 7–331 Requests for Additional Information

LEC may request additional information from the complainant, the complainee, or any appropriate source to assist resolution of the matter.

#### 7–332 Time for and Response from Complainee—Complaint Stage

Within 30 days of reception of the letter, the complainee may respond in writing to the allegations. The complainee must respond personally and not through a third-party. The LEC Chairman may waive or adjust the time requirement if good cause is shown.

### 7–340 Case Closure for Insufficient Evidence

If it becomes clear that insufficient or competing evidence raises substantial doubt about the occurrence of ethical violation, then LEC will close the case. It this action is taken, LEC shall promptly notify both complainant and complainee of its decision and reasoning.

#### 7–341 Reopening a Closed Case

A case closed for insufficient evidence may be reopened upon the receipt of new evidence significant enough (as defined by section 7–310 ff. above) to justify reopening the matter within a reasonable time from the reception of the original complaint.

#### 7–342 Alternative/Supplementary Action May Be Recommended

LEC reserves the right, whether a case is closed or stays open, to recommend alternative or supplementary action—referral to any relevant professional association, denomination, state licensure board, administrative agency, or any other appropriate body to hear the complaint.

### 7–350 Case Resolution by Mutual Agreement

LEC may pursue case closure through a pre-formal agreement with the complainee that is restorative and corrective. By discussion, prayer, reasoning together, and negotiation, LEC will seek to resolve the matter in a way that serves the best interests of both the AACC and its members.

#### 7–351 Structure of Agreement

Such agreement will usually clarify misunderstandings, direct corrective action, establish a time-frame for renewal of ethical relations and proper trust, define a fair assessment of these objectives, or any combination of these things. This agreement shall be signed by the LEC Chair and the complainee and shall be disclosed to the complainant, the complainee, and anyone else agreed to by the signatories.

### 7–360 Cause for Formal Case Review

If the matter cannot be closed or resolved as defined above and in the judgment of LEC sufficient cause exists to pursue the matter further, LEC shall then decide that "cause for formal case review" exists, so shall rule, will notify the applicable parties, and then move prayerfully to the next level of adjudication.

## PR7–400 Formal Case Review Procedures

### 7–410 Selection and Operation of Case Review Sub-committee

LEC shall form a three-person sub-committee (sub-com), chaired by the Chair or Vice-chair, to hear and resolve a formal ethics complaint. This sub-com shall be given sufficient authority and the necessary resources to resolve the matter, consistent with these ethics and rules, in a just and timely manner. Sub-com recommendations shall be forwarded to and accepted by LEC when 2 votes of the sub-com exist.

### 7–411 Presentation of a Charge Letter

The complainee shall receive a formal charge letter from LEC, detailing the alleged wrongdoing, the specific code sections implicated, and the supporting evidence. The letter shall instruct the complainee as to the manner and time for response to allegations. Any supporting materials that LEC will use to assist its review shall be copied and sent with the letter.

### 7–412 Time for and Response from Complainee—Review Stage

The complainee has 30 days from the letter date to respond to the allegations, either in person or in writing. The complainee must follow all charge letter instructions and rules. Any waiver of time and action requirements must be made, in person or in writing, within the 30-day time frame. Legal counsel or other help may be consulted and can attend the case hearing for consultation but cannot speak directly for his or her counselee at the hearing—this representation must be done directly by the complainee.

### 7–420 Documentation, Review of the Evidence, and Recommendations

Additional documentation may be sent to LEC by the complainee within the 30-day period. LEC will, within this 30-day period, forward any additional information it receives to the complainee. LEC will review the case and render a judgment no later than 120 days from the date of the charge letter. One of four recommendations will be made to LEC by the sub-com and the appropriate parties notified of this decision.

### 7–421 Recommendation to Dismiss Charges

If the sub-com finds (1) no evidence or very weak evidence of violation, or (2) has insufficient evidence to render an informed judgment, or (3) finds a slight violation that has been or is in process of being corrected, it shall recommend that LEC dismiss the charge(s).

### 7–422 Recommendation to Educate and Repair

If the sub-com finds a more weighty violation, or a pattern of violation that is not too serious, and there is evidence of some correction, it may elect to recommend the complainee educate him or herself and repair the violation. Notification of such action will be communicated to the complainee and complainant only.

### 7–423 Recommendation to Reprimand and Suspend

If the sub-com finds a more serious violation, or a pattern of continuing violations with no repair started, but the likelihood of correction and restored practice is significant, it may recommend that LEC reprimand and suspend the member, with instructions for possible reinstatement. Such action, and the violations related to it, will be communicated to AACC members in official publications.

### 7–424 Recommendation to Terminate Membership

If the sub-com finds a very serious violation, or a pattern of continuing serious violations, especially after being challenged to change, and the likelihood of correction or value of it is slight (compared to the harm done), it may recommend to LEC that membership in the AACC be terminated. Such action, and the violations related to it, will be communicated to AACC members in official publications.

### 7–425 Agreed Resignation of Member

A member of the AACC may elect to resign his or her membership, or LEC may elect to offer such resignation to the member prior to termination of membership. Such action, and the violations related to it, will be communicated to AACC members in official publications.

### 7–430 Final Ruling of the Law and Ethics Committee

Recommendations for case disposition from the sub-com shall be heard and accepted by LEC. LEC rulings, tracking the recommendations of the sub-com, shall include sufficient information and instruction to satisfactorily achieve the stated objectives of the LEC ruling. Except in the case of termination of membership, all rulings by LEC at this stage shall be final, with no consequent appeal.

### 7–431 Limited Discretion to Modify Sub-committee Recommendations

LEC shall retain limited discretion to modify the recommendations of the sub-com if there is good reason to find that such change will yield a more just and restorative outcome. This discretion shall be used sparingly, and only in cases where there is a general consensus for such change among LEC members.

## PR7–500 Formal Appeal Hearing Procedures

### 7–510 Complainee Election of Formal Appeal—Termination Cases Only

Appeal of rulings by LEC shall be allowed only in case of termination of AACC membership.

### 7–511 Time and Documentation

Both LEC and the complainee shall receive and argue from the same materials that formed the original judgment, plus any additional materials that are deemed necessary to support the appellate challenge. No hearing will take place within 30 days of the receipt of all relevant documents by both LEC and the complainee.

### 7–512 LEC Represented by the Chair or Vice-chair

LEC shall be represented by the Chair or Vice-chair of LEC (the other will sit on the appeals panel). They shall be responsible for arguing the case to the appeals panel to support the LEC ruling.

### 7–520 Standards and Conduct of the Formal Appeal Hearing

There shall be one appeals hearing only, on a date and at a place that is most convenient for the appeals panel, whose ruling shall be final as to all matters concerning the case. The appeals panel will review the appeal and render a judgment no later than 30 days from the date of the appeals hearing.

### 7–521 The Appeals Panel

Appeals shall be heard by a five-person panel, consisting of the LEC Chair or Vice-chair (whoever is not representing LEC in the appeal) and at least two other LEC members (not those hearing the original action). Other panel members, if needed, shall be invited from the National Advisory Board.

### 7–522 The Appeals Standard—Unjust Result

The appellate panel must rule against the termination of membership if the complainee can show substantial evidence that (1) the sub-com panel or a member of it showed a clear intent to harm the complainee, or (2) that findings of fact or application of the ethics code were clearly erroneous, or (3) the application of termination was a clearly excessive and punitive sanction.

### 7–523 Representation by Self or with Legal Counsel

The complainee shall represent and speak for him or herself in all appellate actions, though they may choose to retain legal or other counsel who may help the complainee before and during the hearing.

### 7–524 Retention of Legal Counsel by the AACC

LEC may elect to retain legal counsel, or any other expert help it deems necessary.

### 7–530 Final Order of the Appeals Panel

The appeals panel shall rule, by at least 3 votes, either to uphold the prior LEC ruling or to reverse it. Upholding the rule will end the matter for the AACC. A reversal will lead to a dismissal of the prior ruling and an order for a new case review hearing with at least 2 new panel members on the sub-committee.

## VIII. Procedures Following Action by Churches, Courts, and Other Bodies

### PR8–100 LEC Authorized to Act Independently or With Others

#### 8–110 Litigation, License Revocation, or Other Disciplinary Action Not a Bar to Action by LEC

LEC reserves the right to proceed with an ethics action even if the member is engaged in litigation, license revocation, or other disciplinary action for the same or similar issues.

#### 8–111 LEC Election to Stay Process Pending Resolution

LEC reserves the right to suspend an ethics action until case disposition in another legal or disciplinary forum is completed. Any delay in action by LEC shall not waive jurisdiction and any time constraints shall be suspended until the action is begun or resumed.

#### 8–112 Retention and Referral of Jurisdiction to Other Bodies

LEC reserves the right to refer a case to another recognized body for action, and to cooperate or work jointly with another tribunal. Any referral to another body shall not constitute waiver of jurisdiction by LEC, nor shall LEC be barred from acting on its own following referral.

### PR8–200 Bases for and Procedure of a Show Cause Hearing

#### 8–210 Five Bases for a Show Cause Hearing

An AACC member may be directed by LEC to show cause why official action by LEC should not be taken if the member is sanctioned for misbehavior substantially related to his or her professional or ministerial tasks, in the form of (1) conviction of a criminal offense, (2) a malpractice judgment, (3) a malpractice settlement of $25,000 or more, (4) a license revocation or suspension action, or (5) any church, denominational, or any other official organizational act of expulsion, suspension, or de-ordination.

*8–220 Notice by LEC and Response of Member*

Upon receipt from LEC of a show cause letter, the member will have 30 days from the letter date in which to respond. The member may show cause based on either the unjust result standard (see section 7–522 above), or the lack of due process in the other proceeding.

*8–230 Review of Prior Action and Recommendation*

The LEC Chair or Vice-chair will review the evidence and prior proceeding and determine whether just cause exists to challenge its rule. If so, a recommendation will be made to start a formal case review on the merits according to the procedures of this code. If cause is not shown, a recommendation of termination of membership will be made based on the finding of the prior proceeding.

*8–231 Stipulated Resignations*

The AACC and the member may stipulate and agree on the resignation of the member. Whether termination or resignation, the result will be published in official AACC publications.

*8–240 Final Order of the Law and Ethics Committee*

Recommendations for case disposition shall be heard and accepted by LEC. LEC rulings, tracking these recommendations, shall include sufficient information and instruction to satisfactorily achieve the stated objectives of the LEC ruling. All rulings by LEC in a show cause hearing shall be final, with no consequent appeal.

## FINAL ENCOURAGEMENT

May God be exalted, the Holy Spirit invited, and Jesus Christ be seen in all of our counseling and helping endeavors. If done, our counselees and parishioners will be blessed and not harmed, their wounds will be healed, their sins forgiven, and they will be given hope for the future. If done, we will participate in a wonderful adventure—one that will likely never grow old or stale—and we will fulfill our call to excellence and ethical integrity in Christian counseling.

### *End of the 2004 Final Code*

# Appendix C

# Intake Form

## PERSONAL INFORMATION INVENTORY

Please complete this inventory as carefully as possible. Answer each item that applies to you. All information you provide will be treated confidentially and will become part of your record. If you have a question about a particular area, please put a mark by it and ask your counselor when it is complete.

## DEMOGRAPHIC INFORMATION

Name: _____ Date: _____

Home address:_____

_____

Phone (Home) _____ (Work) _____ (Cell) _____

S.S.#: ___ - ___ - _____ Sex: __ Date of Birth: _____ Age: _____

E-Mail Address:

Occupation:_____ Hour Per Week: _____

Employed By: _____

Referred Here By:_____ Phone: _____

Referral's Address: _____

Emergency Contact: _____ Phone: _____

Contact's Address: _____

## MARRIAGE INFORMATION (Circle One)

**Single**      **Engaged**      **Married**      **Separated**    **Divorced**

**Remarried**  **Living Together**  **Widowed**

Please list your relationships below. List your children beginning with the oldest. (Place a check by the child's name if from a previous marriage.)

| Relationship | Name | Age | Grade/Occupation |
|---|---|---|---|
| SPOUSE | _____ | ____ | _____ |
| EX-SPOUSE | _____ | ____ | _____ |
| CHILDREN | _____ | ____ | _____ |
| (or siblings if | _____ | ____ | _____ |
| under 18 yrs.) | _____ | ____ | _____ |
| | _____ | ____ | _____ |
| MOTHER | _____ | ____ | _____ |
| FATHER | _____ | ____ | _____ |

What Year Married?: _____ How Long Did You Date?: _____
How Did You Meet?: _____
Did Your Parents Approve of Your Marriage? _____
Spouse's Parents?: _____
Have You Ever Been Married Before?: _____
Number of Divorces? _____ How Long Divorced? _____

## FAMILY INFORMATION

Father Living? Yes____ No ____ Mother Living? Yes ____ No ____
If so, where? _____
What kind of relationship do/did you have with your father? (Circle One)
**Excellent　　Good　　Fair　　Poor　　NonExistent**

What kind of relationship do/did you have with your mother? (Circle One)
**Excellent　　Good　　Fair　　Poor　　NonExistent**

Did anyone else have a key role in your upbringing? (If so, who and why):
_____
_____
How many children are/were in your family? (Brother and Sisters) ____
What child are you by number? (Circle One)
**Oldest ❑2nd　❑3rd　❑4th　❑5th　❑6th　❑Youngest　❑Other**

## EDUCATION

Highest Level/Grade of Education Completed:
　　　　　❑**Not Complete　❑HS　　❑Some College　❑AA Degree**
　　　　　❑**College (Major:_____ )　❑Graduate (Major: _____ )**

How well did you do in elementary school? _____

How well did you do in HS? _____

How well did you do in College? _____

How well did you do in Graduate School? _____

## RELIGION/FAITH

Religious Affiliation: _____

Church/Synagogue Name: _____

Circle Your Level of Church Activity:     **Active**          **Inactive**

Briefly describe how important your faith is to you: _____

_____

_____

Do you want a Christian counseling approach?   ❑Yes ❑No

Do you want the counselor to pray with you?     ❑Yes ❑No

## HEALTH

Health Status: ❑Excellent   ❑Good   ❑Average   ❑Poor   ❑Very Poor

Height: _____ Weight: _____

Have you **gained** or **lost** any weight in last six months? (Circle One) How Much? _____

Describe any physical problems you have that require medication or physical care: _____

_____

_____

Are you currently under a doctor's care? _____

(If yes, please describe)_____

_____

Physician's Name: _____ Address:_____

_____

If you are currently taking any medication please complete below:

| **Name of Medication** | **Dosage** | **Date Prescribed** | **By Who** |
| --- | --- | --- | --- |
| _____ | _____ | _____ | _____ |
| _____ | _____ | _____ | _____ |
| _____ | _____ | _____ | _____ |
| _____ | _____ | _____ | _____ |
| _____ | _____ | _____ | _____ |

Have you ever used drugs other than for medical purposes? _____
(If yes, what and when) _____
_____

Please describe your use of alcoholic beverages:
　　　**❏Never   ❏1–4 Times Year   ❏1–2 Times Month**
　　　**❏1–2 Times Week   ❏4 Times Week   ❏Daily**
What medical and emotional problems existed in your family in which you
grew up? _____
_____

Have you previously had counseling/therapy?     Yes                 No
When? _____
With Whom? _____ For How Long? _____
Why Did You Stop? _____

## PRESENTING PROBLEM(S)

In your own words, briefly describe the main problem that prompted you
to seek counseling at this time: _____
_____

How long have you faced these problems? _____
Have there been times when the problems got better or disappeared?
❏Yes ❏No
If so when? _____
What do you think helped?_____
_____

Were there times when the problem was especially bad? ❏Yes ❏No
When? _____
What made it bad? _____
_____
_____

Are there other people who play a role in:      ❏ Causing your problem?
　　　　　　　　　　　　　　　　　　　　 ❏ Helping your problem?
Briefly explain:
Please check any of the following that are currently troubling you. Put **two**
checks by those items that are most important. You may add any comments
you would like:

___Abortion/Adoption

___Adjustment Problems

___Anger/Temper

___Anxiety (worry)

___Apathy (the "blahs")

___Assertiveness

___Bitterness (Resentment)

___Breathing Difficulty

___Change of Lifestyle

___Child Abuse

___Children (Discipline)

___Children (School)

___Communication

___Concentration

___Confusion

___Death of Loved One

___Dependent On Others

___Depression

___Divorce

___Dizziness

___Eating Problems

___Envy (Jealousy)

___Exhaustion

___Failure

___Family Conflict

___Family Violence

___Father

___Fatigue

___Fear

___Finances

___Forgiveness

___Frustration

___Guilt

___Health

___Headaches

___Homosexuality

___Honesty

___Impotence

___Inability To Relax

___In-Laws

___Irritability

___Loneliness

___Loss of Interest

___Loss of Pleasure

___Lust

___Mother

___Marriage

___Memory Difficulty

___Muscle Tension

___Occupation Issue

___Opposite Sex

___Overactivity

___Perfectionism

___Pride

___Rape

___Rebellion

___Rejection

___Religion/Spiritual Issues

___Repetitive Ideas

___School Problems

___Separation

___Sex

___Sexual Abuse

___Shy/Awkward

___Single Parenting

___Sleep Problem

___Spouse Abuse

___Stomach/ GI Disturbance

___Stress

___Substance Use

___Substance Use In Family

___Suicidal Thoughts

___Suspiciousness

___Troubling Memories

___Troubling Habit

___Trust

___Underactivity

___Unfairly Treated

___Unusual Experiences

___Wish To Hurt Someone

___Withdrawal

How did you hear about this counseling program?_____

# Appendix D

# Informed Consent Form

For many people, counseling is a new experience. New situations naturally lead us to have some misconceptions about what to expect. This information may answer some of your questions and help you to use these services more effectively. In addition, this document contains critical information that you need to know about your counseling. Please read this material carefully. You must **SIGN the final page**, verifying that you have read and understood this material. Please **bring the signed form with you**, but **keep the document for future reference**.

## THE PROCESS OF COUNSELING

Participating in the counseling process is voluntary. We respect your decision to seek counseling and know that it may be the most constructive step that you have taken thus far. Your willingness to share your difficulties and concerns demonstrates courage, wisdom, and resourcefulness on your part.

Counseling is a cooperative venture with responsibility resting on both the counselor and the counselee. Your first session, or intake, will be structured to help your counselor understand the problems you are facing. You may also be asked to take one or more assessment inventories to more quickly and thoroughly understand you and the problems you are facing.

The counseling approach that I utilize includes the whole person: body, mind, and spirit. The goal of counseling is to bring renewal and to enhance the quality of life for the counselees that this practice serves. Because each counselee is a unique individual with unique struggles, no one course of counseling will apply to everyone. In general, however, the beginning stage of counseling involves clearly identifying the issues by which you are troubled. The second stage involves gaining insights into patterns of emotions, thoughts, and behaviors related to your problems. These insights will help you begin to make needed changes. In the last stage, you will be encouraged to actively apply and solidify new insights and skills to facilitate change in yourself and your life situations.

The duration of counseling depends on many factors unique to your particular situation. My objective is to provide you with the most effective form of therapy in the most cost-efficient manner. Experience shows that those who are most motivated to work on their problems, follow their counselor's advice, and complete homework assignments see the greatest improvement most quickly.

## TRADITIONAL AND CHRISTIAN-ORIENTED COUNSELING

While this practice offers a traditional approach to counseling, some people are interested in a Christian-based approach that respects their Christian beliefs and values. This practice, therefore, offers its counselees the opportunity to have a Christian approach that is biblically sound and consistent with a Christian worldview. The approach incorporates prayer, the spiritual disciplines, and biblical truth to help counselees utilize their spiritual resources in dealing with their concerns in a way that brings honor to God. Please inform your counselor of your interest in this approach.

## CONFIDENTIALITY AND HIPAA

**All communication between you and your counselor will be held in the strictest of confidence**. In fact, your right to confidentiality in therapy is required by law. Title 8.01, Chap. 14, Article 4(8.01–400.2) of the Code of [your state] allows the counselee to claim privilege in civil action, over those communications with a licensed counselor involved in a professional relationship. It is important for you to know that there are ethical and legal exceptions to the confidentiality privilege. Information can be disclosed in only the following situations: you have given **written consent** authorizing disclosure to another individual or party; **child/elder abuse or neglect is suspected**; if you are a **danger to yourself or to others;** and to appropriate medical authorities in the **case of an emergency**. In addition, when **filing for insurance**, the insurance company may need full access to your files to verify information they require for reimbursement.

In addition, the Health Insurance Portability and Accountability Act (HIPAA) is practiced and followed by this office. First, the HIPAA Privacy Rule (45 C.F.R. parts 160 and 164) permits disclosure for treatment, payment, health-care operations or as authorized by the patient, court orders, serious threats to health and safety, workers 'compensation laws, and reporting on victims of domestic violence or abuse as required by law. If disclosure needs to be made, you will receive notice.

Occasionally counselors decide that they need to consult with a colleague or obtain supervision from another mental-health professional in order to serve you better. Every effort is made to protect counselee privacy (e.g., withholding names, not revealing information). If your counselor desires consultation or supervision, you will be informed of that decision and have the right to refuse.

## APPOINTMENTS

Your initial appointment will be scheduled for one hour, unless other arrangements have been made. Subsequent appointments are **scheduled for 45 to 50 minutes** to allow the counselor time between appointments to make and/or review notes in preparation for the next session. **You may need to obtain authorization from your insurance company for any sessions that exceed one hour or for more than one session per week**. When sessions extend beyond the normal time frame or "outside the session" work (i.e., extensive phone calls, reading or writing letters and/or reports, or reviewing previous therapy history), you will be billed at the hourly rate proportional to each 15 minutes of the hour utilized.

Typically, your counselor will schedule to see you weekly during a standing appointment time. This will be "your time" reserved just for you. However, because you may need to change your appointment from time to time, please confirm your next appointment at the end of each session. Changes in appointment can be made by phone; however, priority will be given to those with standing appointments.

**You may cancel an appointment** without charge by calling at least **twenty-four (24) hours** in advance. Please try to call as soon as you know you must cancel. Emergency situations will be evaluated on an individual basis. Except in emergency situations, appointments canceled less than 24 hours in advance, or missed without notification **will automatically be charged at full-fee charge**. Insurance companies do not pay for charges incurred for missed appointments, thus it is your responsibility to pay.

Late cancellations prevent your counselor from being able to schedule this time with other counselees in need. Two consecutive cancellations of any kind may also lead to the forfeiture of your standing appointment time and the need for you to find a new time.

## FEES AND PAYMENTS

This practice has attempted to set fees at a reasonable level and are moderate in comparison with the prevailing rates in this area. The normal fee for a 45–50 minute session is $_____. Intake sessions (i.e., the initial session) are $_____. Since **fees are rendered for the counselor's time**, shorter or longer sessions are prorated. Phone calls, apart from scheduling issues, are billed at $_____ per 10 minutes. Costs for testing vary with the individual test; if your counselor discusses with you the benefit of taking a particular test, the cost will be discussed with you at that time.

The legal system is not conducive to effective counseling. Since counselors seek to remain neutral, there is little benefit for those seeking to sue the counselor in litigation. For that reason, this practice has placed its **court costs at $_____ per hour**. Any time traveling to and from court will be billed at the cost for normal sessions ($_____ per hour). In addition, you will be billed for any costs related to travel including, mileage, meals, parking, and hotel costs.

All fees for services are **due and payable on the day of the service being rendered**. You may pay by check or cash. If there is a financial problem, please discuss it prior to your session. A payment plan can be arranged to accommodate almost anyone, but those who ignore their obligations will not be accommodated. A monthly **5 percent surcharge will be added to the balances** of inactive counselees who are not regularly paying on their balance. In addition, delinquent accounts in which there is no or minimal activity may be handed over to a credit service or a "Warrant of Debt" will be issued through the General District Court. In either case you will be billed for the additional charges (e.g., cost of credit service, court costs) as well as this office's time involved in the matter. A minimum of one therapy hour ($_____) will be charged.

## INSURANCE

Unfortunately insurance coverage cannot be guaranteed because policies vary among individuals and companies. Your insurance policy is a contract between you and your insurance company. Thus **verifying coverage and payment of fees is ultimately your responsibility**. If you have questions about coverage, contact your insurance company or agent.

Managed-care policies require preauthorization before initiating therapy. **Obtaining pre-authorization is your responsibility.** Failure to do so will result in your having to pay the full session fee; regardless of whatever lower rates your insurance carrier may have established with this practice.

Any financial settlement (including liability claims) is solely a matter between you and the insurance carrier. Therefore you will need to make full payment while you await settlement on your claim.

Please bring your insurance information with you, including the addresses of the claim office.

## ADDITIONAL INFORMATION

[Put information about yourself here]

*Thank you for choosing this practice to serve you.*

**Respectfully,**

**Dr. John C. Thomas**

# VERIFICATION OF READING AND UNDERSTANDING THE ORIENTATION TO THE COUNSELING SERVICES GUIDE

I, _____ hereby sign below, verifying that I have read the ORIENTATION TO THE COUNSELING SERVICE material. I fully understand my rights, and financial and other responsibilities related to participating in this service.

_____          _____

Counselee Signature                                                        Date

_____          _____

Witness                                                                    Date

# Appendix E

# Informed Consent Form for Recording Sessions

To provide the highest quality service to our counselees, we need to continually evaluate our counselors. The best approach for evaluating our counselors and helping them to develop their skill level is to audiotape the sessions. These tapes will be used only for the express purpose of evaluation and education of our center counselors. All tapes will be erased following use for its stated purpose.

I understand that such tape recording will not occur without my prior knowledge or consent. I also understand that I may revoke this consent at any time.

_____          _____
                Counselee Signature                                      Date

_____          _____
                Counselor Signature                                      Date

# Appendix F

# Counseling
# Authorization Form

I, _____, an applicant for
services, or I, _____, a representative
or guardian of the above-named applicant for services authorize
_____ to provide mental-health related services.

### CONFIDENTIALITY

Your identity and any information shared by you will be held in the strictest confidence. The right to release information about you belongs to you.
No information, including the fact that you are being seen by this office,
will be released to anyone without your written consent.

Exceptions to this policy are made as a result of legal requirements to
report:

1. The abuse and neglect of a child or a dependent adult.
2. Imminent danger of harm to yourself or others.
3. In cases of court involvement, your treatment record may be
   obtained by a judicial order.
4. Information regarding your involvement in treatment (i.e., dates
   of treatment and billing record) may be released if legal collection action becomes necessary by this office.
5. Information regarding to your treatment, dates of services,
   diagnosis and treatment plans will be released to your insurance
   company if you choose to have this office file your insurance
   claims.

## I HAVE READ AND UNDERSTAND ALL OF THE ABOVE.

_____          _____
          Counselee/Caregiver Signature                           Date

_____          _____
                    Witness                                        Date

# Appendix G

# Release of Information Form

**TO:** _____

_____

_____

_____

**Counselee Name:** _____

**Parent/Guardian:** _____

**Counselee's Birth Date:** _____

**SS Number:** _____

**State Purpose or Need for Release:** _____

_____

I, _____ hereby authorize _____to (circle one or both of the following) obtain and/or release information regarding myself or my above-named dependent. You may forward the said information to the address on the form. It is further understood that this can be revoked at any time in writing, and unless otherwise specified hereafter, it automatically expires one year from the date of my signature.

Signed: _____Date: _____

Parent/Guardian: _____Date: _____

Witness: _____Date: _____

**Revocation:**

Signed: _____Date: _____

Parent/Guardian: _____Date: _____

Witness: _____Date: _____

# Appendix H

# Financial Information Form

**If you have insurance**, complete the necessary insurance sections and read and sign the statement of understanding. You will also need to present your card so that a copy can be made. **If you do not have insurance**, please read and sign the statement of understanding.

Insurance Carrier: _____

Telephone: _____

Claims Address: _____

Insured Name:_____Date of Birth: _____

Insured ID #: _____ Group #: _____

Employer Name: _____ Policy #: _____

Patient's Relationship to Insured: Self __ Spouse __ Child __Other ____

**(If additional coverage, please complete this section)**

Policy Holder:_____ ID #: _____

Plan Name: _____

Address: _____

Telephone: _____

Policy Number: _____ Group #: _____

## STATEMENT OF UNDERSTANDING

I hereby authorize this practice to release information to my insurance carrier to process any and all claims for services rendered. I also authorize direct payment to this office. *I understand that I am financially responsible for any balance not covered by my insurance.* (This includes any services rendered that were not preauthorized by your managed-care company and any missed appointments or late cancellations [24-hour notice]. Such services **will** be billed at normal practice rates, rather than contracted rates with your carrier. Balance is **due in full 30 days** after insurance company response. A 5-percent surcharge will be added monthly to inactive balances at the discretion of this practice.)

*I, _____ understand that the fee is for the time of the appointment. Payment is requested at time of service,* unless prior arrangements have been made. In the event that my account is turned over for outside collection or to the General District Court for a "Warrant in Debt," I agree to pay all costs related to collection (e.g., court fees, collection fees, attorney fees) plus office time for processing your statement (a minimum of $_____).

I have read and agree to the conditions of this practice. I understand the financial policy and agree that I am responsible for payment.

Signature: _____ Date: _____

Witness: _____ Date: _____

# Appendix I
# List of Feeling Words

| Anger | Joy | Sadness | Pride | Confusion |
|---|---|---|---|---|
| Annoyed | Cheerful | Depressed | Boastful | Aimless |
| Abhorred | Ecstatic | Dejected | Capable | Awkward |
| Antagonistic | Enthusiastic | Despair | Confident | Baffled |
| Bitter | Euphoric | Disgusting | Envious | Capricious |
| Bothered | Excited | Dismayed | Esteemed | Conflicted |
| Disgusted | Exhilarated | Distraught | Fulfilled | Doubtful |
| Exasperated | Festive | Grief | Hard-Hearted | Fickle |
| Furious | Fortunate | Helpless | Head-Strong | Foggy |
| Frustrated | Glad | Hopeless | Idolized | Honored |
| Hateful | Happy | Listless | Insensitive | Indecisive |
| Infuriated | Joyful | Loathed | Jealous | Lost |
| Mad | Liberated | Melancholy | Lustful | Misguided |
| Provoking | Strengthened | Miserable | Oppositional | Puzzled |
| Rageful | Wonderful | Moody | Respected | Stunned |
| Vengeful | Zealous | Sulky | Selfish | Uncertain |

| Hurt | Fear | Loving | Peaceful | Fearless |
|---|---|---|---|---|
| Abandoned | Afraid | Accepted | Calm | Bold |
| Agony | Anxious | Acknowledged | Carefree | Brave |
| Betrayed | Apprehensive | Adorning | Comfortable | Capable |
| Disappointed | Cowardly | Affirmed | Easy-Going | Committed |
| Disillusioned | Frightened | Amorous | Encouraged | Courageous |
| Embarrassed | Inhibited | Aroused | Free | Determined |
| Guilt | Nervous | Attractive | Gratified | Devoted |
| Heart-Broken | Overwhelmed | Benevolent | Light-Hearted | Enterprising |
| Homesick | Panicky | Caring | Quiet | Gallant |
| Humiliated | Paranoia | Consoled | Relaxed | Hardy |
| Inadequate | Scared | Empathy | Relieved | Industrious |
| Lonely | Shaky | Flattered | Restful | Powerful |

| | | | | |
|---|---|---|---|---|
| Mistreated | Suspicious | Fond | Safe | Resolute |
| Pity | Terrified | Friendly | Secure | Revitalized |
| Rejected | Threatened | Glamorous | Serene | Secure |
| Shameful | Worried | Tender | Tranquil | Self-Reliant |

| Humbled | | | Interested | |
|---|---|---|---|---|
| Content | Grateful | Satisfied | Absorbed | Excited |
| Convicted | Heroic | Sorry | Concerned | Fascinated |
| Encouraged | Modest | Spirited | Curious | Inquisitive |
| Foolish | Reassured | Sullen | Engrossed | Intrigued |
| Generous | Remorseful | Thankful | Entertained | Protective |

# Appendix J
# Symptoms Survey

Please fill out the following survey as carefully and honestly as possible. The more I know about you the better I can assist you in reaching your goals. Rate your experience of each of the following symptoms on a scale of 0 (not at all) to 10 (always). On the reverse side of this form, please describe any symptoms rated at a 6 or higher.

## INDIVIDUAL SYMPTOMS

1. Persistent sad, anxious, or empty mood most of the time_____
2. Feelings of hopelessness, pessimism, and low self-esteem_____
3. Feelings of guilt, worthlessness, helplessness_____
4. Loss of interest or pleasure in hobbies and activities that once gave pleasure_____
5. Insomnia, early-morning awakening, or oversleeping_____
6. Weight loss or gain_____
7. Decreased energy or fatigue_____
8. Panic and anxiety symptoms_____
9. Suicidal thoughts or plans_____
10. Uncontrollable cluttering of sad, negative thoughts_____
11. Social isolation, fear of people, things, certain tasks_____
12. Inappropriate social behavior, brash, rude, unkind_____
13. Irritability and impatience_____
14. Feeling disconnected, alone, unwanted, unloved_____
15. Feeling shame and inadequacy_____
16. Racing, cluttered thoughts causing constant distraction_____
17. Inability to complete tasks and easily distracted_____
18. Impulsive or immature decision-making_____
19. Unable to concentrate on school work unless with one-on-one attention_____
20. Failing grades, inability to function in work or school, disruptive, defiant, disorganized_____
21. Fidgety, in constant motion_____
22. Loud, disruptive, self-centered_____

23. Inability to trust people_____
24. Difficulty making or keeping friends, demanding own way, poor loser, insecure_____
25. Exaggerated emotional response/mood swings_____
26. Perfectionism_____
27. Disordered eating_____
28. Obsessive or compulsive thoughts or actions_____

## MARRIAGE QUALITIES

(If you are not married, write about your parent's relationship while you were growing up in your family of origin.)

1. We have a solid triangle of love based on commitment, intimacy, and passion_____
2. We choose to see the good in each other_____
3. We care about meeting each other's emotional needs_____
4. We protect one another and our relationship_____
5. We have fun together regularly_____
6. We are each able to take personal responsibility_____
7. We feel safe to share our hurts, concerns, and feelings with each other_____
8. We confess to one another and forgive one another_____
9. We embrace and accept each other's differences_____
10. We listen to one another_____
11. We resolve any anger between us before we go to bed at night_____
12. We do not blame each other_____
13. We validate our partner's perspective even if it is different from our own_____
14. We take time to nurture our marriage and connect with one another regularly (e.g., weekly date)_____
15. We understand and employ "fair fighting"_____
16. We love each other for who we really are and we do not desire or expect an ideal partner_____
17. We have left our family of origins and have cleaved to one another (our loyalty is with our marriage partner and not our family of origin)_____
18. Our sexuality is fulfilling for both of us. We can talk openly about our needs and desires_____

## PARENTING QUALITIES

(If you are not a parent, write about your experience with your parents while you were growing up in your family of origin.)

1. Children are treated in a loving, patient manner _____
2. Children are soothed when afraid, understood in their needs, listened to and heard in their grief_____
3. Children are supported as unique individuals and are encouraged to have their own feelings, tastes, and opinions_____
4. Parents have a healthy, loving relationship and utilize firm, fair, and consistent rules, limits, and consequences
5. Family time is encouraged and there are many family rituals, traditions, and times of regular emotional connection_____
6. Children are held accountable to meeting standards of performance and parents agree on these standards. Parents have clearly communicated these standards and the consequences for not following them. BOTH parents follow up on the consequences consistently_____
7. Parents model an appropriate response to authority_____
8. Parents model that they are imperfect and that being imperfect is normal and OK. When they fail, they admit it and say "I'm sorry"_____
9. Both parents have resolved their own family-of-origin issues_____
10. Both mother and father are safe and available_____
11. Children are never shamed, emotionally abandoned, or abused_____

## FAMILY QUALITIES

1. Communicates and listens_____
2. Affirms and supports one another_____
3. Teaches respect for others_____
4. Develops a sense of trust_____
5. Has a sense of play and humor_____
6. Exhibits a shared sense of responsibility_____
7. Teaches a sense of right and wrong_____
8. Has a strong sense of family in which rituals and traditions abound_____
9. Has a balance of interaction among members_____
10. Has a shared religious core_____
11. Respects the privacy of one another_____
12. Values service to others_____
13. Fosters family table time and conversation_____
14. Shares leisure time_____

15. Admits to and seeks help with problems_____
16. Able to share feelings_____

## PHYSICAL HEALTH

1. When and where have you had your last full medical examination?

2. Have laboratory examinations been done in which electrolytes, thyroid function (full screen), liver enzymes, and hematological indexes were determined to be within normal limits?

3. Are you currently taking any medications (including over-the-counter medications)? What is the name of the medication, the dosage, the purpose for taking it, and the duration of use?

4. Do you have a family history that includes family members with any of the symptoms you are currently experiencing, or any other mental-health problems?

5. For how long have you had these symptoms?

6. Have you had any previous treatment (including counseling of any kind) for these or any other symptoms that were medical or psychological? If yes, please explain. Include any diagnosis or treatment process you received.

7. General Health:

8. Physician's Name, Address, and Phone Number:

9. Date of last physical or doctor visit:

10. Any recent changes in (please explain):

    A. Sleeping patterns (over or under sleeping, hardly sleeping for three or more consecutive days):

    B. Eating habits:

    C. Behavior:

    D. Mood swings:

    E. Energy level:

    F. Weight:

    G. Tension level:

    H. Describe any significant medical problems/conditions/symptoms:

11. Do you have a history of substance use? Do you currently use alcohol or drugs? If yes, please describe your daily, weekly, and monthly use. Please be honest. In order to help you, I need accurate information in this area.
12. Do you exercise regularly? If yes, what is your regular exercise pattern (what, how much, how often)?

## SPIRITUAL LIFE

Please describe your spiritual/religious values, beliefs, and practices and how important these are to you. Be specific.

## LIFE MAP

On the back of this form, create a life map that includes the following information about you:

- Life themes: things that keep coming up/have significance in your life
- Destiny markers or turning points
- Spiritually significant experiences
- Supportive relationships
- Identity variables: gift mix, your calling, your aspirations, your personality, interests and your passions in life; the things that make you, you.
- Painful life experiences
- People who encouraged you (heroes)
- People who hurt or abused you (villains)
- Traumatic experiences/wounds
- Future hopes and dreams

# Author Index

610

# Subject Index

# Scripture Index